SAN FRANCISCO

Frame-up

The Incredible Case of Tom Mooney and Warren Billings

BY *Curt Gentry*

W · W · NORTON & COMPANY · INC ·

New York

To W.K.B.
and all the other
forgotten men

Altogether, it is the most amazing story
I have ever had anything to do with. When
all is known that I think can be known,
it will be shown clearly that the State
before an open-eyed community [conspired]
to murder a man with the instruments that
the people have provided for bringing about
justice. There isn't a scrap of testimony
in either the Mooney or Billings cases
that wasn't perjured, except that of the
man who drew the blue prints of Market
Street.

FREMONT OLDER TO UPTON SINCLAIR

Contents

Illustrations

Frame-up

Prologue: Preparedness Day 1916

1 P.M.

THERE IS a San Francisco legend that no hot spell lasts more than three days. This was the third day, and many in the vast crowd lining both sides of Market Street, waiting for the parade to start, were unconsciously listening for the hoarse-voiced cry of the fog horns, the sound which would announce that cooling waves of billowy white mist were rolling in from the Pacific through the Golden Gate.

This was one explanation for the strange tenseness of the crowd. There were others.

Although San Francisco sits in solitary splendor on the tip of its own peninsula, with water lapping on three sides, it is one of the least isolated of American cities. World events have a way of converging upon it.

Even though the United States was not yet a participant in the European war, it was as close as the munitions ships in the Bay, several of which had recently, after leaving this harbor, suffered mysterious explosions for which German agents had been blamed. Indeed, the war was as close as the parade itself, sponsored by advocates of "Preparedness."

This was not the only war being fought, nor the only cause of disquietude. United States troops were massing along the border at Nogales, awaiting only the arrival of General "Black Jack" Pershing before marching into Mexico to hunt down the bandit-revolutionary Pancho Villa. (Some unsympathetically called it "Hearst's War," charging that the publisher, who had been largely responsible for precipitating the invasion through his papers, was really interested only in protecting his vast landholdings south of the Rio Grande.) There was a large Mexican community in San Francisco; like the Germans, whose numbers were also not inconsiderable, many had mixed loyalties. Just three weeks earlier, on June 30th, a man identified by the conductor as a Mexican had left a suitcase-enclosed bomb in the washroom of a San Francisco bound Southern Pacific passenger train. It exploded shortly after the train pulled into Oakland, blowing a huge hole in the side of the car, breaking all its windows, and injuring 14 people, although none fatally. Police believed the explosion to be the work of a Mexican revolutionary.

There was the Irish war, blossoming wherever a bit of the old sod was

11

transplanted. The Easter Rebellion was less than three months past. San Francisco had also a large Irish population, virtually to a man unsympathetic to England's plight and incensed over the pending execution of Sir Roger Casement.

And there was the war between labor and capital. This was an old war, but less than a month earlier its battles had left blood and dead men on San Francisco's strike-bound waterfront.

The parade itself was an embodiment of many of these tensions.

In July 1916 pacifism was a fighting issue, and "preparedness" a convenient mask behind which hid all manner of things.

Officially the United States was following a policy of strict neutrality with regard to the European war. Already one heard the slogan that in just four months would assure Woodrow Wilson's re-election: "He kept us out of war." Yet in July the public attitude was still unknown, and Wilson was safely playing both sides. Although it was the Republicans who most strongly cried for Preparedness, Wilson had blunted their argument by advocating it himself, even going so far as to lead one of the Preparedness parades. If this was bad diplomacy, it was also good politics, and 1916 was an election year. In general, however, the Preparedness Day parades were business-sponsored, Republican, anti-administration.

This, at least, was the background of the Preparedness parades that had already taken place in New York City and Washington, D.C. The San Francisco parade was something more. It was an ill-kept secret that the Pacific Defense League, sponsor of the event, was in reality little more than a front for the San Francisco Chamber of Commerce and that the parade itself was to be an "open shop" demonstration conducted under the banner of patriotism. Though old, the labor war had entered a new phase. For years San Francisco had been the most heavily unionized city in the United States. Just one month before, the Chamber of Commerce had organized a "Law and Order Committee" for the purpose of correcting this situation. Many employers had ordered their non-union employees to march in the parade on pain of dismissal.

PATRIOTS' PAGEANT TO CRY: PREPARE! read the banner headline on that morning's San Francisco *Chronicle,* the official paper of the city's business interests, those five words in effect implying that the Democrats, the Progressives, the labor unions who had voted almost unanimously against participation in the parade, the Socialists, the pacifists, and all others endorsing the President's stand were less than loyal. "Little by little, the good nature began to go out of the fight for peace," R. L. Duffus, a reporter for the San Francisco *Bulletin,* would later write. "It wasn't considered harmlessly idealistic to be a pacifist any more; it was dangerous, perhaps unpatriotic."

The *Bulletin* was anti-preparedness. The *News* was uncommitted. The *Chronicle, Call,* and of course Hearst's *Examiner,* were all for it.

If their headlines, lead stories, and editorials were not sufficiently indicative of how the papers stood on this issue, one needed only to examine their forecasts of the estimated number of marchers. The *Chronicle* predicted 200,000 would assert their patriotism, the *Bulletin* guessed it would be about one-tenth that.*

If for most San Franciscans the tension was little more than a vague and indefinable feeling—a combination of many ingredients—for a few it was graphically clear.

The anonymous threats had begun arriving several weeks earlier, shortly after the parade was announced. There had been more than 200, meticulously lettered in the same hand, all mailed in the city, to newspapers, civic leaders, and those prominent in the planning of the parade. Not all who received them took them seriously. One who did was Fremont Older, tall, hawk-like editor of the San Francisco *Bulletin.*

The message to Older began:

"Our protests have been in vain in regards to this preparedness propaganda, so we are going to use a little 'direct action' on the 22nd, which will echo around the earth and show that Frisco really knows how, and that militarism cannot be forced on us and our children without a violent protest. Things are going to happen to show that we will go to any extreme, the same as the controlling class will do, to preserve what little democracy we still have."

Reading on, the editor nearly yielded to habit, blue-penciling the misspelled words.

"Don't take this as a joke or you will be rudely awaken," the message continued. "WE HAVE SWORN TO DO OUR DUTY TO THE MASSES, and only send this warning to those who are wise, but are forced to march to hold their jobs, as we want to give only THE HYPROCITAL PATRIOTS WHO SHOUT FOR WAR BUT NEVER GO a real taste of war. Kindly ask the Chamber of Commerce to march in a solid body IF THEY ARE NOT COWARDS. A copy has been sent to all papers, our duty has been done so far.

"THE DETERMINED EXILES FROM MILITARISTIC GOVERNMENTS, ITALY RUSSIA RUSSIA ITALY Germany Holland U.S."

Older turned the letter over to the police, suggesting they put a watch on the local IWW hall. The police assured the editor that they would investigate and take special precautions to ensure that no violence occurred during the parade, but Older could tell they weren't greatly concerned.

* On the next day, both the *Chronicle* and *Examiner* would give the total number of marchers as 51,000. The official police count was 22,400. The *Bulletin* generously granted 22,458.

One group of men was. These were the members of the San Francisco Chamber of Commerce's Law and Order Committee. The message received by Frederick H. Koster, head of the committee and president of the chamber, was brief enough to go on a postcard. While it bore a different signing and made no specific reference to the parade, it was the product of the same hand, and was explicit enough:

"Your extreme activity in promoting and glorifying militarism, marks you as the most vicious and dangerous 'jingo' of all your brutal, greedy, thieving and war-making class; and the immediate 'extermination' of you and your evil class, is going to be the sole and 'patriotic' duty of the EMPLOYEES LIBERTY LEAGUE."

Few of the hundred thousand people now gathered along Market Street were aware that "a little 'direct action'" had been threatened. To avoid panic, the police had asked the newspapers not to publicize the warnings.

1:15. "Why doesn't it start?"

"San Francisco parades never start on time."

This was true. The announced starting time was rarely the official starting time. Today, although the papers had said the parade would begin at 1 P.M., the actual planned start was 1:30, to allow police time enough to clear the street of traffic. Those who now looked down Market toward the Ferry Building, searching vainly for the head of the parade, saw a long street near devoid of vehicles. They also saw the results of the special police measures, though unaware of them as such. Police stood on every corner, and were scattered out along the blocks in-between. Ropes and cables were put up along much of the street to hold back the crowds. To cross Market at any but a few designated intersections one needed a special pass, of which only a few had been issued, to reporters, photographers, and firemen.

1:25. At the foot of Market Street, parade units were in line on both sides of the Ferry Building, along the Embarcadero, waiting for the starting signal. In addition, a number of other units waited in various sidestreets that led into lower Market, scheduled to fall into place as the main body passed. On one of these, narrow Steuart Street, just a block from the Embarcadero, were units representing the Grand Army of the Republic, their Women's Auxiliary, the Sons of the American Revolution, and the Spanish War Veterans. There were even a few Confederate veterans among the GAR. They marched together in most parades, their common experience now uniting more than dividing them. The uniforms of both were so badly faded that it was difficult to distinguish the blue from the gray.

The main attraction here, however, and the reason so many spectators were crowded into this particular sidestreet, was the bullet-torn battleflag of the Spanish War Veterans, removed from its showcase in the state museum for just this one day. Its presence was of more than ordinary interest because the United States was once again at war with its Spanish-speaking neighbors.

One block away, at the intersection of Embarcadero and Market, police captain Duncan Matheson checked his watch against the Ferry Building clock. At exactly *1:30* he blew his whistle and the first parade unit started up Market Street.

In the lead, riding a spirited bay, was Thornwell Mullally. Although a popular figure in San Francisco society, the former Southerner was cordially hated by labor. A director of United Railroads, Mullally had been instrumental in crushing two strikes of the URR streetcar men—one in 1907, the other just two weeks prior to the parade. The choice of Mullally as Grand Marshal was a direct slap at the unions.

Mullally was escorted by a phalanx of mounted policemen. Behind him was a band, and then the mayor.

At *1:31* Mayor James Rolph, Jr., jauntily stepped off onto Market. Everyone, business and labor included, liked "Sunny Jim." It was generally agreed that although Rolph's executive abilities might leave something to be desired, he was the ideal mayor for parades. Sunny Jim was a showman. In gold-heeled cowboy boots, ten-gallon white Stetson, and frock coat with a camellia in the buttonhole, Rolph was the highlight of any celebration. Today he was waving a small American flag. Flags were the parade's only decoration—tens of thousands of them, small ones held by the spectators, large ones hanging from trolleylines or draped across building fronts.

Mullally passed the mouth of Steuart Street at *1:32*, Rolph at *1:33*.

The heat and excitement were too much for one GAR veteran. Seventy-two-year-old Adam Fox crumpled and slipped to the pavement. His comrades carried him onto the sidewalk while a policeman called for an ambulance.

With all this activity it was not too surprising that only a few people noticed that someone had left a suitcase on the sidewalk next to the wall of the Ferry Exchange Saloon, on the southwest corner of Steuart and Market, behind the crowd at the curb.

Elmer E. Kimberlin, a retired night watchman, was standing near the door of the saloon, talking to an acquaintance, when about 1:30 he saw a man coming up Steuart from Mission Street (one block south) carrying a worn brown suitcase that he set down next to the wall of the saloon, not more than two feet from where Kimberlin was standing. According to Kimberlin, the man "was approximately five feet ten inches in height, weighed a hundred and seventy pounds; he wore a soft black hat turned down all around; he wore dark clothes apparently much worn, was of a very dark skin or complexion" and "was either Mexican or Italian."

Charles F. Johnson, a ship's carpenter and a deputy constable of San Mateo County, saw the same thing, but almost in reverse: he was sure the man was walking from Market down Steuart toward Mission. "In appearance he seemed to be a Mexican or Spaniard, being very dark complexioned, and had a smooth, round face. He was shabbily dressed, about five-feet-seven in height, weighed about one hundred sixty pounds, black hair and wore a dark-color crush felt hat."

William H. Taylor, a seafaring man, was coming out of the saloon when he saw a man shoving the suitcase up against the side of the building. Taylor warned him, "That is a bad place to leave it, my friend, for this crowd is around here and somebody will come along and pick it up." "Don't you touch that suitcase," the man replied. "I know what I am doing." The man then cut across Steuart. Taylor watched him as he went down Steuart to Mission, then turned up Mission toward Spear. Taylor would later recall him as being about "five feet seven or eight, with a mustache, kind of sallow complexion . . ."

M. T. Prendergast, an Oakland gardener who was to march with the Spanish War Veterans, also saw the man place the suitcase on the sidewalk. He described him as "Mexican or Portuguese, twenty-five, dark suit and hat, a hundred and forty-five pounds, five feet eight," with several days growth of beard. Prendergast was sure he was with another man, of medium height and complexion, but what he may have seen was Taylor talking to the man, although Prendergast claimed the pair then went into the saloon together.

There were others who didn't see the man, or men, but who saw the suitcase.

Thirteen-year-old Boy Scout Jimmie McDougal, who was to help carry one of the big flags, noticed the suitcase next to the wall and started to sit on it, but jumped up quickly when it began to sink in. Jimmie assumed the suitcase was empty and had been used to carry flags.

Major W. J. Watson, who was to march with the GAR, also saw the suitcase. He went over and was about to give it an inquisitive kick, when the order came to fall in.

At *1:48* Mullally reached the corner of Third and Market. This was the beginning of "newspaper row," since the city's major papers were all located here in close proximity.

At *1:49* Mullally passed a two-story building at 721 Market. When Mayor Rolph passed it at *1:50* a raucous-voiced young lady, leaning out the window of a credit dentist on the second floor, yelled "Hell-ooo, Mayor Rolph" and waved a white towel. Mayor Rolph was a great favorite of the ladies.

A minute later the mayor passed the offices of the *Bulletin* at 767 Market.

Edgar T. "Scoop" Gleeson and Miss Henrici were on the fire escape outside the fourth floor city room. Both were assigned this spot because it was assumed that if Gleeson, who covered the waterfront and city hall, couldn't recognize a person, Miss Henrici, the society editor, could. Ernest Jerome Hopkins was sitting at a desk just inside the window, acting as rewrite. The pair would call back their observations, which Hopkins incorporated into the revised proof of the afternoon edition. Editor Fremont Older hadn't told his reporters about the threats, but they were conscious that something was oddly askew. As Hopkins later put it, "The outstanding fact, on which we commented, was one I couldn't use, for it wasn't definitely established; it was a matter of impression merely. But we felt it, sensed it unmistakably: that crowd was queerly tense. This wasn't like the civic merrymaking of 1915, the Exposition year; this was like no other public event we had seen. Something was in the air.

"It showed mainly, in the stern quiet of the marchers, and the unaccustomed silence of the crowd as the divisions marched by. The scene had gorgeous color, little sound, little motion . . ."

1:58. On reaching Fifth Street, Mullally halted the parade to give the marchers a short rest. Mayor Rolph stopped about a quarter of a block behind him. Eight stories above Rolph, on the coping of a roof, young Wade Hamilton framed the mayor in his viewfinder and snapped the shutter. It was a cheap Brownie, and Hamilton was very much an amateur photographer; unintentionally he photographed some people leaning over the edge of the adjoining roof, that of the Eilers Music Company Building at 975 Market, as well as the parade stretched out below. Hamilton took two more pictures, one at *2:01,* the other at *2:04.*

At exactly *2:04,* more than a mile back down Market, the Grand Army of the Republic began marching out of Steuart Street, their Women's Auxiliary, the Sons of the American Revolution, and the Spanish War Veterans moving up behind them.

Mounted on his horse, patrolman Francis Gaddy directed the marchers around the ambulance just arrived to take GAR veteran Adam Fox to Central Emergency Hospital. It was parked on the east side of Steuart Street. On the west side, John C. Myer stood in the doorway of his saloon, debating with himself as to whether to join the crowd and watch the parade or tend to business, which was brisk. He was standing less than ten feet from the suitcase.

In the crowd that jammed the sidewalk between the saloon wall and Steuart Street, Mrs. Kingsley Van Loo lifted up her daughter Marie, age seven, to "see the old soldiers." Her son, Richard, nine, stood alongside her, waiting his turn. The Van Loos, from Fresno, had spent the past week in Oakland visiting relatives. They had come over to the city for the parade and to meet Mr. Van Loo, who was to arrive that evening to take them home.

Standing near the Van Loos were Henry J. Claussen, from Alameda; Arthur Nelson, commissary clerk for the Fairmont Hotel; and *Chronicle* reporter Frederick Hinkle.

Reuben J. Vaughan, captain of the river steamer *Sacramento*, was edging his way through the crowd not far from Hinkle. Vaughan wasn't interested in the parade. Unemployed for more than two months by a strike, he was now on his way to the ferry, and thence home to Berkeley and his wife, with the good news that he would be returning to work next week. The Vaughans, with four children of their own plus one recently adopted, had been hard hit by the strike.

2:05. Vaughan passed Lea H. Lamborn, an assayer from Alameda. A widower, Lamborn lived with his daughter. They were to go on a camping trip to Lake Tahoe that evening and Lamborn, having some time to kill, had come downtown to watch the parade.

Vaughan also passed just behind George Lawlor and the Knapps. Lawlor, thirty-three, a lumber salesman from Alameda, had unexpectedly run into his neighbors in the crowd. Howard Knapp, thirty-eight, was in an allied line of work, salesman for a paper company. Lawlor also had two children about the same age as the Knapps' two-and-a-half-year-old son Willie, whom Howard Knapp was now holding in his arms. Hetta Knapp stood between her husband and Lawlor, at the curb, nearest the parade.

2:06. The two ambulance attendants were carefully lifting Adam Fox onto a stretcher; he was conscious and chatting with another GAR veteran who had dropped out of the ranks to look after him . . . The Spanish War Veterans were about 60 feet from Market, their front ranks just opposite the Van Loos . . . Vaughan was still trying to get through the dense crowd . . . Lawlor had just turned to say something to Knapp . . .

Then the sudden roar.

The blast blew off the top of Lawlor's head, threw Lamborn atop Lawlor, sent Mrs. Knapp crashing into the street, hurled Mrs. Van Loo and her daughter Marie to the sidewalk, dumped Adam Fox off the stretcher, toppled like tenpins the front ranks of the Spanish War Veterans, stripped the flesh from the legs of a six-year-old boy, ripped off limbs, riddled backs, arms, and legs, punctured lungs, and scattered bodies, dropping them in bleeding mounds for more than 50 feet. It also knocked over the row of men at the bar inside the saloon, smashed the windows of nearby buildings, and threw both patrolman Gaddy and his horse to the pavement. More than 100 feet away, across Market, a hat containing a piece of skull dropped onto the roof of a building.

For what seemed a full minute but was probably seconds "not a sound

Steuart and Market Streets, San Francisco, minutes after the Preparedness Day bomb explosion. The evidence had not yet been washed away by Lt. Bunner. The figure at far left, leaning against the saloon wall, appears to have lost part of his leg. He had. Fortunately it was wooden.

was to be heard, not a thing to be seen." Dense white smoke obscured everything. Then a few voices broke the stillness—a man moaning "Oh my God! Oh my God!," a child shrilly calling "Oh Momma"—then many screams, as the glass from the upper stories of nearby buildings fell onto the people on the sidewalks below.

For many the silence lasted longer: the explosion shattered the eardrums of those nearest, gave others the temporary deafness of shock.

One by one, people struggled to their feet, trying to understand what had happened.

Captain Matheson, who had been standing on Market Street, with his back to the corner, reacted more quickly than most: "There was a loud report. I instantly turned around. I saw a white vapor rising followed by a cloud of dust." Almost instinctively, out of long habit, Matheson checked both his watch and the Ferry Building clock and determined the time to be *2:06*.

19

Chronicle reporter Hinkle had been standing near the Van Loos: "Next to me a woman, who had been holding up a little white-clad girl to 'see the old soldiers' dropped, horribly mangled. The child shrieked. Something struck me on the breast with a thud. I found two bullets and a small piece of casement blown into my breast pocket."

Acting police lieutenant Charles Birdsall had been standing at the corner: "There was a sudden roar and I was knocked to the ground. The body of a young girl crashed into me with full force . . . I arose, looked down at the girl, and found one of her legs was hanging by a thread. All around the bodies of men and women almost stripped of their clothes lay in horrible grotesque heaps."

Dr. Robert G. O'Connell of San Anselmo, like Captain Vaughan, had been working his way through the crowd toward Market, but was some distance ahead of Vaughan when he felt the concussion: "Turning I saw figures, men and women, crawling and creeping over the sidewalk and in the gutter. A few lay very stiff. A stream of red was slowly surging over the stone walk. Several of the women were staggering in the streets. Their clothes were practically stripped from their bodies."

One man, on reviving from shock, was first aware of a small child crying. "What's the matter?" he asked, kneeling down. The boy, Richard Van Loo, was standing, although his right foot was badly mangled. "Oh, my momma," the boy sobbed. "Where is your mother?" the man asked. The boy pointed to an inert shape. Sure she was dead, the man decided to get help for the boy and his sister, whose legs were bleeding from multiple cuts. When he returned minutes later with Dr. O'Connell, a man was kneeling over Mrs. Van Loo. They thought he was another doctor, administering treatment. Actually he was pulling off her wedding rings and jewelry.

Myer stared unbelieving out the door of his saloon. Inside and outside were complete chaos, yet Myer, who had been closest of all to the point of the explosion, hadn't even one scratch.

In the third rank of the Spanish War Veterans two brothers, who had been marching side by side, looked at each other. With amazement, each discovered the other's face was dripping blood.

In the ranks behind them an aged veteran kept muttering, "It's war, that's what it is, it's war."

At the head of the group, Captain Hyman Meyers surveyed his bloody, broken ranks, made an instant decision, and cried *"Attention! Move out!"* The men did, stepping over the bodies of their fallen comrades, among them Dr. George L. Painter, a prominent Berkeley physician and close friend of Mayor Rolph's, who had been in the front rank, directly behind the historic banner. In uneven rows, they marched out onto Market Street, turned sharply and joined the parade, following Meyers, who

George Lawlor, Mill Valley lumber salesman, one of those killed instantly by the blast. The final count was 10 dead and more than 40 seriously injured.

marched jerkily on two badly lacerated legs.

Police Lieutenant Stephen Bunner was standing about 15 feet from Captain Matheson, staring helplessly at the scene. Matheson ordered him to take care of the injured while he kept the parade moving. Another contingent of marchers was due to arrive by ferry from Oakland and Matheson wanted to make sure the crowd didn't surge across Market, blocking the street. Spotting two plain-clothes detectives who had been on duty watching for pickpockets, Matheson sent them in opposite directions to commandeer whatever vehicles could be found to take the injured to hospitals.

For perhaps five minutes Howard Knapp was stunned, with no recollection. Then, as in a silent dream, for his eardrums had ruptured, he saw George Lawlor's body and thought, "Well, George is gone." Only then did he realize that his wife wasn't beside him. Still holding his son, who had escaped with only a bruised forehead and cut leg, he stepped over the bodies, looking at each to see if it was Hetta's. Unaware that he was himself bleeding from gaping wounds in his shoulder and side, he finally

21

found her among those who had been crowded into the ambulance. He recognized her by the color of her dress.

Bodies seemed to be everywhere, their limbs twisted in unnatural directions. Both the sidewalk and the street were littered with shoes, blown or cut from the feet of the victims. Making a quick count, reporter Hinkle estimated the dead and injured at more than fifty. Moving among them, asking names and addresses of those able to talk, he found many were from outside the city. Included was the Nevada State Superintendent of Schools, a stationer from Los Angeles, a printer from San Anselmo. Yet there was also a longshoreman from the Embarcadero, two schoolboys from Chinatown, an Italian baker from North Beach. Freak accidents abounded. One man near the explosion was thrown down but uninjured, while the man he knocked down, Arthur Nelson, commissary clerk at the Fairmont, was killed instantly. A Spanish War Veteran had half his leg blown off; fortunately it was his left leg, which was wooden. Officer Gaddy had various minor injuries; his horse, a much larger target, was without a bruise.

Captain Matheson had utilized resources at hand. Lieutenant Bunner, who had been on the force for 22 years, was "hardly the man to put in charge of anything," one police reporter later observed. "One look at Bunner and you knew where they got the stereotype for 'cop.' He was big, flat-footed and incredibly stupid." Bunner turned to the "terribly nauseating sight on the sidewalk," his first thought, he later stated on the witness stand, "to get rid of it." He first dispatched a policeman to the fruit stand on the opposite corner to borrow a tarpaulin to cover the dead. Then he attempted to clear the scene of bystanders. Already a crowd of scavengers had moved in, picking up souvenirs, ragged pieces of metal, steel-jacketed bullets.* Bunner attempted to push them back as best he could, but he didn't attempt to pick up any evidence himself or to determine what had caused the explosion. As trucks arrived he supervised the moving of the bodies, but he didn't mark where they had fallen. After all, this was the job of the detective bureau, he was later to explain, "and I'm not a detective."

When the last of the dead and injured had been dispatched to Harbour and Central Emergency hospitals, Bunner sent a policeman to the nearest fire station, where a hose was commandeered. Attaching it to a fireplug, he had the sidewalk washed clean. The horribly nauseating sight was gone, down the gutter with the swirling water. And with it the bomb parts, the bullets, and other evidence.

This simple act would render it impossible ever to accurately recon-

---

* Later the police would have to advertise, asking anyone who had picked up evidence to bring it in. More than 100 people came forth with items said to have been picked up and pocketed at the scene.

struct what happened on the corner of Steuart and Market Streets at 2:06 P.M. on the afternoon of July 22, 1916.

2 ·

Like the earthquake that preceded it by just a decade, the Preparedness Day bombing had its aftershocks.

Oddly enough, at the time of the explosion some in the crowd were listening for the sound of a bomb going off. The *Chronicle* that morning had announced that as soon as the head of the parade reached the reviewing stand at Marshall Square a bomb would explode as signal for all the bands to start playing the national anthem.

Moments after the explosion, those farther up Market heard "a low rumble like distant thunder ricocheting up the artificial canyon of the street." Many bared their heads and started singing *The Star Spangled Banner*.

On the fire escape outside the *Bulletin's* city room, the reporters heard "a muffled roar," and looking in the direction of the sound—lower Market, not upper, where the reviewing stand was located—saw a small column of white smoke rise up and dissipate. They wondered about it, vaguely apprehensive. Two or three minutes later all the phones began ringing and Gleeson climbed back inside. Before the first caller had finished "Scoop" was running down the stairs. Similar scenes were being enacted in all the nearby city rooms. The battle of the Extras was on. Initial reports said a gas main had exploded on Steuart Street and that the dead and wounded might number 100 or more.

For many along the parade route the first intimation of the horror that lay at the foot of Market came when Company K of the California Volunteers passed. Opposite the Palace Hotel, young newsboy George Davis crowded close to the curb to see the famed regimental flag of the Spanish War Veterans. He saw it, and more. Immediately behind was a grizzled sergeant, the entire side of his uniform, from shoulder to cartridge belt, stained a dull red. Limping behind him was a private, face grimaced with pain, hand tightly pressed against his thigh. There followed another soldier holding a blood-soaked handkerchief to his cheek. The audible gasps of the spectators followed the veterans up the street.

Nearly 30 minutes passed before news of the explosion reached the head of the parade. Mayor Rolph ordered an "immediate sweeping investigation," placing Chief of Police White in charge. Immediate it was not. More than an hour passed before Chief White could be located, on the city's golf links, and the better part of another hour before he could reach the scene.

Due to the crowd and the special security precautions, it took Gleeson nearly forty minutes to navigate the nine blocks to Steuart, even though he possessed one of the red cards permitting its bearer to cross police lines. Fortunately for the *Bulletin*, they already had a man on the scene. Stewart Dunbar, hired as a vacation fill-in, had been laid off just that morning and was at Haviside, a ship chandlery on Steuart, buying paint for a surplus whale boat he planned to renovate at the Clay Street wharf. He was walking out the doorway when the blast knocked him back in. Viewing the scene, and assuming that he had been rehired, he quickly called in the first story. When Gleeson arrived, the first loads of wounded had already been taken to the hospital, Dunbar going along with them for eye-witness accounts. The scene was still chaotic. Gleeson was interviewing a policeman when someone brought over a section of steel pipe, found in the crowd on the other side of Market Street. It was, Gleeson and the policeman observed simultaneously, the same kind used by the German agents in their schrapnel bombs. Gleeson picked up some additional pieces of jagged metal as well as some spent brass cartridge cases that had landed outside the perimeter of Bunner's housecleaning. It was probably a bomb, he reported to city editor Carl Hoffman on the telephone, possibly dynamite or dynamite soup enclosed in a lead pipe and surrounded with cartridges, which on impact had mowed down people as effectively as a machine gun.

Hoffman relayed the message to Fremont Older. The editor, a pacifist, looked stricken. "They'll probably blame me for this," he told Hoffman. Just two days earlier, Older had addressed a huge peace meeting in Dreamland Rink, speaking out against this "preparedness nonsense."

His suspicions were quickly confirmed. At the window Older, Hoffman, and editorial writer R. L. Duffus saw an open truck hurrying up the street, its horn blaring. In the back were some half-dozen wounded, on their way to the hospital. On passing the *Bulletin* one of the prone figures struggled to lift his arm and angrily shook his fist.

By this time the Extra race was over. Although the *Chronicle* claimed to have scooped the other papers, by virtue of posting Hinkle's first dispatch on the paper's outdoor bulletin board just ten minutes after the explosion, the *Bulletin* and the *Examiner* had papers on the street about 2:45.

On learning that the probable cause of the explosion was a bomb, policemen had been dispatched to the roofs of all buildings along the parade route to make sure that people had some legitimate reason for being on them. Other bombings were feared. On the roof of the Eilers Music Company Building, opposite which Mayor Rolph had briefly stopped, some dozen people had seen the ambulance going down Market, later returning, and had wondered about it. Among those on the Eilers roof were Thomas J. Mooney, a local labor leader, his wife Rena, who was a music teacher, and two of her relatives. A policeman, William Smith, came up on the Eilers roof about 3 P.M. Mooney asked him what had happened. He said, "They are throwing bombs off the roofs downtown."

Still farther away, in an apartment at 569 Dolores Street, in the Mission District, three people were finishing a lazy, leisurely lunch. Two were easily the most notorious personages in the United States: the anarchists Alexander Berkman and Emma Goldman. For decades, newspaper headlines had accused this pair of everything from corruption of youthful morals to being accessory to the murder of McKinley.

Had the American public been able to observe them as they were now they would have been amazed to find that Berkman was a quiet, extraordinarily gentle man, with a zestful sense of humor and an abhorrence for violence, whether by governments or men. He bore little resemblance to the hot-blooded young immigrant who in 1892 had thought he could settle the Homestead Steel Strike by an *Attentat,* the assassination of Carnegie company manager Henry Clay Frick. The attempt, which Berkman had botched, had merely injured Frick, turned sympathy away from the strikers, and cost the anarchist 14 years in prison.

It is probable that the same viewers would have been greatly disappointed to find Emma Goldman, America's foremost advocate of free love, a rather dumpy, middle-aged matron whose conversation was as much concerned with drama and art as sex and revolution.

The make up of the trio would have confirmed the worst suspicions, however, for the third member of the group was Mary Eleanor "Fitzie" Fitzgerald, a striking girl with red hair, delicate skin, blue-green eyes, and a Celtic temperament. Fitzie was Berkman's current mistress, a role fulfilled in the past by Emma. Emma had been twenty-three when her lover went to prison; she was nearly forty when he was released. Berkman, who during his long imprisonment had dreamed of returning to the girl he left, had never been able to bridge the intervening years. Fitzie was in her early twenties. Contrary to their public utterances about free love, jealousy was not altogether absent; both women called Berkman by his Russian diminutive, Sasha, and both vied for his attention.

Today the mood was bright, however, for Emma, recently released from the New York Workhouse after serving 15 days for advocating birth control, was currently doing what she enjoyed most, traveling across the country on a lecture tour. Proclaimed by even her enemies to be "probably the most effective woman speaker in the country," she had already made a number of lectures in the city, to capacity crowds, on such topics as "Anarchism and Human Nature—Do They Harmonize?" "Art for Life," and "The Family—Its Enslaving Influence Upon Parents and Children." She had canceled another speech, "Preparedness—The Road to Universal Slaughter," announced for the preceding Thursday, on learning that another anti-preparedness meeting, the one at which Fremont Older spoke, was scheduled for the same night.

Sasha was regaling Emma with a humorous account of Fitzie's culinary exploits when the telephone rang in an adjoining room that served as the office for Berkman's revolutionary periodical *The Blast.* He went to answer it.

When he returned, both women, sensitive to his moods, noticed his serious expression.

"A bomb exploded in the Preparedness Parade this afternoon," he said. "There are killed and wounded."

"I hope they aren't going to hold the anarchists responsible for it," Emma cried out.

"How could they?" Fitzie asked.

"How could they not?" Berkman answered, "they always have."

That the telephone call had come from a reporter who had asked Berkman if he wished to make a statement indicated that they were already being associated with the crime.

3 ·

At about 3:30 Captain Matheson returned from the Embarcadero. To his irritation he saw that Bunner had failed to rope off the area. Walking closer, his look changed to incredulity, then anger as Bunner explained what he had done. Matheson's exact words were not reproduced in the trial transcripts. He ordered Bunner to rope off the area immediately, then stayed long enough to be sure that much was done before returning to direct the parade.

What occurred during his absence this time has been variously interpreted. Very simply—without coloration, reconstructed solely from the testimony of the major participants—it was as follows.

Shortly after 3:30, Charles M. Fickert, District Attorney of the City and County of San Francisco, arrived on the scene. He was accompanied by a personal friend, Frederick H. Colburn, a banker and official of the San Francisco Chamber of Commerce. They found, at the spot where the bomb allegedly exploded, a crack in the sidewalk and a slight indentation in the saloon wall.

Fickert ordered a policeman to get some tools. Using a light sledge hammer Colburn broke up the sidewalk, after which the men rooted around in the hole, "looking for evidence" as Fickert later explained. Then, with a crowbar, Colburn pried some of the bricks out of the wall, leaving a gaping hole.

Only then were the official police photographs taken.

At the suggestion of press photographers, other photos were taken also, of Fickert pointing to the holes in the sidewalk and wall. In talking to reporters Fickert had already announced that his office would supervise the investigation.

"The reporters enjoyed kidding Fickert," Gleeson recalls. "They knew that he had only been elected because he knew how to take orders and didn't think too much on his own. They also knew that his sole distinction, one in which he took great pride, was that he had been a guard on the Stanford football team on which Herbert Hoover was waterboy. Not inappropriately, Fickert's teammates had nicknamed him 'Boob.' The reporters enjoyed ribbing Fickert because he never realized he was being kidded."

Bulletin staff writer Charles Brennan was one of the reporters clustered around the District Attorney. "You know, Mr. D.A.," he said, "you solve this one and they'll make you Governor."

Fickert's mouth spread in a wide grin. "You know, men," he said, "I already think I know who did this."

Recalling the incident in the light of later events, Brennan remarked, "I'll never forgive myself for having said that."

About 4:30, as the last units of the parade went up Market Street, Captain Matheson returned and saw the two gaping holes.

"What happened Bunner?" Matheson asked.

"I believe," Lieutenant Bunner replied, "some detectives were here."

4 ·

Shortly after four, the fog moved in through the Golden Gate, breaking the hot spell.

The cloud of fear that rose from Steuart and Market and now overhung the entire city was not so easily dissipated.

San Francisco was in a state of shock. By early evening nearly everyone knew that "the most fiendishly diabolical crime in the history of California" had taken place at the corner of Steuart and Market Streets. What made it especially frightening was its senselessness. Apparently directed at no specific person, it could have happened to anyone. It might happen again at any moment.

Gleeson remained at Harbour Emergency, together with the reporters from the other papers, calling in to the city desk each time another death was added to the mounting toll.

Forty-four people had been injured seriously enough to require hospi-

Before: This photograph, snapped by an amateur photographer shortly after the bodies were removed, shows the actual damage to the saloon wall and sidewalk to be minimal, important in determining whether the bomb was "placed" on the scene in a suitcase or "dropped" from the roof above. District Attorney Charles Fickert was unaware this photograph existed.

Courtesy Bancroft Library

Courtesy Bancroft Library

During: Searching for evidence or destroying it? This photo, taken at a time between the preceding two, appeared in a San Francisco paper on July 23, 1916, and would prove embarrassing to the prosecution. District Attorney Fickert is at far right.

After: The "official" police photograph of the same scene, taken after District Attorney Fickert and Frederick H. Colburn, banker and official of the San Francisco Chamber of Commerce, used a sledge hammer to smash in the brick wall and break up the sidewalk. Introduced in evidence before the Grand Jury to show the bomb damage.

Courtesy Bancroft Library

talization. Nineteen-year-old Pearl Seeman of Oakland, the girl thrown against officer Birdsall, lost her leg; she was only one of a number who would be crippled for life. Of those killed, only two died instantly: George Lawlor, the lumber salesman, and Arthur Nelson, the Fairmont Hotel clerk. Lea Lamborn, the assayer, died soon afterward; his daughter and her family waited more than an hour at the train station, before seeing an Extra and learning that there would be no trip to Tahoe. Hetta Kamp died about 5 P.M. Dr. George Painter died about 6, his friend Mayor Rolph at his bedside issuing a statement that "The fiends responsible for this outrage will be brought to justice" and personally offering $5000 as the start of a reward. Adam Fox died at 8.

There were no deaths Sunday or Monday.

Riverboat captain Reuben Vaughan, whose only injury was a badly mangled right leg, died unexpectedly Tuesday morning. Mrs. Kingsley Van Loo died Wednesday morning; steamship clerk Thomas H. Turnbull, the only bachelor among the victims, died that night. Henry J. Claussen was the tenth and last to die, on Thursday.*

By this time, however, San Franciscans were breathing easier—for just that morning the police had arrested the last two of the five people accused by them of plotting and perpetrating this hideous act.

In a very real sense, these five—Thomas J. Mooney, his wife Rena, Warren K. Billings, Edward Nolan, and Israel Weinberg—were also victims of the San Francisco Preparedness Day bombing, for as later events were to prove, incredible as it might seem, there was no evidence whatever connecting any of them with the crime.

---

* Various accounts of the bombing give the death total as nine or ten, those who cite the lower figure contending that Fox's initial collapse might have been a heart attack which later proved fatal. Inasmuch as the official cause of Fox's death was listed as "shock superinduced by the explosion" he is included here among the victims.

PART ONE

The
Making
of a
Radical

"I suppose the urge to serve the
labor movement was born in me."

TOM MOONEY

1· *Aboard the Red Special*

Tom mooney grew up on the bloody side of the American labor movement, his earliest memories of coal dust and violence.

His mother had come to the United States as a girl of seventeen from Fall Moor, County Mayo, Ireland, following two older sisters. Working as a domestic in Iowa, she met and married Bernard Mooney. Mooney, a native-born American from Indiana, was a coal miner and one of the first organizers for the Knights of Labor. The early years of their marriage were spent largely traveling from one state to another seeking work, since as a result of his union activities Mooney was often blacklisted.

Thomas Jeremiah Mooney, their first child, was born December 8, 1882, in Chicago. When Tom was two, the Mooneys moved to Washington, Indiana, where they lived for the next eight years. Here, during the David County strike, Mooney was shot in the leg by a strikebreaker. Wrenching the gun from his assailant, Mooney shot him in the chest. That night, his leg hastily bandaged but still bleeding, he gathered up his family and their few belongings and hid out in the fields. By this time the family had grown to five, including John, born 14 months after Tom, and Anna, born two years later. The strikebreaker's wound proved less serious than Mooney's own, and when after several days a miner brought word that no charges would be filed, the family returned home, Bernard Mooney with a permanently lame leg. Not long after Tom's tenth birthday, his father died. Although Mary Mooney would always attribute her husband's death to the "scab's bullet," the actual cause was "miner's pneumonia" or TB.

Raffling off her husband's mining tools to cover burial expenses, Mary Mooney moved the family to Holyoke, Massachusetts, where her sisters were living and where she obtained a job in a paper mill, sorting rags. She worked at this 12 hours a day; at night she took in laundry. Although she was, as her husband had been, nearly illiterate, she insisted that her children be educated. Tom attended St. James' Parochial School for four years, before quitting that institution and the Catholic Church simultaneously, in his first rebellion.

While still living in Indiana, Tom, hearing that bags of candy would be

33

given to the children, had taken his brother and sister to a Christmas Eve service at a Protestant church, only to be whipped by his father as a result. The slap of a priest was the final indignity precipitating his break with the Catholic Church. For some time he had been skipping mass because, he later said, he didn't have shoes to wear. When he refused to tell the priest the reason for his absence he was slapped for his obstinacy. Without telling anyone, he quietly left the parochial school and enrolled himself in a public school, this at a time and in a place where it was considered almost a sin for a Catholic child even to speak to a Protestant.

At fourteen he quit school entirely, to go to work in the paper mill where his mother was employed. The job lasted nearly a year before he was laid off during a cutback.

One of his mother's laundry customers was manager of a foundry in Holyoke; she inquired if he might have a job for her son. He took one look at the strong, barrel-chested, 15-year-old, with his thick black hair and Mick brogue and decided to take him on as an iron-molder apprentice. Tom liked the work—liked especially working naked to the waist in the smoke-dark factory, "pouring off," carrying the long ladles full of liquid metal with their showers of sparks—and at the end of four years he asked his employer for journeyman's wages and joined the International Core Makers' Union.*

When his request was refused, he quit and went to work for the Blake Pump Works in East Cambridge. Before long the men in the foundry organized a union and elected Tom shop foreman. The men were making $2.25 a day for nine hours' work, while in another part of the same factory the women, who were unorganized, were being paid $1.10 for ten hours. When the owners attempted to shift part of the men's work to the women, most of the men welcomed the change, feeling it would make their jobs easier. But Tom saw it as a threat to both groups and organized a protest. He was laid off by the superintendent of the core department "to teach him a lesson and make him quit being so aggressive."

These three jobs set the pattern for his next several years, during which he worked at some dozen foundries in Massachusetts, Connecticut, and New York. He was laid off some jobs due to economic conditions, quit others in protest against shop conditions, and was fired from the rest. He was proud, brash, impulsive, not one to moderate either his words or acts. His frequent complaints over speed-ups and wage cuts eventually brought him to the attention of the officials of the International Molders' Union, who marked him as a "comer." Management marked him too, and his name began to appear on blacklists.

---

* Six months later, the union amalgamated with the International Molders' Union and Tom Mooney's membership in the Molders—which he would maintain for the rest of his life—dated from this time.

He turned twenty-one while working on gasoline engines for the Apperson Automobile Company in Waterbury, Connecticut, and voted for the first time—mostly for Socialist candidates. This was due less to political convictions than because his best friend, Peter Peterson, a Swede with whom he shared an avid belief in physical culture, was a moderate Socialist.

In 1907, while working for the Gould Coupler Works in Depew, New York, making the bolsters on which railroad trucks rest, he got his first taste of union politics, running as nominee for delegate to the International Molders' Union convention in Philadelphia, losing by seven votes.

He stayed with the Depew job longer than most, because he wanted to save enough money to go to Europe, which had fascinated him since childhood geography classes. After accumulating about $350 he went to Boston and bought a third-class ticket to England. During the voyage, a fellow passenger gave him a Baedeker, and as Tom later put it, "introduced me to a new world, of man-made beauty." He visited England, Ireland, Wales, Scotland, France, Belgium, spending most of his time in museums, wanting now more than anything else to become an artist. His clothing was cheap, his hands permanently blackened by his trade, but it seemed to him that he had found in art a possible escape from working-class reality.

2 ·

He was standing before a Rembrandt in a museum in Rotterdam, Holland, when a well-dressed man asked to borrow his Baedeker. On handing it back, the man grinned, "I see by your pin that you're a member of the Iron Molders' Union." Tom proudly wore the molders' pin in his lapel at all times.

The man introduced himself as Nicholas Klein, explaining that he had just returned from Stuttgart, as American delegate to the International Socialist Convention. Their conversation lasted for the better part of two days. Peterson's socialism had been a crude, practical idealism; Klein was an intellectual who talked knowledgeably of the movement's historical and philosophical background.

Klein urged Mooney to interest himself in social and economic problems, as well as art, and drew up a list of books. The balance of Mooney's trip—to Germany, Hungary, Switzerland, Italy, Sicily, and the Azore Islands—had a new focus, discovering how the workers of Europe lived.*

* In 1927 San Quentin prisoner #31921 received a letter that read, "The other day I was in an art gallery where I met a young chap twenty years ago. I wonder if that young chap is sorry for the meeting?"
Mooney replied to Klein, "I have never for a day regretted it."

Any lingering thoughts of the artist's life disappeared on his return to the United States. The Knickerbocker Trust Company had failed and the country was in the midst of the "bankers' panic." Hundreds of thousands of workers had been laid off.

Mooney "rode the rods, not the cushions" across the country, looking for work. "I 'saw America' from the bumpers of freight trains and through the smoke and grime of iron foundries in all of its industrial centers," he would later remember. Unable to find more than temporary work in his trade, he harvested wheat in the Dakotas, unloaded bananas on the docks at New Orleans. But mostly he looked for employment that didn't exist—in Boston, Cincinnati, Houston, Vera Cruz, El Paso, Los Angeles, until, moving up California, he arrived in Stockton one evening in March 1908. Broke and hungry, he planned to catch a freight north the same night, but stopped to listen to a soap-box orator, Ed Lewis, an old-time Socialist organizer, and missed the train. The next day he found work in the Sampson Iron Works. On receiving his first week's pay he joined the Socialist Party and subscribed to *Appeal to Reason*. He was twenty-five.

He was not one to do things half-way. His evenings were spent working in party headquarters or selling literature on street corners. Maynard Shipley arranged his debut as a public speaker, by letting him introduce the other speakers. In less than a month he was making speeches on his own, mostly to raise money for Eugene V. Debs' campaign for the Presidency. He succeeded in raising $75 and was elected delegate to the state Socialist convention in San Francisco. At this time, Debs' "Red Special," as his campaign train had been dubbed, came barreling into California and Tom Mooney went to San Jose to meet it.

After Debs' speech Tom climbed aboard the train and introduced himself to the candidate, asking what he could do. Debs assigned him to the literature table. At each stop a table of Socialist literature was set up for those wanting to buy pamphlets. To Mooney this seemed ineffectual. Instead he went through the crowd with a stack of pamphlets, selling them on a personal basis. No one had thought of this heretofore and Debs, as much amused as impressed by the forceful persistence of the young Irishman, asked him to stay on the train as "official party literature agent." Mooney remained on the Red Special from the first week of September until the morning of election day, when the train reached Debs' home town, Terre Haute. Debs, running against Democrat William Jennings Bryan and Republican William Howard Taft, received only 421,000 votes, but during the course of the trip Tom Mooney met most of the leading American Socialists. On election eve, Debs, in a tactful way, suggested that if Tom were really to be effective in the party he would need more education. Following the election Mooney drifted up to Chicago, then national headquarters for the party, where a Socialist newspaperman,

Eugene V. Debs' "Red Special" presidential campaign train, 1908. In the doorway at right, holding the Debs banner, is the party's official pamphleteer, 25-year-old Tom Mooney.

Otto McFeely, tried to get him into the University of Chicago. Failing in this, McFeely introduced Tom to A. M. Simons and his brilliant wife Mary Wood Simons, who outlined a course of self-study. For the next five months Tom Mooney spent 12 hours a day in the reference library at Marshall Field's. Waiting when it opened at ten, he would read until noon, have a nickel glass of beer and plate of free lunch in a nearby saloon, then return and read until the library closed at ten, after which he would spend ten cents for a plate of beans and brown bread. Sundays, when the library was closed, he attended lectures, whatever the subject.

Running out of money the following spring, he again set out looking for work, taking odd jobs in Fargo, North Dakota, Butte, Montana, and eventually finding work in a foundry in Wallace, Idaho, in the heart of Wobbly country.

In November 1909 the city council of Spokane, Washington, alarmed by the growing strength of the Industrial Workers of the World (IWW), passed an ordnance banning street meetings. Since religious groups were specifically exempted from this ban, it was obviously aimed primarily at radicals. Consequently the IWW, the Socialist Party, and a number of labor unions combined in a united "free speech fight." From all over the country radicals came to Spokane to speak and submit to arrest, until more than 600 packed the city's jails.

William D. "Big Bill" Haywood was scheduled to speak in Wallace on behalf of the defendants, but became ill the day before he was to appear. Socialist Tom Mooney and a young lady IWW organizer were chosen to take his place. Standing in the back of a buggy, speaking against the backdrop of a sheer mountain wall, the pair took turns haranguing the listening miners and lumberjacks.

Mooney's co-speaker, Elizabeth Gurley Flynn, would later recall Tom as "a rosy-cheeked, black-eyed, laughing young Irishman . . ." His speech must not in itself have been very impressive, for she later wrote, "Probably I would not have remembered meeting Tom at that time except that he had an accident while I was there. A ring on his little finger caught on a nail in the bannister of a hotel staircase and tore his finger so badly he had to have it amputated."

Perhaps "Gurley" was a more persuasive speaker, for in March 1910 Tom Mooney joined the IWW. Later he would say that he did it solely in protest against the brutal police treatment of the Spokane defendants, and this was apparently true, for he remained a Wobbly only three months, dropping out by letting his membership lapse shortly after the Mayor of Seattle agreed to allow the IWW to reopen their hall and resume street meetings.

By this time, Tom Mooney was active in another campaign. *Wilshire's Magazine,* in an attempt to boost circulation, was offering a round-the-

Music teacher Rena Hermann, about the time she met the motorcycling Socialist. Class war demanded a heavy toll of sensitivity.

Courtesy Warren Billings

world trip to the Socialist who could secure the most subscriptions during a six-month period. With characteristic determination, Mooney signed up everyone he could persuade in Wallace, Mullen, Burke, Coeur d'Alene. Having exhausted this area, he talked some miners into smuggling him aboard a train to Denver and signed up members of the Western Federation of Miners conventioning there.

Returning to California, he found a job in a San Francisco foundry and saved enough money to buy an old motorcycle, which he repaired and used to travel up and down the state, visiting union meetings, collecting subscriptions, and in the process absorbing impressions of the politics of union labor in the Golden State.

3·

In retrospect, it would seem that Tom Mooney was drawn back to California as if by gravity, for it was the one state in which, as Carey McWilliams has noted, labor and management were in "total engagement."

In reality, a good part of the reason was a woman, whom he had met in Stockton in 1908.

Rena Brink Hermann had already lived a more than usually eventful life by the time the young iron molder entered it.

Born on a farm near Kansas City, Missouri, in 1878, to an impractical visionary and his much-harassed wife, Rena had grown up with a fascination for music but little opportunity to cultivate it. While she was yet a child her father had left his wife and two daughters to fend for themselves while he traveled West to sell a gate on which he had secured a patent. This was in the days when the West was still fenceless. He found work as

39

a ranch hand, however, and in 1896 moved his family to Stockton, where he was employed on the ranch of a Mr. Merrill. The Merrills owned a piano. With Mrs. Merrill's encouragement, Rena taught herself to play. Then, with a loan from the same benefactor, she went to San Francisco seeking work in order to save enough money for music lessons. She found a job in a cordage factory, hardly the place for a person with sensitive hands, but she stayed with it. After three long years, just as she managed to reach her goal of $300, she contracted typhoid fever and the money went for medical expenses.

While recuperating at Quartz Mountain, where her father was working, she met a young miner, Will Hermann. Hermann's face had been badly disfigured in a fire and Rena would later come to believe that what she really felt for him was pity rather than love. Following their marriage and return to California, Rena obtained a cheap piano and solicited pupils, eventually earning enough money to attend King's Conservatory of Music in San Jose. She was twenty-six and had been teaching music for several years when she had her first professional lesson. By 1904 she was success-ful enough to open a large, seven-piano studio in San Francisco. It was completely destroyed in the earthquake and fire of April 1906.

She had just started over again when, on a visit to Stockton, she met Tom Mooney at the Merrill home. They were totally unlike and immedi-ately attracted to each other. According to her own account, she told Her-mann of her feelings and he understandingly agreed to a divorce.

In 1910 Rena opened another studio in San Francisco. Working late into the nights, she typed hundreds of letters, soliciting subscriptions for *Wilshire's Magazine*. The studio also served as a meeting place for Tom and his friends, most of whom were, like himself, young union radicals. The group consisted mainly of left-wing Socialists and IWW's, with a couple of anarchists thrown in as if for argumentative purposes.

When the contest finally ended, it was found that the winner was a na-tional union organizer who had signed up his whole union. Tom Mooney had come so close to tying him, however, that the magazine created a sec-ond prize, an all-expenses-paid trip to the International Socialist Congress in Copenhagen.

The two-week Congress, held in the fall of 1910, brought Mooney into contact with some of the great figures in the world Socialist movement: Jean Jaures of France; James Ramsey MacDonald, Keir Hardie and Ben Tillot from England; Daniel DeLeon, William D. Haywood (recently acquitted of the bomb-murder of Idaho's Governor Steunenberg), Victor Berger and Morris Hillquit of the United States; and from Russia a strange-looking, short, stocky man with a large balding head and bulging eyes. Mooney was less impressed with Nikolai Lenin, however, than with the three female delegates: Rosa Luxembourg, Clara Zetkin, and Alexandra Kollontay. He would recall the latter as "the most immaculately dressed woman at the Congress—a fashion plate from Paris."

Following the Congress, Mooney stopped off in England and attended the British Trade Union Congress at Sheffield, then took the boat for home.

Mooney was traveling steerage. A tale is often told that on the return trip Mooney, glancing up at the first-class section and spotting an American Federation of Labor official, with typical belligerence shouted "Why aren't you down here with the working class where you belong?"

Although the tale may be apocryphal, it is true that by this time Mooney was less awed by Gene Debs' moderate form of Socialism than by the militant radicalism of the one-eyed founder of the IWW, who had shocked many at the Copenhagen Congress with his denunciation of the reactionary AFL leadership. Tom Mooney was one of the few who applauded "Big Bill" Haywood's remarks.

He agreed with Haywood about other things. In the foundries where he had worked he had seen how few workers actually were represented by the craft unions of the AFL. By concentrating entirely on the skilled crafts, the AFL had left the rest of the workers unorganized and voiceless. Like Haywood, Mooney favored industrial unionism, the organization of all the workers in an industry. Like Haywood, too, he was beginning to feel that the Socialists were wrong in advocating only political action and disavowing direct action.

It was a more militant Tom Mooney who returned to San Francisco in the fall of 1910.

4 ·

In the November 1910 general election the name of Thomas J. Mooney appeared on the ballot as Socialist candidate for Judge of the Superior Court. He received 5,890 votes, a not unimpressive showing for a candidate totally unqualified for the office. Mooney wasn't disappointed. Like most Socialist candidates, he campaigned less in expectation of winning than for the opportunity of expressing his views.

In May of 1911, together with Austin Lewis and Cloudsley Johns, Mooney founded *Revolt: The Voice of the Militant Worker,* a left-wing Socialist weekly that aimed at revitalizing the Socialist Party in California and hit out strongly at local labor leaders who it charged with selling out their memberships in the interests of political preferment and "industrial peace." The paper, whose first issues drew strong praise from such diverse figures as Jack London, George Sterling, William Haywood, and Eugene Debs, lasted a year, with Mooney serving as publisher and circulation manager. By the time of the 1911 state Socialist Convention, Mooney had become "the lusty-voiced, aggressive, belligerent spokesman of the Socialist left-wing . . ." The description was that of Ernest Jerome Hopkins, who covered the convention for the *Bulletin*. "Socialists, then as now," Hopkins would later write, "lived by and in and for resolutions." In this Mooney was no exception; according to Hopkins, he not only introduced a large number of resolutions of his own, but also blasted any others that smacked of Fabianism.

That same year, when her divorce became final, Tom Mooney married Rena Brink Hermann. And that fall he again ran for office, this time for Sheriff of San Francisco. He received 2,733 votes in the primary, not enough to qualify for the general election ballot, although in November he did receive 30 write-in votes, as accurate a way as any to count his close friends.

By this time he was almost thoroughly disenchanted with the Socialist Party. In reality, Mooney, who now considered himself "a militant unionist and a revolutionary socialist," did not comfortably fit into any of the then existent niches.

The AFL, whose leadership was largely conservative, Catholic, and opposed to socialism in any form, did not welcome militants. The Socialist Party had its own definition of revolutionaries, one far more theoretical and future tense than Tom Mooney's own.

The Socialists believed in political action (running their own candidates for office, advocating legislation favorable to the working class, etc.), but disavowed direct action (a loose term with components running the gambit from strike, primary and secondary boycott, and slowup, to, at the farthest extreme, seizing and taking over the means of production). The IWW believed only in direct action, to the extent that they even refused to mediate before calling a strike. Tom Mooney was convinced that the workers needed both political and direct action to get a fairer share of the goods they produced.

Haywood and the IWW advocated "dual unionism," the setting up of industrial unions to compete with the craft unions of the AFL, these eventually to be merged in "One Big Union" to include all workers, whatever their trade. Mooney did not disagree with the dream, only with Haywood's method of arriving at it. By drawing all the progressives out of the AFL into the IWW, the AFL would be left solely in the hands of the reactionaries. To Mooney dual unionism seemed nothing more than division. Too, he remembered the Knights of Labor and the early struggles of the American Federation of Labor, and however much he disagreed with many of the organization's current policies, he still retained a strong pride in his AFL membership.

In the fall of 1911, young William Z. Foster, returning from a trip abroad imbued with the syndicalist philosophy of the European workers, attempted to persuade the IWW to give up dual unionism in favor of syndicalism. In this he failed, but he did impress Tom Mooney and a number of others. Foster advocated the formation of small militant groups of workers—*syndicats*—to "bore from within" the unions, eventually taking them over.

In 1912 Tom Mooney tried to put this theory into practice, plunging into the intense, and often dirty, warfare of San Francisco union politics.

5 ·

By this time, the scene was already set for a drama in which Mooney would play a prominent part.

In 1912 San Francisco was the most heavily unionized city in the United States. Not only had the unions won significant concessions from management in many of the trades, but they had their own political party, the Union Labor Party, which in the past dozen years had placed two of its own candidates in the Mayor's office. On the surface this bastion of unionism appeared unshakeable. Actually it was suffering from the dry rot of betrayal, complacency, stagnation, and fear, and was dangerously vulnerable to assault.

In 1901 Eugene Schmitz, president of the Musician's Union, had been elected Mayor of San Francisco on a Union Labor Party ticket, the first labor mayor in American history. It soon became apparent, however, that both the party and the mayor were being conducted by Republican political boss Abe Ruef, and after a careful investigation, *Bulletin* editor Fremont Older revealed that Ruef and Schmitz were sharing such grace notes as payoff money from the city's brothel owners. Discordant as these and other *Bulletin* exposés were, they failed to strike a responsive chord in the voters, who continued to re-elect the musical mayor to office.

In 1905 Patrick Calhoun, a colorful financier who had at one time been a confidential agent for J. P. Morgan, bought up a number of San Francisco streetcar companies and merged them into United Railroads, thereby securing a near monopoly on public transportation in the city. He then asked the Board of Supervisors for permission to install overhead trolley lines. Electric streetcar lines being relatively new, the public strongly opposed them, arguing that they were dangerous, unsightly, and would reduce property values. An underground system of conduits was suggested as alternative, but this system was more expensive; Calhoun, who had seriously watered the stock of United Railroads, opposed it. The matter was still pending when, on April 18, 1906, tragedy struck the city.

The earthquake and fire left San Francisco without public transportation. When Calhoun put up overhead lines, ostensibly as a temporary measure to restore service during the emergency, no one opposed him. Less than one month after the fire, however, the Board of Supervisors quietly voted permission to make the system permanent. Upon investigating this sudden switch, Older learned that it had been accomplished by wholesale bribery. Ruef would later confess that Tirey L. Ford, chief counsel for United Railroads, had paid him $200,000. The political boss had given Mayor Schmitz $50,000, kept an equal amount for himself, and distributed the balance among the eighteen members of the Board of Supervisors.

This time the charges hit home. The thought of these men feeding ghoulishly off the city's tragedy aroused tremendous indignation, and the sensational San Francisco graft trials followed. To mention only a few of the incredible developments (the whole story is ably chronicled in Lately Thomas' *A Debonair Scoundrel* [Holt, Rinehart & Winston, 1962]) Ruef attempted to appoint himself District Attorney in order to try his own case; Older was kidnapped by the gunmen hirelings of a United Railroads attorney, but managed to escape this attempt on his life, as well as two others; the home of a leading witness was bombed the night before he was to testify; and the special prosecutor, Francis J. Heney, was gunned down in open court, while the man who replaced him, Hiram Johnson, was catapulted into the Governor's chair.

The graft trials, which lasted three years, made the name San Francisco a by-word for municipal corruption. By the fall of 1909, however, the city had a new Board of Supervisors, Schmitz and Ruef had been removed from the political scene (Ruef to San Quentin), and many prominent San Franciscans were sick of having the sins of their city fathers exposed to public view. Indictments against the "higher-ups," the men Older and the graft hunters most wanted to get—Calhoun, his chief assistant Thornwell Mullally, and Ford—were still pending, however.

In the November election of that same year a former Stanford football star, Charles Marron Fickert, ran for District Attorney against Heney.

Fickert, the son of a Tehachapi rancher, had entered Stanford in 1893 at the age of twenty. Although his academic record was undistinguished, he was, by the time of his junior year, one of the nation's leading football guards. Yale tried to persuade him to transfer there, just before its big game with Harvard. After college Fickert was admitted to the bar, but finding the law less interesting than football, returned to Stanford in 1900 as assistant varsity football coach. In 1904 he received political appointment as Special Assistant U. S. District Attorney in San Francisco; 15 months later, in a cloud of scandal over his mismanagement of an embezzlement case, he resigned. Except for football glories, his had not yet been a notable career.

During the 1909 campaign, it was an open secret that Fickert's chief backer was United Railroads, and Fickert would in later years admit this. At the time Older charged, and fairly conclusively documented his assertion, that United Railroads spent $100,000 just to get Fickert elected.

Elected he was. One of his first acts as District Attorney was to dismiss the indictments against Calhoun, Mullally, and Ford, bringing the graft trials to an end.

In 1910 the Union Labor Party placed another candidate in the Mayor's office, P. H. "Pinhead" McCarthy, Secretary of both the State Federation of Labor and the powerful Building Trades Council and a force in the San Francisco Labor Council. McCarthy's nickname was a misnomer in all but its description of his appearance. McCarthy was a shrewd conservative whose own unions, the building trades, had made significant advances following the earthquake and fire and whose major interest now was the consolidation of these gains. As Mayor, he vowed to make San Francisco again "Paris of the Pacific," interpreted by most to mean a return to open vice, graft, and political preferment. As a labor leader, his chief interest was in "getting along" with management.

California had two major cities, however, one known as "the first closed shop city in America," the other as "Gibraltar of the open shop."

Due in large measure to the rabid efforts of Los Angeles *Times* publisher General Harrison Gray Otis, Los Angeles had been almost wholly successful in resisting the inroads of unionism. To many, Otis, whose supreme military rank was self-bestowed and who so feared radicals and revolutionaries that he kept a small cannon mounted on the hood of his automobile, was a ridiculous figure. Among local employers, however, he was an undisputed power, the man whose Southern California boosterism almost by itself had made Los Angeles a major city. Although not all employers shared Otis' militant anti-union feelings, they had learned not to oppose him.

As a result of this North-South dichotomy, when new business came to California it went to Los Angeles, where, as its Chamber of Commerce proudly advertised, "cheap non-union labor is plentiful." This in turn caused a strong counter pressure, the determination of San Francisco business and community leaders to break the power of unions in their own city.

As far as San Francisco labor leaders were concerned, there was only one satisfactory way to alleviate this pressure: organize Los Angeles. Toward this end, the Los Angeles Metal Trades Strike Committee was quietly formed. Also known as the Committee of 26, its members included such conservatives as McCarthy and "Mike" Casey of the Teamsters' along with radicals such as Andrew Furuseth of the Seamen's Union. A $300,000 war chest was raised and outside organizers brought in, among them two brothers, James B. and John J. McNamara, the latter secretary of the International Association of Bridge and Structural Iron Workers. Not only did the organizing go badly from the start, but in July of 1910 Otis and the Merchants' and Manufacturers' Association effected the adoption of an anti-picketing ordnance, one that would serve as a model for all anti-picketing laws in the United States.

At seven minutes after one on the morning of October 1, 1910, a suit-casebomb exploded in the Los Angeles *Times,* gutting the building and killing 21 men. When the McNamara brothers were arrested and charged with the crime, American labor, in a united voice, cried "frame-up."

The frame-up was an old and well established tactic in the war between labor and capital in the United States. The easiest way for an employer to remove a bothersome strike leader was to have him arrested on another charge and held for the duration of the strike. Such frame-ups numbered in the hundreds, a great many of which were subsequently exposed.

In this conflict single and double agents were common, triple agents not unknown. There were spies in every union worth the name, just as the unions themselves usually tried to plant their own agents among the strikebreakers when a strike was in progress.

The role of the union spy (i.e., the agent for the employers) did not always stop with providing information. Usually hired by the Pinkerton Detective Agency or the local Merchants' and Manufacturers' Association, these men were paid on a piecemeal basis, for information received. Hypothetically, this caused them to try harder, dig deeper for information. In practice, sometimes they created it. Strategically placed inside a union, such an agent was ideally situated to plant frame-up evidence or to foment unrest. It was axiomatic that the most vociferous advocate of direct action in a union was the most probable spy.

"The union spy was hired on the theory that unions were criminal in character," remarks Louis Adamic in *Dynamite.* "Of course, if he found that the union in which he had a membership was not criminal, he instigated or encouraged his fellow members to violent acts, for he kept his job as a spy only so long as he had something to report."

To American labor, the Los Angeles *Times'* bombing seemed a classic example of the frame-up in practice. The 21 dead were all workingmen. The McNamaras were not militants: they were Roman Catholic trade unionists, their most radical affiliation their AFL membership. Samuel Gompers and the rest of the AFL leadership quickly came to their defense, hiring the great "working-class lawyer" Clarence Darrow to represent them. McNamara defense committees were organized across the country, hundreds of thousands of laboring men contributing their time and money. Tom Mooney was especially active in the San Francisco committee.

It was the common belief of most of the rank-and-file that Otis himself had arranged to have the bomb planted, to discredit the unions.

The elder brother, J. B. McNamara, went on trial in October 1911. On December 1st, Clarence Darrow, addressing the court, announced that his clients wanted to change their pleas from not guilty to guilty.

The shock was felt throughout the American labor movement.

The background of this sudden reversal was not long a secret. Muckraking journalist Lincoln Steffens, who felt that both men were guilty and who believed that they both would hang unless something was done, had arranged a "deal." Consulting with both the defense and the prosecution, as well as various community leaders (including Otis and his son-in-law Harry Chandler), Steffens had worked out a compromise. The McNamaras, Steffens argued, were merely tools, not instigators, in the conflict between labor and management. By applying the "Golden Rule" and showing leniency in this case, the employers would not only remove the spotlight of unfavorable publicity from Los Angeles, they would also prove that they were seriously interested in industrial peace.*

The conditions were as follows: If the McNamaras would plead guilty, J. B. would be sentenced to life, J. J. to 15 years, both men to be paroled in the minimum time. There would be no further prosecutions (causing The Committee of 26 to breathe easier). And a statewide conference for the purpose of finding a peaceful solution to the problems of labor and management would be held.

The McNamara case, Steffens believed, would go down in history as an example of "true Christianity in action."

J. B. McNamara did receive a life sentence, while his brother was sentenced to 15 years, but neither would be paroled. Three years later, two other men, M. A. "Matt" Schmidt and Dave Caplan, were also tried and convicted of participating in the crime, Schmidt given a life sentence, Caplan 10 years. Darrow himself was later tried for jury bribery, but acquitted. And the labor-management conference never materialized.

Since the McNamaras only pled guilty and never made confessions, there remained some doubt as to their part in the bombing. A few continued to believe them innocent, also believing that the only reason J. B. had consented to the plea was to save his brother's life. Some felt that an agent of the employers, Ortie McManigal, who turned state's evidence and was released, had talked them into the act. While yet others came to believe that the bomb was intended only to frighten Otis, but that a leaky gas main had resulted in a far greater explosion than anticipated.

In many a California bar it is still possible to provoke an argument concerning the McNamaras' guilt, innocence, or the degree thereof.

---

* Darrow, less an idealist, would later write that the case against his clients was so conclusive that the agreement was the only possible way to save their lives.

On one point there is no disagreement: the effect of the guilty plea.

Among those in labor the expression "frame-up" would never again be so unquestioningly accepted, while to the general public the word "dynamite" would ever after have connotations as explosive as its ingredients. The AFL leadership, who quickly wiped their hands of the case, were thereafter extremely reluctant to give more than token (or resolution) aid to labor defendants in cases where violence had occurred, while the San Francisco labor leaders, as if to prove that they had no part in the bombing, became even more conservative. It wouldn't be enough, however. In the next election McCarthy was soundly defeated, while San Francisco employers used the case, and the change in public sympathy, as an opening wedge in their fight to rid the city of unions.

Rather than "Christianizing" relations between labor and capital in California, the McNamara case marked the beginning of a new era of open warfare as real and as violent as that fought on any foreign battlefield.

For Thomas J. Mooney, it had effects both immediate and long-lasting.

6 ·

When less than a month after the McNamaras' change of plea, Tom Mooney contrived to muster enough support to win election as a delegate from his local (#164 of the International Molders' Union) to the San Francisco Labor Council, that powerful body was for the first time in many years "running scared," more than ever before anxious to maintain peace with management. Controlled by conservatives such as McCarthy, Casey, and Andrew J. Gallagher, the council was unequivocally opposed to any new organizing or other demands that might upset the status quo.

Mooney, who wanted "more organizing, more strikes, and more consideration of the rank-and-file," immediately came into conflict with the conservative council leaders who were quick to label him a "troublemaker" and "hothead."

He was that, and more. Impertinent and discourteous. he egotistically designated himself spokesman for the rank-and-file. When he thought they had been sold out, he said so, bluntly. Inasmuch as the "sell out" charges bore in some cases a certain validity, this earned him few friends among the union leaders, some of whom had "overstepped" in their efforts to establish an amicable relationship with management. Almost a fanatic in his insistence on honesty, whether in the handling of union funds or in the representation of union members, he was quick to see "betrayals." Angered over the council's failure to pass one of his militant resolutions, he was apt to charge its leaders with "class collaborationist policies," or hitting an even more tender spot, accuse McCarthy and the others of betraying their memberships to gain political preferment and "appear 'respectable.' "

Although the council minutes fail to mention it, council members still living recall several meetings that ended in fist fights. Gaining the floor, Mooney would not relinquish it until he had completed his invariably lengthy say. Pacing back and forth like a caged lion, he would roar "My delegates demand this resolution be passed," although everyone present was well aware that the only molders he truly represented were himself and his brother John. While he was frequently supported by other liberals on the council, the conservatives were in the majority. Few of his motions passed.

One old Socialist who knew Mooney in those days recalls, "You could forgive a man any manner or number of sins but Tom Mooney had one bad habit that was unforgivable. Whatever the argument, he was nearly always right."

Although this evaluation was undoubtedly colored by the "Mooney myth" later to grow up around him, there was some truth in it. Some of the betrayals would in time be documented: McCarthy, for example, would be proven to have accepted a bribe of $100,000 from the Pacific Gas & Electric Company. The industrial unionism Mooney advocated would eventually come into being, with the organization of the CIO. But years would pass before either of these things happened. In 1912 Tom Mooney was the wrong person in the wrong place at the wrong time, though with the right ideas. About all he accomplished while on the San Francisco Labor Council was the making of new enemies.

When his six-month term expired that summer he was not re-elected.

After a bitter fight in his local, however, he did succeed, by one vote, in winning election as a delegate to the International Molders' Union (IMU) convention in Milwaukee that fall. The election was unusually important because at this time the molders met only once every five years. At Milwaukee Mooney fought for "a militant industrial union" to include not only the molders but all the other workers in the foundry, just as the coal miners' union included everyone who worked in the mines. Although this resolution, like his others, failed to carry, his fight gained widespread attention. William Z. Foster enthusiastically praised his stand in the *International Socialist Review*, while Joseph Valentine, president of the IMU, felt it necessary both to rebuke and compliment him: "Young man," he told him, "you are too eager, too anxious to accomplish too much in too short a time—but someday you will be president of the International Molders' Union."

Following the convention, Mooney toured the foundries in the East, paying special attention to the new automatic machinery. On reporting back to his local he warned that the machinery would result in the loss of many jobs unless some provision were made to transfer the workers into related fields. For this he was labeled a "calamity howler."

During 1912 Foster had formed the Syndicalist League of North America. Mooney now became the group's leader among the iron workers, chartering four separate locals in a period of about six months. His participation in the league ceased abruptly in early 1913; this time however not due to ideological disagreements but to a new involvement.

To date Tom Mooney's "battles" had largely been internecine, with brother unionists and fellow radicals. With the Frank & Hyman shoe strike, Mooney's militancy was pitted against a different adversary, the employers.

2· Class War in California

L ATE IN 1912 a San Francisco shoe manufacturing firm, G. M. Kutz, closed down. When it reopened several weeks later under the name Frank & Hyman Shoe Company, most of the members of the Boot and Shoe Workers' Union were not rehired; those who were had to take a sharp cut in wages. A "wildcat" strike was called in January, the international union having refused strike sanction. Since many of the union members were also Wobblies (the holding of dual cards was not uncommon), the IWW took over conduct of the strike. Mooney volunteered to take charge of picketing and during the first three months made a name for himself as an innovator.

More than 200 had walked off their jobs. A number of unskilled local workers, plus about 60 strikebreakers imported from St. Louis, had been brought in to replace them. Most of the men, who carried guns, slept in the factory. The women, however, were driven to their homes each night by owner Hyman. Trailing Hyman on his motorcycle, Mooney would learn where the women lived. A strike committee would then call on them, attempting to persuade them to walk off the job. This failing, Mooney employed another tactic—picket lines around their homes. As a result the company was having trouble keeping the factory staffed. Hyman, discovering that Mooney was following him, decided to remove him from the scene.

About this same time there arrived in San Francisco a foot-loose, happy-go-lucky kid from New York, who had hoboed his way across country, intending to join Pancho Villa's revolution in Mexico.

Warren Knox Billings was born July 4, 1893, in Middletown, New York. His mother, of German extraction, had been born on Avenue A in New York City; his father, William Billings, was of pure Massachusetts Yankee stock. Warren bore the names of two Boston heroes of the American Revolution. Theirs was the poor branch of the family, however, and when William Billings died in 1895, he left his wife and nine children destitute. The widow barely managed to support them with domestic work and makeshift quarters shared with a Negro family above a saloon on Water Street. One of the older daughters married a Brooklyn police-

51

man, however, and in 1900 he moved the family to the New Lots section. There was little charity in the gesture: against departmental regulations, the policeman was running an off-duty business, a dairy and truck farm, and he needed the family for both front and labor. His treatment of the children was hard and vicious. By the time Warren Billings was ten he had learned that there were several ways to protest exploitation—fight, strike, or run away—and at various times had tried all three. After graduating from Public School 144 in 1908, he left the farm and worked at a variety of jobs—bellboy, silverplater's helper, errand boy for Tammany in the Wigwam. He was quick and alert, but nothing held his interest for long. About 1910 he went to work in a Brooklyn shoe factory as a pattern boy in the cutting room, and through observation, learned the trimming, shoe, and lining cutters' trades as well. But as with his other jobs, this too was brief. Later, in his maturity, he explained it with a certain detachment: "I always felt that I was being overworked and underpaid, and consequently, I never got along well on any job that I was on."

At night, he played the young tough—drinking, gambling, loitering about the streets in a pack. He was seventeen. He was also 5'4" tall, and his size may have had more than a little to do with his swaggering bravado. His first brush with the law was, ironically enough, a frame-up.

When two of his companions were arrested for possessing stolen property, Billings was pulled in as an accessory and paroled into the custody of his policeman brother-in-law. What he didn't know at the time was that since there was no evidence against him the charges had been dropped and the "parole" was his brother-in-law's invention, to keep him working at home.

When he finally discovered this, he moved out again, this time working as a streetcar conductor on the Brooklyn Rapid Transit. This job was also brief; he was fired for "nickeling," failing to turn in all his fares. After losing what little money he had gambling, he left New York and hoboed his way across country, taking work wherever he could find it, always quitting when he felt he was being exploited. The spirit of adventure was strong in him. On Washington's birthday, 1913, he decided to join the Villa revolution in Mexico and was on his way there when he became stranded in Oakland, California.

On a cold, foggy day in early March 1913, he caught the ferry to San Francisco and went to an employment agency looking for work. He was told that there was a job open for a shoe liner at the Frank & Hyman Shoe Company, which was currently on strike.

"Hell, I'm no strikebreaker," he said in disgust.

His remark was overheard. Outside a man introduced himself by pulling out his red IWW card. There might be a job for him, the man said, if he wasn't afraid to live dangerously. Billings, a venturesome nineteen, was game. He was taken to Woodman's Hall and introduced to Ted Hooper, local IWW secretary and strike leader for the Boot and Shoe Workers' Union.

Hooper came right to the point. They needed a spy to work in the struck factory, to see how many pairs of shoes were being made and for whom—in order that secondary boycotts could be organized. It would be an extra dangerous job, for not only would he be liable to beatings or worse at the hands of the Pinkertons if found out, he could also expect the same if the strikers caught him outside the factory.

Billings, with a boyish grin, said he wasn't afraid.

There was the problem of where to report. Socialist Party Headquarters was suggested but ruled out, on the likelihood that it might be under surveillance.

"We could meet at Tom Mooney's place," someone said.

At this time the Mooneys were living in a house on 15th Street, where Billings was taken and introduced to them all—Tom, Rena, Mary Mooney, John, and Anna. Tom had arranged for his mother and sister to move West several years earlier; John, also a molder, worked in the same foundry as Tom. Almost immediately Warren Billings was adopted as one of the family, and he soon came to look up to Tom Mooney, both literally and figuratively. They were an oddly matched pair. Mooney was thirty, nearly six feet, a stocky restless 190 pounds, with round face, black hair, and thick black brows. Billings was 5'4", 124 pounds, and thin-faced, with sandy red hair and blue eyes, looking much younger than his nineteen years. He was greatly impressed by the militant Mooney, who said what he thought and was uncompromising in his honesty. They met infrequently during the strike, however, for once Billings took the spy job he was locked inside the factory most of the time, while Mooney's own participation was to be short-lived.

Hyman had tried circuitous routes and different cars to shake Mooney. One night in late March, spotting the motorcycle some distance behind him, he doubled back, caught Mooney just as he was going up a hill and tried to run him down. Smashing him to the curb, he stopped suddenly, then threw the car into reverse to back over him. Mooney, quickly rolling aside, suffered only a broken leg and a badly damaged motorcycle. Hyman was later convicted of assault and fined $50, a cheap enough price to pay, since Mooney was temporarily removed from the action.

Meanwhile, Billings had graduated to more dangerous work. He had encountered no trouble getting either the job or the requested information. The factory needed a skilled lining cutter; since only one was employed, every pair of shoes went through Billings' hands. When his information proved reliable, he was given additional tasks: learning which of the scabs were skilled workers and which merely thugs; determining which of the workers might be susceptible to reason, and having found them, trying to convince them that they should "come out." The wrong word to the wrong man meant exposure.

Hyman wasn't the only one to use "direct action." One night after Billings had been working in the factory about seven weeks someone smuggled in several bottles of whiskey and got the guards and strikebreakers drunk. Dawn brought not only hangovers but the discovery that some 480 pairs of shoes had been cut to pieces. Billings arranged for another man to be suspected and fired. The man was innocent. He had been chosen as "fall guy" because he was the best worker in the factory.

Since it was Billings who furnished the whiskey, it was a logical assumption that he also unlocked the doors to let the saboteurs in. Hooper and Mooney decided that since management would soon reach this conclusion, now would be a good time for Billings to quit. The factory would be further hurt by the loss of their only shoe liner.

When Billings returned to collect his pay, three guards grabbed him and started to beat him up, at the same time trying to disarm him. Almost all of the strikebreakers had guns; Billings had a .32 caliber pistol. In the scuffle the gun went off and shot Billings through his left thumb. The bullet hit just above the knuckle, passed through, and struck a guard in the foot. Billings was arrested, charged with assault, and jailed for about three months pending trial.*

He was prosecuted by Assistant District Attorney Maxwell McNutt. When Billings was placed alongside the three beefy guards, each over six feet, the charge was so patently ridiculous that even McNutt agreed to its dismissal.

The strike was settled in May. Since both the workers and the union wages were reinstated, it was proclaimed a victory by both the international union and the San Francisco Labor Council, which had belatedly given sanction. The Labor Council even begrudgingly conceded that Mooney's tactics had played an important part in the triumph.

Had Mooney been a different man, he might have accepted the compliment and said nothing. The strike had added to his stature as a labor leader. Instead, characteristically, he denounced the agreement as a "sell out," revealing what the Labor Council had carefully concealed—that one of the terms of settlement was the addition of an open-shop clause to the contract.

Both Rena and Tom had visited Billings several times while he was in jail. At their suggestion, on his release in June, he moved in with them until he could find employment. Since he was now blacklisted, this took

* *The Labor Clarion,* unaware of Billings' double role, ran an article characterizing him a classic example of the depraved scab, so vicious that he turns on his own.

some time but eventually he obtained a job in another shoe factory under the name Gregory Smith. And gradually, as he became involved in other labor battles, he forgot the idea of going to Mexico to fight for Villa.

2 ·

There was no armistice in the class war, no pause between battles, many of which were occurring simultaneously on a front extending over the whole state.

At the time of Billings' release, one of the San Francisco Bay Area's bitterest strikes was already a month in progress, with Tom Mooney very much involved in it. In May a number of outside linemen belonging to Local 151 of the Electrical Workers had gone on strike against the Pacific Gas & Electric Company (PG&E), a major California utility. This strike too began as a wildcat—P. H. McCarthy, president of the Electrical Workers as well as of the Building Trades Council, had even gone so far as to issue union cards to the scabs—and Mooney, employed in a foundry in Berkeley, went to work for the outlaws in his spare time. Billings, whose job was only part time, soon joined him.

The strike differed from most others in one important particular—the nature of the commodity. While a picket line might halt the distribution of shoes and other items, it had no effect on electrical power carried by high-tension lines.

PG&E supplied nearly all of the electrical power for Northern California. To disrupt service in an attempt to bring the company to terms, a variety of tactics were used, none of which were "officially sanctioned." Strikers would go out at night and throw ropes over the most important power lines; tying the ropes to the bumpers of automobiles, they would then drive off, pulling the lines down. Cow chains would be tossed over two wires, causing a short circuit. And dynamite was used to blow down strategic transformers and power lines in the outlying districts.

As Traverse Clements later observed in *American Mercury,* "While there is evidence to support the contention that dynamite . . . was first introduced in California labor struggles by an employer, it is true that high explosives were handled carelessly, to say the least, by both sides."

Both sides were using dynamite to their own advantage in the PG&E strike.

Three union men, arrested in Berkeley for plotting a dynamiting, were sentenced to San Quentin. The man responsible for trapping them was one Martin Swanson, head of the Pinkerton Detective Agency in San Francisco. Later union officials succeeded in recording the conversation of an ex-Pinkerton, who bragged of having helped frame the men. The

Governor, on hearing this evidence, pardoned all three. Immediately after this, Swanson was dismissed by Pinkerton. Labor leaders—who from the days of the Homestead Strike had more than ample reasons to distrust "The Eye," as the Pinkerton Agency was called—claimed Swanson had been fired for being caught in a frame-up, not for attempting it. Although these particular arrests occurred during the strike, the exposure of the frame-up didn't occur until the summer of 1914, after the strike had been settled. During the whole of the strike, which lasted from May 1913 to January 1914, Swanson was still employed by Pinkerton and assigned to work with R. Cantrell, property agent for PG&E, whose job it was to see that power wasn't interrupted.

As in the shoe workers' strike, Mooney was active in attempting to persuade the workers to come out. A part of Billings' job was investigative —discovering how many guards were placed along certain high-tension lines leading into the city and just where they were stationed. Also, as Billings in later years admitted, on a number of occasions he obtained dynamite for the strikers by burglarizing powder shanties in quarries or on construction jobs.

The strike leaders maintained a headquarters at 1095 Market Street in San Francisco. One afternoon in September 1913, Billings went there to make his report, after which he went downstairs to the Waldorf Bar for a beer. At the bar he was approached by a tall stranger asking if he were Billings. He affirmed it. The man said, "John said you might do a job for me." Billings excused himself and checked with John in the strike office, who said the man was "O.K."

"I want someone to take a suitcase to Sacramento," the man explained.

"What's in it?" Billings asked.

"You don't need to know what's in it. It don't make any difference."

"I'm not talking about the suitcase," Billings replied. "I mean, what's in it for me?"

"Twenty-five dollars and carfare."

"When do I go?" *

This was on Thursday, September 11th. On Saturday the 13th, Billings was given the suitcase and his instructions. He was to catch the train to Sacramento and would be contacted in the train station there.

If Billings did not know what was in the suitcase (he maintains he didn't), it is probable that he at least guessed. The man told him to handle it very carefully.

Tom Mooney was going to Sacramento the same day, in connection with the strike, but he planned to drive up on his motorcycle. He also arranged to meet Billings at the station. The California State Fair was on at

* The above conversation and account of the incident are as Warren Billings later recalled them.

this time and to harass PG&E some of the strikers were planning to blow up several high-tension lines supplying power to the fairgrounds. In an interview conducted some years later, Mooney intimated that he was at least aware of these plans.

Mooney wasn't at the station when Billings arrived, but Billings' contact was. He was told to take a streetcar to the Silver Cup Saloon, a hangout for the electrical workers. On arriving there he was to set the suitcase next to the bar. Another man would then pay him the balance of the money.

Billings followed the instructions, unaware that he had been under police surveillance from the moment he stepped off the train.

On arriving at the saloon, he set down the suitcase. On straightening up, he looked into the muzzles of two guns. The men holding them were Sacramento detectives. Also present were PG&E property agent Cantrell and Martin Swanson.

"He isn't the man," one of the detectives remarked, "but that is the suitcase."

"Yes," Swanson agreed, "that's the suitcase all right."

Opened, it was found to contain 60 sticks of dynamite. In addition, a search of Billings' pockets yielded a pistol and a set of burglary tools. He was handcuffed and placed under arrest.

An accident saved Mooney from the same fate. His motorcycle had broken down en route to Sacramento. By the time he arrived Billings was in custody.

Billings went on trial in November, charged with knowingly carrying explosives on a public conveyance. In defense he argued that since he had never opened the suitcase he hadn't been carrying them "knowingly." The judge, a PG&E stockholder, was unimpressed with the argument, and Billings was sentenced to two years in Folsom Prison. Although he was a minor and would ordinarily have been sent to a youth center, the dynamite possession law specifically stated imprisonment in a "state prison." The judge regretted that he could only give Billings the maximum of two years.

On December 2, 1913, Warren K. Billings entered Folsom Prison. He was twenty years old, and a long way from Mexico.*

* The question arises—was the arrest the result of an informer's tip, or a frame-up? Billings maintained at the time, and continues to do so, that the latter was true, and offers several persuasive arguments for the charge, among them that although the police heard the man in the station instruct him to go to the saloon this man was never arrested.

The remark of the detective about the right suitcase but the wrong man led Billings to believe that he was not the intended victim of the plant. For some years he believed that the man who first contacted him in the bar was the intended victim and had unknowingly passed the job on to him. This man, whose identity Billings later learned, was at that time a PG&E strike leader in Oakland. Later he became prominent in both union and state politics, serving for a time as a State Senator. Much later, however, union officials dis-

3 ·

Less than one month later Mooney was arrested on a charge of felonious possession of high explosives. This arrest occurred in Contra Costa County, where he had been working with the linemen to persuade other PG&E employees to walk out. A total of some 1,700 had done so already, but the strike was faltering and many had returned to work.

This was Delta country. Mooney and two electrical workers—Joe Brown and H. C. "Eddy" Hanlon—had bought an old skiff to go to and from the various meetings. On the morning of December 29th the boat sprang a leak; the men tied it up at a wharf at Point St. Pablo while they went into Richmond for oakum to repair it. That evening a deputy sheriff, finding the boat, searched it and found it empty. Shortly afterward, several PG&E detectives searched it and found a 12-gauge double-barrel shotgun, aluminum-plated for night use; an equally expensive Winchester .30-.30 with a Maxim silencer; a .38 caliber Colt revolver; ammunition for the three guns; 13 dry cell batteries wired in series to an alarm clock; fourteen electric fulminating blasting caps; and a 500-foot spool of wire. On their return that night Mooney and his companions were arrested.*

It was charged that the men were planning to blow up one of the two giant steel PG&E towers that bridged the Carquinez Straits. These towers, 208 feet in height, carried the highest span of high-power transmission wires in the world, their six cables supplying the electrical current for the entire San Francisco Bay Area. If destroyed, the city and all its environs would be blacked out.

The men were held in jail at Martinez, the county seat, for five months while awaiting trial. To assure their conviction two PG&E attorneys, Ralph Jones and John J. Barrett, were assigned to "assist" the local district attorney. As the local paper admitted, their "assistance" amounted to running the prosecution.

Although the San Francisco Labor Council was not overly fond of Tom Mooney, they believed him innocent of the charge and endorsed his plea for funds with which to conduct his defense. For defense attorney,

covered that the man had for some time been secretly in the employ of PG&E—which fact may put a different slant on the incident.

The man, who is still living, has denied that he either contacted Billings or was in any way involved in these incidents. The reader therefore has the choice of either accepting or rejecting Billings' own explanations. All that is clear is that Martin Swanson was implicated in the arrest, and that in the aftermath he did his best to involve Mooney.

* Mooney defense literature, simplifying the story somewhat, would later state that Martin Swanson was present when the men were arrested. He did not appear until the following day. Since he was working with the detectives, this not mean that he was uninvolved, however.

Mooney hired Maxwell McNutt. McNutt's father, a wealthy surgeon, was an extremely conservative Republican. Young McNutt, whose main interest outside the law was in training thoroughbreds, had on being admitted to the bar worked briefly as assistant to San Francisco District Attorney Charles M. Fickert. Disgusted with what he had learned about the conduct of that office, however, he had resigned and entered private practice. Despite his background, he found his sympathies often lay with the labor defendants, as in the Billings assault case. After examining the evidence, he was convinced that Mooney, Brown, and Hanlon were innocent and agreed to defend them.

The jury was mostly composed of farmers, a group not given to radical sympathies. The first trial, however, resulted in a hung jury (6-6), as did a second trial (7-6, with the majority for acquittal). In a third trial, in June 1914, the three defendants were acquitted.

Despite PG&E's best efforts to convict Mooney, the rural juries had been disturbed by several things. One was that no dynamite had been found.* Another was puzzlement over how the unemployed strikers came to possess such expensive guns. But what bothered them most was the prosecution's inability to explain why the deputy sheriff had found the boat empty and the detectives, minutes later, had found it loaded with dangerous weapons.

On walking out of the courtroom Mooney was re-arrested and charged with participation in the Sacramento suitcase incident.

According to Warren Billings, following his arrest Swanson had told him that if he would implicate Mooney in the dynamite possession case his superiors would not only see that he was freed but would "make him a rich man." Even after Billings was in Folsom, Swanson had visited him again, this time, still according to Billings, promising him an immediate parole in return for his testimony against Mooney.

In a preliminary hearing in July the Sacramento charge against Mooney was dismissed because of insufficient showing.

Following Mooney's release PG&E attorney Barrett told McNutt, in the presence of Cantrell and Swanson, "Well, Mac, you got Mooney out of this but we put a red shirt on him and we will get something on him some day."

Although PG&E had failed to convict Mooney, he had been removed from the labor scene for some eight months, during which time the company had won a far more important victory. The strike itself—"betrayed by both McCarthy and Gompers," Mooney would charge, since both the

* The absence of dynamite was odd. It was rumored at the time that a striker, seeing the detectives deposit several boxes of dynamite at the base of one of the towers and suspecting the worst, had waited until they left, then tossed them into the Bay. The story, however, defies documentation.

Building Trades Council and the AFL Executive Committee had sided with the unions that settled independently with the company—had ended in the complete defeat of the outlaws in January.

This was about the time of the exposure of the Berkeley frame-up and Martin Swanson's dismissal from Pinkerton. He was not long unemployed. He immediately went to work for PG&E as head detective, with an office in the company's building at 445 Sutter Street. Nor were these his last battles with Mooney. As Fremont Older put it some years later, from this time on "Swanson tracked Mooney as intently as Javert followed Jean Valjean."

4 ·

During 1914 the frame-up pattern was laid bare for all to see.

Following his acquittal in July, Mooney returned to San Francisco. In September the Merchants' and Manufacturers' Association (M&M) of Stockton, California, declared war on the closed shop. In various trades a lockout of all employees affiliated with labor unions was ordered. A number of the more militant San Francisco labor leaders went to Stockton to help organize the picketing and mass meetings. Among them were Mooney and three of his friends: Edward D. Nolan of the Machinists' Union; Anton Johannsen, organizer for the Brotherhood of Carpenters; and Olaff A. Tveitmoe, secretary-treasurer of the California Building Trades Council.

Returning unexpectedly to his hotel one evening, Johannsen found a man in his room. Although both reached for their guns, Johannsen was faster. The man, Hans Le Jeune, a private detective in the employ of the M&M, confessed that he had been hired by H. C. Brokaw, anti-union campaign manager for the Chamber of Commerce, to place a suitcase of dynamite in the hotel room. A similar satchel was to be placed in the Southern Pacific baggage room and the claim check slipped into Tveitmoe's pocket. Still other suitcases of dynamite were to be planted in a mill and foundry involved in the lockout by a man who bore some resemblance to Mooney.

Several days later, J. P. Emerson, another private detective also working for Brokaw and the M&M, broke into a freight car at the Sante Fe yards at Bay Point, just outside Stockton, and stole some 200 pounds of dynamite. Planting four sacks under scattered railroad trestles, he had the balance in a suitcase when stopped by an inquisitive Bay Point constable.

Not so mysteriously, less than six hours after Emerson's arrest he was freed and all charges dropped. Mooney and Nolan learned of the incident, however, and filed a citizen's complaint and had him re-arrested. Emerson, thinking he had been double-crossed by the M&M, signed a full confession agreeing in all particulars with Le Jeune's. It contained details of other projected frame-ups as well, including rental of a boat in Mooney's name and the filling of it with dynamite.

Brokaw and the members of the executive committee of the M&M—all prominent Stockton businessmen—were indicted on the strength of the two confessions.

Tom and Rena Mooney attended Emerson's trial, Rena filling a notebook with notes on the testimony. Emerson, represented by an attorney provided by the employers' group, now repudiated his confession. Everyone was acquitted.*

5 ·

Folsom Prison is located some 30 miles from Sacramento, at a place known as Repressa. In 1913, when Warren Billings was brought there, Folsom was known as a no-foolishness prison, one of the toughest in America, far stricter than its sister institution San Quentin.

Outside, Folsom was not unattractive—its massive gray-blue walls of native rock overlooking the magnetic blue American River, where gold was discovered in 1848. Inside, it was bleakness personified—the most dominant feature not the buildings or cell blocks but the ugly, gaping cavity that was the granite quarry. Prisoners here had the dubious psychological distinction of knowing they were hewing out the walls that would confine them.

Following his conviction, Billings was escorted to the prison by an erstwhile Folsom guard, who, taking no chances, had him bound in both handcuffs and leg irons. When the much-despised guard brought the much-manacled youth through the yard he was soundly hooted.

On his arrival, Acting Warden Jack Smith asked Billings to name his accomplices in the suitcase case. Billings refused and was assigned to the quarry—usually reserved as punishment. He was to remain there during his whole term.

These two incidents, plus his age, contributed to his quick acceptance by the other prisoners. On his first day in the quarry several of the older cons informally adopted him, giving him some sound advice on the easiest way to serve his time. Mind your own business and don't mix with any

---

* Four years later Emerson was working as watchman for a struck oil company when a $1000 reward was offered for the arrest of anyone observed destroying company property. Emerson set fire to a boxcar, intending to blame it on the strikers. Another watchman apprehended him in the act. He was convicted of arson and sent to San Quentin.

gangs, they told him. Do your work and do it the easy way, by studying the rock before you try to break it. Above all, they warned, don't fight the rock ; if you do you'll be the one to break.

He was paroled on December 22, 1914, having served a year and 20 days. On his return to San Francisco, Mooney took him to Fremont Older, who had a reputation for helping ex-cons. During his prison time Billings had studied bookkeeping at night ; so Older found him a job keeping books for a tailor. Soon he was also keeping the books for the International Workers' Defense League, which was now occupying most of Mooney's free time.

The International Workers' Defense League (IWDL) had been formed in 1912 as an outgrowth of the McNamara case. Although originally there had been branches in a number of cities, by 1915 most had disbanded or merged into the defense committees of the IWW and Civil Liberties Union. Due largely to the efforts of such radicals as Nolan, Johannsen, Tveitmoe, David Milner, Eric B. Morton, and Tom Mooney, who had taken over the job of local secretary, the San Francisco branch of the IWDL had remained extremely active. Composed of the delegates of some 50 unions, its declared purpose was to raise funds for, and agitate for the release of, "class-war labor prisoners." There were many of these across the country, as these were years of indescribable bitterness and nearly every clash left a residue of incarcerated.

There were the Fresno and San Diego free-speech fights ; the Lawrence and Paterson strikes ; the Ludlow Massacre, when the Colorado Militia, firing a strikers' tent colony, burned to death two women and 13 children and machine-gunned 30 miners in the battle that followed ; the Christmas Day Tragedy in Calumet, Michigan, when 73 strikers' children were suffocated in the panic following a false fire alarm. There were the cases of Mother Jones, Caplan and Schmidt, Ford and Suhr, and Joe Hill.

Although the IWDL was active in all these cases, the latter two, both involving Wobblies, were to have a special impact on the future of Tom Mooney.

In August 1913, 2,800 hop pickers on the Durst ranch near Wheatland, California, struck, demanding the pay the advertising brochures had originally promised, the right to purchase food in Wheatland (rather than solely at the ranch commissary where extravagant prices were charged), and better sanitary facilities (there were seven toilets for 2,800 people). Two pickers, Richard "Blackie" Ford and Herman Suhr, both Wobblies, led the strike. During a protest meeting, Durst called in a posse to disperse the pickers and arrest the two leaders. On their arrival a drunken deputy sheriff fired his shotgun, touching off a "riot" that left three dead on each side, one of them District Attorney Manwell. Ford and Suhr were later arrested and charged with Manwell's murder. While awaiting trial

Suhr was so brutally tortured he attempted suicide. Although the prosecution conceded that neither Ford nor Suhr had fired the fatal shot, they were found guilty of having incited the strikers to violence and both were sentenced to life imprisonment at Folsom. When all other appeals had failed, pressure was placed on Governor Hiram Johnson to pardon the men. The Governor did hold a public hearing, in February 1915, but after seven months of procrastination denied the petition for pardon.

"The governor's statement of his reason for refusing to act at this time," wrote Tom Mooney in an IWDL release signed with his own name, "shows him in his true colors, a cowardly cur, despicable beyond recognition and resorting to the cunning, shrewdness, trickery, and cowardice of the average district attorney in prosecuting a case, by only mentioning that portion of the evidence which would to the average unthinking person look more incriminating, and thereby justifying himself in not granting the pardon or even commutation of sentence, the latter of which we would never have accepted as satisfactory to us.

"There are some workers at least, Governor Johnson, who will not accept as final your decision on the Ford and Suhr case, and from now on they will attempt to use the only kind of reasoning that will eventually reach you, and we hope it will be indulged in until Ford and Suhr are out of prison.

"And so if violence is committed, Governor Johnson is responsible for it, as he has closed the last legal or Governmental avenue of action. The workers must act, and they will act until Ford and Suhr walk forth free men vindicated to the labor world as their champions in the greatest cause in history."

The Wheatland riot, observes Carey McWilliams, "is of great historic importance for it marked the beginning, in a sense, of intense labor strife in California agriculture."

It was personally important to Tom Mooney. For Governor Johnson considered Mooney's letter no less than a threat on his life, and in the years that followed, as Governor and then United States Senator, Johnson consistently refused to lend his support on Mooney's behalf—support that might well, on several occasions, have opened prison doors.

Mooney had met Joe Hill, the famous IWW troubadour, just once, when Hill was working at a construction job at San Pedro. He knew even better his songs: "Casey Jones the Union Scab," "Hallelujah I'm a Bum," "Pie in the Sky," and a dozen others that had put backbone into hundreds of picket lines.

In January 1914, while active in an IWW strike in Tucker, Utah, Hill had been arrested and charged with the murder of a Salt Lake City grocer. The evidence against him was wholly circumstantial, but damning none the less: Hill had been shot the same night. Even more incriminating to many was his refusal to provide an alibi explaining his wound. (The semiofficial IWW story was that an irate husband had caught Hill making love to his wife, and that with characteristic chivalry Hill refused to implicate the woman.) Hill was thirty-one, tall, slender, very blond with deep blue eyes, and according to those who knew him best, of a gentle, sensitive nature. He was, in short, excellent martyr material. His arrest, the circumstances of his trial, and his sentence—death by firing squad—aroused labor around the world. Thousands wrote to Utah's Governor William Spry, begging for a reconsideration of the case.

Tom Mooney wrote him too, on behalf of the 53 organizations represented by the IWDL, but his was not a begging letter. After reviewing the case and stating his belief that Hill did not have a fair and honest trial, Mooney said:

"We demand you to act in his behalf. We ask you to pardon him if you are in favor of justice. If you are not in favor of justice, then you can only be expected to be treated as you would treat others. This defense league is on record to do all in its power morally and financially and otherwise to defend Joe Hillstrom, and we are not going to see any working man perish without being revenged, when we are satisfied he was not proven guilty of the crime charged in our estimation . . ."

There was much more.

After several delays, Hill's date of execution was set for November 19, 1915. On November 15th, Mooney appeared before the 35th Annual Convention of the AFL, then meeting in San Francisco. Speaking with great feeling, he urged the adoption of a resolution instructing Gompers to appeal to President Wilson, Governor Spry, and the Utah Board of Pardons to postpone the execution pending a full review of the case. The resolution passed unanimously.

On the 17th President Wilson wired Spry: "With unaffected hesitation but with a very earnest conviction of the importance of the case I again urge upon your Excellency the justice and desirability of a thorough reconsideration of the case of Joseph Hillstrom."

The Governor termed Wilson's action "unwarranted interference."

On the evening of the 18th Hill wrote his last song and sent his friend "Big Bill" Haywood two telegrams. One read: "Don't waste any time in mourning. Organize." The other, equally serious but with a touch of Hill's humor, read: "Bill. It is only a hundred miles from here to Wyoming. Could you arrange to have my body hauled to the state line to be buried? I don't want to be found dead in Utah." He was shot the next morning.

Mooney's letters to Governors Johnson and Spry were bold, brash, perhaps even ill-conceived, but taken in the context of events, understandable. Taken out of this context, however, and placed in another, together with a number of other IWDL letters Mooney had written to such known radicals as Haywood, Mother Jones, Lucy Parsons, and Elizabeth Gurley Flynn—many signed "Militantly yours" or "Yours for the revolution"— they would soon provide evidence that Tom Mooney was a dangerous agitator, capable of murdering, out of pure spite for his own failures, ten innocent human beings.

6 ·

Even more damning would be his friendship with anarchist Alexander Berkman.

Berkman, accompanied by M. Eleanor "Fitzie" Fitzgerald, had arrived in San Francisco in the fall of 1915 intent on starting a newspaper treating the labor movement from the revolutionary viewpoint. The paper, as Berkman conceived it, would be free of any particular "ism," "an open revolutionary forum in the fullest sense."

Among the local militants to whom Berkman broached the idea, Ed Nolan and Tom Mooney were especially enthusiastic. Mooney suggested that Berkman use the name of his old, long defunct paper *The Revolt*, but Berkman eventually decided on another name, *The Blast*.*

The first issue appeared January 15, 1916. It was from the beginning strongly anti-militaristic and anti-preparedness and filled with Berkman's own vitriolic class-conscious prose. Containing such incendiary phrases as "general strike," it probably would have frightened some capitalists had they seen it, but considering its limited circulation, chances are that few, if any, were even aware of its existence.

Although Mooney had at first considered going into the enterprise as a full partner with Berkman, the extent of his actual participation was limited to collecting subscriptions and writing a single article. For that winter Tom Mooney had taken up a task many labor leaders had dismissed as impossible. He had decided to organize United Railroads.

* A more unfortunate choice, from the viewpoint of retrospective history, would be hard to imagine.

3 · Prelude to a Frame-up

By THE end of 1915 Mooney had succeeded in irritating the San Francisco Labor Council; a minor shoe company; the Merchants' and Manufacturers' Association of Stockton; the Pacific Gas and Electric Company and its subsidiaries, the San Joaquin Light and Power Company, the Western Electric Company, and the Sierra and San Francisco Power Company; and the governors of California and Utah.

He now added to his list United Railroads and the San Francisco Chamber of Commerce.

In heavily unionized San Francisco, United Railroads (URR), with its 2200 non-union carmen, stood out as a tempting challenge to an energetic organizer. To successfully organize this powerful corporation, one of the strongholds of the open shop, would be the making of any labor leader.

Yet the risks were also great. One prior attempt had gone down to ignoble defeat.

When Patrick Calhoun's streetcar franchise fixing was first exposed in 1906, the public had quickly turned on him, even the pro-business San Francisco *Chronicle* labeling him a "ghoul." To rally public sympathy to his side, Calhoun pulled off a brilliant coup. Using union spies, he fomented a strike among his own carmen. Suddenly the city, struggling to recover from the holocaust, was again without public transportation. Then dramatically—with the use of professional strikebreakers, and ably assisted by Thornwell Mullally—Calhoun stepped in and forcibly crushed the strike. In the eyes of the public, he became the fearless hero who broke the strike and saved the city.

In 1916 Calhoun was no longer president of URR. After milking the company of some $4 million in an elaborate stock scheme, he had gone on to other things, including bankruptcy. Although URR now had another president, Jesse W. Lilienthal, the company's attitude toward unions remained unchanged. Mullally, in the meantime, had risen to a directorship.

During the winter of 1915 Mooney attempted to persuade W. D. Mahon, president of the Amalgamated Association of Street Railroad Employees, to give him credentials as an organizer, with target URR. Mahon delayed a decision, however, and Mooney went ahead with his preparations.

These were detailed. A nucleus of trusted men within the car barns channeled information on the employees to Mooney. Rena Mooney then meticulously typed this onto file cards, one for each employee, giving his background together with his real or probable sympathies. In addition, a general card was kept on each car barn. One, for example, read:

O.K. 25
May be O.K. 101
Doubtful 56
Will scab 12
No line on them 5
Scabs 44
243

The initial organizing was carried out in great secrecy. Meetings were held in Rena Mooney's studio in the Eilers Building at 975 Market, where Tom and Rena were now living, those attending arriving separately at different times. The card file was carefully hidden in various places, known only to the Mooneys, who were well aware that hundreds of men might be jobless if it fell into the wrong hands. Throughout the spring, preparations went on.

United Railroads was making its own preparations. The URR was riddled with spies. Several were among Mooney's most trusted confidants.

That there were leaks Mooney was aware. By selectively confiding false leads to particular individuals he was able to locate some but not all of them.

During 1915, foundry work being scarce, Mooney had worked as a laborer on the Exposition grounds. He now gave his full time to organizing, the couple living on what Rena made teaching. There were other sacrifices. Because of the importance of the files, Tom and Rena could never leave the apartment at the same time. Mooney did find time to write an article for Alexander Berkman opposing preparedness. Few in labor had come out in favor of it; former Labor Council president Andrew J. Gallagher was one; Mooney soundly denounced him. He hit even harder at the attempt of the Pacific Coast Defense League to establish military training in the public schools in the high grammar grades. "They wanted to take kids out of the cradles and make soldiers of them," Mooney would recall, still angry, years later. The article, which appeared in the April 1, 1916, issue of *The Blast*, did not mention the Preparedness parades. They had not yet been conceived.

Toward the end of spring the pressure began. Everywhere Mooney went he was followed, either by Swanson or one of his operatives.* Several

* In February or March of 1916 Martin Swanson organized the Public Utilities Protective Bureau, a private detective agency whose major clients were PG&E and its sub-

times every hour of the day and night the studio telephone would ring, the caller hanging up as soon as it was answered. Such tactics, which Mooney realized were part checking, part harassment, disturbed Rena far more than him. Finally he complained to Maxwell McNutt, inquiring if there were some legal way Swanson could be forced to stop bothering him. McNutt repeated what Barrett had told him, warning Mooney that if he didn't leave the power companies alone and drop his organizing of the platform men he was going to have trouble. To McNutt, Mooney's current project was madness; Mooney was not even a carman.

Finally, Mahon agreed to grant Mooney credentials as an organizer and $50,000 strike benefits, if he could secure strike approval from the Labor Council. Mooney presented his case but was told to try mediation first. He did; Lilienthal said there was nothing to mediate. Mooney again asked strike sanction but the Council denied it, 80-4. Undaunted, he decided to call the strike anyway. It would be a wildcat, yet he knew that if it were successful both Mahon and the Council would recognize it. An organizational meeting was called for the night of June 10th, at Woodman's Hall. It was Mooney's plan—unannounced but confided to a few associates—that if he received enough support at the meeting, the strike would begin the following day.

On the morning of June 10th the following notice was posted in all URR car barns:

Notice to Employees

This is to inform you that one Thomas J. Mooney, a moulder by trade, but at present unemployed, who was arrested and confined in jail as a dynamiter for his activities during the Pacific Gas and Electric Company's strike in 1913, is at present endeavoring to enroll some of our employes in the Carmen's Union. It is needless to advise you that the company is thoroughly familiar with his every move and takes this occasion to notify you that any man found to be affiliated with Mooney or any union, will be promptly discharged.
United Railroads of San Francisco

Since Mooney had been acquitted of the explosives possession charge, he asked Maxwell McNutt if he could bring criminal libel charges against the company. McNutt urged him to forget it, sure that District Attorney Fickert would refuse to prosecute.

sidiaries. Although United Railroads was not officially one of the bureau's clients, the conclusion is inescapable that Swanson and his operatives were working closely with URR. (Swanson maintained two offices, one in the PG&E Building, the other at 16 Sutter, the same building in which the attorney for URR had his office.) One does not have to take Mooney's word that Swanson was watching him. During the Rena Mooney trial, the only occasion on which Swanson was forced to take the stand, he testified that he had Mooney under "constant surveillance" from June 1 to the afternoon of July 22nd, Preparedness Day.

On the evening of the 10th, the Mooneys rode to and from the meeting with Israel Weinberg, an official of the Jitney Bus Operators' Union.

Weinberg, thirty-two, was not a radical, and his acquaintance with Tom Mooney was slight. His eleven-year-old son was taking piano lessons from Rena Mooney. Rena felt the boy had promise and had been giving him violin lessons at no extra charge. When Rena mentioned the URR organizational meeting to him, he had offered to drive the Mooneys to Woodman's Hall, out on 17th Street.

Weinberg had an interest in the outcome of the meeting. The jitneys were a fleet of driver-owned Fords that competed with the streetcars of United Railroads. By charging only a nickel ("jitney") they provided a major drain on URR revenues, to the amount of roughly 3 million per year. The jitney operators had been much harassed by a few policemen, who, they felt, were being paid by URR to bother them, and a URR-backed move to ban the vehicles from Market Street during rush hours was currently under consideration.

When the Mooneys arrived at the hall, they found some 30 to 40 armed men standing on the other side of the street, apparently placed there to discourage attendance. Martin Swanson was seen with these men at various times during the evening. Despite the intimidation some 200 men showed up for the meeting. Unfortunately, where Mooney was concerned, they were mostly friends or IWW's, who had their headquarters at Woodman's Hall. The actual number of carmen was small and among these the proportion of spies was in all probability large. An error of one of them was to have important ramifications.

The turnout was so disappointing that Mooney was forced to give up the idea of calling a strike the following day. Although it was discussed at length, he did not bring it to a vote.

At about ten o'clock Mooney called a brief recess and adjourned to an anteroom for a conference with several of the men. One of the URR spies, thinking Mooney had left the building, left to convey this misinformation to the men on the other side of the street. He was observed doing so by some of the carmen. The meeting resumed after a few minutes, and continued until 1 A.M., when Weinberg drove the Mooneys home. Mrs. Weinberg, who had gone to the hall to meet her husband, was with them.

About 3 A.M. three electrical towers were dynamited in the San Bruno hills about ten miles south of San Francisco. The towers, owned by the Sierra Light and Power Company, supplied United Railroads' electrical power. The damage was slight. Someone had thoughtfully arranged for alternate power and streetcar service was not interrupted.

Word was circulated that Mooney was responsible for the bombing. On June 30th, nearly three weeks after the incident, San Francisco newspapers carried the following advertisement:

REWARD

Dynamiting of Towers Carrying Current Having Been Done to Cripple the Service of the *United Railroads*

A Reward of FIVE THOUSAND DOLLARS is hereby offered for the arrest and conviction of one or more of the dynamiters.

United Railroads of
San Francisco
by Jesse W. Lilienthal
President

It was fairly obvious to Mooney and his friends that an attempt was being made to kill the strike before it started by railroading its organizer on a phony dynamiting charge. What Mooney couldn't understand—until much later—was why he hadn't been arrested or even brought in for questioning.

If it was a frame-up (there is no positive proof that it was, only supposition) two errors were probably responsible for its going awry. One was that Swanson—who was at the scene minutes after the explosion, where he found a suitcase of unexploded dynamite and a clock-timing device—thought Mooney had left the meeting shortly after ten. Several witnesses saw a man dressed like Mooney carrying two suitcases near the towers about 11 P.M. (Swanson had their affidavits, which he would turn over to Fickert after the Preparedness Day bombing.) At 11, however, Mooney was presiding over the organizational meeting, as some 200 men could verify, having been out of the room only a few minutes, far less time than would have been required for him to go to San Bruno, much less there and back.

The crowning error, however, was probably the belief that Mooney was going to call the strike for the following day. If this was indeed an attempted frame-up, Mooney's change of plans thoroughly frustrated it. Had the strike occurred on June 11th, Mooney almost certainly would have been arrested. As it was, the bombing was meaningless.*

There were other indications that a frame-up was in the air. During the latter part of June, Irish patriot Jim Larkin, on a visit to the United States, stopped off in San Francisco, where he saw Mooney several times. At a picnic held in Larkin's honor a number of off-duty policemen, Sinn Feiners like the honoree, were in attendance. One took Larkin aside and warned him, "Keep away from that fellow Mooney. He is being framed on. Something dreadful is going to happen to him very soon." Larkin didn't take the advice seriously enough to bother relaying it to Mooney. Only after the Preparedness Day bombing arrests did he realize its possi-

---

* Coincidence would often play a startling role in the Mooney-Billings case. The posting of a notice labeling Mooney a dynamiter less than 24 hours before the explosion does, however, seem a little too coincidental.

ble importance. By the time he got the word to him, Mooney was in San Quentin under sentence of death.

Mooney continued his organizational efforts.

Early in July, Israel Weinberg received a copy of the reward notice in the mail. Appended to it was a printed postscript:

> This notice of reward was published in the San Francisco newspapers on Friday, June 30th, for the purpose of apprehending and bringing to justice the depredators who on the night of June 10, 1916, dynamited three steel towers at South San Francisco.
>
> The owner or driver of the automobile which conveyed these depredators to the scene of their crime will do well to communicate this information to Jesse W. Lilienthal, 58 Sutter Street, San Francisco, and he can be assured he will be fully protected.

Weinberg, thinking that this was a routine notice sent to all jitney operators, tossed it aside and promptly forgot it. Unaware that an attempt was being made to connect Mooney with the dynamiting case, it did not occur to him to mention it when, on July 4th, he drove the Mooneys to an anarchist picnic at Colma.

The picnic, organized by Alexander Berkman to raise funds for *The Blast,* was one of the rare occasions on which Tom and Rena left the apartment together. Several nights earlier Rena had taken the URR card file to the home of her sister, Mrs. Belle Hammerberg, for safe-keeping, unaware that she, too, was under surveillance. Probably hoping for a ride, the Mooneys had invited Mr. and Mrs. Weinberg and their son to the picnic, and they had accepted. It was an all-day affair, with—in addition to the inevitable speeches—games and prizes, a complete set of Nietzsche among the latter.

The respite was brief. Although the strike was now tentatively set for July 14th, Mooney had not given up trying to secure Labor Council approval, but he was unsuccessful. Mooney had few friends on the council. Too, his assertion that he could singlehandedly do what the Labor Council itself had thus far failed even to attempt, must have rankled. There were, however, stronger reasons for the refusal of strike sanction. Mooney had to admit that to date he could not claim a clear majority of the carmen. The council had enough to worry about without sanctioning an ill-timed strike against URR. A strike of the culinary workers was in the planning. Even more important, there was open warfare on the waterfront.

On June 1st, the Pacific Coast Longshoremen had walked off the docks in a pay dispute, tying up all waterborne commerce on the West Coast. In San Francisco, as in Seattle, Los Angeles, and San Diego, there was not a business that did not feel the effects of the strike. When scabs were brought in to move the cargo, violence quickly erupted. To cite only one version, the Chamber of Commerce claimed that between June 9th and July 17th, 38 "non-union workers" were assaulted badly enough to require hospitalization, while, during the same period, there were seven "retaliatory assaults" on union men.

Two strikers had been killed, one in Oakland, one in San Francisco. In the latter incident, arousing the greatest indignation, one Thomas Olsen, a striking longshoreman, had been gunned down by one Homer Waters. Olsen had a wife and 13 children. Waters was an ex-convict, a part-time pimp, and an active strikebreaker. He was also a Negro, which fact heaped additional fuel on the explosive situation.

It was war. All that remained was for someone to declare it. This the Directors of the San Francisco Chamber of Commerce did, on June 22nd.

2 ·

Citing the "outrageous conditions" on the waterfront and the "iniquitous demands" sought by the longshoremen, the Directors declared, "While the Chamber of Commerce has never yet opposed and will not attempt to oppose organized labor as such, it cannot without making a vigorous protest against the practices, allow the present attacks upon the commerce of the Coast to go unchallenged . . .

"The Chamber of Commerce favors the open shop and insists upon the right to employ union or non-union workers, in whole or in part, as the parties involved may elect . . .

"*Therefore,* the Chamber of Commerce pledges its entire organization and the resources it represents to the maintenance of these principles and will oppose any attempt on the part of any interest, business or organization which tries to throttle the commercial freedom of San Francisco."

Thus, on June 22nd, 1916, the San Francisco Chamber of Commerce for the first time officially went on record advocating the open shop.

The move was shrewdly timed. Following the death of Olsen by one day, it was obviously intended to shift the blame for his death onto the strikers. On a larger scale, the Chamber—which had long been considering such a declaration—could now claim that the violence on the waterfront forced them to take this stand.

It was war, and all the careful, polite phrases could not disguise the fact.

On July 5, a large delegation from the chamber called on Mayor James Rolph, asking for authority to hire 500 special policemen to protect the movement of goods on the docks. Rolph angrily refused the request, declaring that no one was going to maintain an extra-legal army in the city so long as he was Mayor.

On July 6, Frederick J. Koster, energetic new chamber president,* sent a letter to all the city's merchants, calling a mass meeting for Monday, July 10th, to discuss means of correcting the "intolerable situation" on the waterfront.

Over 2000 merchants attended, packing the floor of the Merchants' Exchange. It was, according to one chronicler, "one of the most dramatic meetings in San Francisco history."

"A condition of lawlessness exists for which there can be no excuse," Koster said in his keynote speech. Means had to be found to stamp out "that disease permeating this community of which the waterfront situation is at present the most outstanding example . . ."

Koster asked that a committee of five be appointed, to be known as the Law and Order Committee of the San Francisco Chamber of Commerce, its stated purpose "to rid San Francisco of anarchistic elements." He also asked the establishment of a special fund to carry this work to a successful conclusion.

For all of Koster's careful protestations that the chamber was not anti-labor, there was not a man present who was unaware that the real purpose of the committee and the fund was to bring an end to the closed shop in San Francisco. Other speakers were not so careful. Fiery old shipping magnate Robert Dollar, never given to moderation in labor disputes, was to utter a challenge that would make labor history. The only way to restore "peace and quiet on the waterfront," Dollar was quoted as saying, "is when they compel us to send one ambulance to the receiving hospital, we send two of theirs." †

As for the fund, within five minutes after the meeting $200,000 had been subscribed; within a week, $600,000; and by year's end the Law and Order Committee was "operating in round figures with a fund of $1 million." ‡

Just sixty years after the hanging of Casey and Cora, the Vigilantes had returned to San Francisco.

3 ·

More than a month after the organizational meeting, Mooney still lacked a definite majority of the carmen. He was sure, however, that he

---

* Koster was a wealthy barrel manufacturer. His own company had always enjoyed excellent relations with labor, a fact that is often brought forth to "prove" that he was not anti-union. His active role in the open shop fight, however, speaks for itself.

† This is the most commonly quoted version of Dollar's remarks. Another version, which appeared in the *Bulletin* the following day, had Dollar saying, "Let's fight! If a peaceful workingman is beaten up by strikers, then beat up two strikers in return."

‡ Both the figures and the quotations are from a San Francisco Chamber of Commerce publication, *Law and Order in San Francisco: A Beginning*.

could win them over by one bold, dramatic move.

Not wanting to take into his confidence any except those in whom he placed implicit trust, he called Billings back to the city from the Russian River, where he was vacationing.

Since his release from Folsom, Warren Billings had worked at a variety of jobs, ranging from apprentice tailor to poker hustling. Prison hadn't tempered his spirit of adventure. Blacklisted in his own trade in San Francisco, he had gone to Denver in 1914 in search of work. While in the mile-high city he heard a rumor that during the Ludlow strike the miners had hidden a cache of guns and ammunition in a mountain cave. Billings found a young boy who supposedly knew where the cave was located, but was unable to pry his secret from him. Thus the Warren Billings plan to storm Utah State Prison and free Joe Hill died aborning.

On returning to San Francisco, he was elected president of the Boot and Shoe Workers' Union. "It was not quite the honor it sounds," he later recalled. "Since all the shoe factories now had open shop contracts and wouldn't hire an official of the union, the union leaders had to be men who weren't working at their trades." Still, for a young man just turned twenty-one and only one year out of prison, it was an important post. He was also one of the union's two delegates to the San Francisco Labor Council. Although he had joined neither the Socialist Party nor the IWW, his labor philosophy was more or less similar to Mooney's own, Tom in effect thus having a spokesman on the council. During his term of office, Billings joined a group of rebels in ousting reactionary Andrew Gallagher as council president and installing progressive young pressman, Daniel Murphy, in his place. For the early part of 1916 Billings had worked mostly as an auto mechanic. When in May the Machinists' Union declared a strike against a number of garages, he had returned to his former trade, posing as a scab while spying for the union. But he had been detected and fired on June 30th.

During this period he was living in a Mission Street boardinghouse run by Mrs. Belle Lavin. The place, tenanted largely by radicals, had a certain notoriety, since the McNamara brothers had stayed there for a short time in 1911 prior to their arrest and Mrs. Lavin had also been arrested and held briefly. On being fired from the struck garage, Billings, Mrs. Lavin, and a friend, Frank Lee, decided to go camping for a few days on the picturesque Russian River, north of San Francisco. When Mooney called, Billings caught the next train back to the city.

The date for the strike was now definitely set. On Thursday, July 13th, as the URR employees left the car barns, Tom and Rena Mooney handed them leaflets announcing a strike the following evening. Both were arrested and charged with the misdemeanor of distributing handbills. Having anticipated this, they were bailed out almost immediately. That it was necessary for Rena to help Tom in this was indicative of only one thing: the lack of open support from the carmen.

Mooney's plan was daring. On Friday evening, July 14th, during the five o'clock rush hour, Billings was to ride downtown on the Geary street-car. Just as it was crossing the intersection on Geary, Kearny, and Market Streets, he was to yank the emergency cord, halting the car and blocking all traffic on the three busy streets. The resultant jam would tie up most of the traffic in downtown San Francisco. The motormen would then desert their streetcars and the strike would be on.

It began as planned. Billings yanked the emergency break, while Rena climbed onto the car and started to fasten a union button on the motor-man. But even before it was in place she was grabbed by detectives, yanked off the car and placed under arrest, charged with disturbing the peace. Only six motormen abandoned their cars; they were replaced immediately by company carmen waiting on the streetcorners.

Every detail of the plan had been known to the company and prepared for. Within 45 minutes the strike was over and traffic moving smoothly.

Mooney's big attempt to prove himself as a strike organizer ended in ignominious failure. That night he managed to raise enough money to meet Rena's bail. Only by chance, or perhaps vanity, had he himself escaped arrest. Shortly before the strike was to begin he had changed from his brown suit to a new blue suit bought especially for the occasion. The detectives were watching for a man in a brown suit.

Elizabeth Gurley Flynn once wrote: "Most of us were wonderful agitators but poor union organizers."

4 ·

"Continued Peace through Preparedness—Join the March of the Patriots—Join, March and Show Your Colors!"

The ads appeared daily, sponsored by the city's leading stores. From the strike to the Grand Preparedness Parade was only eight days.

Even though the strike was over, the telephone calls and surveillance continued. Tired and discouraged, the Mooneys decided to take a vacation. Billings had spoken so enthusiastically of the beautiful Russian River country that they decided to go there. Rena's trial was set for Wednesday the 18th, and a hearing was to be held on Friday the 21st, to determine whether the carmen currently under suspension were to be fired for their part in the strike. The Mooneys decided to delay their departure until after the hearing.

5 ·

Three days after the abortive strike, on Monday July 17th, a large, heavy-set man climbed into Weinberg's jitney and asked the fare to Seven Mile House on the Pacific Ocean. Weinberg told him the rate was $1.25 an hour and that he could probably make it out and back in an hour if the man didn't intend to stay long. The man climbed in and Weinberg drove off.

The man was talkative. "If Mooney would be able to pull off a car strike, you jitney drivers would be doing pretty good."

Weinberg replied that he supposed they would.

"How's business?" the man asked. Weinberg said that it was slow.

"You could make $5000 as easy as that." The man snapped his fingers.

"That will be fine. Tell me how."

"You know Mooney." It was a statement, not a question.

"Yes," Weinberg replied, with just a trace of apprehension, "I know Mooney."

"You know that the towers were blown up, don't you?"

"I don't know if they were or not," Weinberg replied cautiously.

"A few days ago you received a notice from United Railroads offering $5000 for any information leading to the arrest of the fellows that blew up the towers."

Weinberg wondered how the man knew about the notice. "Who are you, anyway? Are you a police officer?"

"No, I'm not a police officer. My name is Swanson. I'm a detective with United Railroads." He showed Weinberg his badge.

According to Weinberg, Swanson then said the $5000, "enough to start you in a good business back East," would be his in exchange for his testimony that he drove Mooney to San Bruno on the night of the carmen's meeting. Weinberg replied that he couldn't testify to that because it wasn't true. Swanson assured him he wouldn't have to admit taking part in the actual bombing, that "it would not take much to convict them, just a little circumstantial evidence," and that if he did testify all they asked was that he be a little vague as to the time. If he was afraid of Mooney, Swanson added, he needn't worry: he would be given protection. Weinberg again said he could not help him.

At this point, Swanson changed his tactic. If Weinberg wouldn't cooperate, steps would be taken to have the Chief of Police revoke his jitney license. Weinberg said he doubted that this could be done, but that if it could he supposed he could make his living in some other manner.

A rare photograph of Tom Mooney's nemesis, utilities corporation detective Martin Swanson. Although actually in charge of the bomb investigation, Swanson's name never appeared in the press.

"We know you took Mooney to the carmen's meeting," Swanson said, "and we know that you took him to that anarchist picnic." Weinberg didn't answer. At the end of the ride Swanson tipped him a quarter and said that he would be seeing him shortly. If Weinberg changed his mind meantime, all he need do was contact Mr. Abbott, attorney for United Railroads. Just his name would ensure Mr. Abbott's seeing him. Weinberg again stressed that he knew nothing and that he hoped Swanson wouldn't bother him again. He then drove to the Eilers Building and told Mooney what had happened.

6 ·

The following day, Tuesday, July 18th, Rena Mooney was convicted of disturbing the peace, given a suspended sentence and released.

The same day Warren Billings was in the PG&E Building, paying his gas bill, when he encountered Swanson. This was their first meeting since Swanson's visit at Folsom. Swanson casually mentioned Mooney, the towers, and the reward. Billings claimed to know nothing about it, since he hadn't been at the carmen's meeting. Having been temporarily blinded that same day during an accident in the garage where he was employed, he had remained in a dark room all weekend, both eyes bandaged. Swanson said he already knew that. Reaching into his pocket he took out a copy of the reward notice, handed it to Billings, and told him to "think it over."

7 ·

The next morning, Wednesday, July 19th, Billings received a telephone call from Swanson, requesting a meeting. Billings reluctantly agreed to go to Swanson's office. This time the detective was more to the point, making substantially the same offer as had been made to Weinberg, with the proviso that in addition to the reward money Billings would have a permanent job in the PG&E garage. Playing along to see how far things might go, Billings said he doubted that Swanson could deliver either the reward money or the job. Swanson then took him to the office of Cantrell, PG&E property agent, where before Cantrell and another man he repeated his offer. Provide information linking Mooney to the San Bruno dynamiting, Cantrell said, and both the money and the job are yours. Billings said he would think it over.

Leaving the building, Billings glanced back and saw that Swanson was following him. He was trying to figure a way to warn Mooney without being observed when he spotted George Speed, local IWW secretary. Speed, a veteran trade unionist who had helped organize the Seaman's Union, agreed to take a message to Mooney while Billings waited in a nearby bar.

On receiving the message, Mooney wrote a note asking Billings to meet him at *The Blast,* and gave it to Speed to deliver. Just that morning the bothersome telephone calls had finally stopped, and as far as Mooney could determine, he was no longer being watched. He had chosen Berkman's apartment for a meeting place, however, in the event the Eilers Building was still under surveillance.

Billings, after reading the note and following a circuitous route to shake Swanson, met Mooney and told him what had happened.

Unknown to both men, their every move had been observed by operatives of the Thiel Detective Agency; Swanson's own operatives, most of whom Mooney now knew by sight, had that same day been replaced by the more professional Thiel men.*

* Whether the Thiel Detective Agency was hired by United Railroads, PG&E, or by Swanson on behalf of one or both has never been made clear. All that is known is that they did have Mooney and Billings under surveillance during this period, and that Swanson had access to their reports.

Mooney's choice of a meeting place couldn't have been more unfortunate. In the trials that followed the Preparedness Day bombing, the prosecution would claim the conspirators had met at the offices of *The Blast* to plot the bombing of the parade.

Later that same afternoon Swanson again climbed into Weinberg's jitney, to repeat his earlier offer. Weinberg just as adamantly refused to help him. "Listen," Swanson said, "I was talking the matter over with Mr. Abbott, and if you don't know enough to secure a conviction, we will pay you for what you do know, and keep your name strictly confidential." Weinberg stopped the vehicle and ordered Swanson out. Swanson angrily handed him a nickel and promised, "I'll get you yet." *

That same evening Mooney and Billings met again in Rena's studio. Billings, his zest for adventure undiminished, suggested that he pretend to go along with the frame-up attempt, then expose Swanson and Cantrell in court. Fortunately Ed Nolan, also present, was more level-headed and quickly pointed out the risks of such a plan. All they could do, Mooney said resignedly, was to wait and see what Swanson tried next.

They didn't have long to wait.

8 ·

The following evening, Thursday, July 20th, there was a mass meeting in Dreamland Rink to protest the Preparedness demonstration. So many attended, more than 5000, that a second overflow meeting had be held outside. Not all present were pacifists. Many were angry employees whose bosses had given them the choice between marching or losing their jobs. Billings attended the meeting, although the Mooneys, who were preparing for their vacation, did not. Fremont Older, who had promoted the meeting through the columns of the *Bulletin,* was one of the featured speakers. Another was Rudolph Spreckles, who, with Older, had been responsible for the graft prosecutions. Still another was William McDevitt.

McDevitt, who ran a bookstore specializing in radical literature, was San Francisco's Commissioner of Elections. Like Captain Dollar, McDevitt was not inclined toward caution. During his speech he recalled that George Bernard Shaw had once been asked how to end war. Shaw's

---

* This and the foregoing conversations between Swanson and Weinberg and Swanson and Billings are taken from the testimony of Weinberg and Billings in the various trial transcripts.

That these conversations occurred was never challenged by the prosecution. During the Rena Mooney trial Swanson admitted that each had taken place substantially as stated. He denied, however, that he had threatened Weinberg, and claimed that in each of these encounters he had stressed that the reward money (and, in Billings' case, the job offer) was in return for truthful information.

advice, directed to new recruits, had been "Shoot your officers and go home." McDevitt's quotation brought amused laughter. Not one of the San Francisco newspapers, reporting the meeting the following day, considered it newsworthy. Later the quotation would be recalled and (1) attributed to McDevitt, cost him his election job; and (2) misattributed to Older, be cited as proof of his complicity in the Preparedness Day bomb plot.

9 ·

In the hearing the next morning the six suspended transit employees were fired for participating in the abortive strike. Ostensibly siding with the men, the San Francisco *Chronicle* observed, "Thomas Mooney, a labor agitator, is partly responsible for the plight of the six accused men . . . Mooney has been repudiated by all of the labor organizations of the city."

The Mooneys had planned to leave for the Russian River after the hearing. However Rena's cousin, Mrs. Martha Timberlake, having come up from Los Angeles for the weekend to visit Rena and Belle, they postponed their departure until Monday.

When Billings had gone on his Russian River trip he had borrowed Mooney's camera. Now that the Mooneys were preparing for their holiday, Tom stopped at Billings' room to pick it up. Billings wasn't there, however, so he left a note that read: "Deliver the camera 18th and Guerrero. Tom."

The address was that of Rena Mooney's sister, Belle. Billings delivered the camera there, only to find that the Mooneys had been detained at Rena's studio, so he dropped it off at the Eilers Building.

The prosecution would soon contend that "camera" was a code name for "bomb."

That same Friday evening, the San Francisco Labor Council adopted an astonishing resolution. Vague rumors had brought it into being— rumors that attorneys would later spend months trying to track down, unsuccessfully.

It read in part:

"Whereas, it has come to our attention that, because united labor is opposed to the fostering of the war spirit by 'preparedness parades,' an attempt may be made by the enemies of labor to cause a violent disturbance during the progress of the parade and charge that disturbance to labor . . .

"Therefore, be it resolved: That in order to forestall any possible frame-up of this character . . . we hereby caution all union men and women . . . to be especially careful and make no other protest than their silent

non-participation . . ."
    A violent disturbance during the parade.
    A possible frame-up.
    It was Friday, July 21st, the eve of Preparedness Day.

PART TWO

The
Making
of a
Martyr

"While there is a lower class, I am in it; while there is a criminal element, I am of it; while there is a soul in prison, I am not free."

EUGENE V. DEBS

4 · Saturday, July 22nd, 1916

L EAVING HIS HOME at 1479 Dolores Street at about 6 A.M., Israel Weinberg drove to the Ferry Building, arriving in time to meet the 6:35 ferry and pick up his first load of commuters. From the Ferry Building he followed his regular route up Mission to Fillmore, and from there to Fillmore and Sutter, the end of his run, and back, picking up and dropping off passengers along the way. After several of these trips he went home and fixed his own breakfast, washing the dishes when he finished, something he was being careful to do while his wife and son were visiting relatives in Cleveland. The postman was due at 11, and he waited for him, hoping there would be a letter from his wife; there had been none for several days and he was worried. The postman arrived late, about 11:45, but there was a letter; they were well but had been too busy to write. He then drove to 29th and Valencia, the end of another of his regular runs, arriving there exactly at noon. Two men jumped in, asking if he could make it to the Ferry Building in time for the 12:20 boat. He would try. Traffic was heavy, however, and due to the number of pedestrians crossing Mission en route to Market to watch the parade the going was slow. After being rerouted several times by the police he reached his destination at 12:25, just missing the boat. Another jitney driver, Schwab, who wanted to stay and see the start of the parade, gave him two passengers for Fillmore and Sutter. Weinberg then drove up Mission to Second, from which he turned onto Market. He continued up Market, picking up a full load at Third Street, exchanging greetings with another jitney driver, Simon Statler, who passed him at Market and Golden Gate about 12:35. Turning off Market at Fillmore about 12:45, he drove to Sutter, unloaded, and picked up several passengers for the trip downtown. He drove back down Sutter, but on arriving at Golden Gate and Market found he couldn't cross Market, the street having been blocked off for the parade. Letting off his passengers, he returned to Fillmore and Sutter, picking up other passengers along the way. There followed another trip downtown over the same route. Mrs. Ida Klotz, a neighbor, tried to hail him at Golden Gate and Taylor about 1:30, but he didn't see her. On his return trip, at about 1:45, he stopped at Mrs. Caplan's clothing store between Fillmore and

Webster. Mrs. Caplan was a friend of Mrs. Weinberg's; the previous day he had told her he was worried about not receiving a letter from his wife. He showed her the letter. On returning to his auto, he met a friend, David Brock. Brock introduced him to his companion, Leon Carasso, who asked if Weinberg could take them to a bookstore on Fillmore Street. He picked up and let off passengers along the way. His last passenger getting off at Grant Avenue, he drove on to the PG&E office, and at approximately five minutes after two, paid his gas bill. Slipping the receipt into his pocket, he then made a trip back to 29th and Valencia, followed by another trip downtown. This time, about 3 P.M., he crossed Market Street at Van Ness and went down Mission to the Ferry Building, where the other jitney operators told him there had been a terrible explosion at Steuart and Market Streets.

Some 20 witnessess—passengers, acquaintances, other jitney drivers—would eventually come forward to support Israel Weinberg's assertion that at no time between 12:45 and 3 P.M. was his vehicle on Market Street.

2 ·

That morning the Mooneys arose about 7:30, Tom working on his strike report to Mahon of the Carmen's Union while Rena unpinned her hair and dressed. By the time she was ready to go out for breakfast, Tom was involved in the report, so she went alone. On her return, about 9:30, he went out for breakfast at Hoffman's Restaurant, after which he went by the Tivoli Theatre, to see what movie was showing that evening. When he returned to the studio, about 10:45, two of the discharged carmen, Nathan Trask and Nicholas Treanor, were there, and they talked about the hearing. While they were talking, two boys were in and out of the studio, fastening an American flag into place across the front of the building. It was an immense flag: dropped into place and secured, it covered almost the whole façade, from the seventh floor to the mezzanine. The Mooneys had intended to watch the parade from the studio windows that overlooked Market—Rena having invited her sister and visiting cousin to join them—but the flag covered all but a part of one window of the fifth-floor studio. Between 10 and 12:15 the boys came in and out a half-dozen times, realigning the flag.

About 11 Rena went downstairs to the Eilers Music Company to return some sheet music and pay the rent. On her return she found that in her absence one of her young pupils, Camille Leger, had arrived with some blackberries and roses for her favorite teacher. As Rena had some shopping to do, she and Camille left the studio about noon, parting on the street. Rena then went to a close-by store, Schwartz and Goodman's, where she bought some underwear for herself, and on to The Clarion, a shop that sold union label goods, where she bought two shirts and a tie for Tom. She arrived back at the studio about 12:20, just as Treanor was leaving. A few minutes later another of Rena's pupils, Rebecca Cutler, arrived, accompanied by her little brother. They had come downtown to watch the parade, and their parents had permitted them to come up to the studio to wish Rena a happy vacation. Trask stayed until about 1 or 1:15. After his departure Rena tactfully suggested that Rebecca and her brother might miss the parade, whereupon they left also. A few minutes later, while taking some garbage down the hall, Rena noticed that the door to the tailor shop was open.

The tailor was moving and Rena was thinking about expanding the studio. She asked Tom if he would like to look at the rooms. Since there were a number of people in the shop, Rena apologized and suggested they come back later but the tailor, Benjamin Kirsch, urged them in. The Mooneys already knew Kirsch, his wife Gertrude, and their little girl Ray, who spent much of her time in the studio. Kirsch introduced them to the others: Sam Green, a fellow tailor, his wife Sadie, and their three children; and Harry Rosenblatt, Mrs. Kirsch's brother. The Mooneys stayed only a few minutes. Going back to the studio, about 1:30, they had less than five minutes alone together when Rena's sister and cousin arrived. They had heard band music playing and were afraid the parade had already started, but Tom, peering out the slit uncovered by the flag, saw that it was a band marching down Market to join the parade. The time the band passed would later be determined to be about 1:35.

Shortly afterward, about 1:40 or 1:45, they heard more music. Tom spotted the head of the parade at about Fifth Street. The elevator wasn't working (it had stopped at 1:40, when its operator went to the roof to watch the parade), so they walked up the four flights of stairs to the roof, arriving at approximately 1:50. As they came onto the roof, John C. Lawlor, an Eilers employee, passed them going down. He had a two o'clock appointment.

There were a number of people already on the roof, some of whom the Mooneys knew by sight if not name, others who would later be identified. There was Lawlor's wife Gertrude; two Eilers clerks, Miss Mendell and Miss Hussy; Mario Cresafulli, a piano tuner, and his wife, together with her mother, Mrs. Julia DeLorenzo, and her sister, Mrs. Busco; and William Balcom, a piano and organ repairman. Wade Hamilton, another Eilers employee, was on an adjoining roof, waiting to take pictures of the parade.

While Rena inspected a flower bed Tom had planted for her on the roof, Tom and the two women found places on the edge overlooking Market. Rena then joined them. When James Rolph came into sight, Mrs. Timberlake asked "Who is that?" Tom replied loudly, since Mrs. Timberlake was hard of hearing, "The Mayor."

Tom then left the roof—the only time during the afternoon—to run downstairs to the studio to get the *Examiner,* so they could identify the units as they passed. While he was gone Rolph stopped opposite the Eilers Building; the time was 1:58. Tom was gone not more than five minutes but brought back the wrong section of the paper. He offered to go back but the women talked him out of it. There is indisputable proof that he was back on the roof by 2:01.

The Mooneys, Mrs. Hammerberg, and Mrs. Timberlake would remain on the roof for the rest of the afternoon, until after 5, when the last unit, an aeroplane float, passed.

In addition to those named, there were others, including another of Rena's pupils, Hilbert Roberts, who arrived on the roof at various times while the Mooneys were still there. Altogether 16 witnesses placed Tom and Rena Mooney on the Eilers roof from about 1:50 on.

With the exception of about five minutes after Rebecca Cutler and her brother left, and another period of about equal duration between their visit to the tailor shop and the arrival of Mrs. Hammerberg and Mrs. Timberlake, the Mooneys were not alone from about 12:20 until after 5.

The Eilers Building, at 975 Market, was about a mile and a quarter—6088 feet to be exact—from the corner of Steuart and Market.

About 3 P.M. a policeman came up on the roof to ask if everyone had a reason for being there. Since everyone either worked in the building or was a friend or relative of someone who did, they assured him they had. The policeman asked Tom is there was any other means of access to the roof and he said No, except for the adjoining roof on the west side. Asked the reason for his questions, the officer replied, "They are throwing bombs off the roofs downtown." *

3 ·

Warren Billings' activities that day were less innocent.

On May 1st some 200 mechanics belonging to the Machinists' Union had gone on strike against seven large auto agencies. Official strike tactics included picket lines and boycotts. Unofficial tactics included the use of

* Few of the people mentioned, the Mooneys included, were aware of exact or even approximate times. These were later determined by a number of means, such as checking the stories against each other, determining the passing times of the parade units, etc. This was further complicated by the fact that not all of these witnesses came forth immediately or even voluntarily. Many had to be sought. Others who were also on the roof were never located. And some, as will be seen, did report to the police, only to have their testimony suppressed.

spies posing as scabs—which Billings had done until detected and fired at the end of June—and sabotage—which was what he was engaged in this Saturday.

Most of the morning Billings had spent at the Labor Temple, working with Ed Nolan, president of the Machinists' local. From about 1:30 P.M., when he went downtown, to shortly after 3, he was engaged in a type of work never openly sanctioned by any union, but not infrequently practiced. At this time all new autos were guaranteed for one year, any necessary repairs in the interim being made at the agency's expense. To harass the dealers, spies inside the struck agencies obtained lists of those autos still covered by warranties; when located, these vehicles were then sabotaged, the dealer having to pay for their repair.

Working his way down the streets north of Market, Billings watched for new Cadillacs, Fords, and Hudsons. In one pocket was a package of cigarette papers; the license numbers were written on one of the sheets. In another pocket was a rubber bulb syringe and a can of paint remover.

About 1:40 he turned into Union Square Avenue (now known as Maiden Lane) where he spotted a new battleship-gray Hudson. The license number was on his list.

Walking into the Reception Bar, he ordered a beer. While the bartender was drawing it, Billings went to the men's room and filled the bulb from the can.

When he returned to the bar the only other customer was leaving, the bartender yelling "So long, Baron," as he went out the door. The German Consul-General Franz Bopp and his staff were currently awaiting trial charged with bombing munitions' ships and other espionage; Billings asked the bartender if the man was Baron Von Schack, one of Bopp's aides. The bartender laughed and said, "Oh, hell no, that's George Baron, the ladies' tailor." Billings finished his beer and left.

A group of pretty girls was marching by on Grant. While everyone watched them, Billings stopped alongside the Hudson, casually reached into his pocket and took out the bulb, and squeezed it. He then moved to the mouth of the alley and joined the watchers. The time was 1:50. The girls, all dressed in white, were employees of Magnins, on their way to join the parade. One girl—later identified as Emma Richter—was late and running to catch up. A man standing near Billings who knew her yelled "Hurry Emma; you'll miss your place in the parade." The man—Bert Wertheimer, proprietor of the Juvenile clothing store—then turned to his companions and remarked that he felt it was unfair to compel employees to march when they didn't want to, as many of the big companies were doing. Just behind the girls was a group of men from Livingston Brothers, also on their way to join the parade. Wertheimer knew the man who was leading them, George Stein, and they exchanged greetings.

At about 2 o'clock, two men came out of a nearby building, got into the Hudson and drove off, apparently not noticing the jagged white streak that ran down the vehicle's side. Billings was thankful they hadn't caught him in the act, for he knew one of the men. He was Superior Court Judge Frank H. Dunne, who had presided over his assault trial. Later Billings would learn that his companion, the owner and driver of the car, was Dr. Robert Patek, Dunne's physician.

Ironically, Judge Dunne would preside over Warren Billings' trial for the bomb murders.

Union Square Alley was three-quarters of a mile from Steuart and Market, where, in just six minutes, these murders would take place.

Billings resumed his quest along other streets north of Market. He found one more car, a Cadillac, but a man and a woman were inside it. The man asked Billings to help him back out into the traffic and Billings, with a broad grin, did so.

About 3 P.M. Billings reached the corner of Sixth and Market where a newsboy was shouting "Big explosion! Read all about it!"

4 ·

"I'm sure Mooney did it."

It was late afternoon. Fremont Older was on the peninsula train. With him was his editorial writer, Robert L. Duffus. Fearing that a mob might turn on the *Bulletin* as a result of its anti-preparedness stand, Older had insisted that Duffus spend the weekend with himself and his wife Cora at Woodhills, their ranch at Cupertino.

"Why Mooney?" Duffus asked.

"Because he's the only labor leader radical enough to do it," Older replied.

Young Duffus would later look back on this day and realize that it marked a turning point not only in his own life but in the lives of Older and everyone on the paper. "The campaigns the *Bulletin* was carrying on were never so idyllic, never so dreamlike, never so inexorably certain to win, after that . . ."

5 ·

Tom Mooney's name, together with that of Warren Billings, was mentioned in two other discussions that night.

One occurred in the office of San Francisco Chief of Police David Augustus White, where a hastily called conference of some dozen officers was taking place.

It was neither a calm nor a dispassionate meeting. The number of dead was mounting, the city in a state of panic over the possibility that this might be only the first in a series of bombings, and Mayor Rolph was demanding that the department, already under fire from the Chamber of Commerce for failing to maintain law and order on the waterfront, immediately arrest the "fiends responsible." On the streets people were saying that if the police didn't act they would. The pressure for a quick solution to the case was already tremendous, and growing greater every hour.

But there were problems that made a quick solution difficult.

One was that the San Francisco Police Department had no "bomb experts." Captain Duncan Matheson, of the traffic squad, who had been standing at the corner of Market and Steuart when the explosion occurred, knew as much as anyone about what had happened. Chief White placed him in nominal charge of the investigation, with officers assigned to help him. (On Monday this group would be officially designated the San Francisco Bomb Squad, the first in the city's history. Among those assigned to help Matheson were Lt. Stephen Bunner, Sgt. Charles Goff, and detectives William Proll and Draper Hand.)

The greatest problem was not the scarcity of suspects but the abundance of them.

There were the German espionage agents, who quite naturally opposed the Preparedness parade. Although the Consul-General and his aides were currently under indictment, the mysterious explosions continued—that same day there had been one in the Hercules Powder Works across the Bay in Pinole. From what could be learned about the parade bomb, it had been similar to those employed by the Germans.

There were the Mexicans, who resented Pershing's invasion. The explosion on the Southern Pacific train was less than a month old and still unsolved.

There were a dozen separate groups, from pacifists to laborites, who for one reason or another opposed Preparedness. All had their fanatics.

There was the anonymous letter writer, whose identity was not yet known.

And there were those who didn't fit into any category, the mentally disturbed and psychotic.

It may be that all these possibilities were at least mentioned, however briefly. By the time the meeting ended, however, Chief White had simplified his task by narrowing suspicion to two groups.

One, of course, consisted of "known dynamiters." Among these were Thomas J. Mooney and Warren K. Billings. Mooney had been tried three times in Martinez on a charge of possessing explosives and had undergone a preliminary hearing on a similar charge in Sacramento. Rumor had it that he was also responsible for the recent San Bruno towers explosion. He was known as a hothead and trouble maker. Billings, a disciple of

Mooney's, was an ex-con who had served time for carrying a *suitcase* of dynamite on a public streetcar.

They were logical suspects; had the police failed to consider them they would have been remiss. They were not the only logical suspects, however, nor for that matter even the most logical. Under the circumstances, however, logic played a minor part in these initial deliberations, and the police had a good reason for giving them special attention. Immediately after the parade, a "confidential source" had suggested to both Chief White and Captain Matheson that Mooney might bear investigating. White had immediately assigned a man to shadow him.

The other group, also logically chosen, was one traditionally associated with bombs and violence, whose two leading spokesmen were at that very minute in San Francisco preaching their revolutionary doctrines. It was Chief White's theory, as reported by the *Examiner* the following day, that "one of the anarchist groups in the city is responsible for the outrage." Detectives were assigned to shadow every known anarchist and to watch their meeting places.

To grant them the fullest benefit of the doubt, it may be that had the police had more time, and had events transpired differently, they would eventually have gotten around to investigating some of the other possibilities. But things didn't happen this way, and both the German and the Mexican leads, as well as a number of others, were dropped without investigation.

As yet unknown to Chief White, his task had already been even further simplified. So much so that his new Bomb Squad was almost rendered unnecessary.

6 ·

Although several days would pass before Chief White and Captain Matheson would be appraised of this fact, the San Francisco Police Department was no longer in charge of investigating the Preparedness Day bombing.

Charles Fickert maintained rooms in the Palace Hotel. At 9:30 that Saturday evening, less than eight hours after the explosion, the District Attorney had a visitor. The caller was Martin Swanson. Little of what occurred during this meeting is known, except that when Swanson left he was no longer head of the Public Utilities Protective Bureau, but on salary as "special investigator into the bomb cases under the District Attorney of the City and County of San Francisco." *

---

* Swanson, by his own admission, made during the Rena Mooney trial, was "constantly employed" by the District Attorney "in and about these cases" from 9:30 P.M. on July 22, 1916, to February 1, 1917.

As interesting as what was discussed in the meeting is the question: How did it come about?

There are three possibilities:

1. Fickert may have called in Swanson because he had prior experience in dynamite cases.

2. Swanson may have volunteered his services.

Either is possible, but neither is probable. Far more likely:

3. Someone sent Swanson to Fickert or suggested to Fickert that he contact Swanson.

Neither Charles Fickert nor Martin Swanson was a free agent.

Fickert, elected by United Railroads as a tool to squash the graft indictments, had, following his fulfillment of this task, remained no less in their control. As the Densmore Report would later reveal, Fickert was mentored by two men representing the business interests of the city, rarely prosecuting even the simplest case without first consulting Frank C. Drew, attorney for the Chamber of Commerce, or Fred W. Henshaw, at this time still a justice of the California Supreme Court, his acceptance of a $410,000 bribe in the Fair will case not yet having been exposed. Fickert was closely connected with the Chamber of Commerce. He was in the debt of PG&E as well as URR, both companies having financially supported his election in 1909 and all his re-election bids since. His loyalties lay with the same utility companies Thomas J. Mooney had fought.

Swanson was employed as an investigator for the utility companies. For him to take a leave of absence from his duties to assist Fickert meant that he had their permission to do so. It is possible his employers may even have suggested it.

This would not of itself necessarily imply anything sinister. It could have been the result of the most civic minded of motives, one of Swanson's employers saying, "Charley Fickert will need all the help he can get in this case. Why don't we call him and see if he'd like to borrow Martin Swanson?"

All this is conjecture. There is nothing conjectural about the importance of the meeting. In effect, the Preparedness Day bomb case was "solved" on the evening of the same day the murders took place. For when Martin Swanson entered Charles Fickert's room he brought with him his own suspects. All that remained was to find enough evidence to convict them.

The San Francisco *Chronicle* for Sunday, July 23rd, made up on the night of the 22nd, contained the following line: "District Attorney Fickert intimated that his office had a suspicion as to the identity of the ringleaders in the bomb plot, but further than that, would make no statement."

The use of the plural, the presumption that this was a large scale plot with several ringleaders, was telling.

Some years later a U.S. government fact-finding group, the National Commission on Law Observance and Enforcement, popularly known as the Wickersham Commission, would make a thorough study of the Mooney-Billings case. After considering this meeting and the events immediately following it would conclude:

"There was never any scientific attempt made by either the police or the prosecution to discover the perpetrators of the crime. The investigation was in reality turned over to a private detective, who used his position to cause the arrest of the defendants. The police investigation was reduced to a hunt for evidence to convict the arrested defendants."

5 · The Arrests

Sunday, July 23

Early Sunday morning the newly formed Bomb Squad began piecing together the puzzle of what had happened on the corner of Steuart and Market Streets.

It was not easy.

There was the suitcase story. A number of people had noticed the suitcase, some even claiming to have seen who placed it there. But there were discrepancies between their stories. Prendergast saw two men, Taylor and the others only one. Taylor said the man had a mustache, Prendergast that he had several days' beard, Kimberlin that he was smooth-shaven. Most of the witnesses described the man with the suitcase as a Mexican. This was certainly a clue. Yet the whole suitcase story might be a false lead. Because of the close proximity of Steuart Street to both the Ferry Building and the Southern Pacific Station, suitcases were a common sight.

Too, there were other witnesses who claimed to have seen an object falling through the air above the crowd just before the explosion. One, Mrs. Janie Compton, watching the parade from her room on the sixth floor of the Terminal Hotel directly across Market, said she saw a man walk across the roof of the saloon. He leaned over the edge, then turned and ran back. The explosion had been almost simultaneous.

The physical evidence was equally confusing. If the bomb was left at the scene in a suitcase—some 25 to 40 minutes before the explosion, according to the witnesses—it had to be a time bomb, triggered by a clock mechanism or an acid fuse. But there were no clock parts in the assembled evidence. This would seem to indicate the fuse bomb. Yet there was another possibility; if the bomb was dropped from the roof, it would probably have been a bomb of the percussion type, one designed to explode on impact. Such a bomb could be of very simple construction, with few parts.

Yet it was also possible that all the clock parts had been washed away. In an attempt to partly remedy Lt. Bunner's bungling, adjacent storm drains were sifted, netting several bullets, a few pieces of metal, and one and one half ball bearings. The bullets were of the same calibers as those found on the sidewalk. There was no proof, however, that the other pieces belonged to the puzzle. Some of the metal scraps, heavily coated with rust, obviously did not, and a nearby garage might have accounted for the ball bearings, none of which had been found on the scene. The drains hadn't been cleaned for six months. Nor was there any proof that all the assorted objects now brought forth by souvenir hunters were actually from Steuart and Market. Publicity can be a very creative force. There were locks from *two* suitcases, but a metal frame for neither—the one part least likely to have been totally destroyed, overlooked, or washed away. The press reflected the confusion: in the *Bulletin* and *Call* the bomb was thrown, in the *Chronicle* and *Examiner* placed.

From the evidence picked up on the corner by policemen and reporters, and from those metal fragments taken from the bodies of the victims,* a probable bomb emerged. It was much as Gleeson described it, consisting of a steel pipe filled with an explosive, then surrounded by steel-jacketed cartridges. These, when the explosive detonated, had sprayed lethally in all directions. More than 50 bullets, spent shell cases, and unexploded cartridges had been found, all steel-jacketed, of .22 and .32 calibers.

Over the next several days the police would interview "scores" of people and assemble a small mountain of possible evidence. Sifting through it, District Attorney Fickert and his assistants would pick and choose, and from their choices the prosecution would form its case. What did not fit their theory they would ignore, discredit (if the newspapers had learned of it also), or suppress. Although the police had obtained affidavits from each, the prosecution would never call Prendergast, Kimberlin, or Taylor as witnesses. Their descriptions of the men they saw did not fit the defendants. Nor did they call Mrs. Compton or any of the witnesses who saw the object falling through the air. These stories contradicted their theory of the bombing.

Only later would it become apparent that they went far beyond this— adjusting testimony to better fit their hypothesis and creating evidence that had not previously existed.

Most of Sunday, Tom Mooney worked on the carmen's report, which he finally finished that night, while Rena spent the better part of the day fashioning a new hat to wear on their trip. It was a large hat with a tan drape, picot-edged, with a red band. It was nearly midnight when she finished pinning on the trimmings.

2 · Monday, July 24

Rising early, the Mooneys caught a jitney to the train depot and bought two round-trip tickets to Montesano, some 50 miles north of San

* Even this was not incontrovertible. At one point the prosecution would attempt to introduce into evidence a number of metal pieces removed from the ashes of one of the victims who had been cremated. A mortician testified, however, that the pieces were fasteners from the coffin in which the body had been burned.

Francisco on the Russian River. They left on the 8:45. Neither their destination nor their departure was secret—Rena had notified her pupils that she was taking a week's vacation and both the building superintendent and elevator boy were given their address. In addition, Rena had written a note to be posted on the studio door; in the rush Tom had forgotten to put it up; it lay on a table inside the studio.

The police were well aware of their whereabouts. Detective Frank McConnell, assigned by Chief White to shadow them, caught the same train.

The announcement in the morning papers that a Bomb Squad had been created and Captain Duncan Matheson appointed to head it, helped relieve some of the tension. Matheson was well thought of. He had a long and honorable record and was known to be scrupulously honest at a time when this was a distinguishing characteristic. His name would add special weight to the bomb evidence; he was not a man one could easily accuse of unfairness. Overlooked in these analyses was one significant fact: Matheson was not a detective; he was a traffic officer.

Later that morning Billings, his face spotted and blotched with a skin rash from which he had been suffering for more than a week, went to Lane Hospital for treatment. Swanson's operatives had him under surveillance. They learned that he had another appointment Wednesday morning.

Meanwhile, Fremont Older was also suffering from some splotches, only these were on his reputation.

Immediately after the explosion Thornwell Mullally had charged that the "incendiary speeches" of Fremont Older and Rudolph Spreckles at the Dreamland Rink peace meeting had "inspired the wholesale murder." William Randolph Hearst's *Examiner,* which aired Mullally's charges, had gone him one better by demanding the immediate arrest of all the meeting's speakers plus all other known or suspected radicals in California.

Although the accusations angered him, Older didn't miss the irony: that because he had advocated peace he was now being accused of violence. But this was standard San Francisco journalism, in which mudslinging, especially at rival papers, had always played a prominent part. Older could answer such attacks editorially. He was not so well prepared for another, less open accusation.

For years Older had delighted in bringing together at his ranch diverse people who seemingly had nothing in common. That they got along so well proved to him, and he hoped to them, something about the human condition. On a typical weekend the guest list at Woodhills might include a reformed prostitute and a society matron, a radical and a banker, a judge and an ex-convict. On one such weekend, Emma Goldman had been among the guests.

One of Older's leading competitors couldn't resist reporting, on his society page, that "Last weekend Mr. and Mrs. Fremont Older were honored to have as their houseguest the well-known anarchist Emma Goldman." Feeling it too good to use just once, however, the rival publisher had ordered it set in type several times a year ever since. Older took it as a mild joke, a barometer to the publisher's pique at the *Bulletin's* gain in advertising revenues. Only now did he become aware that it was less jest than obsession.

Monday afternoon the rival publisher, Fred W. Kellogg of the *Call,* went to Robert Newton Lynch, manager of the Chamber of Commerce, and told him that he had evidence, from a source he couldn't disclose, that the bomb plot had been hatched on Older's ranch by Cora and Fremont Older and Emma Goldman.

The Chamber of Commerce was far from disinterested in the bombing: Koster, for the Law and Order Committee, had already called a mass meeting of the city's merchants for Wednesday night "to consider what steps shall be taken to bring about the arrest and punishment of those responsible." But Lynch knew both Kellogg and the Olders and discounted the story. He made sure that Older heard it, however, and the editor was given still another reason to proceed cautiously in his handling of the bombing.

According to the press, more than a score of men and women had already offered tips concerning the identity of the bombers. By Monday it was beginning to appear that everyone who watched the parade had done so from the same intersection. Those who claimed to have seen suspicious persons were shown, either in the Bomb Bureau or in Fickert's office, photographs of possible suspects, among them police mug shots of Mooney and Billings. There were no identifications.

Among those who came forward that day was one John McDonald, an itinerant waiter, recently released from the hospital and presently unemployed. McDonald said that on Saturday afternoon, while he was standing on the southeast corner of Steuart and Market, he saw a man walking up Steuart Street carrying a very dirty tan leather suitcase. The man set it against the saloon wall and looked inside the door of the saloon. Another man came out and the two talked for three or four minutes. Then the man who had set the suitcase down crossed Market in an easterly direction. The other man remained on the corner for about four minutes, nervously glancing at his watch, the Ferry Building clock, and the suitcase. Then he crossed Market in a westerly direction. McDonald himself proceeded down Market toward the Ferry and was about half a block away when the explosion occurred. Only later did he connect the two events, and after mentioning them to several people, finally contact the police on Monday.

McDonald was taken to the Bomb Bureau and questioned. Officer George L. McCullough took down his statement in affidavit form, which

McDonald signed. Another officer, Peter Hughes, wrote a separate account of the interview for Captain Matheson.

In his affidavit McDonald described the man who carried the suitcase as twenty-five to thirty years old, 5 feet 8 inches tall, weighing about 145 pounds, smooth-shaven, of medium complexion, and wearing a dark blue serge suit and a gray fedora hat.

He described the other man as thirty to thirty-five years of age, 5 feet 7 or 8 inches tall, weighing 145 to 150 pounds, smooth-shaven, of rather dark complexion. He was unable to recall the color of his suit but did remember he wore a brown hat.

Neither description fit Mooney—who was thirty-three, 5'10", 190 pounds, with a full plump face and very noticeable bushy, black eyebrows—or Billings—a boyish twenty-two, with blond hair, normally of very light complexion although on this day his face was broken out in eczema, who weighed only 122 pounds and stood only 5'4".

McDonald's description of the dark complected man was similar to that supplied by Prendergast and Kimberlin, although they had this man carrying the suitcase and McDonald didn't.

One more item in McDonald's statement bears mentioning, the time at which he said he first saw the man coming up the street with the suitcase. This was given as 2:20 P.M., 14 minutes *after* the explosion. This may, or may not, have been a stenographic error.

It is not clear whether Fickert, Swanson, or any of Fickert's assistants were present at McDonald's initial interrogation or whether, on the basis of the affidavits, they decided to call him back for further questioning. What is clear is that the two men McDonald described bore no resemblance whatever to Thomas J. Mooney or Warren K. Billings. Yet, despite this, John McDonald was to become the first of the prosecution's major witnesses, one of that group which the Wickersham Commission would later describe as "a weird procession consisting of a prostitute, two syphilitics, a psychopathic liar, and a woman suffering from a spiritualistic hallucination."

As for the affidavits, they were suppressed, for 14 years.

That evening the *Bulletin* reported the reward total had reached $8000.

3 · Tuesday, July 25

At Montesano, the Mooneys arose shortly after dawn. Tom gathered wood and built a campfire, over which Rena cooked breakfast. McConnell watched, through binoculars, from the bushes some distance away. The detective had spent a miserable night, unaware that the Mooneys had planned to camp out.

In San Francisco, newsboys shouted the *Chronicle* headline $14,100 OFFERED FOR CAPTURE OF THE BOMB FIENDS. Overnight the Chamber of Commerce had boosted the reward total by offering $5000 for "information leading to the conviction of anyone for the bomb outrage."

With only a slight attempt at subtlety, the Law and Order Committee was already attempting to blame labor for the bombing:

"Recent disturbances upon the waterfront were accompanied by violence," read a statement issued by the committee that morning. "Intimidation was practiced on merchants and their employees and an intolerable situation resulted, which led to a mass meeting of businessmen to protest against such a situation. This spirit of lawlessness in the community logically terminated in the damnable bomb outrage on Saturday."

The bombing was now three days old. The fear of additional explosions had died down. Koster resurrected it with a frightening revelation. He told the press that Chamber officials had received another anonymous letter, identical in handwriting to those received before the Preparedness Day parade. It stated that if the Law and Order Committee's announced meeting were not canceled it would be bombed.

The committee would not be intimidated, Koster said. The meeting would be held despite the threat.

That same day John McDonald was moved to a better hotel, assigned a police guard, and given his meals and pocket money.

And that night, as if in answer to the mounting pressure, Chief White announced that the bombers would be arrested within 48 hours.

4 · Wednesday, July 26

Although the eczema on his face had almost disappeared, Billings decided to keep his appointment at Lane Hospital. He was in the waiting room of the clinic shortly before 11 A.M. when he saw Martin Swanson and a number of men coming down the corridor. Reaching into his pocket, he pulled out the package of cigarette papers, and using the piece with the license numbers on it, rolled a cigarette and lit it. It was fortunate, he decided, that he had left the bulb and the can of paint remover in the bushes outside.

Swanson paused beside the door. "The man I speak to will be Billings," he told his companions. He then entered the room, greeted Billings "Hi, kid," and grasped his hand. Officers Bunner and Goff moved in quickly, grabbing Billings' other hand and snapping on handcuffs. While being frisked Billings was told he was under arrest. When he asked on what charge, no one replied. Also present were Fickert and Chief White.

As they passed down the corridor Bunner asked, "Billings, who was

Warren K. Billings (center) shortly after his arrest for the Preparedness Day murders. To the left is police Sgt. Charles Goff, to the right Assistant District Attorney James Brennan, Billings' prosecutor, who later would admit he didn't believe his own witnesses.

that fellow you were talking with?"

Billings, surprised, answered "Don't you know him?"

"No," Bunner admitted.

"His name is Martin Swanson. He's a URR detective."

Bunner wasn't the only man who didn't know Swanson. Captain Matheson would later testify that not until the 26th or 27th did he first meet Swanson, and learn that he had been employed by Fickert and placed in charge of the bomb investigation.

Billings was taken to Richmond Station and interrogated. Although questioned about his activities on July 22nd—as well as other dates—no mention was made of the charges against him.

5 ·

Swanson, together with Fickert, his assistant Edward Cuhna, Lt. Bunner, and Detective Proll then drove to Belle Lavin's roominghouse at

2410 Mission Street, where they searched Billings' room. They found a .32 caliber pistol, a .22 caliber rifle, a half can of .22 short and .22 long cartridges, a jimmy of the type used by burglars, and ten ball bearings.

Swanson also found the PG&E garage job application, which he had given Billings and which he now pocketed.

Mrs. Lavin arrived while the search was in progress and asked to see their search warrants. For reply, she was arrested "on suspicion."

6 ·

At about two that afternoon detective Draper Hand and officer Desmond stopped Israel Weinberg's jitney on Market Street and ordered his passengers out. Weinberg was then frisked and told he was under arrest.

"What am I arrested for?" he asked.

"I don't know," Hand replied. Taking the Union Label from the window of the vehicle, Hand, with a grin, tore it into little pieces, which he dropped in the street.

Weinberg assumed that this was just another part of the police harassment of jitney operators.

His jitney was taken to the police garage, while Weinberg was placed in a cell in City Prison. About a half-hour later he was taken out and questioned by Matheson, Goff, and several other officers regarding his activities on June 10th and July 22nd and his relationship with the Mooneys. He talked freely.

Repeatedly he inquired as to the charges against him, but there was no reply. He was asked for a list of friends and business associates who might put up bail. He gave them the names of his doctor and several officers of the jitney operator's union. The men were never called, although each was investigated. Weinberg was returned to his cell, only to be taken out after a few minutes and questioned again by a different team of officers.

7 ·

While this was taking place, Swanson, Bunner, Proll, and Hughes had broken open the door of Rena Mooney's studio in the Eilers Building. They found the note Tom had forgotten to post. They also found, and seized, a large number of radical books, magazines, and newspapers, including copies of Berkman's *The Blast* and Mooney's own *The Revolt;* considerable correspondence relating to the URR strike; the files of the International Workers' Defense League, including letters from such known agitators as Haywood, Debs, Lucy Parsons, Mother Jones, Flynn, and Berkman, as well as a New Year's card from San Quentin signed J. J. McNamara; two revolvers, one .32 caliber, the other .38 caliber; 15 .32 caliber lead cartridges; 33 .32 caliber steel-jacketed cartridges; and 9 .38 caliber lead cartridges. They also found the notebook in which Rena Mooney had taken down the testimony during the 1914 trial of Emerson, the M&M detective caught with stolen dynamite.

8 ·

Although an attempt had been made to keep the arrests secret, a *Bulletin* reporter learned of the arrest of a man, "name unknown," at Lane Hospital in time to make headlines in the 5 P.M. edition. The article stated—the reporter may have surmised this—that "The man was suffering from injuries which apparently were caused by an explosion."

While Captain Matheson refused to add further particulars, he did issue a statement that the police expected to arrest all members of the dynamite ring within the next 36 hours and that all had been under constant surveillance since the time of the explosion.

9 ·

Promptly at eight, Koster called the meeting in Civic Auditorium to order.

Despite the bomb threat, 6000 people had mustered their courage and passed the careful police scrutiny at the door. There were policemen on the platform, along the walls, at every exit, some 200 in all. In this tense and dramatic setting, speaker after speaker stepped forward to denounce the bomb outrage and to call for an end to the era of lawlessness that plagued the city.

Koster, the keynote speaker, repeated in almost identical words the Law and Order Committee's earlier statement implying that the waterfront strike had "logically terminated" in the Preparedness Day bombing. Stressing that the committee's only concern was to uphold the law, he nevertheless warned that if the constituted authorities could not maintain peace, the people themselves would have to take action as they had done in an earlier time. Koster did not elaborate. It wasn't necessary. Everyone present knew the episode in the city's history to which he was referring.

After unanimously passing a resolution demanding "the relentless pursuit of those responsible" and pledging "united support to the redemption of this city from violence and intimidation and the re-establishment of a law-abiding spirit," the meeting disbanded.

The bomber had not dared carry out his threat.

Neither the drama nor Koster's veiled reference was overlooked in press reports of the meeting. Under the headline SIX THOUSAND BRAVE BOMB—JOIN CRIME WAR, *Call* reporter Edward H. Hurlbut began his account:

"They sat with us last night at the Auditorium, the brooding shades of the Vigilantes.

"The high resolve that consecrated their work sixty years ago, recrudescent, spoke from the lips of the younger generation.

"Grim, stern, patriotic, the sons of the sires of 1856 pledged themselves to carry on in sacred trust the fair name of a great city that these men of an elder time cleansed of stain and dishonor and passed along to us unsullied and glorious, a golden escutcheon without blotch . . ."

It was far from impartial reporting. Heavy with such statements as "Times make the man. Leaders arise when the occasion is large. There was a Coleman in 1856; there is a Koster today" it ended "The Chamber of Commerce is working for all the people, for all classes, for the greater good of a still greater, a more united San Francisco. And this work, this city, by its outpouring in face of death threats, has endorsed and will inexorably support."

Reporter Hurlbut's enthusiasm was understandable. Although few *Call* readers were aware of it, Edward H. Hurlbut was listed on the payroll of the Chamber of Commerce as "Director of Publicity for the Law & Order Committee."

Though less eulogistic, the city's other papers were no more critical. Whatever the private feelings of their editors and publishers about the return of the extra-legal vigilantes, none chose to speak out against them editorially. While the *Bulletin* did feature Mayor Rolph's statement that the police were fully capable of maintaining law and order, it stuck to factual reporting of the meeting. Following the arrests, Fremont Older instructed his reporters to avoid saying anything that might be taken as an implication that the arrested parties were innocent.

Older, like many others, was living with a memory. In 1911, convinced of their innocence, he had launched a campaign in defense of the McNamaras.

10 ·

At about 11 P.M. a raiding party, led by Martin Swanson, surrounded Edward Nolan's home on Angelica Street. Nolan, who had been attending a meeting of his local, arrived home shortly after midnight and was placed under arrest. The house had already been searched, netting only unimportant correspondence. Asked if there was anything in the basement, Nolan said there wasn't. Swanson demanded the key. Nolan gave it to him. The party found Tom Mooney's motorcycle, assorted washer, nuts and bolts, some clay molds, and several boxes and sacks of various powders.

TOOLS, MATERIALS FOR MANUFACTURE OF BOMBS SEIZED, the *Examiner* would headline the find the next morning.

11 ·

Each time Weinberg fell asleep, he would be reawakened, taken to an interrogation room, and under a bright spotlight, questioned for several more hours. Billings, at Richmond Station, was undergoing similar treatment, the officers working in relays through the night.

12 ·

All these arrests, searches, and seizures had one thing in common—they were illegal.

Billings, Mrs. Lavin, Weinberg, and Nolan had all been arrested without the benefit of warrants.

With a single exception, the searches of the various residences also were made without search warrants. The exception was Rena Mooney's studio, and even this search was unlawful inasmuch as the searchers neglected to file a return with the issuing magistrate as required by law.

Also required by law is that owners of seized property be given an itemized receipt for items seized. In no instance was this done. This was important, because except for the distorted stories in the press, the accused would have no way of knowing until their trials just what the raiders would claim to have found.

*Far more important, the arrests were made without any evidence whatsoever connecting the defendants with the crime.**

This is admittedly an astonishing statement. Not until 1930, and the discovery of the original McDonald affidavits, would the defense be able to prove this conclusively.

Of all the witnesses who later connected the defendants with the Preparedness Day bombing, only one had contacted the police *prior* to the arrests. This was John McDonald, whose suppressed statement described two men wholly dissimilar to any of the defendants. The case against the

* This may explain why no arrest warrants were issued, since in order to issue such a warrant there must be at least one complaining witness.

alleged Preparedness Day bombers was formed, in its entirety, *after* their arrests.

On what basis then were the arrests made?

The answer would be long in coming. Though asked this question numerous times in the course of the trials, Captain Matheson would assert that this information was confidential in character and could not be divulged.

Years later he would admit that Chief White had ordered the arrests on District Attorney Fickert's assurance that he possessed more than sufficient evidence to obtain convictions. Chief White, under great pressure to solve the cases, had apparently been so relieved at being handed a ready-made solution that he had not thought to consider it carefully. Captain Matheson did consider it, over a period of time, and concluded finally that the arrests were made with no evidence to support them. One of Fickert's chief assistants, James Brennan, the prosecutor of Billings, would eventually admit that the arrests were made on the sole basis of the defendants' past records and associations.

But both these admissions would not be made until years later, when they were no longer helpful to the accused.

The stories given to the press by District Attorney Fickert's office and the Bomb Bureau were vastly different, however.

13 · Thursday, July 27

POLICE ARREST MAN AND WOMAN FOR BOMB MURDERS

On seeing the headlines in the morning *Chronicle* San Franciscans breathed a collective sigh of relief.

It was premature, however, for there was a sub-head:

THOMAS J. MOONEY, DYNAMITE SUSPECT, SOUGHT BY POLICE

"In a whirlwind round-up the police yesterday swooped down upon the free clinic at Lane Hospital and arrested Warren K. Billings, a man once convicted of dynamiting activities.

"Swiftly following this, a squad of detectives swept into the lodging-house at 2410 Mission Street and there arrested Mrs. Belle Lavin, a woman who five years ago was arrested on the charge of complicity in the Los Angeles 'Times' dynamiting murders . . .

"Close upon the heels of this action the police last night raided the rooms of Thomas J. Mooney, agitator and suspected dynamiter, at 975 Market Street, and carried away all the papers, documents and personal effects belonging to Mooney and his wife, Rena Mooney.

"And in the midst of all this quick-firing action, the police discovered that Mooney, who, they said, had been a known co-worker and associate with Billings, had, with Mrs. Mooney, fled the city; and an imperative order was given to effect his arrest."

In the next paragraph, the "police asserted" that the group also had "criminal knowledge" of the San Bruno dynamiting. There followed a lively account of the radical pasts of the accused, with stress on their dynamiting records.

No mention was made that the charges against Mrs. Lavin in the *Times* case had been dropped for lack of evidence, or that no dynamite had been produced in Mooney's three Martinez "dynamiting trials," or that, despite the best efforts of Swanson and his operatives, there was no proof any of the accused were involved in the San Bruno dynamiting.

The Mooneys had not "fled the city," but the statement that they had was equivalent to a presumption of guilt. (Later the *Chronicle* would say they left San Francisco at 4 P.M. on July 22nd, an accusation as damning as it was untrue.)

Billings' Bertillon description from Folsom Prison was given—age, height, weight, complexion, color of hair and eyes. Under "Scars" there appeared: "Bullet wound across thumb of right hand." This information dated from 1913—the wound, then prominent, had by now all but disappeared, leaving only a slight indentation on the nail of the thumb. There was also a typographical error, perhaps the most important ever to appear in the *Chronicle*. This scar was on Billings' *left* thumb.

The reward offers had now reached a grand total of $17,100.*

The *Examiner's* account of the arrests was more dramatic; it had Billings struggling to escape at Lane Hospital, but captured and subdued. The paper also reported that police had sent out "a nation-wide call for the apprehension of Thomas J. Mooney, an I.W.W. agitator, and his wife Rena . . ."; stated that the evidence found in the Mooney rooms included "a quantity of steel-jacketed bullets, slugs and other missiles identical to those found in the bomb that exploded during the Preparedness Parade"; and described Rena Mooney's transcript of the Emerson trial as "a notebook containing records of explosives stolen from quarries in the Bay Region and of structures dynamited in San Francisco."

"According to District Attorney Fickert and the police," the *Examiner* continued, "the existence of this notebook proves that the Mooneys belonged to an organized group of dynamiters who planned and carried out the systematic destruction of property belonging to corporations having differences with labor."

Even more incriminating was the following:

"A bomb mechanism similar to the one fired during the Preparedness Parade, but intended solely for the destruction of property and not loaded

---

* As a gauge to the public attitude, the fund to aid the impoverished families of the bomb victims finally amounted to only $6700.

with bullets and metal slugs, is also among the evidence that has been obtained by the District Attorney's office."

The implication was that the bomb had been found among Mooney's effects. In reality, this was the bomb Martin Swanson allegedly discovered near the San Bruno towers in June.

In addition to full descriptions of the defendants, the *Examiner* also carried front-page photos of Mooney, Billings, and Mrs. Lavin. The photo of Mooney was an old one, taken in 1912 at the time of his Martinez arrest, and showed him with a long scraggly mustache that he no longer wore.

It was also in the *Examiner* that the first of the host of ghostly witnesses appeared. A Mission Street jeweler was said to have positively identified Billings' picture as that of a man to whom he had sold an alarm clock three weeks prior to the explosion.

The jeweler was never called as a witness in the subsequent trials.

Thus began the first, and in many ways the most important, trial of the Preparedness Parade bombing defendants—the trial by press that would set the community mood under which the jurors would be chosen and the court trials held. Day by day, for months, San Francisco newspapers would carry similar stories—filled with errors, distortions, unproven insinuations, and outright fabrications. In attempting to track down the sources of these stories, the Wickersham Commission would interview the reporters who wrote them. They stated that inasmuch as the defendants were held incommunicado and the prosecution refused to let its witnesses be interviewed, all such stories had to come from one of two sources: the Bomb Bureau or District Attorney Fickert's office.

In retrospect, the stories are almost as interesting for what they do not mention. Although he was present when nearly all of the arrests and searches took place, the name of Martin Swanson appeared in none of the accounts.

14 ·

Among those who read the papers that morning was a Miss Estelle Smith, receptionist for a Market Street credit dentist. On seeing Billings' picture and description she told her employer that she thought he looked like the man with the suitcase who had asked permission to go on the roof of the building during the Preparedness parade. The dentist called Assistant District Attorney Brennan, whom he knew slightly. Shortly afterward, three officers arrived and took Estelle to Fickert's office. Among those present when she arrived were Fickert, Cuhna, Brennan, Chief White, Captain Matheson, Sgt. Goff, and Mayor Rolph. The Mayor greeted her warmly, congratulating her on behalf of the city for her courage in coming forward. There followed several hours of questioning by Fickert, Swanson, and Cuhna.

15 ·

About noon, Tom and Rena Mooney went out on the river in a canoe. They planned to tie up at some shaded spot, swim, and have a picnic lunch. Clad only in bathing suits, they rowed to Monte Rio, one of the many small resort communities scattered along the river. While Tom swam, Rena went to the train station to buy some beer for him and to mail postcards to her students. As a train had just come in with the morning papers, she bought an *Examiner* and took it, folded, back to the boat. They drifted down river and tied up by some willows to eat their lunch. While Tom unwrapped the sandwiches, Rena opened the paper.

"Oh my God, Tom," she cried. *"Look at that!"*

The headline seemed to scream out at them: BILLINGS, WEINBERG, NOLAN ARRESTED: MOONEYS ESCAPE!

They rowed back to Monte Rio and went to the station, where Tom dictated a telegram. Dated 2 P.M and addressed to Chief of Police White, it read:

> Wife and I left San Francisco last Monday 8:45 for week's vacation at Montesano. See by Examiner I am wanted by San Francisco police. My movements are and have been an open book. Will return by next train to San Francisco. I consider this attempt to incriminate me in connection with bomb outrage one of the most dastardly pieces of work ever attempted.
>
> Tom Mooney

As a precautionary measure, Tom sent an identical copy to Fremont Older at the *Bulletin*.

Rather than attempt to row upstream, the Mooneys abandoned the canoe and walked the three miles to their camp, where they dressed, packed, and by hurrying managed to catch the 4:15 train to San Francisco.

Several miles down the line, at Guerneville, detective McConnell and another officer boarded the train, arrested the Mooneys, and removed them from the train at gun point.

These arrests, too, were made without a warrant.

The papers the following day, quoting Chief White, would claim that Mooney's telegram was a ruse, that the Mooneys had bought tickets not to San Francisco but to an intermediate point along the line, and that only on learning that they were planning to escape had he ordered their arrests.

As was subsequently established, the Mooneys bought no tickets at the station, using the return portions of their round-trip tickets, a fact of which Chief White was aware, inasmuch as his officers had confiscated their ticket stubs and obtained statements from the station agent and conductor.

There was never any official explanation as to why Chief White delayed so long in arresting the Mooneys, or why he told the papers they were fugitives when, as Captain Matheson had told the press the previous day, they had been under "constant surveillance" since the afternoon of the 22nd.

One can only surmise that he was giving them ample opportunity to escape if they felt so inclined. As it was, the papers, quoting Chief White, reported their "attempted escape" and "capture" anyway.

16 ·

That day, Billings drew a map for Chief White, showing exactly where he had been on the afternoon of the 22nd. On it he marked those incidents he could remember—the conversation with the bartender about "Baron" in the Reception Bar, seeing the Hudson with the jagged white streak in Union Square Alley, the girls marching by, the overheard remarks. He left out only one detail, exactly what he had been doing at the time. Only then was he told the charges against him.

At about four that afternoon, Weinberg was handcuffed and taken from his cell to his home, where Swanson, Cuhna, Brennan, and Goff were already conducting a search. No incriminating evidence was found. The searchers did find the gas company receipt, which supported a portion of Weinberg's alibi, and which they kept.

While there, Weinberg later testified, Swanson got him aside, out of hearing of the others, and grinning, said, "Didn't I tell you I would get you?"

(Swanson would later deny that he had made any such remark.)

Only then was Weinberg told that he was being held for the Preparedness Day murders.

17 ·

Just about the time the evening papers were going to press, Fickert brought reporters into his office, where he introduced them to Estelle

Smith.

"Garrulous, dramatic, vivid, a born actress," Hopkins of the *Bulletin* would later describe her, "she brought two features the case had badly lacked from the newspaper standpoint: a brand-new change of scene, and sex appeal." And she had a story to tell, one to send shivers up the spines of even the most jaded readers:

About 1 P.M. on the afternoon of Preparedness Day, while Estelle was working in the reception room of the dental office of her employer at 721 Market Street, a young man had come up the stairs and asked permission to go up on the roof to take photographs. He identified himself as a reporter for the *Chronicle* and was carrying "a small black suitcase, or it may have been a satchel. It looked like a photographer's case."

Explaining that she would have to obtain permission from the dentist, who was out to lunch, she invited him to sit down and wait. As he did so she noticed that he was quite nervous and perspiring badly.

"I said, 'What is the matter with you?'

"He said, 'I am sick with the heat.' "

Feeling sorry for him, she dampened a towel and wiped the perspiration from his brow. As she did, he put his hand over hers and she noticed that he had a "mashed thumb . . . his nail is all wrinkled on his *right* thumb . . ."[italics author's].

The suitcase was in the middle of the floor, where a patient might trip over it, and she reached over to move it.

"My God, girl, don't touch that!" he yelled.

"What's the matter with you?" she asked.

"I'm afraid you will strain the lens in my camera," he replied.

Deciding that she might as well let him go onto the roof, she called a friend of her mother's from an adjoining room, one Louis Rominger, and asked him to carry the case up onto the roof, which he did, commenting, "My God, this is a heavy camera."

Sometime later Estelle noticed another man in the corridor and asked him what he wanted. "He was very rude, a repulsive looking man, long mustache. I would say he was a Russian Jew or something that way—a foreigner anyhow . . ." He gave her a sharp reply and an argument commenced. Barring his way to the stairs, she told him "We lease this building—we pay the rent—so I guess we have got a right to say who can come into the building!" If he didn't leave, she threatened, she would call a cop. At that moment a woman came up the stairs, and hearing the argument, told the man to come back down.

Estelle then joined her mother (Mrs. Alice Kidwell), Rominger, and the doctor at the window, as the parade was just reaching their block. Looking out she saw the couple leaving the building and heard the man on the roof yell down for them to come up. They motioned for him to come down and "went on down the street."

About this time Mayor Rolph passed. "I took a towel and I waved it out the window. I said, 'Hell-ooo, Mayor Rolph' as loud as I could. The doctor says to me, 'Gracious me, you have such a mouth, don't holler so loud.' When I walked from the front window to the reception room, this gentleman . . . I had let on the roof . . . he was coming down.

"I said 'What is the matter with you? Don't you want to take the pictures?' He was very agitated. He put the suitcase down. He said, 'No, I am awful sick with the heat.' Then I said, 'Come on in and sit down.' I said, 'Just make yourself at home in our reception room.' He said, 'No, I won't wait, I have got friends waiting for me.' He turned around and shook hands with me. He said, 'Good-bye, girl, you have been very kind to me. I won't take advantage of you.' "

The young man, whom she positively identified from photographs as Warren K. Billings, had then left the building.

It *was* a dramatic story. According to Hopkins, "The city rang, next day, with the gripping narrative of the tender-hearted little dental nurse who had wiped the sweat from the brow of an intending murderer desperate with fear; who had all but lifted in her hands the fatal suitcase . . ."

It was such a dramatic story that apparently none of the reporters thought to ask just what it had to do with the bombing at Steuart and Market, for 721 Market was exactly 4066 feet—or three-quarters of a mile—from the bomb scene.

18 ·

"That Billings was present at the corner of Steuart and Market streets on Saturday afternoon, just before the explosion, has been definitely ascertained by the police," reported the 5 P.M. edition of the *Bulletin*. "They are reported to be certain that Billings left the suitcase there."

As proof of this statement, the police stated that a mechanic had identified Billings' picture as that of the "blotch-faced" man who had warned him of a coming explosion while standing alongside him at the fatal corner.

No such witness appeared in the subsequent trials.

Fickert was quoted as saying of Weinberg, "He drove the plotters from the spot in his jitney"; of Nolan, "Nolan is one of the toughest of the gang. He is able to make the bombs himself"; of all the group, "The evidence against them is conclusive. They are the direct actors."

19 ·

The Mooneys were held in a hotel room at Guerneville until after seven, then driven to the city via a circuitous route, several times changing vehicles, with a number of delays while officers called in for instructions, finally arriving about midnight at Sausalito, where a special ferry was chartered to bring them to San Francisco. On arrival photographers snapped their pictures, which appeared in the papers the following day. Rena was shown wearing her hat.

Taken to the office of the Bomb Bureau they were searched, separated, and interrogated from 12:45 until 4 A.M. Independently they gave to the police as full an account as they could recall of their activities on the 22nd, together with the names or descriptions of people who could verify that they had watched the parade from the Eilers Building roof.

Both repeatedly asserted their innocence; both repeatedly asked permission to consult an attorney.*

In searching Tom the police found several keys; they asked what each fit. He told them, identifying several as keys to the studio, another as a key to Nolan's basement. He kept his motorcycle there, he explained, because the Eilers Building had no garage. The police retained the keys. They also confiscated Rena Mooney's hat.

Tom was then taken to City Prison, where he was held in an isolation cell for 11 days. Rena Mooney was placed in a regular cell that night; the next two days and nights, however, she was locked in a bathroom in the women's branch of the prison, having to sleep on the floor between the tub and toilet. She was then moved to County Jail at Ingleside. Like Billings, Weinberg, Nolan, and Mrs. Lavin, the Mooneys were held incommunicado, allowed communication with no one, including each other.

To their growing list of illegalities, the police now added several more:

None of the defendants were allowed to see counsel; none of them were booked; all were denied the right to prompt arraignment.

Section 825 of the California Penal Code reads:

"The defendant must in all cases be taken before the magistrate without unnecessary delay, and after such arrest, any attorney at law entitled to practice in the court of record of California, may at the request of the prisoner or any relative of such prisoner, visit the person so arrested. Any

---

* Later, in the trials, the defense, in an attempt to confirm that the Mooneys had not changed their stories, would ask the prosecution for the transcripts of their interrogations. In reply, Fickert and his assistants would state that no transcripts had been made. They were discovered nearly 20 years later, when the Bomb Bureau files were reopened. They not only proved the defense's contention, but showed that Tom Mooney had demanded counsel a total of 86 times.

officer having charge of the prisoner so arrested who wilfully refuses or neglects to allow such attorney to visit a prisoner is guilty of a misdemeanor."

During Tom Mooney's trial Captain Matheson was questioned by one of Mooney's attorneys:

Q. You knew that a man arrested without a warrant, you were at once to take him before the nearest magistrate?

A. Yes, I am familiar with that section of the Code.

Q. Then why didn't you do it?

A. In the interest of justice.

Q. In the interest of justice you suspended law?

A. Yes, sir.

Although this was in itself a rather remarkable statement, Lt. Bunner, under questioning re Weinberg's arrest and detention, managed to surpass it, by replying to a similar query:

A. I regard the directions of my superior as sufficient warrant for violating the law.

6 · The Theory

MOONEY'S ARREST put his friends in a difficult position. In coming to his aid they would be courting the risk of arrest themselves.

Admittedly, the number struggling with this problem was not large. In his half-dozen years in the California labor movement, the outspoken agitator had managed to make more enemies than friends. By advocating industrial unionism, he had alienated the leadership of the AFL. By proceeding with the URR strike without Labor Council sanction, he had managed to antagonize the few members of that body he had not already attacked at one time or another. The radicals in his own molders' union were in the minority. The firing of the URR men who heeded his strike call meant that few carmen were now likely to come to his defense. He had also burned his political bridges, having joined and broken with the Socialist Party, the IWW, and the Syndicalists.

For two people, the moral dilemma was acute. Emma Goldman knew the Mooneys and Nolan only slightly; she had never met Billings or Weinberg. But Alexander Berkman knew all the defendants except Weinberg well (he had met Weinberg only once, at *The Blast* picnic), and was absolutely certain of their innocence. "He considered none of them capable of throwing a bomb into a crowd of people," Emma would later write in her memoirs. "His assurance was sufficient guarantee for me that they had no connexion whatever with the preparedness-day parade explosion."

At first the pair anticipated a concerted response from the liberal and radical elements, similar to the immediate protests in the cases of Ford and Suhr and Joe Hill. "Instead we were confronted by complete silence on the part of the very people who had for years known and collaborated with Mooney, Nolan, and their fellow-prisoners."

The silence of organized labor was not accidental. One evening, shortly after the arrests, a delegation from the Labor Council called on District Attorney Fickert in his office. The group, headed by reactionaries Andrew Gallagher and Mike Casey, told Fickert that Mooney had been thoroughly repudiated by organized labor; they asked him therefore to promise that the prosecution wouldn't treat these as "labor cases." Fickert assured them of his compliance. Although the Labor Council's part of the bargain was not spelled out, it was clear to all concerned. If Fickert wouldn't treat them as labor cases, neither would the Labor Council. Although Fickert soon broke his promise, for months after the arrests no mention of the case appeared in *Organized Labor,* organ of the powerful California building trades, or the *Labor Clarion,* official weekly of the San Francisco Labor Council and the State Federation of Labor.

The silence of the radicals had another basis, Emma realized. "The Mc-Namara confession was still haunting, ghostlike, the waking and sleeping hours of their erstwhile friends . . .

"It was a desperate situation. Only Sasha [Berkman] and I dared speak up for the prisoners. But we were known as anarchists and it was a question of whether the accused . . . would wish to have us affiliated with their defense; they might feel that our names would hurt their case rather than do them good."

There was no way for them to consult the defendants. Berkman called John Mooney and learned that the prisoners were being held incommunicado; despite repeated attempts, neither their families nor the lawyers for their unions had been able to see them. Berkman also learned that to date they had been unable to find a lawyer willing to represent Tom and Rena.

Both Berkmen and MissGoldman had already had a taste of the unpopularity of this cause. Prior to the bombing, Emma's lectures had drawn packed houses. On the night afterward there were, as Emma put it, "just fifty people at my meeting, the rest of the audience consisting of detectives." Following Estelle Smith's revelations, reporters had called Berkman asking if he were "the repulsive-looking Russian Jew" in her description.

"But we could not sit by idly and be a party to a conspiracy of silence."

In all her remaining lectures, Emma spoke out on behalf of the defendants, while Sasha began preparing a special issue of *The Blast* dealing with the explosion and the arrests. They did so with a certainty, born of long experience, that it wouldn't be long before Fickert attempted to connect them with the crime.

2 ·

In the meantime, the trial by press continued. On the 28th, the day after the Mooneys were arrested, the stories of their "attempted escape" appeared in all the papers. On this day too, Fickert supplied one important ingredient thus far missing from the case—motive. Fickert was quoted in the *News* as saying that "The explosion was . . . an attempt against the URR employees, who failed to respond to a strike organized two weeks ago. Fickert says he has positive evidence that the bomb aimed at the URR employees exploded prematurely. He declared that he can prove Mrs. Rena Mooney, the organizer's wife in jail as a suspect, was seen at Steuart and Market streets just before the explosion . . . A second bomb was to have been exploded underneath a URR car by Mrs. Mooney according to Fickert."

No mention of this second bomb was made in the subsequent trials. But in the main, Fickert did stick to this motive, improbable as it was. Considered logically, it made no sense. Why should a man try to blow up the men he had been trying to help? Even if one accepted Tom Mooney's motive as vengeance or spite, why would anyone else join him in so senseless a venture?

But the public mood was not inclined toward the logical. Fickert's explanation—that the bombing of the spectators was in a sense an accident, that the bomb had been intended for a specific target but had exploded prematurely—was, for all its basic contradictions, far more believable than the possibility that 10 innocent people had been blown up for no reason whatever.

3 ·

But the public did not have to rely on theories. There were certainties. One was Estelle Smith. Friday morning Estelle was shown the hat taken from Rena Mooney following her arrest, the hat Rena claimed not to have finished making until after Preparedness Day. "It's the same hat!" Estelle exclaimed. "The hat the woman who came up the stairs on Preparedness Day wore!"

Shortly after there occurred a dramatic confrontation in Fickert's office. With the press in attendance, Warren Billings was brought in to face his accuser.

"That's him, that's the man," Estelle screamed.

Billings, taken aback, mumbled that she was mistaken.

"You know you are the man!" she cried. "Why do you deny it? Why, boy, I have a brother of my own, and I wouldn't say this about you if there were the slightest possibility of my being mistaken!"

Estelle positively identified Billings as the young man with the suitcase. Moreover, there was confirmation of her story. Hubbard Wade, a school teacher from Hawaii, stated that he had been present at 721 Market that Saturday and had seen the young man with the suitcase on the stairs. He too positively identified him as Billings.*

---

* Fickert did not allow the press to question any of his witnesses. He either let them recite their stories before the reporters, as in the cases of Estelle and Wade, without interruptions or questions except by himself, or in the case of some of the other witnesses,

Fickert promised the reporters that before the day was over two even more damning identifications would be made, one by Peter Vidovich, an "Alaska mining man" who had also been standing outside 721 Market and had seen Billings; the other by Louis Rominger, the man who "was in the dental office and accompanied the youth with the suitcase to the roof."

Vidovich's identification of Billings took place that day as promised. Rominger's didn't. But so many witnesses against the bombers were now appearing, that the absence of one passed unnoticed.

4 ·

When John Mooney had telephoned, asking him to defend Tom and Rena, Maxwell McNutt had been noncommittal, asking for time to think about it. McNutt had been involved in two major labor cases—the Mooney-Hanlon-Brown trials at Martinez and the Ford-Suhr pardon attempt. Both had hurt his law practice. Such cases not only rarely paid for the expense involved; they usually took a fantastic amount of time and almost invariably lost their attorneys important business and corporation clients.

The man who defended the people accused of the Preparedness Day bombings could anticipate both legal and social ostracism. Although the bombing was now nearly a week old, the horror of it still hung over the city. McNutt had made no attempt to contact either Tom or Rena. He had, however, been following the newspaper stories closely, and against his better judgment, had begun to acquire certain feelings.

Friday afternoon, as he was walking down Sutter Street, Martin Swanson came out of the PG&E building and hailed him, asking what he thought of the bomb cases.

"I think there is too much Swanson," McNutt replied.

"What do you mean?" Swanson asked.

McNutt reminded him of PG&E attorney Barrett's remark, made in Swanson's presence following Mooney's acquittal at Martinez, "Well, Mac, you got Mooney out of this but we put a red shirt on him and we will get something on him someday."

Swanson nodded.

issued statements in their names. From the time they appeared until well into the trials themselves, all his witnesses were kept in hiding. This was done allegedly for their protection.

One cannot help wondering how quickly the frame-up would have evaporated had the press, whatever its prejudices and preconceptions, been allowed just a few minutes alone with the garrulous Estelle. A single question—What is your brother's name?—would, on investigation, have revealed some remarkable things.

"Martin," McNutt said, "you are the man who caused the arrest of these defendants, and the identification is being sought afterwards."

Swanson, according to McNutt, admitted that this was so. Swanson then asked, "Do you think if we keep the private detectives in the background and make the public believe that the District Attorney and the police are prosecuting these cases that we will not get them?"

"Not if anybody is awake you won't," McNutt replied.

"You won't take the case?"

"I am beginning to get interested. Are you going to hang anybody else along with them?"

"Yes, Alexander Berkman."

"Who in the hell is Alexander Berkman?"

McNutt's question indicated how little he knew about the radical movement in America.

Swanson reached into his pocket and took out one of Berkman's pamphlets, which he handed to McNutt, explaining that Berkman was an anarchist.

"Martin," McNutt put the pamphlet in his pocket, "you know perfectly well where the defendants were that day, because Mooney had been to my office, complained to me just before the car strike that he could not move day or night but that he was followed by your men and by you."

Swanson claimed that he had Mooney under surveillance during the parade but that he had lost him "for a few minutes" in the crowd.

After Swanson had gone on, McNutt took out the pamphlet and wrote on it: "Handed me by Martin Swanson opposite 110 Sutter Street in discussion of private detectives with the bomb cases."

But still McNutt made no attempt to see the prisoners.

5 ·

That evening the *Bulletin* carried the story of Estelle Smith's and Hubbard Wade's identifications of Billings. The headlines, however, went to yet another story. According to Fickert, James Crockett, an employee of United Railroads, formerly a PG&E detective, who said he had known Billings since 1913, claimed that he had seen him on the roof of the Ferry Inn minutes before the explosion. The Ferry Inn was a saloon located across Steuart Street from the Ferry Exchange Saloon where the bomb exploded.

The importance of Crockett's testimony was apparent: he was the first witness to place Warren K. Billings at the bomb scene. According to the *Bulletin,* he not only identified Billings by sight, but had also identified a brown coat and hat police had taken from Billings' rooms as those Billings wore at the time.

Crockett did not testify in any of the subsequent trials, for a good reason. The following day a *Bulletin* reporter, interviewing witnesses to the explosion, talked to Frank Doyle, the operator of the filling station next to the Ferry Inn, and from him learned that the only access to the roof of the saloon was by means of a ladder located inside his gas station. Doyle said that on the day of the parade no one had gone up to the roof.

Fickert never mentioned Crockett again.

6 ·

With all these rapidly breaking stories, it was not too surprising that some developments in the case received scant mention in the press.

One was a brief item, date-lined Oregon City, Oregon, that one Chris Lassen, a Dane, had confessed to local police that he had committed the Preparedness Day murders. San Francisco police were reportedly investigating Lassen's confession.

The other was a report from the City Chemist that the materials found in Nolan's basement had been tested and found to be "non-explosive" in character.

Two interesting happenings that Friday did not appear in the paper Saturday, or on any other day.

One was that U.S. government handwriting and photography expert Theodore Kytka had completed his comparison of the anonymous threats and the handwriting samples obtained from each of the defendants and concluded that there was no similarity. With this, the prosecution discontinued its investigation of the threatening letters.

The other was the "confession" of Israel Weinberg.

Weinberg was not a radical. He had never been in jail. He had never been questioned by police. To him the accusation was an unbelievable nightmare, the kind of thing that sometimes could happen in the Russia of his boyhood under the Tsar's secret police but not in the United States.

Since his arrest, his interrogation had been near continuous. Late Friday night he broke.

"Tell me what you want me to say and I will say it," he begged.

Fortunately Captain Matheson was in charge of the questioning. "No, we don't ask you to do that," Matheson replied, and ordered the police to return Weinberg to his cell and let him sleep.

Weinberg, emotionally shaken, told his jailor that he needn't bring him any more meals. He was not going to eat anything until he was allowed to see a lawyer and his wife and child.

7 ·

Over the weekend Martin Swanson led three more raids.

One was on the home of Rena's sister, Mrs. Belle Hammerberg, where Swanson seized Mooney's files on the URR strike, including the card file they had so carefully protected. There is no proof that Fickert or Swanson allowed United Railroads access to this file. But, coincidentally perhaps, shortly afterward a number of carmen listed as "sympathetic" were fired without cause.

The second raid was on the home of Tom's sister, Anna, where, according to Fickert in the *Chronicle,* correspondence was seized that proved Tom Mooney's connection with the bomb plot.

No such correspondence was ever introduced in evidence.

The last raid was on 569 Dolores Street, and it went badly from the start. Swanson, Cuhna, Brennan, and several policemen charged up the stairs only to have Alexander Berkman and Eleanor Fitzgerald ask what had delayed them.

Cuhna bluntly asked Berkman if there were any explosives in the house. To the surprise of the raiders, Berkman admitted there were, and handed them copies of *The Blast* and various anarchist books and pamphlets. Cuhna disgustedly said he was not interested in "mental dynamite." Not at all pleased with Berkman's tone of levity, he shook his finger at him and said, "You know, every suspect we've arrested in this case had a copy of *The Blast* on his person."

Berkman replied that he supposed he should be flattered but that he was really appalled. Since the last issue had come out two weeks before the arrests and run to only eight pages, this could only suggest he had some very slow readers.

While conducting their search (warrantless, one needn't add) the raiders asked more questions. Concluding from them that his visitors were remarkably ignorant when it came to matters philosophical, Berkman explained to them, as best he could, the meaning of "anarchism."

"But," as he later wrote in a humorous account of the raid, which appeared in *The Blast,* "I soon gave up the attempt as hopeless when Detective Swanson, considered the most intelligent of the crew, met one of my arguments with the profound parry: 'It's nonsense to say the land is monopolized. If you got enough money you can buy any piece of land you want.'"

Failing to find anything incriminating, the raiders shifted their attention to Berkman's co-worker. Miss Fitzgerald was very attractive, and considerably younger than her mentor.

"Are you an anarchist?" Cuhna asked her incredulously.

"Why, yes, I have been in the movement for ten years," Fitzi replied.

"You surely don't look like a rabid anarchist," Cuhna said.

"There are no rabid anarchists," said Miss Fitzgerald.

Brennan then, according to Berkman, "discreetly inquired whether we hang our underwear on the same clothesline, and in the next breath wondered why 'such a nice sweet lady with such a good Irish name' could have anything in common with the terrible Anarchists . . .

"In her calm, well-poised manner," continued Berkman, "Miss Fitzgerald replied that she was proud to be connected with the Anarchists; but she has been wondering ever since what had been my association with the District Attorney's office."

After four hours the raiders departed with copies of Emma Goldman's *Mother Earth* and *The Blast,* plus a copy of the latter's California subscription list. While this was admittedly a small catch, the "sensational raid on anarchist headquarters" netted three pages of headlines in the next morning's *Chronicle.* The paper noted that Berkman, the man who had attempted to assassinate Frick during the Homestead strike, had been questioned in connection with the Preparedness parade murders and was under constant surveillance.

8 ·

While this was true, other items in the papers were less so.

Fickert was quoted as saying that the defendants were instigators of the Wheatland hop riots and that they had been involved in the Los Angeles *Times'* dynamiting.

With the exception of Mrs. Lavin's having been briefly held for questioning in the *Times'* case, there was no basis for either charge.

Fickert was also quoted as saying that the alibi of the Mooneys was unsupported by witnesses. By the time this story appeared, at least seven people had voluntarily contacted the police, stating that they had seen the Mooneys on the Eilers roof. The Mooneys, in separate questioning, had given the police a number of names and descriptions of people on the roof. Incredible as it may seem, the defense later established that prior to the time this story appeared, July 31, Fickert had not bothered to contact any of these people.

Fickert was quoted in the *Examiner* as stating that the police were searching Mooney's campsite on the Russian River and that they expected to find the bomb ring's dynamite cache momentarily.

It was not mentioned again.

Fickert was quoted in the *Bulletin* as saying that the 24 sticks of dynamite found in the suitcase were "positively identified by a witness, name withheld, as the property of Warren K. Billings." No such witness ever appeared, although the prosecution did attempt to introduce the dynamite itself into evidence.

Fickert was also quoted in each of the papers as saying that Billings and Nolan had offered to confess if they were granted immunity but that he had refused to consider the offer. Both men later denied any such suggestion and no proof of it was ever introduced in evidence. In fact, within a month Fickert's assistant Brennan would approach a defense attorney and inquire about the possibility of arranging such a deal.

9 ·

There is a certain fallacy in characterizing news treatment of the case "trial by press," for the word "trial" usually implies a hearing of both sides. In this case, it wasn't true. All of the defendants were still being held incommunicado. They could not reply to the charges made against them, and there was no one outside speaking in their behalf. Although Fickert occasionally referred to "alibis," he did so only to say they had been disproven.

Not only were the defendants mute, they were also deaf. Allowed neither visitors nor newspapers, they were unaware of outside developments. Tom Mooney, for example, was unaware that his family had tried to see him every day, his mother twice collapsing when refused permission. Weinberg did not know whether his wife and son were still in Cleveland, wondering why he had not written and sent them money for their return trip, as he had promised to do, or if they had somehow returned to the city and knew of this horrible thing of which he had been accused. If so, was anyone taking care of them? He was their only means of support. Nolan, who had a wife and two children, was similarly concerned.

They were in a vacuum with the only reality questions and accusations.

10 ·

Monday's papers carried some "hard news." Estelle Smith, in a confrontation in Fickert's office, "positively identified" Rena Mooney as the woman who had come up the stairs at 721 Market and later waved to Billings to come down from the roof; and Fickert announced that he would submit the bomb cases to the Grand Jury the following night.

And that day, for the first time, the prosecution tied together the many loose threads and stated its theory of the crime, which would form the basis of the Grand Jury indictment and subsequent trials. The *Bulletin* quoted Captain Matheson outlining the theory as follows:

"The bomb was meant to obliterate the United Railroad employees' section of the parade, probably as an act of vengeance because the platform men did not respond to a summons to strike. The conspirators intended to blow up these men as they passed the building at 721 Market Street. The conspirators had figured they would pass this point at two o'clock and set the bomb to explode at that hour, but a delay in the parade threw their plans awry. Billings was sent to the roof of the building with the bomb, while Weinberg in his auto with Mooney, Mrs. Mooney, and another man not yet arrested waited in the street below. The time growing short they became agitated and decided to hunt the URR paraders and fling the bomb into their midst."

McNutt could not believe what he read. There were three things glaringly wrong with this theory.

One was that you do not throw a time bomb. Had the conspirators intended to throw a bomb, they would have made a percussion-type bomb, which would explode on impact. Not only would this have been much easier to construct, if one threw a time bomb one ran the risk of damaging the mechanism and having it fail to explode. Time bombs were not made to be thrown.

Two, were these people so mad that they would sit in an automobile at the curb while Billings on the roof above them tossed a bomb over them into the paraders? Not only was it possible that the bomb might fall short and land on the auto, but it was probable that even if the bomb landed directly in the center of the street the flying bullets would kill or maim everyone in the auto anyway.

The other discrepancy was so fantastic as to make the entire theory untenable. It was also so apparent that McNutt could not believe the Grand Jury would fail to see it.

It was the prosecution's contention that sometime between 1:40 and 2:06 P.M. Weinberg had driven Mooney and Billings from 721 Market to the corner of Steuart and Market.

To have done so Weinberg would have had to drive down a street already cleared of traffic, directly into and through the parade!

II ·

The list of illegalities continued to grow.

It is customary in criminal cases, as a test of credibility and safeguard against incorrect identifications, to have witnesses identify suspects from a lineup.

The lineup is, at best, a risky method of making identification. It is, however, the most workable method yet devised.

This elementary safeguard was skipped entirely in all the identifications in this case. Estelle identified Billings before reporters in Fickert's office; there was no possibility of mistaking him, as he was the only man wearing handcuffs. Rena Mooney was introduced to Estelle by name in Fickert's office, the uniformed jail matron the only other woman present. Sgt. Goff took McDonald to Billings' cell where Billings was talking to Chief White, and calling him by name, told him to come out of the cell a moment to meet someone. Mooney was alone in his cell when Goff took McDonald up to the cell door and said, "This is your man, this is Mooney." All other identifications were similarly enacted. The Wickersham Commission would later conclude that "personal identification of the defendants was not surrounded by any of the safeguards necessary to accuracy."

Yet, consistently, the newspaper stories emanating from the Bomb Bureau and the District Attorney's office stated that each of the suspects had been identified in a lineup.

7· The Grand Jury

O<small>N THE NIGHT</small> of Tuesday, August 1st, District Attorney Fickert presented the bomb cases to the San Francisco Grand Jury.

Since Grand Jury sessions are secret, closed to the public and press, there is about them an air of mystery. In California, a Grand Jury consists of 19 persons, drawn from a select jury list made up largely of business and professional people. Its purpose is to investigate crime in general, or as in this instance, specific acts of crime committed by individuals. The prosecuting attorney presents his evidence and the Grand Jury determines if there is sufficient information to hold the person for trial, in which case an indictment is returned. One stated purpose of the body is "protection against unfounded prosecution." If the jurors find there is insufficient information to warrant an indictment, charges are dropped.

Proceedings are largely informal. There is no judge, only a jury foreman. Any juror may question any witness.

Although quasi-judicial in nature, the proceedings are governed by certain rules. Witnesses are called into the chambers individually and thus, hypothetically, are unaware of the testimony of other witnesses. According to California law, a witness called before a Grand Jury is not entitled to counsel during his appearance; he is entitled to counsel before appearing, however. Too, as in a trial, the prosecuting attorney is responsible for determining the veracity of his witnesses and is charged with introducing only that evidence admissible in a court of law.

Fickert departed from this with his first witness.

"Call Henry Kneese."

Kneese, City Marshal of the City of South San Francisco, testified to the finding of the bomb near the San Bruno towers on June 11th. While Kneese was still on the stand Fickert turned to a deputy and said, "Bring in the bomb." The deputy brought in a battered suitcase, and very carefully set it on a table in front of the jury box.

Trial transcripts rarely more than hint at the emotions prevalent in a courtroom. The effect on the jurors of the proximity of the bomb— containing 24 sticks of dynamite whose destructive power Kneese was now describing—can only be imagined. The shock must have lasted long

Estelle Smith, one of the principal witnesses against Billings. Only later did the defense learn that the "demure dental assistant" was a prostitute and accused murderess. She recanted her testimony in installments, then recanted her recantations.

after the bomb itself was removed from the room.

Since the San Bruno dynamiting was a separate crime, for which no one was ever arrested or indicted, both Kneese's testimony and the introduction of the bomb into evidence were clearly irrelevant and prejudicial.

Kneese was followed by a coroner who described in detail the wounds of the Preparedness Day explosion victims.

Estelle Smith next took the stand and testified that she and her mother lived at 721 Market Street, in three rooms provided rent-free by her dentist employer. Fickert asked the Grand Jury to keep Miss Smith's residence confidential; she had already received several letters threatening to murder her if she testified, he said.

These letters were never produced in evidence.

Although more detailed, her story was in most particulars the same as

127

had appeared in the press. To her identifications of Billings and Rena Mooney, however, she now added that of Mooney himself, identifying him as one of the men she had seen standing on the sidewalk outside 721 Market. Again, the error still apparently unnoticed by Fickert or anyone else, "I also recognized Mr. Billings by his thumb. Mr. Billings looks like he had a mashed thumb and his nail is all wrinkled on his right hand."

In telling her story, Estelle stated that Billings went up on the roof about 15 minutes before the parade started, that her argument with the woman and the Russian Jew occurred just before Mayor Rolph passed, that "five minutes" after they left the building or "two or three minutes" after Mayor Rolph passed was when Billings came down from the roof and left the building.

Fickert didn't ask Estelle for exact times and Estelle didn't volunteer them. But by using two other facts—(1) the parade started at 1:30, (2) Mayor Rolph passed 721 Market at exactly 1:50, as was later established by photographs—it is possible to assign times to these alleged events.

Thus Estelle placed Billings in the building from about 1:15 (about 15 minutes before the parade started) to 1:52 or 1:53 (two or three minutes after Rolph passed), while Mrs. Mooney and her unidentified companion left the building at 1:47 or 1:48 (five minutes before Billings).

Estelle's mother, Alice Kidwell, followed her on the stand. A portly woman, in her sixties, Mrs. Kidwell testified that while watching the parade from the window overlooking Market she had seen a man (whom she subsequently identified as Mr. Mooney), a woman (whom she subsequently identified as Mrs. Mooney), and a third party (a "dirty-looking man" with "a long, stringy mustache") standing together on the sidewalk in front of 721 Market. She had noticed them because they kept looking up at the window. The woman then left them briefly. When she came back she waved her hand, beckoning to someone on the roof. A few minutes later the man who had gone up on the roof to take photographs (the man Estelle identified as Billings) joined them. They talked briefly, then Mr. and Mrs. Mooney walked away to the left (west) while Billings walked away to the right (east). She hadn't seen what became of the other man. All this occurred, she said, shortly before the explosion.

Several policemen were then called who testified to the prior records of Mooney and Billings. Fickert handled the questioning in such a way as to synopsize the trials at Sacramento and Martinez, so that it appeared Mooney had been tried three times and finally acquitted on the same evidence that sent Billings to Folsom. Matheson, Bunner, Proll, and others also testified to the evidence that had been found at the bomb scene and in the searches of the defendants' rooms. Fickert interrupted one witness to state, "Cartridges of a similar character were found in the possession of two of the defendants, Billings and Nolan." This was at best a half-truth.

No cartridges were found in Nolan's home.

Bunner, in testifying regarding the Billings' search, mentioned the arrest of Mrs. Lavin:

Q. (Fickert) : Who was she?

A. She was a woman who was connected up in the dynamiting case at Los Angeles. She was the one who was harboring Schmidt and Caplan.

This incorrect information was to be the only mention of Mrs. Lavin before the Grand Jury.

It was not to be the only false information, however. Fickert stated, several times, that all of the defendants had refused to make statements following their arrests. With the exception of Mrs. Lavin, who had steadfastly refused to say anything until after seeing an attorney, each of the defendants had made lengthy statements concerning their whereabouts on July 22nd. Stenographic transcripts of all these statements were in Bomb Bureau files. In addition, Billings had drawn a map showing his route that day, indicating places along the way where he had talked to people or overheard conversations. It went unmentioned.

"Call Earl R. Moore."

Moore was a surprise witness, no mention of him having previously appeared in the press. A traffic officer, Moore had been assigned to the 700 block of Market Street on the afternoon of the 22nd, charged with clearing the street of all vehicles prior to the parade. This he had done, he said, except for a lone vehicle parked in front of 721 Market, an "old Ford jitney." Standing next to it, his hands in his pockets, was a young man, "twenty-three or twenty-five years old, about five feet seven or eight inches tall." Moore asked him if he knew the owner of the vehicle. The young man replied "I don't know," gestured vaguely toward the building, and added "He will be here in a minute." Moore reached into the auto and honked the horn. In doing so he noticed the horn button stuck and had to be pried back up. He also noticed a tear in the cushion in the back seat. Moore was then called down the street. This was at "one-forty or one-forty-five." On his return, about ten minutes later, both the vehicle and the young man were gone.

Moore testified that he had subsequently identified Billings as the young man and the Weinberg jitney, which he had seen in the police garage, as the auto that had been parked in front of 721 Market.

Moore said the man he saw was twenty-three to twenty-five. Billings was twenty-two but looked younger. Moore said the man was 5'7-8" tall. Billings was 5'4".

Estelle had placed Billings in the building until at least 1:52. Moore now placed him on the street 7 to 12 minutes prior to this—before, not after, the arrival of the first units of the parade.

"Call John McDonald."

McDonald too was a surprise witness, previously unmentioned in the press.

McDonald now identified Warren K. Billings as the man he had seen at the corner of Steuart and Market with the suitcase, and Thomas J. Mooney as his companion.

No mention was made of McDonald's initial failure to identify the two men, or of the affidavits in which he described two men wholly dissimilar to the defendants.

McDonald now testified that he had arrived at the corner of Steuart and Market at "about twenty minutes to two," and that while standing there, on the east side of Steuart, directly across from the saloon, he had seen a young man "coming down Steuart Street from Mission" carrying a suitcase. The young man, whom he had subsequently identified as Billings, was very nervous and kept looking back over his shoulder, leading McDonald to suspect the suitcase had been stolen. Billings then placed the suitcase next to the wall of the saloon, went in the saloon door and came out with another man, whom McDonald subsequently identified as Mooney. They talked for "a few minutes, a second or two," and then "Billings took a cut right through the parade toward the other side of Market Street as though he was going back to the Ferry Building." Mooney then went back to the saloon door and looked in. Returning, he looked at his watch and then at the Ferry Building clock. He did this several times. "Then Mooney took a cut across the street this way [indicating] as though he was going across to Drumm Street [northwest]. Then I started down Market Street and I got as far as the Alameda Coffee House when the explosion occurred." Only later, McDonald said, did he connect the two events and go to the police.

There was no mention of a vehicle in McDonald's statement or testimony (nor had there been in the testimonies of Estelle Smith and Mrs. Kidwell) nor any explanation as to how Mooney had managed to arrive before Billings.

In the all-important matter of time, McDonald, with his "a few minutes, a second or two" was even more vague than Estelle.

In his original affidavit, however, McDonald had been specific, stating that the explosion occurred "ten minutes" after the man he now identified as Mooney left the corner. The explosion having taken place at 2:06, this would have been 1:56. Subtracting *at least* another five minutes to allow for the occurrence of all the things McDonald had described as happening, this would have placed Mooney and Billings at the scene at 1:51—a minute *before* Billings left 721 Market to join the Mooneys on the sidewalk three-quarters of a mile away.

The Grand Jury, of course, knew nothing of McDonald's affidavit. But District Attorney Fickert did.

He also knew that the next testimony he took was wholly false.

"Call Peter J. Hughes."

Officer Hughes described the arrest of Nolan and the items found in his basement, Mooney's motorcycle, some clay molds, a sack of nuts, bolts, and washers . . .

Mr. Fickert: These are similar to the washers that were found in the vicinity of the explosion.

No washers had been found in the vicinity of the explosion.

Hughes: There was also some plaster of paris found there, another box containing saltpeter, and I think it was a bag of yellow clay and another bag of powder—looked like black powder.

Fickert let Hughes' testimony stand as he gave it. Yet as early as July 28th, Fickert knew that these materials were non-explosive, for on that day the *Chronicle* had carried the report of City Chemist Wilbur Kellogg that all these materials "were of a non-explosive character."

Later the defense, under court supervision, would have these materials analyzed, finding that they were exactly what Nolan had claimed at the time of his arrest: a sack of clay he was using to perfect a new welding technique; 20 pounds of Epsom Salts, which his mother-in-law was using for medicinal baths; a small quantity of flashlight powder; and a large sack of ordinary flour.

Officer Michael V. Burke then took the stand and testified to finding the key to Nolan's basement on Tom Mooney's person: "He could go in and out of the basement at will." Burke also testified regarding the basement search and finding the nuts, bolts, and washers.

A Grand Juror: They are no use for any purpose?

A. Good for making bombs.

Nolan was a machinist. Nuts, bolts, and washers were among the tools of his trade.

Hubbard Wade took the stand and testified that he was positive Billings was the man he had seen going up the stairs to the dental offices at 721 Market Street. He also said he saw a woman, "one who resembled Mrs. Mooney, although I couldn't swear it was her, at the foot of the steps." Also a man, who he couldn't say for sure was Mooney. The time wasn't mentioned.

A few minutes after midnight, Thomas J. Mooney was called and the Penal Code read to him. Mooney had not yet seen an attorney; he was unaware, until taken in the chambers, that he was to appear before the Grand Jury. He had been awakened a few minutes before, bore several days growth of beard and was wearing the same clothes in which he had been arrested.

There followed a brief argument between Mooney and Fickert, Mooney stating that he was willing to testify if he could first have counsel.

Mr. Fickert: But just answer the question now whether you want to testify or not.

A. I have been held in detinue ever since I have been arrested and I have not been allowed to get in touch with anybody at all, and I want to get counsel in the matter so that my rights will be thoroughly protected. I have nothing to fear whatever.

Q. Do you want to testify now?

A. I would like to have counsel first, as I told you. If I had counsel first I would be glad and willing to come before the Grand Jury and testify. I think that is only a fair test as to my rights, and I think they ought to be upheld in this matter . . .

Q. The question is whether you want to answer these questions here or not?

A. As I said, I would be glad to testify before the Grand Jury, but I would like to have counsel. I am entitled to it.

Q. You can't have counsel in here.

A. I know, but I could have counsel before I went before the Grand Jury. I don't like to be obstinate in this matter. I want to be fair. I have nothing to conceal whatever.

Q. Well, then, why don't you give us a statement?

One of the jurors, obviously antagonistic, interrupted to ask Mooney why, if he was innocent, he refused to testify.

But at least one juror was sympathetic to his position.

A Grand Juror: The gentleman has not refused to testify. He said he wanted counsel first.

Mr. Fickert: It is a question for him to determine, not his counsel.

The Grand Juror: The fact of him not having counsel kind of puts a different light on it, doesn't it? . . .

Mr. Fickert (to Mr. Mooney): There is no use arguing the matter. Do you want to testify or not?

A Grand Juror: Do you want to make a statement or not? Do you want to make a statement or do you refuse to make a statement?

A. I don't refuse to make a statement.

Fickert: It is one thing or the other . . . You either testify or you do not testify now. It is entirely up to you. We can't arrange for lawyers and all that kind of stuff.

Mooney was taken from the room and Warren K. Billings brought in. Billings also had not seen an attorney and refused to testify for the same reasons.*

"Call Israel Weinberg."

Weinberg had seen an attorney, the previous afternoon. Having five

---

* Independently, it should be added. The defendants were still separated, each in a different jail.

times attempted and failed to get permission to see his client, Weinberg's attorney, appointed by the Jitney Operator's Union, obtained a court order from Judge Cabannis ordering the police to grant the interview. But Weinberg, who only then broke his fast, was too weak to talk more than briefly. The attorney assured him that his family was in the city and that they were being cared for. He also strongly advised him to refuse to testify before the Grand Jury, as was his prerogative. Weinberg, however, didn't agree. He had nothing to hide.

Asked if he was willing to testify, Weinberg answered, "I am willing to answer every question you wish to ask me," and was sworn.

Fickert questioned him about the June 10th URR organizational meeting ("Isn't it a fact that on that night you took the men Billings and Mooney to the place where the Pacific Power Plant was blown up?"), the July 4th *Blast* picnic ("Do you remember attending an anarchist picnic at Colma?"), and briefly, Preparedness Day, skipping back and forth from one event to another in such a way that Weinberg had trouble following.

But he did manage to get out, piecemeal, his alibi for July 22nd; a statement that he knew the Mooneys only slightly, as a result of his son's music lessons; and a denial that he had ever met Billings or Nolan.

He admitted that the horn on his vehicle sometimes stuck and that there was a tear in the rear seat cushion. He denied, however, that his jitney had been parked before 721 Market at any time on Preparedness Day.

Much of the questioning was irrelevant, and considering the mood of the times, prejudicial.

Q. Do you know Emma Goldman?

A. Yes, sir. I have seen her.

Q. You have received letters from her?

A. I didn't receive any letters from Emma Goldman.

Q. You didn't see a letter written to Mr. Nolan by Emma Goldman stating that she would be in the city at this time?

A. No.

One such letter was found during the search of Nolan's home. It was an invitation to Emma's lecture on art. Weinberg had already stated he had never met Nolan.

Q. Do you know what the meaning of "Red" is in your parlance?

A. No.

Q. Do you know what the meaning of "Direct Action Boys" is?

A. Well, I don't know. It depends the way a fellow thinks about it.

Q. Isn't it a fact that among the "Reds," as you call yourself, that Mr. Billings and Mr. Mooney are known as "Direct Action Boys"?

A. I don't know.

Fickert asked Weinberg if he had ever received any mail at Mooney's home. Weinberg said he hadn't.

Q. Would you be surprised to see a lot of letters found in his place that were addressed to you?

A. Yes, sir. I would like to see them.

No such letters were ever produced.

"Call Rena Mooney."

Like her husband, Rena had not yet seen an attorney and had not been informed that she was coming before the jury. Awakened shortly before, she had been brought directly here, not even allowed a comb with which to straighten her hair. She was quite willing to testify. But under Fickert's questioning she fared even worse than Weinberg. Whenever she attempted to name someone who could verify their presence on the Eilers Building roof Fickert interrupted.

Q. Isn't it a fact that both you and Mr. Billings—you and Mr. Mooney did not go up on the Eilers Building until after three o'clock that day?

A. We went up right after when I tell you.

Q. Isn't it a fact you came in about three o'clock wearing a light-colored hat?

A. No.

Q. And you changed that to a dark hat and went up on the roof?

A. No, I went up with my sister, my cousin, and my aunt and Mr. Mooney right away.

Q. Isn't it a fact that you came up about three o'clock into the Eilers Building and met a Mr. Dunne there?

A. I did not. I was on top of the building.

Q. And you were perfectly cool and calm when you came on top of that building?

A. Yes, sir.

Q. You would be quite surprised if some of those people say you were not there, wouldn't you?

A. Yes, sir.

Mr. Dunne was never called as a witness. No one on the Eilers roof that day ever denied the Mooneys were there.

"Call Edward Nolan."

Nolan's attorney, appointed by the Machinists' Union, had finally been given permission to see his client that afternoon, after threatening to get a court order. Five minutes later he was told that his time was up.

Nolan now refused to testify until allowed more time to consult with his counsel. The Grand Jury proceedings were brought to an end.

It was, then, Fickert's contention that the principal defendants had gathered at 721 Market for the purpose of throwing a time-bomb from the roof into the ranks of the URR employees; that a delay in starting the parade had thwarted their plans; that they had then driven on down

Market, in Weinberg's jitney, in search of the marchers and failing to find them, their time running out, had been forced to leave the bomb in the crowd at the corner of Steuart and Market Streets and flee.

Apparently neither the discrepancies in this theory, nor the conflicting testimonies of Fickert's own witnesses, were obvious to the Grand Jury.

At 2:15 on the morning of Wednesday, August 2nd, they reached their decision.

No evidence against Belle Lavin having been introduced, she was released from custody.*

Against each of the other five defendants—Thomas J. Mooney, Rena Mooney, Warren K. Billings, Edward Nolan, and Israel Weinberg—the Grand Jury returned eight separate indictments of first degree murder.

2 ·

In at least one account of the Mooney-Billings case it has been suggested that District Attorney Fickert was more sinned against than sinner, that in his singleminded attempt to obtain convictions of Mooney and his associates as a step to the Governor's chair he unwittingly accepted at face value the bogus testimony of a variety of witnesses created by the $17,100 reward. In short, that Charles Fickert was himself deceived.

An honest look at Fickert's case before the Grand Jury should dispel this assininity.

None of the witnesses had placed Edward Nolan at either 721 Market or at Steuart and Market. The evidence against him consisted solely of his friendship with Mooney and the "explosives" found in his basement. Possessing the City Chemist's report, Fickert knew there was no real evidence to connect him with the crime. But he prosecuted him nevertheless.

The prosecution's entire case rested on the testimony of a single witness, for only one witness had placed Mooney and Billings at Steuart and Market. This was John McDonald, and possessing his original affidavit, Fickert knew he was lying.

There was much more. But all of this was incidental to one other fact. When Fickert took the bomb cases before the Grand Jury on August 1st he knew, positively, without doubt, that Tom and Rena Mooney couldn't have been at either 721 Market or Steuart and Market at the times charged. On July 31st, the day before the Grand Jury met, Wade Hamilton had turned over to Fickert's chief assistant, Edward Cuhna, the photographs

---

* Whether her arrest was calculated or merely incidental to the search of Billings' room is unknown. Its effect, in terms of publicity, was important, since it provided a link in the public mind between the Preparedness Day bombing and the dynamiting of the Los Angeles *Times*.

he had taken on the roof adjoining that of the Eilers Building the afternoon of the parade, photos which, had Fickert examined them closely, would have revealed the Mooneys, Mrs. Hammerberg, and Mrs. Timberlake on the edge of the Eilers roof at the time Tom and Rena were alleged to be at Steuart and Market, more than a mile away.

8· The Stage Is Set for Conviction

NOT UNTIL after the Grand Jury returned its indictments did Maxwell McNutt decide to take the case.

The parade had been much photographed. McNutt and his assistants began collecting pictures, from the newspapers, wire services, professional and amateur photographers. By the time McNutt was finally allowed to see Mooney, a week after the Grand Jury met, he had more than 200 photographs. He had also begun collecting affidavits from paraders and spectators who stated that, with the exception of a single, plainly marked Press Car (a large Lozier), and the ambulance that had been called for Fox, no other vehicle had driven down Market from shortly after one to the time of the explosion. McNutt tried to obtain a list of the traffic officers stationed between the two points but Captain Matheson refused to supply it.*

Of the several thousand people assembled along those eight blocks, marchers and spectators, Fickert had not produced one who claimed to have seen a third automobile pass!

Important as this was, McNutt didn't rely too heavily on it. That Fickert's story had been accepted so unquestioningly by the press and Grand Jury indicated a public not inclined to skepticism.

To the photographs, McNutt's assistants added newspapers, a copy of every edition published in the city from the time the Preparedness Parade was first proposed. Those of July 21st and 22nd, which gave the parade route and the positions to be occupied by the various units, were given particularly close scrutiny, since it was Fickert's contention that a change in the stated starting time of the parade, from 1 o'clock to 1:30, had frustrated the bomber's original plans.

Was it possible for Mooney and his associates to determine where the URR unit would be at a certain time? If the parade had started on time, would the URR carmen have been anywhere near 721 Market at 2:06

---

* Matheson eventually gave him the names. At the Rena Mooney trial 18 policemen who had been stationed between 721 Market and Steuart and Market would testify that, except for the above two vehicles, no automobile had gone down Market between 1 and 2:30 P.M.

P.M.? Proof of both points was essential to Fickert's thesis.

From the newspapers, charts were drawn up showing when each of the witnesses had been first mentioned in the press and what their statements were—for comparison with their Grand Jury testimony.

From the mass of photographs, which soon grew to more than 500, plus considerable movie footage, the defense made still other charts. There were, in addition to the Ferry Building clock at the foot of Market Street, a number of street clocks along the route, sometimes several to a block, which appeared in the photo backgrounds. Each was checked for accuracy. Using these as guides, the defense was able to establish the exact time the various units passed specific points and from this the rate of march computed (between 205 and 215 feet per minute).

Among these photos, three were to prove especially important. One, taken by an amateur photographer, showed the bomb scene as it was immediately after the explosion, before Fickert and Colburn began "digging for evidence." Another, which had appeared in the *Chronicle,* showed them at work. The third photograph had been taken from the north side of Market just as Mayor Rolph was passing 721. A street clock established the time as 1:50 (this was later verified through other photographs, eye-witness testimony, the rate of march from known points, etc.) The photo, much magnified, showed someone waving what appeared to be a white flag from the window of the second floor dental office. This tended to support Estelle Smith's story that she had waved a towel at the Mayor when he passed. The photo also showed a man sitting on the corner of the roof above. At his side was a black object which appeared to be a camera case. There were also several other men on the roof; they would have to be found. One thing the photo didn't show was a vehicle parked on the street in front of 721 Market.

If this part of Estelle's story was true, what of the rest? Although familiar with the workings of Fickert's office from his three years there, McNutt doubted that the stories of Estelle Smith, her mother, Hubbard Wade, and Officer Moore were wholly fabricated. It was his belief, and that of the other defense attorneys, pending the discovery of evidence to the contrary, that each of these people had seen some person or persons but that they were mistaken in their identifications. If they had seen other people, then those people had to be found.

This was only a small part of the task confronting the defense. Every person named in the alibis of the defendants had to be located. As many people as possible who had been at the corner of Steuart and Market shortly before, during, and immediately after the explosion must be interviewed. (The 40 injured, many of whom were naturally hostile, provided only a start.) A background check had to be run on each of the major witnesses. There were thousands of questions to be asked of hundreds of people and only a few to ask them. What was McDonald's background, for example? Who were his friends and associates and what had he told them? Because of the importance of his testimony, McNutt hired detectives to follow McDonald wherever he went, asking them, if possible, to gain McDonald's confidence.

There were also the newspaper stories, packed with false leads. But each person or reference had to be tracked down.

It was a job for an army rather than a few attorneys. There wasn't enough time, help, or funds to do all that had to be done. Fickert was rushing the bomb cases to trial before public indignation subsided. Over defense objections, he requested and obtained September 11th as the starting date of the Billings trial. He had, wisely, decided to try Billings first, since he was an ex-convict with a prior dynamite conviction. Also, with equal astuteness, he chose to try him on the indictment for the murder of Mrs. Van Loo, a mother with two children.

There were obstacles and setbacks each step of the way, some, McNutt and his associates felt, intentionally placed in their paths.

To prepare for the trials, it was essential that McNutt obtain a transcript of the Grand Jury proceedings. As defense attorney he was entitled to this by law. But there was an unusually long delay—more than two weeks, while the notes were allegedly being transcribed—which he did not believe accidental.

Essential witnesses had disappeared or been taken into hiding. Alice Kidwell, Estelle's mother, could not be located. A key witness to Billings' alibi, a bartender with whom Billings claimed to have talked, had two days after Billings' arrest (and one day after Billings mentioned him to the police) quit his job and moved, leaving no forwarding address. Some of the witnesses who had told the press of seeing a man or men with a suitcase, such as Taylor and Prendergast, could not be located.

Limitations were placed on the number of times the attorneys could consult their clients, and then just as mysteriously removed.

Fickert refused to supply the defense with a list of his witnesses. There was no law that said he had to; it was a matter of common legal courtesy. There would be no such niceties in these trials.

Much of this was anticipated. What wasn't was the indifference, even open hostility, of the one group on which they were most dependent for aid, labor itself.

The initial defense team consisted of Maxwell McNutt, Edmund H. Lomasney (an attorney sent to Billings by the Shoeworkers' Union), and his partner, John G. Lawlor. Of the three, Lawlor was the youngest, and because of his background (raised south of Market, he had hoboed, read law at night to pass the bar, and worked as a newspaperman as well as a lawyer) the most sympathetic to the defendants' philosophy. A number of other attorneys were asked to assist. One was William Haggerty, former Labor Council president. As a prominent labor leader and attorney for Nolan's local, #68 of the Machinists' Union, Haggerty was a logical choice. Haggerty not only refused to serve as counsel but issued a statement to the press that under no circumstances would he defend Nolan or any of the other Preparedness Day bombers. This "betrayal," as Mooney predictably characterized it, was only slightly offset by the local's voting $1000 for Nolan's defense, the only sizable early union contribution.

From many approached by McNutt came a standard reply: "Remember the McNamaras."

The defendants had already been tried in all the major San Francisco papers and found guilty. Except for the *sub rosa* assistance of a few reporters who thought Fickert's case weak, this important avenue of information was closed to the defense. McNutt, at one point appealing to Fremont Older for assistance, had been told: "Mooney's guilty. Let the bastard hang!"

2 ·

Only one San Francisco paper was quick to come to the defense of the accused.

"This conspiracy to eliminate the best labor men of San Francisco is the prelude to a bitter campaign to exterminate the unions," Alexander Berkman wrote prophetically in *The Blast*. "The case of Nolan, Mooney et al is really a fight for the open shop . . ."

Comparing these arrests to those that followed the Haymarket tragedy, with revolutionary gusto Berkman cried, "The enemy is athirst for blood: it is planning to transplant to San Francisco the gallows of 1887 when five of Labor's best and truest friends were strangled to death in Chicago . . . It is the solemn duty of every lover of liberty and friend of Labor to hasten to the rescue. Action is necessary—quick action—immediate, to prevent the planned diabolic outrage. Agitation and funds are needed at once. Publicity is necessary to enlighten the people about the bloody vengeance Capital is scheming. No stone must be left unturned to expose the vile conspiracy of the bosses and to tear Labor's prisoners of war from the rapacious maw of the bloodthirsty masters . . ."

If the lives of the bomb defendants were to be saved, Berkman and Emma believed, a defense committee would have to be organized, and quickly. Berkman asked that contributions to the defense be sent to the offices of *The Blast,* but this was only a stopgap measure. Emma, Sasha, and Fitzi might be arrested momentarily and *The Blast* suppressed. Someone capable had to be found to take charge.

Robert Minor was in Los Angeles, staying at the home of writer Upton Sinclair. Berkman wired him, asking that he come to San Francisco immediately to head the defense.

Minor was then thirty-two, a giant of a man, extraordinarily handsome, with bushy black eyebrows, dark piercing eyes, and a deep commanding voice.

Although descended on his father's side from General John Minor, Jefferson's presidential campaign manager, and on his mother's from Sam Houston, his childhood in San Antonio was spent in poverty. Leaving school at fourteen and home at sixteen, he had for several years followed the half-hobo, half-migratory worker existence common to most Wobblies. He had a genius for drawing, however, and from a start on a San Antonio paper, he moved, at twenty, to head cartoonist on the St. Louis *Post Dispatch,* where he introduced a bold, new style in American cartooning. Instead of pen and ink and thin lines and crosshatching, he used thick charcoal or grease crayon and heavy black lines and shadows, much as Herblock does today. By 1911, when he turned twenty-seven, Robert Minor was the highest paid cartoonist in the United States.

A Socialist since 1907, a trip to Europe in 1912 to study art brought him in contact with the anarcho-syndicalist philosophy of the studios and garrets of Montparnasse and Montmartre. By the time he returned to New York to work for the *World* he was, according to Theodore Draper, "a full-fledged, outspoken anarchist. Bill Haywood was his hero and Alexander Berkman his bosom friend and teacher." Like his mentor opposed to killing in any form, his anti-war cartoons were savagely satirical. When Pulitzer's policy shifted to pro-preparedness in 1915, Minor, choosing convictions over salary, moved to the Socialist *Call.* There followed a stint in Europe as a war correspondent. When Berkman's telegram reached him in Los Angeles, he had just returned from covering Pershing's comic-opera search for Pancho Villa in the wilds of Mexico and was ready to try something new. He caught the first train north, although as he later admitted, he had never heard of any of the Preparedness bombing defendants. There is a legend, somewhat cruel but not necessarily untrue, that on stepping off the train in San Francisco he gave a speech to the press asserting his belief in their innocence.

It was to be Minor's baptism as a political organizer. "The Mooney-Billings case was much more than a landmark in the development of one future Communist," observes Draper. "It was a crisis of conscience for Minor's generation of radicals. Not a few young men traced their active participation in the radical movement to righteous indignation at the plight of Mooney and Billings." That they did so was due, in no small part, to the important role Minor played.

Of the experience Minor himself would later write, "The last under-pinning of respect for the 'democratic' social organization was knocked out of me by the Mooney case."

It did not take him long to familiarize himself with the case. In his first article, which appeared in the September 1st issue of *The Blast*, behind a Robert Minor cover, he wrote perceptively:

"There is evidence against these men, charged with murder—but evidence of what sort? In events of such justified excitement, thousands of different sorts of 'evidence'—of any sort you want—can be found in the rumors and growing imaginations of a terror-stricken crowd. By forming a set theory and sticking to it, building it up on what plastic-minded witnesses may be induced to contribute—and by carefully excluding all testimony that may show that your damnable pet theory is false (even eyewitnesses have in this case been discarded for circumstantial evidence)—you may prove anything you want."

Minor's initial task was rendered somewhat easier by the existence of an organizational framework. Although Swanson and the police had seized and still possessed the files of the International Workers' Defense League, of which Mooney had been secretary, the organization, composed of elected representatives from various unions, still existed and Minor took it over. The first defense committee consisted of Minor, Berkman, Goldman, and Fitzgerald. An office was rented and staffed with voluntary help.* Dozens, then hundreds of letters—typed on borrowed typewriters, mailed with postage bought from donations collected at Emma's meetings —were sent to unions and radical groups in all parts of the country, appealing for aid. Under Berkman's tutelage, Minor spoke at union meetings, organized a mass protest rally for the eve of the Billings' trial, and wrote press releases, reviewing the evidence, exposing for the first time Swanson's backstage role, and hitting out at labor's "conspiracy of silence."

"These cases are not of mere local importance. Our own efforts will not be sufficient to defeat the conspiracy of Big Business. The case is of country-wide significance. It will require a national campaign of agitation to prevent the terrible crime planned by the masters of San Francisco . . .

"Let no friend of Labor lull himself into self-satisfied inaction with the hope that these men will get a fair trial, and that their absolute innocence guarantees an acquittal. The stage is set for conviction. You might as well expect decency in a brothel as to hope for justice at the hands of the ex-Pinkertons and Burns bloodhounds in the District Attorney's office, all mad with the scent of the $21,000 reward . . ."

* For some time Minor was the only paid staff worker, receiving $15 a week for living and traveling expenses.

At first these press releases appeared in only a few anarchist publications (*The Blast* and *Mother Earth*), Socialist papers (the *World* in Oakland, The *Northwest Worker* in Everett, Washington), labor papers (*The Tri-City Labor Review,* published in the East Bay), and one literary outlet (Margaret Anderson's *Little Review*). Later they would be printed up as leaflets, and still later, incorporated into pamphlets on the case.

At first there was only scattered, limited response, mostly from followers of Berkman and Goldman. Two of their wealthy friends made sizable early contributions: Mrs. J. Sergeant Cram of New York City sent $500; Los Angeles oil heiress Aline Barnsdall sent $2000 to help secure counsel.

Gradually, through the efforts of the anarchists, the names J.J. and J.B. McNamara began to fade, to be replaced by those of Tom and Rena Mooney, Edward Nolan, Warren Billings, and Israel Weinberg.

Thus the case developed on two fronts—McNutt handling the legal defense, Minor the publicity.

3 ·

As the Billings trial drew nearer, a vast amount of information accumulated in McNutt's office. Facts, fictions, rumors that could be either, purposely planted lies—all had to be evaluated, put into perspective.

A quick check of officer Moore's past, for example, revealed that prior to joining the police force he had worked as a strikebreaker for United Railroads. Was this important or merely a coincidence?

Police Chief White had worked for PG&E. Relevant or irrelevant?

Attempts to check into Estelle Smith's past fell against a closed door. McNutt could discover nothing about her activities prior to the time she went to work for the dentist about two months before the bombing. All he had was a suspicion that she was not the wide-eyed innocent she pretended to be, an awareness that she dressed expensively for a $9-a-week dental assistant, and a rumor that her duties went considerably beyond helping her employer pull teeth. If true—and it would, McNutt knew, be difficult to prove—what possible bearing did it have on her testimony?

Other decisions were larger and might materially affect the outcome of all the cases.

Was the bomb planted or thrown? There were two sets of witnesses, those who saw an object falling from above, those who saw the suitcase. In effect, the prosecution had taken the least likely part of both theories, with their time bomb that was to be thrown.

Should the defense make a full-scale attempt to discover what the police obviously hadn't—the real perpetrator or perpetrators of the crime?

Mooney adamantly insisted that they should. McNutt, feeling that this was after all the responsibility of the police, and aware that this could take a large part of the defense's limited resources and manpower and still quite possibly net nothing, decided against it. McNutt won out, although this wasn't to be his last argument with Mooney, who had his own ideas on how the defense should be run.

There were questions without answers. What type of bomb? The prosecution hadn't even said whether nitroglycerine or dynamite was used. Who was the man with the mustache seen by Estelle? Had she, perhaps, described Mooney to Fickert from the newspaper photo which showed Mooney with a mustache? Or was the "Russian Jew" groundwork for the involvement of Alexander Berkman?

There were the "tips." McNutt, for example, received an anonymous message from a man who identified himself only as a San Francisco policeman. He told him that an Eilers Building employee named Wade Hamilton had turned over to Fickert a number of photos that showed the Mooneys on the Eilers roof during the parade, giving them an ironclad alibi. Lawlor, already looking for the photographer, whom Rena Mooney vaguely remembered seeing, called on Hamilton but found him uncooperative. Since he refused to give the defense a set of prints, McNutt was forced to ask the District Attorney's office for them. Fickert ignored the requests.

There was the evidence found in the searches. This, at first glance, looked incriminating. McNutt had to prove that it wasn't.

Billings said the .22 rifle and ammunition found in his room belonged to his friend Frank Lee, who had left them with him following their camping trip. Lee verified this, saying he had bought them at Shrieve and Barber's. This was also verified through the firm's purchase records and a statement of the clerk who had waited on Lee. Billings was unable to recall just where he had purchased the .32 caliber pistol but knew that it was bought about the time he was posing as a scab in the shoe strike. The only .32 caliber ammunition he possessed was that which was in the gun. The 10 ball bearings, Billings said, had been used in his work as a mechanic in the Cadillac garage and had been in his pocket when he was fired after being found out as a spy.

An old .38 caliber revolver had been found in the Mooney studio; this Mooney said he had purchased some years before. (No .38 caliber cartridges had been found at the bomb scene; only .22 and .32.) Also found there had been a .32 caliber pistol, loaded with lead cartridges; a handful of extra ammunition of the same type; and some 30 steel-jacketed cartridges of the same caliber. The latter were similar to those found at the bomb scene. Mooney said that he had borrowed the gun and cartridges from a friend to bring home an $800 collection from an IWDL Ball at four o'clock one morning, and this was also verified.*

That both Billings and Mooney had some cartridges similar to those used in the bomb could help as much as hurt the defense. For it was unlikely that had they made the bomb they would have left this incriminating evidence in their residences.

Too, this was the West. The possession of firearms was still common and accepted. It did not appear that the prosecution could tie this evidence to the bombing, but the defense could not be sure.

McNutt had other problems, the largest of which were the past records of Mooney and Billings. Although their prior "dynamiting activities" probably wouldn't be admissible into evidence, they had been given wide coverage in the press. How could he make it clear to the jury that there was a great difference between the use of dynamite on isolated electrical towers during a labor dispute and the bombing of a crowd of innocent people watching a parade?

Another problem was Billings' alibi. The day after his arrest Billings had given the police a detailed statement of his activities on the afternoon of Preparedness Day, together with a map showing where he had talked to the bartender, overheard various conversations, etc. He had told the same story and drawn a similar map for McNutt.

What Billings neglected to mention to either the police or his attorney was what he had been doing in these places at these times. Billings would later say that he felt an admission of having been engaged in sabotage would do nothing to help his case. Also, he didn't want to "squeal on" the Machinists' Union official who had assigned him the job.

If McNutt suspected his client was lying, he never admitted it. But he must have been aware that Billings' seemingly meaningless wanderings would not strike a jury as very convincing.

Not the least of McNutt's problems was the fact that someone was leaking information to the prosecution.

Among the attorneys asked to assist the defense was one active in affairs of the Labor Council. Although never sympathetic to Mooney before this, the man offered to help, whereupon McNutt turned over to him considerable information, most of it dealing with McDonald. One man McDonald saw frequently was a pharmacist whose main business was supplying drugs to addicts. From this the defense surmised that Mc-

* Lest the careful reader accuse the author of suppressing evidence at this point, it should be noted that the "makes" of the cartridges found at the bomb scene and in the searches never became an issue in the trials. If the makes had been the same, Fickert would surely have used this fact; had they been dissimilar, McNutt would have stressed this. As it is, one can only conclude that probably some were of the same make and some were not, so that neither side stood to gain by interjecting this issue.

Donald himself might be an addict. Though as yet without proof, they had collected a number of affidavits relating to the pharmacist's activities.

In an attempt to learn the whereabouts of the prosecution's witnesses, McNutt had a detective watching the District Attorney's office. Only he, Lomasney, and Lawlor were aware of this. Late one night, shortly after the attorney had joined the defense, the detective saw him entering Fickert's office. The visit, McNutt knew, might be wholly innocent, relating to another case. But the defense attorneys hadn't time to take chances. The following day they asked him the purpose of the visit. His only reply was that he had decided to withdraw from the defense. The same day the pharmacist disappeared. (He did not return to the city until the trials were over.)

There was no proof the attorney had betrayed his client's trust. He was, however, among those on the Labor Council who later strongly opposed taking a stand on behalf of the defendants.

His departure didn't stop the leaks. Several times as soon as the defense learned of the existence of a witness that witness dropped out of sight. One of the most important witnesses for the defense was Spanish War veteran M. T. Prendergast, whose description of the man with the suitcase didn't tally with McDonald's. Prendergast had gone to the police but had been told his testimony wasn't needed. He had also talked to the press, however, and the defense was finally able to track him down and obtain an affidavit. Shortly thereafter, Fickert told the papers "the story of M. T. Prendergast, a former soldier and now a gardener of Oakland, that he saw a swarthy man who looked like a Mexican plant the bomb at Steuart and Market Streets was the result of efforts to throw the authorities off the track and aid those in custody." *

Coincidence? The defense attorneys thought not. Failing to find the source of the leak, they decided they might as well take advantage of it.

The trial by press hadn't ended with the Grand Jury indictments. Throughout August Fickert continued to issue daily statements. Many were prejudicial distortions of the evidence, others false leads apparently intended to throw off the defense. The latter bothered McNutt most, since each required time-consuming investigation.

Though McNutt pretended to be acting in great secrecy, everyone connected with the defense was told, in confidence, that McNutt was compiling a list of Fickert's erroneous press statements, to be submitted to the state bar association as basis for disbarment proceedings.

Abruptly, two weeks before the Billings trial, Fickert stopped talking to the press.

* Prendergast had reported to the police the same day as the bombing, before any arrests were made. Fickert was in effect charging that he was part of the plot.

4 ·

Between the Grand Jury and the Billings trial there were four important breaks in the defense's favor, three due to careful investigation, the fourth to the wildest sort of coincidence.

As a matter of course, defense attorneys interviewed all employees of the two buildings adjoining 721 Market. In the offices of the Uhl Brothers at 717 Market they hit paydirt: four young men who had been on the roof of 721 Market during most of the parade.

Since 717 was a tall building, and 721 only two stories high, the roof of the latter was the more advantageous spot from which to view the parade. About 1:30 P.M. Uhl employee Alphonse DeCaccia had climbed onto the roof of 721 from a window in 717. There were already there two girls, one about fourteen, the other about sixteen, and sitting some distance away, in the northwest corner of the roof, a young man of twenty-eight or thirty. "He had a kodak grip—a black grip about two feet long and a foot wide" and "wore a khaki serge Norfolk belted suit with trousers of the same," DeCaccia later testified.

About 1:40 another Uhl employee, William Crump, joined DeCaccia on the roof. By this time the young girls had gone. Crump also saw the young man.

About two, DeCaccia and Crump saw their friend Henry Pincus standing on the sidewalk in front of 721 Market. Whistling and waving they caught his attention. Pincus, waving back, asked how they reached the roof. DeCaccia yelled down directions. While this was going on several women and men standing near Pincus looked up to see what the yelling was about.

Shortly after Pincus joined them they spotted another friend and fellow employee, Tracy Barrett, and went through the same yelling and waving. Barrett also came up via the window of 717.

DeCaccia was on the roof until 4:30, most of the time in company with one or more of the others. The man with the camera, he said, left about 4:15. He saw him get up and walk toward the skylight of 721 but, looking back at the parade, hadn't seen him go down.

All four had seen the young man. Pincus hadn't noticed his face, but DeCaccia, Barrett, and Tracy had, and later, on being shown Billings, each stated that he was not the same man. Since three of them had only seen the photographer sitting, they were unsure of his height. DeCaccia, who had seen him walking toward the skylight, said he was a little shorter than himself. DeCaccia was six feet.

Realizing the importance of their stories McNutt and Lawlor checked them carefully. By this time the defense had obtained several photos of 721 Market and had them blown up.* One or more of the youths was in each and readily identifiable, wearing the clothes they said they had worn that day. The same blowups showed the young man with the camera case was wearing a belted suit of a material resembling khaki. Except for De-Caccia, who had climbed onto the roof before the parade started, each of the boys had been asked what unit of the parade was passing when he arrived on the roof. Checking their answers against the charts giving the passing time of the units, the defense attorneys were able to verify the approximate times given as correct.

It seemed probable that what Mrs. Kidwell had actually seen was Pincus yelling and waving to DeCaccia on the roof.

But if the young man with the camera case was the same one Estelle Smith claimed to have seen, then she was lying about his having left the roof shortly after Mayor Rolph passed, for DeCaccia placed him there until 4:15.

One of the most surprising things about this testimony was that no one had questioned the four boys earlier. From this and many similar incidents it seemed to McNutt, as it would later to the Wickersham Commission, that Fickert had made little if any attempt to verify the stories of even his own witnesses.

At the risk of giving away part of his evidence, McNutt distributed copies of a blownup photo of the young man to all the newspapers in California, together with a reward for information leading to his identification.

About the same time the defense also found Thomas Doidge. An engraver, employed by the International Film Corporation, Doidge said he had been standing next to the lamp post in front of 721 Market from 12:15 to 3:15.

"About ten or fifteen minutes after the traffic on Market Street had stopped [police would testify that the street was cleared of streetcars and nearly all vehicular traffic by 1 P.M.] an automobile drove in there right in front of me," Doidge later testified. The driver got out—Doidge having to step aside to get out of his way—and went into one of the buildings. A few minutes later officer Moore, whom Doidge knew by name, walked up "put his hand on the car and looked over to me and said, 'Here, you will have to get this car out of here.' I did not answer him and he says to me 'Is this your car?' I says 'No sir.' I says 'The driver has gone in the building here' and with that he took hold of the horn and honked four or five times." Shortly after Moore left, the driver came out and drove away. He was alone.

* Eventually six photos were obtained, taken at 1:45, 1:50, 2:00, 2:10, 2:14, and 2:50. The young man with the camera case was in each.

Before the Grand Jury officer Moore had described the man he talked to as about 5'7 or 8" tall. Billings, whom he had identified as the same man, was 5'4". Doidge was 5'7".*

The third break concerned John McDonald. The defense had learned a great deal about him, though far from as much as they wanted to know. They knew that he had spent most of his life wandering about the country, occasionally working as a waiter but more often than not unemployed. They knew that ten days before Preparedness Day he had been released from the hospital after a series of stomach operations and that when he went to the police with his story he was broke and had been living off the free lunches in saloons. They also knew, through tailing him, that he made occasional visits to Fickert's office, and that almost daily he visited the office of Frank Drew, attorney for the Chamber of Commerce and a close friend of Fickert's. What went on in these various meetings they could not learn. All attempts to gain McDonald's friendship had failed. Everywhere he went he was accompanied by a detective. He had also, at first, been very suspicious and extremely careful what he said around others.

But McDonald was not tight-lipped by nature, and it wasn't long before the impulse to visit his former acquaintances and do a little boasting became irresistible.

To C. L. Logan, another waiter from whom he had bummed meals, McDonald bragged that Chief White had patted him on the back and said, "Mac, if you stick to this story, you can go back to Baltimore or Detroit on the cushions with a nice piece of change in your pockets."

He told the same story to Colonel Requa and another Salvation Army official, to whom he also confided that he was now set up in a good hotel, getting his meals and three dollars a day for expenses, and having a fine time.

Sitting in a barber chair, getting "the works," he bragged to barber Frank Sumney that he was the star witness in the bomb case and that "When those fellows go over the road and I get my divvy, back to the East for me."

"Do you have to wait until the end of the trial?" Sumney asked.

"No, I am getting three dollars a day right along and I won't have to wait until the trial is over."

All these statements the defense would document with sworn affidavits, to be introduced in evidence.

The chief break came from an unexpected source, Folsom Prison.

---

* Unknown to the defense (for another 20 years) officer Moore's original traffic report on the incident was in Bomb Bureau files. The height discrepancy was in it. Too, in the report Moore said the young man's hair was dark. Billings' hair was a sandy red, Doidge's black.

Less than two weeks before the start of the Billings' trial Lawlor received a message for Billings, smuggled out of Folsom via the underground. It was from one of Billings' former friends, who was now, the note said, the cellmate of Daniel J. Kidwell, Alice Kidwell's husband.

The defense had already learned that Kidwell was in prison, serving a two year sentence for a 1915 forgery conviction in Ventura County, but had not considered the information relevant. According to the note, Kidwell had recently received a letter from his wife telling him that she had struck a deal with the District Attorney and police, who had promised to release Kidwell on parole provided she testified against the defendants. What, the convict asked, did Billings want him to do about the letter?

Lawlor, via the underground, quickly sent back a brief reply. "Steal it."

Lawlor received it less than a week before the start of the trial. It read:

> San Francisco
> September 2nd

My dear Hubby:

I arrived here this P.M. The officer subpoenaed me for the trial and sent for me. I am very tired. Now, sweetheart, as soon as you receive this put your name up on the calendar, [for parole] do it right away. The authorities are going to let you out and maby in a few days and maby by the 16th. Have got work for you in the Wricon Iron Works, anyway at 4 dollars a day, maybe more. Captain Matheson and the District Attorney went to see two of the Board [parole board] this A.M. and will see the others at Sac [Sacramento]. Now you do as I tell you and you will be free in a few days and we will be so happy. I got a housekeeping room this eve. Will have a place of our own so have courage and if you are ever asked any questions, tell the truth, don't be afraid, just be honorable that is all. I know I am needed for awitness and they are helping me by getting you out. They told me to write this to you and you put your name on the calendar just as soon as you get and you will be home in a few days. Now, sweetheart, I want you to do this at once. With love and kisses I will soon have my darling man.

> Your wife,
> Alice Kidwell
> Ad. 2255 Van Ness Ave.

P.S. Do not delay for we expect to have a private meeting to get you out. Yes, Yes, I am so glad.

By various subterfuges, samples of Mrs. Kidwell's handwriting were obtained and experts consulted who verified that she had written the letter. As quietly as possible, the defense checked to see if such a request had been filed with the parole board: one had, by James Brennan, Fickert's assistant.

The defense said nothing about the letter to the press. They planned to let Mrs. Kidwell take the stand and tell her story, after which the letter would be introduced in evidence and Mrs. Kidwell impeached.

5 ·

It was beginning to look as if the defense had a good case. The defense attorneys knew, however, that Fickert had probably not placed all his witnesses or evidence before the Grand Jury. Lacking a list of the witnesses, they could anticipate surprises. But there was still another reason for optimism. One day in late August defense attorney Lawlor encountered James Brennan on the street.

Brennan told Lawlor that if he could get Billings to make a confession implicating Mooney, he would see that he was freed and given a share of the reward.

Lawlor asked Brennan if he had any evidence.

Brennan replied that yes, of course they did.

"Then what in hell do you want a confession for?" Lawlor asked.*

* When McNutt related this incident during the Billings rehearing, Brennan admitted that it had taken place as stated but insisted he had only been kidding.

9· The Astonishing Plea

I WANT Mr. Fickert's servants here tonight to repeat this to him: a man can be murdered as easily and more safely with a legal rope than with a bomb," Minor shouted to the crowd assembled in Dreamland Rink on the eve of the Billings trial. "What do you want, people—fourteen victims instead of nine? Do you want innocent men, or the guilty?"

Despite the mood of the community, this first mass protest meeting drew 3000 people. Only $168 was collected, but such meetings rarely paid their way except in publicity.

On leaving the platform Minor was handed a subpoena to appear as a prosecution witness. Similar summonses had been issued for Alexander Berkman and Emma Goldman, but both had managed to avoid being served. Fickert had no intention of calling any of them. He too was interested in publicity.

2 ·

The courtroom was packed an hour before the trial began. Those waiting for a glimpse of the "bomb fiends" were not disappointed: Billings, Mooney, Weinberg, and Nolan were brought in handcuffed, only Rena Mooney being spared this indignity. Tom and Rena embraced. Rena had been moved from Ingleside into the women's section of City Prison several days before. Although from his cell in the men's section Tom could hear the music of her violin, this was their first sight of each other since their arrests, one and one-half months earlier.

For a murder trial, the case of The People *vs.* Warren Billings proceeded at an amazing pace. By adjournment the first day 11 jurors had been picked; by the end of the second day the prosecution had completed its opening statement and was well into its case.

San Francisco at this time had the "professional jury" system, that is, jurors were not picked at random from the voter registration lists but were politically nominated for permanent tenure on a select venire list. It was a minor political job; there was no age limit, and each juror was paid

The Billings trial. From left to right: James Brennan, Billings' prosecutor; Edward Cuhna, Mooney's prosecutor; Lt. Stephen Bunner; and Charles M. Fickert. Along the other side of the table are defense attorneys Edmund Lomasney, John Lawlor, and Maxwell McNutt, and their client Warren Billings. In the dock behind them are Billings' co-defendants; left to right, Israel Weinberg, Edward D. Nolan, and Tom Mooney.

$2 per day. In effect, as one prominent attorney observed, this system made the jury "a refuge of the old, the infirm, the unsuccessful."

Since the number of jurors on the list was small, the personal history of each was well-known. Theoretically, since this information was available to both the prosecution and the defense, it was claimed to favor neither. In practical operation, however, it heavily weighted the prosecution's odds, since the juror who frequently voted for acquittal knew that he faced the risk of a preemptory challenge and the loss of his $2 per day.

Eight of the 12 Billings jurors had no occupation other than jury service. Only one of the 12 was under sixty. The jury foreman, Hugh Fraser, was eighty-three, had been a professional juror for 10 years, during which time he reputedly had never voted an acquittal unless directed by the court to do so. That McNutt accepted him was indicative of the quality of those rejected.*

---

* Billings did not want to use Fraser; McNutt did. Time proved Billings right. In 1936, 20 years after the trial and long after Fraser's death, a letter from him was found

There were no radicals on the jury. That radicalism was to be a major issue in the case was indicated by two questions Brennan asked each prospective talesman: "Have you been at any time, or are you now, connected with any organization of Anarchy? Have you ever been, or are you now, a subscriber for, or a reader of, the publication known as *The Blast?*"

McNutt had his own questions: "Do you know a private detective named Martin Swanson? Are you now, or have you ever been, or do you have any relative who is, employed by United Railroads or the Pacific Gas and Electric Company?"

Frank H. Dunne was the presiding judge. A valiant fighter during the graft trials, he had aged greatly since, grown cantankerous and impatient. To date he had shown no indications of radical bias; he had himself, for a time, been a Progressive. The prosecution was represented by District Attorney Fickert and his assistant James Brennan. Maxwell McNutt, Edmund Lomasney, and John Lawlor represented the defense.

Brennan delivered the opening statement for the prosecution:

"We expect to show that away back in the early part of 1913, the defendant in this case and Thomas J. Mooney and others, entered into a criminal conspiracy that had for its purposes and objects the terrorizing of people opposed to their particular view of social conditions, the obstructing and perversion of justice and the destruction of life and property.

"And we hope to show, in furtherance of this conspiracy, and to show the scope of that conspiracy, and the purpose of that conspiracy, that in 1913, the defendant, Warren K. Billings, blew up some towers belonging to a corporation down in San Bruno, and . . ."

And so it went. At least seven prior dynamitings were credited to Billings; there was no evidence supporting any of them. It was stated that Mooney had paid Billings $50 to take the suitcase to Sacramento; no evidence of this had been, or ever was, produced. It was claimed that while Billings was working as a mechanic at the Ford factory he told his fellow employees, "how he had tossed a bomb in the city of Chicago, and received two hundred and fifty dollars for it; he told how he had blown up certain towers and received two hundred dollars for it, and the day that he left the Ford factory he went to some of his fellow co-employees, some fifteen of them, and showed them a vast amount of money that he had; he said that he was going to the City of New York for the purpose of tossing a bomb there." The employees would remain nameless.

The rules covering opening statements permit considerable latitude.

in the Bomb Bureau files. Dated July 23, 1916, the day after the bombing, it was addressed to Mayor Rolph and asked that a law be passed to drive all anarchists out of the city. Fraser stated that if he personally could be of service in this direction, he was available. For some reason the Mayor's office had forwarded the letter to Chief White; the receipt for it was signed by Captain Matheson.

Since neither side is absolutely certain as to what will or will not be allowed into evidence, it is possible that some allegations made in the opening statement will remain undocumented in the trial itself. The charge in
this case was murder, however, not conspiracy, and the prosecution must
have been aware that evidence of conspiracy (if such evidence existed)
would be inadmissible, as would testimony regarding alleged crimes other
than that for which the defendant was being tried.

Had this happened only in the opening statement of the Billings' trial
it might be credited to over-enthusiasm on the part of Brennan. It was
common to all the bomb cases, and to the closing as well as the opening
addresses, leading the Wickersham Commission to conclude that it was
deliberate and clear evidence of "unfair prosecution." In a great number
of instances, the Commission noted, "the prosecution either in its opening
assumed that it could prove facts which it had no reason to believe that it
could prove, or in the closing referred to facts that it definitely had not
proved. The multitude and similarity of the incidents, and especially the
persistence of the references in later trials to incidents whose irrelevance
had been shown at the earlier trials, exclude the notion that it was
through inadvertence that the prosecution came to defy accepted standards of fairness."

McNutt immediately objected to the conspiracy charge, but Dunne de-
ferred a ruling, and not until the trial was in its fourth day did he have
the jury taken out so that he could hear arguments from the lawyers.

While waiting, the jury took a secret ballot and voted 10-2 to hang the
prohibition amendment. They also elected Charles Evans Hughes to the
Presidency over Wilson by 9-3.

After hearing Brennan's plea for introduction of the conspiracy evidence, Judge Dunne asked him, "Surely you are not trying to prove a general conspiracy against the whole world?" Brennan said that was exactly
what the prosecution wanted to prove, by showing that the defendants
had conspired together to overthrow the existing social order. Dunne
ruled the conspiracy evidence inadmissible, and when the jury came back
in, told them to disregard it. "We will introduce conspiracy evidence in
another way," Fickert told the press.

He tried, the following day. Not one to let a good thing go unrepeated,
Fickert attempted to introduce into evidence a suitcase-bomb allegedly
found at Tanforan during the latter part of June. McNutt objected and
Dunne sustained the objection. But while arguments on the point were
being heard, the suitcase sat in plain view on a table a few feet from the
jury. Judge Dunne told the jury to disregard it; as with the other conspiracy evidence, this was easier ordered than done. (Even Dunne kept
glancing at it nervously.)

The first several days went much as the defense attorneys had anticipated. Descriptions of the deaths of the victims were sufficiently detailed to send one reporter from the room, his hand to his mouth. As McNutt knew it would, the testimony regarding the cartridges and the ball bearings found in Billings' room had its impact on the jury. Questioning the policemen regarding the arrests and searches, however, McNutt was able to establish Martin Swanson's presence at these events and to make it clear that the defense considered Swanson's role of prime importance to the case.

Then the surprises came, in batches.

One was the introduction of an alternate motive. To reporters Fickert had said that the defendants had assembled at 721 Market to toss a bomb at the URR men who would be passing at 2:06. McNutt, through photographs and charts, was ready to prove that even had the parade started on time, the carmen would have been nowhere near 721 Market at 2:06. Now Fickert said that the defendants had gathered there to throw the bomb because Preparedness Day headquarters was located just across the street. It was as improbable as the URR motive—Market Street was 120 feet wide, which would have required some olympian throwing—but it caught McNutt unprepared.* As did the testimony of some of the witnesses.

Officer Moore testified as he had before the Grand Jury. McNutt, saving Doidge until the defense presented its case, dwelt on the height discrepancy in Moore's identification of Billings.

While McNutt was questioning Moore, two women entered the courtroom, surrounded by a phalanx of detectives. "The prosecution calls Mellie Edeau." The older of the two now took the stand. Brennan explained to the court that because of her religious beliefs Mrs. Edeau could not take the oath.

A gray-haired, stern-faced woman, Mellie Edeau identified herself as an Oakland seamstress. She spoke with almost fanatical conviction.

On the afternoon of the 22nd, she testified, she and her daughter Sadie had been standing on the sidewalk in front of 721 Market. They had first noticed Billings shortly after they arrived there, at 1:20, waving from the roof of the building to someone in the crowd. He was holding a brown suitcase in his right hand and leaning so far over the edge he made them nervous. They had next seen him standing next to the curb talking to officer Moore, at "about 1:30 or 1:35." She had recognized Billings, Mrs. Edeau said, by his pale face. He was wearing a brown suit and gray hat.

In her early twenties, Sadie Edeau was a frailer copy of her mother. She corroborated her mother's story in every detail.

On cross-examining the pair, McNutt tried to cast doubt as to the times and identifications, but the women only stuck more firmly to their stories.

---

* Fickert, however, never returned to this theory—which made the trip to Steuart and Market unnecessary. Apparently he simply tossed it in for good measure.

The next witness, according to the *Chronicle,* "was anything but a passive witness." Estelle Smith walked around the platform until ordered to sit down, argued with the attorneys, and addressed most of her remarks to the judge.

Estelle's story was the same as that given before the Grand Jury—until she reached the point of Billings' departure from 721 Market.

Q. About what time was that?

A. I should say it was between half after one and about twenty minutes to two or something like that; I can't swear definitely as to the time; I can't make a positive statement to your Honor about the time . . .

It was immediately apparent to the defense that Estelle was attempting to change her testimony. Before the Grand Jury she had stated that her last conversation with Billings had taken place *after* Mayor Rolph had passed, i.e., after 1:50.

It was an important change, for it gave Billings and the others time to travel to the bomb scene. Estelle's earlier testimony had, in effect, been an alibi for Billings.

McNutt, on cross, approached the point gingerly:

Q. Now, after you had seen the Mayor pass and waved the towel, you had some further conversation with Billings, didn't you?

A. It may, as I tell you now, and as I told the Chief of Police at the time, it may be that I saw Mr. Billings before the Mayor passed or after . . .

Approaching from a different direction, McNutt asked,

Q. Now, everything you testified to, in point of time and otherwise, before the Grand Jury, was correct?

A. Not the time. I said then, and I say now, I am not positive about the time.

The questioning grew heated, Estelle snapping back her answers angrily. The old men in the jury box looked at her with undisguised sympathy.

Wade, the school teacher from Hawaii, was next. He had been standing on the sidewalk just outside 721 Market, looking at the dental exhibit in the glass display case, trying to decide whether to have his teeth fixed then or later, when a man carrying a suitcase brushed past him and went up the stairs. As he turned at the top of the stairs Wade got a good look at his face. Thinking he was another patient, Wade had decided to postpone his visit to the dentist.

On cross-examination, Wade testified that the suitcase was reddish-brown in color, that Billings was wearing a dark gray suit and a soft, dark hat.

The prosecution called Peter Vidovich. Vidovich was not exactly a surprise to the defense. The *Examiner* of July 29th had carried an item reporting that Vidovich, an "Alaska mining man" had identified Billings the previous day, confirming the identifications of Wade and Miss Smith. Vidovich had not appeared before the Grand Jury, however, and defense attempts to locate him in the interim had proven futile.

Vidovich testified that he was leaving the dentist's office just as Billings came up the stairs, that he had stepped aside to let Billings pass him in the hall, and that he had had a good close look at his face.

McNutt asked him to describe the man he had seen. Vidovich said he was two or three inches shorter than himself (Vidovich was 6'1"), was wearing a "dark-light" suit with fine stripes, and carrying a black suitcase. Yes, it was dark in the hallway, Vidovich admitted. As for the time, McNutt elicited from him "It was maybe 12:05 to 12:15 that I saw Billings." This was fully 45 minutes or more before Estelle and Wade placed Billings on the scene.

It was late Friday afternoon. Judge Dunne adjourned court until Monday morning. Fickert told the assembled reporters that the guards around the Edeaus were for their protection against possible assassins, that all his witnesses were now being closely guarded night and day "to forestall the workings of feared outside influences."

On Monday John McDonald took the stand. McDonald made a number of changes in his previous testimony. The defense missed none of them.

Before the Grand Jury, McDonald had placed his arrival at Steuart and Market about "twenty minutes to two" and had given the impression that Billings had arrived shortly afterward. Now he said that when he first saw Billings "near as I can remember it must have been eight to ten minutes to two" and that Billings had put down the suitcase "at about two o'clock."

Thus, by Estelle's having Billings leave sooner, and McDonald's having him arrive later, the conflicting Grand Jury testimony was resolved.

Before the Grand Jury, McDonald had the two men leaving the scene thus: "Billings took a cut right through the parade toward the other side of Market Street as though he was going down to the Ferry Building . . . Then Mooney took a cut across the street this way [indicating] through the parade as though he was going across to Drumm Street."

Market Street was roped off, however. Only those with special passes being permitted to cross the lines. And the police didn't let anyone cut through the parade itself except at designated intersections. Steuart and Market was not one of them. McNutt had affidavits to this effect.

McDonald now testified that he hadn't seen which way the men had gone, that he had lost sight of both in the crowd.

McNutt hammered away at these contradictions. By reaffirming McDonald's position on the opposite side of Steuart Street, 65 feet away

"That's one of the men I saw with the suitcase." John McDonald, itinerant waiter, pointing the finger of accusation at Warren Billings during his trial in 1916. Five years later McDonald would sign a full confession admitting to being coached in perjury by Swanson, Fickert, and others.

from the saloon, he raised the question of whether he could have seen any of the things allegedly witnessed. For McDonald was a short man, only a little taller than Billings. And there was a dense crowd on the sidewalk nearest McDonald; a parade unit with dozens of American flags on tall standards forming in the street itself; and another dense crowd on the opposite sidewalk. Did McDonald expect the jury to believe that he had looked over or through all these groups and actually seen little Billings walking along with a suitcase, glancing nervously over his shoulder, then leaning down and placing the suitcase against the saloon wall?

McNutt moved on to the reward. Had he told anyone that he was going to make "a nice piece of change" on this, that when it was over he would be able to ride back to Baltimore "on the cushions," that he was already getting a hotel room, meals, and $3 a day? McDonald denied having made such statements. McNutt promised to prove otherwise.

"The prosecution calls John Crowley."

Crowley, an odd looking little man who behaved nervously on the stand, said that he was an auto mechanic and that he knew Billings from the auto mechanics' strike. On the afternoon of the parade, he said, he had seen Billings standing outside the garage where he worked, at Steuart and Mission (one block south of the bomb scene). He had seen him there both before and after the explosion, Crowley said. Had anything unusual happened which caused him to notice Billings, Brennan asked? Yes, Crowley replied, when the explosion occurred one of the bands, thinking it was the signal to play, had launched into *The Star Spangled Banner* "and everybody took their hats off but the defendant and the man that was with him." Ordered by a bystander to remove his hat, Billings refused and walked off in the direction of Howard Street (another block south).

McNutt remarked that Billings' conduct was rather odd behavior for a man hoping not to be noticed.

When had he first seen Billings at Steuart and Mission, McNutt asked? "I seen him there I guess it was between, I am positive sure it was one fifty-five, standing about three feet from which I was."

This startling answer, in complete contradiction to McDonald's testimony, made McNutt more venturesome. Brennan had failed to ask Crowley several key questions. McNutt, sensing a trap, had been undecided about asking them until now.

Had Billings been carrying anything? No, Crowley replied. He didn't have a suitcase? No, he didn't have a suitcase. What about the other man, McNutt inquired, what did he look like? He was "tall and dark," Crowley answered, "Spanish or Mexican." It wasn't Mooney then? No, Crowley was positive sure it wasn't Mooney.

Crowley's story so contradicted McDonald's that McNutt couldn't understand why the prosecution had called him. One of McNutt's assistants began an immediate background check on Crowley.

"The prosecution calls Louis Rominger."

Rominger was an important witness. In Estelle Kidwell's initial story to the press, she had mentioned his having helped Billings carry the suitcase to the roof. On the 28th Fickert had told reporters that Rominger was expected to identify Billings later that afternoon. He had not been mentioned again, and he had not been called before the Grand Jury, but the defense had seen nothing suspicious about this, assuming that Fickert was saving him for the trial.

The defense knew only two things about Rominger, neither of which was very helpful: one, that he was an ex-private detective from Spokane;

the other, that he had been sharing Mrs. Kidwell's bed and board since her husband's imprisonment at Folsom. The relationships of the various witnesses at 721 Market were becoming involved.

Rominger confirmed Estelle's story that he had carried the camera case to the roof. He had seen the young man clearly and positively identified him as Billings. He had seen Billings later talking to a man and woman on the street and had seen him walk away from them in the direction of the Ferry Building.

What time did these events occur, McNutt asked? Rominger wasn't sure. What had Billings been wearing? A suit and hat, Rominger said, but he couldn't describe them. How had he identified Billings then? By "a small scar on his head" and "his thumb looked like it had been mashed." McNutt had no further questions; he knew enough now to cast doubt on Rominger's identification.

The defense expected Mrs. Kidwell to be the next witness. The purloined letter was ready for introduction into evidence. Instead the state rested its case.

3 ·

The prosecution's failure to call Mrs. Kidwell wasn't the defense's only disappointment that day. The court had ordered the prosecution to turn over to the defense copies of the photographs taken by Wade Hamilton on the Eilers Building roof. Because of the prosecution's reluctance to produce these photos, McNutt was sure they would be important. The copies he was now handed, however, were so badly blurred and out of focus that it was impossible to positively identify any of the people on the roof or to determine just which parade units were passing.

The defense had a strong case, McNutt told the press. And would completely refute every allegation made by the prosecution.

The defense called Alphonse DeCaccia to the stand. Except for his height, DeCaccia bore a startling resemblance to Billings, so much so that the newspapers referred to him as "Billings' double." Wearing the same clothes as on the day of the parade, a brown suit and gray hat, DeCaccia stood on a chair to demonstrate how he had waved to the boys in the street. In evidence McNutt introduced photographs in which the young men and the photographer both appeared.

Thomas Doidge took the stand and related his conversation with officer Moore.

Billings' friend Frank Lee testified that the .22 rifle and cartridges found in Billings' room belonged to him, that they had taken them on their Russian River trip for target practice.

The .32 caliber pistol was identified as one purchased by Billings in 1913 when working as a pretended scab in the shoe factory.

That .22 and .32 caliber cartridges had been found both in Billings' room and at the bomb scene proved nothing, McNutt asserted; probably half the jurors had similar ammunition at home.

The ball bearings in Billings' room, McNutt said, dated from his prior employment as an auto mechanic. They also proved nothing, since those found in Billings' room were Cadillac ball bearings, 3-16 size, and the one-and-a-half ball bearings found in the storm drain at Steuart and Market were Ford ball bearings, 5-8 size.

McNutt let the burglar's jimmy go unmentioned.

"The defense calls Warren Billings."

Billings went through his alibi step by step; it was so detailed as to include the makes and models of cars he had seen. The effect of this detailed testimony on the jurors remained to be seen. A *Chronicle* reporter thought it convincing enough to disprove the prosecution's whole case. But at least one reporter, Ernest Jerome Hopkins of the *Bulletin,* had doubts that he later expressed. "I know it was in my own mind, at the time, that friends from outside might have visited Billings and told him of these happenings."

As best he could, McNutt attempted to eradicate any such impression by establishing that Billings had been held incommunicado from the time of his arrest until after the Grand Jury met, and that he had, immediately after his arrest, made a detailed statement to the police similar to his present testimony. Upon court order, the police produced the map Billings had drawn. Fickert denied, however, that there were any copies of Billings' original statements and McNutt had to rely on the map for evidence.

McNutt then had Billings stand before the jurors with his hands out as if carrying a suitcase and wearing the hat the police claimed he had worn that day. Several of the jurors said they noticed that Billings' left thumb-nail was slightly crinkled, but most of them couldn't see it until the hand was held up before their faces. As for the scar on Billings' forehead, which Rominger claimed to have seen, it was hidden by the hat he said Billings had been wearing. Even without the hat, the scar was so faint that most of the jurors were unable to see it, even when Billings stood directly in front of them.

Brennan's cross-examination of Billings was severe, but Billings stuck to his story.

Other witnesses testified to the various events Billings described in his alibi. Dr. Patek took the stand, and saving the defense the embarrassment of questioning Judge Dunne, said that he had a battleship-gray Hudson, that he and the judge had parked on Union Square Avenue at about 12:30 P.M. on July 22nd, that they had driven away at about 2 P.M., and that there was a jagged white streak on the side of the vehicle. Emma Richter, Bert Wertheimer, and George Stein testified to the other events and remarks Billings claimed to have seen and overheard. None recalled seeing him, however, and the bartender remained among the missing.

The following day Tom and Rena Mooney took the stand and testified to their activities on the afternoon of the parade. They were followed by some dozen others, Mrs. Hammerberg, Mrs. Timberlake, Eilers employees, etc., who placed them on the Eilers Building roof from about 1:50 until after 5.

Four businessmen testified that they had been standing approximately where McDonald said he had been standing and that the crowd was so dense McDonald couldn't have seen the things he claimed. All the witnesses the defense had thus far located, who had seen the man or men with the suitcase, testified that they had given their statements to the police, had been shown pictures of Mooney and Billings, and having failed to identify them, had not been recalled. Their descriptions of the men they saw did not fit any of the defendants.

McNutt then called the Salvation Army officials, the barber, and the others to whom McDonald had talked about the reward.

Using photographs and charts, McNutt presented the heart of his case, his "battle of the clocks," attempting to prove through photographic evidence that it was impossible for the defendants to have traveled from 721 Market to Steuart and Market in the time allotted.

And point by point, McNutt indicated the changes of testimony, the improbabilities, the discrepancies in the testimonies of the prosecution's witnesses. Crowley contradicted McDonald, McDonald contradicted Estelle, Estelle contradicted Vidovich. The descriptions by Moore and Vidovich not only failed to describe Billings, but failed to agree with each other.

The prosecution's witnesses, McNutt showed, had Billings in three different places at the same time. They had him wearing four different suits of clothes and two different hats. They had him both without suitcase and with it, and in the latter category, the cases covered a spectrum from yellow to black and came in five different sizes.

Wednesday afternoon the defense rested its case. The following morning rebuttal evidence was heard. Officer Moore reaffirmed his identification of Billings, as did Estelle and the Edeaus. One of the detectives guarding McDonald denied that the money conversations had taken place. On re-direct, however, McNutt made him admit that he had been guarding McDonald on only one of the occasions alluded to, the incident in the barbershop, and that he had not been close enough to McDonald to hear what he said.

That afternoon District Attorney Fickert, who thus far had played a secondary role to his assistant Brennan, delivered the prosecution's closing argument. The conspiracy evidence had been excluded; Fickert referred to it. The evidence regarding other alleged Billings bombings had been excluded; Fickert mentioned them again.

Some highlights:

"Gentlemen, the case here is far more serious than any other case that was ever submitted to any jury. It is not a question of this defendant against Mrs. Van Loo; that unhappy woman is at rest; those orphan children must go through life, thinking of the scenes that were enacted here. But here, gentlemen, was the offense: This American flag—this American flag was what they desired to offend. They offended that by killing the women and men that worshiped it. Here is another photograph of Mrs. Van Loo dying on the streets of our city, and in a feeble hand she holds the American flag, and if that flag is to continue to wave, you men must put an end to such acts as these. So far as I am concerned, no personal consequences are going to swerve me one jot from my sworn duty. What are personal consequences, what are political consequences at a time like this? Gentlemen, the very life of the Nation is at stake. No foreign foes were on our land at this time, but some traitor, some murderous villain, who, with his associates, perpetrated this crime, and, to disgrace the flag, they took the life of this unfortunate woman . . .

"It was done on a day—it was done for a purpose. It was done not to murder the people, the unfortunates who were there; it was done—they were merely an incident—the crime was against the flag; the crime was against the Constitution of the United States; the crime was against the laws of this government. It was done by men who believed in fear, who figured they could by intimidating people, put through certain propositions that they believed in . . .

"Gentlemen, when you leave the jury box I want the message to go down to Merced—where the innocent, unfortunate children of Mrs. Van Loo reside—that the man that murdered their mother has met his just punishment. I want your verdict to be such that when little Willie Knapp grows to manhood he can say that, 'When my mother was foully slain on the streets of San Francisco, she had citizens decent enough to mete out a just punishment.' It is not only the life of Mrs. Van Loo and the other children that we are concerned with, but it is the very life of this Republic . . ."

Fickert, who spoke for an hour and a half, concluded by asking that this "cowardly hyena," "this contemptible animal," be found guilty of murder in the first degree with a recommendation of the death sentence.

4 ·

Exactly what happened that night will probably never be known, even though Assistant District Attorney Brennan would, four years after the trial, issue a detailed statement regarding it.

According to this statement, following Fickert's closing, Brennan told Fickert that he would publicly withdraw from the case if the death sentence was urged. "Had I been a juror sitting in the case, and heard the evidence which I myself presented," Brennan would state, "I could not and would not have voted for Billings' conviction . . . None of these witnesses—Estelle Smith, the Edeaus—I would regard as credible had I been on the jury . . ." Inasmuch as Brennan's statement was not made for four years, or until after most of his major witnesses were proven to have committed perjury, this explanation is open to some doubt.

What happened in court the next day was part of the record. McNutt spoke for more than an hour, closing for the defense. He was followed by Brennan, who, to the astonishment of nearly everyone present, asked that the jury find Billings guilty but with the recommendation of life imprisonment.

There are three possible explanations for this startling change:

1. That Brennan, as he stated in 1920, felt the state had failed to establish its case and that "Imprisonment for life would . . . give Billings an opportunity to prove his innocence."

2. That Brennan, as he told reporters after he made his closing statement, felt that Billings was "only a puppet" and that by recommending leniency in his case Billings would be encouraged to turn states' evidence against Mooney and the other bomb defendants, in which case, Brennan said, he would be the first to petition the Governor for Billings' release.

or

3. That Brennan believed the prosecution's case so weak that to ask the death penalty meant risking acquittal, which would weaken all the other bomb cases, while by asking only life imprisonment the jury would have less hesitation in finding Billings guilty.

Saturday, September 23rd, 11 court days after the trial had begun, and two months and one day after the Preparedness Day bombing, Judge Dunne delivered his final instructions to the jury. They went out at 10:52 A.M.

Those in the press box took their usual 25-cent pool. Most of the money was on a disagreement. Only a few thought there would be either an acquittal or conviction in the first degree. None believed it possible that the jury would heed Brennan's suggestion of a lesser finding. Life imprisonment for the murder of ten people? Ridiculous.

Meanwhile, in the jury room, the first ballot was 8-3 with one blank; the second, third, and fourth ballots, 8-4. A short discussion revealed that their disagreement was not a question of guilt or innocence, but the penalty. This was resolved. By now it was nearly lunch time, however, and they agreed to put off the final ballot to have lunch at the city's expense. Two hours later they returned, voted again, this time 12-0, and at 2:52 P.M., three hours after going out, returned with their verdict:

"Guilty of murder in the first degree—with a recommendation of life imprisonment."

A veteran police reporter collapsed with a heart attack.

"The story of young Billings didn't seem to sound honest," one of the jurors told the press. "It did not pass muster."

"His story did not carry conviction at all," remarked another.

Said still another, "His story didn't ring true."

10 · A Vested Interest

"WE DO not know Billings and have no sympathy whatever with the doctrine he is said to preach as a remedy for our ills," wrote James Mullen, conservative editor of the *Labor Clarion*. "We do not know whether he is guilty of the crime with which he is charged, but it is our firm conviction that the verdict returned by the jury which sat in the trial was entirely unwarranted by the evidence . . ."

Mullen's editorial was a microcosm of the shock felt by the community at large. It jarred preconceptions. How could a jury find a man guilty of mass murder—and then give him less than the death sentence? The Billings verdict raised doubts, and with them the disquieting thought—if the defendants weren't guilty, then the real bombers must still be at large.

Not everyone shared this concern. Hearst's *Examiner* called it "an American verdict by an American jury" and a hopeful beginning to the end of the tyranny and violence of the IWW, sentiments that were reflected, in differing degrees, by the *Chronicle,* the Los Angeles *Times,* and the Sacramento *Bee.* Even those in whom the verdict engendered doubts were not enough disturbed to countenance McNutt's "frame-up" charges. In his closing in the Billings trial, McNutt had charged that the District Attorney's office "picked out the easiest man to convict, then went out and hunted up evidence that applied to him."

Immediately after the jury returned its verdict, McNutt released Alice Kidwell's letter, together with proof that Brennan had approached at least one of the parole board members on Kidwell's behalf. Brennan admitted making the plea, claiming that since both Mrs. Kidwell and Estelle Smith were living in fear of assassination, Kidwell's release would give them added protection and save the city the cost of a bodyguard. Not an altogether convincing explanation, but as far as the San Francisco papers were concerned, it sufficed. Both the charge and the answer were buried on the inside pages.

Talk of a frame-up, observed the *Call,* was "folly, and worse than folly." "To my knowledge," observed *Bulletin* editor Fremont Older, "there is no such conspiracy."

But the evidence was rapidly accumulating.

167

2 ·

The prosecution's case began to fall apart even before Billings was sentenced.

Two days after the trial, on September 26th, businessman William C. Kerch, bothered by what he knew to be perjured evidence, went to the defense and told them his story.

Kerch had been with Rominger when he helped the young photographer to the roof and also when he went to the police. On July 29th, Assistant District Attorneys James Brennan and Harry McKenzie had driven the two men to Richmond Station, and taking them to Billings' cell, asked whether he was the man they had seen.

Both said they had never seen this boy before—the man they saw was older, at least 5'9" tall, and bore little resemblance to Billings.

Neither Rominger nor Kerch appeared before the Grand Jury. Both were subpoenaed by the prosecution for the Billings trial. Kerch was not called. Rominger was. To Kerch's amazement, Rominger took the stand and positively identified Billings.

If Kerch was telling the truth, Louis Rominger had committed perjury. And the prosecution had introduced testimony that it knew to be false.* McNutt immediately filed a motion for a new trial on the basis of newly discovered evidence.

Now the defense knew why there had been no follow-up story on the promised Rominger identification.

Serious doubts about the credibility of another of the prosecution's witnesses, as well as a clear reflection on the prosecution's handling of the case, came to light when the defense learned the past of John Crowley. It was not pretty.

A background check revealed that Crowley had a long police record for deviate sex acts, larceny, and other offenses. In 1910 Crowley had been arrested during a police raid on a Barbary Coast house inhabited by female impersonators. A physicians' examination disclosed that he was suffering from advanced syphilis of the penis and rectum. In April 1911 he had married a seventeen-year-old girl, communicated the disease to her, then abandoned her. That July, District Attorney Charles M. Fickert had signed a complaint charging Crowley with wife abandonment. Convicted, he had been given two years probation on condition he pay his wife's support and medical expenses. There was also an instance where Crowley had perjured himself in a legal action. At the time he had testified as a prose-

* On October 29, 1917, Assistant District Attorney Harry McKenzie signed an affidavit admitting that Kerch's statement was correct.

cution witness against Billings, he was on probation for watch-stealing.

In a criminal case the calling of a witness by either side is an implied representation that the witness is worthy of belief.

Missing witnesses now began reappearing.

Retired seaman William Taylor, one of the witnesses who had seen a man with a suitcase, contacted the defense. After he had gone to the police with his story, he said, they had put him on the Stockton boat with instructions to stay away from the city until they called him. The call never came.

Elmer E. Kimberlin was now located. Although he had received two stomach wounds, severe injury to his eyes, and various internal injuries from the explosion, Kimberlin had—like Prendergast and Taylor—immediately reported to the police. He too had not been called in the trial. Also, like Prendergast and Taylor, on being taken to see the defendants he said there was no resemblance to the man with the suitcase.

By now the defense had found five witnesses to the falling object: Mrs. Janie Compton, who had seen the man on the saloon roof; Dr. J. Mora Moss, a prominent physician who was marching with the Sons of the American Revolution ("I happened to look toward the building and saw a black object falling through the air. It was twelve or fifteen feet from the ground, from a foot to fourteen inches in length, and three and a half to four inches in diameter and black in color. It disappeared behind the people standing on the sidewalk and a violent explosion immediately followed."); Mrs. Fannie Dahl, who had suffered facial wounds from broken glass ("I was trying to cross Steuart Street at Market coming from the direction of the Ferry. The parade was going on. I saw something black flashing before me, then I heard the explosion and saw the smoke."); Charles F. Hollfender ("I was standing on Market Street near the south car tracks opposite the fruit stand on Steuart. Something seemed to flash by me on the left side."); and Mrs. Maud Masterson ("I was looking in the direction of the saloon . . . Immediately before the explosion I saw an object like a balloon falling.").

Three of these witnesses had taken their stories to the police and had been told that they would be called back for further questioning; none were. The prosecution's efforts to suppress these stories magnified their importance in the eyes of the defense, which was now beginning to accept the theory that the bomb had been dropped. Mrs. Masterson, for example, had told her story to Fickert on his arrival at the bomb scene. He had refused, however, to give her name and address to the defense until required to do so by court order. Shortly after Mrs. Compton talked to the defense, she was called upon by a man who tried to persuade her not to testify at Tom Mooney's trial, now pending. Didn't she realize that if she helped these murderers, her husband's position might be jeopardized, and her own social standing affected? Mrs. Compton told him that her husband worked out of Chicago, that it was unlikely his employers had even heard of the case. As for her social standing, she was new in the city and had none. From photographs, she identified the man as Martin Swanson.

Too, there were dozens of new leads, many of them false. One the defense thought belonged in the crackpot category was a letter from an Italian in Los Angeles, filled with obscenities, obviously written by a near illiterate. But on the basis of its contents the defense wrote to the Los Angeles Police Department requesting a copy of the police record of a woman known variously as Miss and Mrs. Estella Moore, Estella Smith, and Estelle Smith.

In reply, they were informed that this information had been labeled "confidential" at the request of the San Francisco Police Department.

Lawlor went to Los Angeles to investigate.

3 ·

Following the Billings verdict, McNutt had made the usual motion to set aside the verdict as against the weight of the evidence. Judge Dunne now denied the motion. On the morning of October 7, 1916, Warren K. Billings appeared before the judge and was sentenced to "imprisonment at the state penitentiary at Folsom, California, for the rest of your natural life."

4 ·

Weary from her long lecture tour and her imprisonments in the various free speech and birth control fights, Emma Goldman was taking her first vacation in eight years. No sooner had she arrived at her sister's home in Provincetown, however, than she received a wire from Berkman telling her of Billings' conviction. A barrage of letters and wires followed. How could Emma think of rest, Berkman indignantly demanded, while Tom Mooney and his comrades were facing death? He urged her to go to New York immediately in search of a prominent attorney to defend Mooney. McNutt had failed to save Billings. Outside help was needed. Detecting an unusual tone of desperation in Sasha's letters, Emma terminated her vacation.

Frank P. Walsh, a Kansas City attorney long associated with labor and Democratic politics, former chairman of the Federal Commission on Industrial Relations and editor and publisher of the Kansas City *Post*, was in the city running President Wilson's New York campaign headquarters.

Following the arrests, Walsh had wired Berkman $500, asserting his belief that the defendants could never have committed the crime attributed to them. Emma called on Walsh at Wilson headquarters.

Important as he knew the case to be, Walsh told her, he was engaged in a much greater crusade—election of the man who had kept America out of the war thus far and who now represented the country's only hope for peace. Walsh not only regretfully declined her plea, he made one of his own—that Emma prove that she and the other anarchists were true champions of peace by working for the defeat of Hughes.

Emma, to whom political action was anathema, later wrote in her memoirs, "I left Walsh with a feeling of impatience at the credulity of this radically minded man and his co-workers in the Wilson campaign. It was additional proof to me of the political blindness and social muddle-headedness of American liberals."

Persuasive as Emma Goldman could be, she could not find an attorney willing to defend Tom Mooney. She informed Berkman of her failure. He replied that as soon as possible he would come East to see what he could do.

5 ·

Berkman and the defense committee had other problems closer to home. One was the attitude of California labor toward the case.

The conflict erupted on the floor of the State Federation's convention in October, when Nolan's union introduced a resolution calling for the full support of organized labor. Nolan, Mooney, Billings, and the others were being prosecuted solely for their past activities in the labor movement, the resolution stated, particularly their parts in the URR, PG&E, and machinists' strikes; therefore this was a labor case and should be treated as such.,

The resolutions committee derided this claim, stating that "no one at this time is attempting to connect labor with the bomb outrage."

A bitter fight ensued: Hugo Ernst of the waiters' union, from the first on the side of the bomb defendants, opposing the committee report; Mike Casey of the Teamsters, Thomas Tracy of the Printers, and Paul Scharrenberg, secretary of the State Federation, supporting it. The committee report—which mildly criticized the verdict in the Billings case as not being consistent with the evidence and recommended that all unions contribute to the defense "to assure the defendants fair trials," while at the same time reiterating that this was not a labor case—passed 38,196 to 4,226. The San Francisco Labor Council promptly referred its request for funds to the executive committee, "the graveyard of good causes." Before long Mullen was editorializing in the *Labor Clarion* that San Francisco unionists were "not the least interested or disturbed by the pending fate of the defendants" since "this is not a labor case."

Events were already proving otherwise. Using the Preparedness Day bombing as the opening wedge in its fight to abolish the union shop in San Francisco, the Law and Order Committee of the Chamber of Commerce now secured a tremendous victory over the unions.

The role of the Chamber of Commerce in the Mooney-Billings case has been much debated, ranging from the claims of some that Martin Swanson, acting on behalf of the Law and Order Committee, actually planted the Preparedness Day bomb to a complete denial on the part of chamber president Frederick Koster that his organization had any interest in the bombing. In reaching the truth an independent viewpoint seems in order. Robert Edward Lee Knight, in his book *Industrial Relations in the San Francisco Bay Area,* observes:

"In the ensuing months and years, Frederick Koster repeatedly stated, with evident sincerity, that the Chamber of Commerce never attempted to exploit the Preparedness Day bombing for the purpose of arousing anti-union sentiment. Yet almost from the moment of the bomb blast, the chamber acquired a vested interest in this crime which it could not bring itself to relinquish. Having immediately interpreted the bombing as a manifestation of labor violence, San Francisco business leaders clung to this interpretation. Although not explicitly charging the labor movement with responsibility for the crime, they pointedly referred to the bombing in the same context as disorders in labor disputes . . . The committee's intense interest in the case, and its dogmatic insistence upon the guilt of the defendants, could leave little doubt that it considered the prosecution to be significantly connected with its own effort to counteract the power of San Francisco labor."

Shortly after the bombing, the Law and Order Committee began circulating an initiative petition to place on the November ballot an anti-picketing ordnance nearly identical to that passed in Los Angeles. Full-page ads were run in all the papers. "There is no such thing as peaceful picketing," they read. "Picketing is an instrument of violence. It is Un-American. It hurts a city by bad advertisement, leads to crime, and does labor no good."

Election day was November 7th. From the 4th through the 6th, 400 telephone girls, in "the largest single campaign in the history of the telephone company," called every registered voter in the city, urging "Vote Yes on Ordnance 8 and prohibit picketing." As the nation went to the polls to re-elect the man who "kept us out of war," the most heavily unionized city in the United States voted in landslide proportions to make picketing a crime.

The four-month-old Law and Order Committee took full credit for the victory, as well as for the fact that during the same period the San Francisco chamber had increased its membership from 2,400 to 6,313, becoming the largest Chamber of Commerce in the United States.

Later that same month, in Baltimore, leaders of the San Francisco Labor Council told John A. Fitch, reporter for *Survey* magazine: "Some people have been indicted on a charge of murder. They happen to be trade unionists. But their plight has nothing to do with that fact. This is not a labor case."

6 ·

Fortunately for the defendants, many outside California disagreed. Through the bulletins of the IWDL and the personal efforts of Goldman, Berkman, and Minor, awareness of the plight of the defendants spread. In October, *Literary Digest* became the first large national magazine to take notice of the case, devoting three pages to the frame-up charges. Minor, traveling to Seattle, succeeded in arousing strong union support there. Lucy Robins did much the same thing in Chicago.

The efforts of Lucy Robins provide a glimpse into the informal manner in which most of the Mooney-Billings defense committees were born, as well as a not unhumorous view of the problems arising any time labor and the various radical groups attempted to unite in common effort.

Mrs. Robins (later Lucy Robins Lang) was an unusual young lady. A friend of Berkman's, she had been active in labor and radical causes since her teens. Moreover, she possessed considerable mechanical ability. With Warren Billings' help, she had designed an auto-house, progenitor of the modern house trailer, equipped not only with living accommodations, but also a portable printing press. Whenever the urge hit them, she and her husband Bob traveled across country, doing printing jobs wherever they stopped.

On learning that they were planning to go East, Berkman urged her to stop off in Chicago to see John Fitzpatrick and Edward Nockles, president and secretary of the Chicago Federation of Labor. Through Berkman, both men were already familiar with the case and aware of the need for immediate action. However, "Big Ed" Nockles explained to her on her arrival, leaders of the CFL they could go no further than the rank and file was willing to go, and the rank and file was lethargic. If Mrs. Robbins could organize a defense committee, and build up sentiment for the accused, then they could act. Canceling her trip and taking a part-time job as a waitress in a Loop restaurant, Lucy began organizing. Stollar Tobinson, president of the influential Workers' Circle, had been suggested as a possible chairman. Arriving at the Workers' Institute she asked a young man in paint-daubed overalls where the president's office was located.

"Right on top of this ladder," Tobinson replied.

Lucy informed him that he was chairman of the Chicago Mooney Defense Committee.

"Is there such a committee?" he asked.

"There will be when you appoint it," she replied.*

Deciding that the quickest way to arouse interest would be a mass meeting, the pair picked out those radicals they felt would draw the largest crowd. These were three in number: "Big Bill" Haywood, Alexander Berkman, and Jim Larkin, the Sinn Feiner now marooned in the United States by the war.

After many refusals, an auditorium was rented, that of the Hebrew Institute. On hearing that Berkman would be a speaker, the Institute withdrew its permission, declaring that Berkman had disgraced the Jewish people with his attempted assassination of Frick and that he would never be permitted to cross their threshold. This led to a boycott of the Institute by Jewish labor leaders, a boycott against the boycotters by the *Jewish Daily Forward,* and a protracted fight within Chicago's Jewish community that was still rife long after the case was drawing thousands to Chicago Coliseum.

Larkin, convincing friends on the Chicago police force that Mooney was being persecuted because he was Irish, finally obtained a hall above an Irish saloon on North Clark Street.

At this point another problem arose. Larkin was willing to speak, as was Berkman, who planned to stop off on his way East, but Haywood, with an antagonism born of many ideological battles, refused to appear on the same platform with the anarchist.

Failing to persuade him by other means, Lucy used psychology, wondering, aloud, if this was the *real* reason he didn't want to speak.

Glaring at her out of his one good eye, Haywood demanded "What do you mean by that?"

"Out on the coast they say you're scared since your own trial. You don't want to get mixed up in any more labor cases."

"God damn it, I'll speak!" Haywood shouted, jumping up and waving a clenched fist. "I'll speak to those bastards and tell them plenty."

He did, along with Berkman, Larkin, and William Z. Foster. Following the meeting, the Chicago Mooney Defense Committee was officially launched with a banquet of hot dogs and beer in the saloon downstairs.

---

* Following the 1917 revolution, Tobinson would return to Russia where, under the name Krasnoschokov, he would become President of the Far Eastern Republic (Siberia).

7 ·

From Chicago, Berkman went to New York. In less than two weeks he enlisted the support of nearly all the Jewish needle trades plus a half-dozen other unions, and persuaded the United Hebrew Trades, the largest and most influential Jewish central labor organization in the country, to call a mass meeting in Carnegie Hall to protest "California's big business conspiracy."

Through Mrs. Cram, Berkman also approached former congressman W. Bourke Cockran, the highly paid Tammany lawyer and Democratic party orator, asking him to defend Mooney when he came up for trial. Cockran replied that there wasn't enough gold in the world to make him defend these men if they were guilty. Berkman gave him a copy of the Billings trial transcript, telling him to read it and make his judgment solely on the basis of that.

Preceded by the usual afternoon demonstration in Union Square, the December 2nd rally in Carnegie Hall drew a mammoth crowd who heard Frank P. Walsh, Max Eastman, Max Pine, secretary of the Hebrew Trades, Arturo Giovannitti, poet and labor leader, and Goldman and Berkman present an impassioned plea for aid to the frame-up victims. $1000 was collected, an unheard of amount for such a meeting. John Reed caught the theme when he wrote, in the December issue of the *Masses,* "His Honor the District Attorney doesn't yet realize that the Labor Movement of the United States is past the stage where its champions can be slaughtered with impunity."

Cockran finished the Billings transcript. Declaring to Berkman that never before had he seen so gross and monstrous a travesty of justice, he volunteered his services without fee. McNutt and Cockran were close friends. It was arranged that Cockran would go to California toward the end of December; Tom Mooney's trial was to start early in January.

By now the juggernaut that would be known as the Mooney Defense was moving full steam, with defense groups in most of the major cities. The one in Kansas City, for example, was organized by Berkman and headed by young radicals Earl Browder and James P. Cannon. (One would in time head the Communist Party in the United States, the other the Trotskyite opposition.) Robert Minor, working closely with ex-pamphleteer Mooney, and fighting with him over every sentence, wrote and published the first pamphlet on the case: *The Frame-Up System.* Over the years, newly revised with each major development, it would go into some dozen editions and more than three million copies, under such

Mooney-chosen titles as *Fickert Has Ravished Justice* and *Justice Raped in California*. By the time the Mooney trial started, contributions to the defense were averaging $3500 per month.

This success was not without its dangers. As the staff of volunteer workers increased, so did the number of informants. Nor were the contributions themselves always free of suspicion. Already Berkman had ferreted out, and refused, two contributions made in the name of (and probably without the knowledge of) organizations connected with the German government, the easiest way, as the United States now moved ever closer to war, to discredit the organization.

8 ·

The letter that sent Lawlor hurrying to Los Angeles was from the owner of a cheap house of prostitution who claimed that the woman who now called herself Estelle Smith had once worked in his establishment.

Using unofficial channels, Lawlor obtained a copy of Estelle Smith's police record. It was lengthy. In a typical entry, at 11:30 P.M. on Saturday, May 30, 1914, officers Kirby and McAffee raided a disreputable house at 300½ South Los Angeles Street where they arrested four girls and one customer. One of the girls was Mrs. Estella Smith, who gave her age as twenty-five, her place of birth as Kentucky, her occupation as housewife, and was released on $100 bail, which she forfeited. Investigating further, Lawlor found it to be a $1.50 house.

Prostitution arrests were not the only dealings of the "demure dental assistant" with the police. On April 10, 1913, Estelle had been arrested and charged with the murder of one Irene Smith. Through newspaper files, interviews with policemen and others involved, Lawlor pieced together the sordid story. For some time Estelle, then using the name Moore, had been carrying on an incestuous relationship with her half-brother Morris Bohannon. Bohannon, however, became infatuated with a chorus girl named Irene Smith. Learning of this development, Estelle, accompanied by her uncle James L. Murphy, called on Miss Smith, apparently for the purpose of persuading her to stop seeing Bohannon. But Bohannon was there when they arrived, and an argument broke out. There are two versions of what then happened, but one indisputable fact: someone put a bullet in the stomach of Irene Smith. Both Estelle and Murphy were indicted for the murder. The charges against Estelle were dropped in July 1913, however, when Murphy testified that she had taken no part in the slaying. Murphy was convicted and sentenced to 12 years in San Quentin.

It was the opinion of several people Lawlor contacted, including a po-

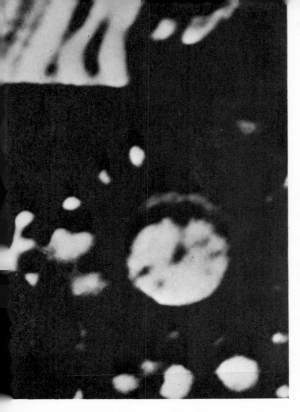

One of the Wade Hamilton "alibi photos," which placed Rena and Tom Mooney on the roof of the Eilers Building at 975 Market at the time they were allegedly placing the bomb at the corner of Steuart and Market, more than a mile away. The District Attorney's office first suppressed these photos, then supplied the defense with blurred prints that did not show the street clock. Greatly magnified, the clock disclosed the time to be 2:01 p.m.

lice captain, that Estelle had killed Irene Smith and that Murphy had been persuaded to take the rap for her. Murphy, the captain pointed out, had no motive.

By the time Lawlor returned to San Francisco he had a sizable dossier on Estelle, including such items as the affidavit of a social worker, Miss Suzanne Dean, who first met Estelle when she was in jail on the murder charge and had seen her frequently after that, when brought in on prostitution charges. According to Miss Dean, Estelle's "reputation for truth and veracity was very bad, and she was generally reputed to be utterly depraved and beyond the reach of any good influence."

Had Fickert made a deal with Estelle for Murphy's release, similar to the Kidwell arrangement? The defense suspected he had.

McNutt released the information on Estelle to the press.

Mrs. Alice Kidwell, Louis Rominger, John Crowley, Estelle Smith. McNutt knew these witnesses wouldn't be called in Tom Mooney's trial.

9 ·

The principal break in the case came less than a month before the trial was to start. It concerned the photos taken on the Eilers roof. Even after seeing the blurred prints, McNutt was not convinced that they were unimportant. Fickert had tried too hard to keep them from the defense. McNutt was now operating on the theory that if the prosecution attempted to suppress evidence, it must be defense evidence.

Another attempt was made to obtain Hamilton's copy of the prints, with a court order. Hamilton now said he had destroyed his only copies. Hamilton's lack of cooperation didn't surprise the defense, who had learned that his employer was an active member of the Chamber of Commerce, and perhaps more pertinently, that his YMCA roommate worked in the offices of PG&E. A court order was finally obtained requiring the District Attorney to turn over both the negatives and prints to Theodore Kytka, U.S. government expert on handwriting and photography.

On December 16th, in the presence of police photographer Blum, Kytka took the $2\frac{1}{2}''$ x 4 negatives and magnified them 144 times. Examining the prints, McNutt and Lawlor found that not only did they show, clearly and distinctly, the people on the Eilers roof, but that across Market Street there was the round shape of a jeweler's street clock. Magnified 200 times, this gave the times the three photos were taken.

The first photo, taken at 1:58, which included only a part of the roof edge, showed Mrs. Hammerberg, Mrs. Timberlake, and Rena Mooney, the latter holding her hat to her head. It was a dark-colored hat. Tom Mooney was not in this photo.

He was in the second and third photos, however, which were taken at 2:01 and 2:04, and which also included Rena and the others.

Here was clear proof that McDonald was lying or badly mistaken, since he had placed Mooney at the time of the second photo, 6088 feet away, at the corner of Steuart and Market.

Examining the blurred prints the prosecution had furnished the defense, Kytka remarked that the only way such bad copies could be made from such clear negatives was through intentional distortion—such as photographing the pictures over and over again. McNutt had him put this information in writing.

Was Fickert unaware that the photos gave the Mooneys an ironclad alibi? The defense felt sure he was not, not only from his reluctance to produce them, but from a question he had asked Rena Mooney during the Grand Jury proceedings. He had asked—or rather charged—that she had first worn a light colored hat on the day of the parade, then changed to a dark hat before going onto the Eilers roof.

McNutt had five-foot enlargements of the photos made up for courtroom use. Anticipating Fickert's strategy, he then tried every way conceivable to disprove them. The effort was unnecessary; the prosecution never disputed their authenticity.*

By the time Cockran arrived in California, McNutt and Lawlor had established a case strong enough, they felt, to win Tom Mooney an acquittal.

---

* Some years later a San Francisco newspaper did attempt to discredit the photos, announcing that they had hired experts who would prove that the shadows in the photos disproved the times on the clocks. The shadows verified the times, however, and the paper quickly dropped the subject.

11 · America's Dreyfus Case

MANY SAN FRANCISCANS began the year 1917 by reading the love letters of Alexander Berkman.

On going East, Berkman had turned editorship of *The Blast* over to Miss Fitzgerald. At 10 A.M. on Saturday, December 30, 1916, Fitzi again had the honor of entertaining Swanson and Assistant District Attorney Cuhna, this time accompanied by detectives Draper Hand and Mike Burke. Drawers and files were ransacked, papers and subscription lists seized. Fitzi picked up some letters. Cuhna asked what they were. Fitzi replied that they were personal letters and didn't concern the District Attorney's office. "Get them," Cuhna ordered. According to the press, "a desperate struggle ensued." It was brief; twisting her arms behind her back, Hand and Burke forced her to drop the letters. They were to her from Berkman, and of a decidedly personal nature. A search of the files also netted a number of love letters Emma Goldman had written Berkman during his long imprisonment.

With a good sense of timing, Fickert held back the story for two days. Typical was the *Chronicle's* screamer headline on Monday, January 1st: 'BLAST' IS RAIDED FOR BOMB PLOT EVIDENCE—DISTRICT ATTORNEY, SEEKING TO STRENGTHEN CASE AGAINST THOMAS J. MOONEY, SEIZES PROPERTY OF ANARCHIST PUBLICATION

According to Fickert, the office of *The Blast* was the place where the bomb plot had been hatched, and letters had been discovered in which Mooney, Nolan, and the other defendants threatened to stop the Preparedness parade by violence.

No quotations from these particular letters were released—probably because the letters didn't exist—but excerpts from the other letters were, the intimacies of America's foremost free love advocates more than compensating.

Two days later the trial of Thomas J. Mooney began.

2 ·

There was a changed mood in the courtroom. In September of 1916, when Billings went on trial, it still seemed Wilson could keep the United States out of war. By January of 1917, participation looked inevitable and peace talk was just short of treasonous.

The trial opened to a packed courtroom on Wednesday, January 3rd, with Judge Franklin A. Griffin presiding. A former secretary to Governor Hiram Johnson, now in his third term on the Superior Court bench, Griffin was a large man with broad shoulders, iron-gray hair, and keen, inquisitive blue eyes. Mary Mooney, embracing Tom when he was brought into the courtroom, comforted him and herself by saying that surely no Irishman with blue eyes would go along with "framing-up" her son.

It was, with a single exception, a contest of large men: the defendant, his attorney, the District Attorney—all were big men. Only Fickert's chief assistant, Edward A. Cuhna, who was to handle the prosecution, was of small stature. But Cuhna, a former Stanford debater, was young and energetic, and as *Bulletin* reporter Hopkins saw him, seemed tremendously excited at the chance to "put one over on the great Bourke Cockran." According to Miriam Allen DeFord, Cuhna regarded Fickert "with the worshipful admiration of a freshman for a senior who is also a football star."

Cockran was sixty-three. The great moments when he had mesmerized Democratic national conventions and Congress with his silver-throated oratory were past. Hopkins saw him as "an aged lion, rather weary, seeming at outs with the unaccustomed atmosphere of antagonism; perhaps unwilling to descend to the usual tactics for getting en rapport with a San Francisco jury." He left most of the questioning of the prospective witnesses to his associates McNutt and Lawlor, who had had experience with criminal cases. Cockran himself hadn't.

As for the defendant, Tom Mooney was, Hopkins observed, "self-contained, at times smiling, cynical; a man without faith in courts or legal justice, essentially vindicated in his mental position if courts and justice went wrong . . ."

A full two weeks were spent in choosing the jury, 177 talesmen being called and sworn. The result was not a "professional" but a "blue-ribbon" jury, made up largely of small businessmen ranging in age from twenty-one to seventy. The only excitement during these first days occurred when McNutt, representing Berkman and Miss Fitzgerald, asked the court to return their private correspondence, inasmuch as it had been illegally obtained, no return having been filed on the warrant. Cuhna objected. Judge Griffin had the correspondence examined, found nothing relevant to the case at issue, and ordered its return.

Cuhna delivered the prosecution's opening statement:

"We will offer evidence in this case, gentlemen, to show that some time prior to January first, 1916, this defendant, Thomas J. Mooney, entered into a general enterprise, or undertaking, or conspiracy with a number of other citizens—including Alexander Berkman, M. E. Fitzgerald, E. M. Morton, and Edward D. Nolan, and others—this general proposition—of bringing about an uprising or revolution of those persons in this State of California who were not owners of property, generally speaking those who worked. That this conspiracy had for its object confiscation of private property and the destruction of the Government; that in order to bring about the object of this conspiracy, the people in question in this case organized themselves together into an organization, known as the 'Blast-ers' . . . and some time prior to January first, 1916, or about that time, they published and circulated an announcement in San Francisco and other places, of the purposes of their organization; that they began the publication of a newspaper in San Francisco known as the 'Blast'; that in that newspaper, they announced the purpose of their conspiracy and the business of their conspiracy and what they were doing and what they intended doing . . ."

The aims of this revolution, Cuhna said, included overthrowing the American Federation of Labor, taking over the factories, closing the banks, weakening America by fighting Preparedness, and advocating such direct action as assassination of the President. The people would prove, Cuhna promised in his four-hour opening, that Mooney and his fellow anarchists "hated the government and the labor unions and the church." *

Berkman, probably recalling more than a few ideological disputes with Mooney the socialist, Mooney the IWW, and Mooney the syndicalist, would remark wryly: 'Mooney was to be, in spite of himself, made an anarchist."

3 ·

There were, Cockran and McNutt knew, only two ways the prosecution could overcome the alibi provided by the Eilers roof photographs: dispute their authenticity, difficult to do considering that they had been in the hands of the District Attorney's office since they were first developed; or change the testimony of their major witnesses so Mooney could

* San Francisco was heavily Catholic. Earlier Fickert had released to the press an extract from a letter of Mooney's in which he stated that he had little use for "priests and other skypilots."

plant the bomb and still have time to get back to the Eilers roof to have his photograph taken at 2:01.

The prosecution chose the latter course. To maintain this hypothesis, however, it was essential for the prosecution to establish that the bomb was a time bomb, preset for later detonation.

With the prosecution's first witness, coroner David Stafford, this theory suffered a damaging blow. On cross-examination Stafford remarked that most of the wounds on the bodies of the victims were on the neck, back, and legs and were downward slanting, indicating, Stafford said, that the bomb had fallen behind the crowd and probably exploded in the air before hitting the sidewalk. Stunned, Cuhna did his best to qualify this on re-direct, but the point was made.

During the Billings trial no clock parts had been introduced. The prosecution now produced three brass rings, identified as the winder for the time, the winder for the alarm, and the carrying ring at the top of a clock. All had been found by one Lyndback, a waiter, on the roof of the Alameda Cafe. On cross-examination, Lyndback contradicted himself a number of times, but he finally said that he had found the rings on three separate occasions, the first more than a week after the police had searched the roof for evidence. The defense would later establish that the rings were from two different clocks and gave no signs of having been through an explosion.

A piece of brass, said to be the pole of a dry-cell battery, was shown to be a spark-plug top. This was found on the corner of Steuart and Market several days after the explosion.

A small green coil of insulated wire, alleged to be the coil of a dry-cell battery, was expertly identified as the retardation coil from a telephone switchboard. This was found near the scene two days after the explosion.

Several small pieces of fabric were introduced that may, or may not, have been a suitcase. Three metal pieces, allegedly from the same suitcase, were later identified, by a suitcase manufacturer, as a lock from a suitcase, a clasp used exclusively on handbags, and a part from neither, finally identified as a piece of a baby carriage.

Witness after witness, point after point went to the defense.

Cuhna attempted to introduce in evidence a photo of the bomb-site damage taken after the rooting. Cockran objected, producing the real photo of the damage, of which the prosecution was still apparently unaware. As a result the prosecution was forced to call Colburn to the stand, to explain why he had knocked in the wall and smashed the sidewalk, and Bunner, to explain, as best he could, why he had washed the evidence away.

Officer Moore stuck to his earlier identification of Billings—but Cockran made the most of his erroneous estimate of Billings' height, as well as his statement that the young man he saw didn't have a suitcase.

The discrepancies in Vidovich's description were also stressed.

In the Billings trial Wade had stated that he was standing on the sidewalk outside 721 Market scrutinizing the display case when Billings passed him and went up the stairs, that on reaching the top Billings had turned, thereby allowing Wade to get a good look at his face.

McNutt, on cross-examination, asked Wade to mark on an enlarged map the spot where he stood. McNutt then proved that from where he said he was standing Wade couldn't have seen the top of the stairs.*

Before the Grand Jury and in the Billings trial three people had testified to seeing the Mooneys as well as Billings at 721 Market: Alice Kidwell, Estelle Smith, and Louis Rominger. Discredited by the defense, none of these witnesses were called in the Mooney trial. By removing their testimony, however, the defense helped the prosecution as much as hurt it, for by eliminating Estelle, the time was again left open.

Sadie Edeau took the stand. During the Billings trial the Edeaus had testified that they had first seen Billings on the roof, then later talking to officer Moore. Neither had mentioned the auto, the Mooneys, Weinberg, or anyone else. The times had been vague.

"About half-past one," Sadie now testified, she and her mother had been standing in front of the Kamm Building, just west of 721 Market, when they noticed Billings on the roof. A few minutes later he had appeared on the sidewalk, whereupon a man and a woman who had been standing in the doorway of the Kamm Building stepped out to speak to him. Sadie had noticed this couple earlier, in part because of the woman's hat, and had later identified them as Tom and Rena Mooney. There was an old five-seated Ford jitney parked next to the curb. While Billings and the Mooneys were talking, officer Moore had walked up to it. Leaving his suitcase with the Mooneys, Billings went over and spoke briefly to officer Moore. Moore had then honked the jitney horn a few times, and getting no answer, had walked away. As soon as he left, another man, identified by Sadie as Israel Weinberg, walked up to the jitney and began cranking it. It failed to start. Observing this, the Mooneys and Billings, the latter having reclaimed his suitcase, started walking down Market Street in the direction of the Ferry Building. Weinberg then got the jitney started and drove off in the same direction. Although this was the last Sadie saw of them, the implication was clear that Weinberg must have then picked up the trio and driven them to Steuart and Market. "All that I saw occurred between half past one and twenty minutes to two," Sadie testified. "At the time they left it was between twenty-five and twenty minutes to two."

Cockran cross-examined her.

* In the Rena Mooney trial, Wade changed his position, placing himself in the passageway instead of outside.

Q. Now, Miss Edeau, will you tell us why you didn't mention Mr. Mooney and Mrs. Mooney and Israel Weinberg and the Kamm Building and that automobile and the man cranking the automobile, and the automobile starting toward Third Street at any time during the trial of the Billings case?

Her reply was devastating in its simplicity.

A. Yes, I was never asked anything about them on the witness chair.

Q. Were you asked what you saw that day?

A. I was only asked what I saw Billings do.

Mellie Edeau told the same story, at times with almost identical wording—"This all took place between one thirty and twenty minutes to two." But there was one addition. While Sadie was watching the trio walk away, Mrs. Edeau had seen another man, a dark man with a stubby mustache who "looked like a laboring man," climb into the back of the vehicle just before it drove off.

Cockran had Mrs. Edeau indicate on a map exactly where they had been standing when they first saw Billings on the roof. Mrs. Edeau pointed to a spot directly in front of the Kamm Building. Cockran then produced a photo showing that if they had stood where she said, they couldn't have even seen the roof of 721, since they would have been standing under the Kamm Building awning. Mrs. Edeau changed the position to the middle of the sidewalk.

Q. Did you see anything about a reward in the papers?

A. No, sir. Such a thing as that would not appeal to me . . . I would like to swear I am not after the reward.*

Though Cockran had scored a few telling blows, this round went to the prosecution. But the crucial testimony was not that of the Edeaus. It was that of John McDonald.

Before the Grand Jury there had been a time conflict between the testimonies of Estelle Smith and John McDonald. During the Billings trial an attempt had been made to resolve this, with Estelle having Billings and his associates leave 721 Market sooner than aforesaid, and McDonald assigning them a later arrival at Steuart and Market.

The prosecution was now faced with the opposite problem. In order for Mooney to be on the Eilers roof at 2:01 the timetable of events at Steuart and Market had to be moved back again.

During the Billings trial, McDonald had Billings arriving at Steuart and Market at "eight or ten minutes to two" and setting down the suitcase at "about two o'clock." Billings' walk to the door of the saloon, Mooney's emergence, their conversations, Billings' departure, Mooney's

---

* On December 8, 1919, Sadie and Mellie Edeau each filed a claim for one-fifth of the reward. By this time, however, their testimony had been wholly discredited, and their claims were denied.

lengthy wait as he repeatedly checked his watch and the Ferry Building clock, then his disappearance in the crowd—all these things had occurred after Billings set down the suitcase at 2. But Mooney had been photographed more than a mile away at 2:01. If the Eilers photos were to be explained away, McDonald would have to change his testimony as to the time.

He tried. Under Cuhna's questioning he stated, as earlier, that he had arrived at Steuart and Market at about 1:40.

Q. How long after you arrived there . . . was it that you saw Warren K. Billings coming up with the suitcase, about?

A. Well, it must have been about—I don't know—I guess about five minutes.

1:45. A small enough change, but in this instance every minute counted.

As to the time the succeeding events occurred, McDonald was now vague. And there was one new addition to his testimony. Before, McDonald had left the scene just after Mooney. Now he stood around awhile, several minutes, maybe longer, watching the parade, before leaving and walking down Market to the Alameda Cafe, where he heard the explosion.

McDonald was literally stalling for time, time for Mooney to leave the scene, travel the distance to the Eilers building and be on the roof when the camera snapped.

On cross-examination, Cockran crucified McDonald, nailing him firmly to his previous testimony. McDonald squirmed, cried out, said first he had been mistaken, then hesitated and reconsidered. Despite almost constant objections from Cuhna, Cockran didn't let up until suddenly McDonald broke, blurted out that his previous testimony as to the time had been correct. Cuhna, dismayed, jumped up and objected. It did no good; McDonald had made his choice; he stuck with it.

Q. You stated in the last trial when you say your recollection was quite as good as it is now, that you saw Billings place that suitcase in that spot at two o'clock.

Mr. Cuhna. Just a moment.

Mr. Cockran. About two, didn't you?

A. Yes.

Q. About two o'clock, you mean as near as you can tell; you don't mean on or about?

A. I mean about as near as I can tell to two o'clock.

Q. You don't want to qualify it now?

A. I don't change it.

Q. You have stated, to the best of your recollection then, and the best of your recollection now, it was about two o'clock.

A. Yes.

John McDonald was finished as a witness. But to make sure, Cockran drove in one last nail. There was another fixed time to which McDonald had committed himself, the time of the explosion, 2:06. McDonald said he had just reached the Alameda Cafe when the explosion occurred.

The Alameda Cafe at 7 Market, Cockran established, was approximately 80 feet from where McDonald claimed to have been standing.

How long had it taken him to walk that distance, Cockran asked? McDonald said it had taken quite awhile, that he had been ill, just out of the hospital, and that he could only walk at "a snail's pace."

Cockran told him to stand and walk to the door of the courtroom, "as slow as you can possibly walk." Cockran timed his progress with a stopwatch. McDonald seemed barely to move his feet. It took him 33 seconds to cover the distance, which, as Cockran pointed out, was 50 feet—five-eighths of the distance from the place where he claimed to have been standing on Steuart to the door of the Alameda Cafe.

"No further questions."

Only one person had placed Mooney in the vicinity of the bomb scene. With the introduction of the Eilers photos, the defense felt sure, the last remnants of the case against Thomas J. Mooney would vanish.

It had been an interesting trial. Cockran had even managed, with no effort whatsoever, to make the District Attorney look ridiculous.

At one point Fickert claimed that Weinberg had driven the Mooneys to an anarchist picnic where a dangerous explosive was to be given away as a prize. He couldn't pronounce it, Fickert said, but it was spelled "N-i-e-t-z-s-c-h-e."

"The District Attorney thinks Nietzsche is a bomb!" Cockran exclaimed.

Puzzled, the Stanford graduate sent one of his assistants for an encyclopedia.

"Nietzsche," he now declared triumphantly, "was a bad man who associated with Richard Wagner!"

4 ·

Cuhna. We call Mr. Oxman.

Cockran looked at McNutt inquiringly. McNutt raised his eyebrows; he had never heard of Oxman.

The man who took the stand was in his mid-fifties; gray-haired, he had the rugged, deeply tanned face of a man who has spent most of his life outdoors. Frank C. Oxman was, Cuhna's questioning brought out, a wealthy cattleman from Durkee, Oregon, whose business occasionally brought him to San Francisco. He had been here, as a matter of fact, on

July 22nd last, arriving between 12 noon and 1 P.M. on the train from Portland. What had he done immediately after his arrival, Cuhna asked. Oxman replied that he had checked into the Terminal Hotel, then gone out to look for a bite to eat. All the restaurants being crowded, however, he had stopped at a fruit stand on the southeast corner of Steuart and Market and bought some fruit.

Q. I will ask you if on that afternoon after you arrived here in San Francisco you saw the defendant here, Thomas J. Mooney, on that corner or around that corner?

A. Yes.

Q. I will ask you if shortly after you arrived here in San Francisco you saw the defendant, Israel Weinberg?

A. I saw that gentleman over there, yes [indicating].

Q. What was that gentleman doing when you saw him?

A. Driving an automobile.

Q. Tell us what kind of automobile it was.

A. An old Ford.

Q. Did you see the defendant, Warren K. Billings?

A. I don't know his name. I saw the little auburn-haired boy over that way [indicating].

Q. Did you see the defendant here, Mrs. Rena Mooney?

A. The lady, yes.

There was complete silence in the courtroom as Cuhna asked him to tell the court what he had observed.

Unhurriedly, Oxman said that he had just crossed Steuart to the southwest corner, munching the fruit while he walked, when an automobile pulled up and stopped a few feet away on Market. Weinberg was driving. Mooney was with him in the front seat, his arm out the window, grasping the handle of a suitcase resting on the running board. Billings jumped out of the back seat and took the suitcase. Another man—"he had a stubby mustache and looked like a workingman"—climbed out after him and took the suitcase from Billings. Oxman was right in their way and Billings rudely shoved him aside, causing him to remark to the little fellow, "You are a pretty smart boy that will push a big fat man." Billings then set the suitcase against the wall of the saloon. Mooney, in the meantime, had left the car and slipped inside the saloon. When the two men returned he came out and told Billings, "Give it to him and let him go; we must get away from here; the bulls will be after us." Billings handed the man something, Oxman couldn't see what it was—presumably money—and the man crossed the street and disappeared into the crowd. Mooney and Billings then talked briefly, Mooney glancing at his watch and the Ferry Building clock. Meanwhile, the auto with Weinberg and Mrs. Mooney had turned the corner and started down Steuart. Mooney and Billings climbed in; the auto drove off down Steuart toward Mission. Oxman had then walked across Market to his hotel, arriving there at "fifteen minutes to two o'clock." All this, everything he had described, had taken no longer than five or six minutes.

According to one reporter present, "All of the assurance, all of the air of bravado, all of the self-confidence had left the faces of the five defendants. Their attorneys sat almost cowed by the turn of events."

Cuhna. Your witness, Mr. Cockran.

Cockran arose slowly and began his cross-examination. Leading Oxman through his story again, Cockran asked him the exact time he had seen the automobile.

A. I ain't going to testify as to minutes.

Q. It is very important to get you to fix the time as close as possible.

A. I don't know how long I was on that corner before going across to go to the hotel.

He did know that he had arrived at the hotel at exactly 1:45, because he was expecting a telephone call from a Miller and Lux cattle buyer at 2.

Cockran questioned him as to his identifications, establishing, as with previous witnesses, that Oxman hadn't picked the defendants out of a line-up, but had been taken to see each one separately in his cell. But as for the positiveness of his identifications, he was firm. Each question by Cockran only elicited additional confirming details; for example, "When I saw Mrs. Mooney in the automobile she had a red band on her hat, the hat was a dark material. I think it was gray."

How could he be so sure about such minute details so long after the day in question?

He was a cattleman, Oxman explained tolerantly, as if to a dude. In his business a man had to notice little things, like brands, differences between one cow and another, and such.

What caused him to notice these people in the first place?

The queer, nervous way they were acting, Oxman said, had made him think they were thieves who had stolen the suitcase, emptied it of its contents, and then were trying to dispose of it.

Suspecting they were thieves, why hadn't he gone to the police immediately.

He wasn't sure, he said. And, he replied straightforwardly, he hadn't wanted to become involved.

Cockran pounced. He hadn't been sure they were thieves even after hearing Mooney allegedly say "We must get away from here; the bulls will be after us"?

A. I didn't know what the meaning of "bulls" was. I never heard a policeman called a "bull." I am a cattleman. We call a male cow a bull.

Judge Griffin had to gavel for order.

The year was 1917. Many were beginning to realize that "the West that was" was no more. Oxman was straight out of the frontier tradition: his grammer wasn't polished, he used no fancy words, but he was honest, forthright, as open as the land. Cockran was an Easterner, a Tammany lawyer brought in to meddle in a strictly local case. Their confrontation was classic. It was obvious where the jury's sympathy lay.

What about the auto, Cockran asked. How could he be so sure it was Weinberg's?

He had been taken to the police garage and had identified it, Oxman replied.

But how could he be sure it was the same auto, Cockran persisted.

He would regret having asked this question for the rest of his life.

A. I seen it when it went off, and I took the number of their automobile.

Q. Oh, you did.

A. I supposed, probably the next morning it would be in the newspapers.

According to one reporter, Cockran was like a fat little rabbit who has chanced on a rattlesnake. He knew it was deadly, he knew he should run away, but he could only stare at it in horrified fascination.

Q. You took the number of the automobile?

A. Yes, because I am in the stock business—

Q. I understand that—

A. I was going to answer the question that in my country—

Q. Don't let me interrupt you. You say you saw the number of that automobile.

A. Yes.

Q. You took it down?

A. Yes, sir.

Q. Do you mean to tell us that you had the number of that automobile in your possession?

A. Yes, I have it now.

Q. Let me see it.

A. (Witness produces paper) It is right here.

Oxman handed Cockran a wrinkled yellow telegraph envelope, on the back of which was penciled, "Ford No. 5181—Think stolen grip—S.F. Jul 22nd."

The trial of Thomas J. Mooney would last two more weeks. Cockran would point out that Oxman's testimony contradicted that of McDonald in almost every particular, from the defendants' manner of reaching and leaving the scene to the time itself. Witnesses would testify that no vehicle other than the official photographer's car and the ambulance had traveled down Market during the parade. Of the many thousands who lined both sides of the street, the prosecution wouldn't produce one person, other than Oxman, who claimed to have seen such a car, and this included the paraders assembled at Steuart and Market into whose ranks the vehicle allegedly turned. Cockran would emphasize one important discrepancy in Oxman's story—he stated that when the auto arrived the paraders were marching out of Steuart onto Market, but this had occurred not at 1:40 but 2:04. Cockran would introduce 16 witnesses who placed the Mooneys in the Eilers building or on its roof on July 22nd. The Wade Hamilton photos would be introduced, together with damning testimony regarding their suppression. Swanson's attempts to bribe Billings and Weinberg into testifying against Mooney in the San Bruno case would be testified to, and left unchallenged by the prosecution. The court would force the prosecution to produce the PG&E employment application given by Swanson to Billings, then seized in the search of his rooms. The witnesses who said they had seen the placing of the suitcase but whom the prosecution had neglected to call would be called now, by the defense, to give their descriptions, which did not fit the defendants. The witnesses to the falling object would testify as well. The prosecution would be forced to admit, in effect, that none of the items found in the searches of the defendants' rooms connected them to the bombing. Cockran would prove, using handwriting expert Kytka, that Oxman had originally written "Jan" on the envelope, then erased and written "Jul" over it, an indication that he might well have noted the license plate after being shown the vehicle in the police garage. Cockran, in a brilliant closing address, would make the prosecution's whole theory of the jitney trip down Market through the parade look ridiculous. Fickert would deliver a closing equally brilliant, until the *Bulletin* demonstrated, with parallel columns, that he had cribbed several hundred words from a speech by Daniel Webster.

And yet all this wasn't enough. Against it stood the testimony of the man the newspapers described as "the honest cattleman from Oregon," reluctant to come forward because he didn't want to become involved, too rich to be interested in the reward.

5 ·

Because, less than three months later, Charles M. Fickert would attempt to minimize the importance of Oxman's testimony, insisting it had no real effect on the outcome of the case, it is necessary to establish how much impact his testimony did exert on those present.

Every San Francisco newspaper covering the trial said that Oxman was *the* witness against Mooney. On the day after his appearance, the headlines read: *Chronicle*—RANCHER RIDDLES MOONEY DEFENSE; *Examiner*—RANCHER SHATTERS DEFENSE IN BOMB TRIAL; *Call*—OREGON MAN SENSATION AT TRIAL.

There was in the courtroom that day a writer who had sat through both the Billings and Mooney trials and who was thoroughly convinced both men were guilty. In an article entitled *Frame-Up or Square Deal?*, in *Sunset Magazine,* Colin Irving Spangler wrote:

"There were about one hundred and twenty witnesses summoned by the state. Oxman was worth all of the others put together. His was the clinching argument, the convincing force, the overbalancing weight necessary to a conclusion of guilt against Mooney . . .

"Without Oxman, had I been a juror, I might have returned a verdict of acquittal in the Mooney case, but with his testimony, under my oath, I would have been forced to convict."

Assistant District Attorney Cuhna, on the day after the verdict was returned, told the press that although he considered the other witnesses important, Mooney stood convicted on Oxman's testimony alone.

But there was a still better judge of Oxman's effectiveness. In a letter to Governor William D. Stephens, dated November 19, 1918, Judge Franklin A. Griffin would state:

"Oxman was by far the most important of these witnesses. His testimony was unshaken on cross-examination, and his very appearance bore out his statement that he was a reputable and prosperous cattle dealer and land owner from the State of Oregon. There is no question but that he made a profound impression upon the jury and upon all those who listened to his story on the witness stand, and there is not the slightest doubt in my mind that the testimony of Oxman was the turning point in the Mooney case and that he is the pivot around which all of the other evidence in the case revolves."

6 ·

On the afternoon of February 9th, Judge Griffin delivered his charge to the jury. It was, the press wrote in a tone almost of complaint, exceedingly fair to the defendant. When the jury went out at 3:03, Mooney turned to Cockran and said, "They'll convict me." Cockran was so sure they wouldn't that he kept an appointment to deliver a lecture that night and so wasn't present when the jury filed back in at 9:35.

There was no need to wait for the verdict to be read. Jury foreman William MacNevin, spotting Fickert, grinned and drew his finger across his throat in a slitting motion.

Mooney turned, and reaching across the railing, grasped his mother's hands and whispered, "Don't cry, mother!" just as MacNevin stood and said, "We, the jury, find the defendant Thomas J. Mooney guilty of the charge of murder in the first degree."

No one said anything, waiting for MacNevin to continue. He didn't. There was no recommendation for life imprisonment.

"My brother! My brother!" Anna Mooney screamed in a hysterically high voice. "Tom! Tom!" sobbed Mary Mooney as Tom tried to take her in his arms. A deputy forcibly separated them. Anna fainted, as did Mrs. Weinberg, and both had to be helped from the courtroom. There were tears in Fitzi's eyes; there was anger in Robert Minor's. In the Billings trial Fickert had tried unsuccessfully to have Minor ejected from the courtroom, but had been overruled by the judge, and during both trials Minor had sat in the press box representing *The Blast*. As he moved forward to say good-bye to Mooney, Lieutenant Brunner grabbed his arm, and twisting it behind his back, pushed him through the crowd and out the courtroom door.

There had been ten ballots, jury foreman MacNevin told the press, but only on the question of whether Mooney was to be given the death sentence. His guilt had been agreed to from the start.

Rena was in her cell when told, as were Billings and Weinberg. Reached by the press just after having completed his lecture, Bourke Cockran was stunned and would say only that they would appeal. Through his last interview with his client the next day he seemed unable to comprehend that Mooney had actually been convicted. The same day he caught the Overland East. En route, some of his old fire returned and he wrote Mooney:

"I think it can be clearly shown to all reasonable men that we are in the presence of another Dreyfus case. The only difference being that the object of the French perversion of legal procedure to perpetration of the very crimes which courts are organized to prevent, was exclusion (by force and threats of force) of Jews from the Army, while the object of your prosecution for the crime repugnant to every element of your nature, it is to drive laborers from organizing by killing a man who has the temerity to urge some of his fellows to form unions for their own protection . . .

"I have reached the deliberate conclusion that the appalling judicial crime committed against you will never be allowed to reach the consummation which induced its perpetrators to plan it . . ."

Sentencing was set for February 4th. Tom Mooney wrote a speech for the occasion. In it he said, "I do not know why life, as we workers have to live it, is sweet, but it is. I do not know why one should wish to prolong this unceasing battle, but I do. Because of this feeling which may be little more than a man's instinct to live, I would have uttered one final protest

—futile there is no doubt, but not without avail, I trust, in the ear of the public, which when permitted to know the truth is always committed to justice.

"I am under sentence of death. Whatever may be the legal equivocation, the crime of which I have actually been convicted is not that of having thrown a bomb into a throng of innocent people . . . but that of having striven with what strength I had for the alleviation of industrial wrongs that labor has suffered, and the establishment of the rights which naturally belong to labor. I do not believe—I cannot believe—that because I have exercised the simple privilege of a human being I must meet death on the gallows. The fury engendered by industrial strife may defeat justice in a given locality, but so deeply imbedded in the hearts of the people is the desire for justice that it must inevitably find expression in a court of review. In that faith I am content."

Judge Griffin didn't let him deliver it. The occasion was difficult enough for Griffin already, as it was the first time he had been called upon to sentence a man to death.

"It is the judgment of the court and the sentence of the law in this case that you, Thomas J. Mooney, be delivered by the Sheriff of the City and County of San Francisco to the warden of the State Prison at San Quentin to be by him executed and put to death on the 17th of May, 1917, in the manner provided by the law of the State of California."

Griffin had dispensed with the traditional wording, which ended "that you be hanged by the neck until death, and may God have mercy on your soul."

7 ·

To prosecutor Edward A. Cuhna, it was an auspicious beginning. That night in the bar of the Palace Hotel he proposed a toast, overheard by a *Bulletin* reporter, "To Charles M. Fickert, the next Governor of the State of California and . . ."—there was a modest pause—"to Ed Cuhna, the next District Attorney of the City and County of San Francisco."

To Emma Goldman, all the omens were grim. Tom Mooney had been convicted and sentenced to death. In Everett, Washington 74 IWW's were on trial for their lives, accused of a crime of which they themselves were the chief victims.* The United States had become a military machine,

* On Sunday, November 5, 1916, 250 Seattle IWW's chartered the *Verona* to take them across Puget Sound to Everett, where a free speech fight was talking place. As the ship approached the dock it was riddled with the gunfire of some 200 citizen "deputies," killing 11 Wobblies and seriously injuring 31 others. Two deputies were also killed, apparently in the crossfire of their fellows, and 74 of the IWW's were arrested and charged with these murders. No like charges were pressed in connection with the murders

moving with frantic haste toward war, running down everyone who stood up to protest.

"The political sky in the United States was darkening with heavy clouds, and the portents were daily growing more disquieting . . .

"Then, unexpectedly, the light of hope broke in the east. It came from Russia, the land tsar-ridden for centuries. The day so long yearned for had arrived at last—the Revolution had come!"

It was the February Revolution.

The Tsar had been deposed and a provisional government instituted under Alexander Kerensky. Though Emma would be one of the first to grow disillusioned with what was happening to *Matushka Rossiya,* these events were to have a profound effect on the radical movement in America, and not least of all, on the fate of Thomas Mooney.

of the workers. Fred Moore, later counsel for Sacco and Vanzetti, defended the men. all 74 finally being acquitted in May 1917.

12 · The Fall of an Honest Cattleman

MORE THAN 2000 miles from San Francisco, in the small town of Grayville, Illinois, the owner of the Manhattan Pool and Billiard Parlor read the newspaper stories of Tom Mooney's conviction and wondered what he should do about it. For Ed Rigall had in his possession evidence which could save Mooney's life.

Unknown to the defense, Grayville was Frank Oxman's home town. He had lived there for more than 40 years before deserting his wife and children and running off with another woman.

Rigall's story, as he would later tell it, went as follows:

In December of 1916, he had received a letter from Frank Oxman. It had come as a surprise, since Rigall, though acquainted with Oxman's son, knew the elder Oxman only slightly and hadn't seen him in more than 10 years. Too, there was bad feeling between the families. Some years earlier, Oxman and Ed Rigall's father had been partners in a land fraud scheme for which they had been taken to court; Rigall's mother had always blamed Oxman for her husband's involvement.

Oxman's letter was in an envelope of the Hotel Terminal, 60 Market Street, San Francisco, and was postmarked San Francisco, December 14, 1916, 1:30 A.M. The letter itself was on two sheets of hotel stationery. It read:

> Mr. Ed Riggall
> Grayville, Ill.
> Dear Ed:
> Has been a long time since I hurd from you. I have a chance for you to cum to San Frisco as a expurt wittness in a very important case. You will only hafto answer 3 to 4 questions and I will Post you on them. You will get mileage and all that a witness can draw probly 100 in the clear so if you will come ans me quick
> [second sheet]
> in care of this Hotel and I will mange the Balance it is all O.K. but I need a witness Let me know if you can come Jan. 3 is the dait set for trile Pleas keep this confidential.
> > Answer hear
> > Yours truly
> > F. C. Oxman

Rigall had never been to California and this seemed a good chance to see it, expenses paid, $100 in the clear. On December 18th, he wired Oxman "Will come. Wire transportation and expenses."

A second letter from Oxman arrived a few days later. On the same hotel stationery, it was dated December 18, 1916, and it read:

> Dear Ed:
> Your Telegram Received I will wire you Transportation in Plenty of time also expce money Will Route you by Chicago Omaha U.P. Ogeden S.P. San Frisco. I thought you can make this trip and see California and save a little money—
> [second sheet]
> As you will be aloued to collect 10¢ Per Mile from the stake which will Be about 200 I can get your expence and you will only hafto say you saw me on July 22 in San Frisco and that will be easey dun. I will try and meet you on the way out and talk it ovr the state of California will pay you but I will atend to the expces The case won't come up untill Jan. 3 or 4 1917 so start about 29 off this month.
> [third sheet]
> You know that the silent Road is the one and say nothing to any Body the fewer people no it the Better when arrive Register as Evansville Ind little more mileage.
> Yours truly
> F. C. Oxman
> Will you want to Return by Los Angles can Route you that way

There was a third letter, dated December 25, 1916, this one to Ed's mother:

> Mrs. J. D. Rigall
> Grayville
> Dear Mrs. Rigall:
> As I am sending Ed transportation tomorrow 26 it might be that I can use you also about the 10 if so I can obtain you a ticket that you can see California if you would like the Trip adress me care this hotel tell F.E. to say nothing until he see me Can probly use a Extry witness Been a long time I dont see you
> Yours truly
> F. C. Oxman

Mrs. Rigall, who distrusted Oxman, urged her son not to go, but Oxman had already wired the price of the ticket plus $27. Rigall arrived in San Francisco on the evening of January 7th, and per Oxman's instructions, registered at the Terminal Hotel under the alias "L. O. Charles, Evansville, Indiana." That night he saw Oxman who told him about the Mooney case. In a few days he was to be a surprise witness; all he wanted from Rigall was testimony that he had seen him in San Francisco on Saturday, July 22nd.

"I was in Niagra Falls on the 22nd of July," Rigall protested.

"Well, you were here as much as I was," Oxman replied.

The next day Oxman took him to Steuart and Market and went through the testimony he was to give. Deciding it might be a good idea if Rigall testified that he too had seen the Mooneys, Billings, and Weinberg, he briefed him on what they looked like and were alleged to have done. All this proved too complicated for Rigall, who said he could never remember it. Oxman then asked if he had any friends back home who would be interested in making some money by testifying. Rigall mentioned a paperhanger in Chicago who might. "He is a union man," Rigall added. "He won't do," Oxman replied.

Rigall stayed in San Francisco for three weeks. During this period he had frequent consultations with Fickert, Cuhna, Swanson, and Bunner, who also saw that he was properly entertained. In the company of Estelle Smith, Fickert once took Oxman and Rigall to the Cliff House for dinner. On another evening Fickert and Rigall got drunk together in the bar of the Palace Hotel. Fickert also obtained for Rigall a guest card entitling him to all the privileges of the exclusive Olympic Club, of which Fickert was a member. Repeatedly, Fickert had asked him to try to remember: Hadn't he seen Mooney, Billings, Mrs. Mooney, Weinberg, and the jitney? Rigall said no. "Well," Rigall quoted Fickert as saying on one of these occasions, "perhaps you and Mr. Oxman had better go back to the hotel and refresh your mind." Back at the hotel, Oxman told Rigall that if he testified as Fickert suggested, he would get a good piece of the reward. Pulling out his checkbook, Oxman offered to write out a personal check for $250. Rigall refused. He was, he said, edgy about testifying at all. And he didn't like being registered under an assumed name and address. Oxman explained that this was to make it more difficult for the defense to track him back to Grayville. However, if it really bothered him, he could change his registration. Rigall did.

The Mooney trial was now in progress. Bunner arranged for them to attend one day in order to have a good look at the defendants. Oxman thought it might be a good idea if they also saw Weinberg's jitney, whereupon officers Hand and Bunner took them to the police garage. Oxman noticed that it didn't have license plates. Hand said they had been taken off and were being held by the police custodian but that he could arrange for them to be shown, which was done. Up to this time Oxman had said nothing about having copied down the license number. It was Rigall's impression that Oxman's producing of the number on the stand was as great a surprise to Fickert and Cuhna as to Cockran.

During this period Oxman also introduced Rigall to Estelle Smith,

Wade, and Vidovich. Several of these meetings ended in arguments over how the reward was to be divided. At least twice, Rigall said, he had been with Oxman when he asked Fickert exactly how much his share would be. Both times Fickert told him not to worry about it, assuring him there was plenty of money "higher up" and he would be taken care of.

Oxman was due to testify on the 25th, with Rigall following him on the stand. On the afternoon of the 24th, Rigall told Bunner that he couldn't testify, that he hadn't been in San Francisco on July 22nd, that he hadn't, in fact, ever been in California before. Bunner, not too greatly disturbed, said he thought Rigall had better tell Cuhna or Fickert. That evening Rigall and Cuhna talked privately in a Hall of Justice room. As Rigall recalled the conversation, it went as follows:

"Now Ed," Cuhna said, "I want you to tell me what you know about this case. This is a big case, this is the first big case I was ever in, and it means a whole lot to me."

"I realize that," Rigall replied, adding "I like you Cuhna, you are a good fellow, and that is why I don't want to lie to you."

"Now Ed," Cuhna said, "I want you to come clean with me."

"All right," Rigall replied. "You came clean with me and I will come clean with you. I never was in San Francisco and I don't know a damn thing about the case."

Cuhna replied, "If that is the case we won't use you."

Rigall then told Cuhna that he had already spent some of his own money, over the $27 sent him by Oxman.

"Oh, well, will a hundred and fifty dollars put you in the clear?"

Rigall answered affirmatively. Cuhna told him to come to Fickert's office during the noon court recess the following day and he would be paid. Cuhna then asked, as if in afterthought, how Oxman had sent for him in the first place. By letter, Rigall replied. Did he have it with him, Cuhna asked. No, it was back home in Grayville, Rigall declared, but he could send it. Do that, Cuhna said.

The next day Rigall went to Fickert's office for his money. Both Fickert and Cuhna were present. Fickert started to write out a check but Cuhna stopped him, suggesting it might be better to make payment in cash. Fickert went into the outer office; a few minutes later he returned with $150—two $50 bills, eight $5 gold pieces, and $10 in silver. He then asked Rigall to do him a favor. The cross-examination of the witnesses had taken longer than expected; Oxman wouldn't be taking the stand until tomorrow. He would appreciate Rigall's staying over another day to lend Oxman moral support. Rigall agreed. Oxman testified on the 26th, and that night Rigall caught a train back to Grayville.

This was Rigall's story.

After learning of Mooney's conviction, Rigall told it to Claude O. Ellis.

Ellis was an attorney and the Mayor of Grayville. Ellis asked Rigall whether he had proof his story was true. Rigall produced the Oxman letters, his train ticket stubs, and the Olympic Club guest card (issued on January 17, 1917, at the request of Mr. C. M. Fickert). Ellis, according to his version of these events, then suggested they obtain additional verification of Rigall's having been in San Francisco. On February 12th, Rigall sent a telegram to Edward A. Cuhna, Hall of Justice, San Francisco:

> Congratulations on your conviction. Think my evidence will get party new trial. F. E. Rigall.

Cuhna fell for the trap. The same day he wired Rigall in Grayville:

> Cannot understand your telegram. You told me your friend was thoroughly trustful and reliable. We have plenty of other witnesses and conclusive evidence supporting his testimony. Am astounded at your suggestion you have testimony to help defendant. It is your duty to reveal to me at once any and all facts you have because I certainly want defendant to have a new trial if he is entitled to it. Wire me collect all details at once. Explain in detail your telegram and your attitude. Be careful and fair because any witness who has testified falsely in this murder case must himself be prosecuted for murder . . . Wire immediately to me at Olympic Club San Francisco California.
>
> Edward A. Cuhna

Both Rigall and Ellis are now dead. It is possible to say what the Mooney defense took pains to hide while both men were still living—that neither man was particularly anxious to right a great legal wrong.

Rigall would state that he had never intended to testify, that he had played along with Oxman and Fickert only to learn the extent of the conspiracy. Giving him the greatest benefit of the doubt, it seems far more probable that Rigall felt he had found a "good thing" and rode it as long as he could.

As for Ellis, his motives emerge clearest in what he failed to do. Although Mooney's execution date was less than three months away, the attorney made no move to contact the Mooney defense. He simply locked the letters and other documents in his safe and waited.

Considering this, the telegram he instructed Rigall to send Cuhna seems less a testing of Rigall's story than a request for bids.

2 ·

While Rigall and Ellis were playing their game, two more of the prosecution's key witnesses were impeached.

Shortly after Mooney was sentenced, an investigator for the defense called at Foreman & Clark, the Oakland men's clothing store where Mrs. Edeau had been working at the time of the bombing. She had left this job shortly before the Billings trial.

Did any of the employees remember her? Yes, Mrs. Muriel Stewart, one of the tailors, did. Had Mrs. Edeau mentioned anything about her activities on Preparedness Day, the investigator asked. Yes, on July 27th,* Mrs. Edeau had told her, and two other tailors, that she had been standing on the corner of Steuart and Market just before the explosion occurred and had seen two men—

At Steuart and Market?

Yes, and had seen two middle-aged men put down a black suitcase with white trimmings against the saloon wall. Had she told the police, the tailors asked her. No, she replied, she didn't want to get involved. But after much urging she finally relented, that afternoon taking time off to see Oakland Police Chief Peterson. She hadn't come to work the following day. When she returned the day after that and they asked her what had happened, she said a policeman had taken her to San Francisco to identify the suspects but that they weren't the same men, they were too young.

Mrs. Stewart's statement was taken down and notarized. After a brief search, the two other tailors were located. Both—Thomas J. Stout and William Burgess—verified her story. Armed with the three affidavits, defense attorneys called on Walter J. Peterson, Chief of Police of Oakland, California.

Chief Peterson seemed relieved to see them, insisting that if they hadn't contacted him, he would have contacted them, that he had been thinking of little else since the Mooney verdict.

Peterson then called in one of his officers, William H. Smith. McNutt and his associates listened in astonishment to the story they told.

Mrs. Mellie Edeau had come to see him, Chief Peterson said, on the afternoon of July 27th, 1916, with her story of having seen two middle-aged men with a suitcase on the corner of Steuart and Market just before the explosion. Chief Peterson had called Fickert, who suggested Mrs. Edeau be brought over the next morning to see if she could make identifications. Officer Smith arranged to pick her up at her home.

She wasn't ready when he arrived, officer Smith explained, and while waiting he had talked briefly to her daughter Sadie. He asked if she too had seen the men, but she replied that she knew nothing about it.

On arriving in San Francisco, Sergeant Goff had taken Mrs. Edeau and officer Smith to the cells of both Billings and Mooney. According to Smith, Mrs. Edeau said, "Those are not the men I saw. They are too

* This was after the suitcase stories had appeared in the press.

young. I have never seen either of these men in my life."

Smith had made a memorandum to this effect in his notebook:

> Jul 28, .16.
>   Took Mrs. Sadie Edeau of
> 4106 Bayo St. to S.F. to see
> if she could identify Tom
> Mooney and Warren K. Billings
> as men she saw with suit case
> at Market and Steuart St.
>   She failed to identify them.*

This memorandum was also incorporated into officer Smith's official report to Chief Peterson.

Considering it just another false lead, Peterson and Smith forgot the incident. Mrs. Edeau did not appear before the Grand Jury. Reading a newspaper account of the Billings' case, however, officer Smith discovered that both Mrs. and Miss Edeau had identified Billings, stating not that they had seen him at Steuart and Market, but at 721 Market Street. Smith told Chief Peterson. Peterson agreed it was odd, but decided Fickert must know what he was doing. The two policemen did nothing.

Shortly after the start of the Mooney trial, officer Smith encountered Mrs. Edeau in Oakland and questioned her about the change in her testimony. Yes, she admitted, she had changed her story, but District Attorney Fickert had shown her some photographs of 721 Market, and pointing out two figures in the crowd that looked like her daughter and herself, had convinced her she was mistaken as to her location. As for Billings, she was sure now she had seen him. Smith didn't attempt to hide his skepticism.†

A day or two later Chief Peterson received a call from Fickert asking him to send officer Smith over to see him. According to Smith, Fickert told him he wanted him to take the stand in the Mooney case, testifying that Mrs. Edeau had identified Mooney and Billings. Smith said he couldn't do that, since it wasn't true. He showed Fickert the entry in his notebook, which Chief Peterson had suggested he bring along. "You keep your damn mouth shut," Fickert said. "You'd make a damn good witness for the defense." On returning to Oakland, Smith had reported the incident to Chief Peterson.

When the two Edeaus took the stand in the Mooney case, they testified not only to having seen Billings, but Mooney, Mrs. Mooney, Weinberg,

---

* Officer Smith confused the names of the two women in his report. It was the mother, Mrs. Mellie Edeau, he took to San Francisco.

† Mrs. Edeau did not explain to Smith just how this second meeting had come about —whether she had called on Fickert or whether he had sent for her. Nor, according to Smith, did she mention having identified anyone except Billings.

and the laboring man with the stubby mustache as well.

When Mooney was sentenced to hang, Peterson and Smith decided they would have to contact the defense.

They hadn't, however, until the defense contacted them.

McNutt obtained their affidavits and Peterson and Smith agreed to accompany them to the home of the Edeaus, where they confronted Mrs. Edeau with their evidence. Wild-eyed and scarcely rational, she told them Yes, she had failed to identify Mooney and Billings the first time, but a voice in her heart had told her they were guilty. Too, on looking at them a second time, she had seen the brown eyes of her dead husband and knew this was a sure sign of their guilt.

Didn't she realize that both she and her daughter could be tried for perjury, one of the attorneys asked. No, she slyly replied, they couldn't; they hadn't taken the oath.

The attorneys now recalled that both women had refused to take the oath on grounds it was against their religious beliefs.

The defense attorneys decided not to release the Edeau story for the time being, hoping that on consideration one or both women might decide to tell the truth.

3 ·

The defense learned of the Oxman-Rigall letters through a combination of accident, fear, and greed.

Shortly after the Mooney trial, a Fresno woman notified the defense that she had known Oxman many years ago, when he lived in Grayville, Illinois. The defense already had investigators in Oregon, checking into Oxman's background there. (They learned that he was exactly as represented, a wealthy cattleman.) Since this new lead could be false, rather than hire more investigators, they contacted Ed Nockles, of the Chicago Federation of Labor, and asked if he could send some men to Grayville to make inquiries about Oxman. Nockles arranged for two men to make the trip.

They arrived in early March. On checking into the local hotel they began asking questions about Frank C. Oxman.

Mrs. Rigall ran the hotel.

When the investigators entered the pool hall—always a good source for local gossip—Ed Rigall, without waiting for them to identify themselves, sure that they were San Francisco detectives sent by Fickert, told them "I guess I know what you fellows are here for." He refused to answer any questions about Oxman, he said, until they had talked to Mayor Ellis. Mystified, for they hadn't even mentioned Oxman's name, the investigators went along to the Mayor's office.

Mayor Ellis, informing them that he represented Rigall, explained that he knew all about Rigall's trip to San Francisco and Oxman's attempt at subornation of perjury. Reaching into his desk, he brought out photographs of the letters.

Only after reading them did the two men explain that they represented the defense. Ellis, apparently undisturbed by this development, stated his terms.

That night the investigators called Nockles with the news of their almost unbelievable find. Nockles in turn contacted Frank Mulholland, attorney for the International Association of Machinists, who had been hired to represent Ed Nolan. The negotiations dragged on for several weeks. Ellis wanted $10,000 for the letters and Rigall's testimony. The defense had trouble raising this amount but finally obtained a cash loan from the President of the International Association of Machinists.

Edwin V. McKenzie, a young attorney who had recently joined the Mooney defense, arrived from San Francisco to conduct the final negotiations, in the LaSalle Hotel in Chicago. Aware that if the letters were bought their effectiveness would be decreased, McKenzie tried to persuade Rigall and Ellis to turn them over voluntarily. The argument lasted all one night, until, at eight the following morning, the two men wearily agreed.

McKenzie's persuasiveness may have been responsible for the victory. But it was probably aided by fear. A few days before, Ellis' office had been burglarized, his desk and files ransacked. Nothing had been taken. Ellis had moved the Oxman materials elsewhere. But it was an indication that someone would go to extreme lengths to obtain this evidence.

Ellis did not come out of the negotiations entirely empty-handed. He was, about this same time, hired as an attorney for the Mooney defense. There is no record of what he was paid.

On April 6, 1917, F. E. Rigall signed an affidavit telling of his adventures in the city by the Golden Gate, and "Big Ed" Nockles was handed the Oxman letters.

That evening President Woodrow Wilson appeared before the Congress in Washington. He said: "It is a fearful thing to lead this great peaceful people into war, into the most terrible and disastrous of all wars, civilization itself seeming to be in the balance. But the right is more precious than peace . . ."

4 ·

Once possessing the letters, there was the problem of how best to use them. It was too late to make them the basis of a legal appeal to

Mooney's sentencing; the time limit for such an appeal had already expired. This left two alternatives, appealing to the Governor directly or through the press. The defense decided on the latter course. It was also agreed that if any San Francisco newspaper editor would agree to publish them it was Fremont Older of the *Bulletin*. The almost legendary Andrew Furuseth, weather-worn founder of the Coast Seamen's Union, was in Chicago at the time. Furuseth agreed to return to San Francisco and approach his old friend.

Walking into the editor's office, he came directly to the point.

"Mooney didn't plant that bomb, Older."

Older frowned and waved his ever-present cigar. "Let's not go into that, Andy. Why be foolish? Mooney's as guilty as hell."

"He was framed!" Furuseth asserted, and told him of the letters. Older asked to see them. Furuseth promised they would be brought to him the moment Rigall and Nockles arrived in San Francisco.

By some manner, word of Rigall's imminent arrival had already reached the District Attorney's office. Fickert called in Lt. Bunner and ordered him to Oakland to meet all incoming trains from the East. Rigall would be on one of them, Fickert told Bunner, with some important papers Fickert wanted. Bunner was to bring Rigall and the papers directly to his office, whatever the hour.

Bunner, unhappy at being assigned such a task, complained to his superior, Captain Matheson. Matheson told Fickert that Bunner had better things to do, that if he wanted a messenger boy he should hire one. Fickert told him to forget it.

Fearing just such a move, the defense had Rigall removed from the train at an earlier stop and brought into the city secretly on the morning of April 11th. Within two hours the letters were in the hands of Fremont Older, who turned them over to a handwriting expert to verify their authenticity.

All this placed Older in an extremely difficult position. He was far from a free agent on the *Bulletin*. Since assuming its editorship in 1895, he had experienced repeated arguments with the paper's owner, R. A. Crothers, an aged conservative who disapproved of Older's politics, his sensationalism, his crusades, everything about Older, in fact, except his remarkable ability to increase circulation. As a partial check on Older's enthusiasms, Crothers had made his young nephew Loring Pickering a co-owner. To Older's infinite disgust, Pickering edited his copy, changed his editorials, rescinded his orders. Neither Crothers nor Pickering, Older was sure, would permit publication of the letters—that is, if he asked them first.

Too, Older disliked Mooney personally. He was an opinionated loudmouth who did what he thought was right and damn the consequences. Almost the only good thing Older knew about him was that he was honest, scrupulously so, a quality not resident in all California labor leaders. Older personally had been slandered and his peace efforts misrepresented as a result of the Preparedness Day bombing and for this he had blamed Mooney. Yet if Mooney were innocent . . .

Too, Older had just turned sixty. He felt he was too old for new crusades, especially one that would net only enemies.

Older had an unusual talent—many felt it was a dangerous defect—the ability to change his mind once it was made up. For years he had fought to expose San Francisco graft and bring city political boss Abe Ruef to justice. For this he had gained the enmity of "the best people." Once Ruef was in San Quentin, however, no longer powerful but a broken man, Older saw him differently; declaring that he was no more than a pawn of the higher-ups who used him—men such as Calhoun and Mullally—he started a campaign for Ruef's release. By so doing he alienated most of the people who had fought alongside him in the graft crusade.

The expert verified the letters as written in their entirety by Oxman.

Informing only a few essential people of what he was doing, Older had the letters set in type and himself wrote the headline to appear above them. After reading the proofs, he ordered the printing of a special edition. It reached the streets that evening—long after the publisher and his nephew had gone home for the night.

From his office Older could hear the newsboys on Market Street screaming FICKERT FRAMED THE MOONEY CASE—MOONEY PLOT EXPOSED.

5 ·

One of the first calls was from Fickert's chief assistant, Edward A. Cuhna. In what Older would later describe as "a very frightened voice," Cuhna asked if they could meet privately. Older, who kept a suite of rooms in the Palace Hotel, suggested they meet there at eight Friday evening.

Older had the edge and knew it: Cuhna had no idea how much he knew. Older had reprinted only a portion of Rigall's story.

It now occurred to Older that if the Rigall disclosures exercised such a profound effect on the prosecution, some of the prosecution's witnesses might react similarly.

The following day Older, together with one of his reporters, Charles Brennan, defense attorney McKenzie, and officer Smith, called on Mrs. Edeau. Although she admitted them to the house, once they were inside she ran to the bedroom, took a revolver from a bureau drawer and declared that she would shoot them all. Smith succeeded in disarming her, while Older tried his best to soothe her. All they wanted was the answer to one simple question. How did she explain the contradiction between her original statement, that she was at Steuart and Market, and her trial testimony, that she was at 721 Market?

There was no contradiction, she averred. Both statements were true. "While I stood at Steuart and Market in the flesh, my astral body was at 721 Market Street."

6 ·

Promptly at eight the following evening, Assistant District Attorney Edward Cuhna knocked on the door of Fremont Older's Palace Hotel suite. According to the editor's account of the meeting, Cuhna was "panic-striken, desperate," moaning that his career was finished, in the ashcan, that he could never live this down. "I got into the heat of the fight," he told Older, "and went from one thing to another, and finally got all balled up, lost my head—and this is the result!"

Older heard him out, then assured him that he was not out to "get" anyone, that all he wanted was justice, a new trial for Mooney. Greatly relieved, Cuhna promised to do everything in his power to see that Mooney got a new and fair trial. He didn't know how Fickert felt, however. Older suggested that he talk to him and find out.*

7 ·

That weekend Older succeeded in locating Estelle Smith.

The time was advantageous. Just a few days before, on April 10th, Estelle's uncle, James Murphy, convicted of the same murder with which Estelle had been charged, had been granted a full commutation on condition that he leave California.† Perhaps now Estelle would feel free to

---

* The above is drawn from Older's account of the meeting, which subsequently appeared in the *Bulletin,* in a sworn affidavit, and in Older's memoirs. Cuhna denied almost everything about the meeting except that it had taken place. He most strongly denied promising to secure a new trial for Mooney. During the next week there were at least five meetings at which Cuhna stated substantially the same thing in the presence of Older, defense attorneys McNutt, Lawlor, and McKenzie, and attorneys Harry Stafford, Thomas O'Connor, and Nathan Coghlan, three impartial mediators agreed to by both sides.

† Murphy, convicted of a capital crime, was commuted after serving only three years, 6 months, and 17 days of his sentence. Over the years the defense endeavored to prove that, as in the case of Mrs. Kidwell and her husband, a deal had been made whereby Estelle would testify in return for Murphy's release. The time interval between Estelle's testifying and Murphy's release was average for parole request considerations. One state parole board member allegedly admitted to a defense attorney that Assistant D.A.

talk.

Estelle, tricked into meeting Older, angrily told him she had nothing to say. That was all right with him, Older said. However he had instructed one of his reporters to lock the doors of the Palace Hotel suite and not return for an hour, so they might as well talk about something. For example, female intuition. Older vowed he had great respect for it; he had always thought women were a lot wiser than men. That's why it surprised him that Estelle hadn't realized Oxman was lying.

She had, Estelle said; she'd been onto Oxman from the start! Why, she could tell him things about Oxman . . .

Older could, when he desired, be one of the most charming and diplomatic of men. He was also a remarkably good listener, less interested in voicing his own opinions than in hearing what others thought. By the end of the hour Estelle was ready to dictate her confession. Sensing that Estelle enjoyed an audience, Older called the *Bulletin* to send over several reporters and a stenographer.

This was to be the first of a number of partial recantations Estelle would give Older over the years. It became a standard joke in Older's city rooms that the editor had missed his true calling, that of father confessor.

Estelle's rambling statement was, as later events disclosed, made up of equal parts of truth, exaggeration, and justification. Winnowed down, Estelle said that she hadn't identified Billings, Mooney, or Mrs. Mooney when Fickert first showed her their photos, but that Fickert had kept working on her to make positive identifications. "Fickert at one meeting brought in a lot of photographs of mangled bodies and spread them out before me. 'Don't you,' he said to me, 'want to find the ones who are guilty of this?' " He had assured her, she said, that there was abundant evidence proving these people guilty. He had also revealed his knowledge of her past record and insinuated it wasn't too late to reopen the Irene Smith murder case—that there was no statute of limitations on murder. Swanson too had emphasized this point. "Swanson said if I didn't look out I'd find myself across the bay," i.e., in San Quentin. Estelle had made the identifications.

She had been firm on the time from the start, she said. She had told Fickert and Swanson that the young photographer hadn't left until after 1:50. However, just before she was to appear on the witness stand, "They told me to let the time be open, 'on or about' the time, they said. They said they wanted to give Billings the benefit of the doubt. I testified on or about and after Billings was convicted I went to them and told them that if I had testified ten minutes to two it would have saved him. Fickert told

Brennan had made such a request, but due to political considerations the man refused to sign an affidavit to this effect and declared that if subpoenaed he would deny it under oath.

me I had done the right thing."

Yes, Fickert, Cuhna, and Swanson had rehearsed her in the testimony she was to give. No, she had never talked much about her testimony with Captain Matheson. The first time she had been taken to see these people and had hesitated to identify them, Matheson had taken her aside and told her that unless she was absolutely positive of her identification, not to identify them.

Yes, she had been suspicious of Oxman. He had called on her several times, always to discuss the reward. He was curious to know how much she had already received. She told him nothing. "He said, 'You're silly to work here for twelve or fifteen dollars a week. If this case were in Oregon the reward would be three or four times as much. Did you see Weinberg downstairs?' 'No,' I said. 'Wouldn't you testify that you saw him for a check in four or five figures?' he said. I asked, 'Who sent you to me—Fickert?' He said, 'No, not Fickert, but men higher up than Fickert.'" Estelle said she had then gone to Fickert and complained that Oxman had attempted to bribe her. His only reply had been, "Oxman is a queer old duck."

Yes, she suspected the Edeaus too. The mother and daughter had come up to the dental office one day, ostensibly to inquire about dental plates. While she was getting out samples "I heard her say to her daughter 'Swanson says there are three windows here, I only see two.' I told her Swanson was right and pointed out to her how a partition shut off one window from view."

This was the gist of Estelle's confession. As Older was undoubtedly aware, it largely absolved Estelle of any wrong-doing, while at the same time casting doubts on the testimony of the other claimants to the reward.

Despite a warning from Crothers and Pickering that he was to drop the Mooney case immediately, Estelle's confession made headlines in Monday's *Bulletin*.

8 ·

The two judges most concerned with the Oxman disclosures reacted differently to them.

On reading the letters, Judge Griffin called a conference of the attorneys for the prosecution and defense. On the basis of the letters alone, Griffin declared, Mooney deserved a new trial. Unfortunately, once he had turned down the last appeal the matter had passed out of his jurisdiction.

"Technically—" Cuhna started.

"I don't want any technicalities," Griffin interrupted. "This is no time for technicalities. A man's liberty is at stake."

There was only one thing that could be done, Griffin said, that was for the District Attorney to go to state Attorney General U. S. Webb and "confess error," requesting the case be referred back to the Superior Court. This would again place the matter in Griffin's jurisdiction and he could then automatically grant Mooney a new trial. When Cuhna didn't reply, Griffin added, "If the District Attorney does not take this action, it will be my duty to do it myself."

Older went along with McNutt when he took the letters to Judge Dunne. He and Dunne were friends of long standing, having worked closely together during the graft prosecution. McNutt wanted Dunne to issue a warrant for Oxman's arrest. Dunne's reaction was unexpectedly hostile. The letters could be perfectly honest and innocent, he declared. Amazed, Older pointed out the portion where Oxman had suggested Rigall register from a town farther away in order to collect more mileage. Was that honest, Older asked. "Oh, that's a thing that anyone might do," Dunne replied. Dunne flatly refused to issue the warrant. It was for Older a small foretaste of how unpopular this cause was going to be.

There were other, stronger indications.

Pressure on Older had begun immediately after he published the Oxman letters. From Crothers he learned that the Law and Order Committee had called a special meeting in one of the city's banks to discuss the most effective way of silencing him. An advertising ban on the *Bulletin* had been suggested, and the move had carried with only one dissenting vote. The dissenter was the president of a leading department store. While he agreed that Older should be censored, he didn't want to give up an advertising outlet that reached 100,000 people. When he refused to withdraw his advertising, his leading competitor was forced to do likewise. Within minutes the proposed ban was in pieces.

Still, Crothers said, to placate the committee, both he and Pickering had to appear before them and promise that thereafter the *Bulletin* would publish nothing about the Mooney case.

Older's reply to Crothers, if there was one, does not appear in Older's autobiography. Instead he writes, "I continued then with even greater activity."

9 ·

For a week after Rigall's arrival, secret negotiations were held between the prosecution and the defense, with Cuhna and Older acting as go-betweens. The meetings were tension-charged. During one, Cuhna had offered his hand to defense attorney McKenzie and McKenzie had refused to take it, saying "You are a murderer." Older managed to cap their

Frank Oxman, the "honest cattleman" from Oregon, whose testimony sent
Thomas J. Mooney to a San Quentin death cell. This photograph was
taken in San Francisco County Jail in 1917, after Oxman's arrest for
attempted subornation of perjury.

tempers if not soothe them, but though Cuhna professed his anxiousness to help Mooney, few agreements were reached. Fickert did, however, through Cuhna, promise to have Oxman brought back to San Francisco. He arrived on the 17th, immediately closeting himself with the District Attorney.

To date, McNutt had been unable to obtain a warrant for Oxman's arrest. That day he walked into the police station and found Captain Matheson, his brow scowled in concentration, reading a huge volume of Krafft-Ebing.

"What in the world are you doing?" McNutt asked.

"I'm trying to find an explanation for Frank Oxman," Matheson replied.

When able to stop laughing, McNutt asked Matheson if he were mad enough to sign a complaint against Oxman charging him with attempted subornation of perjury. Matheson was. Police magistrate Matthew Brady issued the warrant and Oxman was arrested the next day.

McNutt decided to press his luck. Pointing out that there was, as Matheson knew, no evidence whatever connecting Edward Nolan with the crime, he wondered if Matheson would do what he could to see that Nolan was released on bail. Matheson, who claimed he had protested Nolan's arrest from the start, made a formal complaint against his continued detention and Nolan was released that same day—after nine months in jail—under $2000 cash bond. Although Fickert refused to drop the indictments, Nolan was never brought to trial. Upon his release he immediately went to work for the International Workers' Defense League on behalf of the other defendants.

10 ·

Charles Fickert never set down a chronicle of his thoughts and feelings during this period. It is probable, however, that he was worried. He, at least, had good reason to be, for he had done a very stupid thing and although no mention of it had yet been made, he must have feared that the defense was aware of it.

The day after Mooney's conviction, a woman had contacted the defense, stating that she had seen Oxman some distance up Market Street at the time he claimed to have been at Steuart and Market. She was in error, but the defense at the time believed her, using her statement as the basis for a new trial motion and at the same time releasing it to the press.

Fickert, asked to reply to the charge, had told reporters that he was undisturbed at her revelation since he had three eyewitnesses to Oxman's presence at the bomb scene, including a "John Regal, who was prepared to take the stand and corroborate, detail by detail the testimony of the Oregon cattle man."

Fickert's statement had appeared in the *Examiner* of February 14, 1917, and in the *News, Bulletin,* and *Chronicle* of February 15. This was nearly three weeks after Rigall allegedly told Cuhna he hadn't been in San Francisco.

Apparently the defense overlooked this item, for, important as it was, no mention of it was made in the Oxman proceedings. This is just as strange as the fact that Fickert mentioned "Regal" at all, since Cuhna had received and replied to Rigall's telegram just the day before Fickert made his statement. But then Fickert reacted strangely under pressure. And it is possible he saw Rigall's wire for what it was and felt they might still come to terms.

II ·

The day Oxman was arrested, Fickert suggested, through an intermediary, a secret meeting with Older in a private room in the Olympic Club that evening.

Also present were Cuhna; McKenzie for the defense; and two neutral attorneys, Stafford and O'Connor.

Pacing the floor nervously, Fickert declared he was as amazed as the defense at the Rigall disclosures and said of Oxman, "I'll hang that son of a bitch!"

McKenzie reminded him, none too gently, that attempted subornation of perjury, like being a labor organizer, was not a hanging offense.

O'Connor jovially, but with point, ventured that Oxman couldn't be charged with murder unless Mooney was hung first.

There were two questions before them, Older said. Tom Mooney was scheduled to be executed in just 29 days. What did they intend to do to stop the execution? Second, what was to be done about the Rigall disclosures?

Ignoring the first question, Fickert said he wanted to present the Oxman matter to the Grand Jury for investigation. Older and McKenzie, declaring that the Grand Jury was under Fickert's influence and that only a whitewash would result, demanded a trial for Oxman with a full public airing of the charges. The impartial attorneys agreeing with the latter course of action, Fickert unhappily consented. He would see that Oxman was tried, and after some further discussion, he agreed to request a new trial for Mooney.

McKenzie, in turn, agreed that if this were done frame-up charges would not be pressed against the District Attorney's office or a recall move started.

The meeting adjourned at 10 P.M. What happened during the next two hours is not known. Older would later state his belief that those "higher up" persuaded Fickert to change his mind, promising him their full support.

Shortly before midnight that night Fickert, contrary to his promises, appeared before the Grand Jury and (1) requested that they conduct an investigation of Rigall's story; and (2) asked that he personally be placed in charge of the investigation.

The Grand Jury deliberated briefly, deciding affirmatively on the first request but, since the District Attorney's office was itself under criticism in this matter, negatively on the second. It was agreed that the state Attorney General be asked to appoint a special prosecutor to bring the matter before them.

12 •

The defense learned of Fickert's about-face the next day. They also learned that he had asked Samuel M. Shortridge to defend Oxman. Shortridge (who later became United States Senator from California) was one of the highest paid attorneys in the state. He also happened to be the personal attorney of John D. Spreckles, Jr., foreman of the Grand Jury.

Oxman was arraigned before Judge Brady on April 23rd. Representing Fickert's office, Assistant District Attorney Louis Ferrari requested an adjournment of the proceedings until after the Grand Jury had met and made its investigation. Judge Brady denied the request and bound Oxman over for trial. The undercurrents in the courtroom erupted in a fist fight between Assistant District Attorney Brennan and defense attorney McKenzie. The men were separated and the fight declared a draw.

The battle over Oxman was also a draw. Judge Brady asked the Grand Jury to withhold its investigation until the court proceedings were completed. His request was denied.

If there was any mystery over Fickert's current position, it disappeared on the 24th. In a statement covering several columns of small print, Fickert characterized the events of the past few days as an elaborate plan to create sympathy for Mooney and Billings, "a formulated policy of those blood-thirsty anarchists to escape punishment for their crimes." Quoting liberally from back issues of *The Blast*, with the implication that Mooney was author of the remarks,* reviewing all the old charges and

---

* These out-of-context quotations were grouped under the headings: Religion, Patriotism, Our Flag, Our Preparedness Parade, His Principles of Action, and His Love of Country.

throwing in a few new ones (while in custody one of the defendants had dictated a confession admitting 72 separate crimes committed by the Mooney gang, Fickert said), he declared that the IWDL, composed as it was of foreigners, reds, and direct actionists, should be known as the "Murderers' Defense League" and accused Fremont Older of being the "murderers' advisor" and of having guilty foreknowledge of the bombing. He admitted his single interview with Older, but said that despite Older's threat to launch a recall move against him, he had refused to go along with his plan to free the blood-splattered pair, and denied vehemently that he had agreed to a new trial for Mooney. He threw in everything except an explanation of the Oxman letters.

Fickert's charges appeared in all the morning papers on the 24th. That evening, in the *Bulletin,* Fremont Older printed a full résumé of all the meetings with Cuhna and Fickert, telling who had attended and what had been said, making it clear, for those who wanted clarity, that either Fickert or a half dozen other people were lying.

Reading Fickert's statement and realizing that the District Attorney had no intention of contacting the state Attorney General in Mooney's behalf, Judge Griffin wrote a letter to Webb. Characterizing Oxman the most important witness produced by the prosecution, he told of the discovery of his letters to Rigall and pronounced them of "undenied and undisputed" authenticity.

"As you will at once see, they bear directly upon the credibility of the witness and go to the very foundation of the truth of the story told by Oxman on the witness stand. Had they been before me at the time of the hearing of the motion for a new trial, I would unhesitatingly have granted it." Urging Attorney General Webb to take the necessary legal steps to return the case to his jurisdiction, Griffin concluded: "I fully appreciate the unusual character of such request coming from the trial court in any case and I know of no precedent thereof. In the circumstances of this case, I believe that all of us who were participants in the trial concur that right and justice demand that a new trial of Mooney should be had in order that no possible mistake shall be made in a case where a human life is at stake."

Griffin wrote to Webb on April 25th, 22 days before Tom Mooney's scheduled execution. As yet unknown to him, three days earlier there had occurred in Russia an incident which would place the Mooney case on front pages around the world and transform it into an international *cause célèbre.*

13· The Petrograd Incident

LINCOLN STEFFENS and war correspondent William G. Shepherd were talking with American Ambassador David R. Francis when they first heard the angry voices and went to the windows. Outside, a crowd of hundreds, then thousands, then tens of thousands, turned from Litneny Prospect onto the street in front of the Embassy, loudly chanting over and over the same phrase.

"Muni! Muni!" the Ambassador repeated. "Who or what is Muni?"

Francis, a former governor of Missouri, new to the diplomatic service, had only a scant knowledge of Russian. After a few perplexed minutes, Shepherd guessed that they might be referring to Tom Mooney, the California labor leader under death sentence for a Preparedness parade bombing.

Francis opened the door and, through an interpreter, told the mob that he would convey their protest to his government.

"Who is Muni? What crime committed?" Ambassador Francis cabled Secretary of State Lansing.

"Who is Muni?" The question was repeated in a number of American city rooms. In its account of the incident, *The New York Times* reported the demonstration was "said to have been due to the alleged killing in America of an anarchist named Mooney."

In the interest of accuracy, the Socialist New York *Call* fared only a little better, placing Mooney correctly but displaying a woeful—while then common—lack of knowledge of Russian affairs by crediting the outburst to German propagandists, particularly one "Nikolai Lenine, a Russian radical, who recently returned from exile in Switzerland through Germany" and who was said to have roused the mob to frenzy by declaring that America, in its hatred of Socialism, had murdered the prominent Socialist leader Thomas J. Mooney.*

Other stories followed. And—as the result of a message Emma Goldman

---

* Recent research by George F. Kennan and others indicates that Lenin and the Bolsheviks were not involved in the demonstration, that it was conducted by an anarchist faction in Petrograd. While Mooney was still living, however, he believed Lenin was responsible for the protest, as indicated in a letter he wrote to Joseph Stalin.

216

had sent to her anarchist comrades in Petrograd—many in the United States learned of the Mooney-Billings case for the first time.

Observed the *New Republic*, "Is it not a remarkable commentary upon the attitude of the American press toward labor that one of the most significant and dramatic events in the history of organized labor in America should have come to the attention of American newspaper readers through a mass meeting in Nevsky Prospect?"

As with many of Emma's other innovations, this mass demonstration of the Russian workers would be extensively copied in the years ahead.

14· We Unanimously Commend
Charles M. Fickert

A{.PRIL WAS} a busy month.

With the disclosure of the Oxman letters, agitation in behalf of the defendants increased tenfold. The British Labor Party, through its secretary, the Honorable Arthur Henderson, M.P., denounced the frame-up and demanded a new trial for Mooney. The Netherlands Federation of Labor protested to President Wilson through its Ambassador in The Hague. In the United States mass circulation magazines of all and no political shadings suddenly discovered "America's Dreyfus Case." As the date of Mooney's execution drew nearer, defense committees were organized in most major American cities and protest meetings took on an evangelical fervor. At one a young girl was so moved by Bourke Cockran's impassioned plea that she wrenched her most precious possession off her finger and threw it on the stage. A shower of coins followed the thin gold band. New York theater goers found it impossible to avoid the hundreds of factory girls who waited outside the lobbies selling pamphlets and "Free Mooney-Billings" buttons. Similar scenes occurred outside ballrooms in a half-dozen cities. In Seattle labor staged a 10-minute strike protesting Mooney's hanging. The Salt Lake City Labor Council passed a resolution urging two sanctions the very mention of which frightened business more than any other: a boycott of all California products and a nation-wide general strike. Radical factionalism seemingly disappeared in a united front as Haywood, Debs, and Goldman mentioned Mooney and Billings in every public speech. Contributions to the defense passed $10,000 per month.

And in San Francisco the plight of the defendants suddenly became a labor case.

On April 27th, the San Francisco Labor Council passed a resolution charging that Mooney and Billings were the innocent victims of a monstrous frame-up and demanding District Attorney Fickert's removal from office.

On April 28th, the Law and Order Committee of the San Francisco

Chamber of Commerce took three-quarter-page boldface ads in all of the city's newspapers except the *Bulletin,* reminding the public of the horrible deaths that had occurred on July 22nd, warning that "those very forces that made the bomb outrage of Preparedness Day possible have been taking full and measured and unscrupulous advantage of you to spread again their doctrine of anarchy, their intimidation of courts and elected officials," and pledging the Law and Order Committee's full and complete backing of the District Attorney. In a meeting on April 25th, the ads said, the committee had voted to provide the District Attorney with "the services of such counsel and such other services as may be necessary to the end that there may be no miscarriage of justice."

2 ·

Judge Brady's attempt to complete his preliminary hearing on the Oxman matter met with repeated delays. On April 30th Oxman's attorney, Samuel Shortridge, requested a postponement so that witnesses to Rigall's character could be brought from Grayville. Brady reluctantly granted the delay, complaining that it was beginning to appear that Shortridge was stalling for time in order that the Grand Jury could meet and reach a decision before the court did.

That is apparently what Shortridge intended, and exactly what happened. That night the San Francisco Grand Jury began hearing evidence in the Oxman case.

To conduct the investigation, Attorney General Webb had appointed a former Superior Court judge, Robert M. Clarke.

For each charge there was an explanation:

Oxman testified that while standing on the corner of Steuart and Market on July 22nd a young man had greeted him by name. Failing to recognize him, Oxman said "You have the better of me, young man." "Why, Mr. Oxman, you remember me," the boy said, "I'm Ed Rygals. I used to know you when you shipped stock from Grayville to Chicago." Oxman still couldn't place him, but thinking about it later he decided that he must have heard wrong, that the boy must have said "Ed Rigall" and that he must have been a son of his old acquaintance Jim Rigall.

Recalling the encounter later, he had told District Attorney Fickert that there was a boy back home who might be able to support his testimony. Fickert had suggested he write to him. Oxman did so. He admitted writing the letters. They were genuine. Only they weren't complete, he said. That first letter had three pages instead of two, and on the third he had written a postscript, which, as near as he could remember, had read "P.S. If you were not in San Francisco on July 22 cannot use you as witness. Wire answer. F.C.O."

Clarke took out the first Oxman letter and held up the second page. Why, he asked, had he used a third sheet for the postscript when there was on the second sheet, below his signature, a space 1½ inches long and 6¼ inches wide, more than ample room for the message?

He hadn't known how long the postscript would be, Oxman said.

What of the letter to Mrs. Rigall, Clarke asked. Had he thought he had seen her in San Francisco too?

No, Oxman replied, he had thought she could be a character witness.

Why, if he thought he had seen Rigall on the 22nd, had he begun his first letter to him, "Has been a long time since I hurd from you"?

It was just a polite phrase.

Why, if he thought he had seen Rigall in San Francisco, had he said in his second letter, "I thought you can make this trip and see California?"

Oxman's reply was interrupted by a juror's question.

If he were being perfectly honest, just how did Oxman explain the passage in the letter suggesting Rigall register from Evansville, Indiana, instead of Grayville, Illinois, to get a "little more mileage"?

Oxman replied that "if the fellow had registered from Evansville, Indiana, and testified, these anarchists couldn't trace him as easy and poison his well, as they did mine . . ." *

Oxman further stated that the moment Rigall arrived in San Francisco he knew he wasn't the same boy and that he had told Fickert as much a day or two later. No, he had never discussed the reward with Estelle Smith, because he hadn't known there was a reward.

Fickert also took the stand. Oxman had told him on January 8th or 9th—the first chance they'd had to speak after Rigall's arrival—that Rigall was not the same young man. Fickert said that he and Cuhna had decided that since Rigall was already in San Francisco, he might as well stay and keep Oxman company. It would give Oxman some additional protection and that way Rigall would be available if the defense wanted to call him as a witness. Fickert admitted paying Rigall's round-trip fare and $27 over; he also admitted paying him $150. Since the state had called him to California he felt obligated to cover his expenses. As for Oxman's own testimony and background, he had checked into them very carefully before calling him to the stand. He had "proved up" the stories and backgrounds of "all" the state's witnesses before using them, because he knew the defense was trying to plant spies among them.

Earlier Captain Matheson and Lieutenant Bunner had been called to the stand to testify to the train-watching episode. Fickert, now ques-

---

* Oxman wrote Rigall more than a month before he took the witness stand. Inasmuch as Oxman's testimony came as a complete surprise to the defense, it seems rather unlikely that Emma, Sasha, or their associates had gone to Oregon at this time to poison his well.

tioned on this, claimed he had only asked Bunner to put Rigall under surveillance to see where he went on arrival.

On May 3rd the Grand Jury, with a 14-3 vote, reached its decision:

> TO THE PUBLIC: After a careful and conscientious investiga-
> tion covering every phase of the charge of subornation of perjury,
> preferred against F. C. Oxman, conducted by this jury under the
> able direction of Robert M. Clarke, Assistant Attorney-General, we,
> the jury, find no cause for criticism of the District Attorney's office in
> connection with the bomb cases, and we unanimously commend
> Charles M. Fickert for the able and fearless manner in which he has
> performed his duties to the people of the State of California in con-
> nection with these cases.
>
> JOHN D. SPRECKLES, Jr.,
Foreman
Thomas J. Dillon,
Secretary

The next day special prosecutor Clarke issued a statement disagreeing
strongly with the Grand Jury's verdict. The leading jurors had been antagonistic to his presentation from the start, Clarke charged. Witnesses
whose testimony he deemed important—such as Estelle Smith, who had
signed an affidavit charging Oxman with attempted bribery—had not
been called as he requested. The evidence, he said, had been "overwhelmingly sufficient" to indict Oxman.

Judge Brady, who had heard much the same evidence in his preliminary
hearing, thought so too, and had Oxman bound over for trial on the
charge of attempted subornation of perjury.

Older characterized the Grand Jury's verdict a "whitewash," noting
that three-quarters of the jurors belonged to the Chamber of Commerce,
while its foreman was on the governing body of the Law and Order Committee.

The Grand Jury's verdict *was* a victory for law and order, Fickert declared. He could now proceed with the trials of Rena Mooney and Israel
Weinberg, whose convictions would prove, once and for all, the guilt of all
the bomb defendants.

3 ·

The President was disturbed by the events in California. Protests had
been filed with American embassies in half a dozen countries. The Petrograd incident had been repeated in Rome, Paris, London, New York,
Chicago, even on Boston Commons. Every paper he picked up appeared
to have some mention of the Mooney case.

Woodrow Wilson would probably have been surprised had he known how greatly Alexander Berkman and Emma Goldman were influencing his thinking.

Immediately after the Petrograd incident Berkman had foreseen the importance of interesting the President in the case and had sent Ed Morgan, an old Wobbly friend, to Washington to lobby in Mooney's behalf. Emma, who thought Morgan good-hearted but "fearfully long-winded" had believed this a wasted effort. But she was wrong, as she soon admitted. "Ed Morgan proved a wizard. In a short time he succeeded in getting more publicity for our purpose than we had got in months. His first step in the capital had been to find President Wilson's favorite morning papers, his second to bombard them with news items about the agitation in Russia over the San Francisco frame-up. Then Morgan button-holed influential officials in Washington, made them familiar with the happenings on the Coast, and enlisted their sympathies." One of these was the President's most trusted advisor, Colonel Edward M. House.

As a result, wherever he turned, Woodrow Wilson encountered the name Mooney.

Too astute a man not to recognize such well-laid plans, the President nevertheless realized the importance the Mooney case was rapidly assuming, both in the United States and abroad.

The situation in Russia was mercurial, the Prince Lvov-Kerensky government unstable. It was essential that no new incident disturb the fighting fervor of the Russians.

It was also essential to the war effort that labor and management in the United States maintain a working truce for the duration, however uneasy it might be.

On May 11th, six days before Mooney's scheduled execution, the President sent a telegram to California's Governor William D. Stephens. It read:

> I hope that in view of certain international aspects which the case has assumed you will not deem me impertinent or beyond my rights if I very warmly and earnestly urge upon you the wisdom and desirability of commuting the sentence of Mooney or at least suspending its execution until the charges of perjury lodged against the witnesses in the case are judicially probed to the bottom. Such an action on your part would I can assure you have the widest and most beneficial results and greatly relieve some critical situations outside the United States.
>
> Woodrow Wilson

Consulting with his advisors Governor Stephens learned that since Mooney's original appeal was still in the courts, the date of execution would automatically be allowed to pass unheeded. Stephens wired the President that same day that Mooney's sentence was "stayed indefinitely by appeal pending in state supreme court."

The President wrote a personal note of thanks on the 14th: ". . . It relieves a rather serious anxiety."

May 17, 1917, Mooney's first scheduled execution date arrived and passed almost unnoticed.

For the defense the postponed crisis was replaced by others more immediate.

4 ·

One was bias on the bench.

On April 30th Judge Dunne had granted a postponement in the Weinberg case. It was a routine motion, but in the course of granting it Dunne had felt compelled to comment on the frame-up rumors by stating that in his opinion Billings had been justly and properly convicted, not only upon the state's evidence but by "his own statement, which was perjury so palpable and plain it would not have deceived a jury of children." Furthermore, he added angrily, "I find out also that every crooked, cowardly, blackguard lawyer who is going around this community with a letter of marque in the shape of a license to practice can be permitted to obstruct the administration of justice, to cloud the issue, to raise a doubt in the minds of decent people as to where they are at in all these matters."

In May the trial of Rena Mooney was assigned to Judge Dunne.

The defense immediately challenged Dunne's right to preside, charging that he had already declared his belief in the guilt of the accused. By California law the decision was submitted to Dunne himself for consideration and he overruled it, on the ground that he had expressed belief in the guilt of Billings only, and Billings was not on trial. When even the *Chronicle* felt compelled to criticize this logic, Dunne, yielding to pressure, excused himself. He did not admit bias, however, and he accepted the prerogative allowed him by law of choosing the jurist to replace him. He chose Judge Emmet Seawell, who was reputedly anti-radical, and on May 21st the trial of Rena Mooney began in Judge Seawell's courtroom.

There was an interesting innovation—two juries. The second group of 12, who sat with the audience, was a "silent jury" composed of trade unionists appointed by labor organizations. Their stone-faced presence was a constant reminder of labor's interest in the case.

For prosecutor, Fickert used another young assistant, Louis Ferrari. Although more polished, Ferrari used much the same tactics as his predecessors. There were repeated references to conspiracy and radicalism. Rena Mooney, Ferrari stated in his opening, had been "seized by the frenzy of anarchy and worships at the shrine of dynamite." "This little music teacher," he went on, "sometimes ran to playing the dynamite chord on an anarchistic fiddle . . ."

Both Dunne and Griffin had excluded the conspiracy evidence. Seawell allowed it, and the prosecution introduced everything it had. True to its promise, the Law and Order Committee provided the services of an eminent attorney, Charles W. Cobb, to assist Fickert in his prosecution.

Yet the weakness of the prosecution's case was soon apparent. Fickert was forced to use both Estelle Smith and the Edeaus as witnesses. Although Seawell cautioned the defense that he wouldn't permit "ungentlemanly questions" about Miss Smith's background, her past was now common knowledge and she fared badly both in the press and on the stand. Several times she hysterically accused people in the audience of "making faces" at her.

Her presence was, in a way, ludicrous. In presenting her as a witness, Fickert was vouching for her truthfulness and credibility. But Estelle in her *Bulletin* confession had said that Oxman tried to bribe her. By using her, Fickert was in effect discrediting Oxman.

But Fickert was now too desperate to consider such logical niceties. Wade, Vidovich, and McDonald again testified. Though their recitations should by now have been well rehearsed, each attempted minor but significant revisions. The Edeaus testified, and were impeached by the testimony of former Oakland Chief of Police Peterson (now a Captain in the Artillery), officer Smith, and the three tailors. Sadie Edeau was further discredited when she admitted on cross-examination that she had signed a statement identifying the defendants even before being taken to see them. Oxman was not called, and not a single witness placed Rena at the bomb scene. There was one new witness, Samuel Samuels, a longshoreman who claimed to have sold Mrs. Mooney a small quantity of nitre prior to the explosion. But Samuels was discredited when it was shown that he was unable to identify even his own brother in a lineup.

The trial ran over into July. Only one thing enlivened the proceedings, the calling of Martin Swanson to the stand. Swanson admitted discussing the San Bruno dynamiting with Billings and Weinberg as well as offering Billings a job in the PG&E garage, but claimed that both Billings and Weinberg had approached him first, implying they had information to offer. He denied using the reward money as bait. He also admitted that he had been employed by the District Attorney's office since 9:30 on the night of the bombing, but denied that he was out to get Mooney or anyone else. All this the defense had anticipated. But Swanson made one unexpected admission. He announced that he and his detectives had kept the defendants under constant surveillance from before the URR strike in

June until the afternoon of the explosion, when they had eluded his operatives in the crowd.

It occurred to the defense that if Swanson had indeed had the Mooneys, Billings, Nolan, and Weinberg under surveillance on the 22nd then he must have known they were innocent even while arranging for their arrests!

But the big moment in the Rena Mooney trial took place outside the courtroom. The not-so-mysterious "repulsive-looking Russian Jew" with the "stubby mustache" was finally identified. On the night of July 14th, just after the defense had called its last witness, District Attorney Fickert appeared before the San Francisco Grand Jury to ask for and receive an indictment of Alexander Berkman, on the charge of murder in the Preparedness Day bombing.

5 ·

The United States had been in the war three months. Society girls were pinning yellow feathers on the backs of ununiformed young men of draft age. Quakers were being arrested for refusing to sign draft registration forms, IWW's for carrying their red cards. The Post Office Department was preparing to suppress the *Masses, Mother Earth, The Blast,* and 12 other periodicals. And in New York, on July 9th, Emma Goldman and Alexander Berkman were convicted of conspiring against the draft and sentenced to two years in prison, after which they were to be deported.

The specific charge, advising young men not to register, was bogus, for in their speeches both had taken special care to emphasize that such a decision had to be a matter of individual conscience. But their opposition to the war was open and a matter of record.

Less than a week after their convictions, Fickert wired New York's Governor Whitman requesting Berkman's extradition on the murder charge. Certain that if Berkman were returned to San Francisco he would be convicted, no matter how insufficient the evidence against him, Fitzi, Lucy Robins, and their friends organized a labor defense committee to approach the Governor, requesting a refusal of Berkman's extradition. They soon secured powerful support from the United Hebrew Trades, the Amalgamated Clothing Workers, and other unions.

Released on bail pending her appeal, Emma joined the fight. Wartime censorship was in effect but she sent a coded message to Louise Bryant, John Reed's wife, in Moscow: "Uncle is sick of same disease as Tom. Tell friends." Mass demonstrations for both Berkman and Mooney followed almost immediately in Petrograd and Krondstadt.

Bail was not raised for Berkman. Recalling the illegal extraditions of

Mollock, Haywood, Moyer, Pettibone, and the McNamaras, it was feared that Fickert might try to kidnap him and take him to California.

6 ·

"If the thing were done that ought to be done," assistant District Attorney Edward Cuhna told John Fitch in an interview for *Survey,* "the whole dirty low-down bunch would be taken out and strung up without ceremony.

"They ought to be in jail on general principles . . . If I knew that every single witness that testified against Mooney had perjured himself in his testimony I wouldn't lift a finger to get him a new trial."

Recalling the first raid on *The Blast,* Cuhna said "I should have murdered Berkman. My only regret is that I didn't."

The Rena Mooney trial was obviously going badly.

7 ·

The two juries went out on July 24th. The labor jury was back within an hour. The regular jury took an additional 50 hours. But both reached the same verdict.

"Oh, if you could have been here, you'd have been as crazy as the rest of us," defense worker Madeline Gazza wrote Lucy Robbins. "Just picture us waiting fifty-one hours for the verdict, everyone on the verge of a breakdown, the tense faces of relatives and friends worn to bags of bones as they fainted and cried. Then everyone went crazy with joy, laughing, crying, hugging and kissing everyone in sight including the newsboys, who were shouting 'Rena Mooney Acquitted!' "

Rena had been in jail just two days short of a full year. As she was leaving the courtroom, a deputy worked his way through the well-wishers, grasped her arm and informed her that she was under arrest for the Preparedness Day murders. Stunned, believing this could only be some cruel joke, Rena was told she had been rearrested on Fickert's orders. The Grand Jury had originally returned eight indictments against the defendants, one for each of eight of the bomb victims. Fickert announced to the press that he would retry Mrs. Mooney on all eight if necessary to secure a conviction.

This was not "double jeopardy," according to Fickert, for though the crime and the evidence were the same, the indictments were separate.

It's like a mad nightmare, Fremont Older told friends: Tom Mooney begging for one new trial to prove his innocence; Rena Mooney, proven innocent, might well have seven more trials to prove her guilt.

There were a few hopeful signs. The recall move against District Attorney Fickert was gaining momentum. And on July 30th Attorney General Webb, ruling favorably on Judge Griffin's request, filed a consent with the California Supreme Court, asking that body to reverse the judgement against Mooney and remand the case to the lower courts for a new trial.

8 ·

The hope was short-lived. On September 11th, in what was to be the most important single legal decision in the Mooney case, the one against which all other appeals would flounder, the California Supreme Court denied the Griffin-Webb motion for a new trial.

The court had no other choice, it observed. Under California law the court was only able to consider matters of error which appeared in the trial proceedings. There was, as the decision noted, "no provision of law by which newly discovered evidence may be presented to this court in the first instance." In other words, even if every witness in the Mooney trial subsequently confessed perjury, the courts would be unable to reverse the verdict inasmuch as those confessions did not appear in the trial record.

The trial record included the actual transcript of the trial and the appeals. California had a statute of limitations, after which no new appeals could be made; this was ten days after sentencing. Rigall and Ellis, by holding back the Oxman letters for nearly two months, had made it impossible for Mooney's attorneys to use them as basis of an appeal to set aside the verdict.

This did not leave Mooney without a means of relief, the Supreme Court noted; it only meant that the courts themselves could not act. "The remedy in such cases," the decision concluded, "rests with the executive. He alone can afford relief."

In short, the fate of Tom Mooney was now in the hands of the Governor of California.

9 ·

That same month Frank C. Oxman went on trial on charge of attempted subornation of perjury. The outcome was a foregone conclusion, the newspapers frankly stated, as Oxman was being tried before Judge Dunne, who had already remarked publicly that there was nothing incriminating in the letters from Oxman to Rigall, and the prosecution was being handled by assistant attorney general Ray Benjamin, a close personal friend of District Attorney Fickert's.*

Shortridge did not call his client to the stand. Instead he hammered at Rigall's checkered past, which included running "short cards," a bootlegging conviction, and a charge of white slavery. Although the latter charge, involving the transportation of a sixteen-year-old girl across a state line for immoral purposes, had been dropped, its mention was enough. Prosecutor Benjamin failed to bring out the fact that when one is looking for perjurers, as Oxman was, he isn't likely to choose people of unblemished reputation. The letters themselves were only cursorily discussed.

The newspapers were right. Oxman was acquitted on the 28th, and the verdict heralded as an endorsement of Fickert's handling of the bomb cases.

---

* Benjamin would later, as a state senator during the years of the red scare, author California's first Criminal Syndicalism Law. Still later he would become one of Herbert Hoover's most trusted advisors and a power in the national GOP.

15· The Second Bomb

As September 1917 drew to a close it was apparent to the President that the situation had worsened, both in the United States and in Europe.

The war was going badly.

In Russia there were ominous signs of still another revolution, with the attendant possibility that the new government might decide to withdraw from the war completely, or worse, join in common alliance with Germany.

In the United States industrial unrest had reached a new high. With the attempted extradition of Alexander Berkman, agitation over the Mooney case had increased. In Butte, Montana, IWW organizer Frank Little had been lynched from a railroad trestle. In Bisbee, Arizona, armed vigilantes had kidnapped 1200 striking copper miners and "deported" them across the border, leaving them in the desert, without water or food. In Chicago, Haywood and 165 other IWW's had been arrested and charged with sedition. Samuel Gompers, the rotund, affable President of the American Federation of Labor, had already called on Wilson, unofficially, informing him there was an excellent chance the AFL would pass a strong resolution at its annual November convention condemning the San Francisco frame-ups and demanding new trials for Mooney and Billings. He also warned the president that radicals had aroused a great deal of sentiment for a general strike in behalf of the defendants, which if brought about, would immediately paralyze the U.S. war effort.*

The President took several steps by which he hoped to lessen the unrest. He sent Colonel House to Albany to discuss the Berkman extradition matter with Governor Whitman. And he appointed a Mediation Commission, composed of representatives of both labor and management, to look

---

* Radical criticism of Gompers, never slight, had intensified with his failure to take an open stand on the Mooney case. Without his endorsement, many AFL unions refused to contribute to the Mooney defense. "Gompers is so busy running the war that he has time for nothing except to appoint upon his committees labor's bitterest enemies," John Reed wrote in the last unsuppressed issue of the *Masses*. "I suppose that as soon as Tom Mooney and his wife are executed, Gompers will invite District Attorney Fickert to serve upon the Committee of Labor."

into the Bisbee incident and the Mooney case. Secretary of Labor William B. Wilson was chosen to head the commission. For its other members the President appointed John F. Spangler, of Pennsylvania; Verner Z. Reed, of Colorado; John H. Walker, of Illinois; E. P. Marsh, of Washington; and as the commission's legal representative, a bright young lawyer from Harvard named Felix Frankfurter.

2 ·

The President called the members of the commission to the White House.

Wilson "gave us a cold, short, high-minded few minutes' talk, which was the staple of his meetings with people on the whole," Frankfurter later recalled. "He got off some generality about the importance of industrial peace, all beautifully couched, perfect sentences. It could all be taken down. Even his speech was copperplated like his handwriting. He said, 'There's one more matter I want this commission to look into and, as the lawyer of the commission, Mr. Frankfurter, this will be particularly your concern. That is the Mooney case which is greatly disturbing to our Allies, Russia, and Italy. When you get to California, I hope you will look into that and report to me about it.' "

Frankfurter had been out of the country for several months on war work. The name Mooney meant nothing to him. He assumed, from the President's remarks, that the man was either a Russian or an Italian. A great believer in "prepared improvisation," however, he decided to learn all he could about the case prior to his arrival in California.

"I was wholly innocent of all the terrific feelings that the Mooney case had released and the state of mind of the community" he later admitted "so that in my innocence I wired out to a classmate of mine, a very good lawyer, 'Would you be good enough to get together for me all the documents, the record, and prepare a statement for me of the situation?'

"I got back a telegram expressing great regret that professional duties would preclude his doing so. I thought, 'He's a busy lawyer,' and I then wired to another fellow and then another fellow." Finally Frankfurter succeeded in finding a young attorney willing to assist him. By the time the Mediation Commission left Arizona for California in mid-October Frankfurter was aware that they were walking into an explosive situation.

3 ·

As a result of the efforts of Fitzi and Lucy, a delegation of more than 200 labor leaders called on Governor Whitman in Albany. Morris Hillquit, Socialist candidate for Mayor of New York City, served as spokes-man for the group.

More than a year had passed since the Preparedness Day bombing, Hillquit informed the Governor, during which time no attempt had been made to arrest Berkman through he was readily accessible and had in fact been questioned several times and his offices searched. His attempted ex-tradition at this late date appeared to be nothing more than a grandstand play on the part of Fickert to influence the Rena Mooney and Israel Weinberg trials and to counteract the growing sentiment for his recall. The delegation, representing more than 100,000 union men, and voters, re-spectfully requested the Governor to refuse Fickert's extradition request.

Governor Whitman told the group that he would wire the District At-torney, asking for a copy of the Grand Jury proceedings against Berkman, and base his decision on the evidence.

Whitman wired Fickert for the Grand Jury minutes. Fickert, obviously surprised at this unforeseen development, replied that the minutes were "secret" and declined to send them.

Whether moved by the arguments of the labor leaders, the behind-the-scenes persuasiveness of Colonel House, the assumption that Fickert had no real evidence on which to indict Berkman, or the awareness that the federal government already had Berkman in custody, Whitman denied the extradition request. It was, Emma felt, a great victory. Berkman was free to stay in prison.

4 ·

In the meantime, events were occurring rapidly in California.

The move to recall Fickert from office was gaining momentum.

On October 30th, Alice Kidwell, now estranged from her daughter, signed a full recantation of her testimony, in the process clearing up many of the remaining puzzles in the 721 Market Street stories.

Estelle *had* talked to a man and a woman in the hallway, Mrs. Kidwell said. The man and his wife had come up from the street during the parade and the woman had used the toilet at the end of the hall. Estelle, seeing her coming out, had raised a ruckus. "We don't furnish toilet paper and water for everybody that passes by," she had yelled. "You'll just have to fork over a dollar or I'll call a cop." Embarrassed, the man had paid her and the couple had left.

(It was not surprising they had not chosen to come forward with the story.)

As for the incident of Estelle's sponging the young man's forehead, it just hadn't happened, Mrs. Kidwell said. She herself had been in and out of the office during this period and had observed no such incident. Estelle had not mentioned it to her until after her initial talk with Fickert, Cuhna, and Swanson.

There was much more—Fickert, Swanson, and detective Hand rehearsing Estelle, Rominger, Wade, and Vidovich in their testimonies, asking them to change details when their stories didn't jibe; the Edeaus visiting the dental offices to familiarize themselves with the layout of the building; Oxman's dates with Estelle, until the dentist warned him to stay away; the arguments over the reward; Estelle's complaints that Fickert had promised her $1000 and had gone back on his word. She and Rominger had been forced to change their identifications and perjure themselves, Mrs. Kidwell claimed: Estelle had threatened to have Fickert bring adultery charges against them unless they went along with her story.

Israel Weinberg was brought to trial. It took the jury just 20 minutes to find him not guilty. He too was rearrested immediately and held without bail pending retrial on the other indictments.

On November 27, 1917, the same day as Weinberg's acquittal, Warren K. Billings reached the end of his appeals.

Following Billings' conviction McNutt had made the usual motions, which had been denied. He had also made a motion for a new trial on the basis of Rominger's perjury; Judge Dunne had denied this motion also, stating that Rominger was not an important witness. On September 5th, the District Court of Appeals affirmed the conviction. A petition for a rehearing was denied on October 2nd and on November 5th the California Supreme Court denied petition for leave to appeal to that court. On the 27th Billings was returned to Folsom Prison to begin serving his life sentence. Mooney remained in the County Jail in San Francisco, pending the result of his initial trial appeal, which was now before the State Supreme Court.

5 ·

To remove an elected official from office in California a given percentage of registered voters must sign petitions demanding a special recall election.

The move to recall Fickert had begun in April, shortly after the disclosure of the Oxman letters, with the organization of the Union Labor Recall League. Chief backers of the league were Older, labor leaders Paul Scharrenberg, Daniel Murphy, and Hugo Ernst, a group of liberal ministers, and those in the Mooney defense.

"The people leading this fight against me are the anarchists," District

Attorney Fickert charged dramatically. "Their main reason for wanting me out of office is that they fear prosecution. There were more than a hundred people concerned in the Preparedness Day bomb plot, and it is this anarchist element which fears me, that seeks my recall."

By the end of May 5,000 signatures had been collected, by midsummer 15,000, more than enough—if the majority were valid—to force the calling of an election.

Fickert fought the election with every resource at his disposal, including the open support of the Law and Order Committee. Petition solicitors were beaten and their petitions destroyed. As soon as the required number of signatures was filed, Fickert appeared before the Grand Jury, asking for indictments against the solicitors, charging them with falsification of signatures. The indictments were voted. Fickert also took the petitions to court, in the hope they would be invalidated.

As the campaign entered its final months, labor's unanimity over the Mooney-Billings case came to an abrupt end.

Wartime hysteria over radicals had reached a new peak and labor was far from immune to the panic. In October the State Federation of Labor voted to expel IWW's from all AFL unions. During the same convention a resolution was proposed affirming belief in the innocence of Mooney, Billings, and the other defendants. It passed with a single dissenting vote, that of Arthur Brouillet, president of the San Francisco Labor Council. In arguing against the resolution Brouillet charged that Mooney's labor supporters had "guilty knowledge" of the Preparedness Day bombing, a statement which Fickert quickly picked up and used with great effect in his campaign.

Brouillet, of the Retail Clerk's Union, held a salaried position in the state Republican administration. He was also the attorney believed by the Mooney defense to have leaked defense information to District Attorney Fickert. Even after the Oxman disclosures, Brouillet had continued to oppose labor support for Mooney and Billings.

On the basis of his statement at the state convention, the pro-Mooney delegates on the San Francisco Labor Council demanded Brouillet's ouster as president. Charging specifically that Brouillet had made baseless slanders against reputable union men in order to obtain political preferment, he was brought to trial before the council in November.

It was the same battleground, the same battle Mooney himself had fought, one that would be fought over and over again, locally and nationally, until the merger of the AFL-CIO: the industrial unionists vs. the trade unionists; the liberals vs. the conservatives; the actionists vs. the conciliators; the seaman and allied unions (represented by Furuseth, Scharrenberg, Kidwell, Murphy, and Ernst) vs. the building trades and teamsters (McCarthy, Casey, McLaughlin, Gallagher, and Brouillet).

But this time the pro-Mooney forces were in the majority. By a vote of 95-46, Brouillet was ousted as president.

In terms of labor unity, it was a costly victory. Brouillet, with McCarthy, Casey, and others formed the Union Labor Fickert League, declaring themselves, through their organ the *Labor Clarion,* against "Reds, pacifists, seditionists and avowed anarchists."

This division in labor hurt the recall forces. So did a split in their ranks over who should succeed Fickert as District Attorney. Two candidates were running—Charles A. Sweigert and Frank P. Haynes.

But the acquittals of Rena Mooney and Israel Weinberg hurt Fickert even more. And in early November the California State Supreme Court ruled the recall petitions valid. It ordered a special recall election in December.

On November 17th, Fickert received a surprise endorsement, in the form of a telegram printed on the front page of the *Chronicle.*

It read, in part, "I am informed that an effort is being made to recall you because you have successfully prosecuted the anarchists who during the Preparedness Day parade killed ten persons and injured sixty others.

"If such be the fact, I not only feel that the issue between you and your opponents is that between patriotism and anarchy, but I also feel that all who directly or indirectly assail you for any such reason should be promptly deprived of their citizenship . . ."

The telegram was signed "Theodore Roosevelt."

Older was shocked. Together with Hiram Johnson and Rudolph Spreckles, he had been a founder of the Progressive Party in California and a close personal friend of Roosevelt's. It was Roosevelt who had furnished the anti-graft crusaders with their special prosecutor Francis J. Heney and who had done so much behind the scenes to support their efforts.

Older felt sure the telegram was bogus. But its authenticity was soon established, together with an explanation of how it came about. Older learned that a Fickert supporter, Charles F. Hanlon, former president of the Pacific Coast Defense League, the organization that had fronted for the Chamber of Commerce in organizing the Preparedness Day parade, had appealed to Alexander P. Moore, publisher of the *Pittsburgh Leader* and a founder of the Progressive Party, assuring him that Fickert, fighting the fight of "patriotism vs. anarchy," was in desperate need of Roosevelt's big stick. Moore approached Roosevelt and the telegram followed.

Older, Spreckles, and numerous other "old friends" wired Roosevelt, explaining that he had been misinformed, stressing that this Charles Fickert was the same man brought in as District Attorney by big business to squash the graft indictments. In his wire Roosevelt had referred to the five "anarchists" and "assassins." Older explained that none of the de-

fendants were anarchists, that all except Mrs. Mooney were trade unionists, and that—contrary to his apparent belief that all five had been found
guilty—two had been acquitted while the charges against another would
probably be dropped.

It was a different Roosevelt from the man Older remembered who replied to a member of the recall league, "I am sorry to say that all the
information I have is to the effect that the excellent gentlemen connected
with your league are being used simply as a shield behind which the enemies of Americanism, the friends of Germany, and the advocates of
anarchy and disorder, can punish Mr. Fickert, because he had had the
courage to attack the assassins who committed wholesale murder of innocent people with dynamite . . ."

The former President *had* changed. Long out of the political limelight,
more often caricatured than consulted, "Teddy" had embarked on a new
campaign, his last, becoming one of the nation's foremost "red-hunters."

There were more wires, all of which were published. In pain Older read
"Fremont Older and the IWW and the 'direct action' anarchists and
apologists for anarchy are never concerned for justice. They are concerned
solely in seeing one kind of criminal escape justice, precisely as certain big
business men and certain corporation lawyers have in the past been concerned in seeing another kind of criminal escape justice."

"It is," Roosevelt said, "the Hearsts and La Follettes, and Bergers, and
Hillquits, the Fremont Olders and Amos Pinchots and Rudolph Spreckles
who are the really grave danger. These are the Bolsheviki of America . . ."

Fickert added his own charges—Spreckles was a subscriber to *The
Blast,* the Fremont Olders had entertained as house guests Emma Goldman and Alexander Berkman—but to be most effective he needed only
quote the ex-President.

Yet, despite Roosevelt's entry into the local scene, support for Fickert's
recall appeared to be growing.

In late November Fremont Older heard a rumor. Although in publishing it in the *Bulletin* he disguised its origin, it came from a highly reliable
source in the police department. It was to the effect that Fickert strate-
gists had "decided to stage a camouflage dynamite explosion at a psychological moment in the recall campaign for the purpose of shocking the
public mind into a state of sympathy with the district attorney."

As the campaign entered its last two weeks the rumor was forgotten in
the charges and countercharges.

The recall election was scheduled for Tuesday, December 18th.

Shortly after midnight on election eve, a bomb exploded outside the
east wing of the Governor's mansion in Sacramento. Although this part of

the gubernatorial mansion was unoccupied, the blast demolished a brick wall and wrecked several rooms. Headlines screamed from the morning editions:

GOVERNOR STEPHENS HOME DYNAMITED
EXECUTIVE AND WIFE ESCAPE UNHURT

GOVERNOR'S LIFE ATTEMPTED
HOME AT CAPITAL DYNAMITED

That day San Franciscans went to the polls; by a majority of more than 20,000 votes they affirmed their support of Charles M. Fickert.

The final tally was Fickert, 46,451; Sweigert, 26,057; and Haynes, 1684. It was estimated by the Registrar of Voters as many as 35,000 who otherwise wouldn't have bothered to vote did so because of the bombing.

In what was in many respects a restaging of the Preparedness Day aftermath, 53 Sacramento IWW's were arrested and jailed. No evidence connecting them with the explosion was ever produced and none were convicted of the bombing. Three died while in custody; the others were eventually prosecuted by the federal government for violating various wartime sedition laws. Again, no immediate attempt had been made to find the actual bomber.

In June of 1918, Thomas McGowan, a former federal detective assigned to investigate the bombing, charged that he had found evidence linking the District Attorney's office with the explosion but that this evidence had been suppressed. The evidence was circumstantial and no charges were ever filed.

This evidence was to the effect that a Swede by the name of Clawson had been given employment as a watchman on the Capitol grounds late in November; that in establishing his whereabouts on the night of the explosion he was later proven to have lied; and shortly after this he had quit his job and disappeared. It may well have been wholly coincidental —although the Mooney defense thought not—that Clawson was a former Swanson operative and that he had been seen talking with Swanson in Sacramento hours before the explosion.

This was not to be the last time a bomb would figure prominently in a Charles M. Fickert election campaign.

Following the election, Fickert sent a wire to Roosevelt at Oyster Bay, Long Island: "Patriotism has triumphed over anarchy."

With Fickert's successful defeat of the recall move, the Fickert-for-Governor talk moved out into the open.

6 ·

Arriving in San Francisco in October, the Mediation Commission was able to witness firsthand, through the recall fight, the extreme feeling engendered by "The Mooney Case," as it was now most often called. Intending to stay only a week, the Commission found the case far more complicated than anticipated and remained nearly two months, going over the trial transcripts and interviewing all the major participants. It was a quiet investigation, conducted without fanfare and with a minimum of publicity. The willingness of the local press to accede to this last request was in itself frightening.

The bitterness amazed the committee.

In talking to a prominent banker Felix Frankfurter first heard a statement that would be echoed repeatedly in years to come: "We have the right men on the wrong evidence."

Yet Frankfurter found unexpected pockets of Mooney support. One evening, in the company of a small select group of men, he dined with Archbishop Hanna. One of the most influential Catholic prelates in America, the Archbishop was deeply committed to the famous encyclical of Leo XIII, Rerum Novarum. With a strong sympathy for the lowly and disadvantaged, he was a leader in housing reforms and other measures to raise the living standards of the working class. Following dinner, while lingering over brandy and cigars, Frankfurter noticed that, as if by prearrangement, the other men drifted out of the room, leaving the host and the lawyer alone. The Archbishop then told him of the attempts of the employers to suppress unionism in California and said, "I know Tom Mooney very well. He and his family were parishioners of mine. Tom is a bad man, but he didn't do this."

In talking with others, Frankfurter heard similar sentiments, as well as some of the "Mooney stories" already making the rounds. One of these, which may or may not have had some bearing on the Archbishop's attitude, was that Mooney always made a point of using the term "Mr." when addressing priests.

"Mooney is the center of the case," Frankfurter concluded; "the other defendants have significance only because of relation to him."

Frankfurter felt that Mooney was a strange martyr. Even those closest to him and most convinced of his innocence found him unbearable at times. He was self-righteous, opinionated, demanding. Robert Minor, after working a year for the defense committee at a salary of $15 a week, exhausted and dispirited from fighting with Mooney over every decision, had quit and gone East. Following his departure, Ed Nolan became secretary of the International Workers' Defense League (IWDL). But there was friction even between Mooney and Nolan. Though behind bars, Mooney insisted on having a voice in everything that was done in his behalf, from approving the wording in mailing appeals to selecting headquarters workers. Some months earlier Mooney had organized a new defense group, the Tom Mooney Molders' Defense Committee (TMMDC), ostensibly set up to work solely within the unions. It was, from the start, Mooney's vehicle, run personally from the County Jail, and gradually, whether intentional or not the TMMDC took over many of the functions previously handled by the IWDL.

To many, Tom Mooney was already a symbol of labor's martyrdom at the hands of capital. But those who knew him saw the man, human in all particulars. From time to time glimpses of his personality made their way even into those media most strongly championing him. *The Nation:* "He has a genius for antagonizing people." The *New Republic*: "When a district attorney in an American city begins to hunt for evidence wherewith to convict a prisoner whom almost everybody dislikes and almost everybody thinks is guilty, he is almost certain to find it." Robert L. Duffus, Older's editorial writer, would later write: "Tom Mooney wasn't appealing, not at first sight, perhaps never. I have wished that prospective martyrs, or real martyrs, could always be angelic, good-mannered, and good company, but often they are not. Tom Mooney wasn't."

Bourke Cockran's comparison of Mooney to Dreyfus amused Frankfurter for its unintentional aptness. Dreyfus, according to his acquaintances, was one of the most objectionable men who ever lived. One day his great champion Clemenceau was alleged to have screamed, "Captain, if you think we are doing all this for you, you are crazy. We are doing it for France!"

Although from his statements and letters it was clear Mooney was well aware he was important only as a symbol of labor's struggle, he was not without human attributes. Frankfurter, calling at the jail to interview him, was kept waiting a lengthy period. He was finally told by a jailor that Mooney had wanted to shave before seeing him.

Frankfurter thought Mooney vain. Yet he was probably unaware that Mooney had been taken before the Grand Jury unshaven and unkempt.

Some time after his return to the East, Frankfurter would suggest to a group of California lawyers that they prove their mettle and petition the Governor for Mooney's release. One, a whimsical Scot, agreed to do so on one condition—that Mooney be paroled in Frankfurter's custody. Frankfurter would characterize this "an amusing suggestion."

But, foreign as the Massachusetts lawyer found Mooney to his own background and temperament, toward the case itself he harbored no reservations. Even the business members of the commission—Spangler and Reed—were appalled by their findings.

The commission's conclusions and recommendations were unanimous. Frankfurter was given the task of drafting the report to the President.

16. My Dear Governor Stephens

SOME OF the seeds planted by Emma and Sasha were bearing strange fruit.

In November, as the Russian Revolution mounted to its awesome climax, John Reed hitched a ride to the front in a bomb-laden truck. As the bombs rolled back and forth, crashing against the sides, the driver, learning that Reed was an American, inquired solicitously about the health of Mooney and Berkman.

In January, shortly after Felix Frankfurter completed the Mediation Commission's report to the President, the Kronstadt sailors held a mass meeting before the American embassy in Petrograd, where they declared that Ambassador Francis would be kidnapped and held captive until Mooney, Billings, Berkman, and the other American "political prisoners" were released. If Mooney was executed, they said, Ambassador Francis would be executed too. While Francis' aides dispatched a strongly worded protest to Lenin, and hastily cabled Washington for instructions, the Ambassador went into hiding.

2 ·

Secretary of Labor Wilson personally delivered the Mediation Commission's report on the Mooney case to the President.

It was not the Commission's task to decide whether Thomas J. Mooney and Warren K. Billings were innocent, the report stated, but to determine whether "a solid basis exists for the feeling that an injustice was done . . ."

Systematically, in prose almost as polished as the President's own, Frankfurter reviewed the history of the case from Mooney's battles against the utility companies to the California Supreme Court's present impasse.

On the basis of their trial transcripts alone, it could not be said that either Billings or Mooney had been tried unfairly, the Commission stated. But when all four trials were considered, together with the impregnating

240

atmosphere of guilt in which the trials were conducted, "the dubious character of the witnesses, the subsequent revelations concerning them, and the conflict in the testimony of the same witnesses as the need for change in the testimony developed to fit new theories of the prosecution or new evidence by the defense" it became apparent that adequate grounds for a feeling of disquietude existed, one which "leaves the mind in the greatest uncertainty as to the complicity of the accused."

"The utilities against which Mooney directed his agitation, or who suspected him of mischievous activity, undoubtedly sought 'to get' Mooney," the report bluntly charged. "Their activities against him were directed by Swanson, a private detective . . ."

That Oxman was guilty of attempting to suborn perjury there could be no doubt—his letters alone, irrespective of Rigall's testimony or the Grand Jury's verdict, were clear proof of this. And, the Commission noted, "When Oxman was discredited the verdict against Mooney was discredited."

The Mooney case has put the United States on trial in the court of world opinion, the commission concluded. ". . . the feeling of disquietude aroused by the case must be heeded, for if unchecked, it impairs the faith that our democracy protects the lowliest and even the unworthy against false accusations. War is fought with moral as well as material resources. We are in this war to vindicate the moral claims of unstained processes of law . . . These claims must be tempered by the fire of our own devotion to them at home.

"Your Commission, therefore, respectfully recommends in case the Supreme Court of California should find it necessary (confined as it is by jurisdictional limitations) to sustain the conviction of Mooney on the record of the trial, that the President use his good offices to invoke action by the governor of California and the cooperation of its prosecuting officers to the end that a new trial may be had for Mooney whereby guilt or innocence may be put to the test of unquestionable justice. This result can easily be accomplished by postponing the execution of the sentence of Mooney to await the outcome of a new trial, based upon prosecution under one of the untried indictments against him."

3 ·

Six days later, the President wrote Governor Stephens:

THE WHITE HOUSE
WASHINGTON, D. C.
January 22, 1918
MY DEAR GOVERNOR STEPHENS:

Will you permit a suggestion from me in these troubled times, which perhaps I should feel hardly justified in other circumstances?

The suggestion is this: Would it not be possible to postpone the execution of the sentence of Mooney until he can be tried upon one of the other indictments against him, in order to give full weight and consideration to the important changes which I understand have taken place in the evidence against him?

I urge this very respectfully, indeed, but very earnestly, because the case has assumed international importance, and I feel free to make the suggestion because I am sure that you are as anxious as anyone can be to have no doubt or occasion of criticism of any sort attach itself to the case.

Cordially and sincerely yours,
Woodrow Wilson

When several days had passed with no response, the President made public the Mediation Commission report.

4 ·

Reactions were mixed. Labor applauded the President's action. Most of the larger Eastern newspapers called it an unprecedented interference with states rights, but agreed generally that due to special circumstances and wartime conditions, the action might be justifiable.

The reaction in California was less qualified. The San Francisco *Argonaut,* in words similar to those used by a dozen other papers, called it ". . . an obvious intrusion and an impertinence, and it should be treated as such." "Freeing convicted murderers in order to placate anarchists and captious laborite-leaders is carrying even the exigencies of war too far," cried the Los Angeles *Times.* "Is Samuel Gompers running this country —railroads, wheels of justice, and all?"

Individual responses were no less strong. Judge Dunne, who had previously wired ex-President Roosevelt, praising him for his courage in coming to the defense of Fickert, asked "What did you expect of Bolsheviki Frankfurter?" Charging that the Mediation Commission had only consulted defense witnesses,* District Attorney Fickert declared emphatically "I will not become a party to turning loose upon the community in

---

* For a thorough refutation of Fickert's charges, see the James M. Beck—Felix Frankfurter correspondence in the January 18, 1922, issue of the *New Republic.*

this crisis a band of guilty anarchists, murderers and traitors on the recommendation of any Commission."

Few failed to comment. One did: the Governor of California, who let the President's letter go unanswered.

17· Fickert For Governor

THE GOVERNOR of California was a colorless, inoffensive man who had assumed his august office in consequence of a gentleman's agreement.

William Dennison Stephens, a former Los Angeles grocer, had been serving his third term in Congress when, in 1916, Governor Hiram Johnson decided to run for the United States Senate. Needing Southern California support, Johnson offered Stephens an attractive gamble. Because of the death of its occupant, the office of Lieutenant Governor was open. If Stephens would resign from Congress, Johnson would appoint him Lieutenant Governor. Then, if Johnson was elected Senator, Stephens would automatically succeed to the governorship. Stephens liked the odds. He agreed, Johnson won his Senate seat, and on March 15, 1917, William D. Stephens became the 24th Governor of the State of California. Although a Republican and an ex-president of the Los Angeles Chamber of Commerce, he was considered mildly liberal; during his first ten months in office, he hadn't noticeably offended anyone.

The Mooney case threatened to spoil that record.

Before him were the President's request, Mooney's application for a pardon, District Attorney Fickert's vituperative brief explaining why Mooney's request should be denied, and thousands of signatures to petitions for the pardon of Mooney and Billings pending new trials. (Inasmuch as the greatest number of these petitions originated outside California, they probably played little part in Stephens' deliberations.)

The problem was simple. 1918 was an election year.

If he let Mooney's sentence proceed to execution, the Governor would alienate the President, cause further labor unrest in California and elsewhere, and quite possibly trigger international complications affecting the war effort.

If, on the other hand, he pardoned Mooney, he would alienate those corporations and newspapers whose support he needed to win election, thereby providing Charles M. Fickert with an explosive election issue. Although Fickert had not yet officially announced his candidacy, it was common knowledge that he intended to run against Stephens for Governor in the Republican primary in August.

The problem, though real, wasn't pressing. The California Supreme Court had yet to rule on Mooney's appeal. Meanwhile Stephens did the only thing that seemed safe under the circumstances—nothing.

2 ·

Charles M. Fickert also had problems, some of which, ironically enough, were the result of his successes.

The California Supreme Court had upheld Fickert, ruling against defense motions that to try Rena Mooney and Israel Weinberg again would place them twice in jeopardy. But it was a double-edged victory.

Originally the eight indictments against the defendants had been divided between three judges, three each being given Judges Griffin and Dunne and two to Judge Cabaniss. But as the second trial of Weinberg approached, all of Fickert's key witnesses had been impeached or discredited. Fickert asked for a postponement; Judge Griffin, in whose courtroom this indictment was to be tried, denied the motion. Unwilling to risk another acquittal at a time when his political future was at stake, Fickert was forced to drop the indictment.

Another setback followed shortly afterward. In March the California Supreme Court ordered the release of the prisoners on bail. Weinberg was released on the 22nd on a cash bond of $15,000, Rena on the 30th on a $5000 bond. The music teacher and the jitney driver had each spent one year and seven months behind bars. One by one, Fickert was forced to drop all indictments against them except the two remaining before Judge Dunne.

All at once it apparently occurred to someone in the District Attorney's office that Tom Mooney's pardon and new trial plea rested on a single factor—that there were still untried indictments pending against him. Lacking these, Mooney could not be retried. And without a pending retrial, Governor Stephens would be forced to deny his pardon. Quickly, Fickert and staff moved to drop the remaining Mooney and Billings indictments. Informed of the move, and realizing its import, the defense as suddenly found itself fighting to keep the charges against the pair alive.

3 ·

The rapidly occurring events in the Mooney case placed another man in a difficult position. It was one in which, however, he was without free choice.

On March 1st the California Supreme Court denied Mooney's appeal, made before the Oxman's disclosures, thereby reaffirming his conviction and sentence. Upon Judge Griffin fell the odious task of resentencing to death on the scaffold at San Quentin a man he felt unfairly convicted. On May 29th, Griffin ordered the execution "on a day not less than sixty days and not more than ninety days from this time." In early June, Griffin himself had to sign the death warrant, specifying the new date, Friday, August 23rd.

That evening, a court attendant, entering the judge's chambers, found him still in his robes, his head in his arms on the desk, his shoulders shaking with quiet sobs. Even more quietly, the attendant left the room, closing the door behind him.

4 ·

President Wilson wrote a third letter to Governor Stephens. And a fourth.

These too went unanswered.

5 ·

The Mooney defense had its own problems. Many of its most impassioned battlers had dropped out of the case, involuntarily.

In February the United States Supreme Court had ruled the draft act constitutional, by so doing affirming the convictions of Emma Goldman and Alexander Berkman. Berkman had been returned to Atlanta Federal Penitentiary, Emma to Missouri State Prison at Jefferson City, to serve out their two year sentences. Deportation would follow their release. Long a dying movement, anarchism had become almost extinct in the United States.

"Big Bill" Haywood and nearly the entire leadership of the IWW were on trial before Judge Kenesaw Mountain Landis in Chicago.* There were not enough unimprisoned Wobblies left in the United States to mount an effective protest strike.

Nor were the federal arrests confined to anarchists and IWW. In Eureka, California, a man was sentenced to five years at hard labor for criticizing the President, on the testimony of his daughter.

In June, Socialist Eugene Debs, after speaking at Nimisilla Park, Canton, Ohio, on behalf of Mooney, Billings, and the IWW's, was arrested and charged with sedition.†

---

* Ninety-eight of the 100 Chicago defendants were convicted. Twenty of the most prominent, including Haywood, were fined $20,000 and sentenced to 20 years in prison.

† Convicted in September, Debs, sixty-two, was sentenced to 10 years in prison.

The defense had gained one very effective worker. Following her release, Rena Mooney went to work full time for the committees. Basically a shy person, she learned to overcome her timidity. Recitals for her pupils had given her some training in stage presence; she traveled from city to city speaking before labor groups on behalf of her husband and Warren Billings.

At Tom's suggestion, nationwide protest rallies were being planned for July 28th, the second anniversary of his arrest. Local committees had to be organized, halls rented, speakers found, publicity arranged, along with the hundreds of other myriad tasks behind the scene of each successful meeting.

Day after day Rena drove herself to exhaustion, as if trying to forget how fast August was approaching.

6 ·

Charles M. Fickert officially entered the California governor's race on June 13th, his campaign slogan "Patriotism or Anarchy," his platform "the complete suppression of sedition on the home front." As qualifications for the job, he cited the successful prosecutions of the Preparedness Day murderers and the nation-wide suppression of the IWW, which he claimed had occurred on the basis of information supplied to the federal authorities by his office.

Few days passed without revelations of a new and sinister plot, more subversives in government, or new proof of Mooney's guilt. There was evidence, Fickert said, that Mooney, Berkman, and Goldman were agents of the Kaiser. Federal handwriting experts have definitely proven, he claimed, that Mooney had written and mailed the letters threatening violence during the Parade.

Next to Fickert, the incumbent was a colorless campaigner. Campaign advertisements characterized Governor Stephens as "a solid, substantial, safe and sane executive." A remark from one of his more inspired speeches served as his campaign slogan: "Lincoln said, 'It is not best to swap horses while crossing the river.' "

But the crowds went to see neither Fickert nor Stephens, but showman "Sunny Jim" Rolph, San Francisco's genial Mayor, running on both the Republican and Democratic tickets.

For decades California had been a one-party state. No Democrat had occupied the gubernatorial mansion since James H. Budd left office in 1899. In 1910, when the Democratic party was making a successful comeback in other parts of the country, California went Progressive with Hiram Johnson.

One of the legacies of the Johnson regime was California's unique cross-filing system, whereby a candidate for public office could run in the primaries on whatever ballots he chose without stating party affiliation.

Intended as a means of ending one-party rule in California, cross-filing had cemented it. It also shifted emphasis from the November general election to the August primary. For example, a candidate who won both the Republican and Democratic nominations in August was automatically assured election in November.

The 1918 primary election was scheduled for August 27th, four days after Mooney's execution. It appeared that no matter what the Governor did about the Mooney case, Fickert was bound to profit.

7 ·

Shortly after nine on the morning of July 17th, an auto pulled up to the alley entrance of the County Jail. Thomas J. Mooney was deposited inside. In order to avoid a demonstration, his family had not been notified. Handcuffed and heavily guarded, he was driven to the ferry slip, where the auto pulled onto the 10:05 for the trip across the Bay to Sausalito. On board, he was allowed to walk around; some of the other passengers, recognizing him, wished him luck. From Sausalito, the auto drove through the purple hills of Marin County, passing through San Rafael and Kentfield, before turning off onto the barren, wind-swept peninsula where Mooney first saw the high, gray, turreted walls of San Quentin Prison. When they arrived at the outer gates at 11:30, Sheriff Finn removed Mooney's handcuffs and released the prisoner into the custody of Captain of the Guard Charles Gulliver. The auto returned to San Francisco.

What followed was routine. Taken through two more sets of gates into a detention room in the prison proper, the prisoner was searched and his head shaved. He was given a bath and while still naked searched again, this time by a guard wearing a rubber glove who probed his body orifices to make sure he had no concealed weapons or narcotics. He was issued one set of underwear, socks, shoes, a blue denim suit, and a number—31921 —and his photograph and measurements taken. He was given a brief lecture by Warden James A. Johnston and handed a pamphlet entitled *Rules & Regulations for the Government of Prisoners* and told to read it.

The rules, written in a style that can only be described as YMCA-inspirational, contained such instructions as "Breathe through your nose. Brush your teeth every day. Chew your food before you swallow it. If smoking hurts you, stop smoking. If you have bad habits, stop them now. Keep clean. Keep your body clean; keep your speech clean; keep your clothing clean; keep your cell clean."

Courtesy San Quentin Prison and Kenneth Lamott

San Quentin Prison, as first seen by newly arrived convicts.

San Quentin's morning bucket brigade. Convicts carrying their night buckets from the Stones to the Rose Bowl. Although this photo was taken about 1910, all that had changed at the time of Mooney's arrival were the uniforms, prison drab replacing stripes. A gate can be seen on the second tier, separating the six easternmost cells from the rest. This was Murderer's Row, where Mooney was held pending execution.

Courtesy Roy D. Graves and Kenneth Lamott

Much of the pamphlet, dealing with the ways a prisoner earned time off his sentence, wasn't applicable in this case.

He was then assigned a cell.

Only in his cell assignment was prisoner 31921 given special treatment, befitting his sentence. He was assigned to cell #20 in the "Stones." The Stones, the prison's oldest cell block, built in 1854, was a three-tiered building, each cell door opening onto a gallery. Cell #20 was on the second floor on the north side of the building in a special section popularly known as "Murderer's Row."

The cell itself, originally built to hold two prisoners but used solitary for those awaiting execution, was 8 feet long, 4 feet wide, and 7 feet tall in the center where the roof was arched like an old covered wagon or burial crypt. It contained a metal cot with a cotton mattress, one sheet and one blanket, a wash stand, a water bucket and a slop bucket for use as a toilet. There was a single light bulb hanging from the ceiling. The light was dim since the current was kept low to avoid suicide attempts. The walls were stone two feet thick. The door was made of solid steel, rather than bars. A small slit near the top—2″ by 8″—provided ventilation and a limited view of the prison wall. The door was secured by four separate outer locks.

For most of the prisoners the routine was unvarying. Lockup and head count were at 4:30 P.M. At 9 P.M. a bugle blew taps. At 6 A.M. an alarm bell rang; the prisoner had 15 minutes to arise, wash, dress, make his bed, and be standing at the door properly attired, his slop bucket in his right hand, when the locks were pulled back and the door opened. Prisoners were then marched down the outside stairs to the garden, in the midst of which was a huge concrete receptacle known as the "Rose Bowl," where the buckets were emptied. The prisoners then scooped a ladle of chloride of lime into the buckets and returned them to their cells. Then, by cell block, they marched out again to breakfast, which usually consisted of black coffee, sorghum molasses, three slabs of bread, and beans. Those prisoners who had jobs, in the jute mill or elsewhere, were then marched to work. The other two meals usually included more beans and some form of stew.

For most prisoners, the only change in this routine was on Sundays and execution days. There was no work on Sundays and only two meals, the prisoners, at this time, being locked up in their cells following the two-o'clock feeding. On execution days, all prisoners were returned to their cells after breakfast, to prevent any attempt to halt or protest the execution.

By tradition, executions were on Fridays. The condemned remained on Murderer's Row until the Wednesday preceding, at which time he was moved to a death-watch cell located in another building and situated a few feet from the gallows.

For the condemned, the daily routine prior to these last days varied slightly in that they marched and ate separately and were returned to their cells immediately after breakfast each day, to be taken out again only for the next meal.

It struck Tom Mooney as ironic that he had to go to San Quentin to find a community where everyone observed the eight-hour day.

8 ·

Under sponsorship of the AFL, more than 500 mass meetings were scheduled for July 28th, the second anniversary of Tom Mooney's arrest.

On the night before the demonstrations Governor Stephens proved that while he might be a colorless campaigner, he had another valuable attribute. Calling reporters to the Executive Mansion in Sacramento, he announced that he had granted a postponement of Mooney's execution until December 13th.

It was not a political move, he told reporters; the briefs in the case were so voluminous that he would need that much time to study them before reaching any decision.

For a nonpolitical move, it was shrewdly timed, not only taking much of the immediacy and force out of the labor demonstrations the following day but also effectively removing the Mooney case as an election issue. The new date was more than a month after the November elections.

Stephens' procrastination pleased no one, but more important, it offended no one greatly, as either execution or pardon would surely have done. There were two exceptions:

"Had I been Governor of California," Fickert said, "I would have met the Mooney issue squarely, irrespective of personal or political consequences." Without the Mooney case as an issue, the papers flatly stated, Fickert didn't have a chance.

"The Governor is a damned coward," Mooney yelled angrily when Warden Johnston brought news of the reprieve to his cell. "He's using me as a political football!" The following day the IWDL issued a more tempered statement in which Mooney was quoted as saying that he hoped the Governor had acted in accordance with the wishes of the President rather than for political expediency. Maxwell McNutt also issued a statement, diplomatically praising the Governor for his action. This seemed no time to offend the state's chief executive.

9 ·

Primary election day was Tuesday, August 27th; Governor Stephens was a heavy favorite. In the first returns Rolph showed unexpected strength, however, and shortly before midnight he claimed victory. But, as is often the case in the Golden State, the votes from heavily populated Southern California were slow in being tabulated; with the final count the next day Stephens won the Republican nomination by a 22,000 vote plurality.

The complications engendered by California's cross-filing system were never so apparent as in the 1918 election.

Rolph had won more votes than Stephens, and lost the election. Rolph had led the Democratic ballot with 74,955 votes and had come in second on the Republican ballot with 146,990 votes, for a combined total of 221,945. Stephens, who cross-filed on the Republican, Progressive, and Prohibition ballots but not the Democratic, had won on all three but trailed Rolph in the totals.

Stephens was first on the Republican ballot, however, with 168,942 votes, and this gave him the Republican nomination.

Unfortunately for Rolph, he too was a Republican. The election rules stated that a candidate who failed to win his own party's nomination could not qualify for any other. As a result, the Democratic party was without a gubernatorial candidate on the November ballot, automatically assuring Stephen's re-election.

Mooney partisans could point to the election results with satisfaction. Judge Griffin, much criticized for his stand on the case, had been re-elected by a vote of 66,000, drawing the second highest vote of the five candidates for the four judgeships. And Fickert had gone down to overwhelming defeat. Of the nine candidates for governor, Fickert placed eighth, with a vote of 13,259 or less than $1\frac{1}{4}$ percent of the total electorate. In San Francisco he had received only 2,194 votes. Tom Mooney had done better when he ran for Sheriff.

Impartially considered, however, the Mooney case probably had little effect on the results. Griffin was an incumbent, and thereby almost automatically assured re-election. Although the case had undoubtedly cost Fickert labor votes, most of labor voted Democratic, and Fickert had run only on the Republican ballot.

To all intents and purposes, Stephens, in granting Mooney a temporary reprieve, had made it impossible to ascertain the potency of the case as a political issue.

If all of this had any effect, it was as an example to Stephens' successors.

18· The Densmore Report

In the summer of 1918 the publishers of the *Bulletin* flatly ordered Fremont Older to drop the Mooney case.

It was, Older told his wife on returning home that night, virtually an order to let Mooney hang.

Older suffered through his decision. When he took over the *Bulletin* in 1895, it had been a failing newspaper with a net circulation of 9000; in the nearly quarter century since, he had built it up to 111,000. The *Bulletin* had laid bare the San Francisco graft scandals. With its support, Hiram Johnson had been able to break the Southern Pacific's long domination of California politics. To many, Fremont Older and the *Bulletin* were synonymous.

Older was nearly sixty-two, too old to start job hunting, or so he felt. In him, despite his successes, the fear of unemployment was still strong.

"I was living the darkest hours of my entire life," Older wrote later. "Only my most intimate friends knew I had been stopped. I kept it secret, hoping that I might yet find some way to continue the fight." When finally able to sleep at night, according to his wife, tears would course down his face and sobs would wrack his body.

On July 16th, the day before Mooney was moved to San Quentin, Older wrote his letter of resignation.

Crothers, on receiving it, is said to have cried "How could he!", then, brightening a little, adding, "Well, anyhow, I'll save $10,000 a year on his salary."

As Evelyn Wells points out in her biography of Older, the *Bulletin* was soon losing $125,000 a month.

Word of Older's resignation reached William Randolph Hearst in New York. Over the years there had been few issues over which Older and Hearst had not fought. Hearst's response was simple and direct, a wire reading: "Come to the Call and bring the Mooney case with you."

At this time only a few people were aware that Hearst owned the San Francisco *Morning Call* as well as the *Examiner*. Older traveled East to talk to his old adversary. Hearst promised him editorial freedom, while reserving the right to offer criticism whenever he felt like it. In August 1918 Older became editor of the *Call*.

In the years that followed, journalists sometimes accused Older of having sold out to Hearst. To such comments, Older simply replied, "The Mooney case would have died years ago if it hadn't been for William Randolph Hearst."

Still, it must have been a bitter pill to swallow.

Except for the Oxman letters, all the major revelations in the Mooney case would first break in the pages of the Hearst-owned *Call*. One of the biggest of them was now under way, although Older himself had as yet only a glimpse of it.

2 ·

In moving to the *Call* Older had taken along a number of readers (with the announcement of Older's editorship the *Call's* circulation jumped from 99,000 to 103,000, in one year it would be leading the *Bulletin* by 12,000) as well as part of his former staff, who had a loyalty rare in city rooms.

One of these men, city hall and waterfront reporter Edgar T. "Scoop" Gleeson, who had turned down a high pay offer on a New York paper to follow Older, came across a puzzling little piece of information. A man was following Charles Fickert everywhere he went. The man, though apparently a detective, was unknown to any of Gleeson's contacts. Gleeson told Older.

Over the years Older had learned a great deal about Charles M. Fickert. Some of it was fairly common knowledge—that Fickert was a "chaser," sometimes patronizing two or three prostitutes a day. What wasn't well-known was that Mrs. Fickert knew of this and was considering suit for divorce. Older assumed that the man was collecting divorce evidence. Still, he wasn't sure. He arranged to have Gleeson and several other reporters work in shifts, shadowing the man shadowing Fickert.

Older soon had a caller, George Parson, chief aide of J. B. Densmore, Director General of the United States Employment Service, who asked him to call off his bloodhounds. Older refused to do so unless given a good reason why. Parson gave it.

Under instructions from Secretary of Labor Wilson, Densmore had been ordered to make a thorough investigation of the Mooney frame-up charges. Densmore, Parson, and several other aides had arrived in the city that summer, beginning their investigation in complete secrecy. After almost two months of futility, operatives posing as telephone repair men had finally succeeded in planting dictaphones in Fickert's office. Since that time, all of Fickert's conversations had been monitored by two or more operatives, and full transcriptions made.

Parson was carrying a large and bulky package. It contained, he said, transcripts of all conversations recorded to date. Older, not attempting to conceal his excitement, asked to see them. Parson said he had been authorized by Densmore to show them to Older—certain conditions provided. One was maintenance of complete secrecy until such time as Secretary Wilson decided to make the report public. Older agreed.

Still holding the package, Parson recounted the difficulties in gaining access to Fickert's office and planting the microphones. Understandably proud of his work, Parson explained how the microphones worked—new innovations that enabled them to pick up not only conversations in the room but the other end of the line too. Even after the dictaphones had been planted, there had been problems. The District Attorney's office was in a huge room on the fourth floor of the Hall of Justice. Fickert's desk sat in the southwest corner of the room, between two large windows, one facing south on Merchant Street, the other west on Portsmouth Square. For dictaphone purposes the location was by no means ideal. Police sirens, clanging streetcars, tooting automobiles, shouts of Chinese children playing around the Robert Louis Stevenson statue in the park opposite, street noises of Kearny and Merchant, Fickert's squeeking chair—all had been picked up on the sensitive instruments. Furthermore, when the Mooney case was discussed, Fickert, Swanson, and the others often talked in low voices, some distance from the dictaphones, making it impossible to distinguish clearly what they said.

Older impatiently grabbed the transcript. After reading it for only a few minutes he knew that he had in his hands some of the most explosive material set down in cold print.

There was a little bit of everything. Fickert crudely attempting to entrap a woman in adultery, apparently to force her to testify that she had seen Rena Mooney at Steuart and Market. Fickert fixing cases with the notorious bail-bondsman and political power, Pete McDonough, in return for contributions to his gubernatorial campaign. The patriotic Edward Cuhna frantically pulling strings to avoid the draft. Fickert's frequently obscene conversations as he made appointments with prostitutes or arranged trysts with his semi-permanent liaisons, a dancing teacher, a secretary, and her roommate, whom he took alternately on weekend trips.

Thomas Mulhall (a Deputy U.S. Marshal, on the evidence in the Mooney and Sacramento IWW cases): "You know, if this thing ever breaks, we will go down hill so fast that all hell won't save us."

Fickert: An indistinguishable grunt.

*   *   *

Fickert: "That *s*—— —— — *b*—— Griffin! It it wasn't for him we would have had Mooney shoved right off at the end of the trial."

*   *   *

A Los Angeles Burns' agent, offering his services to Fickert: "I can frame the damndest lot of stuff you ever heard of."

Fickert: "If this thing comes to trial again, I am going to have four or five private investigators."

*   *   *

Some of it Older read with mixed feelings. There were a number of conversations between Fickert and a labor leader from Martinez, Fred Nixon, president of the Oil and Gas Workers' Union, indicating that Nixon was leaking Mooney defense information to the District Attorney. Older, pledged to secrecy, could do nothing to stop the leak.

And so it went, page after page. One of the highlights was a conversation between Fickert and Cuhna that had taken place on September 18th. It indicated just how desperately the pair were trying to get Rena Mooney:

Cuhna: "Chief, if you can get a witness who will put Mrs. Mooney at Steuart and Market, I don't give a damn if you put her there in a balloon."

Fickert: "I think we can put her there in a taxicab. It looks as though we have the witness."

Cuhna: "If you have Chief, I will put that *s*—— —— — *b*—— [sic] Mrs. Mooney on trial again and I will convict her by every rule of the game."

The transcripts left little doubt as to the identity of the "higher-ups" over Fickert in the Mooney case. Before making any kind of decision relating to the case, Fickert would call one of two numbers, Douglas 726 or Douglas 1272. The first number was the unlisted office phone of Frank C. Drew, attorney for the Chamber of Commerce; the second that of F. W. Henshaw, until recently a Justice of the California Supreme Court.

That Henshaw was no longer sitting on the bench was due solely to Fremont Older.

The story behind Henshaw's resignation was the sort that perhaps could happen only in California.

3 ·

It began with two has-beens of religious bent.
William J. Dingee, an erstwhile wealthy financier, broke and in ill

health, had gone to Sam Leake, seeking a cure for his illness.

Leake, once a well-known lobbyist, politician, and confirmed drunkard, had—in a well-publicized conversion—been "cured" by Christian Science and had since set himself up as a mental health practitioner.

Leake told Dingee that he couldn't be healed until he cleaned out the mess in his subconscious. Dingee took Leake's advice, wrote out a full confession of his "sins," and gave it to Fremont Older. This occurred in 1917.

While Older probably found most of Dingee's sins rather mundane, one stuck out like a newspaper headline: a statement that California Supreme Court Justice Frederick W. Henshaw had accepted a $410,000 bribe to change his decision in the Fair will case; Dingee, at the time a close friend and business associate of Henshaw's, acting as intermediary between Henshaw and the Fair heirs.

When silver king James G. Fair died in 1894 he left an estate estimated at $45 million and a number of wills. The case had been years in litigation. On reaching the California State Supreme Court the justices had ruled 4 to 3 against the Fair family. The court however inexplicably granted a rehearing in 1901 and this time, due to Henshaw's changed vote, the estate went to the heirs.

This was a serious charge, Older cautioned Dingee. Did he have any proof? He did—a record of the dates and amounts of the checks paid to "J. Brown," alias Henshaw; a list of the dummy bank accounts used; a signed affidavit from Henshaw's bookkeeper; plus two sets of Henshaw's personal books that recorded the passing of the $410,000.

Older confronted Justice Henshaw with the evidence. The justice, in shock, begged Older not to make it public. He was an old man; he would die if sent to prison. His family would be humiliated. Older was convinced that Henshaw was the "Machiavellian influence" behind Fickert, the spokesman for the utility companies in whose behalf he had so often, as a Supreme Court justice, ruled with favor. He felt sure it was Henshaw who had originally proposed Fickert to the utilities as a malleable attorney certain to drop the graft indictments if elected.

Older offered Henshaw a deal. He too was getting old; with the passage of years he had less desire to hurt anyone. If Henshaw would (1) resign from the Supreme Court, giving whatever reason he desired; and (2) disassociate himself from Fickert and the Mooney case completely, he would, in return, not make the information public.

Henshaw had agreed. He had immediately resigned from the court, stating that he wanted to devote all his time to war work. But, as the dictaphone transcripts now proved, he had failed to keep the second half of the bargain. It was apparent from the telephone conversations that Fickert made no move in the Mooney case without first contacting

Henshaw or Drew. Conversations also indicated that the two men had either written or approved the briefs submitted by Fickert in the bomb cases.

This, Parson now told Older, was one of Densmore's reasons for bringing the transcripts to his attention. Densmore knew that Older had the Dingee-Henshaw documents; he wanted to embody them in the text of his report to the Secretary of Labor, to prove the background and connections of the men who framed Mooney. In return for Older's documents, Densmore would allow him to publish the report in its entirety—every word recorded by the investigators.

Having clear proof that Henshaw had broken his promise, the editor opened his safe, took out the documents, and handed them to Parson.

4 ·

The investigation continued. Any time he could spare from his desk, Older went to one of the rooms where the monitoring was taking place and listened in on the conversations. He heard his own name often, together with that of the President, Frankfurter, and others. Fickert, like an elephant, retained his hatreds, even down to separate jurors in the Rena Mooney and Weingerg trials, whom he was now trying hard to discredit.

On November 11th the war ended in Europe. Even in San Quentin there were jubilant demonstrations. In Oakland the shipyard workers, marching in the Armistice parade, held aloft a huge banner: "We are celebrating, but we have not forgotten our fellow worker, Tom Mooney."

Others hadn't forgotten. On November 19th, Judge Griffin, unaware of the Densmore investigation, wrote an impassioned letter to Governor Stephens, begging for a new trial for Mooney. Judge Dunne, on hearing of the letter, was said to have sworn that he would never speak to his former friend as long as he lived.

December 13th was less than a month away. To date the Governor had made no move to interfere with the carrying out of the sentence. Densmore decided to terminate his investigation. He made two copies of the completed report—which included the dictaphone transcripts, the Dingee-Henshaw revelations, and a copy of the Grand Jury minutes of the Oxman "whitewash." One copy was sent to Secretary of Labor Wilson, the other given to Fremont Older.

This time Older had no hesitation. The Densmore Report, he would later say, was the greatest scoop of his career.

He guarded it covetously. On the morning of November 22nd, guards were placed outside the *Call's* press room; the printers could neither leave nor phone out. The entire report was set in type, complete to the names and telephone numbers of Fickert's girl friends, the only editing the use of dashes in place of profanities. Older planned to release the story in the 12:15 P.M. Final Home Edition.

Shortly after 11 Older's telephone rang. It was the Secretary of Labor. He had just received his copy of the Densmore Report and was frightened by the extent of the revelations. "Don't publish it until I have time to think things over," he said.

"You can't stop it now," Older replied. "It's on the press." He quickly hung up.

Waiting impatiently, Older grabbed the first copy that came off the press, then slipped out a side entrance of the building, fearing that at any moment he might be enjoined and publication stopped.

The headline—in big, black, bold type 2½ inches tall—could be read a quarter block away:

FICKERT IS TRAPPED
BY U.S. DICTAPHONE

5 ·

The Densmore Report was one of the journalistic sensations of the decade. It aroused indignation around the world and was read into the *Congressional Record* in its entirety, covering 158 pages of small print. It did not, as Mooney defense literature would later state, conclusively "prove" that Fickert framed the Mooney case, but it raised serious doubts regarding his conduct of the office of District Attorney, as well as of his handling of the case.

In California its effect was, to understate, unbelievable.

The San Francisco Grand Jury, in a hastily called session, demanded an immediate investigation—to determine if Densmore could be tried for malfeasance of office or some other charge.

The Downtown Association threatened to file a suit charging Densmore with slander of the City and County of San Francisco.

None of the other San Francisco papers dared print the report in its entirety, even though Older generously gave them permission to do so.

No action against Fickert or Henshaw was ever taken. The statute of limitations had expired on the Fair bribe and the San Francisco Grand Jury failed to find Charles Fickert guilty of any impropriety.

And Older was soundly criticized by many for his effrontery in casting discredit upon the state's highest tribunal.

He was not long in learning Charles M. Fickert's personal reaction.

Walking through the lobby of the Palace Hotel two days after the report was published, Older encountered Fickert and one of his assistants, Fred Berry, emerging from the bar. *"You son of a bitch!"* Fickert yelled and swung. A number of years separated Fickert from his football days but he did have the edge of 16 years on Older. Fickert's first two punches failed to connect. The third caught Older on the right side of the head and dropped him heavily to the floor. Fickert raised his foot to kick him in the head but Berry parried the blow.

"Older's dead!" someone screamed in the *Call* press room, located just across the alley. *"Fickert just killed him in the Palace Hotel!"*

Grabbing whatever weapons came to hand, the printers and pressmen ran into the Palace lobby en masse. Fortunately Fickert had departed the scene. Although police ordered them out, they refused to leave until taken to Older, who had been helped to one of the hotel rooms. Grinning, albeit painfully, he told them to quit making asses of themselves and go back to work. Only later, on calling home, did he learn that someone had notified his wife of his death.

Fickert, relating his account of the skirmish to a *Chronicle* reporter, explained that he had hit Older only after the editor had reached into his rear pocket for a gun. Older's friends, who knew the editor had refused to carry a gun even when his life had been threatened during the graft cases, failed to see any humor in the charge. But the aging pacifist did.

6 ·

On the evening of November 28th, 1918—Thanksgiving Day—Governor William D. Stephens read a long prepared statement to reporters, one in which the name Berkman appeared almost as often as that of Mooney.

There was no question in his mind of Mooney's guilt, the Governor said, but since certain revelations following the trial had raised doubts in some minds, and since particularly he had been requested—earnestly and repeatedly—to take action by the President of the United States, he had decided to commute Thomas J. Mooney's sentence to life imprisonment.

On learning of the Governor's decision, Warden Johnston went to Mooney's cell to inform him. "I went inside the prison and told Mooney the good news," the warden later recalled. "Mooney was not grateful to the governor for preventing his hanging. On the contrary, he was belligerent, and he berated the governor for not granting him a complete pardon."

Mooney immediately sat down and drafted a letter to the Governor, refusing the commutation:

"Governor Stephens: It is my life you are dealing with. I demand that you revoke your commutation of my death sentence to a living death. I prefer a glorious death at the hands of my traducers, you included, to a living grave. I am innocent.

"I demand a new and a fair trial or my unconditional liberty through a pardon. If I were guilty of the crime for which I have been unjustly convicted, hanging would be too good for me. Then why commute my sentence to life?

"Labor everywhere: I say to you tonight, as I said the night that the Chamber of Commerce jury returned the death penalty verdict against me, that my hope, as well as the hope of Billings, Nolan, Weinberg and Mrs. Mooney, is in the solidarity of organized labor. I shall never depart from that statement . . .

"I refuse to accept the commutation. I now appeal to you again to act, and the sooner the better."

Because it contained aspersions upon the integrity of the state's chief executive, the warden censored the statement, refusing to issue more than excerpts to the press.

Bourke Cockran was less fettered: "The Governor's action in the Mooney case embraces so completely every possible stupidity for which any opportunity was afforded him that it amounted to inverted genius. Never before to my knowledge has a public officer written himself down an ass so conspicuously and with such complacency. How any man who believed Mooney guilty could have commuted his sentence is inconceivable."

To Felix Frankfurter, the commutation "made no sense, none at all." By the evidence Mooney was either guilty and should be executed, or was innocent and should be freed, or if there were still doubts, he should be retried and those doubts resolved.

The Governor, in his statement, had partly foreseen this objection. "The logic that a man is either guilty or innocent and that necessarily, if the maximum penalty is not justified, pardon should follow, does not hold either in theory or practice. It has been no uncommon thing for executives in granting clemency to entertain doubt sufficient to save men from the gallows, but not of that degree of reasonable doubt that the law resolves completely in favor of a defendant." The Governor ignored entirely the third possibility—the one for which the President, the Mediation Commission, labor, and Mooney himself had asked—a retrial.

To Mooney's family the decision was, however wrong, a relief. Emma Goldman, who heard the news in Missouri State Prison, felt similarly. It was a travesty of justice to immure a man for life who had been proven innocent by the state's own witnesses, she observed, yet she couldn't help feeling that it was in some respects a victory, one for which Sasha deserved the largest measure of credit.

Labor's anger over Stephens' "betrayal" and "cowardice" was so heated that a call went out for a nationwide general strike, to begin on December 9th. The intensity of this anger was measurable: the usually conservative San Francisco Labor Council came within one vote of granting strike sanction. Only the Teamsters opposed the walkout.

Both the practical and the passionate held forth in Tom Mooney's nature. Aware that without adequate preparations such a hastily-called move could only result in failure, Mooney personally requested postponement of the strike.

The *Call* protested Stephens' action; most of the other California newspapers lauded it, agreeing with the *Chronicle* that the "Governor had pursued the proper course in disposing of the case."

But the Mooney-Billings case wouldn't stay disposed of. By all logic and precedent, Stephens' move, by negating its immediacy, should have crushed the spirit of the Mooney defense. It didn't.

PART THREE
31921 & 10699

"We may as well be candid and kindergartenish with you. The reason that Mooney and Billings are in prison is because a majority of the people of the state of California want them there and the Supreme Court and the Governor dare not disobey that majority. It is quite beside the point whether or not they are guilty of the particular crime of which they were charged and convicted. The question is: Are Mooney and Billings the sort of people we want to run at large? We have decided this in the negative and we have them locked up. We intend to keep them there, despite all fulminations from Greenwich Village."

THE COLFAX, CALIFORNIA *RECORD*

19· The Red Raids

IN PARIS, Woodrow Wilson was pleading for the establishment of justice throughout the world.

In Chicago, representatives of 1100 unions were asking that it be given to just two men in California.

The idea for the Mooney Congress came from Seattle, a hotbed of Mooney agitation. Both Tom Mooney and Ed Nolan had eagerly seconded the idea and the International Workers' Defense League, in conjunction with the Chicago Federation of Labor, had scheduled it for January 14–17, 1919.

Officially known as the National Labor Congress on the Mooney Case, its stated purpose was the creation of a united labor front to free the California defendants.

The result was far different.

The war was over. With the end of wartime production, unemployment and the cost of living had risen sharply. Many veterans returned home to find their former employers had no intention of hiring them back. Labor unrest, partly suppressed for the duration, had broken out in new intensity. While Samuel Gompers counseled "patience" and "moderation," radicals of every persuasion were emboldened by events in Russia. To some on the American Left, the Mooney Congress appeared a golden opportunity to wrest control of the AFL from Gompers and the conservatives. Others had larger dreams. Observed Crystal Eastman in the *Liberator*: "Many delegates came with a great shining hope that this Mooney Congress might be the beginning of the Revolution in America."

To hold the congress to its express purpose, its chairman Ed Nolan, backed by Nockles, Fitzpatrick, Andy Furuseth, Alexander Howat, and E. B. Ault, limited accredition to delegates from unions of the American Federation of Labor, the Railroad Brotherhoods, and the Amalgamated Clothing Workers. On arriving in Chicago, Socialists, IWW's, and others were informed that as such they couldn't attend. "But," as one delegate observed, "I heard of none going home." Almost all also carried AFL cards. Gompers did not openly discourage AFL attendance, but, as important, he didn't encourage it.

Shortly after Mooney's conviction, Lucy Robins had attempted to see Gompers on Mooney's behalf. Frustrated in this, she had sent him an angry wire accusing him of both dictatorship and cowardice. Amused by her brashness, Gompers granted an interview during which he showed her what she would later describe as a huge folder of correspondence relating to the Mooney case. Looking through it she was amazed to discover that it was Gompers who had persuaded the President to appoint the Mediation Commission, Gompers who had stirred up the movement to impeach Fickert, that "The victories we thought we had won had actually been achieved by the masterly hand that had pulled wires behind the scene." Lucy became one of the aging labor leader's most devoted partisans and the relationship between them was very close. Frankly put, she became Gompers' mistress.*

Prior to the Mooney Congress, Gompers expressed his feelings on what he knew would be the central issue of the meeting—a general strike. "It would destroy all that American labor has won in fifty years," he told her.

Apparently made aware of Gompers' feelings, many key AFL officials did not attend the congress, including most of the Californians. Remarked Eastman: "The most cautious conservative at the Mooney Congress was a radical; [he] would have been a 'red' at any AFL convention."

The sessions were stormy, the debates factionalism personified.

Shall we use more political action or shall we abandon political action entirely and resort directly to economic weapons such as the boycott and the general strike?

If a general strike, should it be for the release of all political and class war prisoners or for Mooney alone—with the thought that once feeling our power we can use it for anything we want afterward?

In either case, should the strike start on May 1st, labor's own day, or on July 4th, America's Independence Day?

These were some of the questions. But mostly there were resolutions, some two hundred, only a few dealing with the Mooney case, often ten or more delegates clamoring for the floor at the same time. Resolved, that there be no restrictions on passports and visas to Russia. Resolved, that a new labor organization be formed along industrial lines. Resolved, that all unions should merge nto "one big union." Resolved, that our troops be

---

* For this reason some of her claims regarding Gompers' role in the case deserve examination. Gompers did clearly play an important part in the formation of the Mediation Commission; his conferences with Wilson may well have been a factor influencing Wilson to write to Governor Stephens; and he probably had a hand in the Densmore investigation. There is no evidence, however, that he was behind Fickert's recall and much evidence indicating that he wasn't. Because of the McNamara case, Gompers largely confined his activities to behind-the-scenes, and with the above exceptions, it is difficult to determine just how significant they were.

withdrawn from Russia. Resolved, that the peace pact be submitted to the voters for approval. Resolved, the creation of an American workers' soviet.

One by one Nolan gaveled them down as having no bearing on the purpose of the convention.

Finally a platform was adopted dealing with the case. It was a curious hybrid of political and economic action: (1) a delegation of five, including Furuseth and Fitzpatrick, was to ask the U.S. Congress for federal intervention in the case, on the ground that Mooney had been denied "due process" of law under the 14th Amendment; (2) heavy publicity was to be directed toward the California legislature to effect a change in the state's penal code whereby new evidence discovered after a trial could be used as the basis for a retrial; and (3) if neither of these methods succeeded in effecting Mooney's release, a referendum would be held, all unions participating, on the question of whether a nationwide general strike—"the first general strike on behalf of human liberty"—should be called, to start on July 4th.

The moment the platform was passed, Nolan declared the meeting adjourned, over the vehement protests of most of the delegates. It has been suggested by at least one observer that had he not done so the American Communist Party might have been born in January of 1919 rather than the following September.

But the prospect of a nationwide general strike—in which all workers would simultaneously lay down their tools and all industry automatically cease—was in itself sufficiently frightening.

America soon had a sample of what it would be like. On January 21, 35,000 Seattle shipyard workers struck for higher wages. On February 6th, 60,000 workers in other industries walked off their jobs in sympathy.

The Seattle general strike lasted just four days. On February 10th, Mayor Ole Hanson brought in 3000 soldiers and policemen, and to avoid bloodshed the Seattle Labor Council ended the strike. There was no violence and all essential services were maintained; but few of the press stories included these two facts. To many the strike was a fearful portent of the rampant anarchy and revolution that was waiting just over the horizon. And with the Mooney Congress and the Seattle general strike the curtain raised on the drama to be known as the great Red Scare.

2 ·

The first act occurred on the day before May Day, when some 30 people—among them, John D. Rockefeller, J. P. Morgan, Federal Judge Kenesaw Mountain Landis, U.S. Attorney General A. Mitchell Palmer—

received an unexpected package. Each was seven inches long, tube-like, and bore as return address "Gimbel Brothers, New York City." And each contained a single stick of dynamite, rigged in such a way that when the package opened sulfuric acid would ignite two dynamite caps and set off the charge. A Negro maid in the home of a former Georgia Senator opened one and lost both hands.

One of the packages was addressed to Charles M. Fickert, another to Edward H. Cuhna.

1919 was an election year for San Francisco's District Attorney. Fickert had strong opposition for the office, in the person of police magistrate Matthew Brady, who had announced his candidacy in January. Although no official charges had been filed against Fickert as a result of the Densmore Report, it was generally assumed that he would be voted out of office in November. He had already announced that, due to ill health, he might not seek reelection.

The bomb changed his mind. Neither Fickert nor Cuhna was in the District Attorney's office when the packages arrived. An assistant had started unwrapping one when a policeman, leafing through the *Bulletin,* commented jocularly "Better be careful. Mayor Ole Hanson, up in Seattle, got a package just like that and it contained a bomb." The assistant very carefully set it down.

To Fickert the bomb was a clear mandate that his crusade against murderous radicals had to be continued, even at the cost of his own personal well-being. The bombs were a part of a nationwide conspiracy, Cuhna told the press, financed by the International Workers' Defense League. Shortly thereafter, Fickert announced his candidacy for reelection.

On May 1st, riots broke out in Boston, New York City, and Cleveland as police and citizens stormed into the streets to break up May Day labor parades. (REDS RIOT IN EASTERN CITIES, read the *Chronicle's* headline.)

Fear was upon the land. The Mooney general strike, newspapers predicted, would be the beginning of the Bolshevik revolution in America. In many cities gun sales zoomed, as citizens prepared to defend their homes and loved ones.

3 ·

At least one man knew that such fears were probably groundless. By now it was apparent to San Quentin prisoner #31921 that there might well be no general strike.

Immediately after learning of Mooney's commutation, Warden Johnston had moved him from condemned row to another cell in the Stones. The next step had been assigning him to a job that neither discriminated against him nor showed favoritism. As Johnston later admitted, this posed a special problem. "There were many radicals in the prison. IWW's shading from parlor pink to blood red were being received under the law against syndicalism. They were a strange assortment. The group included honest but discouraged migatory workers ready to join any industrial movement, half-baked theorists, well-read liberals, mild-mannered pacifists, and hell-raising fire-brands constantly stirring strikes and sabotage. I didn't want to place Mooney where he would be tempted to agitate or where he might be accused of inciting trouble."

Johnston assigned him to a solitary job, operating a hoisting engine on a bluff behind the new prison overlooking the bay. The engine furnished the power for operation of a tramway on which materials were hauled from the wharf to the warehouse.

As the warden soon discovered, Mooney was far too busy agitating outside the prison to foment unrest within.

Between 4:30 lockup and 9 o'clock taps, Mooney became a different man and cell #155 in the Stones was transformed into headquarters for the International Workers' Defense League and the Tom Mooney Molders' Defense Committee.

"Mooney is the embodiment of energy," the warden observed with unconcealed admiration. "He looks like a locomotive. He is built like one. He has the power to pull a heavy load. He keeps several propaganda machines in motion . . . Rena Mooney, his wife, Anna Mooney, his sister, John Mooney, his brother, each have a part to perform." As did Mary Mooney, his mother, and Belle Hammerberg, Rena's sister.

Warden James A. Johnston was an advocate of the "new penology." While warden at Folsom, he had abolished corporal punishment. Since coming to San Quentin, he had eased many restrictions. Two in particular were very important to Mooney: mail and visitors.

"Like all the 'big shots,' Mooney had a large mail and many visitors. Letters, telegrams, and cables came to him from all quarters of the globe. Most of the messages were from persons he didn't know, but who were for the 'cause' or, as so many signed themselves, 'for the revolution.' I let him have all the communications and publications except those radically derisive or anarchistic."

More important than the letters Mooney received were those he sent.

Mooney was a model prisoner. He stayed within the rules—but he also learned to stretch them to their limits. At most a prisoner was allowed to write 10 letters a week—Mooney wrote 10, some of them, directed to Rena and Nolan, running 15 to 20 pages, singlespaced. These contained explicit instructions for what he wanted done. They were not suggestions, they were orders. One man and one man only ran the defense committees.

Friends were allowed to visit once every other month, relatives twice a month, attorneys as often as necessary, permission having to be obtained. With several attorneys, numerous friends and five relatives all active in the defense, his visitor's days were busy.

There were other ways to stretch the visitor's rules. Ella Reeve Bloor (Mother Bloor) mentions one in her autobiography *We Are Many:* "Each time I visited Mooney, I took four or five young people with me. One would send in a request for John J. McNamara, another for Matthew Schmidt, etc. Then I would ask for Tom Mooney and we would all sit together along the line and talk together. We had many wonderful conferences there. Mooney was nearly always cheerful but I used to fear sometimes when I saw his pallor that he would never come out alive."

Under the rules governing California penal institutions, prisoners were not allowed to see California newspapers. It was an old rule, its origin forgotten, although San Quentin historian Kenneth Lamott believes it was probably intended to prevent prisoners from receiving coded messages through the want ads. But, inconsistently, newspapers from Oregon, Nevada, or any other state could be received. Mooney subscribed to a number, including *The New York Times* and the New York *Sun.*

He kept himself fully cognizant of what was happening outside. By spring it was apparent that the July 4th general strike was in trouble. In April, the *American Federationist,* official organ of the AFL, denounced the strike in an article entitled "No Room for Destructionists in Our Movement." In June, Rena appeared before the AFL convention at Atlantic City, pleading for support from the delegates. It was a conservative convention. On the defensive because of the Bolshevism charges, it advocated more stringent immigration laws and voted against recognizing Soviet Russia. As for the Mooney case, the general strike proposal was soundly defeated, the IWDL criticized for its handling of the case, and the Committee on Resolutions reported out an emasculated motion requesting the Executive Committee "take steps" to secure a new trial for Mooney. It was the weakest of the Mooney resolutions yet passed.

In a desperate effort to save the faltering protest, Mooney, through Nolan and the IWDL, proposed a new plan: a general strike starting July 4th and lasting only five days. If this failed to secure his release, there would be a second five-day strike beginning on Labor Day. And if this too failed, on November 19th, the first anniversary of Mooney's commutation, all workers would walk off their jobs and remain off indefinitely.

Though he had an ingrained distrust of "labor mis-leaders," as he called them, Mooney had an almost mystic faith in the rank and file. He appealed to them now, asking *individual* unions members to send in their strike votes. Thousands of ballots poured into IWDL headquarters in San

Francisco. "The whole business would have been funny if it hadn't been insane," Lucy Robins observed, resigning from the IWDL.

But to a great many in labor it appeared just possible that Mooney's mad plan—a direct appeal to the masses—just might succeed.

4 ·

About 11:15 on the night of June 2nd, a blast shook the nation's capital. Opening the door of his house, young Assistant Secretary of the Navy Franklin D. Roosevelt almost stumbled over a mangled torso. The bomb, which had exploded on the front steps of the house opposite, that of U.S. Attorney General A. Mitchell Palmer, had been so powerful that even after all the bits of human wreckage were assembled, it was impossible to determine whether one or two men had been carrying it when it exploded prematurely.*

Throughout June, with the explosion of some half-dozen bombs in various cities, the fear grew to hysteria. As the terror mounted, its focal point became fixed, the July 4th general strike in behalf of the San Francisco dynamiter.

REIGN OF TERROR PLANNED (Chicago *Tribune*), *STOLEN EX-PLOSIVES TO BE USED* (San Francisco *Examiner*), PLANS FOR WIDESPREAD VIOLENCE AND MURDER (Cincinatti *Enquirer*).

As Independence Day dawned, 11,000 New York City policemen were placed on special duty, assigned to guard all public buildings, the Stock Exchange, and the homes of the prominent. Their ranks were augmented by hundreds of deputized citizens. In Chicago, two infantry companies, the entire police force, and 1000 volunteers were placed on alert. Similar precautions were taken in Boston, Philadelphia, Seattle, San Francisco. In Oakland all known radicals were incarcerated for the day as an "insurance device."

"What happened," Robert K. Murray observes in his exceptional study *Red Scare*, "was anticlimactic. Independence Day came and went . . . The Mooney general strike with its attendant bombings and bloodshed simply failed to materialize. Even in the two areas of the country where

---

* In 1920, the Bureau of Investigation took two anarchists into custody as suspects in the bombing. No warrants, writs, or formal charges of any kind were ever filed against them. One was deported; the other, Andrea Salsedo, was held incommunicado in the New York office of the Bureau and allegedly tortured by federal agents in an attempt to exact a confession. Shortly afterward, under circumstances still unexplained, Salsedo fell from the 14th floor of the building.

Just after the arrest of the two men, their Massachusetts comrades sent a young man to New York City to investigate the brutality charges and to agitate in their behalf. Many would later claim that the man, Boston shoeworker Bartolemeo Vanzetti, was marked for special attention by the Bureau from this moment.

one might have expected some disorder, none was forthcoming. In both Seattle and San Francisco the day passed quietly except for the usual sound of exploding fireworks."

But the fear remained. And one man found a way to channel it. As historian Arthur Schlesinger, Jr., put it, Attorney General Palmer "generalized his own experience into a national emergency."

Later Palmer himself described the beginnings in a speech: "Like a prairie-fire, the blaze of revolution was sweeping over every American institution of law and order. It was eating its way into the home of the American workman, its sharp tongues of revolutionary heat were licking the altars of the church, leaping into the belfry of the school bell, crawling into the sacred corners of American homes, seeking to replace marriage vows with libertine laws, burning up the foundations of society . . ."

The Red Scare was on.

5 ·

The President, with larger concerns, did little to check it.

Failing to muster enough Congressional support to obtain ratification of the League of Nations, Woodrow Wilson also took his case directly to the people. Through Columbus, Indianapolis, St. Louis, Kansas City, Butte, Tacoma—the crowds were large and demonstrative. Wilson reached Seattle on September 15th. The mammoth parade began auspiciously.

In *When The Cheering Stopped* Gene Smith describes what then happened:

"He was standing up in the car waving a tall silk hat . . . when with terrifying suddenness all the noise and cheering ended. Standing by the curb in long lines were men in blue denim working clothes. Their arms were folded and they stared straight ahead, not at the President, but at nothing at all. They did not hiss or boo but motionless, noiseless, simply stood there. In their hats they wore signs saying RELEASE POLITICAL *PRISONERS* . . . From the street over which the motorcade had come there were heard the bands playing and the crowds noisily breaking up, but where the IWW's were there was not a sound but the put-putting of police motorcycles. The President was standing and smiling when he first reached the IWW's, but in a flash his smile vanished and a flabbergasted look came over his face. He stood in the terrible silence for two blocks, the hand holding his hat hanging by his side, and then he sank down onto the car seat beside the First Lady. He put his tall hat on his head, a little to one side, and it seemed that he sat in a crumpled-up way. His face was white."

It lasted for six, silent, terrible blocks and would in time become known as "the Seattle treatment."

Ten days later, in Pueblo, Colorado, he stood up to speak, stuttered, stammered, and began crying. It was the last time Woodrow Wilson would address the people of the United States as their President.

6·

"The American Flag or the Red Flag; that is the issue in the campaign for District Attorney."

Everything about the campaign for District Attorney was familiar. Charles Fickert had the backing of the Republican Party, the San Francisco Civic League, a labor splinter group, and A. P. Giannini. Matthew Brady had both the Democratic Party and Union Labor Party backing. Fickert again used the Mooney case and the telegrams from the late Teddy Roosevelt. Brady had the Densmore Report. Fickert accused Brady of being soft on radicalism. Brady charged Fickert with prostitution of office.

Fickert attempted one last grandstand play. On October 1st Alexander Berkman was released from Atlanta. Emma Goldman had been released from Missouri State Prison several days before. As Berkman walked through the prison gate, San Francisco detectives attempted to place him under arrest. But federal immigration authorities, also waiting, stepped in and exercised their prior claim.

Despite newspaper attempts to generate enthusiasm ("It is not too much to say . . . that upon the election or defeat of Mr. Fickert will depend the verdict of the country on the question of whether the people of this city prefer to live under statute law or mob law," observed the *Chronicle*) the campaign was lackluster. On November 4th only a small proportion of the registered voters turned out. It was enough to defeat Fickert, "the man who stood practically alone against the IWW," by a vote of 48,136 to 40,166.

Although Brady made no public promises, his labor support was given largely on assumption that if elected he would retry Mooney on one of the remaining indictments, several of which Mooney's attorneys had managed to keep open.

7·

The first of the federal "red raids" took place three days later, on the second anniversary of the Russian Revolution. Although nominally headed by Attorney General Palmer, the actual planning and execution were carried out by Bureau of Investigation director William J. Flynn and his twenty-four-year-old assistant John Edgar Hoover, who headed the General Intelligence or anti-radical section of the bureau.

In simultaneous raids in 18 cities, 450 "radicals" were arrested. Aliens were held for deportation; citizens were turned over to local police for appropriate action.

The "practice raid," as it came to be known, touched off a number of strictly local raids, many of them conducted by veterans.

One of these occurred in Centralia, Washington, on the 11th, the first anniversary of Armistice Day, when a parade of American Legionnaires stormed the IWW hall. The Wobblies defended themselves, killing three of the attackers, but eventually were captured and jailed. That night there was a power failure in Centralia. When the lights came on again IWW leader Wesley Everest, himself a veteran, had been removed from jail. Everest was responsible for one of the deaths. He was taken out of town and castrated. "For Christ's sake, men," he begged, "shoot me— don't let me suffer this way!" Everest was hung from a bridge. The rope was too short, he was able to clutch the planks with his fingers. The Legionnaires stomped on them until he let go. Still he didn't die. Pulled back up, he was then dropped with a longer rope, but continued to struggle. Only after being dropped a third time and being riddled with bullets did he finally cease moving. The body was cut down the next day and thrown into the cell of the Wobblies so that they could stare at the foot-long neck. The official coroner's report listed the cause of death as "suicide."

On December 21st, while Flynn and Hoover watched, 249 "aliens" were placed aboard an obsolete transport, the *Buford,* and deported. Among them were the United States's two most famous anarchists. Alexander Berkman had never taken out citizenship; Emma Goldman's had been re-voked by an especially created technicality. Nicknamed the "Soviet ark," the ship's destination was Russia.

On January 2nd, 1920, some 10,000 men and women were arrested in federal raids in 70 cities.

20· Tom Mooney's Monthly

THE NATIONAL hysteria passed. Plans to launch a "veritable fleet of Soviet arks" failed when Louis F. Post, Assistant Secretary of the Department of Labor, canceled 1,547 deportation warrants on the ground that they were illegal. In almost all cases that went as far as the courtrooms, the raids themselves were found to be unlawful. Somewhat belatedly, it was revealed that a good number of those arrested weren't radicals at all.

While one would like to say that public indignation or the return of common sense ended the red scare, the probable cause was indifference. The threat had simply failed to materialize. Though stormy, the transition to peacetime had now taken place. With A. Mitchell Palmer's unsuccessful attempt to capture the Republican nomination for the Presidency in 1920, the American public became aware that it had been used. When Palmer and Hoover claimed to have discovered another May Day plot to kill high government officials, blow up buildings and start a general strike, the announcement was treated with more amusement than concern. The public had lost interest.

In all except one state, that is. By virtue of the criminal syndicalist law passed under Governor Stephens, some 500 persons were arrested and 264 convicted in California between 1919 and 1921. Among them was the socially prominent suffragette Anita Whitney, who in February 1920 was sentenced from 1 to 14 years in prison.

In California the red scare lasted a long time. As late as 1924, 60 criminal syndicalists were sent to San Quentin.

2 ·

With certain inevitability, interest in the Mooney case began to wane.

As early as the Mooney Congress, Crystal Eastman had written in *The Liberator:* "The Mooney case was such an old story. It was not easy to be excited about it anymore." As the Twenties began, there was little roaring about this old injustice. Mooney received few letters, even fewer visitors.

In many months financial contributions dropped below postage costs.

Following the Mooney Congress, the Seattle Labor Council, unhappy with the "conservative" stand of the IWDL, had set up a special committee to collect defense funds in the Pacific Northwest. At the time Mooney had strongly protested, arguing that unless funds were collected through one central group they could not be adequately accounted for, that this doubled office rental and other expenses. Between March and October 1919, the committee collected $9,684.37. When the Seattle Labor Council asked for an accounting it was discovered that $8,783.80 had been spent for "salaries, expenses and other incidentals." The ensuing scandal, much publicized, particularly by Fickert and the Los Angeles *Times,* as "the Mooney racket," reduced contributions to the legitimate defense groups to a trickle.

On May 20, 1920, Edward D. Nolan announced that the International Workers' Defense League had been officially disbanded. The Mooney defense would be taken over by the Tom Mooney Molders' Defense Committee, with Rena Mooney its secretary. Nolan moved to Southern California. Israel Weinberg had long since moved East, to Cleveland.

Although Nolan gave no public reason for deactivating the IWDL, he and Mooney had been quarreling over defense strategy ever since the failure of the general strike. Over the succeeding years Nolan occasionally wrote warm letters to Rena, but there were no letters or visits to Tom and in closing his letters to Rena, while he always sent love to other members of the Mooney family, one name was conspicuously absent.

Robert Minor also wrote to Rena rather than Tom, declining Tom's suggestion that he return to San Francisco and write a book on the case. He was too busy. The IWDL had finished itself at Chicago, Minor said, when it chose the conservatives over the radicals. The Mooney case could have played a great role in the proletarian revolution in America, but "a sudden, blighting narrowness of vision wrecked it." Minor's major interest now was Russia.

Upton Sinclair published a novel, 100%—*The Story of a Patriot,* which, Sinclair stated in an addenda, paralleled in its main outlines the case of Tom Mooney, and this, plus Sinclair's suggestion that readers send a contribution to the Mooney defense, led to a brief resurgence of interest. But for all practical purposes, so far as the general public was concerned, the Mooney case was dead.

Mooney, however, was determined to resurrect it. Considering his circumstances, he chose a rather remarkable way to do it. He decided to publish a newspaper.

The first issue of *Tom Mooney's Monthly* appeared in August 1920. Full newspaper size, running to six pages, it was far more professional than *The Blast* or Mooney's old paper *The Revolt.* In the upper corners of the front page were photos of Mooney and Billings. While the motto of the San Francisco *Chronicle* was "100% American" and that of Hearst's *Examiner* "America First," *Tom Mooney's Monthly* was "One Hundred Per Cent for Toilers in Jail and Out."

The masthead listed Tom Mooney as "Directing Editor," Warren K. Billings as "Silent Partner," and Rena Mooney as "Business Manager." As for its credo, Mooney stated it succinctly in the first issue: "I want to make TOM MOONEY'S MONTHLY the most powerful voice of militant labor in the United States." In an accompanying letter, Tom Mooney made it clear that he alone was "responsible for every word in it."

Upon Rena, however, fell most of the burden of bringing the words to print. Tom dictated most of the text to her on visiting days. The paper was then printed in San Francisco. This led to a curious situation. Since prisoners weren't allowed to see California newspapers, Mooney wasn't permitted to view the fruit of his labors. Although aware that this was a unique situation, Warden Johnston wasn't about to grant an exception that could establish a precedent. What is most surprising is that he did nothing to restrict Mooney's visiting privileges, since the paper pulled no punches. In its first issue Mooney demanded that all good union men "blacklist all republican candidates because the republican party in control of the California State administration is responsible for the continued incarceration of Mooney, Billings and other labor prisoners . . ."

Perhaps state officials felt that suppression of the paper would reactivate interest in the case. It seemed unlikely to go beyond a few issues.

Only a portion of the paper dealt with the Mooney case. There were articles on trends in the union movement, exposés of other "frame-ups," an attempt to revive interest in the McNamara and Ford and Suhr cases, attacks on the Klan and the American Legion, an appeal for assistance to the Centralia and Everett prisoners, a plea for support of the general amnesty movement. *Tom Mooney's Monthly* was one of the first newspapers to champion the cause of Nicola Sacco and Bartolomeo Vanzetti. Most Americans—including the intellectuals—wouldn't hear of the plight of the two anarchists for another six years, after all their appeals had failed.

Tom Mooney's Monthly was a direct appeal to the rank and file. And it elicited an amazing response. The initial issue was 20,000 copies, the second issue 45,000. Unions might neglect to pass Mooney resolutions, but apparently their members hadn't forgotten the man in San Quentin. Early issues brought in hundreds of letters, many heavy with misspellings or unlettered expression but each conveying in its own way the sentiment of one laborer who wrote "I liked it awful well." By November Rena was able to tell advertisers "We have the most complete list of radicals, liberals, trade-unions, and union members in the United States." Probably only J. Edgar Hoover could have disputed this claim.

The number of paid subscriptions, however, remained small. And it is probable that despite its initial popularity it might have gone a few issues and then expired had not more sensational developments brought the Mooney case back into national prominence.

3 ·

On September 7, 1920, Peter Vidovich, who had testified to seeing Billings in the hall at 721 Market, died in a charity ward of Bellevue Hospital in New York City, where he had been taken by the Travellers' Aid Society when he claimed to be destitute. It was discovered after his death that he actually had savings of more than $83,000. Only now did the Mooney defense also learn that Vidovich had a criminal record in Alaska, for petit larceny.* Of the state's ten major witnesses in the Mooney-Billings case, Vidovich was, to date, the fifth proven to have a criminal past. Although Mooney, in his newspaper, made much of Vidovich's background and the probable fascination the reward must have held for the miser, Vidovich's testimony had already been substantially discredited of itself, through its inherent contradictions and inconsistencies.

This was minor, however, compared to the confession of detective Draper Hand.

There is some mystery as to how Fremont Older persuaded Draper Hand to talk. Older himself attributed Hand's sudden recantation to pangs of conscience. Considering Hand's character—he was something of a dandy and very much a bully—and particularly his silence while Mooney awaited execution, this appears improbable. Hand had several times been charged with unnecessary brutality and other breaches of departmental regulations. It is possible that Older learned of some wrong-

---

* Denied access to the files of the San Francisco Police Department, the defense was unaware until much later that in the year before his appearance as a witness Vidovich had twice been questioned in child molesting cases, apparently because of a habit of loitering around school grounds and public park restrooms. Neither instance led to a conviction, but they may provide a possible explanation for his coming to the attention of the District Attorney's office.

Cell #155 in the Stones, housing America's most famous prisoner. From this windowless, unventilated headquarters—8' long, 4' wide, and 7' in height—Mooney directed his 22-year campaign for freedom. The photograph on the wall is of Mother Mooney. Legal briefs and correspondence files occupy most of the "extra" space.

Courtesy San Quentin Prison and Kenneth Lamott

doing on Hand's part and used it accordingly. This, at least, is the theory of one of Older's former reporters who, though he still possesses the greatest respect for his one-time editor, notes in a letter to the author "If he felt that the conviction of Mooney and Billings was a fraud, he wouldn't have refrained from promising, bribing, or doing any other single thing, to have justice served."

But talk Hand did, on November 12th.

Draper Hand was a member of the prosecution inner circle. He had been in charge of all prosecution witnesses in the bomb cases. He had personally arrested Weinberg and had been present at many of the interrogations.

Oxman had never seen Weinberg's auto, Hand said, until the night he and Bunner took Oxman and Rigall to North End Station to view it. Oxman had admitted as much to him. While there, Oxman had climbed into the vehicle to see if a man sitting in the front seat could hold a suitcase on the runningboard. He had shown Oxman the license plates at Cuhna's suggestion. Oxman had copied the number on the back of an envelope. Although he couldn't be sure, Hand assumed it was the same envelope later produced in court.

Oxman had, on several occasions, as much as admitted that he was committing perjury, observing that if his statements didn't make sense it was because he was following the program laid out for him by Martin Swanson.

One of his duties, Hand stated, had been to rehearse the witnesses in their testimony and to work out, with Swanson, Fickert, and Cuhna, any discrepancies. (This coincided with earlier statements by Mrs. Kidwell, Rigall, and Estelle Smith.) Both the Edeaus had admitted to him that they knew nothing about the case, as a result of which both had to be more carefully coached than the others.

Following the trials, Hand said, McDonald had approached him with the information that he was broke and that "Unless I get a job I am going to spill everything I know to Fremont Older." Hand told Fickert and a job was found for McDonald in Tracy, California.

There was more than a bit of the theatrical in Older. After obtaining Hand's signed statement, he sent "Scoop" Gleeson to bring Mayor Rolph to the editor's office. Gleeson told the Mayor that Older had a surprise for him; he didn't reveal its nature. "Sunny Jim" entered grinning. As Gleeson closed the door behind the man who had "a constitutional antipathy for nasty messes," Hand, one of San Francisco's finest, began his recital. The famous smile froze. When Hand finished, the red-faced Mayor bolted from the room without a word. For nine years he wouldn't speak to Older.

But it gave Older the headline he wanted—MOONEY FRAME-UP

BARED TO ROLPH—and the *Call* put out an extra edition that afternoon.

It brought unexpected results.

Estelle Smith, who had disappeared from sight along with most of the other witnesses following the Weinberg trial, to reappear only occasionally when a house or massage parlor was raided, now materialized with a statement that she was no longer sure that the man on the roof was Billings. This was a less than startling disclosure, but the following day Fickert's former assistant James Brennan called on Fremont Older. He also wanted to make a statement.

Brennan, now a candidate for the state legislature, perhaps felt it advantageous to clarify his role in the Mooney-Billings case.

"If Hand admitted the witnesses were framed it was probably a fact," Brennan told Older. "I took the witnesses the police department furnished and tried to make a case against Billings." He now told Older (as recounted earlier) why he had requested life imprisonment rather than the death sentence for Billings. Though he claimed to know nothing of the actual frame-up details, he did know that he had disbelieved his own witnesses. "Had I been a juror sitting in the case and heard the evidence which I myself presented," Brennan stated, "I could not and would not have voted for Billings' conviction. There was the element of doubt. There was wanting the final link in the chain forging Billings to the crime."

One part of Brennan's statement bears full quotation:

"Like all prosecutors," Brennan said, "I was blind to all but the pursuit—the chase which would end with the conviction of my quarry.

"I was cursed with the psychology of the prosecution. To my mind, and it is in the mind of every district attorney and his assistants, conviction is the only goal.

"Unconsciously, and with no wrong intent, the prosecutor retains the facts which further his case. Others, perhaps vital to the proof of innocence of the accused, are cast aside. He is a keen-scented hound on a trail. He has become obsessed with his case. Given the slightest evidence supporting his theories, which he has already framed in his own mind, he weaves these into a web of circumstances which are ofttimes damning to the accused, and against which even the innocent may not be able to stand."

Fremont Older had another scoop, and as he later stated, it only cost the *Call* several of its largest advertisers.

On the other side of the continent, another man read a newspaper account of Draper Hand's confession. He was so disturbed by it that he wrote Duncan Matheson a letter.

21· The Forgotten Man

"I GUESS YOU will be surprised to hear from me," John McDonald wrote Captain Matheson from Trenton, New Jersey, on January 11, 1921. "Well, Captain, what is all the fuss about Mooney again? I just seen a little piece of paper. It said that Draper Hand told Mayor Rolph that he knew it was a frame-up.

"Has Hand gone crazy. I will say if I was on my death bed and the last words from me, would be that he is guilty, and that what I swore to was nothing but the truth . . ."

Within a month, John McDonald would confess that he had committed perjury.

McDonald's reappearance ended months of tantalizing frustration. McDonald had disappeared shortly after the last of the trials. An investigator from the Chicago Federation of Labor finally located him in a Baltimore hospital, and on instructions from Nockles and Fitzpatrick, won his confidence. Professing ignorance of the San Francisco cases, he listened as McDonald told him about them. At first it was only the "official" story. Gradually, however, as their friendship ripened, McDonald confessed everything. His new friend tried to persuade McDonald to "come clean," arguing that the true story was bound to come out someday and that it would go better for him if he confessed first. McDonald seemed convinced. But, on his release from the hospital, he again disappeared. By itself, the investigator's report of the confession was worthless.

Aware that the defense had been searching for McDonald, Matheson showed the letter to Older. The Chicago investigator, an Eastern reporter representing the *Call*, and Robert Minor located McDonald in a hotel in Trenton, where he was working as a waiter. They found a frightened but uncommunicative man. Shown Brennan's statement, he appeared even more fearful. On their second visit he was gone.

The following day he appeared at Bourke Cockran's office at New York City, where he said he wished to make a statement of his part in the Mooney case. Cockran was in California. His secretary, ignorant of earlier developments, suggested that he contact Frank P. Walsh, now active in

282

the Mooney defense.

Several days passed. Meanwhile, Minor and the others, learning of McDonald's appearance in Cockran's office, were afraid that he had changed his mind and this time disappeared for good. But on February 7th he suddenly appeared in Walsh's office.

There was no bargaining. Walsh said he could pay McDonald nothing other than expenses to California and back. He did promise him, however, that he would arrange for immunity in return for his testimony before the Grand Jury.

McDonald dictated a detailed statement.

He told of having seen two men with a suitcase at Steuart and Market and of going to the police with his story. When he tried to describe the two men, District Attorney Fickert replied that they were of no interest to him: "Tom Mooney is the son of a bitch we want." Whereupon Fickert had described Mooney and Billings in detail. Over the next several days, Fickert, Swanson, Hand and others had worked on him to make adjustments in his descriptions. Following the arrests, he had been taken to Mooney's cell to see him. En route back to the D.A.'s office, Fickert had said "Well, you saw Mooney; that is undoubtedly the man; isn't it?"

In words similar to those used by Estelle in her second confession, McDonald quoted Fickert to the effect that his testimony was only corroborative, that the prosecution already possessed sufficient proof of the guilt of the men in question. Like Estelle, McDonald justified his perjury. He had been ill, just out of the hospital after a serious operation, frightened by Swanson's threat to imprison him for concealing evidence. Fickert had arranged his move to the Alpine Hotel at state's expense; had given him money for meals and entertainment; and had told him, "Now there is a reward of $17,500 for the conviction of these people, and when I put them away I will see that you get the biggest slice."

Finally, just before the Grand Jury met, McDonald had weakened. Fickert himself had coached him as to his testimony.

But even then they weren't satisfied. They had kept after him to identify Rena Mooney, Nolan, and Weinberg also, and to claim that he had seen them step out of Weinberg's auto. McDonald had refused.

Shortly before the Mooney trial, Fickert told him not to worry about his testimony, that they now had a man worth over $100,000 who would back up anything he said. McDonald asked how this was possible if the man didn't know what he was going to say. Fickert told him not to worry about it. That day he met Frank Oxman for the first time.

Just before McDonald was to take the stand in the Mooney trial, Cuhna had taken him into a private room and instructed him "You had better make the time that you saw the man set the suitcase at 1:30 instead of 1:50." McDonald didn't know about the Eilers photos, but guessed there was some good reason for the time change. He had tried, but Cockran had caught him in the attempt; fearing that he might be tried for perjury, McDonald had stuck to his earlier statement.

Before the Rena Mooney trial, Cuhna had said the defense was going to ask him if he had seen an auto at Steuart and Market and he was to answer "Yes, I think I did. I think it was a Ford." The question was asked, but he didn't answer as instructed. When he left the stand Cuhna angrily demanded "Why in the hell didn't you tell them you saw a machine? It would have been all right."

From July 1916 to October 1919, the prosecution had paid all his living expenses. Although often promised a share of the reward, he hadn't received any sizable amounts. When he needed pocket money he was given $10 or $20, either by Fickert or an assistant, or by the secretary in the office of Frank Drew, attorney for the Chamber of Commerce.

After the trials, when the stipends stopped, he had threatened to go to Fremont Older and tell the truth, unless given a job, and a job had been found for him in Tracy. Eventually, when the reward money failed to materialize, he had worked his way back East.

McDonald told everything, though one item was omitted from his formal recantation. He was not, as the defense had long contended, a "dope addict." The several stomach operations and his sometimes jerky movements were the result of cerebro-spinal syphilis, which he insisted had finally been arrested in 1916.

"I am thoroughly satisfied that McDonald has finally told the whole truth in the matter," Walsh wrote to Older in sending him a copy of McDonald's statement, "and it would seem incredible that the Governor could longer refuse a pardon of the defendants."

McDonald was returned to California to testify. The Grand Jury refused to grant him the customary immunity. The defense, bound by Walsh's promise, could do nothing. McDonald returned to the East.

On May 2, 1921, Mooney's lawyers applied to Superior Court Judge Louderback to vacate the judgment against Mooney by a common law writ *audita querela,* or a writ in the nature thereof. This was an old English common law remedy, originated in 1337 in the reign of Edward III to gain the release of an imprisoned bishop. It had never been used in California. Ground for the motion was that the District Attorney and other persons had engaged in a conspiracy to pervert justice. The Oxman-Rigall letters, the Smith, Kidwell, and McDonald affidavits were submitted as evidence. On May 27th, Judge Louderback denied the motion saying that the writ sought was not available under the law of California. He noted, however, that "had there existed a condition whereby the Court could have tried this issue upon its merits, the application would have been granted."

Mooney, with no illusions of success, again applied to Governor Stephens for a pardon.

2 ·

In 1917, shortly after Older published the Rigall letters, a group of *Bulletin* reporters were sitting in a newspaper hangout drinking and discussing the case. Why, they wondered, had Oxman risked criminal charges to obtain verification of his story?

"What," one suddenly asked, "what if Oxman wasn't even in San Francisco at the time?"

It was such a logical explanation that they had overlooked it. Hadn't Oxman told Rigall, "Well, you was here as much as I was"?

With Older's enthusiastic permission, they pursued this new hypothesis.

During the Mooney trial Oxman had testified that he came to San Francisco by train from Portland. The defense had already investigated this. A train from Oregon had arrived at about the time he stated. When shown pictures of Oxman, several of the train's crew thought they recalled him getting on in Portland. One, however, believed he had gotten off at some point before Sacramento, but couldn't be sure. The questioning took place nearly 10 months after the incident. Any recollections so old were suspect. It was impossible to check out each town along the line.

At the time Oxman first testified there were rumors that he had been seen in several other places on July 22nd. Each of these had been checked out but without success. One, Woodland, in Yolo County, north of Sacramento, was on the route from Oregon. Older suggested that they check it again, more carefully this time.

Defense attorney McKenzie and a *Bulletin* reporter (who for reasons which will become apparent must go unidentified here) made the trip.

On the Byrns Hotel register for July 22, 1916, the day's first entry was "F. C. Oxman, Portland."

The clerk remembered Oxman; he had stayed there several times previously, but hadn't been back. As best he could remember, Oxman had checked in about 7:30 that morning, breakfasted in the hotel, and then left, without using his room.

This was little help. Woodland to San Francisco was three hours by train—sufficient time to reach the city before the parade.

Then they heard a rumor. One of the people questioned recalled that a woman in the telegraph office had gossiped to friends at the time of the Mooney trial that Oxman couldn't be telling the truth because he had received a telegram in Woodland about noon that day.

They found the woman. Afraid of losing her job for her indiscretion, she refused to talk.

The telegraph records could be subpoenaed, but there was no proof, beyond gossip, that the telegram existed.

There was another young lady in the telegraph office. The reporter, though a family man, was on the trail of what could prove to be a sensational story. The courtship was brief and torrid; a few nights later he was in the telegraph office reading the office copy of the telegram. The text, relating to cattle business, was uninformative; what was important was a penciled notation that after attempting to locate Oxman at the Byrns Hotel, the messenger had been sent to the residence of Earl Hatcher, where the wire was delivered at 12 noon. Unfortunately, Hatcher, not Oxman, had signed for it.

In one of those coincidences abounding in the Mooney case, the reporter's undercover work proved unnecessary. At about this same time, an attorney who had done some business with Earl Hatcher told Fremont Older in confidence of Hatcher's admission to him that Oxman was in Woodland, not San Francisco, at the time of the bombing. The attorney's statement, in itself a breach of ethics, wasn't admissible evidence, but it did indicate the next step: to get Hatcher to talk.

Earl Hatcher proved uncooperative. He admitted to knowing Oxman and to sometimes selling him cattle and sheep, but would make no further statement.

This investigation had taken place between Oxman's appearance before the Grand Jury in April 1917 and his trial for attempted subornation of perjury that September. During the latter event, Hatcher had appeared as a defense witness to testify that Oxman had been in Woodland on the 22nd, but that he had caught the 9:08 train for San Francisco.

Older felt sure that Hatcher was lying. For the next four years he worked on both him and his wife, attempting to persuade them to tell the truth. Then, shortly after the McDonald confession, which for a time appeared to reopen the case, the Hatchers contacted Older. They now wanted to tell the truth.

Their story was simple.

Oxman had arrived in Woodland on the morning of July 22nd on the overnight train from Portland and had called Hatcher at about 7:30 A.M., shortly after checking into the hotel. At about 9 they had gone out to look at some stock Hatcher wanted to sell. Since it was nearly noon when they finished, Mrs. Hatcher had prepared lunch for them at the Hatcher home. After lunch, Oxman had taken a nap on the couch. Earl Hatcher had awakened him shortly before 2 and walked with him to the train station where Oxman caught the 2:15 for San Francisco. It arrived in the city at 5:25 P.M.

Nine minutes after the Preparedness Day bomb exploded, Frank C. Oxman was boarding a train 90 miles away.

Only two witnesses had placed Mooney and Billings at the scene of the bombing: John McDonald and Frank C. Oxman. There was now no evidence whatever linking Mooney and Billings to the explosion.

According to Hatcher, at the time of the Rigall disclosures Oxman had called on him and said, "Earl, I believe they are going to put the old man in the pen unless you stand by me." Hatcher, who valued Oxman's friendship, and perhaps even more his business, had agreed to testify that Oxman left Woodland at 9:08.

Older had another scoop.

In May of 1921 both the Hatchers appeared before the San Francisco Grand Jury and told their stories. That body, faced with two contradictory statements by Earl Hatcher, preferred to believe his 1917 testimony and voted not to return an indictment.

3 ·

In June 1921, John Mooney, on his way to the AFL convention in Denver, stopped off at Folsom Prison and asked to see Warren K. Billings. Denied permission, he was told that Billings was not allowed to see visitors. John Mooney was well aware of this: the purpose of his visit had been to make the denial official. In Denver he appeared before the convention, telling the delegates that for nearly four years Warren Billings had been held incommunicado at Folsom, allowed to see or correspond with no one except his attorney and then only after obtaining special permission from the State Board of Prison Directors. During all this time he had been assigned to hard labor, on the prison rock pile, and denied most of the privileges accorded other prisoners.

For many delegates the name "Warren Billings" must have been a faint echo from the past. For years it had been simply the "Mooney case."

Upon a unanimous vote, the AFL Executive Council wired Governor Stephens demanding that Warren Billings be accorded equal treatment with other prisoners, including visiting and mailing privileges.

In August Billings received his first visitor since leaving San Francisco County Jail, a reporter for the *Call*.

The reporter had expected "the forgotten man in the Mooney case" to be a colorless drab, worn old before his time, spiritless and embittered by confinement. Instead, although he had just turned twenty-eight, prisoner #10966 looked a freckled, boyish twenty. He had a sharp, clear mind, an overabundance of animated enthusiasm, and a quick wit.

Being in Folsom had its advantages, Billings told him. Startled, the reporter stared at him as if he were mad.

"In prison I accomplish more than I would outside, I study here, law, Latin, English, Spanish, composition. I have more to do than I have time."

Lockup at Folsom was at 4 or 4:30, depending on the season; taps at 9; this gave him at least four hours a day to study. "Outside the poor working stiff falls into his bed after work, too tired to read, too tired to want to read."

"But the man outside is constructive in his work," the reporter interrupted.

"So am I," Billings laughed. "I work on roads . . ."

No, he had no bitterness over Mooney's place in the spotlight. As the Mediation Commission put it, "Mooney is the center of the case; the other defendants have significance only because of relation to him." If the utility companies hadn't been out to get Mooney he wouldn't have been arrested.

The next day Rena visited him, their first meeting since the trials. They talked for three hours. After this they corresponded frequently. "Of course, I knew that you hadn't forgotten me and that you had always been working in my behalf as well as Tom's," Billings wrote shortly after her visit, "but you might realize that I am not one to be contented with even the efforts of every one of my friends as long as I myself am doing nothing." It was apparent that Warren K. Billings now intended to exercise a voice in the defense.

The contrasts between the leading actors in the Mooney-Billings drama were sharp.

Mooney was a loner, with few close friends; Billings got along with almost everyone, from the newest "fish" to the prison's oldest resident, "Indian Dick," transferred to Folsom when it opened in 1878 after having spent an unremembered number of years in San Quentin, for scalping six Chinese.

Mooney avoided entanglement with the IWW's, allegedly because he felt that word of such associations would prejudice his case. Inconsistently, or rather with a consistency that was Mooney's own, his closest friends were Los Angeles *Times*' dynamiters J. B. McNamara and Matt Schmidt, for whom he had battled as secretary of the IWDL.* Billings, who unlike Mooney had never been an IWW, associated mostly with the Wobblies. Jimmy Price, Blackie Ford, and Dick Suhr, of the Wheatland hop case, worked with him in the stoneyard, where in their rest periods they leveled some land, put down topsoil, and made a garden in the midst of the bleakness.

* The youngest brother, J. J. McNamara, was released from San Quentin on May 10, 1921, after serving his full sentence. J. B. McNamara and Schmidt, like Mooney, were lifers.

Courtesy California State Department of Corrections

Folsom Prison, home of Warren Billings from age 23 to 46. The first years were spent in the quarries in the foreground, breaking rock used to build the walls that enclosed him.

Mooney subscribed only to those newspapers that he felt had given the case fair coverage. Billings, now allowed mailing privileges, subscribed to *The New York Times,* the *Philadelphia Public Ledger,* and the Chicago *Tribune,* to get balanced coverage.

Mooney almost religiously obeyed the rules. "If I ever get out of here" Billings frankly told an interviewer "it will not be because of good conduct marks but because I never deserved to be here."

Still, Billings was rated a "first class" prisoner. His crew of five in the stoneyard, known as "Billings' gang," was considered one of the prison's best work crews, for they were always busy. "To tell the truth," Billings admitted some years later, "we had a system." One man was assigned to watch the guard. When he turned their way they worked, hard; when he turned away they stopped.

Mooney was never "one of the prisoners" at San Quentin. Kenneth

Lamott observes "Prison generates a hostility to a noted prisoner, one who stands outside the accepted way of doing things. The innocent man, the political prisoner, the 'frame-up' victim, etc., are distrusted, looked on as 'squares.' They are outside the criminal society." Billings, however, was "one of the boys."

Over the years several people commented on an odd phenomena. Most of the prisoners at San Quentin assumed that Mooney, for all his protestations, was guilty. Although he rarely discussed his own case, the convicts at Folsom *knew* that Billings was innocent.*

His spirit seemed unbreakable. But then, as he observed some years later, "When I first went back to Folsom, I felt reasonably sure that I would have a good opportunity of securing justice in the next few years. I didn't have any conception of how long it would take, but I couldn't see why an innocent man should expect to be kept in jail for any length of time."

4 ·

On December 23rd, 1921, Rena jubilantly wrote Billings: "Debs is free at last and I almost grabbed the paper out of the hands of the first man I saw in the street with one tonight. One more victory to the credit of labor."

The movement to declare a general amnesty for all political and labor prisoners—supported by the IWW General Defense, the Socialist Party, and the National Civil Liberties Union—had started even before the end of the war, but it was not until the end of Warren Gamaliel Harding's first year in office that he granted amnesty to Debs and 23 others. Mooney and Billings were not among them. But Debs' release brightened their sixth Christmas behind bars.

Eugene Debs was sixty-six, his health broken.

"My dear Tom," Mooney's old hero wrote him. "I have thought of you a thousand times, you who have been more brutally maltreated and who have been compelled to suffer more than any of us.

"I am sure that I need not tell you that my heart is still in prison and will be there until the last, the very last of the political prisoners and the class war prisoners is liberated. It will be some time before my physical condition will allow me to take the platform but meanwhile I shall do what I can with my pen and in every other way I know to increase the agitation and to augment the demand and pressure for your release and

---

* Mooney was so addicted to the use of the phrase "But I'm innocent," that one day, during a visiting period, J. B. McNamara in exasperation commented, "Thank God I'm not."

that of Billings as well as all others who are in prison serving the working class . . ."

It was a long letter. Debs recalled with awe all they had been through since their days of campaigning together.

"How my heart has ached for your dear Rena and for Billings and his dear ones . . . You and I have had our trials, but we also have had our blessings. We have the noblest of wives, who have passed through the fire with us or rather for us without ever wavering for a moment in their loyal devotions and their tender ministrations . . .

"I am not saying good cheer to you, dear Tom! You do not need it for you are winning every day and your day of liberation and complete victory is drawing near . . ."

Debs would not live to see it.

22· The Mooney-Billings Split

By MID-1922, when Governor Stephens announced his candidacy for reelection, more than a dozen labor delegations had called on him demanding the release of Mooney and Billings. The judge who tried Mooney (Griffin), Billings' prosecutor (Brennan), the current District Attorney of San Francisco (Brady)—all had written strong letters to the Governor, urging either a new trial or release.

In addition, new evidence had come to light.

Richard W. Smith, the policeman who had spoken to the Mooneys on the Eilers roof shortly after the bombing, was finally located. Throughout the trials the defense had attempted to learn his identity, without success. The prosecution had implied he didn't exist. Smith now admitted that Fickert had suppressed his testimony.

In July 1922 Mrs. Carrie MacNevin sued her husband for divorce. William MacNevin had been foreman of Tom Mooney's jury. To the surprise of the Mooney defense, Mrs. MacNevin filed an affidavit stating that her husband and prosecutor Edward Cuhna had been acquainted before the Mooney trial and that they had met almost nightly during the trial to discuss the effect of particular testimony on the jurors. MacNevin had offered suggestions as to how certain jurors could best be reached; Cuhna had told MacNevin stories about Mooney's past dynamiting activities, which though inadmissible as evidence, were introduced informally by MacNevin into conversations with the other jurors. After the trial, Mrs. MacNevin charged, her husband had bragged that he was responsible for Mooney's conviction and that he had made a number of powerful business contacts as a result.

The last place one might expect to find truth is in a divorce action. But a substantial part of Mrs. MacNevin's story was later corroborated by her brother and an attorney present at several of the secret meetings. Checking further, the defense discovered that prior to the Mooney trial MacNevin had been removed from the Real Estate Board because of an alleged fraud; after the trial he was reinstated.

Despite labor pressure, Stephens declined to act on the Mooney pardon appeal. With Stephens' announcement of his candidacy for reelection,

Mooney, against the pleas of his advisors, decided to throw his support behind Stephens' chief opponent in the August Republican primary, Friend W. Richardson.

Mooney's logic was simple. The Democratic candidate couldn't win, and Stephens, by past performance, had proven he had no intention of acting favorably on the pardon petition. With Richardson, there was at least a chance.

That it was a remarkably slim chance seemed clear to almost everyone except Tom Mooney. Friend William Richardson, a newspaper publisher and former state treasurer, was leader of the conservative wing of the state Republican Party. He was known to be hard-boiled on penal matters and an advocate of capital punishment. Since Stephens during his term of office had urged an increase in corporation taxes, most of Mooney's professed enemies were now backing Richardson, who had vowed to end the Johnson-Stephens Progressive regime in California.

"Mooney has sold out," organized labor charged. "Tom Mooney is only interested in one thing—Tom Mooney." Some of Mooney's most fervent partisans dropped off the defense committee.

It was difficult to evaluate the power of *Tom Mooney's Monthly*. That it was reaching the rank and file there was no question. By August 1922, more than 500,000 copies of the paper had been printed, but even this wasn't an accurate gauge of its influence, as in each issue Mooney urged "At least 10 different workers should read this paper—Keep it in continuous circulation." Its effect in the election was an unknown factor.

It was a strange election. Richardson's candidacy, observed the San Francisco *Examiner,* was supported by Catholic priests and the Ku Klux Klan, by the reactionary Better America Foundation and Oakland laborites, by San Francisco saloon tycoon Gus Olivia and the Anti-Saloon League, and by the Los Angeles *Times* and *Tom Mooney's Monthly*.

Stephens ran on both the Republican and Prohibitionist tickets, Richardson on the Republican ticket alone. Richardson won the Republican nomination by a large majority; Stephens won the Prohibitionist, but duplicating Rolph's feat of 1918, was disqualified because he had failed to carry his own party. In November, Richardson defeated his Democratic opponent by a sizable margin.

Tom Mooney had the satisfaction of knowing he had backed a winner. He began work on a new pardon petition.

Shortly before Stephens left office Older appealed to him to act in the Mooney case, but this was one of the problems Stephens was apparently only too glad to bequeath to his successor.

2 ·

As prisoners, Mooney and Billings were allowed no direct correspondence. In 1922, with Rena Mooney acting as intermediary, the two reached an agreement regarding disposition of their cases. Billings agreed to let Mooney press his pardon petition first; successful or unsuccessful, Billings would follow suit. There were several good reasons for this course, the most important that Mooney's petition could be granted directly by the Governor while Billings, a second offender, by law had to have approval of both the Governor and the State Supreme Court. Billings asked only that he be kept informed on developments.

He was patient and his requests were few. The Mooney defense put money in his prison account so he could buy the few purchasables available from commissary stores: tobacco (Duke's Mixture), soap, and towels. Allowed to correspond, he could now order certain items from outside. In January 1922 he wrote to Rena asking her to buy him a first baseman's glove. Baseball was not only good exercise, he explained, but one of the best ways to keep warm on cold days in the yard. His request was urgent. Every race or faction in the prison had its own team. He was organizer and manager of the "Wobblies," who had a big game coming up against the "Jews." There followed detailed instructions on how to differentiate a first baseman's mitt from others.

Rena found the correct glove, and the warden let him have it in time for the game.

"The Wobblies beat the Jews 14–12," Billings wrote in thanks.

"Outside of that everything is much the same and I am still working in the stone-yard. Just now I am cutting part of a memorial monument to be set up in San Rafael in honor of the heroes of the World War and it is a rather particular job."

Much of Rena's time was spent on the road, speaking before various labor groups. In her stead, she sent a young girl from the defense committee to see Billings.

Her appearance shocked him. She wears too much lipstick, he complained to Rena. "You see—I've been away so long that the 'modern flapper' is about as strange to me as a factory girl would be to the Prince of Wales. Stranger probably."

In his next letter he asked for various legal papers, suggesting, casually, that if Rena was busy, perhaps the same girl could bring them.

Warren Billings' interest in the outside world was returning. Now, whenever a whole month passed without a letter or visit from Rena, he would fire off a polite but peppery: "What if anything is going on in regard to the case—outside of routine work ?''

That Rena sometimes failed to answer such questions was probably due as much to a reluctance to admit the truth to herself as to hide it from Billings.

In March 1923 no issue of *Tom Mooney's Monthly* appeared. When the April issue came out in May, it was cut to four pages. Although Rena finally notified subscribers that the paper had been "temporarily suspended" in order that all available time and funds could be devoted to the preparation of Mooney's pardon appeal, no further issues appeared. *Tom Mooney's Monthly* had lasted two years and nine months; 581,500 copies had been distributed. Its demise was due less to labor's irritation over Mooney's support of Richardson than to a near complete absence of contributions to the defense. What Rena didn't admit to Billings was that by 1923 the Tom Mooney Molders' Defense Committee was only a shell, manned by relatives and a few close friends. For support, it was almost totally dependent on organized labor, i.e., the AFL. And that support was not forthcoming.

A whole generation of radicals, for whom the Mooney case was the class struggle personified, had passed from the American scene.

John Reed was dead, entombed in the walls of the Kremlin. Emma Goldman and Alexander Berkman were displaced persons, wandering Europe in search of a country. On arriving in Russia and discovering that the Bolsheviks had imprisoned most of the anarchists, the aging lovers had been among the first of the American radicals to proclaim the betrayal of the revolution. In 1921, "Big Bill" Haywood, released on bond pending appeal of his 20-year sentence, had skipped bail and fled to Russia, to the shame of his IWW comrades who remained behind to serve out their time.

Fremont Older remained committed. In Chicago, "Big Ed" Nockles continued to raise as much money and interest as he could: often his checks made the difference between whether Rena did or did not eat. And Debs, although in rapidly failing health, embarked on a lecture tour, rarely failing to mention his imprisoned comrades Mooney and Billings, and Sacco and Vanzetti. On March 1, 1923, Bourke Cockran died, following a party to celebrate his sixty-ninth birthday. Several weeks earlier, acting on a premonition, he had set his estate in order. Calling Frank P. Walsh to his office, he had asked him to take over as Mooney's attorney if need be.

To Walsh the Mooney case had long been a "cause." He wrote Mooney: "Your case is the one thing pending in America which makes my blood boil every time I think of it. It is absolutely incomprehensible how any such thing could take place in America—any place."

Mooney had a plan. He would make his pardon petition to Governor

Richardson so formidable a document that the Governor could not possibly refuse it. It would include notarized copies of all the trial transcripts, the recantations, the perjury evidence. As important, Mooney wanted to obtain letters from everyone connected with the case, asking for his release. "The average man does not care what I say about my conviction," he wrote Walsh, "but he will sit up and take notice when the Judge, Jury, Police and Prosecutor say that we were unjustly convicted . . ."

Ten of his 12 jurors were still living. In September he wrote to each, enclosing a copy of Judge Griffin's letters to Governor Stephens, asking that in light of new evidence uncovered since the trial they write to Governor Richardson requesting his pardon. Two replied immediately with the requested letters. Mooney now began working earnestly on the other eight.

That September the International Molders' Union, meeting in convention at Cleveland, in a show of faith voted Tom Mooney a delegate to the AFL convention the following month.

The AFL convention, in Portland, was less satisfactory. Replying to a request for financial support for the Mooney defense, California labor leader Paul Scharrenberg took the floor and charged that although thousands of dollars had been collected for Mooney and Billings, no public accounting of these funds had ever been made. This wasn't true, Rena hotly answered. A detailed financial statement had been issued in January 1918, accounting for every penny collected to that date.* Since then, financial statements had been issued once a month.

The background of the charges regarding the Mooney finances and Scharrenberg's "betrayal," as Mooney would characterize it, were complex. But basically they arose from Mooney's distrust of the California AFL leaders and his stubborn insistence on running his own defense, even from San Quentin. Earlier, some officers of the State Federation had approached Mooney with a plan to take over the Mooney defense. This way agitation in his behalf could be timed not to conflict with other labor demands. Mooney refused to consider the idea, fearing indefinite sidetracking.

As for finances, Mooney could point to the Seattle committee as evidence of what could happen when fund raising was not tightly controlled by one body. Scharrenberg and the others, however, pointed to it as

---

* The following is a summary of the financial statement of the International Workers' Defense League, August 1916–January 1918:

Income:		Expenses:	
Donations	$97,745.52	Legal account	$58,984.56
Book Sales	10,480.09	Publicity	27,660.03
Total	$108,225.61	Organization	19,115.55
			$105,760.14
		Balance on hand	$2,465.47

evidence of their charge—although an AFL group, and not the IWDL or TMMDC, was responsible.

Too, there were some expenses that Mooney did not want to justify publicly. Over the years a considerable amount had been spent tracking down leads to the real perpetrators of the bombing. Many labor leaders opposed this course of action, feeling it might prove to be a Pandora's Box.

To some, Tom Mooney's insistence on managing his own defense committee meant he was "power mad"; others, fewer in number, saw him simply as a man unwilling to release his fate into the hands of men he distrusted.

Over the protests of some of the California delegates, the AFL convention voted to beseech Governor Richardson to pardon Mooney and Billings. But no funds were voted for the defense.

3 ·

Tom Mooney to Judge Griffin, January 13, 1924:

"I have suffered imprisonment for the past seven and a half years with as much fortitude as any man could under the same circumstances. The new Governor has been in office for one year. I have tried to be patient . . ."

Warren Billings to Rena Mooney, same date:

"I have a Swede girl in Minnesota, a German girl in San Mateo, two German Jew girls in Boston and numerous others of doubtful age all over the country on my correspondence list . . ."

Captain Matheson to Tom Mooney, January 25, 1924:

"I am convinced beyond any question of doubt that your rights were violated and that you were entitled to a new trial . . ."

Sergeant Goff to Tom Mooney, April 12, 1924:

"With the two vital witnesses [Oxman and McDonald] discredited I think the only fair thing to do is to state that I do not think you had a fair and impartial trial as guaranteed by the Constitution."

4 ·

In the spring of 1924 Rena Mooney disappeared. Only Tom, Belle, and Fremont Older knew her whereabouts. Using an assumed name and changing her appearance slightly, Rena got a job as a schoolteacher in Baker, Oregon. For more than three months she collected information regarding the background and habits of Frank C. Oxman. As an investigator, she proved far more talented than those hired by the defense. She learned, for example, that Oxman had married his first wife, Katie O'Bryan, on April 24, 1880, and his second wife, Clara M. Warrick, on April 19, 1904—but that not until January 17, 1910 had he bothered to obtain a divorce from Katie.

She discovered that he had fathered an illegitimate child by his Mexican serving girl.

More relevant to the Mooney case, she found that Oxman had committed perjury in a trial prior to Mooney's. In August 1914, one John Spain had brought suit against the Oregon, Washington Railroad and Navigation Company, asking damages for unlawful ejection from one of the company trains. Frank C. Oxman had come forward as a witness for the railroad, stating that he had seen Spain drinking a bottle of liquor on the train. To lend support to his story, Oxman had offered to produce his traveling companion as witness—one Edward Rigall of Grayville, Illinois.* The railroad decided that Rigall's testimony wouldn't be worth the expense of bringing him to Oregon. Oxman did so testify in two trials, but the jury, choosing to believe Spain, had awarded him damages.

By the time Rena returned to San Francisco she had more than a dozen affidavits regarding Oxman's character ("I would not believe Oxman under oath . . ." "I know his reputation for truth to be bad . . ." "I would doubt his word in any business transaction . . ."). There was also some evidence that "the honest cattleman," who at the Mooney trial so memorably evoked the vanishing West, had added to the size of his herds by a little brand changing.

Shortly after this, Mooney obtained an affidavit that totally discredited Frank C. Oxman. It came after eight years of frustrated effort.

When Fickert appeared before the Grand Jury during the Oxman proceedings of 1917, he had been asked how Oxman was obtained as a witness. He stated that he had heard from two different men that Oxman had told them of seeing the bombers. These men were Frank Woods, the station agent at Durkee, Oregon, and William Hough, secretary of the Western Meat Company, who had done some business with Oxman. Hough's company was represented on the Law and Order Committee, and Hough himself was a close friend of Drew, the Chamber of Commerce attorney. Although Fickert didn't admit as much, the defense assumed it was Drew who had brought Hough's statement about Oxman to Fickert's attention.

According to Fickert, when he first attempted to contact Oxman, he learned that he was in Kansas City on business. Instead of sending Cuhna or Swanson, Fickert had employed the William J. Burns Detective Agency to interview Oxman there and on October 26, 1916, Oxman made a short statement to a Burns operative.

* Rigall denied ever having been in Oregon.

All this the defense had known since 1917, but every effort to obtain a copy of Oxman's original statement from either Fickert, Cuhna, or the Burns Agency had failed.

This affidavit was important for two reasons. If it differed significantly from Oxman's testimony in the Mooney case it would indicate that he had committed perjury. Secondly, if such was the case, it would prove that Fickert had known Oxman was perjuring himself.

Since the statement had been made *after* the Billings trial, which received wide coverage in the press, the defense assumed that many of the details would be correct. But, as Mooney wrote Matheson early in 1924, Fickert's "studied effort to keep it from us for these past seven years is the very best proof that it is in our favor."

In 1923 a Burns operative offered to pilfer the statement from the files of the Kansas City office for $2500; as proof that the statement existed, he quoted several lines from it. But Mooney had angrily turned down the offer, declaring that the defense could neither afford nor would buy testimony. In August 1924, one of Mooney's New York attorneys, who was owed a favor by a Kansas City attorney, who was owed a favor by someone in the Burns office, succeeded in obtaining a copy.*

It was everything the defense had anticipated, and more.

In the Mooney trial Oxman stated he came to San Francisco from Portland; in the affidavit it was Willows, California; in reality, as the Hatcher testimony had already established, it was Woodland.

In the Mooney trial the suitcase was on the runningboard of the vehicle; in the affidavit it was in the back seat.

In the Mooney trial Mooney, Billings, and the Russian Jew had all left the vehicle and stood together on the corner talking; in the affidavit Mooney remained in the car with his wife.

In the Mooney trial Mooney had said to Billings, "Give it to him and let him go; we must get away from here; the bulls will be after us"; in the affidavit "I noticed them talking in a foreign language, and I could not understand what was said."

In the Mooney trial Oxman, unable to get into a restaurant, had bought some fruit at the stand on the southeast corner of Steuart and Market and was eating it when the car pulled up; in the affidavit there was no mention of the fruit stand, and Oxman went to a restaurant.

In the Mooney trial Oxman said that after these people left the scene he had gone to his hotel to await a telephone call, arriving there about 1:45; in the affidavit he went to a restaurant, had lunch, and was just paying his check when he heard the explosion.

Before the Grand Jury Oxman testified that when he made his original

* Not until 1936, however, did the defense succeed in obtaining a notarized copy. By this time it was too late to use it against Oxman.

affidavit he did not know the names of any of the people he saw and that he had not seen any of the newspaper stories concerning the Billings trial; in his affidavit he used proper names throughout.

In his affidavit Oxman described Mooney as sandy-haired, medium height and build, light complexion, with blue eyes (observed from 25 feet away, while Mooney was sitting in the car). This description may have fit many men, but Tom Mooney wasn't one of them.

Interestingly enough, nowhere in his affidavit did Oxman mention the parade. He crossed Market, back and forth, with apparent ease, as if the parade hadn't yet started or had already passed by.

Not one statement in the affidavit held up under careful inspection.

Oxman had perjured himself. And Fickert had known it from the start.

5 ·

Following his defeat in 1919, Charles M. Fickert had moved to Los Angeles and entered private practice. He was not successful. In 1921 there had been a rumor that the Governor might appoint him to a state job. Following a host of labor complaints, that rumor died. There was now talk that Fickert was considering a political comeback. That the Mooney case played some part in his plans was evident. Warren Billings wrote to Lena Morrow Lewis: *

"Fickert has been here 4 or 5 times. He said that he could and would get me a commutation of sentence if I told him the truth about how the bomb was transferred from 721 Market Street to Steuart and Market Street but when I told him that the truth of the matter was that I didn't know any more about it than he did and probably not as much he acted as though he thought I were lying. So after I had told him the truth I asked him to write me a letter recommending me for a commutation. He balked at that . . . and said he would be back in September. Since he will not accept the truth from me I suppose it is incumbent upon me to tell him some sort of a lie if I want him to do anything for me—well if I knew any good ones I'd tell him the damndest 'big lie' he ever heard but I don't seem to be very good at it—that's why I tell the truth, most of the time.

"This business of using a life sentence as a method of third degree is quite a novelty though . . .

"All of this seems to mean that I am to be kept in prison until I do confess to a crime which I didn't commit—and if I did confess—how the hell could I expect to get out?

* Mrs. Lewis, one of Billings' most regular correspondents, was a longtime Socialist organizer, who frequently ran for Congress on the Socialist ticket.

"Good—then I'll stay here. If the world outside is full of that kind of S.O.B.'s—people who have that sort of psychology—then I belong in Represa."

"Speaking of lying to get out of prison," Billings resumed in a later letter, "I would of course if it were possible but in this case it isn't.

"Now if anyone could lie fast enough to explain to Fickert how they carried a suitcase 4066 feet starting with it at 1:51 and getting to the 'finish line' at either 1:50 or 1:52 they would break all known records for both lying and traveling. I admit I'm a 'fast guy' but I must decline the honor of any such record as that."

6 ·

James A. Johnston, warden at San Quentin since 1913, had been closely identified with the Johnson-Stephens regime. In a number of ways, some subtle, most not, Governor Richardson made it clear that Johnston's resignation would not be looked upon with disfavor. He submitted it in November, 1924, and was replaced by Frank Smith, the Governor's son-in-law. Shortly after taking over, Smith transferred Mooney to a better job, steward in the Officers' and Guards' Mess (O&G). It was a *bonaroo* job that gave him better food and allowed him to wear white denims instead of prison gray. Characteristically, Mooney was not at first happy with the change—it gave him two less hours per day for his letter writing campaign.

The letters had become almost an obsession. There was a paragraph in the rules for pardon that read: "In application based upon newly discovered evidence, the evidence must be such as would probably have produced an acquittal on a second trial." It seemed to Mooney that if he persuaded all his original jurors to reverse their verdicts he would fully meet this provision and force the Governor to grant his petition.

His letters to the jurors were only the visible part of the campaign. Most of the work took place outside the prison and had to be done by others. Years had passed since the original trial. Many of the jurors and witnesses had moved elsewhere (Weinberg, on moving to Cleveland, had been badly shaken when he encountered the Edeaus on the street) and had to be located. When a juror failed to reply, Mooney issued a challenge: "Name the witness that gave the testimony that you still believe is sufficient to hold me to strict accountability for the crime of murder." He then, in letter after letter, accompanied by document after document, discredited them. His letters were followed by personal (and often more tactful) visits by Rena, Belle, John, and even his aged mother. Mother Mooney spoke with such a brogue that even the Irish sometimes had trouble understanding her, but Tom knew her appearance generated sympathy, and he used it. He used everyone, and frankly admitted it. "If I were outside I'd do it myself, but I'm not outside and I can't." A magazine reporter who wrote a favorable piece on the case, as did John Fitch of *Survey*, often found himself inundated with requests to interview former witnesses, secure affidavits, copy transcripts, look for newspaper clippings, have photos made. The heaviest burden fell on Mooney's family, however, all of whom had to support themselves as well as carry out his requests.

On visiting days he would dictate pages of explicit instructions for Rena. The tasks were rarely simple enough, nor the hours of the day long enough, for her to accomplish everything. On her next visit, he would go over the list again, often berating her for things undone. In the past, Rena had rarely taken a drink; Billings, while still free, encountered trouble persuading her to take even a beer. Now, at the suggestion of one of the defense workers, she had several drinks each night before bed, to induce relaxation and sleep.

Tom was not only a demanding, but often an insensitive taskmaster. To Belle: "I know you are doing your very best, but . . ." To Rena: "Everybody up on their toes for the next four weeks, and going." To younger brother John: "What seems to be the matter with you—I wrote you asking that you visit me last Friday or Saturday—here it is Tuesday and you have not seen fit to come as yet." But he was sometimes thoughtful, using money from his prison account to order them small gifts, a tennis racket for Belle's daughter, a bracelet for Rena. And in his rough way, he tried to be tender: "Belle—I have sure run you ragged, got you peeved, and I imagine almost exasperated at the way I pushed you into and on and on in this work until you are almost at the breaking point. Never mind, Belle, you know what the 'Good People' say—your reward will come in Heaven. I hope not. If I can, I will try to bring some of it at least to you in this world—the only one we are quite sure about."

Belle had suffered from Tom's conviction and imprisonment as much as his immediate family. Her husband, a petty steamship official, threatened divorce unless she disassociated herself from the Mooneys. Belle, who knew that her sister and brother-in-law were innocent because she had been on the Eilers roof with them, had refused. A divorce had followed.

7 ·

Like Mooney, Billings now had a new job. After seven years in the stoneyard, he was transferred to the prison shoe factory, where because of his prior experience, he soon became assistant foreman. At nights he continued to study law, grammar, and Latin, with Russian "thrown in for recreation." He joined the American Correspondence Chess League, often keeping as many as 20 correspondence games going at the same time, with such opponents as students at the University of California. His record of wins was growing phenomenal, but then, belittling his accomplishment, he noted that he had fewer distractions than those outside. He drew— sketches and Christmas cards. And he tried his hand at writing short stories.

Yet his impatience with the Mooney defense was growing. "Yes, I've thought some about starting a new line of action," he wrote Lena Lewis, "but every time I get ready to begin I am requested by certain people in San Francisco to 'lay off' as they are about to institute one kind of campaign or other and don't wish me to interfere by trying to do anything for myself." He was working on two possibilities, he said, a pardon appeal and a writ of habeas corpus.

His new visiting and correspondence privileges—restricted as they were compared to those at San Quentin—only intensified his taste for the things he was missing. He rarely complained, but little things sometimes touched off moods of longing.

Mrs. Lewis wrote telling him to take care of his health and to eat plenty of fresh fruit. Easier said than done, he replied; his last fresh fruit had been two oranges and an apple at Christmas. "I haven't had a pear in four years—a banana in over six years, nor a pomegranite, persimmon or grapefruit since 1917. I haven't had a peach, apricot or a plum since last July or August although I did have apple pie for dinner today (canned apples) and stewed dried prunes for supper last night. If I tried to live on raw fruit around here my life would be a short and not very merry one."

More and more in his letters he referred to the seasons.

And, about 1925, he fell in love. It came about gradually. Among his correspondents was Dr. Mary Rudolph, a strong-willed woman, who against great opposition had become one of Tennessee's first women physicians. Their correspondence had commenced in 1921, shortly after the Rudolphs moved to San Francisco. Dr. Rudolph's husband was a member of Ed Nolan's former local, No. 68. Because Dr. Rudolph was an invalid, her letters to Billings were written by her young daughter Josephine. By 1925 Josephine was visiting Warren as often as a non-relative could.

Billings' patience was wearing thin. It seemed that absolutely nothing was being done to effect their release.

The mass meetings, the fund appeals, the magazine articles, the militant demands for worker support—all had, at Tom Mooney's insistence, virtually stopped. Mooney was banking everything on his pardon appeal to Richardson. By the end of 1925, seven of the jurors had written to the governor requesting his pardon. Not content with just the juror letters, he had also written to Fickert and Cuhna, and the Edeaus, asking the first pair to admit that there was no longer a case, asking the second to clear their consciences and tell the truth. They were not begging letters, but neither did they express Mooney's true feelings.

It was ironic. Mooney had discontinued direct action to concentrate almost entirely on political action. And in so doing he was following the AFL policy of mediation and conciliation.

It was also bitter gall. On January 21, 1926, Mooney began hemorrhaging and was rushed to the prison hospital where his condition was diagnosed as critical—a perforated stomach ulcer. Newspaper reporters set to work revising his obituary, but he pulled through. He was hospitalized 16 days, the loss of which he greatly resented. Upon his release, there were several relapses, accompanied by long periods of depression. He was often "down in the dumps," he wrote Nockles. "My reserve energy is about depleted and am in no position to resist ordinary matters that any healthy and normally nourished body should."

Everything depended on Governor Richardson.

8 ·

Friend W. Richardson, already characterized as "California's most reactionary governor," was in the fourth year of his term. At no time, either before or after his election, had he indicated in any way that he would consider a pardon for Mooney. Indeed, in matters of penology he had proven himself uncompromisingly strict. He had granted only 11 pardons, four commutations of sentence, three reprieves, and five restorations of citizenship, the lowest record of any governor since the 1850's. Announcing plans to seek reelection, he had given as one of his three campaign planks the maintenance of law and order through crime suppression and a refusal to interfere with the sentences of the courts.

But Mooney firmly believed there was a good chance. It may be that he accepted as significant something that was in reality coincidental. Frank Smith, Richardson's son-in-law and warden of San Quentin, believed in his innocence. He had admitted this to Mooney, although forbidding him to mention it publicly.

As the 1926 election approached, Mooney decided not to embarrass Richardson by pushing his case as a campaign issue. He would delay submitting his pardon appeal until after the August primaries.

Warren Billings' patience snapped. Since 1921 he had been attempting to obtain a notorized copy of McDonald's confession from the Mooney defense, but Rena and the others had given various excuses for not producing it. Since the document was basic to any action he might take, Billings was sure it was being withheld on Mooney's instructions, to make it impossible for him to take any action on his own that might conflict with Mooney's plans. After several angry letters, Billings now broke with Mooney and organized the Warren K. Billings Committee for Pardon.

In this he was encouraged by Fremont Older, one of his most frequent visitors, friends such as Madeline Wieland, a former IWDL secretary who headed the new committee and who felt that Tom had never done right by Warren, and by various California AFL leaders. Paul Scharrenberg had visited Billings for the first time in 1926 and was surprised to find that he wasn't the "wild-eyed radical" he expected. "I've never considered myself a wild-eyed radical," Billings told him with a grin. "I've always considered myself a progressive trade unionist." Both Older and Scharrenberg felt that if Billings submitted his petition there was a good chance Richardson might reduce his sentence to 30 years, making him eligible for parole in several more years. Billings didn't want a parole, however, he wanted a pardon.

Mooney's first reaction to the break was less angry than guilty. Warren had a much harder lot at Folsom than he did at San Quentin, he wrote his correspondents; he'd always known that. But everything he had done had been for both of them. He now asked only that he be kept informed of Billings' plans.

But he didn't send Billings the McDonald confession. And in closing a letter to Belle soon afterward he postscripted, "You should also pay a visit to Warren Neglected Billings."

Richardson's reelection seemed assured. His main opponent in the primary was his lieutenant governor, C. C. Young, a former Progressive. However shortly before the election, Hiram Johnson, seeing in Young a chance to revive the Progressive movement in California, returned to his home state and campaigned actively for him.

By a margin of only 15,272 votes, Young captured the Republican nomination.

Although disappointed at first, Mooney began to feel that this would help rather than hurt his cause. Richardson was now free to act without political pressure.

But he was also beginning to have doubts. On October 26th, he wrote his mother: "In every visit you ask me 'Tom will they let you out?' Mother I do not want to now, nor never did want to build up any false hopes for you, to be later crushed to earth should I be denied a pardon." Three days later, he was back in the hospital.

In November, Young easily defeated his Democratic opponent.

By the time Mooney submitted his pardon petition, in early December, he had letters from nine of the ten still living jurors. The lone holdout, surprisingly, was not MacNevin, the foreman, who had written the ninth letter, but J. W. Miller, a retail hardware store proprietor, who even after several months of *daily* letters from Mooney and frequent visits from his relatives, had refused to be stampeded. The pardon petition consisted of a letter, the official petition, eight fat volumes containing 343 separate exhibits, and a final volume summarizing the contents of the other eight.

Cuhna hadn't answered, nor had the Edeaus. Fickert had, and his letter, wherein, among other things, he accused Mooney of masterminding the 1919 attempt to bomb him, was the only unfavorable document in the petition.

Christmas was the traditional time for gubernatorial pardons. As Mooney's eleventh holiday season behind bars approached, his moods alternated between hope and despondency. Christmas arrived and passed. On December 29th, a guard let Mooney see a copy of a San Francisco paper reporting that Richardson had "passed the Mooney buck" to Young. Richardson had not even acknowledged receipt of the petition.

In his final message as Governor, Richardson stated: "Executive clemency should not be exercised to defeat the ends of the law, to override the verdicts of juries or decisions of courts. Only by strict enforcement of the laws and the elimination of sentimentalism in meting out punishment can law and order be maintained."

Through his four years in office Richardson had never implied otherwise.

23· *California Is the Battleground*

CLEMENT CALHOUN YOUNG, the new Governor of California, was a former schoolteacher who had written a text on English poetry. He was also a man of many promises.

Few California governors-elect seemed better prepared for the office than Young, whose background included, in addition to 14 years as an English teacher at San Francisco's Lowell High, a number of years' business experience and 10 years in the state assembly, with one term as speaker and eight years, while lieutenant governor, as presiding officer. A former Progressive who had changed his registration to Republican, he remained committed to many of the Progressive principles, was considered semi-liberal, and was a close friend of Fremont Older's.

As soon as Young was inaugurated, Mooney wrote to him renewing his pardon petition. He also wrote to Older, asking him to pull out all stops on publicity. The long period of diplomatic silence had gone against the grain: he wanted action now, and fast. "I want a public hearing so all can see and hear as they can in a trial which is being presented in support of my pardon petition."

But Older urged patience. At least give the new governor enough time to review the new petition, he advised; of all the governors who had considered the case, Young gave the most promise of doing something. Older begged Mooney not to act hastily. Griffin reiterated the plea.

There were hopeful signs. Young replied to Mooney's letter, something no other governor had done, informing him that he would review his pardon appeal as soon as the current legislative session had ended.

Mooney waited. In the interim he attempted to heal the breach between himself and Billings. Belle was put to work contacting any still living Billings' jurors. Rena, who had now reopened her studio, was urged to visit Billings as often as possible. But Mooney could not resist the temptation to use the new Billings committee, dumping upon it typing chores for his own group, sending its members on continual errands. Too, there was conflict over finances. Through Madeline Wieland's efforts, a Chicago union had promised to vote $100 for the defense of the two men. She informed Mooney to this effect, cautioning him not to write to the union

307

until after the funds were voted. But write Mooney did, suspiciously inquiring if the money had already been sent to the Billings' committee, and if so, asking that an equal amount be sent to his defense committee. Miss Wieland lacked Billings' patience. After several like incidents she angrily wrote to Mooney, "I must state here and now that there is darn little cooperation or interest or anything else coming from your committee to help these cases along . . . unless I know what's what I don't intend to do anything more on your case."

Mooney wasn't content to wait for Young's readiness to act. He urged Older to try to put pressure on the governor through his chief advisors, Senator Hiram Johnson, *Chronicle* columnist Chester Rowell, and A. P. Giannini, President of the Bank of Italy. Older replied that Rowell and Giannini were doubtful and that there was no possibility of Johnson's acting: "Hiram has not forgiven you for a letter he says you wrote him threatening his life many years ago, and there is no use trying to change his mind. The best we can get from him is silence."

In June of 1927 Young pardoned Anita Whitney. Mooney interpreted this as a very good sign, but a strong barrage of press criticism indicated otherwise.

"I may be wrong in my conclusions. I hope I am," Older wrote to Mooney on the 22nd after visiting the Executive Mansion. "But I think Governor Young has nothing better in mind than parole for you and Billings."

"My dear Older," Mooney replied. "Death will claim me first in San Quentin prison . . . This is my reply to the suggestion of parole . . .

"P.S. What I have said is my view and concerns me only. Warren must speak for himself. What he does will not change me."

Older contacted Billings. "I will not consider a parole," he replied. "I would prefer to remain in the penitentiary to that. I want complete vindication."

Even though he stated that he considered the idea of granting parole to two innocent men unthinkable, Older begged Mooney not to reject it completely. "I do not blame you for feeling the way you do about parole. I am sure if I were in your place I should feel entirely as you do. But I don't think it is advisable to close all doors . . ." It was just possible, Older said, that parole might be the only alternative offered, and "in the event of that being your only way out, probably you ought to take it." Older enlisted the support of others whose advice Mooney respected—Ed Nockles, Roger Baldwin of the American Civil Liberties Union, M. J. Keough, President of the International Molders' Union, and H. L. Mencken of the Baltimore *Sun,* who for the past several years had been writing vitriolic editorials on the case.

Mooney found himself explaining, in letter after letter, that "Parole is for the guilty."

"I could not consider such a compromise of principles, my conscience would not permit it," he wrote Keough. "I am in the right. I have been grievously wronged. I am absolutely innocent. I will not accept anything short of Pardon."

Do you realize what parole would actually mean, he asked his correspondents? It would mean that he could not choose his place of residence or his associates, that he couldn't accept a job or travel more than 50 miles without permission, that he couldn't vote or drink or drive a motor vehicle or run for office, that he would be under surveillance and would have to report regularly to a parole officer, and that this one man would have it in his power to return him to prison for the rest of his life for any "alleged" infraction of the rules. In short, he would be no freer than now.

"A pardon is a remission of judgment. It has no 'strings' attached to it. The pardoned man cannot be shunted around by the police as an 'ex-convict.' The pardon is the act by which the State recognizes its mistake and unconditionally releases the victim wrongfully imprisoned."

Too, practically speaking, he wouldn't be eligible for parole for another three years—the time in San Francisco County Jail not counting toward the required 12 years for a lifer. It was, in short, just another delaying tactic.

"If it were just a matter of being released from this prison I should have left here long ago—via 'French leave,'" he wrote Older. "This case is nothing but a symbol of the times. That I am one of the actors in it is a mere accident and I must not be considered personally, but the big thing involved here is the principle underlying this structure—the perversion of the instruments of justice to defeat the very ends for which they were organized."

The parole rumor became semi-official.

At Older's suggestion, Rowell had written to Governor Young. Young replied:

". . . it seems to me that this matter [the Mooney case] has been threshed over so frequently that it would be unwise to reopen it just now.

"I have always taken the attitude that in a state such as ours, with the very liberal parole system we possess, the ordinary procedure of release from prison should be first through parole, and, later, after the parole term had been served and the prisoner had subsequently demonstrated his right attitude toward the social order, that a pardon and restoration of citizenship should follow.

"It would please me very much if you could aid me in getting this idea across to the friends of Mooney. I should hate to see a request for a pardon which I cannot grant, but I believe that at the proper time the other avenue of release may properly be invoked."

A few understood Mooney's stand. Upton Sinclair, who had been arrested during the Red Scare for reading the Declaration of Independence in public, wrote "I have your letter and I will, of course, do everything in my power to help in the petition for your pardon . . . Needless to say I sympathize with your position and wish you the best of luck."

But many wrote in a vein similar to H. L. Mencken, who observed, "I admire your refusal to accept a parole. But I can't get rid of the feeling that it is rather quixotic. After all, the important thing is to get out of prison. It seems to me that pardon is just as patronizing as a parole . . ."

2 ·

The cell blocks at San Quentin were dark and deathly quiet. There had been no sound since taps except the prison generators and an occasional spastic cough. No one was sleeping. In San Quentin, it was a few minutes after nine on the night of August 22nd, 1927. In Charleston, it was a few minutes after midnight on the 23rd, and in San Quentin, as in Folsom, Alcatraz, Leavenworth, Times Square, Piccadilly Circus, and the Left Bank, this was the time people were conscious of, as millions silently observed the deathwatch for the shoemaker and the fish peddler.

The Sacco-Vanzetti, Mooney-Billings cases had been closely connected from early in the decade. *Tom Mooney's Monthly* had been one of the first radical publications to take up the cause of the anarchists, against the advice of friends who thought Mooney could only hurt his own case by so doing. On taking over the Boston defense in the fall of 1920 Fred Moore had written to Rena asking for all pamphlets "tending to show the method used by the prosecution in Tom's case," to which, the attorney noted, the Sacco-Vanzetti case "bears striking resemblance." The Robert Minor cover of the first Sacco-Vanzetti pamphlet *Are They Doomed?* bore the subtitle *The New England Mooney Case*, the first fund appeal was headed *Shall There Be a Mooney Frame-Up in New England?* In many respects, Moore and his successors had patterned their defense after Mooney's own, perhaps even too closely, for as John Nicholas Beffel wrote Rena following the guilty verdicts in the South Braintree case, ". . . in the end we found that we were up against the same forces which you people had to fight all these years." Rena, acting on Tom's instructions, sent Moore the complete mailing list of *Tom Mooney's Monthly* plus the confidential list of the largest individual and union donors. Mooney wrote to Governor Fuller, explaining, from his own particular position, how a miscarriage of justice could occur. He also wrote Alexander Berkman in Paris, urging him to organize a monster demonstration to greet the 50,000 American Legionnaires conventioning in that city during the summer of 1927. "Make it a genuine salute—a memory that they will always cherish—if you do it right they should come home feeling ashamed of themselves." Berkman did organize the protest—there were hundreds of Sacco-Vanzetti, Mooney-Billings banners—but as to its effect Mooney was perhaps overly optimistic.

Although as prisoners the principals in the two cases couldn't correspond directly, messages of encouragement were exchanged through their defense committees, and in one of his last interviews Vanzetti begged a reporter, "See if you cannot do something for Tom Mooney. Tom is a sick man. He will die in prison soon if something is not done for him."

The parallels were striking, from the common occupation of Sacco and Billings to Felix Frankfurter's intervention in the cases. The trials had all been conducted against a background of hysteria. Murder was the charge against all principals, but radicalism was the silent issue. Both sets of defendants lacked a motive for their alleged acts. Both had unimpeachable alibis. In both cases the police had passed up obvious suspects. ("Must we prove somebody else guilty in order to prove our innocence?" Sacco had cried; "Mooney and Billings didn't do this!") The sole evidence against each was the identification of witnesses who had revised and re-revised their testimony to fit newly discovered facts. The most important witnesses had criminal pasts (each case had its prostitute) and had later confessed perjury or been discredited. Both cases were complicated by a prior conviction of one of the defendants. And in both cases, a law prohibiting the courts from considering newly discovered evidence had placed their fates in the hands of the Executive.

Judge Webster Thayer even bore an uncanny resemblance to Judge Frank Dunne.

But at 12:10 A.M. on August 23rd the parallels ended. Mooney, in cell #155 of the Stones, heard a sound that began as a low moan and grew to a great sob, then ended in a long moment of silence, followed by the deafening metallic clatter of hundreds of tin cups banging against steel doors, the traditional prison method of protest. Nicola Sacco had been pronounced dead. Seven minutes later a guard listening to a radio again relayed a message down the tier of cells, with identical response. Bartolomeo Vanzetti too was dead.

"Dear Comrade Mooney," Mary Donovan wrote Tom, shortly after delivering the funeral eulogy. "I am writing this so that you may know immediately that we, the committee and I, individually, will do everything possible to help you.

"It will be carrying out the wishes of Vanzetti and Sacco—for Vanzetti planned if released to go to you and Billings immediately to offer his services to be used in any manner you might see fit . . ."

If the Mooney-Billings case had influenced the handling of the Sacco-

Vanzetti defense, the ultimate fate of the two men had an even stronger effect on Tom Mooney, leaving him with a deep distrust of gubernatorial advisory committees, white-collar intellectuals, and Communists.

3 ·

During the last months of the Sacco-Vanzetti case, an Advisory Committee, made up of influential citizens, had been appointed to look into the case and advise Governor Fuller. About the same time, Guido Marks, Roger Baldwin's representative on the West Coast, suggested that Mooney adopt a similar tactic with Governor Young. Mooney had briefly considered the idea.

The Sacco-Vanzetti Advisory Committee, however, had found no reason to reverse the court's judgment. With the failure of this last appeal the two men had been executed.

Apparently horrified at how close he had come to accepting Marks' suggestion, Mooney wrote Walsh, "The out come in Mass. would seem to make this a very unwise expedient and I will not do it."

From this time on, Mooney never quite trusted the American Civil Liberties Union.

His distrust of the American Federation of Labor, though of longer standing, was given new impetus that fall. In October 1927 the AFL held its annual convention in Los Angeles. For months Mooney supporters had worked on a strong resolution demanding that Governor Young pardon the two men. Sponsored by the San Francisco Labor Council, and passed by 126 California unions, the resolution was referred to the Executive Council for action. This was the first time since 1916 that the AFL had failed to pass a Mooney-Billings resolution.

For nearly a quarter of a century the AFL had been dominated by one man, Samuel Gompers. Although Gompers had never done as much for the California defendants as Mooney believed he should have, he had at least worked behind the scenes in their behalf. But in 1925 Gompers died and the scramble for succession ended with the election of ex-miner William Green, a man Arthur Schlesinger, Jr., aptly describes in *Crisis of the Old Order* as "the lowest common denominator among the contenders . . . A comfortable man with the air of a small-town banker, rimless glasses on a placid face, a large gold watchchain in his vest, and a diamond ring on his finger, an Odd Fellow and an Elk, Green brought the Harding virtues to the leadership of American labor."

Never representing more than a small minority of American workers, those of the skilled crafts, the AFL during the 1920's had steadily lost membership. And with the loss its leadership had grown even more cautious and conservative.

The resolution would have passed had Green wanted it passed; of this Mooney was sure.

There were apparently several reasons for killing it. Governor Young was one of the convention speakers; he had at least three more years in office and the California leaders did not want to risk embarrassing him. Weighing the Mooney case against labor's other needs in the state, the Californians had no trouble deciding which was to them more pressing.

To Mooney, however, it was a clear and outright betrayal: the AFL had in effect told Governor Young that regardless of what he did or didn't do concerning Mooney and Billings, they wouldn't protest. Mooney personalized the blame: several California labor leaders had already received remunerative appointments from the Governor—Scharrenberg, for example, was on the State Board of Harbor Commissioners.

But the convention's action, coupled with Young's parole talk, raised an even greater fear in Mooney. Ordinarily, referral to the Executive Council for action meant no action at all. However this recommendation was oddly worded: "The committee is of the opinion that the general purpose of the resolution can be accomplished by instructing the President and the Executive Council to use their judgment as to the procedure best calculated to bring about the release of Mooney and Billings . . ." Mooney saw this as no less than a plan to take over his defense. Green and the Executive Council could now ask the Governor to parole the two men and the embarrassing Mooney case would be done. Either that or "They hope to place us in an awkward position—making it appear that we do not want out of prison—that we are posing as martyrs to the cause."

"I will leave this prison a free man or a dead man," Mooney wrote Walsh, "the AFL and the Executive Council and Mr. Paul Scharrenberg notwithstanding."

Although Mooney was quick to see betrayals, there was evidence that his suspicions in this instance were correct.

"I was terribly disappointed at what happened at the AFL convention in Los Angeles," Older wrote Mooney sympathetically. "Isn't it a strange situation? Captain Matheson trying to get you out, and the AFL trying to block it. I would not have believed that the case would ever have got into such a situation as it is."

The remarks Mooney most appreciated, however, came from Baltimore. "The attitude of the California Labor Leaders doesn't surprise," Mencken wrote. "I distrust the whole outfit. They are scabs at heart."

4 ·

Like all holidays, Thanksgiving Day 1927 was eagerly awaited at Folsom Prison. There would be no work, movies would be shown during the morning in the big hall, and a turkey dinner was to be served at noon.

The prisoners never ate it. For six men had awaited this day even more impatiently than the rest. About 11:10 A.M., while the movie was in progress, the group, led by North Beach robber "Black Tony" Brown, captured a guard and made an escape attempt. The alarm was quickly sounded. Guards on the catwalks and in the guard towers that overlooked the auditorium, thinking it was a riot, began firing through the windows into the packed hall. Some of the bullets were dum-dums, which exploded on impact. Billings had been sitting next to one of his chess partners; the partner's head was blown off. In front of him, another head exploded, and the ear of another friend vanished. There were more than a thousand prisoners in the hall.

Billings and those closest to him dived behind a table. But when the bullets ricocheted beneath it, he climbed on top and threw down books from the library shelves to make a fortress. By the time he finished, others had crowded into the space and he was left exposed on top. Looking out the window he could see a gun barrel aimed directly at him. Fortunately this guard didn't fire.

The Folsom Thanksgiving Day "riot" of 1927 left 16 dead: 2 guards, 14 convicts. The escapees were not among them; they had moved into the rotunda before the first shots were fired into the hall.

Following this incident there was a shakedown of the whole prison. The shoe shop yielded a straight razor, about four dollars in cash, and several pairs of handsewn shoes. Billings was responsible only for the shoes, which he had made for a couple of Wobblies due for release, but he took responsibility for the other contraband. For the next six months "I was a land anchor artist," he recalls, the pick-and-shovel crew being used as a form of punishment.

As a result of the riot, all movies and ball games with outside teams were canceled and tighter restrictions imposed.

Oddly enough, it was in part due to the "massacre" (as the prisoners called it) that Billings became unofficial prison watchmaker.

When Billings first arrived at Folsom, prisoners were not allowed watches, on the theory that they might use them to time guards on their rounds. By 1919 the rule had fallen into desuetude and Billings was given back his old dollar watch, confiscated on arrival. It no longer worked, however, and there were no provisions for repairing it, the possession of

Ralph Pekor's painting of "The Last Supper," Folsom Chapel. For his models Pekor used convicted murderers: Simon was Los Angeles "Times" dynamiter J. B. McNamara; Bartholomew was Capone lieutenant Ralph Shelton; James was cop-killer Val Salata. Second from right is Matthew, alias Warren Billings.

tools being worth a month in solitary. Billings had taken a large tenpenny nail, flattened it with a stonecutter's hammer, borrowed a file, filed it square on the end, and made a screwdriver out of it. Before long he was repairing watches for other prisoners, and when he liked them, the guards. To clean a watch, however, he needed watchmaker's oil, and this had to be brought in through the underground. The warden, who knew what Billings was doing, chose to look the other way. Billings, for his part, made little attempt at secrecy. Although his letters were censored, he wrote one correspondent, "Every time I need anything I have to order it through the underground system and the system here is not a good one. It breaks down too often."

The situation was ridiculous. Whenever one of the prison clocks stopped, a guard would give Billings a pass to the area, where he would surreptitiously fix it. The height of absurdity was reached when he was given the new warden's watch to repair.

It was a stupid rule, and Billings was determined to change it by forcing it into the open. Following the Thanksgiving affair, he was interviewed by a reporter for the *Call*. Deciding that this was as good an op-

315

portunity as any to bring his business above ground, he told the reporter of his watch repair activities and of his difficulty in obtaining such essential tools as jewelers' cement, tweezers, watch oil, and an eye loop. On reading the *Call* article a Market Street jeweler, Bob Meyers, sent Billings a package containing all these items and several others.

Meyers, whose shop was at 719 Market, had been interested in the Mooney-Billings case from the start. Among those who had seen the young man on the roof at 721 Market, he had been taken to Billings' cell and asked to identify him. Meyers realized at once that Billings was not the man in question and said so. Draper Hand, however, had attempted to persuade Meyers that he was, and Meyers was still indignant.

The package was returned, stamped REFUSED. Angrily, Meyers went to the *Call* and threw the package on Fremont Older's desk. "The *Call* said Billings needed these, so the *Call* can see he gets them."

One Sunday shortly afterward, while all the men were in the yard, the warden walked up to Billings, and without a word, handed him the package. Billings became unofficial prison watchmaker. It was not a pass line job, it entitled him to no special privileges, and it didn't take him off the shovel detail, but it did enable him to work at something he enjoyed.

5 ·

In part because of the Folsom "riot," in part because of a recent change in wardens, there were now tighter restrictions at San Quentin also. Following Richardson's defeat, his son-in-law had resigned as warden, to be replaced by former sheriff "Big Jim" Holohan.

Holohan had a reputation for being as rough a lawman as any in the Old West. Once during an espionage case one of the accused had gone berserk in the courtroom and killed his co-defendant. Holohan quickly drew and drilled him with a single shot. His toughness was really a myth, Holohan once admitted to Clinton Duffy; that was the only man he had ever killed in his life. But it was a myth Holohan apparently enjoyed fostering, by his practice of wearing two six-shooters.

Holohan's attempts to be a "tough warden" were as strange as they were episodic. For example, every Christmas the International Labor Defense sent each of the "class war prisoners" a parcel containing a package of cigarettes, bar of chocolate, bath towel, bar of Ivory soap, and bar of toilet soap. Holohan allowed the prisoners to receive only the bath towel; he sent the other items, including the cigarettes, to an orphanage.

Many of the restrictions affected Tom Mooney. "There's no such thing as a 'political prisoner,'" Holohan told one visitor. "These boys are all convicts."

Visiting rules were restricted to limit a non-relative or attorney to one visit per month. Outgoing letters were limited to one each day containing no more than two pages of written matter. Many of Mooney's letters were now returned to him stamped RETURNED—CENSORED—NOT AL-LOWED. But the same letter, retyped and remailed several days later, would often go through. The phrase "Soviet Union" was objectionable; "Russia" was acceptable. There was a rule that prisoners could not receive newspaper clippings—an offshoot of the ruling forbidding them to see California newspapers. For some years the clipping rule hadn't been enforced; Holohan reinforced it, but said that if the clipping was typed it was acceptable. Frequently he would announce a new rule, only to drop it several days later. The convicts never knew where they stood. Gradually Holohan let the prison lapse back to the old "con-boss" system of bully boys and homosexual informers.

"As an executive," Kenneth Lamott notes, "Holohan's abilities were better suited to a Salvation Army band than a prison . . ."

Two pages, however, were more than sufficient for Mooney to tell William Green that under no circumstances would he accept anything less than a full and complete pardon.

"I hope I shall never have to tell the real true story of why resolution No. 49 was sidetracked at the Los Angeles convention," he wrote the AFL president on January 2nd, 1928, "but if your actions and those of the Executive Council are other than genuine in my estimation I shall not hesitate to broadcast them to the world.

"Our case has been a political football in California politics long enough and from now on I am going to strongly object to it being further used in that respect, especially by the labor politicians of California. They are not going to get away with their betrayal of labor men in prison in order to hold tight to their political posts in California.

"We have spent almost twelve years in durance vile, and this primarily because the Labor Leaders of California (with a few exceptions) not only did not want us out, but secretly did everything in their power to help bring about our down fall and are now hoping and working for our continued imprisonment. Fraternally, Tom Mooney."

Green's reply arrived two and a half months later, in the form of a brief question: "Will you advise me if you still maintain the position that you will not 'under any circumstances accept a parole, but that you insist upon a complete pardon'?"

6 ·

In January 1928 Governor Young told Fremont Older that "I am inclined to think that Mooney is innocent." In subsequent weeks, the governor told at least four other persons, including U.S. Senator Hiram

Johnson, that he would probably pardon Mooney. One person he told was his wife, who circulated the story widely. Again, Older counseled patience.

But Mooney would have none of it.

"Every cause needs a spokesman—we lack that now . . ." Mooney wrote to Walsh, urging him to come to California and publicly present his pardon petition to the governor. Older was growing old and not thinking very clearly, Mooney said; McNutt and McKenzie were able attorneys, but not first rate. The case needed fire; Walsh would "give it the color it formerly enjoyed."

Mooney now wrote to Lippmann, Villard, Mencken, the *New Republic,* the New York *Telegram,* and numerous others asking them to pull out all stops on publicity. For several years he had refused all requests for interviews; now he solicited them.* He began work on a new pamphlet, which he planned to circularize to every voter in California. He decided to reorganize his old defense committee, dormant for a number of years, and began looking for someone to head it. And he gave the American Civil Liberties Union his somewhat qualified permission to organize a national committee of liberals.

The National Mooney-Billings Committee was Roger Baldwin's idea. When it was first proposed Mooney had reacted coolly, in part because reluctant to have another group collecting funds for the defense, in part because, like most working trade unionists, he distrusted liberals and intellectuals. Now cut off from formal union support, however, he approved the idea. Within a short time Baldwin mounted an impressive roster of names, which included Harry Elmer Barnes, Clarence Darrow, John Dewey, Morris L. Ernst, Norman Hapgood, Arthur Garfield Hays, Morris Hillquit, Fannie Hurst, Philip La Follette, Sinclair Lewis, Alexander Meiklejohn, H. L. Mencken, Lincoln Steffens, and Rabbi Stephen Wise.

Sometime earlier, Felix Frankfurter had written to Fremont Older suggesting that someone write "a complete and lawyerlike work on the Mooney case, so that all the facts could be had within the covers of a single book . . . I think that is very important for Mooney's sake, and very important for truth's sake, for history's sake." Henry L. Hunt, an attorney and former mayor of Cincinnati, who headed the new ACLU committee, volunteered to write it and began work.

In 1926 Older's autobiography *My Own Story* had been published, with several large sections devoted to the case. "Search criminal history back, down through the Dark Ages, and a more glaring and cruel case of injustice cannot be found," he wrote. "Anyone who has a tendency toward pessimism, and in his gloomiest moments declares the human race incapable of any real progress, can find in the Mooney case some justifica-

---

* Norman Thomas was one of the first to arrive, representing *The Nation.* "Mooney can stand prison better than we can stand having him there," he wrote.

tion of his belief." The book received wide distribution; there is no evidence that Mooney ever acknowledged its existence to Older. He did tell one visitor, shortly after it appeared, that Older should have consulted him before writing it, that he had expressly told Older he wanted no publicity at this time.

Fortunately Baldwin, like Older, has learned to expect neither praise nor encouragement from Mooney. "National and International influence is secondary and will play little or no part in the deliverance of Billings and myself," Mooney wrote Baldwin. All a California governor is interested in, Mooney said, is California votes. "California is the battleground."

After numerous postponements Frank Walsh arrived in August. Governor Young agreed to see him in Berkeley in an open hearing. Walsh, one of the great lawyers of his time, lived up even to Mooney's expectations: his "beautiful, impassioned" plea was so moving that several California newspapers previously antagonistic to Mooney now rallied to his cause. Many who had grown disheartened by the long, drawnout quest for justice felt a rebirth of dedication. Following the hearing Governor Young told the group he was convinced that they believed Mooney and Billings innocent. He added that "up until this time" he had believed them guilty. He promised to give the matter his closest attention.

Almost everyone present was jubilant over the governor's remarks. Only Older and a few of the reporters present seemed to realize that Young's was an equivocal statement—that it could mean anything. What bothered Older most was that it conflicted with what Young had told him personally in January.

"What a changed feeling in general," Mooney wrote Older on September 5th. "The whole atmosphere seems to have cleared up—and I feel that I can safely say that things look much brighter today than at any time in the past twelve years. As to the final outcome, I have not the slightest doubt, but how long that will take is a question. I do however believe that there is still much hard work to complete the job so well begun and nearly finished."

Walsh's eloquent plea was only half the reason for Mooney's renewed enthusiasm: Mary Gallagher had appeared on the scene.

24 · Enter Mary Gallagher

MARY Gallagher was a buxom, attractive redhead in her mid-forties. Indiana born, she had been active in the IWW and various radical causes for most of her life. She had known Tom Mooney in the "old days," had visited him while in California working on the criminal syndicalism cases in 1923, and they had exchanged Christmas cards and occasional letters since.

Mooney, in his search for someone to head his new defense committee, had briefly considered Mary Gallagher and rejected her; he hoped to find someone without a radical background. He assigned her several difficult errands in Los Angeles, however, and was so amazed at her success that he offered her the job. She took it—at a starting salary of $10 a week plus traveling expenses—and within a very short time she had the Tom Mooney Molders' Defense Committee completely reorganized and running.

A $100 loan from Mother Mooney's savings was used to rent a San Francisco headquarters. A $500 donation from Clarence Darrow paid for stationery, postage, and typewriter rental. Between September 1, 1928, when she started work, and December 5, 1930, when she "broke" with Mooney, $46,041.47 was collected for the Mooney defense, a remarkable figure considering a good portion of it was collected after the Depression was underway. In soliciting aid she appealed to, and received donations from, such unlikely sources as Miss E. B. Scripps, Hollywood producer Paul Bern (who brought Douglas Fairbanks, Jr., along to one of the Mooney rallies), the students at Barnard College and Columbia University, and Peggy Guggenheim Vail ("I am glad at last to be able to do something about Mooney," she wrote from Paris, enclosing a check for $2000. "I've always wanted to. This is the first time I have been asked to. Thank you!").

Mary Gallagher was, as Tom Mooney soon realized, a rare person who had the ability to stimulate others to action. She was equally at ease before a labor council or a ministerial alliance. Before long there were seven full-time workers in the San Francisco office, a branch office in Southern California, and several full-time representatives on the East Coast.

She was a phenomenally hard worker. Every night Mooney would send her a special delivery letter from San Quentin, detailing her activities for the following day. More often than not she spent from 15 to 18 hours carrying out these tasks and handling the multitude of details Mooney hadn't foreseen.

She was also a charmer. She arranged mass meetings and persuaded Judge Griffin to speak, something he had previously declined to do because of his position on the bench. Her charm even had its effect on Warden Holohan, who lifted restrictions on the number of pages per letter a prisoner could write, and who, although she wasn't a relative, allowed her to visit Mooney twice a week. She would be waiting when the visitor's room opened at 8:30 in the morning; sometimes she didn't leave her chair, even for a glass of water, until 3:30 in the afternoon. Mooney was indefatigable, she later recalled, but she wasn't. Sometimes she left the prison in such a state of exhaustion that a massage was necessary to return the circulation to her aching body.

Work on the new pamphlet was begun. Mooney dictated its contents, making constant changes as it took form. Printers were solicited for the lowest bulk rate. Mooney personally examined paper samples, chose the type face, handled the layout. When Mary went ahead on her own with some detail, however commendable, she received a sharp rebuke. Their original agreement was simple. She was to take her orders from him and no one else and obey them without question, and she was to keep an accurate accounting of every penny received and spent so there could be no criticism of their handling of funds.

Articles on the case again began to appear regularly in such media as the *Manchester Guardian,* the London *Times, The New York Times* and the New York *Herald Tribune.* The *New Republic* and *The Nation* agreed to run fund-appeal ads at half rate, to be paid for after donations came in, and before long Mooney badgered similar deals with *Survey Graphic, New Masses, Labor Defender, Monitor, Outlook, American Mercury,* and others. These ads, each containing some portion of the discredited testimony, proved so successful that Mooney even considered running them in the *Saturday Evening Post,* although "for this I know I will forfeit [Matt Schmidt's] friendship for the rest of my life . . . If he wants to call a man some vicious name, he will say 'Oh he is a Saturday Evening Post Reader.' "

Whenever a celebrity visited San Francisco, Mary Gallagher would pay a visit. Often this resulted in a public statement—Jane Addams of Hull House: "What are the people of California going to do for Tom Mooney?"; Nicholas Murray Butler, President of Columbia University: "Your California is very beautiful as a country, but very backward as a state" —or, in the case of William Allen White, who took a set of the documents back to Kansas with him for study, more editorials.

As if these activities weren't sufficient, she spent several weeks in Oregon on a new Oxman lead. Mooney had learned that following a close brush with death Oxman had joined the Catholic Church. Mary Gallagher persuaded a priest in Baker, Oregon, to write to Oxman asking him to see her, so that as a fellow Catholic she could appeal to him to clear his conscience. Oxman didn't reply. When Mary Gallagher attempted to see him anyway, he threatened to have her arrested for trespassing.

This led to the most unlikely of all the Mooney letters: "What kind of a Christian are you, Frank Oxman?" Mooney asked. "When you eat and drink of the sacrament unworthily you eat and drink damnation to your own soul . . . Frank Oxman, your tongue may be stilled next Christmas. It may be too late. You may not be on pleading terms and praying grounds with God. Take it now—your chance to cleanse your soul."

Not the least of Mary Gallagher's accomplishments was the fact that she got along with Tom Mooney so well and for so long.

2 ·

It was not altogether smooth sailing.

One of Roger Baldwin's reasons for advocating formation of the National Mooney-Billings Committee was that he felt Mooney was ignoring Billings. "About Billings," Mooney had replied to one such complaint, "Everything I do, I have him in mind, and am as anxious for his welfare as for my own, but at times it might seem from a distance that I am somewhat indifferent to his lot—this, in reality is not true. For five years I have had Mrs. Hammerberg working continuously on my petition—in the petition is everything favoring Billings that could be expected of any one and more than even Billings or his friends thought I would have put there . . ."

The announcement of the reorganization of the Tom Mooney Molders' Defense Committee drew immediate fire from a number of people, including Baldwin and Norman Thomas.

"Everything I do is calculated to work equally for Billings—the name 'Tom Mooney Molders' Defense Committee' is purely tactical . . ." Mooney found himself repeating in letter after letter; it was, his correspondents felt, not a satisfactory explanation. Everything was Tom Mooney. Rallies were held on the anniversary of *his* arrest, *his* commutation of sentence, *his* birthday.

Mooney even found it necessary to justify himself to his sister Anna: "Warren must be in another one of his moody spells. I do wish I could do more for him than we have been able to—never does any one come to see me, but that I ask them to call upon him also. I know he has it much harder than I, and I have all these years thought and felt the same way about him and have dreamed of the day when I might be in a better position to make his lot easier. He is a prince of a boy—they don't make them any better."

When the first copies of Mooney's new pamphlet, *Governor Young: Pardon Tom Mooney—Innocent,* appeared in May 1929, Norman Thomas took one look at the title, another at the two photos of Mooney on the cover, read it in its entirety, and then wrote Baldwin that he was "greatly disgusted and so were others to find that Tom Mooney's pamphlet almost ignored Billings. Reference throughout is to 'me.' Mention of Billings is almost incidental."

The two photos had a history of their own. As a result of their publication, Mooney's letters were cut back to two pages and his visits restricted to 20 minutes each.

To many in the American labor movement Tom Mooney was a symbol. They bore an image, however, of the hefty, blackheaded young Irishman depicted in photographs taken at the time of his arrest. But Tom Mooney was now in his mid-forties. His hair was totally gray. As a result of frequent ulcer attacks, he had lost some 50 pounds. And his teeth had all been extracted. In 1928 Mooney had persuaded the prison photographer to take a picture of him as he then was, to be sent to the International Molders' convention. The photo did not receive widespread attention, however, until it appeared on the new pamphlet and committee stationery opposite a picture of him taken in 1916. The contrast was startling: it was almost impossible to believe that the gray, sallow, sunken-cheeked wraith on the right was the same man.

Warden Holohan was inundated with letters and wires protesting his brutal treatment of Mooney. Holohan, in response equally angry, charged that Mooney had removed his dentures just before the picture was snapped. Mooney denied this, and the photographer supported him, but the warden ordered an investigation. A photographic expert was called in to examine all available photos of Mooney: his report, never made public, was that Mooney was not lying—his plates had been in when the picture was taken.

Mooney regretted the furor as much as Holohan, since he had made it a firm rule never to criticize his treatment nor to discuss publicly conditions inside the prison. (When one reporter published a story attributing critical statements to him he quickly repudiated it, proving from prison records that he had never been visited by the man.) Since the controversial photo was taken, Mooney had gained back 20 pounds. He agreed to sit for new photos, which Holohan distributed to the press.* Mooney partisans continued to believe that he had been badly mistreated, his de-

---

* However, he continued to use the "before and after" photos on all of his letterheads and pamphlets until the case came to an end.

tractors that he was a fraud. Few saw or commented upon the obvious—
that more than a dozen years in prison changes any man.

Less ludicrous was Mooney's continuing battle with the Communists.

The International Labor Defense (ILD) had been organized in June
1925 to "protest the continued imprisonment of class-war prisoners." Its
letterhead committee bore the names of such obvious non-Communists as
Clarence Darrow, Socialists Eugene Debs and Upton Sinclair, California
liberal churchman Robert Whitaker, feminist Alice Stone Blackwell, and
IWW poet Ralph Chaplin.* The ILD, however, was a Communist front,
one of the earlier and longest lasting, as well as one of the most profitable
sources of revenue for the general party coffers. Actual control of the ILD
was held tightly by its National Secretary, always high in party counsels.

It has often been charged that the ILD did nothing for the 106 class-
war prisoners whose causes it espoused. This was not true. Every month
each was sent $5, a special prison newsletter, and the ILD magazine
Labor Defender. At Christmas each received $25 and a package of
assorted items; in addition, their families were sent $50, plus $5 for each
child. This was, to a great many of the prisoners whose cases had been
less publicized than that of Mooney and Billings, no small contribution.
In addition, somewhat later, the ILD provided legal counsel in a number
of cases.

The bulk of the money collected in the name of the prisoners, however,
was channeled to other uses. From the Communist Party viewpoint, there
was nothing dishonest in this: anything helping to liberate the toiling
masses from the yoke of capitalism aided the labor prisoners at the same
time. Nor was this an uncommon practice—most charities and many
churches collected money in the name of a specific project but applied it
to their general fund.

In its *Monthly Bulletin* for December 1926 the Sacco-Vanzetti Defense
Committee had complained of repeatedly asking the ILD for an accounting of funds collected in the names of their two defendants, but of receiving no satisfactory reply. Shortly after this, the Moscow press reported
that American Communist leaders had reported raising half a million dollars for the Sacco-Vanzetti defense. These two statements were much publicized, various newspapers charging the Communists with "getting rich"
off the plight of the two men.

From the few references in Mooney's letters it is apparent that he
didn't place much credence in the charges.

From its inception, the Mooney-Billings case had been one of the ILD's
major causes. Through August 1927, however, most of the ILD activity
had been concentrated on the Sacco-Vanzetti case. In September 1928 the

* Many were used without permission. It took Sinclair nearly a year to have his name
removed, while Debs was listed long after his death.

spotlight refocused on California. That month the ILD announced that the Anita Whitney branch of the ILD had been renamed the Mooney-Billings branch; a few days later there was a Communist attempt to introduce an hysterical class war Mooney-Billings resolution at the State Federation of Labor convention. Both moves angered Mooney, who wrote President Keough of the International Molders' Union that he was absolutely opposed to Communists collecting funds in the name of Mooney and Billings and using them for their own purposes.

By January it was apparent that the Mooney-Billings case was being used as the basis for an intensive nationwide fund-raising campaign. "This has got to stop," Mooney complained in a letter to Roger Baldwin, "or I shall have to do the thing that I do not want to do—make public statement and give it general circulation throughout the entire country. This charge was leveled against them in the Sacco Vanzetti case and from the way things are now shaping up in our case, it seems with some foundation to it."

That Mooney's complaints were directed to Keough and Baldwin—neither of whom was associated with the ILD—indicated his reluctance to act. Many of Mooney's most ardent early supporters had become Communists—among them Robert Minor, William Z. Foster, Elizabeth Gurley Flynn, Mother Bloor, "Big Bill" Haywood, James P. Cannon, and Earl Browder. Too, with the AFL unions unable to contribute directly to the defense, he was reluctant to alienate any part of the radical movement. Nevertheless, on January 13, 1929, he wrote Alfred Wagenknecht, secretary of the ILD: "From all over the country come reports to us from various sources that branches of the ILD are holding Mooney-Billings Dances, Balls, Bazaars, Picnics, meetings and debates . . . Your organization has been conducting an intensive drive for funds, and the burden of their appeal is based upon the desire to defend and free Tom Mooney and Warren Billings—yet not one cent of this money is sent to the Tom Mooney Molders' Defense Committee that is handling the actual defense of Mooney and Billings."

It was a warning; when it brought no reply Mooney considered stronger action. When a Catholic publication, the *Monitor,* ran an article stating that all Mooney-Billings contributions should be sent to the ILD, Mooney wrote the editor and protested that this organization was definitely not authorized to collect funds in their name. "They want to use the case for their own ends," he wrote. "Just as soon as I get word from my co-defendant Warren K Billings . . . I will make a public announcement of my attitude towards the ILD and its relations to this case. I shall ask them to drop my case entirely—issue no literature, statements, and above all else, not to collect any funds in my name or the name of my case."

The statement wasn't necessary, however, for as soon as the *Monitor* published Mooney's letter the agitation subsided.

It didn't cease entirely, however.

"They have as little brains as it is possible to have and still remain out of the Bug House," Mooney wrote Mary Gallagher in March, commenting on an ILD leaflet that distorted the facts of the case.*

Again in July 1929 ILD activity caused Mooney to comment, "The less they have to do with our case the better I like them."

3 ·

Despite such ephemera, during 1929 the Mooney-Billings case gained new momentum.

On February 25th, the 12th anniversary of Tom Mooney's sentencing, some 2000 people attended a mass meeting in San Francisco's Knights of Columbus auditorium to hear the man who sentenced Mooney to hang say: "The Mooney case is one of the dirtiest jobs ever put over and I resent the fact that my court was used for such a contemptible piece of work . . . Tom Mooney is innocent and ought to be pardoned . . . I regret that the Governor takes so long to act."

In March the National Mooney-Billings Committee published Henry L. Hunt's 445-page book: *The Case of Thomas J. Mooney and Warren K. Billings: Abstract and Analysis of the Record Before Governor Young of California.* It was, as Frankfurter had suggested, a lawyerlike work; unfortunately it lacked the human element present in Frankfurter's own book on the Sacco-Vanzetti case. In short, it was an impressive legal document—a labor of some three months of concentrated effort—but not very effective propaganda, and Mooney did not bother to write Hunt acknowledging its receipt. The American Civil Liberties Union, however, sold a sizable number of copies at $2 each.

In March Estelle Smith gave Fremont Older her fullest confession to date. Much of it was repetition, but there were some new details.

Prior to and after the Billings trial the defense had been unable to locate Estelle. McNutt had assumed that Fickert was hiding her outside the city. Much of this time she had been in a hospital in a strait jacket, she now confessed, attempting to cure her morphine addiction. She had been under the influence of narcotics throughout the Billings trial, taking

---

* Among other things, it was claimed that Mooney and Billings were among the founders of the ILD, since they had been active in its forerunner, The International Workers' Defense League. This peculiar genealogy overlooked two rather pertinent facts: (1) there was a gap of five years between the demise of the IWDL and the birth of the ILD, and (2) the IWDL had fought the first Communist attempt to take over the American labor movement at the National Mooney Congress in Chicago.

morphine tablets at each recess.

The young man photographed on the Eilers roof was her dentist-employer's illegitimate son, she now claimed. Which was why he had never come forward in response to the newspaper plea.

There were also some new charges.

Oxman had offered her a bribe "in five figures" to identify the man in the hall as Mooney.* She had once overheard Swanson coaching the Edeaus and had mentioned it to Fickert; he had told her to mind her own business. In her original statement to Fickert she had told of seeing a drunken man playing a flute or tin whistle in front of 721 Market at the time of the alleged incidents. Later Fickert had told her to leave the tin whistle story out of her testimony, as he was saving that for the Edeaus. The mother and daughter had later testified to such an incident.

"Had I been normal I never would have identified this man as Warren K. Billings."

In May U.S. Senator Thomas D. Schall of Minnesota wrote a dramatic defense of Mooney and Billings, which appeared in the influential magazine *Plain Talk* under the title "Why Is Mooney in Prison?" Roger Baldwin had interested Schall in the case.

That same month Harry Emerson Fosdick, Francis J. McConnell, head of the Federal Council of Churches, Harry Sloan Coffin, president of the Union Theological Seminary, and a number of other prominent theologians wrote to Governor Young demanding the immediate pardon of Mooney and Billings. These men had also been contacted by Baldwin, and persuaded by Hunt's lawyerlike work. In California, Governor Young sat stone-faced while his own pastor, Dr. Oswald W. S. McCall, said from the pulpit of the First Congregational Church in Berkeley: "I maintain that if the state can put an innocent man in prison and keep him there and justify the doing of the same, and refuse to be sensitive and quick in response when the prisoners are not guilty—then this doctrine and practice is more darkly sinister in its character and more far-reaching in this respect than any doctrine Mooney ever stood for."

That month, too, the first 37,000 copies of Mooney's new pamphlet appeared. It was still a long way from the 2,300,000 needed to reach every California voter, but it was a start.

On June 19th the Mooney-Billings case erupted on the floor of the United States Senate. Requesting and being given permission to speak, Senator Gerald P. Nye (North Dakota) observed that one of the few subjects the new President discussed in his inaugural address was law enforcement. Yet "there exists today in President Hoover's own State of California a situation which admittedly is casting disrepute on our entire

* That Estelle failed to mention this in her earlier affidavit regarding Oxman raises doubts about the authenticity of much of the rest of her current confession. Her narcotics addiction and hospitalization were established, however, by hospital records.

judicial system . . . I refer to the case of Tom Mooney and Warren K. Billings."

Speaking for nearly an hour, Nye summarized the significant developments in the case over the 13 years the two men had been incarcerated, quoting from Judge Griffin's letters, the court records, the recantations, and paying particular attention to the discrediting of Oxman.

When he finished, Senator Schall added his endorsement. He had had all the transcripts of the case read to him, the blind Senator said, "and I want to say that I think Tom Mooney is as innocent of the crime of which he was convicted as any man in the Senate."

Mr. Shortridge (California): "Mr. President, may I put a question to the Senator from North Dakota?"

Permission granted, Shortridge thought it pertinent to elicit the fact that the pardons of Mooney and Billings were now under consideration by the present Governor of California. "There is just one fact which might interest the Senate," the junior senator from California added. "That fact is quite apart from the question of the guilt or innocence of Mooney and Billings. The Senator in his statement referred to certain witnesses who testified against these defendants, and made the comments to which we have just listened. One of those witnesses was a man from Oregon. His name was Frank Oxman. He was a witness on the trial, as I recall, of Mooney. In any event, he was afterwards arrested and prosecuted in the courts at San Francisco. I defended him, and the jury very promptly acquitted him . . ."

Mr. Nye: "Is it not also true that since the trial of Mr. Oxman there has been disclosed evidence which was not then available with relation to Mr. Oxman's personal case?"

Mr. Shortridge: "I really do not know."

Mr. Nye: "I think that is the fact."

Mr. Shortridge: "I have not heard of any such development. There may be such; I do not know."

Mr. Nye: "I think that upon further evidence the presiding judge now bases his contention that Oxman was guilty of perjury."

Senator Burton K. Wheeler (Montana) then took the floor to ask that the letters of Griffin, the jurors, and the others on this, "one of the foulest conspiracies ever perpetrated in this country," be read into the *Congressional Record,* concluding, with barbed civility, "it was not on account of the innocence of Oxman that he was acquitted, but because of the cleverness of his counsel."

Mr. Shortridge: "I thank the Senator very much."

In August the National Mooney-Billings Committee issued its own pamphlet on the case, *The Story of Mooney and Billings,* a short, factual chronology of the main events in the case from 1916 to the present.

Mooney did not like it. He felt its sale would interfere with "my own pamphlet." He demanded an accounting of the funds received by the American Civil Liberties Union, threatening to repudiate the committee if such was not immediately forthcoming. When a sizable amount of money from the pamphlet sale was turned over to the TMMDC he expressed his thanks by commenting, "On the whole I do not have much faith in Liberals in the matter of funds. They do not give like the Unions do." Fortunately Roger Baldwin had a great deal of patience.

In August Judge Griffin and Fremont Older went to Los Angeles, where they spoke in Trinity Auditorium to an overflow crowd of more than 5000. The meeting place and heavy advance publicity had been paid for by heiress Aline Barnsdall, who had renewed her participation in the case. It was, according to Older, "the greatest mass meeting I have ever seen in my life." Mooney, reading transcripts of the speeches, noted that though not a professional public speaker, Older spoke with such emotion that he "stirs the audience every time he speaks." Mooney was given to writing such things, but rarely to the person who would most have appreciated them. This was in a letter to Baldwin.

But it was Griffin's speech that moved both the speaker and his audience to tears as he told how it felt to know that you have sent an innocent man to prison. Mary Gallagher had a stenographer transcribe the speech and rushed a copy to William Randolph Hearst at San Simeon. He was so impressed that he ordered it run on the front page of all Hearst papers the following day.

In September Governor Young confided to Fremont Older and several others that he would probably pardon Tom Mooney and Warren Billings "in the very near future."

4 ·

Older told Billings, Mooney, and Mary Gallagher in strict confidence. Mary Gallagher foolishly told the press that she personally believed the Governor would pardon Mooney by Labor Day. The Governor's office announced that any decision on the case was at least three months distant.

Although this sort of irresponsibility irritated Mooney more than any other, his anger was short-lived. He was too elated.

On September 18th he wrote to Martin Eagan, "To me at this writing from all sources of information and the 'feel' and 'color' of things, the case is won—just when we will be pardoned is a matter of—well we will say hours—days—weeks—months—yes maybe years—but it is won right now."

Billings was not so optimistic. The governor could not grant a pardon unless a pardon request was before him, and his petition, unlike Mooney's, was not yet completed. For eight years Mooney had stalled on the McDonald confession. "Opposed to presentation of Billings petition before decision in my case," Mooney had wired Mary Gallagher at one point; "In any event our committee will not under any circumstances pay counsel fees for presenting such petition." Billings had gone ahead and prepared his petition by himself, without legal aid. Older appealed to Mooney to give Billings a notarized copy of the McDonald confession.

"If Billings presents his case now," Mooney wrote Older, "that gives him [Young] a reasonable excuse to delay the case for another year as he has for three years in my own case—thus will he be brought to the election time . . ."

Older insisted, however, threatening to make public Mooney's procrastination. Finally, after eight years, Billings received a copy of McDonald's confession.

Shortly thereafter the governor announced to the press that he did not have a pardon application from Billings and that "It would be unfair for me to act on the Mooney case before I could consider Billings' plea." They were, he said, "parallel cases."

Now Mooney couldn't wait for Billings to finish his petition. "It is not a correct or perfect legal document that is freeing us—it is an awakened or an aroused public opinion," he wrote him through the defense committee, urging him to hurry and not waste time on legal niceties.

"We have won our case in the minds of the masses of the people— and it is only a matter of time before we will be pardoned," Mooney wrote Older on October 9th. "I feel that I will be able to take to freedom like a duck takes to water—with self respect, poise, grace and dignity. I have no axes to grind, no old scores to clean up, but just want to find my place in the big world outside. Victory will be all the sweeter because of the long delay and the desperate struggle to obtain it."

He begged Older to let him know the big day.

Older advised patience.

Mooney selected the material and had himself measured for his "coming out" suit. On the 24th he learned that Billings had nearly finished his petition and would submit it the following week. "How happy that news made me," he wrote Mary Gallagher. "I am getting ready for the big day in earnest . . ."

His letter to Mary Gallagher on October 26th was short "so that I can put in several hours on my junk pile—straightening out things for the HOME COMING.

"My intoxication still continues—Ye Gods, what exhuberance of joy and happiness prevails within me these days . . . How lovely it will be to be out in the free air again . . ."

In November Billings submitted his petition. On the 19th Governor

Young submitted it to the California Supreme Court for an opinion, asking that they act with all due haste. Two days later, in a surprise move, the Governor announced that he was referring Thomas J. Mooney's petition to his Advisory Pardon Board for investigation and recommendation.

Some reporters observed that this might well be the prelude not to action but further inaction—that what Young had actually done was to remove the responsibility for decision from his own shoulders. Normally Mooney would have been the first to suspect the governor's action, but he was too excited. "Dear," he wrote Mary Gallagher on the 25th, "I do not share your fears and apprehensions nor pessimism about the late action— I understand it—the only objection I have is to the delay . . ."

On December 2nd there was an unexpected surprise. J. W. Miller, the holdout of the 10 still living Mooney jurors, wrote to Governor Young asking him to pardon Tom Mooney.

Then came a new rumor, that Young had asked the two groups to stall on the petitions.

"It is too evident that he does not want to pardon me," Mooney wrote Senator Schall on the 7th, asking the prospects of a Congressional investigation of the case.

On December 14th Young announced that he had asked the pardon board to consider Mooney's petition at their next meeting, on the 16th. "What a surprise—that announcement in last nights paper and over the air between 7 and 7:30 from the Governor's office. I might yet eat my turkey dinner at home on X-mas . . ."

The board met on the 16th and took up the Mooney plea. On adjourning they announced that they would have to delay action until a later date, due to the voluminous transcripts.

"I just received absolute information that everything is all right," Older wrote Mooney the same day. "The Board of Pardons will render a favorable decision; so will the Supreme Court. So it is only a matter of a short time. No one can say just how many days, but it won't be long until you and Billings will be free, and for God's sake don't do anything at this time to create ill feeling toward yourself."

On the 19th Mooney wrote Older that his letter of the 16th, pleading for patience, disgusted him. "Can't we get down to brass tacks on this fight and expose him and his shams—it is pure political cowardice—let's call it that."

Apparently Older learned something that indicated his "absolute information" was less than reliable, for he now did much the same thing that he had urged Mooney not to do. He ran a long editorial in the *Call-Bulletin* * charging Governor Young with reneging on his word and with intending to procrastinate until after the August primaries.

---

* In 1929 Hearst bought the failing *Bulletin* and gave it back to Older, the two papers merging as the *Call-Bulletin*.

The editorial restored Mooney's confidence in Older. "My plan now is to wait a reasonable time for a decision and then failing to obtain one, withdraw my petition from further stalling by this Governor, and urge his defeat and the election of a man courageous enough to do simple justice to the citizens of the state." So Mooney wrote Older on the 23rd. Older never received the letter; the warden returned it to Mooney, objecting to the above remarks. The objection wasn't surprising inasmuch as the warden was one of the members of the Advisory Pardon Board.

On December 25th Tom Mooney had his turkey dinner in San Quentin prison.

Yet the press continued to print rumors, one to the effect that the governor intended to pardon Mooney and Billings before the end of the year—now only days away.

Governor Young's reply to Older's letters and editorial appeared in the *Chronicle* on the 31st. Whether he acted on the Mooney case before or after the primaries next August, the governor said, he would not be influenced by political considerations. He didn't resent Older's impatience, he observed; he had known Fremont Older a long time; he was aware that he believed in the innocence of Mooney and Billings, just as "I am not yet convinced as to the innocence of these men . . ." But he did feel that Older was going too far in implying that the California Supreme Court would be less than fair in arriving at its decision. "The proper disposition of these cases is a duty too sacred to justify attack by those who would seek to use it as a political football."

" . . . this," Mooney wrote Mary Gallagher on New Year's Eve, "after three years of stalling and deliberately evading a decision.

"Oh what's the use of it all—all I can do now is to wait as I did before."

25· People Should Be Told About It!

IF TOM MOONEY is not freed, he should, by rights, be taken out of prison by force!"

The hulking giant in the wrinkled suit who delivered this pronouncement to the press at the Mark Hopkins Hotel, nervously twisting his handkerchief as he did so, was one of America's best-known novelists.

Theodore Dreiser had "discovered" Tom Mooney.

Such discoveries were usually neither spontaneous nor accidental. A well-run defense committee functions much like the headquarters of a political campaign. The distinguished names that adorn the letterheads rarely volunteer their endorsements. They are carefully courted and cajoled. Often, as in Dreiser's case, it is a long courtship. For more than two years Mooney and his defense committee had been working on the author.

By now the procedure for soliciting aid from a name personality was well defined. Mooney would write to the person directly, appealing for help. Such an appeal, coming from behind the walls of San Quentin Prison, was not easily dismissed. Then from the defense committee a second communication, containing the major documents of the case (the current pamphlet, the Mediation Commission Report, the Densmore Report, etc.), would follow. If there was any response—and often even if there wasn't—this would be followed by a personal visit from a representative of the defense committee—Belle, when she was still active, or Mary Gallagher, or if the person lived outside California, by a person prominent in that area. Whenever possible someone known to be a friend of the person was used. Dreiser was appealed to, for example, through his secretary and several of his women friends.

In 1929 Dreiser had finally responded with a letter affirming his belief in Mooney's innocence, a $5 contribution, and a letter to Governor Young demanding Mooney's pardon.

In May of 1930, Dreiser, on a trip to the West Coast, visited Mooney at San Quentin.

For months Mooney had worked to bring this meeting about. Sundays, in the yard, he and J. B. McNamara had read *An American Tragedy* aloud

333

to each other. Yet Mooney's anticipation was based even more on two other books, neither of which Dreiser had written: *The Life and Times* of *Émile Zola* and Zola's own *J'Accuse!* Mooney had long been fascinated with the Dreyfus case and Zola's part in it.*

"What the Mooney case needs is an Emile Zola," Mooney had written to several of his correspondents, "one who can and will risk his reputation as well as his life to arouse and shock the conscience of the people into the enormity of the crime being done by the very agents supposed to prevent its occurrence."

Mooney's longing for a Zola was also a reproach to Fremont Older, who knew Mooney well enough by now to see it as such. "Dreyfus never told Zola what he could or could not write," Older remarked to one of his reporters on the way back from visiting Mooney at San Quentin. "But, on the other hand," Older said, as if immediately sorry for letting his feelings show, "Dreyfus was only on Devil's Island for 12 years; Mooney and Billings have been on theirs for nearly 14."

Mooney and Dreiser looked at each other over the partitioned visitor's table. Neither was what the other had expected. Mooney was neater and in better health than Dreiser had anticipated, and Dreiser's strange habit of continuously wringing his handkerchief unnerved Mooney. But the uneasiness quickly passed. Mooney, simply and with deep feeling, told Dreiser his story, observing that his one desire was to get out and go back to work in the cause of labor. Dreiser pointed out—he was not the first to do so—that in prison Mooney was a figure of international prominence, but that once freed he might be quickly forgotten. Mooney said he realized this but still wanted out.

"Tom Mooney," Dreiser declaimed, "you are the personification of a great issue!" Mooney looked startled, then burst into tears, moving the equally emotional Dreiser to the verge of same.

This happened occasionally—once during a visit by Debs shortly before his death, another time during a visit by Foster. Mooney hated to show weakness, but try as he might to control them, his emotions often overwhelmed him.

Dreiser angrily called on Governor Young and demanded Mooney's release. Young patiently explained to his fellow-author that "the wheels of justice are already moving in the Mooney case."

Dreiser had a number of irritating habits, one of which was to explain a matter as if his listener were totally unfamiliar with the subject. Re-

* In 1927, on learning that Dreyfus was still living, Mooney asked Berkman to see him to speak out on behalf of Sacco and Vanzetti, also Mooney and Billings. Dreyfus, still a conservative army officer, refused, observing that he had a firm policy never to comment on current events. However, just before the executions of Sacco and Vanzetti he did relent slightly, with a brief statement that read: "When doubt exists, it is fighting providence to commit the irreparable."

porters who had covered the Mooney case for years were not impressed on being told what it was all about by a man who had arrived in San Francisco the day before.

Dreiser requested an audience with William Randolph Hearst. Request granted, he drove to San Simeon, where Hearst cordially welcomed him and took him on a tour of his baronial estate. Over lunch, charmingly presided over by Miss Davies, Dreiser told the publisher all about the Mooney case. Hearst (probably without a trace of a smile) promised to look into the matter.

Dreiser evidently expected his California trip to accomplish more than it did. In Oregon he told a reporter that he had tried to free Mooney but had failed; "William Randolph Hearst promised me he would do it and now we'll see." It is also likely that Dreiser read a great deal more into Hearst's remarks than was there.

The matter continued to enrage him, however. On returning to New York he called on Roy Howard and told him about Mooney. This visit, at least, did accomplish something: in October the Scripps-Howard chain began a campaign for Mooney's release.

George Jean Nathan once remarked of Dreiser, "One always finds Dreiser surprised and amazed at what has long been familiar to most persons." The occasion for this remark was an incident on the same trip, when Dreiser saw the Grand Canyon for the first time. "People should be told about it!" he said enthusiastically.

Yet Dreiser's fresh, though naïve, indignation was a tonic Mooney desperately needed.

There was one more irritation about the trip, insofar as Dreiser was concerned. Sinclair Lewis had discovered Mooney first. In March he had driven up from Carmel with Lincoln Steffens to visit Mooney, McNamara, and Schmidt as background research for a labor novel he anticipated writing.

It was perhaps fortunate that the two meetings were not closer timed. Lewis believed that Dreiser had, consciously or unconsciously, plagiarized a goodly portion of one of his wife's books. He also undoubtedly resented Dreiser's ungentlemanly bragging about an affair with Dorothy Thompson in Moscow. Even more basic to their ill will, however, was the fact that the two men were leading contenders for the 1930 Nobel Literature Prize. The next time they met was in New York, after the prize had been given to Lewis. On this occasion Lewis accused Dreiser of plagiarism and Dreiser slapped Lewis' face.

San Quentin was spared this bit of literary histrionics.

It is probable that Lewis' claim to Mooney predated Dreiser's not by months but years. There is some evidence that Lewis may have first seen Mooney when he was the radical grain of sand in the San Francisco Labor

Council. Lewis, together with William Rose Benét, sat in on several council meetings at this time, and Mark Schorer, is his biography *Sinclair Lewis: An American Life,* observes that the radical labor leader Steve Manton, of Benét's Pulitzer Prize winning *The Dust Which Is God,* was apparently patterned after Tom Mooney.

Mooney had first written Lewis in 1928, about the same time he wrote Dreiser. In reply, Lewis had asserted his faith in Mooney's innocence but noted that due to other obligations he could do nothing for him at present. During the meeting with Mooney, he explained that his labor novel, once it was completed, would probably do a great deal toward securing his release.

Although both men remained interested in the case, and Dreiser would soon play a larger part, Mooney was still without his Zola. He did hope, for a time, that Lewis' labor novel would indeed be a means for his salvation, but as Schorer makes clear, the book was just in the "talking stage" and Lewis never did get around to writing it.

2 ·

Mooney's hopes continued to rise and fall.

In May of 1930 Marcet Haldeman-Julius came to San Francisco to interview Mooney for a series of articles in *The American Freeman.* On her arrival, the attractive wife of Emanuel Haldeman-Julius (the Girard, Kansas, publisher of the *Freeman,* best known by the general public, however, for his Little Blue Books) plunged right into the drama of the Mooney case.

Mary Gallagher took her to San Quentin to see Mooney. When the two women gave their names to the guard, they were told to report to the warden's office immediately. Fearful that something had happened to Mooney, they hurried there to find a call waiting from Fremont Older.

You can tell Mooney, Older told Mary, that I have definite, though unofficial, word that the Supreme Court has reached a favorable decision on the Billings case. You can tell Tom that it is now only a matter of time before he and Billings are released.

"I shall never forget my feelings as I watched Tom Mooney hear this news," Mrs. Haldeman-Julius later wrote. "Hope and disbelief contended in his face."

There was reason for both. In the past the referring of the case of a twice-convicted felon to the State Supreme Court had been little more than a formality. Usually the court did not even open the records but acted favorably simply on the basis of the governor's request. Against this, however, were 14 years of defeated hopes.

Skeptical now of anything but proven facts, Mooney told Mrs. Haldeman-Julius on her next visit, "You will see! He put off granting the pardons until after August—and if he doesn't grant them by then, we will be here another four years . . . I don't want my friends to relax their efforts until we are walking out of the gates of San Quentin and Folsom."

But they already had. Sure that the release of the two men was imminent, Mary Gallagher and the defense committee discontinued the current campaign. A new printing of *Governor Young: Pardon Tom Mooney— Innocent* had been scheduled; wishing to do nothing now that might offend the governor, Mary canceled it and halted the mailing of copies already on hand. Some of the paid staff workers were laid off. All this was done without Tom's knowledge.

Fremont Older's source of information this time was not the governor but a justice of the California Supreme Court. He was soon to discover that even men so highly placed could be cruelly vicious in attempting to settle an old score.

On July 4th, Warren K. Billings' thirty-ninth birthday, Governor Young announced that two days earlier the California State Supreme Court, by a 6 to 1 vote, had declined to recommend Billings' pardon.

Even considering the Densmore Report, the court's opinion was easily the most remarkable document born out of the Mooney-Billings case.

Oxman and the Edeaus were thoroughly discredited, the court admitted. Considering John McDonald's earlier testimony and his confession, however, the court chose to believe the earlier testimony, inasmuch as the confession seemed "to have been inspired by McDonald's reiterated sense of injury and complaint against the police and public officials of San Francisco because he failed to receive the reward which he claims to have been promised by them . . ."

Yet the court was satisfied that even without the testimony of McDonald, there was still evidence to prove that Billings had been on the scene "carrying a suitcase of the general dimensions and color of that which contained the time-bomb which exploded at said time and place." (Just what evidence proved this was unstated: only McDonald and Oxman had placed Billings at the corner of Steuart and Market.)

It was Billings' past associations, however, which constituted the greatest evidence against him, the court said. "The record sufficiently shows that prior to and at the time of his conviction of his former offense he was the friend and associate of an organized group of persons, men and women, who were actively engaged in plotting and even executing crimes of violence against both property and persons not only during labor disputes but generally as a means of uttering their protest against both the political and industrial forms and movements of modern society . . .

"There is sufficient in the record before us to show that the deliberated and fiendishly prepared-for crime of Preparedness day [was] in all human probability conceived and carried forward to its execution by the same group of evilly-disposed individuals, whose friend and associate Billings for several years had been and into the inner councils of which he was wont to come and go."

In the Mooney and Billings trials, Fickert and his associates had tried to introduce the conspiracy theory, judging the defendants guilty by association with Goldman, Berkman, and others. In both instances the trial judges had excluded such evidence. The California Supreme Court now based its decision upon it.

The report concluded, in one of the most astonishing opinions ever issued from the high bench:

"It is fairly inferable from his past and present affiliations that Warren K. Billings was familiar with the plot and plans of this group of his most intimate associates, and this being so it is an almost irresistible conclusion that if Warren K. Billings did not himself prepare and plant the deadly time bomb of the Preparedness Day disaster, he and his intimate associates and co-defendant, Mooney, know and have always, both before and since the occurrence of that tragedy, known who did prepare and plant that bomb, and the deadly purpose for which it was prepared and planted.

"Yet there has never come from the lips of either of these defendants, or from out the inner circle of their associates, the slightest tangible hint or aid to the public officials as to anyone else which might lead to a discovery of the real perpetrators of this revolting crime, if these two defendants were not the guilty ones . . ."

In brief, the California Supreme Court, with a single dissenting vote, declared that if Mooney and Billings were not themselves guilty of the Preparedness Day bombing, they were guilty of knowing who the perpetrators were; and since they had withheld this information from the police, they belonged exactly where they were.

The court's decision raised a storm of indignation. The New York *Evening World* called it "a disgrace to American civilization . . ." "An incredible document," observed the *New Republic* in an article entitled "Prejudice Speaks from the Bench." *Outlook* characterized it "A shocking decision . . . Never before have we seen such preposterous reasoning from a high State or Federal tribunal."

But in California, the only place where opinions counted, insofar as Governor Young was concerned, feelings were other. "This paper has never wavered in its firm belief in the guilt of the two," noted the influential Sacramento *Bee.* The inquiry, said the San Francisco *Chronicle,* has "cleared off much of the fog obscuring the truth in the Mooney case."

And the Los Angeles *Times,* with an excellent example of its famous logic, concluded that McDonald "may actually have committed perjury but his declaration that he did so, taken at face value, is the strongest presumptive evidence that he did not."

Governor Young denied Billings' pardon request. And the following day, July 7, 1930, the Advisory Pardon Board, acting on the assumpiton that the two cases were "parallel," denied Thomas J. Mooney's application for pardon. (In at least one important particular Mooney's case differed from Billings': Mooney's alibi was established by photographs and 16 unimpeached witnesses.)

On July 8th, Governor Young accepted the Board's recommendation and denied Mooney's pardon. He did not bar the door entirely, however, declaring that if McDonald or any of the other witnesses was willing to recant publicly before the State Supreme Court he might be willing to ask for a rehearing.

Perhaps Young's remark was intended as a pacifier. Duncan Aikman once described Young as "A soothing type of politician, who had never yet faced an opportunity without trying to conciliate it." It seemed a safe promise: Mooney's attorneys had already told the Governor that McDonald was probably dead.

There began a frantic nation-wide search for John McDonald; the Scripps-Howard papers plastered his picture on their front pages together with a $500 reward notice. One of their own claimed it. On the 12th an alert Scripps-Howard reporter recognized McDonald in the drunk tank of a Baltimore jail. Ed Nockles took the next train from Chicago to Baltimore to bring him back to California to testify before the State Supreme Court. The statute of limitations on his perjury had now expired.

On the 13th the California State Federation of Labor endorsed Governor Young's reelection bid.

Now that McDonald had been found, Billings' attorney submitted a petition for rehearing, which the Supreme Court granted on the 27th. That same day Mooney again refiled his pardon petition, which the Governor again referred to his Advisory Pardon Board.

The primary elections were five weeks away and the Mooney-Billings case was again wide open.

3 ·

The Billings pardon rehearing lasted four weeks. It was, as one reporter aptly described it, "a huge tragic farce."

In at least one detail John McDonald had lied to Frank Walsh in 1921. His syphilis had not been arrested. The John McDonald brought to California by Nockles was a sick, slobbering old man with the mentality of a moron. In the words of the court itself, "a more abject spectacle of debased and degenerated manhood was never before presented to a body of judicial and quasi-judicial investigators."

On the stand McDonald wept, cringed, contradicted himself repeatedly. Then, when wholly tied up in his contradictions, he would thrust them all aside by screaming "Lies! Lies! It was all lies!" At one point he charged that he had been put "under a spell," at another he whimpered "Go ahead. Crucify me."

Since the Supreme Court was not meeting in an official capacity but as a non-judicial fact-finding commission, ordinary rules of conduct were suspended. It was to be far more informal than anyone anticipated. Although the stated purpose of the rehearing had been to examine McDonald, the court, to the surprise of petitioners' attorney, now called Estelle Smith to the stand.

The reason was quickly apparent. Estelle now recanted her recantations. She had been under the "unnatural influence" of Fremont Older. He just wouldn't leave her alone. Not that she disliked him, she quickly added, she was very fond of him. Why, he had given her a string of pearls and other gifts. You might say she really loved him, Estelle said, with an attempted blush. He had been *so* good to her.

Her recantations were in themselves strange. Estelle had signed two confessions in 1917, one in 1918, another in 1920, and still another in 1929. She recanted a bit of each. She was now sure that Billings was the man she had seen. But she didn't deny that Swanson had coached the Edeaus. She denied the tin whistle story but, on cross-examination by Walsh, admitted that it could be true. She denied that Oxman had tried to bribe her into identifying Mooney as the man with the woman in the hall, but didn't deny that Oxman had tried to bribe her into identifying Weinberg. And she admitted the story in her mother's affidavit about forcing the man to pay her $1 after his wife used the lavatory, which contradicted her own testimony in all the trials.

She chattered incessantly, not even the justices being able to stop her. Since this was a quasi-legal hearing, she could refuse to answer questions without fear of contempt, and she freely did so. Not until her second day on the stand was Walsh able to pin her down to a single straight answer. Her performance ranged from histrionics to outright flirtatiousness. Asked her present occupation and place of residence, she turned to the justices and replied cutely, "I'd rather not say here on the stand, but I'd be glad to tell you gentlemen privately."

Fickert and Cuhna were present, but both Billings and Mooney had been denied permission to attend. This was only one of the handicaps under which the defense operated.

Billings was represented, against his express wishes, by Edwin V. Mc-Kenzie. Prior to the rehearing, McKenzie, as Billings' attorney, had publicly repudiated the frame-up charges, averring they would play no part in the proceedings. Some interpreted this as a means of "getting the rats to abandon the sinking ship." But McKenzie had done this without the approval of Billings or Mooney. For this and other reasons Billings discharged McKenzie as his counsel and requested that he be allowed to represent himself. The court, denying the request, appointed McKenzie to defend him. Walsh had hurried out from New York to defend Mooney's interests. But since this was a hearing on Billings' petition and McKenzie's unauthorized action had closed the door on some of the most vital testimony, his course of action was limited.

An even greater handicap was the open hostility of the court. Of the seven justices, only one, William H. Langdon, could be called a mild liberal. Five of the justices were from small towns. At this time California Supreme Court justices were elected, not appointed; two, justices Preston and Schenk, were up for reelection in November. Preston, with the seeming acquiscence of the others, conducted most of the questioning. Acting "as both judge and prosecutor," Lillian Symes wrote in *Harper's,* Preston "displayed a bias that amazed even newspaper men, and generally put on a performance that has probably never been equaled in our judicial history."

The proceedings were so informal that once when Walsh tried to make an objection Preston ordered "You keep your snoot out of this."

Cuhna was called to the stand. Preston's questions, nearly all dealing with radicalism, ranged as far afield as Cuhna's opinions on the guilt of Sacco and Vanzetti, the McNamaras, Haywood and Pettibone, and the Haymarket dynamiters. Every bit of innuendo that had been inadmissable in the trials was now introduced, along with a complete file of *The Blast.* Excerpts from a letter accusing Mooney of planting the bomb were read into the record. When Walsh asked to see the letter, he was denied permission. He could not even determine whom it was from, or to whom, or when mailed—until reading it in its entirety in the *Chronicle* the following day. It was anonymous, its "facts" easily refuted.

During the questioning Cuhna made several statements only less astonishing than the fact that a Supreme Court justice concurred with them.

"I didn't have any particular theory as to 721 Market Street," Cuhna said. "I was satisfied that Mr. Mooney should be convicted upon his activities alone . . ."

"In other words," interposed Justice Preston, "they ought to be convicted of aiding and abetting, whether they put the suitcase down there or not?"

"Absolutely!" Cuhna replied. "At that time I was willing to have Mr.

Mooney even hung on that theory."

The court's ruling that it would consider any relevant evidence of whatever sort (excluding frame-up evidence) aided Billings and Mooney in
one particular. With a court order their attorneys were authorized to go
through prosecution records relating to the bombing. At this time they located only a part of the Bomb Bureau's files, stored in the basement of
the Hall of Justice, but contained there was McDonald's original affidavit, made two days after the bombing, in which he described having
seen two men wholly dissimilar to Mooney and Billings.

The affidavit, suppressed for 14 years, was one of the most important
pieces of evidence yet uncovered, for it indicated not only that McDonald
had perjured himself but that Fickert knew it.

In an ordinary courtroom this by itself would have been enough to discredit McDonald's testimony. But introduced as evidence in the rehearing
it caused not even a stir among the judges.

4 ·

By now it was apparent that this was not a rehearing but a trial, and
the real defendant neither Billings nor Mooney, nor even Goldman nor
Berkman, but Fremont Older. Finally called to the stand, he was sub-
jected to a barrage of slanders, insults, and insinuations, ranging from im-
plications that he had guilty knowledge of the bombings to the quite un-
subtle charge that he had seduced Estelle Smith in order to persuade her
to change her story.

It was evident that the court had not forgiven Older for exposing Justice Henshaw.

"Through it all," a rival editor was forced to admit, "he responded with
cool dignity."

Cora Older begged her husband for a chance to take the stand to
corroborate his explanation of the string of pearls. Older refused to subject her to Preston's insults.

"A friend who was importing these artificial pearls from Japan sent me
a dozen strings," Mrs. Older explained to Evelyn Wells. "I didn't care for
them, and told Fremont to take them to the office and give them to the
office girls. He kept them on the desk, and offered a string to any of the
secretaries and telephone girls who happened in to the office.

"Not all of the strings had been disposed of when this woman dropped
in to see him, as she often did. She admired them, and he waved his hand
at them and said 'Help yourself.' That is the romantic history of the
string of pearls."

Fremont Older was seventy-four years old; although already legendary in many respects, no one could quite imagine him "skirt chasing," and particularly not after Estelle Smith, who had aged much less gracefully than the white-haired editor.

Yes, they had crucified him, Older admitted after stepping down from the stand. But even that could be taken as evidence that "human nature has improved a little. Once they would have boiled me in oil for daring to say I thought Mooney innocent."

Almost as an afterthought, the court decided to hear Warren Billings, and went to Folsom Prison for that purpose. He was interrogated for five hours, largely by Justice Preston. And, considering the harshness of the inquisition, he fared remarkably well, observed an *Examiner* reporter, telling his story, whenever Preston would let him do so, in a convincingly straightforward manner.

Preston began by stating that it seemed strange that Billings had waited 14 years to assert his innocence. Billings replied that he had always said that he was innocent, and explained the circumstances under which he had agreed to let Mooney submit his pardon application first.

Q. In other words, you have rested for nearly fourteen years, or more than thirteen years on a conviction that you deem unjust without a whimper until this petition was filed, is that right?

A. Well, I would hardly say it was without—

Q. Well, without effort, then.

A. It had been without any great effort on my part, but that was usually due to the advise that was given me.

Q. That is just what I am trying to get at, are you staying in prison and refusing a parole because you are attempting to aid any particular class of our citizens?

A. No, sir.

Q. Are you trying to promote any particular moral, social or other purpose by remaining in prison without applying for a parole?

A. No, sir.

The bulk of the questioning was similar, dealing not with the events of Preparedness Day—barely mentioned—but with Billings' radicalism. In question after question Preston—apparently under the impression that the American Communist Party was in existence in 1916—attempted to get Billings to admit that he had been and was a Communist, that once released he would attempt to overthrow the government. Billings, however, stated flatly, "I never was in sympathy with Communism . . . I consider myself nothing more, and nothing less, than a trade unionist."

But Preston persisted.

Q. If you had it in your power tonight to reform the government, what would you do first?

A. What would I do first?

Q. Abolish the Supreme Court, I guess, would you?

A. No, sir. I think the first thing I would do would be to elect a Democratic Governor, a Democratic President, and a Democratic Senator.

This was obviously not the answer Preston wanted.

On August 20th, six days before the primary election, the court recessed until "sometime in September." Mooney could say "I told you so," and of course did. The Billings petition had been a disaster and Young had adroitly managed to procrastinate through a whole four-year term in office.

5 ·

What was not anticipated was that Mayor James Rolph would defeat Governor Young in the Republican primary. Campaigning from one end of the state to the other in a chartered airplane, dressed in silk hat and cowboy boots, "Sunny Jim" managed to upstage the colorless Young by 20,000 votes.

Mooney could now claim that Young had been defeated because of his cowardice. Even the *Chronicle* and *Call-Bulletin* agreed, though for opposite reasons, that Young's stalling with the Mooney case had probably cost him the election. Observed the San Rafael *Independent* during the campaign: "Today's prayer, O Lord! Give us a Governor with intestinal fortitude."

But the Mooney case was only one of several issues. The most important was even simpler. Young was a "dry," Rolph obviously "wet," and California was sick of Prohibition.

September came and passed and the Supreme Court still hadn't reconvened. Neither Mooney nor Billings was hopeful. "It seems," Miriam Allen DeFord observed in the *New Republic,* referring to McKenzie's repudiation of the frame-up charges, "that the defense, in its desire to save the Preparedness Day frame-up victims at any cost, has unwittingly closed the prison doors upon them forever."

On November 4th Estelle Smith was arrested in a Chinatown bordello raid and James Rolph was elected Governor of California by the largest margin in the history of the state.

On December 1st the Supreme Court announced its decision. It was, in all essentials, the same as that given in July. By a vote of 6 to 1, the court advised the governor to reject Billings' pardon plea. This he did the following day. The Advisory Pardon Board then announced that it would be unable to complete its investigation of Mooney's petition during Governor Young's term of office.

The only dissenting vote, both in July and December, was that of the only San Franciscan and the only Catholic on the court, Justice William H. Langdon. This was the same man who, a quarter of a century earlier, Mayor Eugene Schmitz had picked for District Attorney on his Union Labor ticket, only to discover, once Langdon was elected, that he had mistakenly chosen an honest man who had no compunctions against trying Schmitz for graft.

"Considered either as an argument of an advocate or as a judicial review of the evidence," Langdon now wrote, "the consolidated majority report is unsound and indefensible. It is unsound because its conclusions are not founded upon established facts. Suspicions, conjectures, unwarranted inferences, irreconcilable inconsistencies, and admitted perjuries are treated as facts. It is indefensible because it appeals to passion and prejudice.

"One-fourth of the report is devoted to anarchistic propaganda and the bad character of the petitioner. The trial court properly held these matters were not admissible. It is manifestly improper to inject them into this inquiry . . .

"The requirement of the majority that the petitioner prove his innocence, either by establishing an alibi or by identifying the perpetrator of the crime, is unreasonable and unwarranted. A perfectly innocent person may be unable to prove an alibi. And it is preposterous to demand of the accused that he place his finger upon the real culprit in order to exculpate himself. Although Billings has presented an alibi, it is unnecessary for us to consider it. When the chain of proof is destroyed he needs none.

"I do not know," Justice Langdon continued, "whether Billings is guilty or innocent of the crime. I do know that there has been a failure of proof to such an extent that there is now not even the semblance of a case against him. Upon the record now before us a recommendation for executive clemency cannot justly be withheld."

Point by point Langdon's opinion refuted the majority report. In years to come it would become a law school "must," a classic example of a great dissenting opinion. It is probable that even if Mooney and Billings could have known this, they would have drawn little consolation from the knowledge. They were now halfway into their 15th year in prison with no prospect of release.

6 ·

One by one they had all betrayed him, or so Mooney felt.

Organized labor, as represented by the AFL, had done it repeatedly. Every year now, with predictable regularity, the State Federation of Labor passed a weak resolution calling for their release and took more potshots at TMMDC finances.*

The politicians had betrayed him; even Matthew Brady, elected District Attorney on a promise to reopen the Mooney case, had proven "spineless," "anemic," his sole contribution a single letter to the governor.

Baldwin, with his National Committee, seemed intent on running the whole show.

Older had betrayed him, counseling "patience," "caution," "don't do anything foolish," all the way through Young's term in office.

Even his co-defendants had betrayed him, Billings by listening to Older and Scharrenberg and submitting his pardon petition contrary to their agreement, the others by resuming their lives while he and Billings still remained behind bars. In writing Billings in September 1929, urging him not to present his petition, Mooney had remarked "I would not do to you as W—later N—and still later R has done to us both—deserted our case." Weinberg had moved to Cleveland, Nolan to Los Angeles, and Rena had returned to teaching music. As the number of pupils grew, her visits and her work on the defense committee had necessarily slackened.

But Mary Gallagher's betrayal had been the worst, because he had been in love with her.

Although there had been hints in earlier letters, Mooney first confessed it to her in a letter written on November 18, 1928, less than three months after she had taken over as secretary of the TMMDC. The letter itself was also the best explanation of "why":

"Your honesty and integrity in my estimation is beyond and above question . . . Your ability to carry out plans and instructions is wonderful—Your eagerness for the work at hand is marvellous and your self sacrifice in the promotion of our case is so beautiful and lovely that I can not help but just fall right in love with you."

Three days later he wrote that he was glad he had "unbosomed myself —unashamed and unabashed—confession is good for the soul."

She was everything he wanted and needed—a one-woman defense committee, wholly dedicated to the cause, with feelings so strong that they could rekindle in others a desire to right his old wrong.

Although she was already married, she hadn't discouraged him. In one of his letters to her he recalled her own first confession, a dream she had had of an oh-so-sad looking fellow in a gray overcoat with his arms out-

---

* Impartially considered, these were in the main unwarranted. At the 1931 convention, for example, Scharrenberg charged that in a period of just four years and two months the Mooney defense groups had collected $162,069.19.

This was true. But the total was reached by combining the figures for two peak periods of Mooney agitation more than a decade apart—August 1916–January 1918, $108,225.61, and September 1928–May 1931, $53,843.58. That the Mooney defense committees supplied accurate figures on which Scharrenberg could base his accounting was in itself the best refutation of his charges.

stretched. She had run to him and put her head on his shoulder. The dream had caused her to hitchhike from Los Angeles three times to see him, because she knew he needed her.

"I will ring off for the present Mary dear with a great big heart full of love for you . . ." "Can't get rid of jubilant happy feeling—that good things are in store for us. Two reasons—one is my improved health and the other is yourself . . . Love, love, love aplenty."

It went through almost all the stages. Mooney obtained a Victor Grafonola and records—his two favorites were "Mary," with Jess Crawford on the organ, and "Baby Your Mother Like She Babied You Back in Your Baby Days" ("It brings tears to my eyes every time I play it"). With a certain inevitability, Belle and Mary clashed. Mooney immediately sided with Mary (Belle has "the faculty of interfering with my plans if she does not agree with them"). There were criticisms too of Rena ("If music lessons will get me out I sure will be out soon"). And also inevitable, considering the circumstances, there were in time suspicions and fits of jealousy regarding Mary herself ("What were you doing Sat. Eve.—debauching—drinking?") and arguments ("So you too are going to save me in spite of myself are you?" Mooney wrote, but did not mail the letter). It ended, and began again, a half-dozen times.

Gossip is ever an evil thing but when it makes its way through prison walls it can kill. In order to supplement her meager income (the name Mooney was not one with which most parents wanted their children associated), Rena had taken in boarders. At some unknown time Mooney heard that Rena's relationship with one of them was more than casual. Whether this was a factor in his falling in love with Mary, or a later justification, is unknown. He first mentions it in a letter to Anna written in September 1929, a year after Mary's appearance. Those who were closest to Rena believe the gossip at the time totally unfounded.

No word of this state of affairs reached the general public. Older knew, as did Mooney's family, and Belle and Rena must have known or at least suspected. Billings too had heard, through his own defense committee.

Whatever might be said or felt about Mooney's brief and ill-fated romance, it restored his desire to live and secure his release. And when it ended late in 1930, after the "subversion" of Mary Gallagher, it plunged him into bitter despair. It was, without doubt, the final straw precipitating his permanent split with the American Federation of Labor.

7 ·

In 1929 Mooney had considered publishing a pamphlet, to be handed out at the State Federation convention. Titled *What the California State*

Federation of Labor Has Done for Mooney and Billings Pardon from September 1928 *to September* 1929, it was to consist of a cover and four blank pages. At the time, wiser counsel had prevailed. But now no one, including Ed Nockles, could dissuade him from his current project, a pamphlet that ran to 52 pages, none of them blank. It was no less than a detailed exposé of the selling out of the rank-and-file by California labor "misleaders."

Labor Leaders Betray Tom Mooney was, and remains, a curious document, a strange mixture of facts and feeling. Originally Mooney had intended using Billings' name in the title. However Billings, learning of its content, had quickly repudiated it, insisting that Mooney run a disclaimer to the effect that it did not express his sentiments.

It named names—columns of them—and gave dates and details. In this, time was in Mooney's favor. A number of labor leaders reluctant at first to come to his defense had over the years been caught with their hands in the wrong pockets. The labor leaders who had campaigned for Fickert, the secret deals, the backstage machinations at the state convention, the refusal of certain unions, such as the Teamsters, to contribute one cent to the defense—all made their way into the pamphlet, which also drew from Mooney some of his best oratory: "In California justice is like a corpse that stinks and offends the nostrils of the entire world . . . If I were given a choice of submitting my case for solution to a jury of 12 major labor leaders of San Francisco, or 12 members of the Chamber of Commerce, I would choose the latter . . . I would much rather face avowed enemies than treacherous and iniquitous 'friends.' "

Four pages dealt with the "subversion" of Mary Gallagher.

"In March 1930, after 18 months of harmonious agreement, Mary Gallagher's devoted services to Tom Mooney were suddenly subverted, and, instead of continuing the effective work of the committee, she sought completely to change the policy of the defense in defiance of the direct orders of Tom Mooney."

One of the earliest workers in Mooney's behalf had been George Kidwell, of the Bakers' Drivers Union. As Kidwell rose in the labor movement, he became associated with John O'Connell of the Teamsters' Union and others on the San Francisco Labor Council. It was Mooney's contention that this group "schemed to gain her confidence and, in time, subvert the Defense Committee."

For what actually happened one must read between the lines.

A letter from the Tom Mooney Molders' Defense Committee, with the famous "before" and "after" photographs of Tom Mooney.

Author's collection

Tom Mooney
Molders' Defense Committee

FORMED BY MEMBERS OF
INTERNATIONAL MOLDERS UNION NO. 164

▼

TOM MOONEY—DIRECTOR

⟨⟨⟨ 203

PRINTED ON UNION MADE PAPER

P. O. Box 1475
San Francisco

California State Prison,
San Quentin, California,
January 1, 1931.

DEAR FRIENDS AND FELLOW UNIONISTS:

The Tom Mooney Molders Defense Committee has enclosed a 52 page pamphlet entitled "LABOR LEADERS BETRAY TOM MOONEY" with this letter. For fifteen years I have hesitated to tell this story, and much as I regret it, I cannot remain silent any longer.

The rank and file of the Trade Unions have always believed in my innocence. They have worked for me and have given their nickels, dimes and dollars to help my defense. But their desires and wishes have been subverted and sabotaged by the Labor leaders. The "leaders" of the A. F. of L. have always told the politicians in public office to ignore any protest coming from the unions in my behalf.

There has never been a single major labor leader in California who honestly and sincerely urged any Governor of this state to pardon me. If the leaders of the American Federation of Labor in California, and in the whole country, were "right" I would not now be in prison. I would never have been convicted. I might never have been arrested. I could not have been "framed".

Everyone now knows that I was railroaded to the "pen" for life through one of the rankest frameups in this country because I was active in the labor movement. Such a fate inevitably awaits any union men or women who dare become militant. That is why my defense is your best protection. The labor leaders will oppose all action that might be taken by any union trying to help me. They will say it is against the laws of the A. F. of L. The corrupt labor politicians in the trade union movement passed these laws especially to prevent me from securing a defense fund. Without funds no defense is possible.

Every National and International Union, and all their affiliated Locals can donate funds to the Tom Mooney Molders Defense Committee if they wish. The A. F. of L. has no power over these organizations. They are absolutely autonomous. Only Central Labor bodies, State Federations of Labor, and Local Federal Labor Unions directly chartered by the A. F. of L. are prevented from donating funds for my defense.

What is your local union going to do? What will the individual members of your union do? I want every member of Organized Labor to read "Labor Leaders Betray Tom Mooney." I want your local union to buy a copy of this pamphlet for each of its members. Write or wire Governor James Rolph and demand my unconditional pardon. My Defense Committee is now preparing a pamphlet which will give all the facts about this monstrous frameup. Send the Committee a substantial donation so that thousands of pamphlets exposing the frameup can be printed. I urge you, I plead with you, I implore you not to forget what I have endured these past fifteen years. Use your imagination. Can you picture what fifteen years of prison life means to an innocent man? Fifteen years—that means 790 weeks, more than 5600 days. And to a man in prison every day seems like a month, every week like a year. My twenty-nine years as a continuous, active member in good standing of the International Molders Union entitles me to a hearing and a defense. Will you help me?

Sincerely and fraternally yours,

Tom Mooney

31921

THIS COMMITTEE IS THE ONLY ORGANIZATION AUTHORIZED TO COLLECT FUNDS FOR THE DEFENSE OF TOM MOONEY

"By a process of cajolery, flattery, and craftiness Kidwell gradually won Mary Gallagher's complete confidence. Constant attention to her wants, subtle compliments, invitations to the theatre, to dinner, to 'parties,' extended motor trips, convinced Mary Gallagher, who was harassed from overwork caused by the many difficult problems confronting the defense, that George Kidwell was a trusted friend, and that *his* policies were the most sagacious and should be followed. Thus it was that the labor leaders, through Kidwell, succeeded in superseding Tom Mooney as Director of the Defense Committee . . ."

As a result, Mooney charged, the agitation against Governor Young was discontinued; pamphlets were not sent to voters; no fight was made against Governor Young during the primaries (indeed, just after Young first denied Mooney's pardon, Mary Gallagher had issued to the press a statement that despite Governor Young's action, Tom Mooney felt he should be reelected, as a new governor would need more time to study the case) ; fund-raising ceased; and the entire work of the defense committee was disrupted.

"September 4, 1930, Mary Gallagher took a trip East and attended the Convention of the International Brotherhood of Teamsters as a guest of George Kidwell. She did not even make a request that this very wealthy International Union give a donation to the defense. Neither did she ask that a resolution demanding the pardon of Mooney and Billings be passed by the convention . . ."

"It is," Mooney wrote, "one of the real tragedies of this case that so splendid a woman as Mary Gallagher should have been so evilly influenced by the degraded, corrupted and degenerated labor leaders."

But the pamphlet was a great deal more than a simple outgrowth of jealousy and frustrated love. It was a revolutionary document, which in conclusion called upon the rank-and-file to wrest control of the AFL from its present leaders. Appearing as it did in January of 1931, as the Depression grew ever darker and as Green and the other AFL leaders seemed incapable of anything more than mouthing the pallid platitudes of Herbert Clark Hoover, the pamphlet seemed to many no less than a call to arms.

It cost Mooney the permanent enmity of the American Federation of Labor. But it won to Mooney's side nearly the entire American Left. "It seemed at the time," one Socialist recalled later, "that if the Depression was ever to end, there would have to be a revolution, and if there was ever a man to lead it, that man was Tom Mooney.

"Perhaps," he added, "the Depression had made us all a little mad."

26 · A Hippodrome Performance

I T BEGAN with a parade. What could be more appropriate, Mooney supporters felt, than that it end with one?

Again James Rolph led it. But this was January 5, 1931, the place Sacramento, and the occasion the governor-elect's inaugural parade.

Before the procession had advanced more than a few blocks a sign two stories in length dropped from a wire strung across the street, falling directly in front of Rolph. Edged in black, its large letters read: MOONEY IS INNOCENT. CALIFORNIA JUSTICE IS DEAD. PARDON MOONEY AND SAVE THE NAME OF CALIFORNIA.

While Rolph was seated on the reviewing stand, a covered wagon drew up before the platform and stopped. Rolph smiled and waved. The cover on the side of the wagon dropped to reveal: IT'S A CRIME TO KEEP MOONEY IN PRISON.

At a time when everyone was looking at the capital building a huge flag suddenly unfurled from its dome: JUSTICE IS DEAD IN CALIFORNIA. FREE TOM MOONEY.

It was as though a chorus had shouted: Try as you may, you can't avoid the Mooney case.

Yet there was reason to hope that the new governor would not avoid it, but would act favorably on the pardon petition.

Rolph had grown up South o' the Slot, in labor's own Mission District. (He was known as "Mission Jim" long before he became "Sunny Jim.") His shipping firm had always been fair to labor. And, back in August 1916, as Mayor, Rolph had written a scathing letter to Frederick J. Koster which began: "Permit me to say, in the first place, that neither you nor the Law and Order Committee of the Chamber of Commerce has earned, by any conspicuous devotion to law and order, the right to lecture me or the Police Department. On the contrary, the attitude and the activity of you and your particular group have done much, in my opinion, to engender the industrial unrest and class hatred, culminating on a few occasions in turbulence and violence, which have lately distressed this community . . ."

Written only a month after Preparedness Day, this was a brave decla-

351

ration. But since then much had happened. Rolph had lost his personal fortune, becoming dependent upon the large corporations for election support. Too, there had been a tremendous scandal in 1924 when Rolph turned San Francisco's municipally owned $100 million Yosemite Park power project over to privately owned PG&E. Both Hearst's *Examiner* and Scripps' *Daily News* had yelled bribe and named an amount.

Yet even before Rolph took office there were rumors that he intended to free Mooney and Billings, and some of these came from Rolph's closest associates.

Mooney was himself hopeful. But he vowed never again to play the silent role. In his new pamphlet he not only called for political pressure on Rolph, in the form of letters, telegrams, petitions, and mass demonstrations, but he demanded economic sanctions as well. BOYCOTT ALL CALIFORNIA PRODUCTS, he urged labor around the world, and though that movement had been slow to start, it was gaining momentum, as were other defense efforts.

Following Mary Gallagher's departure, Tom's sister Anna took over as Secretary of the TMMDC, while Aline Barnsdall donated $1000 a month to keep the defense moving until fund-raising could begin again.

In February, Mooney resubmitted his pardon application.

In March, the National Mooney-Billings Committee published *The Scandal of Mooney and Billings,* with excerpts from the Billings pardon rehearing.

By April the roster of those calling for Mooney's release included such prominent names as Albert Einstein, H. G. Wells, Rupert Hughes, and Bertrand Russell.

In May, Lillian Symes' "Our American Dreyfus Case" appeared in staid *Harper's Magazine.* The same issue contained an interesting editorial comment:

"We trust that the leading article of this issue will be widely read, both in California and elsewhere.

"So far the Mooney-Billings case has received little national publicity, except in magazines especially directed at 'radical' or 'liberal' readers—as if fair-minded conservatives had any less concern for American Justice. The Editors."

In May, too, *Precedent,* a play by I. J. Golden, opened on the stage of the Provincetown Theatre on McDougal Street in Greenwich Village. Burns Mantle of the *Daily News* called it "one of the few impressive dramas of the year"; John Mason Brown of the *Evening Post* found it "one of the most affecting productions of the season."

"Being frankly a propaganda play," Brooks Atkinson wrote in *The New York Times, "Precedent* makes no pretension to being sound drama. But the astonishing thing about this exposition of the *cause célèbre* of

Tom Mooney is the strong appeal it has in the theatre."

Six telescoped scenes in the opening act showed how the Queen City Railroad Company conspired with a friendly District Attorney to frame Delaney, a labor organizer, for the Preparedness Day bombing. Fickert, Estelle, Oxman, Griffin, Older—all were recognizable. The last act closed with the commutation of Delaney's sentence to life imprisonment. But there was an epilogue, set in 1931, showing Delaney waiting in his cell at San Quentin, and Fremont, the crusading newspaper editor, hatching new schemes to get him out.

While admitting that he knew nothing about the actual case on which the play was based, Gilbert Gabriel of the *Morning American* noted "it is certainly within my province to report that it had me believing, aroused me, yanked me out of a nice spring langour, and made me want to do things about it . . . On the way out I stepped hard on a capitalist's instep and only glared at him when he begged my pardon . . ."

By mid-summer more than 500 ministers—backed up by such publications as *Zion's Herald, Christian Century,* the *Epworth Herald,* and *Commonweal*—had asked for the release of Mooney and Billings. The Southern California conference of the Methodist Episcopal Church, the Federal Council of Churches of Christ of America, the National Catholic Welfare Council, the entire law faculty of the University of Oregon, law professors at both Stanford and the University of California, governors, senators, and members of the House of Representatives had joined the growing throng.

As had the Communists.

In July Frank Oxman died. Mooney haunted him "half-way to purgatory," the priest who administered last rites urging him to cleanse his soul by publicly confessing his part in the Mooney case. But Oxman died silent, and with him went the answer to why he had committed perjury.

That Oxman had committed perjury there was no doubt. The Hatcher testimony, plus Oxman's Kansas City affidavit, proved it. Only his motive, which had so long perplexed reporters, remained a mystery. If not for money, why?

A guess has been ventured by some close to the case, based on what was known of Oxman's character and the manner in which the prosecution first learned of him. Fickert heard of Oxman's tale from at least two separate sources, Frank Woods, the station agent at Durkee, and William Hough, secretary of the Western Meat Company, to both of whom Oxman confided that he had seen the bombers.

Oxman, arriving at the Ferry Building at 5:25 on the afternoon of the 22nd, would have been caught up in the crowds still gathered around the bomb scene just a block away. He must have seen the headlines, heard the talk—it would have been difficult for him to avoid either. Frank Oxman was quite a raconteur. It is possible that, during his several days in the city, he may have bragged a little about how close he had come to getting blown up, just to hold his own in the conversations (as Maxwell McNutt once remarked, it appeared that everyone in San Francisco had watched the parade from one corner). Telling the story in the smoker on the way back to Oregon, the tale may have grown a little, until, upon reaching "the sticks," he had actually seen the men with the suitcase. It would have been a fine story—up to the time the Burns' operative confronted him in Kansas City and asked what he had seen.

Oxman had already committed perjury once, in the John Spain case, for no other apparent reason than to ingratiate himself with the railroad. The Preparedness Day bombing brought him into contact with people even more influential.

While admittedly the above is conjecture, it would seem to be a good guess. It is predicated upon a slight fallacy, however. Because Frank Oxman was comparatively wealthy, many automatically felt that he was not interested in the reward. There is no evidence, however, that rich men are less desirous of obtaining money than poor men.

Whatever the answer, Frank Oxman took it with him, and he was not the first of the major participants to do so. The one man who in all probability could have shed more light on the frame-up than anyone, detective Martin Swanson, had died several years earlier. Although immediately after his death Mooney arranged to have his former offices searched to see if anything incriminating had been left behind, nothing was found.

In October there were mass meetings in San Francisco and Los Angeles. The Los Angeles meeting marked the beginning of a massive Mooney-Harlan-Scottsboro appeal inaugurated by the International Labor Defense in collaboration with International Red Aid. It also marked the return of violence to the Mooney case. Some 10,000 protestors, assembled in Pershing Square, were dispersed by police using tear gas and billy clubs, some 50 of the more active were arrested.

In a message from Mooney, read at the meeting, prisoner 31921 called for an international boycott of all California products and all California tourism, and boycott and picketing of the 1932 Olympic Games, to be held in Los Angeles.

By now many California business leaders believed they were feeling the effect of the boycott on goods (although the actual cause may well have been the worsening Depression). The tourism threat was in itself empty, as Mooney realized; in 1931 few workers were taking vacations in California. There were now armed guards at her borders to discourage migrants with insufficient funds from adding to her relief rolls. But the possibility that the Mooney case might be used to embarrass California in the eyes of the world while the spotlight shone on the Olympic Games caused some, who had otherwise ignored the case, to seek a means of terminating the unfavorable publicity.

A prominent Los Angeles businessman, who claimed to be spokesman for an influential group of his fellows, approached one of Mooney's attorneys with a proposition: If Mooney would publicly promise to take no part in labor activities once released, the group would exert pressure on Rolph to see that he was pardoned.

Mooney's reply is unprintable.

Yet even the proposition could be taken as an encouraging sign.

2 ·

Dandies reigned on both sides of the continent.

On the afternoon of November 19, 1931, Mayor James J. "Jimmy" Walker held a press conference.

"If the pressure of my work will permit," the impeccably-dressed mayor of the world's largest city announced, "I shall go to California as a lawyer and a private citizen and make a final plea for the release of Tom Mooney."

"Why, Mayor, I didn't even know you knew Mooney," one astonished reporter blurted out.

"I have been familiar with the Mooney case for years, and I have absolute and complete confidence in his innocence," the mayor said. A stack of letters and telegrams swamped his desk: these, he pointed out, were requests from labor organizations and individuals begging him to go to California, to speak to his old and dear friend "Sunny Jim" Rolph in Tom Mooney's behalf.

At this moment (an irreverent reporter would later write "almost on cue") a secretary entered and handed Walker a telegram. As he read it to himself, tears rolled down his face.

"Read it for me," he said, and handing it to a reporter, hurriedly left the room overcome with emotion.

" 'Dear Mayor Walker,' " the reporter read. " 'I am eighty years old. Afraid I am breaking down at last. They want to take me to a hospital tomorrow. In the name of God and His Blessed Mother won't you come out to help my boy. It is my last chance to put my arms around him before I meet my God. He has been a good son to me. If you do this for Tom you will have my prayers as long as you live.' It's signed, 'Mother Mooney.' "

There were some so unfeeling as to suggest that Mayor Walker's motives might be a little less than humanitarian. The Seabury investigation was now well underway, and getting very close to home.

"Mayor Walker ought to stay here and plead for himself," observed the *Evening Post*. "It is a sad commentary on American justice that the freedom of anyone should hinge on a 'stunt,' " noted the *Herald Tribune*. "So irregular were the proceedings that convicted Mooney" the Asbury Park *Evening Press* dissented "that even a vaudeville show is justified in attempting to undo them." It was also surmised that Rolph had already decided to free Mooney and Billings and that Walker's intrusion at this time was solely to reap the glory.

All this was mild, however, compared to what many California papers were saying. The *Chronicle,* looking forward not at all to Walker's forthcoming "hippodrome performance," greatly resented the Mayor of New York City "giving States of the Union gratuitous advice on how to run their affairs." It was, many of the papers agreed, "a strictly local matter" and Walker had no business butting his nose into it.

The announcement was not without humorous aspects. It threw the San Francisco Chamber of Commerce into panic. Normally, when so noted a personage as Walker visited the city, the chamber would host a huge banquet in his honor. But in this case . . . Finally, after more than a week of indecisive conferences, the chamber decided to forego the dinner, since Walker was not making the trip in an official capacity.

Accompanied by Frank Walsh and his associate Aaron Sapiro, Walker entrained for San Francisco, arriving on the 24th. Governor Rolph, just as sartorially splendid, was waiting to greet him when he stepped off the ferry, and the pair "two sights to behold," one with a rose in his buttonhole, the other a camellia, rode up Market Street over the Preparedness Day parade route while the municipal band, mounted on a sanitation truck, played "The Sidewalks of New York" and "Happy Days Are Here Again."

Reaching his suite in the St. Francis Hotel, Walker was shocked to read the editorial comment heralding his arrival.

His first call the following day was at 134 Clipper Street, the small clapboard house in the heart of the Mission District where Mother Mooney and her son John lived out their long wait. Mother Mooney broke into tears the moment he entered the door; though long ill and in need of hospitalization, she had put it off until after Mayor Walker arrived.

On the 29th, Walker, accompanied by Walsh, Sapiro, and a horde of reporters, drove to San Quentin where Walker was shown through the prison garden.

"My, this is beautiful," Mayor Walker said. "I'd say it compared very favorably with the garden at Sing Sing." (The Rose Bowl had been covered for the occasion.)

The warden escorted Mooney out. Then, before photographers and newsreel cameramen, the dapper mayor shook hands with "the man he had crossed the continent to defend."

"It's a pleasure to see you," Walker beamed. "You'll soon be free now."

"I seriously doubt it," Mooney replied.

"I think you're wrong about that," Walker ventured, more than a little stunned.

Warden Holohan, with unusual tact, suggested that Walker and Mooney might wish to converse privately, and they adjourned to the warden's office. Mooney's first comment to Walker after the doors were closed was later reported to be, "Say, just how seriously do you take this, anyway?" If true (since only Mooney, his attorneys, Walker, and the warden were present, only Holohan would have leaked it to the press), the two men were on a first name basis by the time they returned to the garden for more photographs. "Good-bye, Tom," the Mayor said; "I'll get you out—just wait and see." "Good-bye, Jimmy," Tom said, with just a trace of resignation.

It was their only meeting. When asked if he intended to go to Folsom also, Walker said he had been asked only to speak on behalf of Mooney.

Governor Rolph had arranged that Walker present his plea to an open hearing December 1st in the San Francisco chambers of the Supreme Court. Choosing this time for a mammoth demonstration in Civic Center outside, the ILD had assembled some 2000 people who chanted FREE TOM MOONEY. Fearing just such "communistic disorders," as the *Chronicle* put it, there was an extra contingent of policemen, some 75 of them, many mounted on horseback. Later the police would say a rioter first struck a policeman, and the protestors would claim a policeman swung first. But swinging their sticks to make a bloody swath through the group, the police ended the "riot" and arrested 25 participants, including Frank Spector, district director of the ILD.

The courtroom was order personified. Former San Quentin warden James A. Johnston, who as director of the State Department of Penology was present in his official role, later described how Walsh, Sapiro, and Walker, "three lawyers as different from each other as winter, autumn and spring" functioned as a well-coordinated team. Although unpersuaded himself, Johnston felt it was a masterful presentation, covering every salient feature. "Their styles differed, but they dovetailed. Walsh was weighty; Sapiro was forceful; Walker was earnest, but at ease, and, at the close, dramatic."

The drama was real, for Jimmy Walker had managed to do the impossible. He read a letter that ended, "In my opinion you are probably right in maintaining it would be to the best interests of the state that executive clemency be granted to Mooney."

The letter, he noted after a pregnant pause, was signed "Charles M.

Fickert."

There was instant bedlam.

Contacted by the press, Fickert admitted that he had signed it but insisted that "the statement cannot be taken to mean I personally am advocating a pardon for Mooney." Later he would, in turn, say that he hadn't signed it; that he had signed it but thought it was another letter which Walker had read to him; and that he had been "misinterpreted."

The real explanation was simpler. The night prior to the hearing Mayor Walker had taken Fickert out on the town and gotten him roaring drunk. His various explanations—all delivered at different times the following day—had come through the haze of a monumental hangover.

Governor Rolph thanked Mayor Walker, promising to give his plea all due consideration, and Jimmy Walker returned East, to learn the answer to his composition "Will You Love Me in December as You Did in May?"

3 ·

WICKERSHAM REPORT ON MOONEY CASE SUPPRESSED ! ! ! !

While Rolph was still considering Mooney's pardon request, the story of the suppressed Wickersham Report on the Mooney-Billings case broke in the United States Senate.

Shortly after Hoover took office, he appointed a National Commission on Law Observance and Enforcement (popularly known as the Wickersham Commission, for its senior member George W. Wickersham). One of its subcommittees—whose members included Judge W. S. Kenyon of Iowa, Dr. Zechariah Chafee, Jr., of the Harvard Law School, Carl Stern, and Walter Pollak—was charged with the particular study of "lawlessness in law enforcement." It was common knowledge in Washington that the subcommittee had chosen, as a classic example of its subject, the Mooney-Billings case.

In due time the subcommittee report appeared, but minus its classic study. Gardner Jackson and Senator Burton K. Wheeler began a quiet investigation to learn whether the study had in fact been made. They learned that it had, only to be suppressed by vote of the full commission. The public reason was that the commission had decided it "was beyond its province to investigate individual cases with a view to making recommendations to their disposition." The private and real reason, Wheeler and Jackson concluded, was that the President was a Californian and 1932 an election year: an unfavorable report on justice in his home state would prove embarrassing.

Wheeler took the floor of the United States Senate and demanded that the suppressed report be made public. This, he observed, was "a public document, prepared at public expense and covering an essential phase of the subject . . . of lawlessness in law enforcement." Backed by Senators Costigan, Cutting, and Walsh, a resolution was introduced and passed requesting the President to produce the report. After a number of delays, the Attorney General sent a copy to the Senate. But, despite public clamor for its release, the report was again suppressed, this time in the Senate Judiciary Committee.

In January 1932 the Scripps-Howard chain obtained a copy of the report's conclusions and published them. Later that year the entire report was privately published in book form under the title *The Mooney-Billings Report: Suppressed by the Wickersham Commission*. It ran to 243 pages and remains the single best study of the case.

It was the opinion of the subcommittee that a grave injustice had indeed been done in California, that Mooney and Billings had indeed been framed through the combined efforts of Fickert, Swanson, and a "weird procession" of witnesses.

Considering the records as a whole, the subcommittee reached these conclusions:

"(1) There was never any scientific attempt made by either the police or the prosecution to discover the perpetrators of the crime. The investigation was in reality turned over to a private detective, who used his position to cause the arrest of the defendants. The police investigation was reduced to a hunt for evidence to convict the arrested defendants.

"(2) There were flagrant violations of the statutory law of California by both the police and the prosecution in the manner in which the defendants were arrested and held incommunicado, and in the subsequent searches of their homes to procure evidence against them.

"(3) After the arrest of the defendants, witnesses were brought to the jails to 'identify' them, and their 'identifications' were accepted by the police and the prosecution, despite the fact that these witnesses were never required to pick the defendants out of a line-up, or to demonstrate their accuracy by any other test.

"(4) Immediately after the arrests of the defendants there commenced a deliberate attempt to arouse public prejudice against them, by a series of almost daily interviews given to the press by prosecuting officials.

"(5) Witnesses were produced at the trials with information in the hands of the prosecution that seriously challenged the credibility of the witnesses, but this information was deliberately concealed.

"(6) Witnesses were permitted to testify at the trials, despite such knowledge in the possession of the prosecution of prior contradictory stories told by these witnesses, as to make their mere production a vouching for perjured testimony.

"(7) Witnesses were coached in their testimony to a degree that approximated subornation of perjury. There is a strong inference that some of this coaching was done by prosecuting officials, and other evidence points to knowledge by the prosecuting officials that such coaching was being practiced on other witnesses.

"(8) The prejudice against the defendants, stimulated by newspaper publicity, was further appealed to at the trials by unfair and intemperate arguments to the jury in the opening and closing statements of the prosecuting attorneys.

"(9) After the trials, the disclosures casting doubt on the justice of the convictions were minimized, and every attempt made to defeat the liberation of the defendants, by a campaign of misrepresentation and propaganda carried on by the officials who had prosecuted them."

For the second time, an impartial U.S. government fact-finding commission concluded that a gross injustice had been done in the Mooney-Billings case.

Just what effect this would have on Governor Rolph remained to be seen.

4 ·

Among friends James Rolph made little secret of the fact that he entertained grander ambitions.

Hiram Johnson had moved from the state capitol to the U.S. Senate and there seemed no reason why Rolph could not do likewise. The Senate seat now held by Shortridge would be up for grabs in 1933.

Yet even before Walker's arrival, there had been other talk, that if Hoover didn't chose to run again, Rolph would make a colorful running-mate for someone like Dwight W. Morrow in 1932. There was scandal in Rolph's past, to be sure, and too many women in his present, but other Vice-Presidential candidates had overcome greater handicaps.

If the United States Senate was his ambition, then to pardon Mooney would be suicide. For he would need business support, and business leaders, for a time seemingly reconciled to the pardon, were now, as the Depression continued, unalterably opposed to his release. The last thing California needed was another rabble-rousing labor leader at large.

But as a Vice-Presidential candidate, the fact that he had pardoned Mooney after three other governors had failed to do so could be a tremendous asset. For by now it was apparent that almost all opposition to Mooney's release was in California itself.

As early as September 1931 Miriam Allen DeFord wrote in *Outlook:*

"Strange as it may seem . . . the fate of Mooney and Billings may rest very largely with the Republican national convention next year."

If indeed this was the way Rolph's mind worked, and there was more than a little evidence in the affirmative, Rolph's hopes were snuffed out early in 1932 when it became evident that neither Morrow nor Coolidge but Hoover would be the Republican candidate. Since both Rolph and Hoover were Californians, there was no chance of Rolph's making the ticket.

(Mooney came closer than Rolph to attaining the office. In December 1931 a number of Socialist Party locals on the East Coast began a movement to place Mooney's name on the Socialist ticket, as a result of which "Tom Mooney for Vice-President" signs appeared in profusion in New York City and elsewhere.)

Following Walker's visit, Rolph did what his predecessors had done before him: he stalled for time, announcing that he would need at least three months to make a thorough study of the case. Some saw this as a hopeful sign; Older, among others, felt that Rolph was only delaying his decision until after the Walker visit was forgotten in order to get full credit for pardoning the two men. Mooney, now almost completely estranged from Older, didn't agree. Angrily he charged Rolph was already guilty of "a year of procrastination." Why should he need more time to study the case? As Mayor of San Francisco, Rolph had led the Preparedness Day parade, ordered the investigation, been present through the trials, the exposés and recantations, including that of detective Draper Hand, whose confession had been made before him.

When Rolph, again following precedent, announced that he was referring the pardon request to his chief legal advisors, Matthew I. Sullivan and Lewis Byington, Mooney knew what the decision would be. Judge Sullivan, so-called because he had served a few weeks on the State Supreme Court on an *ad interim* appointment, was a staunch conservative. Byington had been attorney for Patrick Calhoun when the URR President was tried in the San Francisco graft cases. Shortly after Rolph's announcement Mooney heard that Byington had told a law associate Mooney would "rot in jail" before he would permit his release. True or false, Mooney believed it and refused to call off the products boycott or the proposed picketing of the Olympic Games.

As Rolph's three months began to run out, the campaign for Mooney's release entered a strange phase. There was a barrage of anonymous calls, letters, and telegrams, the mildest threatening "If you fail to pardon Mooney you thereby sign your own political death warrant." The source of these missives was never determined. Older believed they came from the Communists, who he felt were intent on keeping Mooney in prison as a martyr to the cause.* The give-away, Older noted, was the ILD's slogan. If in reality their true aim was to see all class-war prisoners freed, then why was their motto "Long Live the International Labor Defense"?

Rolph himself now provided a clue to his eventual decision. He appointed Charles M. Fickert Attorney to the State Board of Medical Examiners.

It was a minor political post, which paid only $275 a month. Fickert was on the skids and had been for some time. His law practice had failed; he was in ill health and drinking heavily. His last public appearance had been at the Billings rehearsing, the last before that at a banquet for Herbert Hoover shortly after his election to the Presidency. Much had changed since "Boob" Fickert's days of stardom on the Stanford football team. Arriving late and drunk, he had been shunted off to a corner where he couldn't create a disturbance. It was rumored that Hoover had asked Rolph to do something for Fickert, and that the political job was the result. But Fickert was unable to hold even that; he resigned soon after being appointed.

The advisory report was written in its entirety by Sullivan. Weeks before it was released, there were rumors that it merely reiterated the conclusions of the California Supreme Court in the Billings rehearing. When the report was made public, on April 19, 1932, the rumors proved well founded.

Only 10 of the 88 pages of the Sullivan report dealt with direct evidence, and even these avoided the real issues. (In a typical example, Judge Dunne's telegram to Theodore Roosevelt—in which Dunne asserted his belief in Billings' guilt—was given greater weight than Judge Griffin's belief in Mooney's innocence, which the report characterized as "the fulminations of a much younger judge.") The balance was almost entirely devoted to the radicalism of the defendants or their supporters and fully one-fourth, 20 pages, consisted of quotes from *The Blast*. Having proven that the two men were radicals, which no one had ever denied, Sullivan concluded "Their insensate hatred of our present form of government and their fanatical efforts to substitute the red of revolt for the Stars and Stripes impelled Mooney and his fellow conspirators to perpetrate the Preparedness Day outrage." Sullivan did not attempt to prove this charge. Instead he relied on the Supreme Court decision in the Billings' hearing. "If Billings is innocent of the crime of which he was convicted," Sullivan reasoned, "Mooney is innocent. If, on the other hand, Billings is guilty, Mooney is likewise guilty."

* Allan Chalmers, in *They Shall Be Free,* noted that when Alabama's Governor Graves was considering the Scottsboro appeals in 1938 "Telegrams and telephone calls, which the governor described as preemptory and insulting, were received at the moment of the interviews from known Communist leaders in the state."

On only one point did the Sullivan report differ from the Supreme Court. The court had charged Mooney and Billings with making no attempt to find the perpetrators of the bombing. The Sullivan report charged that the Mooney defense had wasted thousands of dollars on such searches—which, considering that both men were guilty, must have been intended solely to frame some innocent scapegoat.

There was slim hope that Governor Rolph would go against the report of his advisors—but at least one member of the Mooney family believed he would. Mary Mooney, accompanied by her daughter Anna, journeyed to the capital on the morning of the 21st to hear Rolph's official announcement. The governor's office was packed with reporters, however, and the two women had to wait in an adjoining room.

They couldn't see Rolph approach the forest of microphones and spotlights, or hear him when he read, in what the wire services described as "a firm and measured voice," his three-page announcement. But they could hear and feel the excitement as the reporters rushed to the phones. One reporter, passing the room, shouted the decision to Anna.

"What? What did he say, Anna? What did he say?"

Anna gently placed her hand on the old woman's shoulder.

"We'll have to try again, Mother. He won't let Tom go."

It was inevitable that someone say it—the Sacramento *Bee* did: "Four Governors of California might be wrong about different things, but it is incredible to suppose that they could all be wrong about the same thing."

27 · Listen to the Rumble

"I<small>N A FIRM</small> and measured voice," Heywood Broun repeated in the New York *World Telegram*. "The Governor had nothing to talk down but the whisper of conscience and the still, small voice of truth. He was louder for the moment. A breeze stirred the leaves. It was nothing. But the wind rises. Pin your ear to the ground, Governor. Listen to the rumble. It is not settled. It is not done. Truth can and truth will be a tempest . . . A lie may live and even wiggle after it has been spiked, but not beyond the sundown."

The rumble heard that spring and summer of 1932 might have been the muttering voices of the more than 12½ million unemployed, the rising wind the increasing talk of revolution.

In Iowa, farmers who had never voted other than Republican blocked off roads with logs and patrolled them with pitchforks to make sure no farm produce went to market until they were guaranteed a price that covered costs of production.

In Kansas, Oklahoma, Texas, Nebraska, in a hundred small rebellions, when the bank foreclosed on a farm neighbors would gather at the foreclosure sale to buy the land, house, and farm implements, for pennies, nickles, and dimes, later to return them to their former owner. There were no other bids. The farmers, carrying rifles and shotguns, made sure of that.

In May, from all parts of the country, and by every method of transportation from feet to boxcars, World War I veterans marched on the nation's capital to ask for the "adjusted compensation" voted them by Congress. When Congress failed to approve early payment of the bonus and the veterans remained camped outside the city in late July, President Hoover, fearing that revolution had indeed come, called out the troops, which, led by General Douglas MacArthur, with the assistance of his aide Dwight David Eisenhower, moved into Anacosta Flats with drawn bayonets, hurling tear gas bombs, burning barracks and shacks. A seven-year-old boy was bayoneted by an overly enthusiastic soldier. One officer, George S. Patton, Jr., rode down a man awarded the Distinguished Service Cross for saving Patton's life in France 14 years earlier. The "mob,"

MacArthur later justified his use of violence, was animated by "the essence of revolution."

The Communists played no part in any of these events; the leadership of the bonus marchers, for example, had been careful to purge Communist Party members. These were symptoms of the times. And MacArthur was not alone in reading into them portents of revolution.

"These conditions in the Kentucky coal fields, Tom Mooney in San Quentin prison, and other incidents that are multiplying are a warning to America," observed *Christian Century*. "The class war is not threatened in this nation; the class war is actually opening. Can its full fury be averted? The passions that gather on both sides of a Mooney case fill us with foreboding."

2 ·

The Communists were not inactive, however.

"The more hell that is raised about my frame-up imprisonment, the greater the protest, the larger the demonstration and the wider the public opinion of mass pressure, the better are my chances for freedom."

By 1932 Tom Mooney was no longer disavowing Communist support; he was welcoming it. From the start of the case, the Socialist Party and the IWW had stood behind the California defendants, even though Billings had belonged to neither and Mooney had broken with each. By the early Thirties, however, they were hollow shells, the most potent force in the American Left the Communist Party. Doctrinaire and financial differences aside, the Communists drew crowds. In 1931, Mooney had given the ILD permission for a combined Mooney-Harlan-Scottsboro appeal, although insisting that an equitable portion of funds collected go to the TMMDC.

Less than a month after ILD entered the Scottsboro case, they had sent Mother Wright, mother of two of the Scottsboro boys, to Europe to speak on their behalf. As a propaganda move, it was remarkably effective.* When, following Mayor Walker's visit, the ILD broached the idea that Mother Mooney, accompanied by one of the Scottsboro mothers, undertake a nationwide tour, Tom consulted with her and granted permission.

Mother Mooney was eighty-four. Unfailingly, when there was a mass meeting in San Francisco, Mary Mooney was on the platform. Shy, frightened by crowds, she did it for her boy. She was, Mary Gallagher once observed, "a sweet little old lady . . . She was always present at

* "So successful did the ILD find Mrs. Wright's tour" Allan Chalmers claims, "that it arranged to have at least eight Mother Wright's appear simultaneously in widely scattered parts of the world."

any meeting which was held in behalf of her son. She took her position on the stage and would take a bow, but she never attempted to make a speech. She was quite inarticulate and timid."

In January of 1932, together with Scottsboro mother Viola Montgomery, she traveled East, appearing in a dozen cities on the way. In Chicago, together with Mother Montgomery and Lucy Parsons, widow of Albert Parsons, she placed a wreath on the Haymarket monument. Arriving at Grand Central Station she was greeted by William Z. Foster; that night she shared the spotlight with Corliss Lamont, son of one of the Morgan partners, as 16,000 packed Bronx Coliseum. Two days later it was a crowd of 50 in a Negro church outside Washington, D.C. Each time she tried to deliver the speeches they had prepared for her, but failed. "My boy Tom is a good lad," she would say, peering anxiously over the lectern at all the strange faces. "He didn't do this thing they say. He is innocent. Please help my boy." Choked with emotion and nervousness she would then falter and sit down, while one of the earnest, dedicated young men of the ILD completed the speech for her.

In Washington she went to the White House to plead with the President for her son. President Hoover couldn't see her; he was too busy. Although the radical press created a furor, the other papers didn't join in until it was learned that Hoover had not been too busy to grant a private interview to Jean Harlow.

The tour continued, concentrating on the heavily industrial cities, until in Detroit, on March 24th, she collapsed with a heart attack. After rallying slightly she begged to be allowed to continue the trip, but Tom canceled it and had her returned to California, where she was hospitalized in a sanitarium a short distance from San Quentin.

In April she left it, against doctor's orders, to go to the state capital to learn Governor Rolph's decision. In late May she resumed her tour, this time accompanied by Negro Communist leader Richard B. Moore. San Diego, Seattle, Great Falls, Denver, Kansas City, to Chicago, in mid-June, where she was to picket the Republican National Convention. But she didn't make it; on the way, she suddenly went blind. Doctors diagnosed her condition as temporary blindness, brought on by great nervous strain, and recommended hospitalization. Four days later, her sight only partially restored (it would never get better) she appeared in Superior, Wisconsin, followed by Duluth, Milwaukee, Ann Arbor, Cleveland (her 25th city), Cincinnati, Youngstown (her 40th city), Pittsburgh, and then East.

She was a tremendous drawing card. And wherever she stopped, she was interviewed. Even though reporters found her brogue "as thick as Irish stew," they were moved by her plea. Observed an Ohio paper: "There is no posing, nothing of the professional campaigner about the woman. She is absolutely sincere." Observed a labor paper in Rochester, New York: "It was a pathetic sight to see the aged Mrs. Mooney sitting behind the vain and cunning Moore while he used her presence, and the tragedy of her son's life, for no other purpose than to swell the membership of the Communist Party."

In California, as the Olympic Games moved toward their dramatic closing ceremonies, four young men and two young women ran onto the field. Thinking they were athletes the crowd applauded; it stopped only on seeing they were carrying FREE TOM MOONEY banners. Arrested, all were later convicted and given six-month jail sentences, while their attorney, Leo Gallagher, was dismissed from the law faculty of Southwestern University. "The Mooney case is beginning to breed martyrs," complained the Los Angeles *Times*.

In October, Mother Mooney sailed for Russia as an honorary delegate to the Congress of International Red Aid. She carried with her a letter from her son to Joseph Stalin.

Initially the State Department had refused her a passport; after loud protests, however, it was granted. On learning that she was to speak in Dublin under the auspices of Mrs. Sheehy-Skeffington, the British Government refused to issue an English visa. But after a stormy session in the House of Commons, it too was granted, and, nervous but smiling, she sailed on the 28th. It was her first ocean trip since leaving County Mayo as a girl of seventeen, 67 years ago.

The letter was to be presented to Stalin in Red Square on November 7th, fifteenth anniversary of the Russian Revolution. In it, Tom sent his congratulations on the anniversary of this momentous event, "beyond any question the greatest happening in the whole history of the world so far as the working class is concerned"; recalled that it was "our beloved comrade Lenin" who had saved his life by leading the militant demonstrations before the American Embassy in 1917; and thanked Stalin, and the other Revolutionary workers of the U.S.S.R. for their efforts "in defense of my fight for freedom, and for the freedom of all class war and political prisoners."

The letter concluded: "All Hail to the Russian Revolution and the Dictatorship of the Proletariat. I'm for it hook, line and sinker, without equivocation or reservation . . . Comradely yours, Tom Mooney, 31921."

Without equivocation or reservation.

Tom Mooney's less public letters—filled with complaints about bungled publicity, inopportune demonstrations, and mismanaged funds—indicated otherwise.

As he had done with many others, Tom Mooney was now attempting to use the Communist Party.

3 ·

That fall the takeover of the Mooney defense began in earnest. It was, as usual, by process of burrowing from within.

A huge Mooney mass meeting was scheduled for November 7th in San Francisco Civic Auditorium. Theodore Dreiser flew out to be the keynote speaker.

On the 6th Dreiser, Lincoln Steffens, Ella Winters, Samuel Ornitz, and Orrick Johns paid a visit to the "infamous trio" at San Quentin. It was the first time Johns, a young Communist recently assigned to West Coast labor defense work, had met the three famous labor prisoners.

Schmidt he found a "big, red-faced jolly dutchman." J. B. McNamara was "lean, rangy, and iron-jawed, but with sparkling eyes and lines of humor in his face." Both looked in the prime of life—Johns couldn't see a touch of prison about them.

"Tom was a somewhat different type. I had seen early prison photographs of him, but he was unlike any of them. He was a short, square, solid man, with white hair, thin to transparency, brushed back, and a bold, glowing look in his eyes. He was dressed in trim white dungarees and open gray shirt, and wore leather sandals."

Even though that same day Schmidt's parole request had again been refused, the talk was as spirited as if at a party. J.B. remarked, "They're moving the arsenal out of the tower over the gate, and building a new arsenal outside the walls, down there by the bay. That's because they're afraid Tom and Matt and me will capture the arsenal some day."

Recalled Johns, "I have never met three more jolly fellows than these three who had spent the best years of their lives behind bars." Altogether the three had served a total of 57 years.

"Well, when are you going to get out of here, Tom?" Dreiser asked.

J.B. answered for him, in a voice that he made no attempt to keep down: "Tom Mooney will get out when he's a bigger nuisance inside than he would be outside. And that means when the unions demand his freedom."

It was a strange meeting, Johns suddenly realized, for it was Lincoln Steffens who had served as middleman between the prosecution and the defense in the Los Angeles *Times'* case, who had persuaded the Mc-Namaras that if they pled guilty the prosecution would honor its part of the bargain. Yet the men appeared on the most cordial of terms.

This was only surface, however. Johns was unaware that following Steffens' visits, J. B. McNamara was given to hilarious cape-swinging imitations of his affections. "Distance lends enchantment," McNamara once told Mooney. "In Moscow Steffens talks of the struggle in San Francisco.

In San Francisco he talks of the struggle in Moscow."

Nor was Steffens exactly betraying his true feelings. In a letter he would describe the same meeting thusly: "Tom Mooney was stating his case, proving his (undoubted) innocence, and as he talked we all felt that he was not only innocent; he had become a righteous bore, an offense with his rights and his wrongs."

Later, at the Mark Hopkins, Dreiser was beseiged by women reporters. One asked him, "Don't you think, Mr. Dreiser, that even if Mooney is innocent, he is a dangerous anarchist and should not be at large?"

"If you mean that," he roared at her, "then you are an idiot, and ought not to be at large."

On Sunday, the 7th, just before the mass meeting, 5000 union members paraded, chanting "Free Tom Mooney" and singing songs by Joe Hill. The meeting itself was a spectacular success, the novelist drawing a crowd of 15,000. By the simple expedient of using their own people to take the collection, every cent collected went to the ILD.

This was the first of a number of mass meetings dominated by the Communists. Orrick Johns, in *Time of Our Lives*, gives a backstage view of how this was done:

"The public probably thought the meetings had simply been called, and the crowds had come to them. On the contrary, they required weeks of preparation, involving very hard work. Small conferences were held at first, months before. These conferences drew in more and more trade unions, socialist, anarchist and liberal elements, until they almost became mass meetings themselves. The Communists never went into one of these meetings without careful planning beforehand. The moves of the hostile colleagues were anticipated at 'fraction' meetings, and district meetings. The best way to cope with the opposition was worked out, and speakers were planted prepared to deal with the controversial points. As a result the Communists usually carried the argument.

"Whatever the methods, the great Mooney meetings were successful, not in setting Tom at liberty, but in bringing thousands of workers and unemployed people into class conscious activity.

"I do not think that Dreiser ever realized the immense amount of work that had gone on before he arrived to take the star part; but he played the star part well, and without him the newspapers would hardly have given us a line."

4 ·

On December 22nd, Mother Mooney returned from her Russian trip aboard the U.S.S. *Europa*. The press came down to the pier to interview actress Marilyn Miller and actor Don Alvarado, who it was said had boarded the wrong ship and gone to Europe by mistake, but Mary Mooney got the headlines, even though they were somewhat contrived. Reporters had two standard questions for travelers to the Soviet Union: How did you like Russia? and, following the answer, If you liked it so much when are you going to move there? To their surprise Mother Mooney replied to the first question, "I didn't like it." Why not, they asked, ignoring Miss Miller and Mr. Alvarado. "Because it's too cold," she replied. MOONEY'S MOTHER DIDN'T LIKE RUSSIA, the headlines read.

Another passenger on the ship found Mother Mooney thoroughly enchanting. In a letter to *The New York Times,* Dorothy Parker observed "She had the manner queens ought to have . . ." The ILD had wasted no time on the trip, Miss Parker noted, holding daily mass meetings in the third-class dining room. But her favorite memory of the voyage was Mother Mooney sitting on deck, wearing an emerald green scarf and a string of shiny green beads and drinking her tea clouded with milk.

Although weary after appearing in Moscow, Rotterdam, Amsterdam, The Hague, Paris, Hamburg, Berlin, London, and Dublin (the only place she really felt at ease), on the 30th Mother Mooney went to Albany to see the new President-elect.

Franklin Delano Roosevelt did not have to see her. It was easily avoidable. But in contrast to Hoover and legion other officials who had dodged like pestilence any and everything connected the Mooney case, Roosevelt did receive her.

Shaking her hand, he apologized for the condition of his study. It was his last day in the Executive Mansion, and he was clearing his desk preparatory to turning the governorship over to his successor, Herbert J. Lehman.

Mother Mooney delivered her brief, carefully rehearsed speech: "I wish you would do your utmost to help my boy, who has been in prison, although he is innocent, for almost 17 years. My boy is a good boy."

Roosevelt answered slowly, and just as carefully: "I feel sure because so many people believe he is innocent that there must be some reason for believing in his innocence. I am unable to take any action as governor."

Louis B. Scott, TMMDC secretary, mentioned that two other governors had written Rolph.

Roosevelt nodded. He knew that. He had been preparing to say that as soon as he left office he would be glad to write to the governor in his private capacity, as a friend, an ex-governor, and President-elect.

Mother Mooney and Scott left with the impression that Roosevelt appeared to be sympathetic personally, but cautious officially. He did write to Rolph, however, the following day, explaining that he was writing in a private capacity, and bringing to his attention Mrs. Mary Mooney's visit.

5 ·

In 1933 the TMMDC spent almost $3000 to organize a Free Tom Mooney Congress, which met in Chicago April 20–May 1. Taken over by the Communists, the Congress, against Mooney's express wishes, organized The National Tom Mooney Council of Action, with headquarters in New York City.

The last thing Tom Mooney wanted was another organization collecting funds and issuing statements in his name. At about this same time, after an almost continuous series of disagreements, he had forced Roger Baldwin and the American Civil Liberties Union to disband the National Mooney-Billings Committee.

Following the Congress, Mooney learned that even though large amounts of money had been collected, the TMMDC had been presented with an additional $2000 in unpaid bills. Mooney demanded an accounting ; all he received was promise of a new fund-raising effort to pay off the debt.

Late in May the ILD and the National Tom Mooney Council of Action held a National Mooney Tag Day, during which Mooney buttons and stickers were sold. Immediately thereafter, the National Tom Mooney Council of Action disbanded. Not only was there no accounting for the monies raised during Tag Day, the $2000 debt remained unpaid.

There was a difference of opinion as to who was using whom.

He fought with them continuously, and broke with them a dozen times. On hearing that the ILD was considering writing a book on the case, he hired Miriam Allen DeFord, at a salary of $25 a week, to write his version. Miriam, the wife of Maynard Shipley, had over the years written some of the most astute articles on the case to appear. But in this effort her talents were largely wasted, for Mooney was not interested in her opinions, only in his own. It was not a happy collaboration. Holohan at this time had forbidden Mooney to be interviewed. Miriam had to reproduce their conversations from memory after leaving the visitor's room. After months of work, during which Mooney made sure she earned her salary many times over, he learned that the Communists had abandoned their projected book, whereupon he lost interest in his own. Miriam De-Ford was not his Zola.

Neither was Ernest Jerome Hopkins, whose book *What Happened in the Mooney Case* appeared in 1932. As one of Older's reporters, Hopkins had been involved since the beginning, and his inside-view remains one of the best studies of the case. Although Mooney was initially more pleased with Hopkins' effort than with Hunt's, it did not escape later criticism.

Nothing being done in his behalf entirely pleased him, but the Communists, who had their own ways of doing things, displeased him most. Yet, again and again, he was forced to seek their aid.

Oddly enough, as the Depression continued, the *number* of contributions to the defense increased significantly. The symbol was changing with the times. No matter how hard a worker's lot, one man had it worst —Tom Mooney. But these individual contributions were quite often nickles and dimes, while the average union contribution for this period was under two dollars. Mooney was reluctant to disavow any support.

In reality, his breaks with the ILD and CP were more shadow than substance. From 1931, there was at least one—more often several— Communists in key positions on the Tom Mooney Molders' Defense Committee.

6 ·

On May 18th, 1933, Thomas J. Mooney was taken aboard a private yacht and returned to San Francisco, to stand trial for the murder of Arthur Nelson.

Returned to San Francisco County Jail, where he had spent the first two years of his imprisonment, Mooney was unable to hold back the great sobs.

"To attempt to free a man by trying him for murder—how strange that sounds!" observed *The Nation.*

Mooney had originally been charged with murder on eight separate indictments. He had been tried and convicted on one, and Fickert, to forestall just such a move as was now taking place, had successfully arranged for six of the others to be dropped. But Judge Griffin had refused to drop the remaining indictment, and on this Mooney was now to be given the new trial he had so long requested.

Except for Mooney himself, practically everyone had opposed the current move. District Attorney Brady had refused to prosecute, saying there was no case, and an Assistant State Attorney General had been appointed in his stead. (Mooney had wanted Charles M. Fickert as prosecutor but he had refused, as had Mooney's second choice, Matthew I. Sullivan.) Defense attorneys opposed the move because acquittal would in no way alter Mooney's present status, while conviction (though offering the possibility of appeal to the U.S. Supreme Court) might place him again in the shadow of the hangman's noose. It was a gamble only Mooney wanted to take.

Liberal periodicals were decidedly hopeful. "Splendid news," *The Nation* called it. Observed *Christian Century:* "It hardly seems likely that, if this man is now acquitted when tried on exactly the same charges as led to his imprisonment, the state of California will go on holding him. It *does* look as though the day of justice for Tom Mooney is at hand."

The courtroom was haunted with old memories, for it was here, in the Hall of Justice, that Mooney had first been tried. The offices formerly occupied by Charles Fickert were just down the corridor. Present, as before, were Rena, Mother Mooney, Anna, and John. But these were among the few familiar faces.

The scene was tense. The trial had been called in April but when police had attempted to clear the demonstrators from Portsmouth Square opposite violence had erupted, and the presiding judge, Louis H. Ward, had granted a month's postponement. The streets and square were quiet now, more than 200 police were patrolling them, keeping everyone moving. But the tension remained. There had been several anonymous threats to kill Mooney "and end the Mooney case once and forever."

Nearly two days were spent choosing a jury. Nearly everyone, at some time or another, had heard of the case and formed an opinion. Surprising, however, was that of those who admitted to such, the majority believed Mooney innocent.

The moment the jury had been chosen, the prosecutor stood and announced that there being no evidence on which to try the defendant, the people requested that the jury bring in a verdict of not guilty.

Angrily Mooney jumped to his feet and demanded to be heard. A heated argument between Mooney and Judge Ward followed. Finally ordering him to be quiet, the judge turned to the jury and instructed them, "There is no evidence here that murder was committed. There is not even a corpus delicti. Hence there is but one course for the court in view of the people's motion. I therefore advise you to return a verdict of acquittal." They did so without leaving the jury box.

Tom Mooney had had his new trial. By nightfall he was back in San Quentin peeling potatoes.

28· Governor Upton Sinclair Frees Tom Mooney

"THE FIRST of January came and the inauguration ceremony took place. The retiring Governor behaved politely, and Sinclair retained no memories of what had been said during the campaign. Immediately after having taken the oath of office, he stepped to the microphone and said: 'As Governor of California my first action is to sign a pardon to Thomas J. Mooney. I commission a messenger to take this document to the warden of San Quentin prison, and obtain Mooney's release. At the same time I offer to him my profound apologies for the injustice which the State of California has done to him for the past eighteen years.' "

*   *   *

So began the most remarkable election campaign in California's history, the EPIC crusade of 1934, with the appearance, in October 1933 (more than a year before the election), of a work of fiction—many believed it to be prophecy—entitled *I, Governor of California and How I Ended Poverty: A True Story of the Future.*

The introductory quotation is from one of its chapters.

Its author, Upton Sinclair, had first risen to fame in 1906 with a novel entitled *The Jungle,* an exposé of conditions in the American meat-packing industry. Over the intervening years he had become one of the most widely read of all American authors, as well as one of the most prolific, his novels, plays, and tracts numbering well over a hundred. As a Socialist, he had also run for office four times, each unsuccessfully: for Congress in 1920, for the U.S. Senate in 1922, and for Governor in 1926 and 1930. This time, however, Sinclair proposed to run as a Democrat. For more than three decades the Democratic Party in California had been extinct. Roosevelt's election in 1932, in which he had easily carried Mr. Hoover's home state, convinced Sinclair that the time might be right for a comeback.

Sinclair's platform, one of the most explicit of any American political candidate, was spelled out in his "novel" and a series of EPIC pamphlets.

While EPIC—the name derived from the initials of Sinclair's campaign slogan, "End Poverty In California"—appears, in retrospect, a mild form of state socialism, when first proposed it impressed many as the epitome of revolutionary extremism. Sinclair advocated, among other things, graduated income and inheritance taxes; state ownership of idle farms and factories to enable the unemployed to produce for their own needs rather than succumb to the largesse of relief; and a pension of $50 per month for widows, the aged, and the physically incapacitated.

At first Tom Mooney, like many other Californians, found it difficult to take Sinclair's candidacy seriously. Most Democrats were suspicious of him. By switching his party affiliation, he had alienated the Socialists. A long-standing critic of Communism, he lacked support from that quarter. He had, as was soon apparent, almost no financial backing except publication royalties and individual donations; the latter, aside from the munificence of a few large donors, such as Aline Barnsdall and Charles Chaplin, were in the forms of dimes and quarters. And he was pitted against one of the most colorful figures ever to fill the gubernatorial seat.

"Sunny Jim" Rolph had proven to be one of California's least effective governors. When forced to face state problems—which was not often, since he avoided them as arduously as he attended rodeos and parades—he acted as if the Depression were a temporary unpleasantness, which if ignored long enough, would one morning be gone. Early in his term he had stated "All California needs right now to bring about recovery is a spirit of confidence and quick response to courageous leadership." But the courageous leadership had been conspicuously absent; as a result the spirit of confidence had faded all too quickly. His failure to deal with agricultural problems had nearly occasioned a recall election. His financial mismanagement had brought the state close to bankruptcy. And there had been the scandals—an investigation of the governor's own fantastically high personal expenses, another of his use of influence to have new roads routed through the expensive property of friends, and the "San Jose incident."

On the night of November 27, 1933, a mob had stormed the courthouse-jail at San Jose, California, dragged two prisoners to the square opposite, and hanged them from the trees. The two men had that day admitted kidnapping and murdering the son of a local merchant; the country was enflamed over the still unsolved slaying of the Lindberg baby. Fearing just such violence, the sheriff had pled for state troops. Rolph not only ignored the plea but gave his stamp of approval to the vigilantes the following day by remarking, "Why should I call out troops to protect those two fellows? The people make the laws, don't they? Well, if people have confidence that troops will not be called out to mow them down when they seek to protect themselves against kidnappers, there is liable to be swifter justice and fewer kidnappings."

Papers across the country had dubbed Rolph "Governor Lynch." "This is the same governor," observed Rabbi Stephen B. Wise, "who keeps Mooney in prison for not committing a crime of violence."

Yet how much all this had affected Rolph's immense personal popularity was not known. As Mayor of San Francisco he had been little more than a "Gorgeous Greeter," but this had not kept him from being re-elected to office for a total of 23 years.

Pleased as he was to have found a candidate who advocated his pardon, Mooney was not, at this time, too greatly concerned with whether Sinclair won or lost. For suddenly a long closed door appeared to have opened.

2 ·

In the spring of 1934 Mooney's legal defense team consisted of Frank Walsh of New York City and John F. Finerty of Washington, D.C.* The pair were badly in need of an able local attorney to handle the day by day developments in the case. He would have to be a man who, like Walsh and Finerty, felt strongly enough about Mooney's innocence to work mostly without fee, and equally important, someone who could get along with their difficult client. A local attorney suggested just such a man, a lawyer named George Davis, who, although still in his twenties and not long in practice, had accumulated a remarkable record of acquittals.

A meeting was arranged, although Davis was not told of its purpose in advance. Few San Francisco attorneys wanted any connection with the Mooney case.

"I hear you are pretty good at pulling them out of the hat," Finerty said after the introductions. "We wonder if you would give us a hand at trying to pull Mooney out of San Quentin."

For a minute Davis was too surprised to speak.

On the afternoon of July 22, 1916, nine-year-old George Davis had been selling newspapers opposite the Palace Hotel. Running to the scene after the explosion, he had seen Lieutenant Bunner washing the sidewalk with a hose, and Fickert and Colburn enlarging the hole with a sledge hammer. Growing up in the Mission District, he had known the name Mooney as a household word. His boyhood ambition to free the man had been partly responsible for his initial interest in the law.

Between that day and this, Davis had had time to go through school in

---

* John F. Finerty had initially been contacted by Warren Billings, after Finerty's eloquent plea in behalf of Sacco and Vanzetti. Finerty also served as counsel for Irish premier Eamon de Valera during his treason trial in England and later, in 1937, would serve as legal counsel for the Joint Commission of Inquiry that conducted Leon Trotsky's counter-trial.

San Francisco, study law at the University of California, serve briefly in District Attorney Brady's office, and launch his own practice.

Walsh asked Davis' personal feelings about the case. Did he believe Mooney was innocent? "Yes," Davis replied, "I always have."

They discussed Davis' record. In 14 murder cases, he had won 13 acquittals, losing only the first. How had he managed this, Finerty asked. Davis explained that he had learned to turn the prosecution's own tricks back on them. Too, in each of these cases, there had been a violation of due process, about which he felt strongly. "And," he added, "there has certainly been flagrant violation of due process in the Mooney case."

Walsh and Finerty exchanged startled looks. "It's an odd remark," Walsh said. "Our minds were moving in that very direction."

George Davis joined the Mooney defense. And from this and subsequent meetings was evolved a plan of action.

Again and again the Mooney case had smashed against two solid walls: one was the reluctance of California governors to grant a pardon; the other was the California State Supreme Court ruling that newly discovered evidence, including evidence of perjury, could not be considered as a legal issue after trial records were closed. There was, however, an authority higher than the Governor and the California Supreme Court—the federal courts. Davis proposed taking the case all the way to the United States Supreme Court in the hope of that high tribunal's finding that through use of perjury and other fraud the prosecution had denied the defendant the "due process of law" promised by the 14th Amendment to the Constitution.

This Amendment read: "No State shall make or enforce any law which shall abridge the privileges or immunities of citizens of the United States, nor shall any State deprive any person of life, liberty, or property, without due process of law, nor deny to any person within its jurisdiction the equal protection of the laws."

Davis hoped to accomplish this by filing a petition for a writ of habeas corpus. Interestingly enough, "jail house lawyer" Warren K. Billings had started work on just such a brief in the 1920's, an opinion report entitled "Habeas Corpus and Why."

What Davis proposed was revolutionary. It also went squarely against the U.S. Supreme Court's long-standing reluctance to interfere with the conduct of the state courts. Yet there was a somewhat negative precedent for such a move. In 1914, when the U.S. Supreme Court had denied review to Leo Frank, Justices Oliver Wendell Holmes and Charles Evans Hughes had dissented, saying "Whatever disagreement there may be as to the scope of the phrase 'due process of law,' there can be no doubt that it embraces the fundamental conception of a fair trial, with opportunity to be heard . . . We are not speaking of mere disorder, or mere irregularities in procedure, but of a case where the processes of justice are actually subverted. In such a case the Federal Court has jurisdiction to issue the writ."

Davis hoped that, after 20 years, a majority of the court might be ready to define "due process of law" and in so doing set Tom Mooney free.

It was a gamble, he told his new client, one requiring time. Mooney was enthusiastic, however.

Davis filed the writ in Federal District Court ("The exceptional cases in which a federal court or judge may sometimes appropriately interfere by habeas corpus in advance of final action by the authorities of the state are those of great urgency, that require to be promptly disposed of . . . The present case is not within any of the exceptions recognized in our former decisions. Petition denied.").

An appeal was then made to the United States Circuit Court ("Approximately eighteen years have passed since the judgment of the state court became final. During all these years petitioner had suffered imprisonment in the state penitentiary . . . The fact that petitioner did not learn of the alleged perjured testimony and of the alleged misconduct of the district attorney who prosecuted him until it was too late to assign same as grounds for a new trial is indeed unfortunate. The petition is denied.").

The long, slow climb to the United States Supreme Court had begun.

3 ·

It was poorly financed, had no formal organizational support, and was looked upon by most professional politicians as just another manifestation of California crackpotism—yet, by early 1934, there was no doubt that the EPIC movement was capturing the imagination of a great number of Californians. More than 800 EPIC Clubs had sprung up over the state.

Republicans refused to take it seriously, but Mooney was having second thoughts. As the campaign progressed he was surprised to discover that Sinclair neither changed his mind nor avoided the topic but reaffirmed his determination to right this old wrong nearly every time he spoke. "I take no stand on the guilt or innocence of Tom Mooney," Sinclair wrote C. K. McClatchy, publisher of the Sacramento *Bee*. "I was not present when the crime was committed, nor have I ever had access to Tom Mooney's heart and conscience; but I do know that he was convicted upon perjured testimony, and that would make it impossible for me to keep him in jail." Sinclair's letter was prompted by a McClatchy editorial stating that Sinclair's promise to pardon Mooney was in itself sufficient to damn him as a candidate.

Although the two men had corresponded for a number of years,

Mooney and Sinclair met for the first time on February 24th, the 17th anniversary of Judge Griffin's sentencing. While waiting for Mooney to enter the visitor's room, Sinclair asked Warden Holohan "Will you allow Tom to have an anniversary cake with seventeen candles?" Holohan, never noted for his sense of humor, didn't smile.

Following the meeting Sinclair described it for the press.

"I told Mooney," Sinclair said, "I was a candidate for the Democratic nomination for Governor and I would pardon him if elected, as my first official act.

"His reply was: 'That's a little hard to believe.'

"I take it from his reply," Sinclair interpreted, "he figured the same interests that sent him to prison would see to it that I met defeat."

Mooney's bad temper didn't dissuade Sinclair from acting in his behalf. In May he wrote an open letter to President Roosevelt, asking him to appeal to Governor Rolph. "I have publicly stated in my book that my first action, if I become Governor of California, will be to pardon Mooney, but that cannot happen for another seven months and Mooney has already spent some eighteen years in prison . . ."

Despite himself, Mooney was impressed, and ordered the TMMDC to do everything possible to aid Sinclair in his campaign. Again Mother Mooney undertook a personal appearance tour, this time pleading for Sinclair's election.

Mooney was still not overly hopeful. Then, on June 2nd, Governor Rolph suddenly died of a heart attack.

California's new governor, former Lieutenant Governor Frank Finley Merriam, was, as a fellow Republican later described him, "at best a mediocrity." Yet, when asked his stand on the Mooney case, he proved himself well-versed in California political tradition. With his eye on the November elections, he observed that not having been duly elected to his present office by a mandate of the people, he did not feel he could in fairness act on Mooney's pardon petition at this time. "During an administration that is authorized by the people, I would feel an added responsibility to study Mooney's case and make a decision."

If Mooney had the slightest hope of Merriam's acting favorably on his petition, it disappeared on July 5th, a day that would go down in the annals of American labor history as "Bloody Thursday."

4 ·

Nearly two decades after the Preparedness Day bombing, San Francisco labor was still smarting from its repercussions. During the Twenties, employers had formed an Industrial Association to finish the deunionizing of the city begun by the Law and Order Committee in 1916. Its greatest success had been on the waterfront, where a company union was established and most of the national unions driven out.

A local of the International Longshoremen's Association had been organized, however, and on May 9, 1934, after the employers refused it recognition, the longshoremen struck. This strike quickly spread to other ports, tying up shipping from San Diego to Seattle.

Warden Holohan sealed off his political prisoners. All letters and telegrams to Mooney, McNamara, and Schmidt from the *Daily Worker* and other papers, asking for their views on the strike, were refused. Outgoing letters were closely censored. And a well-publicized attempt by Harry Bridges and other strike leaders to call on Mooney for counsel was rebuffed.

Yet, despite these precautions, Tom Mooney became one of the strike symbols. Strikers carried Mooney banners. Messages of encouragement, allegedly written by the famous prisoner and said to have been smuggled out of San Quentin, were read at strike meetings.

In early July, the Industrial Association decided to open the port by force, and on Thursday, July 5th, tried to move in truckloads of scabs and goods under police convoy. Starting with tear gas and clubs it ended with gunfire, the death of two pickets and injury to more than a hundred from both sides. This was "Bloody Thursday." That night Governor Merriam called out the National Guard, which marched into the city 5000 strong.

In protest against police brutality, workers from other industries began walking off their jobs. By July 16th they numbered 150,000 and a general strike was officially proclaimed, the first since Seattle in 1919.

Commerce in the Bay Area came to an abrupt halt.

"Here is revolution not only in the making but with the initial actuality," Senator Hiram Johnson wired Harold Ickes.

A Communist Army is marching on San Francisco from the Northwest, the *Chronicle* proclaimed. "Reports," unspecified, "stated that the communist army planned the destruction of railroad and highway facilities to paralyze transportation and, later, communications, while San Francisco and the Bay Area were made the focal point in a red struggle for revolution and control of government."

The proletarian army never arrived, however, perhaps because it never existed, and the general strike collapsed on the fourth day. The longshoremen's strike broke up gradually, with a series of concession on both sides, the union eventually gaining recognition and many of its demands.

These events had their effect on the Mooney case. They clarified beyond doubt where Governor Merriam's sympathies lay. They pushed to the forefront a powerful new figure in the American labor movement, the dockers' leader Harry Bridges. And they introduced into the San Francisco Labor Council a strong and militant element willing to fight for the release of Tom Mooney.

If to some revolution looked imminent in July, by the end of August it seemed to have arrived. For by this time the primary election results were in. Governor Merriam had, as expected, won over his leading opponent, former governor C. C. Young, but only by a slim margin of 5000 votes.

Upton Sinclair, however, not only won the Democratic nomination by landslide proportions, he led all eight contenders for the total number of votes, holding an amazing 100,000 vote lead over Frank F. Merriam.

Everyone now viewed the EPIC movement much more seriously.

5 ·

> The guards are in fear and confusion
> And panic has seized their estate,
> For we've carried a coffin to prison;
> And we're pounding the iron gate.

On Labor Sunday, September 2nd, 1935, Mother Mooney rose early and began cooking a big chicken dinner for John, who was working. The five-hour trip to San Quentin the previous day had tired her more than usual, she admitted somewhat guiltily to her daughter when she called. Anna urged her to cancel her appearance in the Labor Day parade tomorrow, but she said no; she had promised to appear.

> It is only the corpse of a woman,
> A mother of eighty-six years;
> But the powers that be are in terror,
> And gripped with mysterious fears.

When John returned home for dinner she was in good spirits, recalling Tom's excitement over Sinclair's astonishing primary victory. "Do you really think they will let him out, John?" she asked. "I know they will, Mother," he replied, as always. Changing the subject, he asked her what she was going to wear in the parade and she showed him the dress she and Anna had selected.

John returned to work, leaving her alone in the house. About 5:30 a neighbor, hearing low moans, investigated to find her slumped in a chair. Though rushed to the hospital, she died in the ambulance on the way, her last words "Poor Tom."

> We have come to our comrade Tom Mooney,
> Let him bid his dead mother farewell.
> Let him kiss her cold lips and embrace her;
> Then lock him again in your hell.

On hearing the news Tom collapsed "as if hit by a sledge-hammer blow." In shock, he begged to be allowed to attend the funeral. Although never a common practice, it had been permitted on occasion. Warden Holohan referred the request to Governor Merriam, who, apparently fearing a demonstration, stated, "There is no legal way other than a parole or a pardon that Mooney can be released from the prison."

The funeral was scheduled for Saturday, September 8th. That morning a strange procession drove onto the ferry for San Rafael.

> But the guards run about in confusion
> And beg us to leave them alone.
> You must murder or steal or be framed by the boss
> To enter this mountain of stone.

Mooney begged permission to have the coffin brought through the front gate into the yard, but permission was refused and he was ordered back to work in the O&G Mess. From the room where he peeled potatoes a window looked out over the gate.

> They are chasing the men with the cameras;
> No picture must live to relate
> That a coffin came up to the prison
> And banged on the iron gate.
>
> Tom, watching from high in a window,
> Sees them turn us away, and then
> Knows we're taking her off to the funeral.
> He never will see her again.

II

> The sun is high and shining bright,
> And crowds line Market Street
> That feels the now familiar tread
> Of marching worker's feet.

The procession, slowly and somberly, moved up Market. Over 5000 men, mostly from the molders', maritime, and longshoremen's unions, wearing black arm bands with the words "Free Tom Mooney" sewn in white, escorted the coffin to Civic Auditorium, where the "worker's funeral" was to be held.

Members of the Young Communists League carried the coffin down the aisle to the front of the auditorium.

Huge banners reading WE'LL FINISH YOUR FIGHT, MOTHER MOONEY! hung from the balconies. Below them was the speaker's platform, and below that the open coffin. More than 15,000 heard Harry

Bridges, Henry Schmidt, Robert Whitaker, Leo Gallagher, and John
Mooney deliver the eulogies.

> In even ranks the silent men
> Are marching to the grave,
> As only workers march behind
> The coffins of the brave.
>
> And up ahead, bestrewn with flowers
> The honored casket rides,
> Of one who only yesterday
> Was marching by our sides.

III

> She does not smile. Her cold lips set
> Defiantly in death,
> As lips that spake a challenge
> With a warrior's final breath.
>
> This silent corpse that lies in silk
> Knew little silk in life.
> The mills of greed wove coarser cloth
> To garb a miner's wife.
>
> That pale white wrinkled hand in which,
> Ironically, a flower
> Is thrust, once sorted dirty rags
> For twenty cents an hour.
>
> In paper mills that make the page
> On which the rich write lies,
> She toiled and learned the truth that made
> Her orphaned children wise.

IV

> When Tom grew up in labor's ranks
> He gripped and shook the chains
> That bind all workingmen in hell
> To serve a master's gains.
>
> He shouted loud how wealth is made
> By grinding human lives;
> Of riches wrung from toil of men
> And martyrdom of wives.

The owner class went cold with fear.
It drew its sharpest knife
Of treachery and perjury,
And Tom was framed for life.

V

She did not pray to the sky above
Or kneel at plaster shrines,
Or hope for aid from parasites
Who own the mills and mines.

She looked to the strength of the working class,
In its march to victory,
To rip the bars from the cold stone walls
AND SET TOM MOONEY FREE.

After the funeral the coffin was taken back across the Bay, to Mount Tamalpais Cemetery, "within the shadow of San Quentin, her son's living tomb."

VI

Lower her into the narrow grave,
Cover her over with soil.
She is resting with Zetkin and Luxemburg,
And a million heroes of toil.

At graveside, John Mooney asked everyone to raise his clenched right fist and swear an oath with him. Everyone did, in voice so strong that the sound was a roar.

Not your tears, but your fists and your pledges;
Not kneeling, but standing upright;
Bid farewell to a valiant Comrade.
Mother Mooney, WE'LL FINISH YOUR FIGHT! *

6 ·

Upton Sinclair's "novel" proved to be a remarkably accurate piece of prophecy, insofar as the campaign itself was concerned, for between August and November there was conducted in California the dirtiest campaign in that state's rarely spotless history. Blackmail and intimida-

* *Farewell, Mother Mooney* by Mike Quin. Originally published in *The Western Worker*, September 17, 1934. Reprinted by permission of *People's World*, San Francisco.

tion were openly practiced. Thieves were planted in EPIC Clubs to embezzle funds. Sinclair was branded a Communist, an anti-Christ, a racist, and a free lover. Since he was a voluminous writer, it was not difficult to find evidence for each of these charges by using out-of-context quotations from his work. Nor was the Mooney case long absent. To remind Californians what anarchy would result if Sinclair were elected, his opponents purchased large billboards with only this wording:

> Upton Sinclair says,
> "As Governor of California my first action
> will be to sign a pardon for Tom Mooney."

In the same TMMDC letter in which Tom described his mother's death (the first page was a composite photograph of her in life and in her coffin), he branded Merriam "an absolute tool of the bankers and captains of industry" and charged that for calling out the State Militia during the recent strike, the shipowners had contributed $30,000 to his campaign, while PG&E had contributed at least $13,000.

Merriam must at all costs be defeated, he said, and Sinclair elected. Although he personally was not at all impressed with the EPIC plan, he didn't openly say so. He hinted at it, however, when he said, "The Sinclair EPIC plan will be tried. If it fails to satisfy the masses of the people they will march still further to the left, and ultimately to social revolution. They will not die starving without a struggle."

The two months of vilification were telling. With limited financial backing, Sinclair was unable to answer publicly many of the last-minute smears, including a bogus Communist endorsement. In addition, a third candidate, Raymond L. Haight, running on the Progressive ticket, was sure to cut heavily into the Democratic votes. Of equal importance, F.D.R. had declined to give Sinclair his endorsement. If he was to win it it would have to be solely through grass roots support generated by the EPIC Clubs.

On the night of November 6th, 1934, most Californians remained close to their radios as election returns came in. Would California turn Red? This, many felt, was the only issue. As one wit would later remark, "To many Californians radicals were like Negroes. It was impossible to tell them apart." Merriam took an early lead and never lost it. "California voters have overwhelmingly rejected radicalism and socialism in today's vote for Governor," Merriam began his victory speech.

The final tally: Merriam (Republican) 1,138,620; Sinclair (Democrat) 879,557; and Haight (Progressive) 302,519.

Had it not been for the Progressive candidate, Sinclair would probably have been Governor of California and able to fulfill his novel promise.

But the Mooney case was, if nothing else, a chronicle of "might have beens."

Following the EPIC defeat, Sinclair retired to his study to write a sequel, *I, Candidate for Governor of California and How I Got Licked.* Mooney's hopes now returned to the new legal moves.

As a result of the election, a number of Democratic candidates captured minor state offices. One, an attorney elected to the State Senate from Los Angeles County, was a man named Culbert L. Olson.

29· Mooney vs. Holohan

THE UNITED STATES Supreme Court handed down its decision in the case of Mooney *vs.* Holohan in January 1935.

For twenty-eight-year-old George Davis the decision seemed to portend a landmark victory, for, in seeming agreement with Davis' contention, Chief Justice Charles Evans Hughes wrote:

"If a state has contrived a conviction, through the pretense of a trial, which in truth is but used as the means for depriving a defendant of his liberty through a deliberate deception of court and jury by a presentation of testimony known to be perjured, such a contrivance is as inconsistent with the rudimentary demands of justice, as is the obtaining of a like remedy by intimidation."

But for Thomas J. Mooney the decision only meant another delay. For the court also denied the writ of habeas corpus, stating that the petitioner, not having presented this particular argument to the California Supreme Court, had not exhausted all the resources of the lower courts. But it did so without prejudice to a future request.

In effect, the U.S. Supreme Court told Mooney to try again, by making an appeal on these same grounds to the California State Supreme Court. If that court failed to act, there was—the wording of the decision seemed to indicate—good reason to believe the high court would then rule favorably on the request.

Mooney had lost an appeal and won a point, and California justice, though sharply rebuked, was given another chance. Again began the long climb.

The decision had some surprising aftereffects.

On January 23, two days after it was made public, the San Francisco *Chronicle* ran a front page editorial urging Mooney's release.

Rather than have the matter go through the courts again, with all the attendant publicity, the *Chronicle* suggested another solution. "Commute the sentence, without explanation, to the time already served, and turn Mooney loose."

It was common knowledge, the paper said, that Mooney had been offered parole but had refused it. Unlike parole, however, commutation didn't require consent. And in doing this the Governor could end the Mooney case once and for all without implying wrongful conviction.

"Mooney at large on commutation would do no harm that he could not do at large on parole. In fact, the place he can do the most harm is where he is now. Which is a strong practical reason for preferring not to have him there."

Much as Mooney opposed this course of action, he was aware that it represented an important shift in public opinion.

2 ·

On March 3, 1935, Fremont and Cora Older rode to the state capital to attend a flower show. As usual, whenever he went to Sacramento or on to their cottage at Lake Tahoe, Older allowed time for a sidetrip to Represa and a visit with Warren Billings. Although he had been estranged from Mooney for some time, Older remained one of Billings' most frequent visitors. The editor felt a special fondness for the little watchmaker, and on this day he was in an enthusiastic mood, hopeful that the recent legal decision would soon lead to the release of both men.

Billings was less optimistic. He was, he reminded Older, a twice-convicted felon. Even if Mooney were freed, he would still have to have a favorable recommendation from the California State Supreme Court. He was no closer to freedom than he had ever been.

On their return to San Francisco, Fremont Older drove. Although he employed a chauffeur, Older preferred taking the wheel himself whenever possible, and the chauffeur sat next to him, with Cora in the back. They didn't discuss Billings, though he was, Cora felt, very much on her husband's mind. Instead they were talking about a book when the editor slumped forward and his hands slipped from the wheel. Glancing quickly at the speedometer, the chauffeur grasped the wheel, eased Older back, and brought the car to a stop at the side of the road.

The speedometer, the chauffeur later recalled, had read 30.

3 ·

On June 17th the California Supreme Court ruled favorably on Mooney's petition for a hearing on the habeas corpus writ.

George Davis soon heard, through the legal grapevine, an explanation as to why the court had ruled as it had. Mooney would be allowed his day in court; then, when the hearing was finished, the court would deny the petition and the case would be closed. In this way no one could say that

Mooney had not received due process. Or so the rumor went. Carefully considering its sources, Davis believed it to be true, and together with Walsh and Finerty, decided on a new course of action.

Since the hearing would be held in San Francisco, Davis drew up an order asking that Thomas J. Mooney be transferred into the custody of the Sheriff of the County of San Francisco for the duration of the hearing. Chief Justice Waste signed it automatically, probably assuming, as did almost everyone else, that the hearing would last at most a couple of weeks.

It would last nearly a year, during most of which, due to a fantastic set of circumstances, Tom Mooney would walk the streets of the city as a relatively free man.

Mooney was returned to San Francisco County Jail on September 17th. A week later Davis was able to secure the court's permission to have Billings transferred to the sheriff's custody also, as a witness.

This was Mooney's third return to the city since his imprisonment. Warren Billings had not set foot outside the walls of Folsom Prison since 1917.

The court order reached Folsom early in the afternoon. On receiving notification to report to the warden's office, Billings carefully cleaned his watchmaking tools and turned them in, then, with no great haste, reported as ordered. Billings had been appointed official prison watchmaker in 1932.

Folsom's warden, Court Smith, was a huge man, seemingly all muscle and bone. He was known as a "tough" warden, but the word "strict" described him more accurately. He believed in making fair rules and then firmly enforcing them. With Holohan, San Quentin prisoners never knew where they stood. With Smith, the prisoners at Folsom always knew, and over the years Billings had developed a respect for his jailor. It was not entirely one-sided. As they left the prison amid snapping flashbulbs they presented a Mutt and Jeff aspect: Smith was 6'7", Billings 5'4". To reporters, Billings appeared in jovial humor. Noticing one photographer's black camera case, Billings warned him, "Watch out with that suitcase. Estelle Smith may see you and think you're carrying a bomb."

But, as Smith knew, the mood was feigned. Billings was very reluctant to leave Folsom, afraid of the effect of the brief trip on the world he had so carefully constructed in his own mind.

Billings later bared his feelings to a friendly reporter. "The prison world is the smallest world man can know," he said. "For a while I thought I should go mad. Then I began to orient myself to my surroundings by pretending I had been marooned on an island. I sought every kind of job I could find, no matter how small, and ultimately I learned to enjoy the simplicity of my life.

"I'm afraid," he admitted. "I'm fearful of the effect of the outside world on the world of my own creation. All this excitement has broken into my routine. If it meant a chance for me I'd accept it gladly. Since it doesn't, I can only hope I will not find it too hard to reframe my existence along prison lines."

Disdaining the use of either handcuffs or a guard, Smith drove his prisoner back to the city through what, in Warren Billings' eyes, seemed a strange and different world. He was amazed at the roads. Before they had been dirt; now they were smooth and paved. Smith drove at a moderate speed, aware of how frightening 50-miles-per-hour could be to a man imprisoned for more than 19 years. "Won't it go any faster?" Billings asked. After boarding the ferry at the Berkeley slip, Smith took Billings into the restaurant. Billings studied the menu for a full five minutes, while the waitress waited impatiently. "Eat hearty," Smith urged. Finally putting the menu down, Billings ordered a cup of coffee and a piece of custard pie. It was not easy to adjust to freedom of choice.

Going up on deck he looked in wonder at the partly constructed bridge that, when finished, would stretch from Oakland to San Francisco. It was a clear day and he could see the other unfinished span over the Golden Gate. Neither seemed possible.

San Francisco itself, by contrast, appeared to have changed very little.

Several cameramen were waiting when they parked outside the jail. Well over a dozen more were inside, to photograph the first meeting of the famous prisoners since 1917.

"You're looking fine," they said in unison, embracing with wide smiles. Privately each was shocked at the changes in the other. Mooney, taking command of the situation, spoke for them both: "For 19 years we have gone through fire together. We have uttered strong words, but we remain friends. Through the years we have been soldiers fighting together in the cause of the worker, and we are friends today—good friends."

This came as a decided disappointment to the Los Angeles *Times,* which just that morning had editorialized: "Mooney and Billings have not been friendly for some time, and if they get stirred up enough to start telling the truth about each other, the public may learn something."

Later Warden Smith, talking to a reporter, revealed one reason why the split had grown no wider. Occasionally Billings would write a very angry letter. "Those letters all came to my office," Smith said. "I would hold them on my desk until Warren came in Monday morning to set the clocks. Then I'd say, 'You were pretty sore when you wrote this, weren't you, Warren?' and he would say, 'Yes, I'm glad you held it up.' He would then tear them up and throw them in the waste basket."

Mooney and Billings reunited for the first time in 18 years, during the habeas corpus hearing in 1935. Left to right, Billings, attorney George Davis, and Mooney.

Billings anticipated this meeting even more. Warren Billings and his fiancée Josephine Rudolph. Their courtship, by correspondence, lasted 17 years.

4 ·

To preside over the hearing, the Supreme Court had appointed Addison E. Shaw referee. Shaw, a former classmate of Chief Justice Waste, was an elderly retired PG&E lawyer who had never before participated in a criminal case. His duties, as the court originally defined them, were to act as a somewhat glorified notary public, certifying the record. So long as this was his only function, the Mooney defense had no objection.

There was, at the start, little reason to think that this hearing would be anything more than a dull recital of old facts. During the first several weeks it was like an old movie, the story so familiar that one could almost predict each piece of dialogue in advance. But it was a movie in which most of the actors had aged with the print, while others—Bourke Cockran, Mother Mooney, Fremont Older, and a dozen more—had faded from it altogether.

If the first witness, Thomas J. Mooney, had changed physically, neither his philosophy nor his reluctance to take advice had. Against the counsel of his attorneys, he insisted upon making a statement of his personal and political philosophy. *Time* claimed that he had "mellowed," that he was no longer a radical firebrand. He was still a "social revolutionary," he asserted proudly, and he still believed in distributing the wealth and founding a worker's state. It wasn't he who had changed, but the country itself, much in line with his predictions. His views on labor were now just the same as the President's (or, as he put it, "President Roosevelt agrees with my views on labor"). Nor had he lost his fire. "I earned the undying hatred of the big corporations," Mooney said. "Just as they hate Harry Bridges today, they hated me then. Just as they would like to frame Bridges today, they framed me then. They hate any man who is really active in the labor movement. They want every worker to bow his head and take merely what is given him."

Mooney proved his point. He had not "mellowed." He was not a "bitter broken old man." His entire statement was later deleted from the record, at the suggestion of his attorneys, who had wanted to stick to the facts of the case, not reopen the door on the radicalism bugaboo.

Rena followed Tom on the stand. Only now, 19 years later, many of the details of Preparedness Day were vague. She had changed greatly. For the past several years she had been drinking heavily. This, plus the fact that music lessons are one of the first expendables during a Depression, had reduced her income to a mere subsistence level. She was present in the courtroom every day, however, seated in the front row, following every word. During recesses, when they were together, there was no indication that there had ever been any trouble between the husband and wife.

There were other reunions. Israel Weinberg, now a prosperous Cleveland manufacturer, returned to relate the story of Swanson's bribe offer and events that followed it. Edward Nolan, who now had his own business in Los Angeles, returned too. On the stand he proved to be the angriest of the witnesses. He had been arrested, indicted for murder, held for nine months, then released without being brought to trial. Of all the defendants he had never had a chance to answer publicly the vile accusations under whose shadow he and his family had been forced to live. He now had his chance, and he used it.

Maxwell McNutt took the stand to testify to his conversations with Swanson, Barrett, and Cantrell, the suppression of the Eilers photos, and other evidence. McNutt was now a Superior Court Judge in San Mateo County.

Judge Griffin also testified, and met Tom Mooney face to face for the first time since resentencing him to hang. He frankly admitted to never being able to undergo the emotional strain of visiting Mooney at San Quentin.

The prosecution's side was handled by an assistant state attorney general, William F. Cleary, son of William B. Cleary, a famous labor lawyer who had been among the strikers deported from Bisbee, Arizona. It was soon apparent that Cleary the younger did not share his father's philosophy. This pleased Mooney, who wanted this to be a real fight. As Cleary called his witnesses more familiar faces came on the scene.

Billings' prosecutor, James F. Brennan, who in 1920 had issued a statement asserting his disbelief in his own witnesses and in 1926 had written to the Governor requesting a pardon for Mooney and Billings, had now reverted to his original conclusions that both Billings and Mooney were guilty.

Police Captain Charles Goff, who in 1924 had written to the Governor stating his belief that Mooney had not had a fair trial, had also, in the intervening years, changed his mind.

Brennan was now a State Assemblyman from San Francisco, Goff head of the Traffic Squad.

Like a fixed star, Edward Cuhna testified that, if anything, he was more than ever convinced of the guilt of all the defendants. He remained on the stand for several days, talking of Mooney's "known dynamiting activities" and what he now called his deliberate murder of the Preparedness Day victims. After several references to Mooney as a "murderer" and "a man who loves violence," Mooney angrily jumped to his feet. "I am not a destroyer," he said, his voice ringing through the courtroom. "I am a creator, a social builder. The aim and object of my whole life has been to build a new social order which would insure justice to the workers. I abhor violence; the thought of a person being killed, in war or by capital punishment or otherwise, is repulsive and repugnant to my nature. But I have hated and fought injustice all my life, and that is why I am in prison today."

There was a long moment of silence. Even referee Shaw had been loath to interrupt.

One man had changed more than any of the other principals.

"A pitiful wreck," one reporter described him; "only the shell of a man" wrote another. Charles M. Fickert mounted the witness stand slowly. His skin hung loosely on his face, in heavy pouches; his clothing sagged similarly on his wasted body, as if he were wearing hand-me-downs several sizes too large. Partly deaf, he had long been in ill health. His wife had divorced him, charging, among other things, intemperance, habitual gambling, failure to provide, and vile abuse. Behind on his alimony, he had been forced to file a petition of poverty. For the past several years he had been reduced to begging from former acquaintances.

Now that Older was dead one of his reporters revealed something Older would never have admitted publicly while living, that Fickert had come to him seeking a loan and had received it. As Evelyn Wells put it, "Sometimes his friends found it difficult to forgive Fremont Older his capacity for forgiveness."

Roles had now been reversed. From the moment Fickert took the stand, Davis put him on the defensive and kept him there, bluntly accusing him of having guilty foreknowledge of the Preparedness Day bombing. As an elected official of the city, why had he not marched in the parade? Why was he sitting in his office when the tragedy occurred? Was he waiting for word from Swanson that the bomb had exploded on schedule?

Davis used all of Fickert's own tricks, with telling effect, while Mooney's habit of grinning at him across the courtroom reduced Fickert to "insane outbursts."

But in one respect Fickert hadn't changed. "It is close to 20 years now since I prosecuted Mooney for the Preparedness Day bombing," he testified. "Nothing has developed since to change my opinion that he was guilty."

The hearing moved into its second month, and then its third. Walsh returned to the East, followed soon after by Finerty. Davis, who had entered the case as a junior partner—in part because of his strong feelings about Mooney's innocence, in part because of the opportunity to associate with "the great Frank Walsh"—was left in charge of the defense.

Shaw was being paid $50 a day to sit as referee. It was soon apparent that he was in no hurry for the hearing to end. Sometimes court would convene at 11 to recess at 11:15. The fatherhood of one of the assistant prosecuting attorneys, the toothache of another were sufficient reason for a day's recess. Insistent that he be present when deputations were taken, Shaw spent several weeks traveling: to Portland, to listen to testimony concerning Oxman; to Cheyenne, to interview a new witness who, after nearly two decades, had decided to produce a letter from Oxman similar to that sent Rigall; to Grayville, to interview Rigall. The latter was wasted effort. They found a paralyzed old man, in a wheelchair, who could neither see, hear, nor speak. He died shortly after their visit. The trip to Baltimore was also unnecessary. McDonald had been located in a flophouse there. By now his mental deterioration was nearly complete.

All this delay accorded with Davis' defense strategy. He wanted to drag out the hearing as long as possible, introducing into the transcript everything of possible relevance (it would eventually run to 21 volumes, 15,000 pages, more than 5 million words) so that when the California Supreme Court ruled against Mooney the whole story would be in the record, for the appeal to the United States Supreme Court.

It was a tactic that cost Davis most of his legal practice. But he had still another reason for adopting it.

5 ·

Daniel C. Murphy was one of the few California labor leaders convinced of Mooney's innocence from the outset. An original officer of the Tom Mooney Molders' Defense Committee, he had, over the years, been president of the Web Pressmen's Union, the San Francisco Labor Council, and the State Federation of Labor; in more recent years he had served several terms as a State Senator.

In 1935 Murphy announced that he would be a candidate for Sheriff of the County of San Francisco. It was, considering Murphy's background, a step down, but reporters saw nothing markedly significant about it. George Davis did, but he said nothing.

In November Murphy won over the incumbent, Fitzgerald, by a sizable margin.

A few minutes after taking the oath of office, Murphy called George Davis into his office and talked to him briefly. He then sent a deputy for Tom Mooney.

George Davis recalls every detail of the incredible scene that followed.

Tears running down his face, Murphy embraced Mooney and said, "Tom, I know you are innocent. And now you are my prisoner and in my custody." He turned away, staring out the window, as if to compose himself. Turning back, still crying, he smashed his fist down on the desk. "You know and I know and Davis here knows, although he won't admit it, that you will never be freed by the courts. But so long as you are my prisoner, I want you to have some taste of freedom.

"I want you to promise that you will not escape nor embarrass me in any way. If you'll do this, I'll give you the run of the city. All you need be is careful and don't embarrass me."

It was, Davis recalls thinking as he looked at the two blubbering Irishmen, a truly unbelievable situation. As Murphy proposed it, it was also quite legal. Mooney had been remanded into the custody of the Sheriff of San Francisco; so long as a deputy was with him he would still be legally in the sheriff's custody.

Mooney promised. And he walked out of jail a relatively free man.

Over the past several years Mooney's stomach condition had abated, and he had gained back his weight plus about 20 pounds, so that he resembled neither the "before" nor the "after" in his famous photographs. Since the deputy wore civilian clothes and carried neither handcuffs nor a gun, there was little to distinguish them from any two men. That night Tom Mooney dined in one of the city's finest restaurants. He merited not even a second glance. He might have been a prosperous businessman.

There were several close calls.

One day Mooney passed Fickert on the street. Fickert gave an astonished look, then shook his head as if not seeing correctly. The next courtroom session was tense, but Fickert said nothing. Fortunately for Mooney, Fickert had been drunk.

One night, in a restaurant on Fisherman's Wharf, the waiter, an officer of the Waiters' Union, recognized Mooney and asked for his autograph. Mooney signed the menu. Within moments, there was a large crowd around the table. Mooney and the deputy left in a hurry. A similar incident, in the lobby of the Golden Gate Theatre, convinced Davis that something must be done to avoid giving the show away. Amazingly, no reporter had yet discovered what was going on.

An apartment was rented, at 1924 Polk Street, and a cook hired to prepare meals. During the noon recess, Mooney, Billings, and Davis would meet there to plan their courtroom strategy over lunch. After court adjourned and on weekends and holidays, Mooney spent nearly all of his time there. Within a very short time, 1924 Polk became the real, if unofficial, headquarters of the Mooney defense. Several secretaries were put to work answering Mooney's correspondence. Davis would visit the apartment to find Mooney dictating a press release, or a letter to the members of the Tom Mooney Machine Gun Company of the Abraham Lincoln Batallion fighting on the Jarama front in Spain, or making plans for nationwide mass meetings to be held on the 20th anniversary of his imprisonment. One day Davis walked in to find a strange man busily signing Mooney's name to a mountainous stack of letters. He was, Mooney explained, a "graduate of Q [San Quentin]" and "one of the best forgers in the business."

Fund appeals and printed bulletins on the hearings now began appearing with regularity, in the form of letters from "San Francisco County Jail." There was, at this time, a move to free Mooney by act of the California State Legislature; a number of assemblymen and senators visited the apartment regularly for conference purposes. In March 1936 the San Francisco Labor Council initiated a nationwide drive in his behalf, with a slogan proclaiming: "So long as Mooney is in prison no labor union and no American worker is free!" (Were Debs still alive, he wouldn't have minded the borrowing.) Later that year the San Francisco Bay Area AFL Committee for the Freedom of Mooney and Billings was formed. Although San Francisco Labor Council official John F. Shelley was its chairman, Tom Mooney dictated its policy.

Late every night Mooney returned to the cell. He did this apparently less out of concern for Murphy than to be present for interviews should any reporters make morning stop-offs at the jail. Too, during part of this period, in collaboration with Hollywood scenario writer Ben Legere, he produced, in the basement kitchen of the jail, a movie entitled *The Mooney Case*. The film incorporated footage from two previous documentaries,* interspersed with Mooney's narration of his own story, wherein he bluntly accused Charles M. Fickert, Martin Swanson, and the Law and Order Committee of the San Francisco Chamber of Commerce with having planned and perpetrated the Preparedness Day bombing.

The movie ended:

"And so I charge that Charles M. Fickert and Martin Swanson assisted by Edward D. Cuhna, James F. Brennan, Police Chief Daniel White, Officers Stephen Bunner, Charles Goff, Draper Hand, William Proll, Peter J. Hughes, and various other persons, known and unknown, planned, devised, carried out, and executed the conspiracy, various foul crimes including murder and attempted murder, perjury, subornation of perjury, and attempted subornation of perjury, and various and sundry other lesser crimes and violations of law and order, and far-reaching offenses against public welfare.

"And I charge that standing behind these individuals, serving as the connecting link between them and the real instigators of this gigantic conspiracy, were former California Supreme Court Justice Frederick W. Henshaw, Fickert's sponsor and advisor—the brains behind the frame-up gang; Frank C. Drew, attorney for the San Francisco Chamber of Commerce; Hugh M. Webster, secretary to the Law and Order Committee of the San Francisco Chamber of Commerce; Matt I. Sullivan, who since the

---

* The first was produced in 1917, for use in union meetings; the second, *The Strange Case of Tom Mooney*, a two-reeler produced by Brian Foy and introduced by Theodore Dreiser, was released in 1933, but was blacklisted by the major distributors.

death of Henshaw, has carried on as the leading connecting link and mouthpiece of the black reactionary and big business interests that perpetrated and plotted this foul frame-up . . .

"And I finally charge that behind all these stand the barons of a corrupt and vicious social system—the real criminals—the barons of big business, William H. Crocker, banker; Herbert Fleishhacker, banker; A. P. Giannini, banker; Captain Robert Dollar; George Cameron; Frederick J. Koster; Louis F. Byington; Jesse W. Lilienthal; and various and sundry other leading industrialists and representatives of big business.

"These are the guilty parties—all these are the real criminals; all these have committed crimes which brought death and destruction and deep injury, not only to those poor, helpless victims blown to bits by that bomb exploded as a part of their bloody program of preparedness, not only to me and my fellow worker Warren K. Billings, the victims of their foul plotting, but to you, to all of you, as well: you workers and producers of the world who seek only to live in peace with your neighbors and enjoy such comfort and security and happiness as you are entitled to by the useful work which you perform with your hands and brain, the enjoyment of the fruits of your labor which they and their vicious predatory control of all the economic and political processes of the present social system are depriving you of." *

Having failed to find his Zola, Mooney himself had accepted the role.

6 ·

Although Billings was also given fairly wide privileges, much of his time outside the courtroom was spent as legal assistant to the attorneys. His self-study of the law made him a valuable helper. Poring over the voluminous trial transcripts, briefs, appeals, affidavits, and other documents that had accumulated over the years, he would locate particular references sought by the attorneys, and determine which exhibits had been introduced into evidence at the hearing and which remained to be placed in the record.

One evening about seven Davis called at the jail to see his client only to be told Billings had gone to the dentist. This happened several times. "Dentist," Davis eventually learned, was a synonym for "movies."

One day Billings and his warder, deputy sheriff Archie McAllister, were

---

* The movie was never released. Shortly after its completion a TMMDC worker disappeared with all known prints. It was later discovered that he was an employee of the Associated Farmers. Following Mooney's death a single print was found among his effects; it is now in the Mooney Collection at the Bancroft Library, University of California, Berkeley. In 1965 the author attended a screening arranged by Ben Legere and Warren Billings.

not in court following the noon recess. Davis did his best to mask his growing concern. When they finally appeared, nearly an hour late, he worriedly asked Billings what had happened. They had had too many beers with lunch, Billings explained; he had been walking Archie on Marina Green, trying to sober him up.

This informality occasionally reached the point on ludicrousness. One morning McAllister drove Mooney and Billings to the Hall of Justice. It was necessary to park more than a block away. As they were climbing the stairs McAllister discovered he had forgotten something. "Warren," he said, "I left my keys in the car. Would you run back and get them for me?" Warren did. It was not until Billings returned that the trio suddenly realized just how the incident would have appeared had a reporter or a member of the prosecutor's staff entered the building at just that moment.

It was inevitable that a reporter stumble onto the story.

7 ·

The defense was convinced there were more case records than had been found during the Billings rehearing. Even though Charles M. Fickert had taken his files with him on leaving office, most of the Bomb Bureau records remained unaccounted for. Obtaining a court order, Davis and his aides began a thorough search of the Hall of Justice basement. They found the files, which included more than a thousand documents never introduced into evidence.

Among them: Hugh Fraser's letter to Mayor Rolph, written before he became foreman of the Billings jury; officer Moore's original traffic report, in which he described Thomas Doidge, not Warren Billings; the original interrogations of Mooney and the other defendants, which Fickert had maintained were nonexistent; two yellowed letters from Martin Swanson, both dated August 15, 1916, wherein he outlined his theory of the bombing—substantially the same theory used by the prosecution in the trials; and a photograph taken one minute before the explosion, showing a man on the saloon roof—which seemed to reinforce Mrs. Compton's testimony, as well as the defense's contention that the bomb was dropped.

Some items were not then, or ever, located: the original statements of Estelle, Wade, Vidovich, Crowley, the Edeaus, and many of the prosecution's other major witnesses.

As the hearing continued, a number of witnesses who had not previously testified were called, among them a husband and wife who had seen the Mooneys on the Eilers roof, but said that on taking their story to Fickert they were told to stay home until called. They never were. There were other witnesses, with similar stories, none able to explain satisfactorily why they had chosen to remain silent for 20 years.

The most important testimony in the entire hearing, however, came from former police captain Duncan Matheson, now retired, who admitted for the first time that the police had accepted Swanson's theory of the bombing. He also revealed the name of the man who originally pointed the finger of suspicion at Tom Mooney. Shortly after the explosion, on the afternoon of the 22nd, Matheson testified, both he and Chief White had been told "You'd better watch Mooney. He's the man who did this." White had immediately put a shadow on Mooney and his associates. The accuser, Matheson now admitted, had been Thornwell Mullally, Grand Marshal of the parade, prominent member of the Law and Order Committee, and director of United Railroads.

8 ·

Acting on a tip, an *Examiner* reporter began following Mooney when he left the courtroom each day. It did not take him long to discover 1924 Polk. In a short time he had enough evidence for a fantastic scoop. Mooney's privileged state provided the smallest part of it, for in watching the apartment, and quizzing some of its visitors, he had learned that Mooney was busy interviewing prospective gubernatorial candidates for the 1938 election. By now, California labor was seemingly united behind Mooney, to the extent that Mooney believed the rank and file would throw their votes to any candidate he chose. Although hopeful for favorable action by the U.S. Supreme Court, both Mooney and Davis were now convinced that the case, born in politics, would probably have to end the same way, with gubernatorial action.

The reporter wrote up his story and gave a copy to someone connected with the defense. From the reporter's manner it was obvious he was not seeking literary criticism or verification of facts. After several conferences he finally accepted $500 to kill the story.

He was not, however, the only reporter who knew what was going on. A *Chronicle* reporter had learned the facts long ago, but personally sympathetic to Mooney's plight, had chosen not to use them. It is probable that at least two others reporters, one from the *Call-Bulletin,* another from the *News,* also knew and said nothing.

No mention ever appeared in the press.

Mooney had kept his promise to Murphy. He had done nothing to embarrass him. He had resisted the more obvious temptations, such as attending various mass meetings held in his behalf. But there were other temptations he didn't try to resist. One morning when Davis arrived at the apartment, Mooney took him into one of the bedrooms, closed the door, and made a confession.

"I'm in love," he said. "Sounds silly for an old man to say such a thing, doesn't it?"

Davis sat down on the bed and lit a cigar. Mooney explained that shortly after being sent up he had heard rumors about Rena; for a time he had refused to believe them, but finally the evidence had become too blatant to ignore.

Davis warned Mooney that if word of this ever leaked out he might as well count on spending the rest of his life in San Quentin. Mooney nodded impatiently; he knew that; he had no intention of doing anything about it until after his release.

Davis asked if he knew the girl. Mooney answered in the affirmative, and mentioned her name. Davis was not too surprised. She was one of the most active workers on the Tom Mooney Molders' Defense Committee. She was, as the two men talked, working in the outer office. Thinking back, Davis realized he had rarely visited the apartment when she was not there.

On August 18, 1936, the habeas corpus hearings were brought to an end. Mooney had, in effect, had his retrial. Everything of possible relevance to the case had been put into the record, including the considerable evidence gathered over the years concerning the actual perpetrators of the bombing.

Now that the hearing was over it was no longer possible for Davis to justify Warren Billings' presence in San Francisco. He was returned to Folsom on the 20th. His "island" would never again be the same. While in San Francisco he had asked his longtime correspondent, the attractive Josephine Rudolph, to marry him on his release, and she had accepted.

The California Supreme Court now announced that they had empowered referee Shaw to make findings of fact. This included authority to rule on the validity of the testimony and the reliability of the witnesses. Mooney's attorneys strongly objected. Shaw was on the edge of senility. He had slept through much of the hearing. Once, while Fickert was on the stand, a spring had broken in Shaw's chair, throwing him to the floor. "Who fired that shot?" Shaw yelled, crawling under his desk for cover. "Bailiff, find out who fired that shot!" The bailiff found Shaw another chair. It proved just as comfortable, for within a few minutes he was again snoring loudly.

The court stuck to its ruling, however. Shaw's eventual conclusions, which he was in no great hurry to deliver, seemed a foregone conclusion.

By various stratagems, Davis succeeded in keeping Mooney in San Francisco until late spring, 1937. Shortly before his scheduled return to San Quentin, his ulcers flared up again and he was hospitalized for 10 days. On June 17th he was returned to the prison. He left behind one of the best-organized committees in the history of labor defense and he took with him the knowledge that he now had at least three possible avenues of release.

9 ·

San Quentin had changed during Tom Mooney's absence.

On January 16, 1935, while Warden Holohan was entertaining the parole board at lunch in his residence, four prisoners armed with .45—caliber automatics had burst into the room. Holohan, who tried to call for help, was savagely beaten. Using the entire parole board for hostage, the convicts commandeered a car and drove out the gate. Thoughtfully, the four convicts switched clothes with the four board members. At the first roadblock a hastily formed posse shot two of the latter, believing them to be the former. Eventually the escapees were captured.

Holohan had managed to survive both the beating and the resulting investigation but his reign had been ended by another scandal that broke shortly afterward—the discovery, by the Secret Service, that a particularly skillful gang of counterfeiters was using for its base of operations the prison's photoengraving shop. In the aftermath, Holohan resigned (he later became a state senator, his major achievement the passage of a law substituting the gas chambers for the gallows) and was replaced by a "tough warden," Court Smith of Folsom.

Smith brought to "Q" the strictness the "Rock Pile" had known. Among his first acts Smith abolished the con-boss system, and to the delight of most of the prisoners, kicked all the favorites out of their *bonaroo* jobs.

Upon Mooney's return, he was assigned to a cell with three other men and put to work in the vegetable garden. No longer in the pass line, he had to wait in line for his food. His typewriter, papers, books, and other possessions were not returned. He was back only eight days before his ulcer perforated again. He nearly died.

Mooney's collapse resulted in a tremendous outcry from his supporters. In New York, Mayor Fiorello LaGuardia, long a Mooney partisan, demanded an immediate investigation. In Washington, the Honorable Jerry J. O'Connell (Montana) rose in the U.S. House of Representatives to deliver a speech that appeared in the *Congressional Record* under the title "Persecution of Tom Mooney Continues Even Within the Walls of a State Institution." O'Connell charged Warden Smith with inflicting "cruel and unjust punishment upon Tom Mooney that equals medieval torture for downright brutality."

Following his release from the hospital, Mooney was called into the warden's office and asked by the President of the California State Prison Board "what he wanted and what authorities should do to rectify the situation." Mooney, who until now had stuck to prison ethics and himself made no formal complaint, presented an itemized list of grievances.

As a result, he was reassigned to his old cell, single occupancy; his possessions were returned; he was given a job in the prison farm kitchen similar to his old one in O&G; and he was permitted the soft (or so-called "modified sippy") diet his condition required—primarily milk, eggs, and ice cream.

PART FOUR

The End of the Mooney Case

"The truth of the matter is that Tom, like a good many other labor leaders—I should think Harry Bridges is a good example—is a natural dictator."

JOHN F. FINERTY TO WARREN BILLINGS, AUGUST 10, 1939

30. 64% FOR, 36% AGAINST

THINGS HAD changed outside San Quentin as well as in.

In 1931, during Governor Rolph's administration, Assemblyman James L. Quigley (Republican, San Francisco) introduced in the California State Assembly a resolution urging the Governor to pardon Mooney. It had very little backing and was killed in committee.

Three times in 1935, the Mooney case came before the State Legislature. In January five Democratic assemblymen from Southern California introduced a resolution calling for a full and unconditional pardon for Mooney. This too received committee burial. Another resolution, introduced in April by San Francisco Assemblyman James F. Brennan, taking up the *Chronicle's* suggestion, asked not for a pardon but a commutation of sentence to end this "fixed and contentious problem." Despite Mooney's frantic opposition, that resolution passed, 50 to 28. For some time after receiving the resolution Governor Merriam did nothing. Reporters surmised that, despite his reactionary record, Merriam might well free Mooney. He was actively seeking the 1936 Republican Presidential nomination. Mooney's release would give him a more liberal image. Merriam finally remarked that it was unfortunate it was not a concurrent resolution (one passed by both the Assembly and the Senate); nothing more came of it. A final effort by Assemblyman William Moseley Jones (Democrat, Montebello) proposed a change in the laws governing habeas corpus. The bill, if adopted, would have brought an investigation of the Mooney frame-up charges; it was buried in committee.

By 1937, however, the Democrats had a majority in the Assembly and Mooney had solid labor backing. The result was the strongest Mooney resolution to date. Sponsored by Paul A. Richie (Democrat, San Diego) and 26 other assemblymen, it (1) declared that Mooney was innocent, (2) resolved that he herewith be granted a full pardon, and (3) ordered the warden of San Quentin to set Mooney free.

In March the Assembly passed the resolution by a vote of 45 to 28.

What made this singularly amazing was not the popular support it reflected but the simple elementary fact that the legislature did not have power to grant Mooney a pardon. Only the Governor had.

This was a concurrent resolution; on reaching the State Senate it resulted in a bitter debate between two men already recognized as the leading liberal and conservative spokesmen in California, Culbert L. Olson of Los Angeles and William F. Knowland of Oakland. Knowland argued against the resolution for two reasons: Mooney was not innocent and the legislature did not have the power to grant a pardon. Olson debated both points, arguing, on the second, by a round-about logic, that the legislature did indeed possess such power. There was in the State Constitution a provision that read "Neither the Governor nor the Legislature shall have the power to grant pardons, or commutations of sentence, in any case where the convict has been twice convicted of felony, unless upon the written recommendation of the majority of the Judges of the Supreme Court." It was Olson's contention that by exempting the legislature from granting a pardon in this specific situation its power in all others was implied. The resolution was defeated 34 to 5.

Mooney, who studied the vote closely, saw it as a major victory. In California members of the Assembly were elected on a population basis; members of the Senate on a geographical basis—one to each county. The 45 assemblymen who voted for the pardon represented 1,135,441 voters; the 28 who voted against it, only 717,772. As for the Senate, the 5 senators who voted for the pardon represented more voters than the 45 who voted against it combined. Mooney believed this to mean a majority of California voters now favored his release.

He was not the only one who studied the vote and saw in it signs of the changing times.

(Olson's mail volume also indicated heavy support. Knowland received some letters too, nearly 400, 80 to 90% of which, he claimed, contained threats, explicit or implied.)

Encouraged by this showing, a second concurrent resolution, again calling for the immediate pardon of Mooney, was introduced. Adopted by the Assembly by a vote of 42 to 27, it was defeated by the Senate 30 to 8.

The legislature's final attempt to free Mooney took place in March 1938 and was pure drama.

By a vote of 36 For, 30 Against, the Assembly voted to subpoena Tom Mooney to appear there to speak in his own behalf. Though there was some doubt as to the legality of the subpoena, Warden Court Smith complied with it, taking Mooney to the State Capitol on March 10th. For two hours, amid klieg lights, whirling cameras, and popping flashbulbs (a proposal to broadcast the proceedings lost by a narrow margin of 30 to 37), Tom Mooney pleaded his case. The final roll call, late that night, long after Mooney had returned to his cell, was 39 to 35. Failing to receive the necessary majority, the resolution was not adopted.

Attempting to win on a revote, Mooney's supporters went so far as to take a sick senator from his hospital bed and fly him to Sacramento the following day. Mooney's opponents presented Captain Goff, who angrily told the Assembly that Mooney's guilt was well-established. This time the pardon resolution passed, 41 to 29, but the Senate tabled it and it was never brought to a vote.

Although these attempts to grant Mooney a pardon the legislature had no power to grant appear somewhat inane, they did accomplish three things. They added to the considerable publicity the case was again receiving. They indicated that if the legislators truly represented their constituents, a majority of California voters favored Mooney's pardon. And, most important, they brought to the fore a new Mooney champion, Culbert L. Olson.

2 ·

Culbert L. Olson was what might be called "a new native Californian," i.e., someone born elsewhere who has lived in the Golden State more than a decade. In Olson's case the move, from Utah, had occurred in 1920. His involvement in the Mooney case dated back to 1917, however, when as a liberal Democratic State Senator, he had appeared at Salt Lake City labor rallies on behalf of the California defendants. Finding the California political horizons brighter, he had shifted his law practice to Los Angeles, where during the booming Twenties, he specialized in aiding victims of fraudulent business practices and "bucket shop" operators, and politicked, campaigning for Robert M. La Follette. In 1932 Olson helped found the Los Angeles Democratic Club. In 1934, during the EPIC campaign, he wrote the state Democratic platform, served as state chairman of the party, and won election as a state senator. During his term, he worked to build the California Democratic party into a politically cohesive unit, fought the oil monopolists on the tidelands issue, helped to defeat a number of Merriam's legislative recommendations, and—less publicly—planned his campaign for governor.

Late in the spring of 1937, Olson approached George Davis with the information that he was considering making the governor's race and wanted Mooney's support.

Mooney trusted Olson as much as any man; he also believed he had a good chance of being elected. With Davis acting as go-between, a bargain was struck. In return for a promise to throw his labor support to Olson, Mooney was promised that if he had not been freed by the time Olson took office in January 1939, the signing of his pardon would be Olson's first official act. No word of this agreement, of course, was to be released to the press, and it never was. There was some very accurate guessing, however.

That September, a year and two months before the election, Olson officially announced his candidacy.

In October two events affecting the Mooney case occurred: the California Supreme Court denied Mooney's request for a writ of habeas corpus and Charles M. Fickert died. Of the two, Mooney had eagerly awaited one; he truly regretted the other.

After studying the transcript for more than six months, referee Shaw, in a sweeping ruling, found that Mooney was not the victim of a frame-up, that no witnesses had perjured themselves at his trial, and that neither District Attorney Fickert nor any of his assistants had suppressed evidence. Even though the California Supreme Court's adoption of Shaw's recommendation was presumed automatic, it had taken them another 10 months to rule against Mooney's petition, 5-1. Now, finally, Davis could appeal this verdict to the United States Supreme Court, which, from the wording of its 1935 decision, he had every reason to believe would act favorably.

Fickert's death, of pneumonia following a long illness, brought no celebration. With no evidence whatever on which to base his hope, Mooney had never entirely relinquished the dream that Fickert might someday confess the truth of the frame-up.

By the end of 1937 it was possible to measure the change in Mooney sentiment.

In April 1935 a letter to President Roosevelt asking him to "find some way" of "helping to effect the vindication and release of Tom Mooney" had been signed by 13 U.S. Senators and 18 U.S. Congressmen.

In July 1937 a petition to the President requesting a federal investigation into the Mooney-Billings case was signed by 25 Senators and 86 Congressmen. By year's end a move was underway to bring Mooney to Washington to appear before the Congress.*

By this time the only influential California newspapers actively opposing Mooney's release were the Los Angeles *Times,* Knowland's Oakland *Tribune,* and the *Bee* chain (the Sacramento, Modesto, and Fresno *Bees*) owned by C. K. McClatchy. McClatchy was considered a liberal and his long-standing opposition to Mooney perplexed many.

Billings believed his animosity dated from 1913, the time of his arrest on the dynamite transporting charge. McClatchy, a PG&E stockholder, had given the case considerable vitriolic coverage.

Mooney believed that the publisher, a devout Catholic, had never forgiven him for the letter made public by Fickert in which he referred to "priests and other skypilots."

---

* Although nothing came of this, hearings on the case were conducted in both the House of Representatives and the Senate during 1938.

One of the many Mooney-Billings protest meetjngs, this one in San Francisco Civic Auditorium in 1937.

It is also possible that McClatchy simply believed both men guilty.

In December of 1937 Harry Bridges, president of the International Longshoremen's and Warehousemen's Union and West Coast Director of the CIO, stated "Labor is united on the question of Mooney and Billings. We will join together and make common cause against the political and industrial enemies who are responsible for the Mooney-Billings frame-up." From its birth in November 1935, the Congress of Industrial Organizations had been firmly behind Mooney. The Mooney-Billings case now appeared to be one of the few issues on which the AFL and CIO could unite.

By January 1938 there were even clearer signs.

That month Tom Mooney was accorded a full-page photo in *Life,* with the caption designation "America's Most Famous Prisoner."

Of perhaps more import, that same month the American Institute of Public Opinion (popularly known as the Gallup Poll) published the results of its survey on the Mooney case.

Nationwide, 64% of those polled who expressed opinions believed Mooney should be pardoned; 36% believed he should not.

Oddly enough, of this same group, 53% believed Mooney guilty and only 47% believed him innocent. "Maybe he was guilty," an Iowa woman suggested, "but they've kept him there longer than a lot of gangsters."

The breakdown on this question was almost predictable:

65% of the farmers, 60% of the businessmen, and 53% of the profes-sional people believed Mooney guilty.

65% of the unskilled laborers, 55% of the skilled laborers, and 57% of the white collar wage earners believed him innocent.

Belief in his guilt was strongest among older people, Republicans, resi-dents of small towns, and throughout the Southern States.

Belief in his innocence was strongest among young people, Democrats, city dwellers, and throughout the Middle Atlantic States.

What was surprising was California:

Here 52% believed him guilty, 48% innocent. But 55% favored his par-don, while only 45% opposed it.

All of these percentages, however, were based on people who had heard of the case and formed an opinion. Slightly more than half the people in-terviewed hadn't.

When a similar Gallup Poll was conducted just eleven months later, in December 1938, 66% of those who had opinions favored Mooney's release, and only 15% had never heard of him.

The change in these figures was brought about by the most intense year of Mooney agitation yet conducted by his defense. Mass meetings were held almost monthly. Mooney newsletters were issued on an average of every two weeks. On Labor Day, 80,000 organized workers marched down Market Street with, as Anna Louise Strong described it, "the AFL lead-ing, the CIO closing, and a great float demanding freedom for Mooney and Billings rolling along in the space between."

There was another reason. Culbert Olson's campaign for election.

3 ·

Precedent was on Governor Merriam's side and during the early months of the campaign he sat smugly and unconcernedly self-confident behind it: no Democrat had been elected Governor of the State of California dur-ing the Twentieth Century.

But precedent was made in more orthodox times, when there was no functioning Democratic Party in California and no Franklin Delano Roosevelt in Washington. In the elections of 1934, California had resisted the New Deal tidal wave, but only because the Democratic vote had been split between Sinclair and Haight and F.D.R. had declined to give Sin-clair his endorsement. His backing of Olson had been obvious from the start.

There were a number of unpredictables in the 1938 campaign. The largest was the "Ham and Eggs movement," one of the many utopian schemes that sprang up in such profusion in California during the Depression years. Also known as the "Thirty Dollars Every Thursday Pension Plan," it would appear as a proposition on the ballot. Olson publicly took no stand on the issue, saying only that the voters themselves should be given the opportunity to accept or reject it. Merriam opposed it, then personally championed a movement most of his Republican backers thought equally mad—the Townsend Plan. Just how these issues would affect the election outcome was one of the unknowns.

Slightly more predictable was an anti-labor initiative that also appeared on the ballot, providing severe restrictions on picketing, forbidding hot cargo and secondary boycott, and making unions liable for damages incurred in the course of a strike. It was anticipated that this, plus the Mooney case, would bring labor to the polls in record numbers and that few, if any, of these votes would go to Merriam, who although he took no public stand on the initiative, had twice during his term called out the militia to break strikes. Olson denounced the initiative in every public speech.

The Mooney case was the other unknown. During the early months of the campaign it was not even an issue. His stand known from his advocacy of Mooney in the state legislature, Olson saw no reason to mention it in campaign speeches. And Republicans, having studied the Gallup Poll, were well aware that their own ranks were divided on the issue.

At least one thing was in Olson's favor. Merriam had not been a good governor. As H. Brett Melendy and Benjamin F. Gilbert note in their book *The Governors of California,* "Governor Frank Merriam managed the state's administration during some of its most difficult years. He remained faithful to his political philosophy. Unfortunately, Governor Merriam . . . had a static political view more in keeping with the concept of duty held by nineteenth century governors. He was unable to provide the state with the executive ability which was needed during the crisis of the 1930's . . ."

Yet Merriam was self-confident. He had a trick up his sleeve—the old but still remarkably effective tactic of divide and conquer. Through the use of Democratic front men, the Republicans had encouraged several other Democrats to enter the race and split Olson's vote. One of the most important of the men opposing Olson in the primary was a popular labor leader who had the endorsement of the AFL Political League—San Francisco Sheriff Dan Murphy.

Shortly after Murphy's announcement, Olson, worried that Mooney would now throw his support to his old friend, contacted Davis to ascertain Mooney's intentions.

Mooney's reply was a 32-page pamphlet entitled *Tom Mooney's Message to Organized Labor, His Friends and Supporters, and All Liberal and Progressive Voters of California on the 1938 Elections.*

Included was a letter with his endorsement and his reasons for making it. While acknowledging that from early times "Dan Murphy was one of the courageous few who voiced his belief in my innocence," Mooney also recalled that during his eight years as a state senator Murphy had made no move to bring the Mooney case before that body, while Olson, whose record on labor legislation was in no way second to Murphy's, had. His basic reason for supporting Olson, however, was briefly and frankly stated: "I believe that Senator Olson is the only candidate who will pardon me who can be nominated and elected, and I therefore urge my friends to vote and work vigorously for his election."

Murphy, on learning of Mooney's stand, is alleged to have said: "For years I had one great ambition. Now I have two. The first remains to free Tom Mooney. The second is to kick his ass into the Bay." *

In the pamphlet Mooney also picked his own slate of Democratic candidates, all the way down to assemblymen. He did this against the advice of Davis, who pointed out that since many of these offices were contested, he would be splitting his Democratic support. These were the men who had stood up in battle, Mooney said, and the ones who deserved to be elected.

Mooney's special wrath was directed not against Merriam or Murphy but against the Alameda County District Attorney currently running for state attorney general as a nonpartisan candidate. In 1936 "another Mooney case" had broken out across the Bay. Three union men—Earl King, E. G. Ramsey, and Frank J. Connor—were arrested for and subsequently convicted of complicity in the murder of the chief engineer of a freighter docked at Alameda. Many of the unions cried "frame-up" and charged the Alameda County District Attorney, who prosecuted the cases, with perpetrating it. Mooney wrote: "A candidate who must be defeated at all costs is Earl Warren, mouthpiece of the most reactionary political group in this state—the Merriam-Hatfield-Herbert Hoover-Joseph I. Knowland-Harry Chandler crowd. It is this group which has unjustly and bitterly attacked Organized Labor in our efforts to obtain a better life. These are the red-baiters and the tools of predatory corporate interests."

"Warren," said Mooney, "is the Fickert of 1936–37 . . ."

In the weeks before the primary, some 300,000 copies of the Mooney pamphlet were printed and distributed to California voters, at a cost to the Tom Mooney Molders' Defense Committee of about $6000. In addi-

* This remark has also been attributed to at least a half dozen other people, including Mooney's attorney Frank Walsh, indicating, if nothing else, a certain unanimity of feeling.

tion to the precinct work done by its volunteers, the TMMDC contributed $500 to Olson's treasury, picked up a $250 bill for the printing of his program and platform, and paid $395 to sponsor a radio broadcast to Progressives. All this, even though Mooney was sure the United States Supreme Court would free him before Olson had the chance.

The primary took place on August 30th. Olson, opposed by seven other candidates on the Democratic ballot, gathered 42.09 percent of the vote. Murphy ran a poor third.

Olson also won a slight lead over Merriam in the total vote. But because both candidacies had been contested, it was difficult to say which had the real edge.

Merriam, however, was now running scared.

Following Olson's victory, Mooney wired his congratulations. However, he observed, "I seriously doubt if you will have a chance to act on my application for unconditional pardon . . . I think that before the end of the year I shall have been completely liberated and exonerated . . ." Mooney was so hopeful of a favorable decision from the U.S. Supreme Court that he anticipated he might well be released in time to work in the Olson campaign.

4 ·

On October 10th the United States Supreme Court declined to hear the appeal of Thomas J. Mooney.

The denial of Mooney's petition for a writ of certiorari (application for leave to appeal to the court), following as it did the almost promissory wording of the court's 1935 decision, came as a bitter shock to Mooney and his attorneys.

As is nearly always the case in such denials, no reason was given.

Roosevelt was right about the "nine old men," Mooney wrote his supporters. "My only immediate hope lies in the election of State Senator Culbert L. Olson as the next Democratic Governor of California."

5 ·

The last month of the campaign brought other surprises, none of them welcome to Olson or Mooney.

William Green, President of the AFL, wrote M. J. Casey, organizer of the International Brotherhood of Teamsters in San Francisco, urging the reelection of Governor Merriam. Considering the backgrounds of the two candidates, and the importance of defeating the anti-labor initiative,

Green's interference seemed inexplicable except as another example of the "sell out" so often blasted by Mooney. Many of the California AFL leaders (though not all) wrote Green asking him to reverse his decision. He declined to do so.

"Your letter to the AFL organizer of the Teamsters' Union published here today brands you the chief labor faker in the United States . . ." read one telegram. Though the wording sounded familiar, this was Olson's reply to Green's act. Mooney's was even more vitriolic.

As a final nose-thumbing gesture, Mooney, again going against his advisers, resubmitted his pardon application, demanding that Governor Merriam act upon it before November 8th. Merriam declined to be baited. He was, for one thing, doing some baiting of his own.

On October 25th the Dies Committee on Un-American Activities issued a report of its recent investigations in California. Included was testimony charging that all of the top Democratic nominees were either Communists or closely associated with people who were. Harper Knowles, identified as state secretary of the Associated Farmers and chairman of the radical research department of the California American Legion, claimed that Olson knowingly fraternized with Communists. As proof, he cited Olson's advocacy of a pardon for Mooney. Mooney, Knowles stated, was a known Communist.

Merriam, seizing the charges, now lambasted the "radical" Olson, who was supported by the Communists, Harry Bridges, and the CIO (to many the three were synonymous). "Keep California Out of the Red" became the new campaign slogan.

The timing of the Dies Report (it appeared 14 days prior to the election) and the fact that only Democratic candidates were singled out for censure, led rather inescapably to the conclusion that the report was politically motivated. The Dies Committee Report may well have been the final deciding factor in an election already complicated by such issues as Ham and Eggs, the Townsend Plan, Green's endorsement of Merriam, and Olson's advocacy of a pardon for Mooney.

For there was still another charge in the report. One of the committee's witnesses declared that one of the Hollywood celebrities who had allowed her name to be used for Communist fronts was child-star Shirley Temple.

"I am sorry that Comrade Shirley Temple is not here," Olson announced at a Los Angeles meeting the night the Dies Report was made public. "She should be here to aid us in plotting to overthrow the government of the United States of America."

To the chagrin of the Republicans, the campaign of 1938 ended not with a frightened whimper or even a bang, but with the chanting of the ditty:

We're branded RED by Harper Knowles
But we refuse to fuss.
What's good for Shirley Temple
Is good enough for us!

31· Twenty-Two Years, Five Months, and Twelve Days

THE RESULTS were a clear mandate. With 1,391,734 votes to 1,171,019, or with 52.49 percent of the total, Culbert L. Olson had become California's first Democratic Governor of the Twentieth Century.

It was a nearly complete sweep for the slate Mooney had chosen, with a single exception—Earl Warren won the race for Attorney General.

The Ham and Eggs pension scheme had been solidly defeated, as had the anti-labor initiative, labor turning out in record numbers to vote against the measure and for the candidate who championed Tom Mooney.

On the morning after the election Olson met the press in his Los Angeles home and discussed his plans. Asked what he intended to do about the Mooney case, Olson referred reporters to his 1937 senate speech, adding ". . . it must be clear to anyone that I will approach the consideration of Mooney's application for pardon with these convictions, giving opportunity for any and all entitled to a hearing to show cause why I, as Governor, should not pardon him."

"I'm facing the prospect of Culbert Olson's inauguration," Mooney told reporters, "with a smile on my lips and a song in my heart."

He did not add that there was also a doubt in the back of his mind. He had been betrayed too often, had let his hopes and emotions carry him away too frequently, to place complete trust in the promise of any man. The word "hearing" bothered him, but when Davis contacted the governor-elect he was assured it was a mere formality, that the pardon would follow immediately after. Again Mooney began packing.

Liberal magazines and conservative newspapers together greeted Olson's announcement as if the pardon had already occurred. There was a fantastic volume of mail from all parts of the world, most of it congratulatory.

There were a few dissenting voices. Speaking for state law enforcement officers, the newly elected Attorney General wrote Olson: "I trust . . . that in any action you may take on Mooney's application for a pardon you will bear in mind that today law enforcement is, at best, difficult of accomplishment and that you will neither cast any unwarranted reflection upon the agencies charged therewith, nor lend any encouragement to those forces which are opposed to the enforcement of our laws and to the maintainance of security of life and property." In brief, Earl Warren was expressing the hope that if the governor did decide to free Mooney he would not designate him the victim of a frame-up.

Tom Mooney and the Sacramento *Bee* now had something in common. Both were worried about the hearing, although for different reasons.

Damning Olson for even considering a public hearing, McClatchy's editorial said that a private ceremony in Olson's office would be preferable to a "three ring circus." In saying this the paper was not lending its endorsement. On the contrary, the editorial concluded, "the law-abiding citizens of California will not join in these plaudits. They will not assist in that handclapping. Rather will they be thinking of the shame being perpetrated in the name of Justice to laurel and accolade a red handed murderer who richly deserved the gallows."

And outgoing Governor Merriam answered Mooney's attempt to embarrass him with a slap of his own: he denied Mooney's pardon application, thus becoming the fifth California Governor to solemnize that tradition.

November and December were the longest months. Hard news lacking, rumors filled the vacuum. One was to the effect that there was strong pressure on Olson to reconsider his decision. This was countered by still another, appearing in the press, that Olson had already signed Mooney's pardon, which, since Olson had not yet taken office, cast doubt on its legality. Drew Pearson revealed that the Communist Party intended to run Tom Mooney as its candidate for President in 1940.

If true, it would be a genuine draft, for Mooney, apparently feeling he no longer had need of them, was carefully disassociating himself from the Communists. In December, Sam Darcy, former Northern California District Organizer, now in Philadelphia, wrote to Mooney asking him to appear at a Lenin memorial meeting following his release. In his reply on the 12th, Mooney declined the invitation, stating that since his major goal after being freed was to unite labor, he had decided to make personal appearances only under official labor auspices, "and for that reason I would not like to have my tour take on anything in the nature of a political character for the time being, and if I were to speak at a Lenin Memorial Meeting it could not have any other interpretation placed upon it. I have written Bob Minor very fully explaining my position, and he, Earl Browder, Jack Stachel, William Foster and Schneiderman . . . are in complete agreement with me on my future plans." Browder and the others had wanted him to appear at a mass meeting in New York, but he had "nixed it."

Olson's inauguration was set for January 2, 1939. On the afternoon of the 1st, George Davis heard another rumor, from a source too reliable to dismiss, that Olson was considering delaying pardoning Mooney until after he had succeeded in getting part of his platform through the first session of the legislature. A hurried call to Olson brought confirmation: he was considering this, feeling that a short delay might minimize criticism, but had reached no definite decision.

Davis rushed to San Quentin. Warden Smith greeted him warmly, well aware of the active part he had played in Olson's election and perhaps not entirely unmindful that his own position rested on the Governor's pleasure. Davis told Mooney what had happened. Mooney asked the warden for permission to use his office and telephone for the next several hours. Though puzzled (it is unlikely that any other convict had ever made a like request), Smith nodded acquiescence. Mooney and Davis were up most of the night making long-distance calls and sending telegrams. Less than one hour after taking the oath of office, Culbert L. Olson received a delegation of more than 50 top California labor leaders. Led by John Shelley of the AFL and Harry Bridges of the CIO, they formally presented Mooney's pardon application and asked the governor exactly when the pardoning ceremony would take place. Wearily, nearly exhausted after the long campaign, and with a sharp glance at Davis, Olson said that he would schedule the hearing for the following Saturday, January 7th. Later that evening he made the official announcement.

2 ·

On Saturday, January 7, 1939, San Quentin prisoner 31921 arose before dawn and dressed in the chill darkness. His new suit, gray with pin stripes, had been made in the prison tailor shop. Looking through the slot in the door he could see searchlights roaming the walls, but it was still too dark to determine what kind of a day it would be. He made up his cot, then sat down and waited until the cells were unlocked at 6:00, when he left for the last time, marching out by habit, forgetting to look back, to breakfast with Matt Schmidt and the other labor prisoners.

It was a cold day, the sky cloudy. On his way through the yard to the warden's office, the men, marching to work, broke silence and yelled "Good-bye, Tom."

At exactly 7:30 A.M. the gray-haired, fifty-five-year-old man stepped through the last steel door. Over the doorway was an iron horseshoe, turned up so the luck wouldn't run out. A small group waited: Rena, Belle, Anna, John, and another familiar face from the past, Robert Minor. Tom kissed Anna, hugged Rena for a very long time, and posed for

Prisoner #31921, leaving San Quentin for the last time, January 7, 1939.
Even though the horseshoe was inverted, the luck soon ran out.

photographs. Promptly at 8 the group left for Sacramento, the prisoner, George Davis, and Warden Court Smith in the lead car. For this trip he was not handcuffed.

The Assembly Chamber of the State Capitol was packed. People who couldn't get in listened over loudspeakers outside, or over radios at home. The proceedings were broadcast on a coast-to-coast hookup.

They began promptly at 10:30 A.M. There were three people on the speaker's platform, the Governor, Tom Mooney, and George Davis.

Olson, concisely and quite eloquently, reviewed the history of the case. He then paused and asked "Are there any persons present who can give any reasons why Thomas J. Mooney shall not be granted a pardon?"

All over the United States people, sitting beside their radios, leaned forward tensely, as if expecting to hear a voice break the silence. There was none. Olson picked up a piece of parchment and began reading from it. As he neared the end it was clear that he had chosen not to take his Attorney General's advice:

"I have made an extended study of the voluminous records of this case and am convinced that Thomas J. Mooney is wholly innocent of the crime of murder for which he was convicted and that his conviction was based wholly on perjured testimony presented by representatives of the State of California. In view of my convictions I deem it my duty to issue a pardon to Thomas J. Mooney.

"Now, therefore, I, Culbert L. Olson, Governor of the State of California, pursuant to the authority vested in me by the Constitution and Statutes of said State do hereby grant Thomas J. Mooney, San Quentin No. 31921, a full and unconditional pardon of the crime of murder in the first degree and do hereby restore said Thomas J. Mooney to all of his civil rights and privileges as a citizen."

"Tom Mooney," the Governor said, "you are now a free man." Twenty-two years, five months, and twelve days after his arrest, Tom Mooney was handed his full and unconditional pardon.

The Governor had a few more words, however. "In granting this pardon to Tom Mooney I am mindful of the case of Warren K. Billings. Billings was convicted on essentially the same evidence as Mooney. Therefore I feel it my duty to suggest to the Supreme Court that if Billings apply for a review of his case and for recommendation of his pardon, that his application be granted and that the Supreme Court reconsider Billings' case and recommend a pardon."

Mooney approached the microphones. In a voice so filled with emotion that it threatened to fail him any moment, he thanked the Governor and all those who had helped make his release possible.

"I am not unmindful of the fact that this case is, in reality, not the case of an individual charged with the crime of murder. I know that it symbolizes our whole economic, political and social life and all of the forces that go to make it up. I fully realize that those forces are at work, not alone in California, but throughout the world. I understand those common elementary laws that govern all life.

"They are simple. In the biological world, they are conception, birth, growth, decay and death, and those rules also govern in the sociological world; and so it is with our present economic system. It was conceived like we were; it was born, it grew to maturity and now it is in a state of decay, not only here but throughout the world, and in its place, just as in our place, it will be replaced by a new and I hope a better social order.

"And to that end, Governor Olson, I shall dedicate my life and immediately I shall try to make it possible for the State of California to comply with your request—so that it can completely raise its head from the shame in which it held it, bowed, for these past 22 years—by releasing my co-sufferer, co-defendant, and co-worker, Warren Billings."

In a union hall in San Francisco, printer Marvin Sanford, who as a young Socialist had been a delegate to the IWDL on the Mooney case, listened in amazement, not so much to the words as the voice. It was mellow, sweet, remarkably gentle. Someone else, entering the room, asked, "Who's that?" The workers shushed him. "That," Sanford said, tears in his eyes, "is the reincarnation of Jesus Christ."

Mooney called for unity in the American labor movement. "You hear much today about the liquidation of the Jews in Germany and Italy, but we must not forget that that was not the beginning of liquidation in fascist Germany or Italy. The first liquidation was the trade union movement and then the Socialists and the Communists. Now the Jews, then it will be the Catholics and the Protestants, and all of us in a common purpose must fight that reaction that intends to blight our life and the life of all civilized people, and we must establish a real social order wherein people will live for the benefit of one another and not for the profit of themselves at the expense of the other . . .

"I thank you, Governor Olson."

In the audience a group of the first returnees from Spain, members of the Abraham Lincoln Batallion, wept unashamedly.

Well-wishers were so thick that it took Mooney more than half an hour to make his way out of the building and across the street.

From Sacramento a motorcycle escort took him directly to Folsom Prison, where there was an emotional confrontation between the two Preparedness Day defendants. "The fight is on for you," Mooney told Billings. There followed a private meeting of the pair, followed by a reunion with J. B. McNamara, who had recently been transferred from San Quentin to Folsom because of his health. McNamara was now in total time served—28 years—California's oldest convict. Mooney promised to work for his release, as well as those of all labor prisoners.

That evening Tom spoke to a huge labor rally in Southside Park. He had, he told his audience, two immediate objectives. The first was to free Billings. The second "great task to which I intend to dedicate my remaining years is the complete unification and solidification of the labor movement in a progressive, forward-looking, militant organization. Such a unified labor movement must include the AFL, CIO, Railroad Brotherhoods, and all bona fide, independent labor organizations." To many in the crowd it seemed possible that if any man could accomplish this it would be Tom Mooney.

Tom and Rena spent that night in Sacramento. The following morning George Davis, accompanied by actor Melvyn Douglas and his wife, Helen Gahagan Douglas, drove the pair to the Berkeley ferry slip. There was a single stop on the way, at Mother Mooney's grave, where Tom planted a rose bush. Long before, Mooney had said that when released he wanted to walk up Market Street over the route of the Preparedness Day parade, with his head held high, as proof that he bore no guilt for that atrocity. A labor delegation had promised to meet him at the foot of Market. Davis and the Douglases, fearing only some dozen people would be present, attempted to persuade him to postpone his walk.

As the ferry pulled into its slip, they heard a deep rumble.

Davis parked the car and they walked out of the Ferry Building. Mooney stopped, stunned. Almost as if the past twenty-two and a half years had been a dream, Market Street was clear of traffic. Police had roped off the street, and for as far as the eye could see, both sides were lined with people.*

Mooney took off his glasses and wiped his eyes. Then, with a firm stride, he walked straight down the middle of the street between the streetcar tracks. Rena, Davis, Anna, Belle, and John followed, accompanied by the official welcoming committee of 35, which included representatives of all the major American labor groups. It appeared that, for at least one day, Tom Mooney had accomplished his second pledge.

As the group proceeded up Market, crowds fell in behind them. Mooney stopped once, at the corner of Steuart and Market. The old saloon had long since been torn down and replaced by a large modern office building, that of the Southern Pacific. Turning to Davis and Rena, Mooney said softly, "I wouldn't really be surprised if there had never been an explosion."

As Mooney again stepped off the shouting grew louder. Soon it was joined by the whistles of the Ferry Building and ships in the Bay. The combined roar was so loud, newspapers later reported, that residents of Berkeley, nine miles across the Bay, jammed switchboards trying to learn

---

* Another thing hadn't changed. Newspaper estimates of the crowd ranged from 20,000 to a quarter million.

Tom Mooney's triumphal march up Market Street. What followed was tragically anti-climactic. In the front rank behind Mooney are, left to right, starting at the streetcar tracks, Harry Bridges, Belle Hammerberg, Rena Mooney, George Davis, Anna Mooney, John Mooney, and John Shelley.

the cause of the sound.

From the steps of City Hall, Mooney again spoke briefly on the need for labor unity and the need for militant defense of President Roosevelt and the New Deal. The crowd stretched for six blocks.

Exhausted, the Mooneys adjourned to a suite in the St. Francis Hotel. The following day Tom returned to Market Street again, to join the retail clerks in their picket line in front of Kress's Department Store. Before leaving he gave them five of the ten dollars given him by the State of California. The other half he sent to the American Newspaper Guild, striking against Hearst in Chicago.

These were Tom Mooney's finest hours. What followed was anti-climactic, and tragic.

32· Unfinished Business

L ESS THAN eight hours after pardoning Tom Mooney, Governor Olson collapsed while addressing an inaugural barbeque crowd at the State Fairgrounds. He was rushed to the hospital, where doctors diagnosed his condition as nervous exhaustion and recommended complete rest. Although he left the hospital 12 days later, more than a month passed before his first public appearance, and yet another several weeks before he returned to his desk.

Meanwhile Folsom prisoner 10699 waited impatiently.

In mid-January George Davis submitted Billings' pardon petition to the governor's office. With Olson absent, it was—to the chagrin of Billings and Davis—referred to the State Prison Advisory Board, a needless and potentially dangerous step. The board, stating it needed time to study the case, postponed decision until February.

Early that month a representative from Attorney General Warren's office asked Billings if he would be willing to settle for a commutation of sentence. Billings said he would not.

The decision came on the 23rd. By a vote of 3 to 2, the board denied Billings' request.

Those voting against the pardon were Attorney General Warren, Folsom Warden Clyde I. Plummer (former head of the San Diego "Red Squad"), and Clarence Morrill, Chief of the State Bureau of Criminal Identification and Investigation. The two members voting in favor of pardoning Billings were Lieutenant Governor Ellis Patterson and San Quentin Warden Court Smith.

Explaining his vote, Warren claimed to have made a "lengthy investigation" of the case and to have found "no justification" for Billings' release. A major deciding factor, he said, was a telegram from the judge who presided over the Billings trial; he firmly asserted that Billings was guilty and had received a fair trial.

It was apparent that Olson and his attorney general were going to have four inharmonious years.

For Billings, this was a major setback. The board's denial made it extremely easy for the State Supreme Court to deny his request. Davis

426

began exploring other ways of securing the prisoner's release without going through the court.

While this was happening, friends visiting Billings brought him rumors. He wouldn't listen to them at first.

In mid-February Tom Mooney had sent out a mass appeal for financial aid. The stationery was familiar: only now the photo on the left was of Mooney freed, that on the right of Billings still imprisoned.

"As long as my co-worker, Warren K. Billings, remains in Folsom Prison, I am not free. Spiritually I am in prison with him . . . Our greatest immediate task is to bring about the early pardon of Warren K. Billings, who is equally as innocent as myself of this infamous crime . . ." His committee, Mooney noted, was not only penniless but $15,000 in debt, from expenses incurred during the last Supreme Court appeal and the Olson campaign.

"I renew now with all fervor my appeal to you to help in this campaign to gain for Warren Billings his freedom. I implore and entreat and plead with you now as I have never done before at any time in the past 22 years to be as generous as it is humanly possible for you to be, to help me carry on the fight to free my co-sufferer . . ."

It was an impassioned plea, but not everyone was moved.

Why—Billings' friends asked—if Tom Mooney's only interest was to see Billings free, did he still call the committee the "Tom Mooney Molders' Defense Committee"?

The rumors grew more explicit. Mooney was using the money collected to pay off his own debts.

"They're my debts, too," Billings replied to such charges. "After all they were contracted in the name of the Mooney-Billings case, although I had very little to say about it."

Mooney was now wholly a captive of the Communists, Billings was told. It was their strategy to keep Billings in prison as a martyr to the cause.

Sometime earlier one of the West Coast unions had collected funds to secure a well-known Communist lawyer to represent Billings. He had refused the offer, not only preferring Davis but distrustful of the motives behind the act.

Finally, as proof of the financial charges began to accumulate, Billings could ignore them no longer. He wrote to Mooney demanding an accounting for all monies collected in his behalf. There was no reply.

Mary Gallagher was living in Los Angeles. Billings wrote to her on April 24th, asking her to come north and organize a defense committee. This was a sound move, as there were few more capable organizers. It was also, as Billings must have realized, a direct slap at Tom Mooney. She arrived early in May and within a few weeks formed a committee, the

Billings Defense, made up of bona fide union members from the AFL,
CIO, Railroad Brotherhoods, and International Ladies Garment Workers'
Union.

When Olson returned to work, Davis confronted him with his promise.
As a result, on June 28th Olson publicly reiterated his intention of pardoning Billings "if I have the power to do it." Privately he explained to
Davis that two resignations from the State Supreme Court were expected
shortly; if Billings were willing to wait until the new appointments were
made, there would be a much better chance of favorable court action. Although both Davis and his client reluctantly agreed, the attorney continued to seek other ways to secure Billings' release. One plan—admittedly
long range and time consuming and to be undertaken only if all else
failed—was to take the Billings case to the United States Supreme Court
in an attempt to win a precedent-making decision that the use of perjury
in any form in a trial nullifies the decision.

Representatives of the State Federation of Labor called on Billings to
tell him they would be willing to mount a strong campaign for his release.
There was a single condition: that he break with Mooney. Mooney, they
said, was now touring under Communist Party auspices. Not only was the
Tom Mooney Molders' Defense Committee being run by Communists,
they had also succeeded in capturing as a front group the San Francisco
Bay Area AFL Committee for the Release of Mooney and Billings. The
AFL leaders didn't cite their long-standing antagonism toward Mooney
—but that was understood. Billings must disassociate himself from
Mooney if he wanted AFL support.

He was extremely reluctant to do this. Finally, however, when Mooney
persisted in ignoring his demands for an accounting, Billings forced
Mooney to visit him on threat of public repudiation. The meeting was
stormy. Mooney refused to justify his conduct to anyone. Billings told
him that he wanted him to cease all efforts in his behalf, that he wanted
nothing more to do with him.

Later Billings would describe his part in the meeting as "more play-
acting than anything." He was not really mad at Mooney, he would say;
they had been through too much together; yet he had been placed in a
position where there was no other choice.

"The break between Tom Mooney and I is now definite and final and I
am sure his recent activities fully warrant it," Billings wrote his old
friend Lena Morrow Lewis in August.

On the 10th of that month the State Federation of Labor announced a
campaign in Billings' behalf.

Despite Billings' warning, Mooney now embarked on a nationwide
"Free Billings" tour. Finally, on September 12th, Billings wrote a public
letter stating that all matters pertaining to the campaign for his release

were to be handled by the Billings Defense. "Tom Mooney and his 'Tom Mooney Molders' Defense Committee' have been repudiated by me," Billings stated with extreme reluctance, "and are not authorized to solicit funds in my name."

2 ·

Culbert Olson's pardoning of Tom Mooney had made him, for a brief time, the most famous governor in the United States. Letters and telegrams of praise came from every part of the world, from the famous and the unknown, numbering in the thousands. Many were in themselves moving: "Dear sir you. Ar a Wonderful Man. You has plezed the harts of meney million workers in this country, by freen tom Mooney. Good luck to you. Governor Culbert L. Olson."

There were others. Some were anonymous. "You freed a notorious assassin whose infamy is world wide. *You have committed an enormous crime.* Your position was bought with the votes of collaborators of crime. You will surely pay the toll. Payment is already being exacted. (*Let us hope the final one.*) You and your family are accursed. You are held in abhorrence by the whole nonshyster world. Poison gas for Sacramento." Others were signed. One of the bitterest was from Judge Frank Dunne.

Many of those who most condemned Olson did not write. They had other ways of showing their displeasure. In August 1939, at the close of the legislative session, there was an abortive move to recall Olson from office, using as its motto "We want to throw Tom, Dick and Harry—Tom Mooney, Dick Olson and Harry Bridges—out of California politics." While the move failed to gather enough signatures, it indicated that not all Californians were pleased with the governor's action.

More than a month had passed since the filling of the second vacancy on the State Supreme Court, but Olson still had not submitted the Billings petition. In mid-September the State Federation of Labor held its convention. One of the speakers was the governor, who, pressed by the AFL leaders, promised to make a public pledge to seek Billings' release. He spoke for 20 minutes, but said nothing about Billings. As soon as he sat down, State Federation secretary Edward D. Vandeleur, who was seated directly behind him, leaned forward and yanked the governor's coattails. *"Billings!"* he whispered loudly enough for everyone on the platform to hear. Red-faced, Olson returned to the podium and spoke for five minutes on the case, vowing his every intention of bringing it to a happy conclusion. Before adjourning, the convention voted unanimously to go on record in support of Billings' pardon.

The Governor submitted Billings' petition to the California Supreme

Court on October 13th, together with a request that they act favorably upon it. There was some reason to be optimistic: of the present justices, only three from the Billings' rehearing remained and Preston, Billings' inquisitor, was not among them.

Billings was hopeful, but prepared for almost anything.

On the night of Sunday, October 15th, he was called to the warden's office. There was a phone call from Davis. How soon could he be packed, his attorney asked. Giving the matter some thought, Billings guessed a week to ten days. "Sorry," Davis replied. "You'll have to be ready bright and early Tuesday morning. The Supreme Court voted to free you and Olson is announcing it tomorrow."

He then told him what it hurt to say. "It's not a pardon, Warren; it's a commutation of sentence."

For a minute Billings was silent. Then he said, simply and quietly, "I'll be ready."

The ceremony in the Governor's office was brief, with only a few people in attendance. One was Miss Josephine Rudolph, another Mrs. Rena Mooney. Tom had sent a wire of congratulations from Pittsburgh, where he was hospitalized. Twenty-three years, two months, and twenty-three days after his arrest, Warren Billings was handed a paper commuting his sentence to time served. He had been twenty-three years old when arrested; he was now forty-six. Exactly half his life had been spent in prison, more than half considering his first arrest.

"I'm only sorry it's not a full pardon," the Governor said.

"I'm sorry, too," Billings replied. "But I thank you anyway."

"Thus ends the Mooney case," remarked a reporter.

"This case will not be closed until a full and unconditional pardon is granted," Billings said flatly.

Asked what he most wanted now, other than a pardon, his boyishness returned. "A ripe persimmon," he replied. "Boy, do I want a ripe persimmon!"

There were crowds in the streets, and bands playing when they returned to San Francisco. They were not for Billings, however, but part of the Golden Gate International Exposition now in progress. One of the bands, mounted on a truck, was that of Count Basie. The group was playing "One O'Clock Jump."

"What's that, George?" Billings asked.

"That," explained Davis, "is the new musical rage. It's called 'swing music.'"

There were many other things he would have to get used to.

More reporters were waiting in Davis' office. Asked his future plans, Billings said he wanted to marry and to open his own watch repair shop. He introduced his bride-to-be, whom he had courted by correspondence for 17 years. Just when the marriage would occur, he couldn't say. It depended on receipt of his pardon. The commutation had restored none of his civil rights. He could not vote, own or inherit property, obtain a driver's or marriage license. Warren K. Billings was, "by law if not by fact," a dead man.

3 ·

There were those who feared that Tom Mooney, once released, would become a disruptive influence. There were others who felt his role would be creative, that the former iron molder might just be the man to forge together the many dissident elements in the American labor movement.

Both were quickly proved wrong. Tom Mooney's influence lasted just a few days short of one month after his release. On February 4, 1939, San Francisco newspapers announced Rena Mooney's confirmation of a rumor that her husband had asked her for a divorce.

Rena, who had been working for $85 a month as a music copyist for the Federal Music Project since the close of her studio three years before, told the press, "I love Tom Mooney. I love him as much today as I did in 1911 when I married him. And I don't believe he's doing this to me of his own accord. It's being forced on him. They're taking him away from me. They want to make him a propaganda machine."

Asked whom she meant by "they," Rena declined to say.

"I don't know why Tom wants to divorce me. We've been through so much together. He seems to forget and so does everyone else that because of him and my love for him I was tried for murder. I walked to the gallows for him and now he wants to throw me out—to toss aside my years of love and loyalty.

"Without him, there's nothing much left for me. I could, I suppose, walk off the Golden Gate Bridge. Or I could give him the divorce he wants. But I won't."

"Instead," as an acquaintance later put it, "she drank." According to those closest to her, there was, and never had been, any basis whatever to the charge of infidelity leveled against her.

Contacted by the press in Los Angeles where he was currently speaking, Tom Mooney termed the divorce report "an attempt to smear me and thereby injure the labor movement." He denied having asked her for a divorce, but admitted the separation. "The truth of the matter is that the lives of Mrs. Mooney and myself are now and have been for the past sixteen years totally and completely incompatible."

Sixteen years earlier would have been 1923, when Rena Mooney *was* the Tom Mooney Molders' Defense Committee.

Papers around the world quickly picked up the news. The symbol had become the man, and while the rank and file in whom Mooney had placed all his faith and hope might easily have forgiven him bitterness, vindictiveness, and any number of other human qualities, they could never forgive him for deserting the woman who had waited for him 22 years.

Attendance at the Mooney meetings dropped off immediately.

In mid-February, as he was boarding a plane to fly from Los Angeles to a labor rally in Monterey, he was stricken with an acute gall bladder attack. He had suffered an earlier, but less severe, attack at San Quentin in 1937. His stomach ulcers provided an additional complication. He was operated on shortly afterward, his condition announced as "all right for the present." Against doctor's orders, he left the hospital to resume his tour. Scrupulously honest where financial matters were concerned, he was obsessed with the idea of paying off his debts. Following his release from jail in Martinez in 1914, while working as secretary of the International Workers' Defense League, he had endeavored for nearly two years to raise money to pay the legal expenses incurred during his trials, even though there is nothing more difficult than collecting funds for a dead cause. As the crowds now dwindled in size (a number of meetings were canceled for lack of attendance), he became more and more dependent on the Communist Party for support.

His attempt to break with them shortly before his release fooled no one but Mooney himself. At least one of the key figures on the TMMDC was a party member. As was Mooney's sweetheart.

From the early Thirties he had tried to use the Communists, much as he had used everyone else with whom he came in contact. He believed he was using them now. He also believed that with their support he could pay off his debts and effect Warren Billings' release.

If there was any formal written agreement between Tom Mooney and Earl Browder it is no longer among Mooney's papers. In all probability there was an oral agreement, made through Robert Minor or one of the ILD lawyers. Many who were closely associated with Mooney believe—there is no absolute proof of this—it was to the effect that in exchange for his touring the country under the auspices of various front groups, the party would liquidate his financial indebtedness. At any rate, tour he did, accompanied by Robert Minor and other party functionaries.

Even before the divorce announcement, there were indications that his pledge to unite the various elements of American labor was doomed to failure. At his first mass meeting in Los Angeles, the only AFL members on the platform were Tom Mooney and two other members of the Molders' Union.

That summer he went East. One stop was Indianapolis, where the AFL was conventioning. Lacking credentials, he was refused admission at the door of the hall. He remained in the city for several days, haunting delegates, asking that someone place before the convention a resolution that he be admitted and allowed to speak. William Green and other AFL leaders saw that no such resolution reached the floor. They had never forgiven him for his pamphlet *Labor Leaders Betray Tom Mooney*.

On September 17th there was a mass meeting in Chicago, co-sponsored by the Tom Mooney Molders' Defense Committee and the Chicago Federation of Labor. This was one of the few places where he appeared under the auspices of the AFL, and then only because the sympathy generated for him by John Fitzpatrick and "Big Ed" Nockles remained strong.

In early October, in Pittsburgh, his ulcer again hemorrhaged. Determined to continue his trip, he refused to be hospitalized. When, on the 16th, Governor Olson announced that Billings would be freed the following day, Mooney announced the cancellation of the rest of his tour and entered a hospital. When well enough to travel, he was brought back to San Francisco and admitted to St. Luke's Hospital. He never left it.

There followed three more operations, each disclosing a progressively worsening condition. At the State Federation of Labor convention a resolution recommending the appropriation of funds to pay his medical bills was introduced, but never made it out of committee. Bedfast, yellowed with jaundice, in near constant pain, he had little correspondence and fewer visitors. One who came several times was Warren Billings. Another was Rena, whom each time he refused to see. There were a few well publicized visits by party leaders, many of whom were also old friends: Elizabeth Gurley Flynn, Earl Browder, William Z. Foster. Although occasionally mentioned in the *Daily Worker* and *People's World,* he rated little newspaper attention elsewhere. In 1941, when Earl Browder was convicted of having unlawfully applied for a passport using an alias and sentenced to four years at Atlanta, Tom Mooney was made Chairman of the Citizens' Committee to Free Earl Browder.

On March 3, 1942, he underwent his fourth operation, for the removal of an ulcer and part of his stomach. He never recovered, dying on Friday the 6th, all but six months of his three years of freedom having been spent in a hospital bed.

Warren Billings claimed the body for Rena Mooney; funeral arrangements were taken over by Labor's Unity for Victory Committee—composed of the AFL, CIO, and Railroad Brotherhoods. Again, for a day, Mooney made good his pledge. The funeral took place on Sunday, March 8th, in Civic Auditorium. Robert Minor, Harry Bridges, George Davis, and Warren Billings were among the speakers. Rena, John, and Anna were also present. The People's Chorus opened with "The Star Spangled Banner" and closed with:

> I dreamed I saw Joe Hill last night,
>   Alive as you and me,
> Says I, "But you're 10 years dead."
> "I never died" says he.
> And standing there as big as life,
>   And smiling with his eyes,
> Joe says, "What they forgot to kill
>   Went on to organize."

At graveside ceremonies at Cyprus Lawn the following day one of the speakers vowed "We will never live so long that you are dead to us, Tom. You will never be here so long that you do not live in us. Take your well earned rest! We will fight on for you. Hail and farewell, Tom Mooney, great hero of labor!"

But many had already forgotten. Only 5000 attended the funeral, less than half the number appearing at Mother Mooney's last rites. The cortege to the cemetery consisted of no more than 25 cars.

Yet some were reluctant to let go. A Tom Mooney Assistance Committee was formed and funds collected, purportedly to pay his hospital bills and other debts.

His estate amounted to approximately $300. In his will he bequeathed his books and correspondence to the University of California, his personal possessions to his sister Anna and brother John. There was also a provision to "specifically disinherit" any other possible claimant.

His real legacy had already been given.

On the day following his death the San Francisco *Chronicle* editorialized that after his release "Tom Mooney became a simple old man, of no more interest or concern than any other simple old man."

This was cruel, but not totally untrue. He was not old—only fifty-eight at the time he died—and he was not simple—not in the sense that his mind was less than clear. But his view of the world remained simple, and static. To him there were only dualities. There was right and there was wrong, with no shadings in between. People were for him or against him. Friends agreed with him or betrayed him.

Imprisoned on the eve of one war, he was released on the eve of another, into a world that had become highly relative. He never entirely succeeded in bridging the intervening decades. During his years in prison, labor had won many of the battles for which he had once fought—the right to organize, the minimum wage, and the maximum hour law had all become reality in all but a few trades. Most of his old adversaries had disappeared or changed beyond recognition. United Railroads had merged into the city's municipally-owned transit system. PG&E paid employee bonuses and welfare benefits; they also hired public relations consultants to personalize and project the company's human qualities. The Chamber of

Commerce boosted San Francisco as a place where labor and management could work together harmoniously and profitably.

Even the unions had changed. Many now resembled, more than anything else, well-run businesses.

The battles weren't over—the same week Mooney died the municipal carmen debated calling a strike because the company was considering hiring Negro drivers—but they were different battles. Maybe in time he would have fought in them. He never had the chance.

"To the end," the *Daily Worker* wrote, "he believed in the working class revolution."

Perhaps this was saddest of all—not that he was a Communist, for he was never that, not even "warmly sympathetic to the Communist Party" as William Z. Foster would claim, for his relations with them remained stormy to the end—but that he failed to perceive that a revolution had already taken place in the United States, during the years of the New Deal.

He kept his dream, but it was riddled with doubts. For in his last years he was forced to admit the most obvious fact about the rank and file, that the chief aim of the average American worker was not to form a workers' state but to attain the middle-class respectability and comforts that would forever separate him from his former station.

The San Francisco *Examiner,* in describing his funeral, called it "the burial of an era."

Barring only the assassinations of Presidents, it is doubtful that any other murder case in American history had so many important legal, social, political, and international ramifications. The Mooney-Billings case not only covered an era, it contained it, holding in microcosm all the major forces and movements of the times.

Yet "burial" is too final a word, for many of its effects are still felt.

Although it did not personally help Tom Mooney, the United States Supreme Court opinion in the case of Mooney vs. Holohan, together with the decision in the Scottsboro case, Powell vs. Alabama, informally opened the door for the host of other due process and civil rights decisions still making headlines today.

One would like to think that certain other facets of the case had been buried, that certain lessons had been learned. But even before Mooney died there was evidence that this was not true. In much the same climate of mobilized hysteria under which Warren Billings and Tom Mooney had been tried, 110,000 Americans of Japanese ancestry were removed from their homes and placed in barbed-wire internment camps, presumed guilty until they proved themselves innocent, while the Red Scare would be resurrected again and again in the decades that followed.

An era may have been buried, but many of its issues have survived it.

Time wrote of him: "He was never meant to be a martyr."

This, also, was true. But then few martyrs are.

Today Tom Mooney the man is mostly forgotten. Tom Mooney the symbol has proven far more durable. To many in American labor his name is legendary, evoking the figure of an heroic giant, a Prometheus of the working class, struggling to break the chains of capitalistic justice. Which is as it should be, for the symbol, like the injustice which created it, was real. Tom Mooney was cast in the martyr's mold; that there were flaws in the clay made the symbol no less valid, only more vulnerable.

One tragedy of the Mooney-Billings case was, from beginning to end, a human one.

The other was, as Mooney himself realized, bigger than one man or even two.

It is perhaps best that Theodore Dreiser never wrote a book about the case, for he had already used the one title that best described it.

4 ·

Following Tom Mooney's death, Rena eked out a living by taking in boarders and giving piano and violin lessons to a few pupils. She told one of her longtime friends that there was no reason for her to continue living, but she continued to do so nevertheless. One evening Miriam Allen De-Ford found her passed out on the cable car tracks. She helped her up and took her home. Others had similar experiences. About 6 P.M. on August 11, 1952, a boarder in her home at 2023 Pacific Avenue smelled something burning and on entering her rooms found a badly scorched ironing board. Her body was on the floor beside it. She had died at seventy-five, apparently of a heart attack.

Perhaps her best obituary came from one of the least likely sources. "From the beginning," Mary Gallagher once told an interviewer, "she was not the dedicated person he was to the cause of labor. She was dedicated to Tom Mooney . . ."

Mary Gallagher died in 1965. The woman Mooney hoped to marry has never married and still lives in San Francisco.

The same week Mooney was released, Felix Frankfurter was appointed to the United States Supreme Court.

Frank P. Walsh, who for 15 years championed without fee the cause of Tom Mooney, died May 2, 1939, shortly before Mooney made his Eastern tour. For George Davis, the Mooney-Billings case marked the beginning of a notable career as one of the country's best-known criminal attorneys.

Emma Goldman died May 14, 1940, in London, still fighting for the causes in which she believed. Sasha had preceded her. On June 25, 1937, her longtime companion, living in poor health and poverty in Southern France, put a pistol to the side of his head and pulled the trigger. More than 40 years after his unsuccessful attempt to assassinate Frick, Alexander Berkman, "the gentle anarchist," still did not know how to use a gun. He lived on for 48 agonizingly painful hours.

For all his early promise, which was considerable, Robert Minor became little more than a party hack, shifting his loyalties with every change in the official line, railing at unfair prosecutions in America but ignoring the purge trials.

Tom Mooney was unable to keep another of his promises. J. B. McNamara died in Folsom on March 8, 1941, after 30 years in prison. His brother, J.J., died a month later. Dave Caplan committed suicide. Matt Schmidt, eventually released on parole, married a wealthy heiress, and played no further part in the labor movement.

Thanks to Charles Fickert, Martin Swanson, and their associates, for nearly three decades the Mooney-Billings case was, as Ernest Jerome Hopkins once put it, "the nation's foremost manufactory of radicals." Not all remained that. Among those assemblymen whose election Mooney urged in his 1938 pamphlet were two "outstanding liberal leaders." One, Jack Tenney, would as a State Senator head the California Un-American Activities Committee, becoming one of the foremost red-baiters of his time. The other, Sam Yorty, would become Mayor of Los Angeles and during the bitter 1966 California gubernatorial primary fight accuse Governor Edmund G. Brown of being soft on Communism. Too, there are many today who would hesitate to call Harry Bridges a "radical." In 1956, for example, he endorsed Eisenhower.

Yet had Mooney lived longer, the man who probably would have surprised him most was "the Fickert of 1936–37," Earl Warren.

Nearly all the leading actors in the Mooney-Billings drama have now passed from the scene. Belle, John, and Anna are gone. Senator Hiram Johnson is dead, as are Governors Stephens, Richardson, Young, Rolph, Merriam, and Olson.

Death has also claimed Thornwell Mullally, Edward Cuhna, and James Brennan, as well as Captains Goff and Matheson and Judges Griffin and Dunne. Shortly before his death, Brennan, in his third about-face, called for a pardon for Billings.

John McDonald is dead; most of the other witnesses have long since disappeared from view. The reward, incidentally, was never paid. Estelle Smith last made the papers in the Thirties, at which time she had risen to the management of a Sacramento establishment.

In the Fifties, Edgar T. Gleeson, once known by the nickname "Scoop," was seated in a cafe in Ensenada, Baja California, when two women at a nearby table gave him a professional come-hither stare. One looked slightly familiar. Looking closer, attempting to peel off the layers of makeup, he was sure he recognized her. It couldn't be, he thought. She would have been in her late sixties, at least.

5 ·

"The case is closed" wrote *The New York Times* in its obituary of Tom Mooney.

At least one man would have disputed this.

On leaving prison, Warren Billings had two choices open to him. He could go to some other state and start life anew, or he could stay in California—where his legal status was questionable—and fight for his rights. He chose the latter.

Mary Gallagher arranged a Victory Ball in Los Angeles. Enough money was raised to pay off all expenses of the Billings Defense, with $80 left over to help him start a business. In January 1940, he opened a watch repair shop at 1095 Market, one block from the Mooneys' former studio. Although Governor Olson had promised to act on his pardon, Billings was impatient; on March 25, 1940, he and Josephine Rudolph "eloped" to Reno.

Unlike Mooney, Billings did not make a series of public appearances. Shortly after his release he did become active in the King-Ramsey-Connor defense. And the following year he accepted an invitation from David Dubinsky to speak before the International Ladies Garment Workers' Union at their annual convention in New York City. Mary Gallagher, in New York at the time, went down to Grand Central Station to meet his train, only to find policemen stationed at every exit plus two on each staircase. Asking who was expected, she was told, "Warren Billings, who was involved with Tom Mooney in that bombing case, is coming in on the train from California."

"This is terrible," she cried. "Billings is innocent of that crime! They proved that by letting him go."

The policeman broke into a big grin. "Sure, everybody knows that. The 'Little Flower' sent us down to see he got to the convention all right."

In 1942, following Tom Mooney's death, Warren Billings took over as Chairman of the Citizens' Committee to Free Earl Browder, and made a brief cross-country speaking tour. Programs for the meetings at which he appeared noted that although Billings did not agree with Browder's political philosophy, he did feel that he had been given a "bum rap." Browder had been convicted of using an alias on a passport—this was a ruse, Billings said, employed by many movie stars, members of royalty, and other notables without receiving prison sentences. As for his associates, Billings put it bluntly: "Just because the Communists are involved in a good cause is no reason for other people to abandon it."

But for the most part he settled into the routine of work, in his trade and also in the California labor movement. Over the years he held a number of offices, in his own local, #101 of the Watchmakers' Union, and on the San Mateo Central Labor Council. In 1958, he witnessed the fulfillment of one of Tom Mooney's dreams, as a delegate to the California AFL-CIO merger convention.

To the general public "the forgotten man in the Mooney case" has remained just that. Since his release he has made the front page only a few times. Once in 1944, when he voted for the first time. After studying the law, he became convinced that even if he possessed no civil rights in California, he was still a citizen of the United States and entitled to choose his own President. Although he was at first refused permission to register, when he threatened to take the matter to court, the registrar, unwilling to make an issue of his stand, relented, and Billings was allowed to vote for national, although not California offices. He voted for Franklin Delano Roosevelt.

In 1958 he made the papers again when badly beaten and robbed of $11 by a newly released convict. He was, at the time, active in prisoner rehabilitation work, and remained so after the incident.

His repeated attempts to obtain a pardon seldom made the papers.

Although Governor Olson had promised to act on his pardon request when the time was right, apparently he never felt it was, as he left office in 1942 without taking action. During the next ten years Earl Warren was Governor of California, and for the following six years that office was occupied by Republican Goodwin J. Knight. Neither was disposed to act on Billings' petition.

Shortly after taking office in 1959, Governor Edmund G. "Pat" Brown promised to look into the matter. In 1961, while in Sacramento as a union representative to the Governor's Conference on Aging, Billings asked Brown just when he was going to receive his pardon. That December 22nd there was a brief ceremony in attorney George Davis' office, as former Folsom prisoner 10699, age sixty-eight, was handed the official document.

Under California law, there is no provision whereby Warren K. Billings can receive even token remuneration for the 23 years he was falsely imprisoned.

As this is written, fifty years after the Preparedness Day bombing, Warren Billings is living in retirement in San Mateo, California. His hair has thinned and is more rusty than red, but his mind is sharp, his memory clear, and his interests still so numerous as to make the word "retirement" something of a misnomer. Although he closed his watch repair shop in 1959, he remains active in union affairs and currently heads the Northern

California Committee for the Release of Morton Sobell, who he firmly believes was convicted on perjured testimony. He also believes there are, in American prisons today, far more innocent men than most people realize. Even at seventy-three, there is still a boyish quality to his grin.

On October 17, 1964, a quarter of a century after his release from Folsom, his wife gave a dinner in his honor, where he was presented a gold watch fob inscribed "To Warren, who endured much for many." Although the dining room was crowded, only George Davis, Mrs. Billings, and a few others dated from the time of "the case." Most were friends who met him after his release.

Earlier that year, on January 7th, Billings made a rare public appearance on a San Francisco television program. The occasion was historic, and with only a little prodding, he related a few of the many incidents that had occurred during the long course of the case. In closing, the interviewer remarked that Billings had certainly played a memorable role in American history. Billings said nothing, but he did smile. The interview commemorated the 25th anniversary of Tom Mooney's release from prison.

Appendix: Whose Bomb?

L EST THERE be any misunderstanding, this chapter will not provide a conclusive answer to the above question. It will bring together for the first time all the existent evidence—the clues, eyewitness testimony, confessions, theories, accusations, and other data—and from this the reader may draw his or her own conclusions.

*   *   *

To clear the mind of preconceptions, there was for a time a suspicion that the Preparedness Day bombing was an accident.

Shortly after the explosion, it was suggested that the suitcase belonged to one of the victims, mining engineer Lea H. Lamborn, and that it contained dynamite to be used in his work.

This was quickly disproven—Lamborn was an assayer; he was also retired and on his way to a vacation at Lake Tahoe; and this explanation failed to account for the bullets that claimed the lives of most of the victims—but is mentioned as just one of the dozens of theories evolved over the years in an attempt to explain what happened on the corner of Steuart and Market at 2:06 on the afternoon of July 22, 1916.

The physical evidence

The following items were picked up at the scene or nearby by police and reporters: several pieces of torn fabric and two locks, which were apparently the lock of a suitcase *and* a bag; a number of small pieces of twisted metal, none of which were from a metal suitcase frame; a number of unexploded cartridges and exploded bullets of various calibers; several pieces of 4″ wrought steel pipe; and several pieces of a malleable iron cap that apparently screwed over one end of the pipe.

In examining the pipe fragments explosives experts agreed they probably came from a single length of pipe and that the explosion had occurred within the pipe, causing it to burst outward.

The prosecution asserted, and the defense didn't disagree, that the explosive itself was probably placed inside the pipe, the pipe then packed in cartridges and metal scraps.

Of the types of explosives in use at that time, dynamite and nitroglycerine were the most common; in all probability one or the other was used.

Dynamite is an explosive containing some proportion of nitroglycerine. Commercial dynamite comes in paper cartridges 8″ long, from ⅞″ to 1½″ in diameter, and is of varying strengths. A 40% strength, for example, would contain 40% nitroglycerine, 10% wood pulp, and 50% nitrate of soda. Since the length of the pipe was unknown, the number of sticks used could have varied, as could their strength, but from the first photo of the scene (made before Fickert began excavating) explosives experts concluded that certainly no more than a single stick was used, of probably no more than 40% or average strength. It was not a powerful explosion.

Even at that, however, the same experts said that if the bomb had been placed on the sidewalk next to the wall the damage should have been greater than it was. The sidewalk should have been very badly broken. From the photo, however, it was apparent that the bomb only cracked a hole of one or two inches in the sidewalk, abraided its surface, and dented several bricks some distance up the wall. This seemed to reinforce the defense's contention that the bomb was dropped, not placed, that it exploded not on the sidewalk but in the air above it.

But the experts by no means agreed on this point. And Bourke Cockran's success at the Tom Mooney trial in making the coroner admit that most of the wounds appeared downward-slanting was more oratorical than actual, for on cross-examination by Cuhna he also admitted that from the way shoes were blown from the feet it must have occurred at sidewalk level.

Dynamite is most commonly exploded by a fulminate of mercury cap. This is a small copper shell about ⅜″ in diameter and 1½″ to 2″ long, open at one end, closed at the other. In the cap is a compressed charge of fulminate of mercury, usually about 12 grains. This cap may be exploded in several ways.

One is by electrical current, which can be supplied by a dry-cell battery, a wet-cell battery, or a magneto. In this case, the copper shell is loaded with fulminate, two insulated wires run down the sides of the shell, while across the ends of these wires is a very fine platinum wire, barely discernible by sight, and on top of that a small particle of gun cotton. What occurs is not one but a series of explosions: the electrical current causes the gun cotton to ignite, which causes the fulminate of mercury to explode, which causes the dynamite to explode.

No wires or battery parts were found on the scene.

The fulminate cap can be made to explode by a timing device. If an alarm clock is used, usually the alarm key of the clock is supplied with an extension arm, so that when the alarm goes off the key unwinds and in so doing throws the arm over the post or strip of metal or wire, which, when it touches the other wire, completes the circuit.

No clock parts were found on the scene. Lieutenant Bunner's house-cleaning may have been responsible, but even so, one might expect a few parts to survive. Prior to the trial of Rena Mooney, the defense hired U.S. Army explosives expert Colonel Albert Isert to construct two bombs as similar as possible to the suitcase-enclosed clock bomb described by the prosecution. These were set off in the Berkeley hills, in a setting constructed to simulate the cement sidewalk and brick saloon wall at Steuart and Market. After both explosions, the area was littered with clock parts and portions of the dry cell batteries, while the metal frames of both suitcases remained intact.

Dynamite can also be exploded by nitrate, muriatic, or hydrochloric acid in an open vial with a cotton wick. The acid climbs the wick by capillary action, setting the powder on fire, causing the dynamite to explode when the heat becomes great enough. An expert can time this action to the minute.

In all probability, if this was a suitcase bomb, the acid-fuse method of detonation was used.

Nitroglycerine can be created chemically or it can be extracted from a stock of dynamite by the use of warm water. The nitro is heavy and sinks to the bottom; the other material is then decanted off.

In its liquid form nitroglycerine (or "dynamite soup") can be exploded with a cap as described or without a cap by any sudden jarring motion: for example, by being dropped, thrown, or shaken.

If the bomb was made to be thrown or dropped, it is probable that nitroglycerine was used.

There is a way to determine whether dynamite or nitroglycerine is used in an explosion. In the trial of Tom Mooney explosives expert Arthur H. Crane observed that if dynamite was used, "An analysis of the nitrate of soda sticking to the wall could readily be made and would determine whether an explosion of dynamite was had."

Unfortunately no such test was made following the Preparedness Day bombing. To be exact, no such test was even possible once Frederick Colburn had finished using his sledge hammer to smash in the saloon wall. In the photo taken before Colburn arrived, however, there appeared to be powder marks on the wall. From the photo alone, it is, of course, impossible to say whether they contained nitrate of soda.

In summary, from the physical evidence that survived the efforts of Bunner, Fickert, and Colburn, it is not possible to say what explosive was used in the bomb, the manner in which it was triggered, or whether it was placed or dropped.

The physical evidence was not the only evidence, however.

The eyewitness accounts

Three sets of witnesses testified to the events at Steuart and Market. One set, consisting of John McDonald and Frank Oxman, may be eliminated from consideration here. The other two were (a) those who saw the man or men with the suitcase, and (b) those who saw a falling object.

(a) As related in the Prologue, seven people testified to having seen the suitcase. Of these, five saw the man or men who placed it there. There were discrepancies among these accounts: Prendergast saw two men, the others only one; Taylor said that he had a mustache, Prendergast several days' growth of beard, the others that he was clean shaven; and there were differences as to the time, the size and color of the suitcase, and the clothing the man wore. Nor was there agreement as to his build, although this may have been due to the fact that none of these persons were trained in estimating such things: Prendergast said he was 5'8", 145 pounds; Johnson, 5'7", 160 pounds; Kimberlin, 5'10", 170 pounds.

Yet on one point there was general agreement. Four of the five said he was dark-complected: Prendergast, "Mexican or Portuguese"; Kimberlin, "either Mexican or Italian"; Johnson, "Mexican or Spaniard"; Powers, "apparently a Mexican." *

In all probability, the man who set down the suitcase was dark-complected, and probably Mexican or Spanish.

We'll return to this testimony in due course.

(b) As related in chapter 10, four persons—Dr. Moss, Mrs. Dahl, Mrs. Masterson, and Mr. Hollfender—testified to seeing an object fall through the air just above the fatal corner immediately prior to the explosion. Dr. Moss's description was most exact: it was a black object, a foot to fourteen inches in length, three and a half to four inches in diameter, and "It disappeared behind the people standing on the sidewalk and a violent explosion immediately followed." **

In his excellent study, *What Happened in the Mooney Case,* Ernest Jerome Hopkins supplies a possible explanation for this testimony. There is, Hopkins noted, a not uncommon psychological manifestation in cases

---

* If John McDonald's original affidavit is considered, this brings the number to five.

Some half-dozen other people made affidavits to seeing Mexicans with suitcases at various points in downtown San Francisco on the same day, but because none of these was connected to Steuart and Market they have been omitted here.

** Although this perfectly describes the pipe, it obviously fails to account for the bullets. Which raises yet another interesting possibility—that the bullets were in the suitcase and may not have been a part of the bomb.

Courtesy Bancroft Library

Suppressed for 20 years, this photograph shows the Market and Steuart Street intersection just before the explosion. The large flag is that of the GAR, which has just turned out of Steuart onto Market. The arrow points to a figure on the roof of the saloon, his back to the camera. Was this the actual bomber?

involving explosions where witnesses tend to confuse the order of events, where the first thing seen the instant after a violent shock is so firmly etched on the mind as to make one believe it was seen before the shock occurred.

This may explain the testimony of these four witnesses. But it doesn't explain that of Mrs. Compton, who saw a man on the roof.

During the habeas corpus hearings (four years after Hopkins' book appeared), new weight was lent to Mrs. Compton's story with the discovery in the Bomb Bureau files of a suppressed photograph that showed a man on the saloon roof approximately one minute before the explosion.

This photo was taken by Mrs. Charles Braddock from the second floor of the Terminal Hotel (Mrs. Compton was watching the parade from a window on the sixth floor) and was just one of a number of photos taken by the Braddocks that day. Not until having them developed did they notice the figure of the man and contact the police. At 6:50 P.M. on July 28th, two detectives came to the hotel and picked up the print from Mr. Braddock, Detective Elmer J. Esperance signing a receipt for it.

Thus, on the day after Tom Mooney's arrest, the San Francisco Police Department was aware that there had indeed been a man on the saloon roof. There is positive proof that the District Attorney's office was equally aware of this fact. The photo was blown up for use as a courtroom exhibit, but with the top portion, which showed the roof and the man, cut off.

The time of the photo was easily established as 2:05, since the Ladies Auxiliary of the GAR had just turned onto Market with their big flag.

Unfortunately, the photo was taken from some distance away, the opposite side of Market; the background of the print (in which the figure appears) is badly out of focus; and the man had his back to the camera. Even greatly magnified, it is impossible to determine the man's size or to accurately describe his clothing, except that he did wear a hat.

Shortly after the discovery of the print, George Davis succeeded in locating the Braddocks. They were unable to find the negative, which apparently had been discarded some time ago. Had the negative still existed, it might have been possible to obtain a clearer print. Had the defense possessed the photo 20 years earlier, when the saloon was still standing, it would have been possible at least to approximate the man's height.

As it was, all it proved was that one minute before the explosion there was a man on the saloon roof, almost assuredly the same man seen by Mrs. Compton.

His presence there may have been totally innocent. He may have climbed onto the roof for the sole purpose of watching the parade. And he may have walked to the edge and looked over just before the bomb exploded. This would have been a remarkable coincidence, but the possibility must be mentioned.

It is also possible that he was the Preparedness Day bomber.

Keep this man in mind. In due course we'll return to him, and give him a name.

From the beginning to the end of the case, the defense was afflicted with this acute schizophrenia. They had two sets of witnesses, and in effect, two theories of the bombing. Unable to discredit one or the other, they presented both to the juries, who were predictably confused.

The prosecution overcame this conflict by ignoring both sets of witnesses and creating their own. Their theory of the clock bomb which was to be thrown was patently ridiculous. But it was at least *only one* theory, and in the trials of Billings and Mooney, the juries apparently had no trouble accepting it.

The confessions (primary)

On the evening of Preparedness Day, a man appeared in the backroom of an Oakland saloon. Two men sitting at a nearby table noticed him because his clothing was disheveled and he was highly nervous. Like everyone else in the Bay Area that night, the men were discussing the bombing. "I have something terrible on my mind," the man broke in. "I put that suitcase there." The men questioned him. He was so excited that they had trouble making sense of his answers. However, he did say that he hadn't known what was in the suitcase, that he had been paid to put it there, and that following the bombing he had grabbed what was left of the suitcase and run, finally tossing the incriminating evidence into the bay.

This was prior to the appearance of the first suitcase story in the press.

Making excuses, the men went in search of a policeman. By the time they found one and brought him back the man was gone. They described him as tall, seedy-looking, of sallow complexion, and wearing a brown suit and hat.

Four days later, one Chris Lassen was picked up by Oregon City, Oregon, police and held in jail overnight as a vagrant. While there, Lassen confessed to his cellmate J. M. Ghrist that he was responsible for the Preparedness Day bombing. Ghrist told the jailor, whereupon Lassen was taken out and questioned. All he would say was "I was one of twelve in the plot. It was my job to stay around the saloon until the parade started, then go outside and put down the loaded suitcase." Officials could get nothing further from him except that he had hopped a train immediately after the explosion.

According to news accounts of the confession, Lassen was forty-nine, 5'8", had a sallow complexion, sandy hair, blue eyes, and when picked up was wearing a brown suit and hat.

Since Lassen claimed to be a Dane, the Danish Consul was called from Portland. By this time Lassen had added a few details that had appeared earlier in the press, plus one that hadn't. Asked who had told him to place the suitcase, he replied "The Kaiser."

Following a hearing, he was pronounced insane and confined to the Oregon State Hospital at Salem. He remained there until 1920, when released as "cured." Apparently he then drifted to various places. In 1935, while working as a cook on a ranch near Stockton, California, he became ill, went into town to see a doctor, and died in a room in the Windsor

Hotel on February 10th. Both the Stockton *Record* and the Sacramento *Bee* gave his name as C. F. Larsen. But he was the same man, for on his body was found an old letter from the Danish Consul stating his involvement in the case.

Whether he was the same man who appeared in the Oakland saloon is unknown. He would have had to go to Oakland to catch a train for Oregon.

According to the papers, San Francisco police investigated Lassen's confession but wholly discredited it. Whether they sent a man to Oregon or merely talked by telephone to the local police is unknown. There was no immediate investigation by the defense since there was no defense at this time, nor, apparently, did they at any later time consider the confession significant. Warren Billings did, and on his release from prison, attempted to investigate the story—even going through the consulate records in Denmark—but by this time the trail had disappeared.

If Lassen, or Larsen, was the man who confessed in the Oakland saloon, his story had at least two things to commend it: the mention of the suitcase and an explanation for why no suitcase frame was found at the bomb scene.

Weighing against the story, however, was that no one at the bomb scene recalled seeing a man grab a badly battered suitcase and run, and of course, Lassen's insanity.

There is a certain irony here. The mental imbalance that might cause a man to explode a bomb in a crowd of people would render his own confession suspect.

In September 1932, one Paul Calicotte, sobbing that he could no longer live with his guilty conscience, confessed that he had placed the suitcase next to the saloon wall.

Tom Mooney was inclined to doubt this confession, even after it was related in detail and notarized, but others in the defense believed it, and on November 7th, before a packed Civic Auditorium, Theodore Dreiser introduced the man who committed the Preparedness Day bombing.

Calicotte's story was dramatic. In 1916 he was only a boy of sixteen, living with his parents in Oakland. On Friday, July 21st, while walking past the local IWW hall, he was approached by a man who asked him if he wanted to earn $5. Paul did; the next day he was given a suitcase and told to take it to the Alameda Cafe at 7 Market Street in San Francisco, where a man would contact him. The man invited him to lunch, after which he was paid and told to leave the suitcase in front of the saloon. The man disappeared into the crowd. Paul was on the ferry back to Oakland when he heard the explosion. He immediately connected it with the suitcase, but was afraid to tell anyone, because his parents were Seventh Day Adventists and he knew they would beat him for working on Saturday.

It was quite a story. Apparently the idea of the man calmly eating lunch with a lethal suitcase beside his feet, or the fact that Calicotte bore no resemblance to the man Prendergast and the others described, bothered no one except Tom Mooney. The audience was clearly not concerned about the IWW connection: that the arrangement was made outside IWW headquarters only proved it was not the Wobblies, but someone wishing to frame them, who was responsible.

Before long, however, the story grew even better, fuller, and more detailed, and with these details came contradictions and discrepancies, until the defense was forced to admit they had been taken in by someone with a rather great affinity for publicity. There was, for example, Calicotte's habit of handing a photograph of himself to everyone he met.

The confessions (secondary)

In 1936, during the habeas corpus hearings, one George Grimmer testified that in the spring of 1916 he had approached Jesse W. Lilienthal, president of United Railroads, seeking a job. Grimmer had worked as a scab for URR during the strike of 1907. Lilienthal sent him to assistant general manager Melnott McCants. "We can use you," McCants told him. "We've got a number of no-good men in this city whom we want to run out of the state or across the bay." He named Mooney as one and assigned Grimmer to follow him. After several days, Grimmer grew nervous about his assignment and asked McCants "Are you going to frame him?" "Of course not," McCants answered sarcastically. "Nobody likes to hear the word 'frame.' We just want you to be at the same place Mooney is, at the same time, if anything happens." This worried Grimmer even more, and shortly afterward he quit the job. On July 22nd, while riding a downtown streetcar, he heard the explosion and told the conductor "I guess that's going to be pinned on Mooney." A week later, three strange men came up to him. One said, "You've been throwing up your guts about this case. The best thing you can do is to beat it."

Grimmer went to Los Angeles. There, in 1920, he encountered Joseph "Indian Joe" Daugherty, a half-breed who had also been a strikebreaker for URR in 1907. Somehow the Mooney case was mentioned; Grimmer asked Daugherty if he thought Mooney had done it. "Naw, that ——— wouldn't have the guts," Daugherty replied. "He had absolutely nothing to do with it. I could put my hand on the man's shoulder that did it." He put his hand on his own shoulder.

A few months later Daugherty's body was found in a Chicago alley, his neatly decapitated head resting on his chest.

By the time Grimmer chose to tell his story, all those he named were dead. Daugherty's murder, upon investigation, proved to have been the work of a madman who had killed another man similarly; it apparently bore no connection to the Mooney-Billings case. What gave Grimmer's story more than ordinary credence was that over the years he had gone up in the world. At the time he testified he was president of the Los Angeles Civil Service Commission, and void of any discernible motive for dredging up this portion of his past.

Another ex-URR spy testified during the hearing, one George Miller, who had been in charge of hiring the 150 scabs who broke up the 1917 URR strike. (Although this strike had Labor Council sanction and more than $40,000 was spent on organization, it was no more successful than Mooney's 1916 effort.) In 1919, Miller was again employed by McCants and URR, to work in the dual capacity of conductor and labor spy. One day the subject of Mooney came up in conversation. "Miller," said Mc-Cants, "Mooney and Billings are going to remain in prison as long as United Railroads can keep them there. We know they're not guilty, but they're agitators, and their kind of agitation cost us a million dollars in that strike."

The fingerpointings

When the *Call* published detective Draper Hand's confession in 1920, one part was omitted, a charge so sensational that even the Mooney defense was unwilling to accept it, at least at that time, for Hand accused Charles Fickert and Martin Swanson with responsibility for the Preparedness Day bombing.

The original plan, according to Hand, had been to place the suitcase containing a time bomb on the barge *Ajax*, used to ferry strikebreakers back and forth from a ship on which they were staying, and to blame Mooney. One Tony Gomez had been hired to place the suitcase. Gomez hadn't counted on the heavy parade traffic, however; on reaching Steuart and Market and finding that his time was running out, he panicked, abandoned the suitcase, and fled the scene.

Several factors lent weight to Hand's charges. One was that Gomez was a Mexican. And the Mooney defense had long suspected the bombing might have some connection with the bitter waterfront troubles, although the strike itself had terminated on the 17th.

However, Hand later admitted his charge was only hearsay, and still later repudiated this portion of his statement.

Which was perhaps best, as further checking revealed Gomez had died in 1915.

In 1922, William J. Flynn, former head of the United States Secret Service, stated in his memoirs, published in installments in the New York *Herald,* that Mooney wasn't guilty of the bombing. According to Flynn, the Secret Service had known the identity of the real murderer since shortly after the explosion!

Flynn did not name him, but his identity was easily surmised. "We know that he was in full possession of all the facts in the San Francisco bomb plot, for which Tom Mooney and others went to jail," Flynn wrote. "At the time the bombing was perpetrated, he was writing for one of the numerous ephemeral newspapers he either founded or edited. That he was more or less informed regarding the San Francisco affair we gathered from one of his editorials wherein he declared that neither Billings, Mooney, Nolan, Weinberg nor Rena Mooney was guilty."

Bourke Cockran called Flynn, demanding that if he had actual knowledge of the guilty party, he name him and produce his evidence. Flynn admitted that he personally had nothing to do with the San Francisco case. "But this I do know," he said in a later installment, "whoever did it was well known to the editor and he knew it was about to be perpetrated and who was to do the actual work."

Despite his former station, Flynn had a weakness for making unsupported allegations. From his statements it was fairly obvious that he was referring to Alexander Berkman. Berkman did indeed declare in *The Blast* that Mooney and the others were not guilty, but this is the only part of Flynn's charge that withstands scrutiny. Although there were many strong anti-preparedness articles in *The Blast,* most of them authored by Berkman himself, a reading of all issues reveals no hint that Berkman anticipated what happened. It may be safely said that if there had been a shred of evidence linking Berkman with the crime, Fickert would have used it.

About all Flynn's articles proved was that as head of the Secret Service he had a remarkably cavalier attitude toward false imprisonments.

In 1936, while Mooney and Billings were in San Francisco County Jail, they were visited by federal prosecutor H. H. McPike, who told them that the government had "conclusive proof" they were innocent but that he couldn't tell them anything more at the time. He died soon thereafter.

One year earlier, an attorney formerly employed by PG&E told the Mooney defense that while working for the company he had found, hidden in the back of a filing cabinet, a folder containing a complete resume of Martin Swanson's activities on behalf of PG&E. As soon as he had the opportunity, he said, he could "borrow" the file, if they were interested. They definitely were.

That Martin Swanson had been employed by PG&E was an established fact; that some sort of record relating to his employment existed—or had at one time—there was no doubt. That the file contained exactly what the lawyer claimed was highly doubtful, inasmuch as he referred to matters no individual or corporation would be foolish enough to put in writing. Still, unlike many others proffering information, he did not ask for payment. However, there followed numerous delays and evasions until finally, pressed to show the folder, he declared the file was now missing.

In 1928, when Mary Gallagher went to Oregon to appeal to her fellow Catholic Frank Oxman, a close female relative of the cattleman offered to tell the truth about Oxman's part for a "Christmas present from Tom Mooney" of "say, $15,000."

"I am absolutely against any such thing," Mooney wrote Mary angrily. "Just think of the cold blooded proposition—after letting two innocent men lay in prison all these years and accept a Christmas gift from them."

There were many similar incidents, including anonymous letters and telephone calls, the largest number directed personally to Rena Mooney following her release.

Stand on a certain corner at a certain time, she was instructed, and you will be contacted with information as to the identity of the real bomber. Send me $500 c/o general delivery.

Run the following ad in the Los Angeles *Times* on this date.

Some of these people appeared directly with their offers. After many frustrated hopes—and for Rena, wasted hours on lonely street corners, since at first she followed the instructions implicitly whenever possible—the defense established a policy of ignoring all communications that failed to provide some substantiating evidence.

There remained, however, the haunting possibility that one of these just might lead to the answer that would free Mooney and Billings. The most improbable letter had led to the discovery of Estelle Smith's past.

Studying the long history of the case, one is less surprised that Rena Mooney was driven to drink than that she bore so many pressures for so long without even this relief.

The anonymous letters

In one of his shotgun newspaper blasts, Charles M. Fickert claimed that the U.S. Government, in analyzing the threat letters received before the parade, had conclusively proven that Thomas J. Mooney was their author.

Fickert knew better. As he was aware, the letters continued to arrive long after Tom Mooney was imprisoned, well into World War I.

For Maxwell McNutt the letters—the most obvious clue to the perpetrators of the bombing—became almost an obsession. He spent several years and hundreds of dollars attempting to trace them to their source. In this he worked closely with U.S. Postal Inspector Morris, who was in charge of the investigation. After consulting a number of chirography experts, McNutt and Morris were forced to conclude that the letters were not the work of a single person but two, probably a man and a woman. One of the experts, Chauncey M'Govern, author of several works in this field, was hired to investigate further.

Then came the confession letter. Printed in block capitals, as were the earlier missives, it read:

Haywood, Cal.
Dec 4, 1918

To Whom It May Concern:

I wish to state that I have kept one of my fellow men in prison for a deed he is absolutely not guilty of. I swear by all that is high that it was I not Mooney that left the suitcase in the corner. I am an Englishman by birth. Am in this country 14 years. But like many of my country men have never taken out citizens papers because we ar to loyl to old England and all we cair for is your money. On my death bed I will confess as the life of an Englishman is to sweet to be given up to a bunch of American grafters.

Frank Doe for now

Examining it, M'Govern found numerous similarities between the printing in this letter and *some* of the printing in the others, causing him to suspect it was written in its entirety by one of the two persons who authored the other letters. There were further similarities—the throwing in of misspelled words toward the end, a certain style of phrasing, etc. There was also—beyond the stated clues to the person's background, which may or may not have been relevant—one portion perhaps intended as a clue, perhaps an unconscious error that thus became a clue. There was a "Hayward, California" and a "Hollywood, California," but no "Haywood, California." There was a man named "Big Bill" Haywood. This left the remote possibility that the author was an IWW who had unwittingly made this mistake.

After following a number of seemingly interconnecting leads, the trio came up with two people they suspected of authoring the letters, a husband and wife named Frederick and Leone Esmond.

According to a secret file in the records of the U.S. Department of Labor, dated June 25, 1918, Frederick Esmond, "I.W.W. and labor agitator," was born near Manitoba, Canada, January 26, 1880. After living for some years in England, he returned to Canada and in 1909 slipped across the border into the United States, without introducing himself to Customs. For awhile he worked in the harvest fields of Montana. He joined the IWW in Galveston in 1913. His whereabouts in 1916 were unknown but from May to December 1917 he was employed by the IWW Defense League on the Pacific Coast. He was, according to informants, given to uttering seditious remarks and also much worried that the draft agreement between Great Britain and the United States would result in his having to serve in the Army.

As for his female companion (there was some confusion as to their exact marital status), she was described as a "rabid socialist with anarchistic tendencies." Apparently she was also something of a dreamer, as she had gone to Japan in December 1917 in the hope of converting the Japanese to IWW principles.

By the time she returned to the U.S. in May 1918, Frederick Esmond had already been in jail three months, one of the IWW's charged with complicity in the plot to bomb the Governor's mansion. Proof of that charge lacking, he was tried and convicted of violating the immigration act and of teaching the unlawful destruction of property. Although there was some discussion anent deportation, he was confined to Leavenworth Prison instead. Except for the confession letter, mailed that December, the threat letters ceased about the time of Esmond's arrest.

M'Govern visited him in Leavenworth in 1920 and obtained samples of his handwriting, which he felt proved almost conclusively that he wrote not only parts of the threatening letters sent before Preparedness Day, but also the confession letter. He also obtained statements from the prison doctor and others that Esmond was mentally unbalanced.

In 1921, M'Govern and McNutt prepared a case against Leone Esmond, and the San Francisco Grand Jury voted an indictment. Several weeks later it was dropped. No official reason was given but McNutt was convinced that it was feared that indicting her would mean "freeing Mooney."

It may have been this, and it may have been the weakness of their case, since other handwriting experts were less convinced than M'Govern that the Esmonds authored the letters. Too, there was that disturbing detail, the confession letter, which M'Govern said was the work of Frederick Esmond, who was in Leavenworth Prison at the time it was mailed. The smuggling out of letters is common practice in almost all prisons, but this may have caused the Grand Jury to think twice about issuing an indictment against Leone.

Following Frederick Esmond's release, the couple disappeared from sight.

And there, unsatisfactorily, hangs the story of the anonymous letters.

Some miscellaneous "foreigners"

People who depart from the traditional way of doing things make excellent suspects. Among the "foreigners" suspected at various times of involvement in the bombing were the Irish, the Italians, and the Chinese.

Many of San Francisco's Irish were explosive in temperament; many did oppose Preparedness; and, at least in Ireland, there were a few Sinn Feiners who treated dynamite lightly—but the British had no unit in the parade and there was never any tangible evidence linking any Irishman to the Preparedness Day bombing (and this includes, of course, Mooney and Nolan).

In 1916 the Camorra (Black Hand, Mafia, etc.) was active in San Francisco. On Thanksgiving day North Beach restaurateur Gaetano Ingrassia was gunned down on Columbus Avenue after committing the blunder of turning a Black Hand note over to the police. And there was a triple bombing of St. Peter's and Paul's Church some years later which police attributed to a madman and some Italians believed showed the Camorra touch—but this bombing lacked any similarity to that on Preparedness Day, and there was no evidence that the Society was involved in what happened at Steuart and Market.

As for the Tongs, although there would be "incidents" as late as 1961, by 1916 they had been rendered largely inactive. One might also say that the use of explosives did not fit the *modus operandi* of the "hatchetmen," although in a 1914 battle between the Hop Sings and Suey Sings such modern implements of warfare as motor cars and a machine gun were used. The slaughter of innocent people was definitely not a characteristic of Tong killings, however, which remained strictly inter-community affairs.

The Mexican theory

There is a great deal more to support the Mexican supposition.

Just three weeks earlier there had been the incident on the Southern Pacific train. On June 30th, three Mexicans, who looked to conductor W. A. Brooks like itinerant fruit-pickers, boarded the overland number five at Elmira (where there was a branch line connection to the Vacaville cherry orchards). One was carrying a suitcase. They bought tickets to Richmond, but when the train pulled in there Brooks saw only two get off, leading him to suspect the third was hiding on the train, trying to ride farther without additional fare. Just as the train reached Oakland he found him in the toilet of the smoking car and ordered him off. The man jumped before the train came to a full stop; about two minutes later—as described in the Prologue—the restroom exploded.

None of these men were ever caught. There was no proof that the bombing was the work of a Mexican revolutionary or fanatic protesting the United States' invasion of Mexico (the train had no military importance), but local and federal authorities believed this to be the case. About this same time, two Mexicans were apprehended attempting to blow up a U.S. supply warehouse at Nogales. This definitely was linked to the war.

Over the years a number of people have felt that these bombings and the one on Preparedness Day were committed by agents of the same principal. Bourke Cockran, Ernest Jerome Hopkins, George Davis—each of whom had closely studied the case—subscribed to this view.

There is evidence indicating they might be right.

The train bomb was suitcase-enclosed and of the acid-fuse type.

Four of the five persons who saw the man set down the suitcase next to the saloon wall described him as a Mexican.

In addition, there is also something of a motive.

One of the most puzzling aspects of the Preparedness Day bombing was: Why Steuart and Market?

The Mexican theory supplies a possible answer to this question.

In the morning newspapers of the 22nd, and for several days previous, much had been made of the anticipated presence of the bullet-torn battle flag carried by the First California Volunteers. It would be brought from the State Museum and carried by the Spanish War Veterans who, the articles also noted, were to line up in Steuart Street. The Spanish American War was between the United States and Spain, of course, over Cuba, and the current military activity was against Mexico, but many Mexicans had sided with the Spanish in the earlier conflict, and in the mind of a fanatic the two actions against Spanish-speaking peoples might have been merged.

Although this theory has been often advanced, no mention has been made of its inherent fallacy.

The one thing wrong with it—presuming the bomb was intended to go off where it did when it did—was the time. Both the *Chronicle* and the *Examiner* of that morning had announced that the Spanish War Veterans would meet at Steuart Street, ready to march out, at 1:15. The *Examiner* even carried a sub-head:

> EX-MEMBERS
> OF NATIONAL
> GUARD
> MEET AT
> STEUART ST.
> 1:15

The bomber might have anticipated that the parade would start late, as this was nearly always the case, but unless he was a policeman or one of the parade officials, he couldn't have known that it would start exactly 30 minutes late, and even then he couldn't have anticipated that due to unforeseen delays en route, the Spanish War Veterans would begin marching out not at 1:15 or 1:145 but 2:06.

This would seem to dispose fairly conclusively of the contention that the bombing was planned to happen when it did—but this isn't necessarily true. There is the possibility that in sitting on the suitcase young Jimmie McDougal might in some way have damaged the mechanism, thus delaying the explosion. Against this, however, is that the earliest time a reputable witness placed the suitcase on the scene was 1:25, after the Spanish War Veterans were due to have marched out.

Discrediting the flag-bomb link (which is tenuous at best) in no way negates the fact that four people saw a man who looked like a Mexican place the suitcase on the scene.

The German theory

Through 1915, German espionage activities in the United States were incredibly amateurish.

In New York, Dr. Heinrich Albert, in charge of tying up U.S. industrial output, left his briefcase on the Sixth Avenue Elevated, its contents providing the Secret Service with a blueprint of most of his future plans and prospects.

At the German Consulate in San Francisco, from which emanated all sabotage activities on the Pacific Coast, Consul-General Franz Bopp maintained, according to one of his aides, "a regular museum of bombs and similarly deadly instruments." Bopp delighted in taking these out of the safe and showing visitors how they worked. One in particular, a thermos bottle bomb, especially fascinated him; he would take it apart and reassemble it for hours on end. Just as laxly kept in the consulate were records of all bombings and payments to agents. Nor were the agents themselves much more professional. One, as a birthday present for Bopp, blew up a factory at Twelfth and Mission streets. It was such an innocent looking place he was sure it must be secretly manufacturing munitions for the Allies. Actually it was a window weight factory. Another agent, a Dutchman, who also played at being a British agent, collected on nonexistent explosions by simply having bogus newspaper accounts printed and presenting them to Bopp and his aides for payment.

Yet in terms of destruction their activities were markedly successful. There were dozens of explosions in munitions factories and powder works on the West Coast, as many more on the ships that transported their products to Canada for reshipment to the Allies, and numerous effective acts of sabotage—involving the destruction of bridges, tunnels, and trains—in Canada itself.

For a very long period authorities were unable to connect a single German agent to these deeds. "The prepondering reason for this failure" observed Captain Henry Landau in *The Enemy Within*, "was the lack of coordination between the various police authorities and between them and the Department of Justice. This in turn was largely due to the fact that until the Espionage Act was passed the Department of Justice was never quite sure whether an individual case of land sabotage was an infraction of a Federal law; consequently there was a disposition to allow the local authorities to handle the matter. The result was that, since the sabotage agents were constantly on the move from State to State, the individual threads of evidence uncovered by the local police were unsufficient to disclose the identity of the agents . . ."

Although Consul-General Bopp took his orders from von Papen, he also instigated numerous acts of sabotage on his own. In this he was ably assisted by his two aides, Baron E. H. von Shack and Lieutenant Wilhelm von Brincken.

Their chief agent for this period was C. C. Crowley, a former Southern Pacific detective and labor spy, who in turn recruited as one of his assistants Louis J. Smith, an American of German descent. In May of 1915, on learning that a large shipment of powder manufactured in the Hercules Powder Works at Pinole was to be taken to Tacoma on a barge for transshipment to Vladivostok, von Brincken sent Crowley and Smith north to plant time bombs on the barge, the S.S. *Hazel Dollar*, plus three other ships helping to carry the powder. On the 30th, the barge exploded in a blinding flash, a watchman disappearing with it.

Smith had been clumsy in his preparations; when authorities learned that he had purchased 190 sticks of dynamite and 450 feet of fuse a few days before the Tacoma harbor explosion, he was arrested. A prearranged alibi and a lawyer provided by the Germans brought about his release. Smith and Crowley then returned to San Francisco. Smith was compromised, however. Not wanting him too close at hand, in June Bopp hustled the pair off to Detroit, from which point they were to go on into Canada to destroy some trains and tunnels. Unnerved by the close call in Tacoma, they merely fabricated a report of a train bombing, then returned to collect on it. Bopp sent Smith back to Detroit, with orders to blow up two powder works, one at Gary, Indiana, the other at Ishpeming, Michigan. As soon as Smith arrived, however, the assignments were canceled and Bopp refused to supply funds for his return.

Smith found a job in Detroit, but soon became suspicious that people were following him. At first he thought they were Department of Justice agents, but before long he became equally sure they were Crowley's men, intent on doing away with him because he knew too much. On October 28, 1915, he contacted the Department of Justice and offered to turn State's evidence.

That agency had been building up a case against Bopp and his associates for some time, but not until Smith's confession did they have definite proof tying them to specific acts of sabotage. Smith himself disclaimed any actual participation in these acts, and while the Department of Justice was convinced he had actually been involved in a number of them, they were willing to accept this fiction. His confession that he had planted the bomb on the barge (as both the Bopp trial and the hearings of the Mixed Claims Commission in the 1930's would almost conclusively prove he had) would have made mandatory a charge of murder against him.

Shortly thereafter, Bopp, his aides von Shack and von Brincken, C. C. Crowley, and his secretary, Mrs. Margaret Cornell, were indicted on charges of conspiring to violate United States neutrality. All were immediately released on bail, and as would later be proven, quickly resumed their sabotage activities, though now more cautiously, which they carried on through most of 1916.

The foregoing is necessary background. What follows is a series of separate incidents, each in itself inconclusive but in toto constituting the German theory.

*   *   *

C. C. Crowley was not only working for the Germans: he was also working for District Attorney Charles M. Fickert.

Fickert first employed Crowley on July 31, 1914, to work for him in an undercover capacity on various unspecified cases (their nature was never satisfactorily explained), the said employment lasting until February 1915, during which period Crowley rose from a salary of $65 to $100 per month.

Fickert employed him also in May and October of 1915.

And between these dates—five weeks after the sinking of the *Lusitania* —Charles Fickert provided Crowley with a credential that would prove as embarrassing as any letter penned by Frank Oxman.

Typed on Fickert's official stationery, it read:

District Attorney
Hall of Justice

City and County of San Francisco
San Francisco, Cal., June 14, '15.
To the Officials and Officers Throughout the United
States and Canada:

The bearer of this note, Mr. C. C. Crowley, whose signature appears hereon, is a special agent of this office and connected with the Department of Justice of the City and County of San Francisco, State of California.

At present, and for some time to come, he will be especially assigned to the duty of investigating the illicit drug and poison traffic between this city, Canada and the Eastern States, and particularly the shipment of such articles from Canada into the United States. A number of officials here are under investigation for their alleged connection with the illicit traffic in these drugs. As a result Mr. Crowley will have to work secretly in his investigation, and I earnestly request that all officers to whom Mr. Crowley may present this letter will cooperate with him to the ends outlined herein.

Respectfully yours,
C. M. Fickert
District Attorney

This document was made all the more remarkable since:

(1) There was no such thing as a "Department of Justice of the City and County of San Francisco";

(2) The District Attorney of said city and county had no authority to make an investigation of the drug and poison traffic between the United States and Canada;

(3) The District Attorney was not at this time, or ever, conducting such an investigation, nor prosecuting any officials engaged in these activities; and

(4) At the time he wrote this credential, Charles Fickert was not only aware that Crowley was in the employ of the Germans but that he was making the trip on assignment for them.

When this document was made public following Crowley's arrest, Fickert declined to make a statement. His friends, however, provided a simple explanation. Fickert ran his office rather informally, with much mutual exchange of favors. It was probable that Crowley himself wrote the letter, and Fickert, to accommodate his sometime agent, signed it without even reading it. It was inconceivable that Fickert would have written such a letter had he known Crowley was working for the Germans.

This explanation was quickly proven erroneous, when Fickert was called to the stand at the trial of Bopp and the other defendants in the fall of 1916.

Under oath Charles Fickert was forced to admit that he had himself dictated the wording of the letter. He testified, vaguely, that he had been looking into the drug traffic and that since Crowley was making the trip anyhow, it made good sense to ask for his help. But as the questioning grew more specific, Fickert also admitted that Crowley's only "report" on his investigation was a note that he had arrived in Detroit.

Fickert admitted the dates of employment. He was also forced to admit that as early as March 1915 he knew that Crowley was a German agent. This had not prevented him from hiring Crowley the following May and October or from providing him with the credential. And as the questioning went on, Fickert even abandoned his earlier explanation for the document.

Q. Mr. Fickert, did you hire Mr. Crowley to do any work in Detroit for you, or Canada?

A. No, not exactly.

Q. Did he, Crowley, tell you for whom he was going to Detroit or Buffalo?

A. Yes, sir.

Q. For whom?

A. He said for the German Consul.

Q. Did he tell you, Mr. Fickert, on whose behalf or for whom he intended to go into Canada?

A. Yes, sir.

Q. For whom?

A. For the German Consul, or for the German Government. I don't know which.

Fortunately for Charles M. Fickert, this was the trip on which Crowley and Smith merely stayed in Detroit and created a "paper" explosion. Had the credential been used during the Tacoma trip, or when Crowley blew up Victoria Bridge, Fickert himself might well have been indicted. As it was, the letter (which the Mooney defense did not hesitate to use) was to prove politically embarrassing for the rest of his life.

Explanations for the letter range all the way from the improbable suggestion that Fickert was a German agent to the much more likely explanation that he was incredibly stupid. Though what it "proves" is open to debate, a few things can be safely stated:

It helps to explain why Charles Fickert became such a super patriot.

It adds a certain wry humor to his 1917 charge that Tom Mooney and Emma Goldman were German agents.

And it helps to explain why the District Attorney's office was loath to probe to any depth the German theory of the bombing.

*　　*　　*

Although all the German espionage defendants were convicted in January 1917, and sentenced to varying terms of imprisonment ranging from one to three years, only Crowley was immediately imprisoned, Bopp, von Brincken, and von Shack remaining free on appeal until the United States entered the war on April 6, 1917, at which time they were arrested as enemy aliens.

Crowley was imprisoned at McNeill's Island. Also there was Maury Diggs, a young man of prominent family who through various misadventures involving a female just under the age of consent was serving a one year term. Hearing that Tom Mooney had been convicted and sentenced to death, Crowley allegedly told Diggs, "They've got the wrong man. Mooney had nothing to do with it. The fellow that pulled that stunt is safe in Mexico."

On Diggs' release (he later became a successful architect) he repeated Crowley's remarks to Mooney's attorneys.

Contacted at McNeill's Island, Crowley denied any knowledge of the Preparedness Day bombing. He admitted that he and Diggs might have discussed it, and that he might have said the things attributed to him, but insisted that any such statement would have been only conjecture on his part.

Following his release from prison Crowley disappeared. After a long and expensive search—which only Tom Mooney felt worthwhile—a Chicago attorney, Homer Johannsen, eventually found him in Los Angeles in 1927. On July 22nd, Johannsen wrote Mooney:

"Crowley is a man about 70 and I located him at his home, 428 W. 53rd St., Los Angeles. On the surface, at least, he appeared to be a rather kindly old gent and stood fairly ready to talk about the matter. Of course I confronted him with the statement Maury Diggs claims he made . . . Crowley, however, claimed that he never made any such statement and that Diggs and he were enemies. Crowley's wife kept interfering, telling him that he had said enough, etc., so I was unable to get more out of the old man. He did say, however, that he was convinced that you were innocent, but that it was merely a matter of opinion. He says that after you were apprehended he advised Fickert that he, Fickert, was on the wrong track, but that Fickert said he had a perfect case against you, and that he, Crowley, did not feel like interfering further. I believe he is still doing work as a private detective for some large corporation and naturally if he did have more info or was involved in any way, he would keep quiet about it."

Like Smith, Crowley had denied having any part in the barge explosion. To have done otherwise would have been to confess complicity in murder. The same was true of the Preparedness Day explosion. Still, Mooney was unwilling to give up. Over the next several years he sent additional attorneys, Belle, Fremont Older, Ed Nockles, and Mary Gallagher to persuade Crowley to talk—but all were unsuccessful.

*   *   *

It has been stated that through 1915, German espionage activities in the U.S. were less than professional. By spring of 1916 the situation was almost reversed. Due to the recall of Captains von Papen and Boy-Ed, the indictments of Bopp and his associates, and the more coordinated activities of the Department of Justice, the German espionage network was forced to proceed more cautiously. In San Francisco, fewer records were kept; Bopp no longer openly displayed his bomb collection; and the quality of agents changed dramatically. It is possible to put a date—May, 1916—on the latter transformation, as that month Bopp brought together for assignment two men Landau would call "one of the most deadly teams of saboteurs in history."

Lothar Witzke * was born in Posen, East Prussia, in 1895; seventeen years later he entered the German Naval Academy as a cadet. At the start of the war he served aboard the cruiser *Dresden*, which played havoc with Allied shipping in South American waters. When the *Dresden* was sunk, he was captured and interned in Valparaiso. In 1916 he escaped, reaching San Francisco in May on board the S.S. *Calusa*. He was described as well built, athletic, good-looking, with keen blue eyes, fair hair, ruddy complexion, and remarkably successful with the ladies.

Reporting to Bopp, he was assigned to work with Kurt Jahnke, who, since Crowley's "compromise," had been placed in charge of sabotage activities under Bopp's jurisdiction.

Jahnke had been born in Germany in 1882. An American Intelligence report would later describe him as 5'11", 160 pounds, swarthy, pimple-, faced, with blond hair and small weasel eyes. At some date unknown he came to the United States, served briefly in the United States Marines, and by 1915 was, according to von Brincken, who had experience in such matters, "the most dangerous spy in the world."

According to Landau, Jahnke and Witzke "showed special aptitude for secret service work and were of a caliber far superior to the rest of Bopp's agents. So cleverly did they cover their tracks that they were never even suspected during the neutrality period."

Among the dozens of successful bombings attributed to this pair were the destruction of the shipyard at Mare Island and the Black Tom explosion, the latter, perpetrated July 30, 1916, at the munitions docks in Jersey City, New Jersey, cost two lives and damages in the amount of $40 million.

Both Jahnke and Witzke were in San Francisco on July 22, 1916.

At the time of Crowley's alleged remark to Diggs, Jahnke was directing the German secret service network in Mexico.

*   *   *

While imprisoned, Bopp's two aides made confessions of their sabotage activities.

---

* At various times he also used the names Lather Witcke, Harry Waberski, Wabrechty, Capewitcke, Hugo Olson, Pablo Davis, Otto, Robert, Nachel A., and the name under which he was sentenced to death, Paul Waberski.

Baron E. H. von Shack, fearing that Germany might consider him dispensible, wrote a letter that he turned over to his attorney, Theodore Roche, to be released only in the event of his assassination. Although both the Department of Justice and the Mooney defense tried repeatedly to learn the contents of the document, they met with no success; it presumably was destroyed upon von Shack's release and deportation. Although not unfriendly to Mooney, Roche over the years consistently refused to divulge whether the document contained evidence relating to the Preparedness Day explosion.

Having married a wealthy American woman and purchased a large ranch in the Santa Clara Valley, Wilhelm von Brincken was less anxious to return to the Fatherland. He made his confession directly to the Department of Justice early in April 1918. It was from this information that authorities first learned of the existence of Jahnke and began a search for him.

The confession was not made public, but on April 16, 1918, the San Francisco *News* reported that Harry Moffett, the Secret Service agent who questioned von Brincken, had stated to friends that Jahnke was being sought in connection with the Preparedness Day bombing.

Moffett denied this. Mooney's attorneys, through connections in the Department of Labor, learned that Moffett had questioned von Brincken about the Preparedness Day bombing, but that he had denied knowing anything about it. It was learned that he had also denied knowing anything about the Tacoma barge explosion, even though it was proven conclusively at his trial from consular records that he had played a major role in expediting that outrage. Murder charges were involved in both cases.

By this time Jahnke had been definitely located in Mexico, while Witzke had been captured attempting to cross the border. Witzke was subsequently tried for spying on U.S. military installations and convicted, becoming the only German agent condemned to death by the United States during World War I. On May 27, 1920, the President commuted his sentence to life at hard labor.

Jahnke remained in Mexico, operating the German secret service network there. Prudently, he did not try to return to the United States.

In 1920, the *Bulletin*, attempting to duplicate Fremont Older's techniques and win back its lost circulation, ran a number of sensational articles. Among them were the serialized confessions of recently released Wilhelm von Brincken. Posters advertising the forthcoming series announced that it would "Shed New Light on the Preparedness Day Bomb Explosion" and would disclose "Matters in connection with the infamous Preparedness Day explosion that may tend materially to change public and judicial verdicts in respect to Mooney and his associates."

In the first installment, appearing August 30th, von Brincken wrote:

"It should be remembered that I was a soldier, sworn and trained since I was a boy in my teens to obey implicitly all orders coming from my official superiors. Mooney I never met, and I never, in my own mind, connected him or any of his clique with the crime for which he was sentenced.

"When called upon to act as go-between, carrying messages from Bopp . . . to the alleged dynamiters to whom, subsequently, I attributed the Preparedness Day atrocity, I was working, according to my own lights, for my country's cause and in obedience to the highest orders."

The series was carried daily. For weeks after this tantalizing hint there was no further mention of the bombing. To all appearances every childhood incident, every card game von Brincken won, every duel he fought was to be recounted.

The *Bulletin*, now one of the most conservative newspapers in San Francisco, seemed a most unlikely agent for reopening the Mooney case. Before long, Fremont Older heard through his spies, and Tom Mooney reported in *Tom Mooney's Monthly*, that Crothers and Pickering would probably not follow through on their promised disclosures "since the Bulletin is one of the voices of Big Business."

There was even more graphic evidence in the articles themselves. Von Brincken was emerging, by his own account, as an heroic American patriot who, loving his adopted country, had frustrated Bopp, von Shack, and Jahnke every chance he got. One incident, however distorted it may have been, was revealing in the light of what von Brincken later wrote. It told of how Bopp had called him to the consulate one night to ask if there was any dynamite on his ranch; Jahnke needed some. He was to meet Jahnke at seven the following evening in an alley behind the Palace Hotel and deliver it. Although von Brincken had some dynamite, he decided to tell Jahnke otherwise. When they met he asked, "What did you want with it?"

Jahnke replied, "Oh, there is some damned English ship loading acid for the manufacture of explosives in the bay and I want to blow the ship up. I had some 40 per cent dynamite, but it is not strong enough. I want some 60 per cent stuff."

On September 30th, von Brincken declared that concerning the Preparedness Day explosion, "if I may run ahead with my narrative—I had no personal knowledge of any such outrage being premeditated, and knew that no such abominable folly would ever be sanctioned, or even contemplated for one instant, by any German consular official."

Continuing, however, he stated his conviction "that the bomb had been intended for a British ship then lying alongside a wharf here . . ."

In saying this, he wanted to make it perfectly clear that he did not know Mooney or his associates, as none "belonged to a class that I might have mingled with in pursuit of social pleasure."

There was such a ship in the harbor, in fact several, one of them berthed only a block from Steuart and Market.

Another point strengthened this theory: the bullets. If they were not originally intended to claim human lives, as happened, then there must have been some other reason for their inclusion. If the bomb was intended for a vessel or place where powder or other explosives were stored, the bullets would have served to trigger further explosions.

The serial, long relegated to the inside pages, ended on October 26th with von Brincken's own theory of the bombing.

"The Preparedness Day parade was made the occasion of a general holiday. Public interest was centered in the parade itself. Work on the docks was practically suspended, and in the general excitement it was reasonable to suppose that the vigilance of the guards who were protecting the ships would be considerably relaxed. Such conditions, it was also reasonable to suppose, would be seized upon by any person who desired to pay a surreptitious visit to any of those ships as a peculiarly favorable opportunity."

If such a person, von Brincken concluded, "were to have gone down Pine or California street that day" he would have encountered an obstacle—the crowd. It was von Brincken's theory that he cut across Market, started down Steuart, saw this was crowded too, and abandoned the lethal suitcase next to the saloon wall.

This was not a new theory. What made it interesting was that he should route the man down Pine or California, since the German Consulate was located on the corner of Sansome and Pine.

If this was a hint, it remained that. Von Brincken subsequently changed his name to Roger Beckwith, moved to Hollywood and entered the motion picture business. Mooney worked on him as on Crowley but with identical results.

In 1923 the German Government lodged a strong protest against Lothar Witzke's continued imprisonment, after which he was released and returned to Germany. Kurt Jahnke soon followed. During the late 1920's and throughout the 1930's, Germany's espionage activities became a diplomatic issue as the Mixed Claims Commission heard evidence regarding American business claims against Germany for losses sustained via sabotage during World War I. Key issues were the Black Tom and Kingsland explosions. Germany procrastinated, and evaded, finally managing to stretch out negotiations virtually until the eve of World War II. Only a fraction of the claims were paid. In the early Thirties, American investigators succeeded in locating Witzke in Hankow, China, and Jahnke in Germany, but the German government would not permit either to be interviewed directly; speaking for them, it categorically denied their involvement in any illegal activities in the United States.

Bopp, too, remained silent.

*   *   *

For nearly ten years Tom Mooney himself suppressed one part of the German evidence, while impatiently waiting for a man to die.

In 1926, Alfred H. Spink, seventy-five-year-old founder of *The Sporting News*, made an affidavit relating to his knowledge of German consular activities in San Francisco, but insisted that it not be made public until his death.

From 1914 through 1916 Spink and his wife lived on 44th Street in Oakland. Their next-door neighbors were Powell Mertz, former German Consul to the Marshall Islands, and his Countess wife. Mrs. Spink was German also and the two women were close friends. Mertz, somewhat fanatic about his privacy, had no telephone, but frequently used the Spinks'.

During the spring of 1916 there were numerous explosions on the Pacific Coast, and according to Spink, "we discussed them each time they occurred. He told me there was a lot of work being done in this country of which he did not approve . . .

"Whenever an explosion took place, Mr. Mertz not only discussed it with me, but he would call up persons in San Francisco and conduct long conversations." Quite frequently Spink overheard them. "I recall especially that at the time of the Victoria bridge explosion Mr. Mertz had a long conversation with someone in San Francisco in the course of which he inquired as to whether or not someone had returned to San Francisco, leaving the impression on my mind that he was inquiring as to some person who had been at the scene of the explosion in Victoria and perhaps committed the deed."

Mertz did much entertaining, with Bopp and his aides frequently in attendance. Whatever Mertz's real feelings about the sabotage may have been, apparently he didn't share them with Bopp, for Spink noted that "These meetings were in the nature of celebrations, one especially I recall was right after the Victoria explosion . . ."

During the spring of 1916 Mertz became extremely anxious to return to Germany to serve his country (he kept his sword and uniform in the closet, Spink recalls) and was trying to negotiate passage for himself and his wife on the submarine *Deutschland*. A few days before Preparedness Day, Mertz came to Spink and "expressed great anxiety to get away from this country, and especially to get away from Oakland. He said, 'You know, Mr. Spink, there have been some terrible carryings on over here, and I do not approve of them. You know where I stand, and I am exceedingly anxious not to be implicated in any way, or have any of the blame attached to me.'

"Several days before the Preparedness Day parade," Spink continued, "my wife told me that something awful was going to happen in San Francisco. She said that Mr. and Mrs. Mertz had told her, and that Mr. Mertz was exceedingly anxious to get away from Oakland before the occurrence for the reason that he did not want to be implicated in any violent action of any kind. Most of the information I received about this came through my wife . . . My wife said that both Mr. and Mrs. Mertz said that under no circumstances should any of our family be in San Francisco on the day of the parade. I asked my wife if she knew why we were being given the warning and she said that she had asked Mrs. Mertz and Mr. Mertz and that they had said in substance, 'You know what has been going on around here, these terrible explosions, and our warning to you is to keep away.' " The Spinks heeded the warning, and alerted all of their relatives.

"When the explosion took place, my wife and I discussed it, and were convinced that the crime was perpetrated by the same man that caused the Victoria explosion and other explosions of that sort that had been in progress in different places in the United States and Canada and especially those that had taken place on the Pacific Coast."

In Mertz' telephone conversations many persons had been referred to by name. "The name Crowley was one name that was mentioned more than any of the others. The man who was referred to by this name was mentioned frequently and seemed to be the chief actor in the explosions."

The Mertzes did return to Germany via the submarine. Up until the time of the war, and for several years after the Armistice, the two families exchanged letters and packages.

Spink had wanted to go to the authorities with the story immediately, but his wife had begged him not to, wanting to involve neither the Mertzes nor themselves. She died in November 1926 and Spink contacted the Mooney defense in December. In ill health, he asked that his affidavit not be made public until after his death. Mooney reluctantly complied with his wishes—but meanwhile wrote to Roger Baldwin, who was in Europe, and had him contact the German Socialists and try to learn the whereabouts of the Mertz family. They learned that Powell Mertz had died but that his wife was still alive. The German government learned of these inquiries, however, which came at the time of the Mixed Claims investigations, and refused to let Mrs. Mertz be interviewed.

Whether they did so because they felt the information she could have provided would have proven costly to the German government is one of the great unknowns of the Mooney-Billings case.

Spink finally died, and Mooney was able to make his statement public, but, unsubstantiated by other testimony, it proved nothing.

*   *   *

This, with one exception, comprises the evidence in support of the German theory. The other item isn't evidence, but rather the absence of it.

Despite the episode on the New York El (which earned him the nickname "Minister Without Portfolio"), Dr. Albert continued to behave indiscreetly. For example, he kept a daily diary.

This too was seized and decoded by American Intelligence.

Although Albert was meticulous in making daily entries, there were, in the year 1916, two intervals when nothing was written. The pages for July 28th through August 4th were blank: the Black Tom explosion occurred on July 30th. Also blank were the earlier dates of July 22nd through July 25th.

*   *   *

In 1933, confronted with a direct question from a reporter, Count Franz von Papen denied emphatically that Germany was guilty of the Preparedness Day explosion. "Anyway," he was quoted as saying, "that fellow Mooney has been in prison for sixteen and a half years so he must be guilty."

The confession of Louis J. Smith

Louis J. Smith, C. C. Crowley's agent and betrayer, liked to call himself a "soldier of fortune." During the Spanish American War, he joined the Army and deserted, then reenlisted under another name, to be caught stealing tobacco from the commissary and sent to Leavenworth for two years. Upon release he was given 30 days for breaking into a jewelry store. There followed a period of wandering. Up until the time Crowley solicited him for espionage work in the spring of 1915, he worked mostly as a labor spy for various private detective agencies, including Baldwin-Felts.

Following the indictment of the German agents, Smith was paroled into the custody of Federal Prosecuting Attorney John W. Preston, who was handling the German cases (and who later, as a Supreme Court Justice, would be Billings' inquisitor at his rehearing). The Mooney defense believed that in the spring of 1916 Preston found Smith a job as an agent with Martin Swanson. Mooney, on seeing Smith's picture some years later, was sure he had been one of the men shadowing him. Although Smith did work as a scab and spy in several local industrial conflicts in which Martin Swanson *may* have been involved, the defense was never able to establish a connection conclusively.

Among themselves, most of the scabs had nicknames or monickers. One, for example, was known as "The Smasher," another as "Quick Toe."

Louis Smith's nickname, the result of his involvement with the Germans, was "Der Kaiser."

This has prompted at least one person, Warren Billings, to wonder if there might not have been more to Chris Lassen's confession than was generally credited.

*   *   *

Following the trials, Smith returned East. He died in Cleveland on August 26, 1922, from injuries sustained while working on an automobile.

In November 1929, following his article on the Mooney case in *Plain Talk,* Senator Schall received a letter from the National Military Home in Dayton, Ohio. The writer was Frank O. Stephens, an aged veteran who thought the Senator might be interested in learning that an old friend of his, Louis Smith, now deceased, had told him that Tom Mooney hadn't committed the Preparedness Day bombing. Just before his death, Stephens said, Smith had confessed to his sister Dora that he committed the crime.

Senator Schall immediately turned the letter over to the press, who, before Mooney's attorneys could arrange to go to Dayton, succeeded in muddying the waters considerably, one enterprising reporter "capturing" Stephens and holding him for several days so as to have an exclusive. In the detailed statement Stephens eventually made, he said that he had first met Louis Smith in the home of Smith's sister, Mrs. Dora Monroe, in September 1915. At this time Smith was carrying handcuffs and a gun and pretending to be a U.S. Detective. The two men became friends and Smith told Stephens about deserting the Army and being sent to Leavenworth. "He did not have any love for the U.S.A. and the Stars and Stripes," Stephens recalled. Smith also told him that he was not really a detective, but a German agent, on his way to Canada to do some work for the Germans.

Stephens next met Smith in Mingo Junction, Ohio, in March 1919. "We got into a conversation about different things and different crimes that were being committed . . . Smith asked me if I was very well acquainted with the Tom Mooney case, and I told him that I hadn't read much about it, but that I thought it was a terrible crime. Louis J. Smith then made the remark to me that Tom Mooney was not doing his own time. I said, 'Are you sure of that?' and he said, 'I know that I am sure of it, and Tom Mooney did not know anything about it.' "

This was the last time he saw Smith. In November 1922 Stephens went to Dora's home to pay her son Ott for taking care of his hound dogs. While there, Dora told him that shortly before Louis' death he had confessed to committing the Preparedness Day bombing.

When reporters located Mrs. Dora E. Monroe in her mountain cabin near Wegee, Ohio, and told her of Frank Stephens' statement she fainted.

She had been sure Stephens was dead. After recovering she threw the reporters out, at the same time strongly cursing Stephens for breaking his promise to her.

They proved persistent, however, and she finally admitted that what Stephens had said was true.

As she stated in her formal affidavit, shortly before his death her brother Louis "came to me and said, 'I have something dreadful to tell you, sister. It is about a crime I committed. I can't live and keep the secret to myself any longer, and I want some one to know about it before I die. It was me that throwed the bomb in the Preparedness Parade in San Francisco . . . Tom Mooney is innocent. He didn't know anything about it. That is the reason I regret committing the crime so much. It causes my heart to be overburdened with grief to think that a crime I committed got an innocent man in such a situation.'

"I said to him, 'What in God's name made you do such a crime as that?' and he said, he done it for money. He said he needed money very much at that time. I said, 'You must have got a lot of money for committing such a terrible crime as that.' He said that he was promised more than he ever received. He said that he was to get $10,000 for blowing an automobile up in the parade but that all he got was $2000. He said that him and two other men brought the bomb down to San Francisco [from Seattle] in a suitcase.

"They paid him $2000 before he throwed the bomb. They were to pay him the remaining $8000 after he blowed up the automobile. After they arrived at San Francisco, they went to the point the automobile was to go by, but the automobile was not there and they got up on a building to see if they could locate it in the parade. After they got on the building the bomb had just six minutes to go before it would explode. He said he looked out in the street as far as he could see but there was no automobile in sight, and he throwed the bomb out into the street into the parade to keep from blowing him and his companions up. After he throwed the bomb they got down off the building and went down to the Bay and got on a vessel so no one could find them. These two men who were with him refused to pay him the balance of the money because he didn't blow up the automobile as he agreed to do."

Frank Stephens' recollections of Mrs. Monroe's conversation with him in 1922 were markedly similar to her own account.

Mrs. Monroe's son Ott, who had overheard part of his uncle's confession to his mother, also signed an affidavit.

Checking further, the defense learned that Louis Smith had a brother, Alonzo L. Smith, living in Wheeling, West Virginia. They located him to find that Louis had confessed to him also.

"My brother was a n'er do well and never did much work during his life. He always lived off someone else," Alonzo recalled. For awhile Louis had stayed with him and his wife, but had stolen his wife's rings and jewelry and disappeared.

He recalled him visiting them again one August or September—he couldn't remember the year—and that he pulled out a big roll of bills and admitted he was doing spy work for the German Government. "He said that a man named Crowley was furnishing the money and that he was working under him." He told Alonzo and his wife he was making $350 a month and expenses. He told him that he blew up a barge-load of ammo in Seattle—dynamited a bridge in Detroit—burned a government building in Montreal."

Each of these things happened, although Smith was never officially connected with any except the first.

Alonzo and his wife refused to accept his present, saying it was "blood money."

Although there was bad feeling between them, this did not keep Louis from coming to see Alonzo when he was in the vicinity. In April 1916 he came by to borrow $5. This was the last Alonzo saw of him until the following October, when in response to a telephone call, he met him on a downtown street corner; Louis got out of a blue automobile, which drove off, and the brothers went into a restaurant to talk. Louis told Alonzo that Crowley and the other German agents had been arrested and that he was going to testify against them at their trial.

Louis also told him that he was mixed up in a bad bombing scrape in San Francisco. "He then went on to tell me that he threw a dynamite bomb into a parade that was going along the street in San Francisco. He did not tell me the exact date but talked like it was a very short time before this visit. He said that he threw the bomb himself, and that the time he threw the bomb there were two other men with him. He said they were on top of a building at the time he threw the bomb and that he threw it about forty feet out from the building. He said that the bomb killed a bunch of people. The way he expressed it was 'we got a bunch of them.'

"I said to him, 'Louis, you ought not to have done a thing like that.' Louis' answer was 'Well, I was promised to be well paid for it.'

"During the conversation he told me the names of the two men that were with him, and referred to one of them all the time as 'Joe' [Joseph "Indian Joe" Daugherty?]. I am sure that he spoke the name of the other man, and my recollection is that it had a foreign sound, but I can't remember it now. [Chris Lassen?]

"Louis said that the man 'Joe' was the one who was to hand him the money for throwing the bomb . . ." However he had paid him only a portion of what was promised.

"Louis told me that they had two bombs on the roof but he only threw one, and that that same night he threw the other bomb in the bay."

During this confession Louis was very nervous, Alonzo said, and kept looking over his shoulder, afraid of being overheard. After several hours, the blue automobile picked him up; Alonzo never saw him again.

He had remained silent, Alonzo said, because though he hated to see an innocent man in prison, he would have hated even more to see his own brother hanged.

For several weeks these stories created such a journalistic sensation that it seemed public indignation alone would force the authorities to release Mooney and Billings.

In all except California, that is, where only two papers, the San Francisco *Call* and *News,* gave them anything approaching adequate coverage. They rated three or four paragraphs in most of the other papers, plus a *Chronicle* editorial stating that the story was wholly discreditable because Smith was a known liar, that he hadn't actually participated in any bombing. Apparently this was based on Smith's statement to federal authorities that he took no actual part in the barge explosion.

Despite California's attitude, some action might have been forced were it not for one thing: Mrs. Monroe changed her story.

Mrs. Monroe was a mountain woman. Overnight she had become a celebrity, several newspapers and magazines offering her money for exclusive rights to the story of her brother's life. She now decided that the Mooney defense owed her something. Later it would be charged that Mrs. Monroe was "reached" by Fickert and his agents. As far as the author has been able to determine, this accusation was simply conjecture. In 1929 Charles Fickert lacked the power to "reach" anyone. There is evidence, however, that she was contacted by an imaginative reporter who convinced her she had forgotten significant details, the most important that Tom Mooney was standing beside Louis when he threw the bomb. This was—considering her earlier statements wherein Louis explicitly termed Mooney innocent—a novel change. Unfortunately, it also made a certain amount of sense.

There was only one car in the Preparedness Day parade, that of city Supervisor Andrew J. Gallagher. This also served as the official press car, and has been mentioned earlier.

Gallagher was the only major labor leader who had come out for Preparedness. Tom Mooney had attacked him numerous times for his "class collaborationist policies," and once specifically, in Tom Mooney's lone article in *The Blast,* for his preparedness stand.

By the time Mooney's attorneys had cajoled—and threatened—Mrs. Monroe into repudiating her additions, the damage had been done. Although the affidavits comprised the basis for an appeal to President

Hoover and an attempt to reopen the case in court, their effectiveness had been blunted.

There are a number of things wrong with the Smith stories, but before mentioning them it might be well to note the reason several people intimately connected with the Mooney-Billings case still believe them to be true. If Martin Swanson or some other agent acting on behalf of the Law and Order Committee wanted to commit an act to split asunder San Francisco labor the murder of Gallagher would have been it. Too, had this happened, Tom Mooney would have been a prime suspect.

Some of the discrepancies (throwing the bomb 40 feet) may be explained away as exaggeration on Louis Smith's part or credited to the fact that all these stories were second-hand and related some time after the first telling.

Nor is Mrs. Compton's story that she saw only one man on the roof necessarily discrediting. There was only one means of access to the saloon roof, an adjoining building in the process of being demolished. From her vantage point Mrs. Compton didn't see the man climbing onto the roof, but only crossing the roof to the Steuart Street edge. There was a large sign that extended above the building top on Market, and it may be that this hid the other men from view.

There is still another possibility worth mentioning. This is that Louis Smith did not tell his sister and brother the exact truth, that he may have been alone in both the planning and the perpetration. It is not unusual for a man to feel so burdened that he must confess a crime, but still, in so doing, attempt to justify his action. His motive? Smith could have assumed that the Germans would be blamed. They were certainly logical suspects. Smith was due to testify against them in the forthcoming trials; he was to be the key witness. The bombing would have made his testimony even more important, would in fact have made him a hero.

This is pure speculation.

The major fault of the Smith story is that it adopts almost in toto the prosecution's theory of the time bomb which was to be thrown.*

Too, if Smith's target was Gallagher's car, there was no way for him to determine where it would be at a particular minute, as it went up and down Market on no set schedule so that photographs could be taken of the parade. A time bomb would have been illogical under these circumstances.

All the Smith story proves is that Louis J. Smith, for some reason or reasons known only to himself, felt it necessary to confess to both his sister and his brother that he committed the Preparedness Day bombing.

---

* It does eliminate one small portion of Fickert's theory. Although Smith allegedly said the bomb was carried from Seattle in a suitcase, in none of the affidavits is he quoted as saying it was thrown in one.

Labor and/or radical groups

It has been suggested—by no less an authority than the California Supreme Court—that if Mooney and Billings were not guilty of the bombing, someone else in labor or radical circles must have done it.

This is a possibility, and there is evidence that tends to support it: the anonymous threats.

A large number of radical groups—ranging from pacifists to IWW's and anarchists—opposed preparedness. Almost all of San Francisco labor—from the conservatives to the militants—were on record as opposed to the parade itself because of its "open shop" aspects. However, none of these groups, as groups, would have stood to gain anything but trouble by committing such an act.

This does not mean that a single individual of disordered mind wasn't triggered into committing such a mad act by the mood of the times; by the inflammatory utterances of a Berkman in a *Blast* or a McDevitt in a Dreamland Rink, much as the speeches of Emma Goldman were said to have driven insane anarchist Leon Czolgosz to assassinate President William McKinley; or perhaps by something even more personal, word from his employer that he would march or lose his job.

A single insane person, acting on motives understood by him alone—perhaps a radical or a laborite but perhaps unjoined to any group or philosophy—remains, as in the beginning, one possible answer to the horror at Steuart and Market.

Fickert, Swanson, et al

To many in labor the bombing and the frame-up were a single package.

According to advocates of this theory, various persons—usually identified as Martin Swanson working on behalf of the Law and Order Committee of the San Francisco Chamber of Commerce or United Railroads or both—were responsible for both the parade bombing and the frame-up of Tom Mooney.

The evidence for this consists of a motive—discrediting labor; the resolution passed by the San Francisco Labor Council on the eve of Preparedness Day predicting "a violent disturbance," "a possible frame-up" (which may have been simply a defensive measure against the anonymous letters); the fact that—according to Mooney, Billings, Weinberg, and McNutt—Swanson had Mooney under surveillance and was endeavoring to frame him on the San Bruno dynamiting charge; and the use to which the tragedy was put.

This theory has two degrees. Warren Billings, for example, believes that Swanson, possibly using Smith and Lassen as agents, prepared the bomb, with intention of having it disclosed prior to explosion, then implicating Mooney; but that somehow plans went awry. In short, that the actual explosion was an accident. Although Billings certainly harbors no fondness for Martin Swanson, he cannot bring himself to believe that the murders at Steuart and Market were deliberate.

Others are less generous in their views. Mooney—at least for a time—was convinced Swanson and Fickert planned the bombing exactly as it happened.

There is a very good reason to reject at least the latter part of this theory.

Leaving from consideration the question of whether even the most militant "management extremists" would countenance such an act, whether Mooney was important enough to warrant it, or whether Martin Swanson was mad enough to consider it—perhaps its best refutation was voiced by Edward Cuhna when he said "If I'd set out to frame Mooney I'd have done a better job of it."

The prosecution's case against the defendants was so incredible that it is inconceivable anyone could have fabricated it in advance of the bombing. Fickert's premise, his explanation for the explosion, his lack of concrete evidence, his chronicle of events, and his witnesses—it is difficult to see in any of these muddles evidence of advance preparation.

One may see something sinister in the activities of Bunner, Fickert, and Colburn at the bomb scene. One may also, perhaps more realistically, view the same episodes as manifestations of sheer ineptness.

Almost all of the evidence would seem to indicate that Fickert and Swanson and their associates and advisors took a tragic *fait accompli* and shaped it to their own ends.

This is not denying that there was a frame-up; that Martin Swanson was out to "get" Tom Mooney; that both he and United Railroads' director Thornwell Mullally were quick to point the finger of suspicion in his direction; that those who benefited most from the tragedy were the open shop forces; that Fickert, Swanson and their associates, apparently in the belief that they were working in the best interests of the people they represented, suppressed evidence, fabricated it, suborned perjury, and committed a variety of other illegal acts; and finally that they conspired to keep two men in prison long after any shred of evidence as to their alleged guilt had vanished, and that in this malfeasance they were aided and abetted by many of California's business and political leaders, most of its newspaper publishers, a majority of its Supreme Court Justices, five of its Governors, and the indifference of a majority of its citizens.

These would seem to be crimes enough.

*   *   *

Whose bomb?

Chris Lassen's? A Mexican revolutionary's? The Esmonds'? Louis Smith's? Martin Swanson's? Joe Daugherty's? Lothar Witzke and Kurt Jahnke's? C. C. Crowley's? A madman's?

All the known evidence is here. From it the reader may come up with his or her own solution. For what one opinion is worth (and it is only that), the author is inclined toward belief in the German theory, though he admittedly remains bothered by the confession of Louis Smith.

This too is part of the tragedy of the case. For as long as there is no conclusive answer to this question, the file on the Preparedness Day bomb murders can never be marked closed.

Acknowledgments

The following authors and/or publishers generously granted permission to quote from the works indicated: Brewer, Warren and Putnam, Ernest Jerome Hopkins, *What Happened in the Mooney Case;* Houghton Mifflin, James A. Johnston, *Prison Life Is Different;* Alfred A. Knopf, Emma Goldman, *Living My Life;* William Morrow & Company, Gene Smith, *When The Cheering Stopped;* Reynal, Felix Frankfurter recorded in talks with Dr. Harlan B. Phillips, *Felix Frankfurter Reminisces;* Stackpole Sons, Orrick Johns, *Time of Our Lives;* University of California, Robert Edward Lee Knight, *Industrial Relations in the San Francisco Bay Area 1900–1918; and People's World* for use in full of the poem *Farewell, Mother Mooney* by Mike Quin.

Grateful acknowledgment is also made to the Bancroft Library, Kenneth Lamott, Roy D. Graves, San Quentin Prison, the California State Department of Corrections, and Warren Billings for permission to use the photographs in this book.

Special thanks are due the following individuals who contributed recollections, source materials, leads or other courtesies: Mrs. Charles Biddle, Mrs. Warren Billings, Mrs. Helen Bretnor, Miss Marjorie Canright, George Davis, R. L. Duffus, Edgar T. Gleeson, Harry Golden, Philip D. Guthrie, Kenneth Lamott, Ben Legere, Pete Maloff, Sr., Steve Murdock, Harvey O'Connor, Allan Ottley, Mrs. Ann Rand, Marvin Sanford, Mrs. Miriam Allen DeFord Shipley, and John Barr Tomkins.

Extra special thanks are due my agent, Malcolm Reiss, who believed there should be a book on the Mooney-Billings case; my editor, Eric P. Swenson, who proved uncommonly patient while it progressed; my wife Laura, who made it possible; and Warren K. Billings, who not only gave generously of his recollections, papers, and library, but also read the manuscript and offered invaluable advice.

Bibliography

Materials on the Mooney-Billings case may be found in a number of libraries, including the California State Library, Sacramento; the San Francisco Public Library; the International Longshoremen's and Warehousemen's Union Library, San Francisco; the University of Washington, Seattle; the New York Public Library (which also has the Bourke Cockran papers); and the Library of Congress, Washington, D.C.

The major collection, however, is the Mooney Collection in the Bancroft Library at the University of California. Following Tom Mooney's death, all his personal papers, together with the papers and records of his defense committees, came into the possession of Bancroft.

This material consists of 74 *very large* cartons of correspondence and other papers; 84 bound volumes of trial transcripts and legal briefs; a large pamphlet collection; 37 scrapbooks of newspaper articles; and various boxes, bundles, and portfolios containing such items as posters, photographs, courtroom exhibits, Mooney's pardon and will, etc.

The author does not pretend to have gone through all this material: some 25 cartons, for example, contain only financial records of the various defense committees. The most valuable, insofar as this book is concerned, were the trial and hearing transcripts and applications for pardon; two cartons containing carbon copies of all letters written by Tom Mooney while in San Francisco County Jail and San Quentin Prison, 1916–1938; and 23 cartons of correspondence received or sent by the Mooney defense committees for the period 1916–1942.

A detailed key to this collection is available at the Bancroft Library.

In addition, the author drew upon various private collections including those of Warren Billings, Marvin Sanford, and the author's own.

Newspapers

Whenever available, originals or microfilms of newspapers were consulted. In many instances, however, the scrapbooks of clippings kept by Rena Mooney and the other defense workers, now in the Bancroft Library, provided the items sought.

California: Colfax *Record*; Fresno *Bee;* Los Angeles *Times;* Martinez *Standard;* Modesto *Bee;* Oakland *Tri-City Labor Review, Tribune, World;* Sacramento *Bee, Union;* San Francisco *Bulletin, Call, Call-Bulletin, Chroni-*

cle, Examiner, News, People's World, Western Worker.
  Elsewhere: Baltimore *Sun;* Chicago *Federation News, Tribune;* New York *Morning American, Herald Tribune, Daily News, Evening Post, Sun, Times, Daily & Sunday Worker, World;* Seattle *Union Record;* Washington *Post.*

Magazines

Often single magazine articles proved as valuable as whole books. However, due to the number of articles consulted (over 300), space permits only the citing of the magazines themselves.
  America; American Federationist; American Freeman; American Law Review; American Mercury; Appeal to Reason; The Blast; Canadian Forum; Christian Century; Columbia Law Review; Commonsense; Commonwealth; Current History; Harper's; International Molders' Union; International Socialist Review; Labor Age; Labor Clarion; Labor Defender; Labor Herald; Liberator; Liberty; Life; Literary Digest; Masses; Monitor; Monthly Review; Mother Earth; Mother Earth Bulletin; The Nation; National Republic; New Masses; New Republic; Newsweek; Outlook; Photo-History; Plain Talk; Revolt; Revolutionary Age; Scholastic; Screen Guild Magazine; Solidarity; Sunset; Survey; Survey-Graphic; Time; Tom Mooney's Monthly; United Mine Workers' Journal; Wilshire's.

Manuscripts

The following may be found at the Bancroft Library or the University of California library:

Billings, Warren K., *Story of a Rebel.* Tape recorded-interview with Corinne Gilb for the Institute of Industrial Relations Oral History Project, University of California, 1957.

De Ford, Miriam Allen (Mrs. Maynard Shipley). *California's Disgrace: How and Why Tom Mooney Was Framed,* 1938.

Frost, Richard Hindeman. *The Mooney Case.* Unpublished Ph.D. dissertation, University of California, 1960.

——. *The Mooney Case in California Politics.* Unpublished Master's dissertation, University of California, 1954.

Gallagher, Mary. *An Interview with . . . on the I.W.W. and Tom Mooney.* Tape recorded interview with Willa Baum for Oral History Project, University of California, 1955.

Trial and hearing transcripts, appeal briefs, pardon petitions, and related documents

To avoid confusion, the following are listed in chronological order:

San Francisco Grand Jury. *Testimony and Proceedings.* August 1-2, 1916.
Documents Relating to the Trial of Warren K. Billings in the Superior Court and the District Court of Appeals. 1916–1918. 6 vols.
California Superior Court (San Francisco). *People vs. Thomas J. Mooney.* 1917. 4 vols.
——. *People vs. Rena Mooney.* 1917. 6 vols.
——. *People vs. Israel Weinberg.* 1917. 4 vols.
——. *People vs. Thomas J. Mooney,* including documents for writs of error, coram nobis, and certiorari. 6 vols.
——. *Testimony of Mellie Edeau and Sadie Edeau.* 1917.
——. *Documents relating to the Oxman perjury case.* 1917. 5 vols.
McNutt, Maxwell. *Before the Governor of the State of California: Petition for Pardon for Thomas J. Mooney.* San Francisco: Perneau-Walsh, 1918.
——. *Before the Governor of the State of California: Reply of Thomas J. Mooney to brief filed by District Attorney of the City and County of San Francisco against petition for pardon.* San Francisco: Perneau-Walsh, 1918.
Mooney, Thomas J. *Documents concerning petition for pardon to Governor William D. Stephens.* 1917–1921. 4 vols.
San Franciso Grand Jury. *Testimony of E. K. Hatcher and Paul Leake.* 1921.
Mooney, Thomas J. *Documents relating to petition for writ of audita querela in behalf of . . .* 1921–1922. 3 vols.
——. *Petition for pardon to Governor Friend W. Richardson.* 1926. 9 vols.
Affidavits of Dora E. Monroe, Alonzo L. Smith and Frank O. Stephens. 1929–1930.
Billings, Warren K., *Petition for pardon to Governor C. C. Young.* 1930.
Text of California Supreme Court ruling denying pardon to Warren K. Billings. July 2, 1930.
Hearing before Advisory Pardon Board. Documents in relation to Thomas J. Mooney's petition for pardon to Governor C. C. Young. 1930.
McKenzie, Edwin V. *In the matter of the application of Warren K. Billings for a pardon.* Petition for a rehearing. July 15, 1930.
California Supreme Court. *Documents relating to the petition of Warren K. Billings for pardon for which the Supreme Court sat as a non-judicial fact-finding commission for Governor C. C. Young.* 1930. 5 vols.
——. *Re application of Warren K. Billings for recommendation for pardon.* December 1, 1930.
Langdon, Justice William L. *Mr. Justice Langdon Dissents: A New Chapter in the Mooney-Billings Case.* New York: Arbitrator Press, 1930.
Mooney, Thomas J. *Documents relating to application for pardon to Governor James Rolph, Jr.* 1931–1932. 2 vols.
——. *Petition for pardon to Governor Frank F. Merriam.* 1934.
——. *In the matter of application for a writ of habeas corpus.* Abstract of record. San Francisco: Perneau-Walsh, 1935.
United States Supreme Court. *Complete text of Mooney opinion.* Reprinted from *The Recorder.* 1935.

California Supreme Court. *Documents Relating to Thomas J. Mooney's application for a writ of habeas corpus.* 1935–1937. 21 vols.

Olson, Governor Culbert L. *Full and Unconditional Pardon for Thomas J. Mooney.* Sacramento. January 7, 1939.

——. *Commutation of sentence for Warren K. Billings.* Sacramento. October 17, 193?.

Brown, Governor Edmund G. *Full and Unconditional Pardon for Warren K. Billings.* Sacramento. December 22, 1961.

Pamphlets

American Civil Liberties Union. *The Story of Mooney and Billings at a Glance.* New York, 1930.

Benson, Elmer A. *Gov. Benson Decries Injustice to Tom Mooney.* Remarks of Hon. John M. Coffee of Wash. in H.R. February 28, 1928. Speech by Elmer A. Benson at San Francisco, Calif., on December 8, 1937. Washington: U.S. Government Printing Office, 1938.

Bijou Theatre, New York City. *Program for "Precedent."* A play by I. J. Golden, beginning at Bijou Theatre June 29, 1931. New York, 1931.

Blackstone, Robert. *By Their Deeds.* New Orleans: Mooney Defense Committee of Dixie, 1937.

California Legislature. Senate. *Consideration of Concurrent Res. No. 18* (Mooney pardon resolution) March 16 and 17, 1937. Sacramento: California State Printing Office, 1938.

California Mooney-Billings Committee. *The Story of Mooney and Billings.* San Francisco, 1929.

Carrasco, H. C. *Eulogy of Tom Mooney.* Delivered at the dedication of the Tom Mooney Labor School, San Francisco, August 2, 1942. San Francisco, 1942.

——. *A San Franciscan Tells the Story of the Mooney Case.* San Francisco: Railway Employees' Committee for the Release of Thomas J. Mooney. San Francisco. [1935?]

Cellar, Emanuel. *Tom Mooney Should be Pardoned Immediately.* Radio Address of Hon. Emanuel Cellar of New York, May 28, 1938. Reprinted in the *Congressional Record,* June 1, 1938. Washington: U.S. Government Printing Office, 1938.

Central Conference of American Rabbis. *Statement of . . .* Issued June 1932. New York, 1932.

Cockran, Bourke. *The Mooney Case.* Address at Washington, D.C. July 28, 1918; and a Memorial to President Wilson submitted by a labor delegation through the Hon. Bourke Cockran. San Francisco: International Workers' Defense League, 1918.

——. *To the Commissioners Appointed by the President to Investigate the*

Conditions Under Which Thomas J. Mooney Was Convicted of Murder. New York, 1917.

Fickert, Charles M. *Bomb Cases: A Personal Statement from District Attorney C. M. Fickert.* San Francisco, 1917.

Fickert Citizens' Committee. *To the Citizens of San Francisco: At This Most Critical Period in Our Nation's Affairs It Is the Paramount Duty of Every Citizen to Uphold Elected Officials.* San Francisco, 1917.

Gardner, Ellsworth. *Case of the State of California vs. Thomas J. Mooney.* A compilation of evidence. Columbus, Ohio: Stoneman Press, 1933.

Geary Theatre, San Francisco. *Program for "The Criminal Code."* A Play by Martin Flavin, beginning at the Geary Theatre April 28, 1930. San Francisco, 1930.

Haldeman-Julius, Mrs. Anna Marcet. *The Amazing Frameup of Mooney and Billings: How California Has Stolen Thirteen Years from These Labor Leaders.* Girard, Kansas: Haldeman-Julius Publications 1931.

International Workers' Defense League. *Excerpts from the Press Concerning the Preparedness Parade Murders in San Francisco.* Prepared for the attention of the President's investigating committee. San Francisco, 1917.

——. *Justice and Labor in the Mooney Case.* San Francisco, 1919.

Law and Order Committee of the San Francisco Chamber of Commerce. *Law and Order in San Francisco: A Beginning.* San Francisco: H. S. Crocker Co., 1916. [Also known as "The Infamous Scab Book."]

McNutt, Maxwell. *Significant Facts Concerning the Cases: Before the Special Commission appointed by the President of the United States.* San Francisco: Pernau, 1917.

Marcantonio, Vito. *We Accuse! The Story of Tom Mooney.* New York: International Labor Defense, 1938.

Minor, Robert. *The Frame-Up System: Story of the San Francisco Bomb.* San Francisco: International Workers' Defense League, 1916. [The first of the Mooney pamphlets, this reappeared over the years in a number of revised editions under the titles *Shall Mooney Hang?, Justice Raped in California,* and *Fickert Has Ravished Justice.*]

Mooney Molders' Defense Committee, Tom. *Governor Young: Pardon Tom Mooney—Innocent.* San Francisco, 1929. [A later edition entitled *Justice Is Waiting* was published by the Mooney Defense Committee of Southern California, Los Angeles, 1930.]

—— *Labor Leaders Betray Tom Mooney.* San Francisco, 1931.

——. *Mooney "Frame-Up" Exposed: Alice Kidwell Affidavit.* San Francisco, 1917.

——. *Tom Mooney Sends Some Facts to the State Federation of Labor Delegates.* San Francisco, 1938.

——. *Tom Mooney's Message to Organized Labor, His Friends and Supporters and all Liberal and Progressive Voters of California on the 1938 Elections.* San Francisco, 1938.

——. *The Story of Tom Mooney, Molder and Miner's Son.* By a Star labor reporter. San Francisco. [192–?]

——. *A Voice from the Living Grave.* San Francisco, 1930.

——. *Workers of America: Free Your Working Class Leaders Rotting in the Bosses' Prisons. Demand "Amnesty!" for Mooney and Billings and the Imperial Valley Organizers.* San Francisco. [193–?]

Murray, James E. *Tom Mooney and American Justice.* Radio address delivered by Hon. James E. Murray of Montana. Printed in the *Congressional Record* May 17, 1938. Washington: U.S. Government Printing Office, 1938.

National Mooney-Billings Committee. *The Scandal of Mooney and Billings.* New York, 1931.

——. *The Story of Mooney and Billings.* New York, 1929.

Nolan, Edward D. *The Preparedness Day Tragedy.* Oakland: *The World,* 1916.

Nye, Gerald Prentice. *Justice for Tom Mooney.* Speech of Hon. Gerald P. Nye of North Dakota in the Senate of U.S. June 19, 1929. Washington: U.S. Government Printing Office, 1929.

Ocana, Floreal. *El Proceso del Capitalismo: Tom Mooney, Otra Victima de la Barbarie Americana.* Barcelona: Ediciones de "La Revista Blanca." [193–?]

Olin, John Myers. *Review of the Mooney Case.* Its relation to the conduct in this country of anarchists, I.W.W. and Bolsheviki. Facts that every true American should know. [Madison, Wisconsin: 1919?]

Refregier, Anton. *Prisoner 31921.* Introduction by Theordore Dreiser. New York: International Labor Defense, 1934.

Swanson, Martin. *Theodore Roosevelt and the Mooney Case.* Martin Swanson for the first time reveals the true facts in the San Francisco Preparedness Day bomb cases and demonstrates the justness of Theodore Roosevelt's attitude in support of the prosecution of these cases. San Francisco: Allied Printing Trades Council 4, 1921.

Symes, Lillian. *Our American Dreyfus Case: A Challenge to California Justice.* Reprinted from *Harper's* Magazine together with substantiating documentary evidence. Los Angeles: Inter-Religious Committee for Justice for Thomas J. Mooney, 1935.

United States Committee on Public Information. *Report on the Mooney Dynamite Case in San Francisco.* Submitted by President Wilson's Mediation Commission. Official Bulletin. Washington, 1918.

United States Congress. House. Committee on the Judiciary. *Tom Mooney.* Hearing before Subcommittee No. 1 on H.J. Res. 297, memorializing the Hon. Frank Merriam, Governor of California, to grant to T. J. Mooney a full and complete pardon. 75th Cong., 3d sess., Serial 18. Washington, May 11 & 17, 1938.

——. Senate. Committee on the Judiciary. *Report in Mooney-Billings Case.* To Accompany S. Res. 166. Washington: U.S. Government Printing Office, 1932.

——. ——. ——. *Thomas J. Mooney.* Hearing before a subcommittee of the Committee on the Judiciary, U.S. Senate, on S.J. Res. 127, a joint resolution memorializing the Hon. Frank F. Merriam, Governor of California, to grant to Thomas J. Mooney a full and complete pardon. 75th Cong., 2d sess. Washington: U.S. Government Printing Office, 1938.

United States Department of Labor. *Connection of Certain Department of Labor Employees with the Case of Thomas J. Mooney.* 66th Cong., 1st sess., H. Doc. 157. Part 1, "The Mooney Case: A Report Addressed to the Secretary of Labor by J. B. Densmore, Director General of Employment." Part 2, "Exhibit B: Meeting of the Grand Jury of the City and County of San Francisco, State of California." Washington, 1919. [The "Densmore Report."]

——. *Report on House Res. 225.* Letter from the Sec. of Labor, trans. report directed to be made to the House of Representatives, pursuant to H.R. 225. 66th Cong., 1st sess., H. Doc. 209. Washington: U.S. Government Printing Office, 1919.

Walker, James J., Aaron Sapiro, Cyrus B. King, and Frank P. Walsh. *A Review of the Facts in the Case of Thomas J. Mooney for Consideration by His Excellency, Hon. James J. Rolph, Jr., Governor of California.* San Francisco, 1931.

Zimmerman, Charles S. *Mooney and Billings Must Be Freed.* Radio Address, Station WEVD, July 29, 1936, on occasion of 20th anniversary of their imprisonment. New York: Dressmakers' Union, Local 22, ILGWU, 1936.

Books

Adamic, Louis. *Dynamite: The Story of Class Violence in America.* New York: Viking Press, 1935.

Baker, Ray Stannard (ed.). *The Public Papers of Woodrow Wilson: War and Peace.* New York: Harper and Brothers, 1927.

Beatty, Bessie. *Red Heart of Russia.* New York: The Century Co., 1918.

Benét, William Rose. *The Dust Which Is God.* New York: Dodd, Mead & Co., 1941.

Borchard, Edwin M. *Convicting the Innocent.* New Haven: Yale University Press, 1932.

Boyer, Richard O. and Herbert M. Morais. *Labor's Untold Story.* New York: Cameron Associates, 1955.

Broun, Haywood. *Collected Essays of . . .* New York: Harcourt, Brace & Co., 1941.

Bryant, Louise. *Six Red Months in Russia.* New York: George H. Doran Co., 1918.

Burns, William J. *The Masked War.* New York: George H. Doran Co., 1913.

Burke, Robert Eugene. *Olson's New Deal for California.* Berkeley: University of California Press, 1953.

Camp, William Martin. *San Francisco: Port of Gold.* Garden City: Doubleday, 1947.

Cannon, James P. *The First Ten Years of Communism.* New York: Lyle Stuart, 1962.

——. *Notebook of an Agitator*. New York: Pioneer Publishers, 1958.

Chalmers, Allan K. *They Shall Be Free*. Garden City: Doubleday, 1957.

Chaplin, Ralph. *Wobbly: The Rough and Tumble Story of an American Radical*. Chicago: University of Chicago, 1948.

Cleland, Robert Glass. *California in Our Time*. New York: Alfred A. Knopf, 1941.

Cook, Fred J. *The FBI Nobody Knows*. New York: The Macmillian Co., 1964.

Cross, Ira B. *A History of the Labor Movement in California*. Berkeley: University of California Press, 1935.

Darrow, Clarence. *The Story of My Life*. New York: Scribner, 1932.

DeFord, Miriam Allen. *They Were San Franciscans*. Caldwell, Idaho: Caxton Printers, 1947.

Deutscher, Isaac. *The Prophet Outcast*. New York: Oxford University Press, 1963.

Draper, Theodore. *American Communism and Soviet Russia: The Formative Period*. New York: Viking Press, 1960.

——. *The Roots of American Communism*. New York: Viking Press, 1957.

Drinnon, Richard. *Rebel in Paradise: A Biography of Emma Goldman*. Chicago: University of Chicago Press, 1961.

Duffus, R. L. *The Tower of Jewels*. New York: W. W. Norton & Company, 1960.

Duffy, Gladys, with Blaise Whitehead Lane. *Warden's Wife*. New York: Appleton-Century Crofts, 1959.

Flynn, Elizabeth Gurley. *I Speak My Own Piece*. New York: Masses and Mainstream, 1955.

Foner, Philip S. *The Case of Joe Hill*. New York: International Publishers, 1965.

Foster, William Z. *Debs: From Bryan to Stalin*. New York: International Publishers, 1937.

——. *Pages from a Worker's Life*. New York: International Publishers, 1939.

Frankfurter, Felix, recorded in talks with Dr. Harlan B. Phillips. *Felix Frankfurter Reminisces*. New York: Reynal, 1960.

——. *The Case of Sacco and Vanzetti*. Boston: Little, Brown, 1927.

Frankfurter, Marion D. and Gardner Jackson. *The Letters of Sacco and Vanzetti*. New York: Viking Press, 1928.

Friedheim, Robert L. *The Seattle General Strike*. Seattle: University Of Washington Press, 1964.

Friedman, Morris. *Pinkerton Labor Spy*. New York: Wilshire Book Company, 1907.

Goldberg, Louis P. and Eleanore Levenson. *Lawless Judges*. New York: Rand School Press, 1935.

Goldman, Emma. *Living My Life*. New York: Alfred A. Knopf, 1931.

Gompers, Samuel. *Seventy Years of Life and Labor: An Autobiography*. New York: E. P. Dutton, 1925.

Hays, Arthur Garfield. *Trial by Prejudice*. New York: Covici Friede, 1933.

Hicks, Granville. *John Reed: The Making of a Revolutionary*. New York:

The Macmillan Co., 1936.

Hill, Edwin C. *The American Scene*. New York: Witmark Educational Publications, 1933.

Hopkins, Ernest Jerome. *What Happened in the Mooney Case*. New York: Brewer, Warren and Putnam, 1932.

House, Edward M. *The Intimate Papers of Colonel House*. Boston: Houghton Mifflin Co., 1926–1928.

Hunt, Henry T. *The Case of Thomas J. Mooney and Warren K. Billings: Abstract and Analysis of Record before Governor Young of California*. New York: National Mooney-Billings Committee, 1929.

Johns, Orrick. *Time of Our Lives*. New York: Stackpole Sons, 1937.

Johnston, James A. *Prison Life Is Different*. Boston: Houghton Mifflin Co., 1937.

Joll, James. *The Anarchists*. Boston: Atlantic Monthly Press, 1964.

Karson, Marc. *American Labor Unions and Politics 1900–1918*. Boston: Beacon Press, 1965.

Kennan, George F. *Russia Leaves the War*. Princeton: Princeton University Press, 1956.

Knight, Robert Edward Lee. *Industrial Relations in the San Francisco Bay Area 1900–1918*. Berkeley: University of California, 1960.

Lamott, Kenneth. *Chronicles of San Quentin: The Biography of a Prison*. New York: David McKay Co., 1961.

Landau, Captain Henry. *The Enemy Within: The Inside Story of German Sabotage in America*. New York: G. P. Putnam's Sons, 1937.

Lang, Lucy Robins. *Tomorrow is Beautiful*. New York: The Macmillan Co., 1948.

McGurrin, James. *Bourke Cockran: A Free Lance in American Politics*.

McWilliams, Carey. *California: The Great Exception*. New York: A. A. Wyn, 1949.

Markmann, Charles Lam. *The Noblest Cry: A History of the American Civil Liberties Union*. New York: St. Martin's Press, 1965.

Melendy, H. Brett and Benjamin F. Gilbert. *The Governors of California*. Georgetown, California: The Talisman Press, 1965.

Morais, Herbert M. and William Cahn. *Gene Debs: The Story of a Fighting American*. New York: International Publishers, 1948.

Mowry, George E. *The California Progressives*. Berkeley: University of California Press, 1951.

Murray, Robert K. *Red Scare: A Study in National Hysteria 1919–1920*. Minneapolis: University of Minnesota Press, 1955.

North, Joseph. *Robert Minor*. New York: International Publishers, 1956.

O'Connor, Harvey. *Revolution in Seattle*. New York: Monthly Review Press, 1964.

Older, Fremont. *My Own Story*. New York: The Macmillan Co., 1926.

Oneal, James and G. A. Werner. *American Communism*. New York: E. P. Dutton, 1947.

Rolle, Andrew F. *California: A History*. New York: Thomas Y. Crowell Co., 1963.

Quin, Mike. *The Big Strike*. Olema, California: Olema Publishing Co., 1949.

Schlesinger, Arthur M., Jr. *Crisis of the Old Order*. Age of Roosevelt, Vol. 1. Boston: Houghton Mifflin Co., 1957.

——. *The Coming of the New Deal*. Age of Roosevelt, Vol. II. Boston: Houghton Mifflin Co., 1958.

Schorer, Mark. *Sinclair Lewis: An American Life*. New York: McGraw-Hill, 1961.

Sinclair, Upton. *The Brass Check: A Study in Union Journalism*. Long Beach, California: Published by the author, 1920.

——. *I, Candidate for Governor and How I Got Licked*. Pasadena, California: Published by the author, 1935.

——. *I, Governor of California and How I Ended Poverty: A True Story of the Future*. Los Angeles: Published by the author, 1933.

——. *The Lie Factory Starts*. Los Angeles: End Poverty League, Inc., 1934.

——. *100%: The Story of a Patriot*. Pasadena. California: Published by the author, 1920.

Slobodek, Mitchell. *A Selective Bibliography of California Labor History*. Los Angeles: Institute of Industrial Relations, University of California, 1964.

Smith, Gene. *When the Cheering Stopped: The Last Years of Woodrow Wilson*. New York: William Morrow & Co., 1964.

Swanberg, W. A. *Dreiser*. New York: Charles Scribner's Sons, 1965.

Taft, Philip. *Organized Labor in American History*. New York: Harper & Row, 1964.

Tasker, Robert Joyce. *Grimhaven*. New York: Alfred A. Knopf, 1928.

Thomas, Lately. *A Debonair Scoundrel*. New York: Holt, Rinehart & Wilson, 1962.

United States National Commission on Law Observance and Enforcement. Section on Lawless Enforcement of Law. *Mooney-Billings Report: Suppressed by the Wickersham Commission*. New York: Gotham House, 1932. [The "Wickersham Report."]

Villard, Oswald Garrison. *Fighting Years: Memoirs of a Liberal Editor*. New York: Harcourt, 1939.

Wells, Evelyn. Fremont Older. New York: Appleton-Century Crofts, 1936.

Williams, Brad. *Due Process: The Fabulous Story of Lawyer George T. Davis*. New York: William Morrow & Co., 1960.

Wolff, Leon. *Lockout: The Story of the Homestead Strike of 1892: A Study of Violence, Unionism, and the Carnegie Steel Empire*. New York: Harper & Row, 1965.

Index